Developing Literacy in Second-Language Learners: Report of the National Literacy Panel on Language-Minority Children and Youth

Developing Literacy in Second-Language Learners: Report of the National Literacy Panel on Language-Minority Children and Youth

Diane August
Principal Investigator

Timothy Shanahan
Panel Chair

LEA
2006

LAWRENCE ERLBAUM ASSOCIATES, PUBLISHERS
Mahwah, New Jersey   London

Lawrence Erlbaum Associates, Inc., Publishers
10 Industrial Avenue
Mahwah, New Jersey 07430
www.erlbaum.com

Cover design by Tomai Maridou

CIP information for this book can be obtained by contacting the
Library of Congress

ISBN 0-8058-6076-2 (cloth : alk. paper)
ISBN 0-8058-6077-0 (pbk. : alk. paper)
E-ISBN 1-4106-1423-9 (e-book)

Books published by Lawrence Erlbaum Associates are
printed on acid-free paper, and their bindings are
chosen for strength and durability.

Printed in the United States of America
10 9 8 7 6 5 4 3 2 1

Contents

Foreword

Peggy McCardle[1]

National Institute of Child Health and Human Development

Two events preceded and contributed to the establishment of the National Literacy Panel on Language-Minority Children and Youth. In December 2000, an important document was published that shook the foundation of the reading community for monolingual English- speaking students. The report of the National Reading Panel (NRP; National Institute of Child Health and Human Development, 2000) identified five research-based elements that need to be present in any reading approach or program for children whose first language is English to develop the skills necessary to become successful life-long readers (phonics, phonemic awareness, reading fluency, vocabulary, and reading comprehension) and told us what works. The NRP surveyed, analyzed, and reported on the research literature that addressed what had been shown to be effective instruction for those five elements of reading. The NRP, given the enormity of the task before it, made a conscious decision not to include the scientific literature available in the development of language and literacy for those students learning to read in English for whom English was not their first or native language.

In 1999, two federal research agencies published a solicitation for research to address issues of learning and instruction in non-English-speaking children with a stated emphasis on Spanish-speaking children learning to read in English.[2] Researchers enthusiastically responded, and a research network was funded. The new projects took the current information on reading skills and optimal instructional methods for teaching reading as compiled in the report of

---

[1]The opinions and assertions herein are those of the author and do not purport to represent the policies or official position of the National Institute of Child Health and Human Development, the National Institutes of Health, or the Department of Health and Human Services.

[2]Request for Applications number RFA-HD-99-012, in the NIH Guide to Grants and Contracts, July 1999. This document can be accessed at http://grants.nih.gov/grants/guide/rfa-files/RFA-HD-99-012.html

the NRP and sought to determine whether and how those principles and approaches might apply to English-language learners, specifically Spanish-speaking children.

Shortly after the funding of that research network, a distinguished group of experts—researchers in reading, language, bilingualism, research methods, and education—from the United States and Canada were invited to be part of a new panel, the National Literacy Panel on Language-Minority Children and Youth. This panel, funded by the Institute of Education Sciences with funds from the Department of Education Office of English Language Acquisition and the National Institute of Child Health and Human Development (NICHD), was charged to examine and report on the research literature on the development of literacy in children whose first language is not the societal or majority language—language-minority students.

The report of the National Literacy Panel on Language-Minority Children and Youth is important because it establishes a foundation for both current and future research on reading in language-minority students. It offers a rigorously and carefully developed synthesis of the research that preceded the current federal investment in biliteracy research. The panel developed scientifically accepted criteria on which to base their selection and analysis of the literature on various areas of research. In this volume, a well-respected group of experts, bringing together various perspectives, has assessed and evaluated the methodological strength of each study and considered this in reporting and synthesizing the findings of groups of studies. This volume represents a systematic review and synthesis, including all studies that met the specifications of numerous literature searches, to ensure inclusiveness; it thus indexes thoroughly what we know about literacy learning and instruction for language-minority students.

The volume provides background information and summarizes research across broad areas in the well-constructed synthesis chapters: literacy and language development, first- and second- language relationships, the sociocultural context of language and literacy learning, instructional approaches and professional development, and assessment. In addition, it provides more detail on the individual studies in the review chapters. It also includes qualitative research on instruction; whereas effectiveness is more effectively addressed through experimental or quasi-experimental methods, qualitative research can offer an in-depth look at the process of instruction and the context in which it occurs. However, the report clearly separates the summaries of qualitative studies from the experimental and quasi-experimental research so that readers can learn which findings are generalizable.

The value of the volume lies not only in the findings it provides on a crucially important area in U.S. education today, but also in the model the panel set for establishing rigorous criteria for judging research quality across a range of research methods. Through their thorough efforts, the panel discovered that there is a paucity of research available on the topics the researchers and the community deemed most important. Where research reports did exist on a particular topic, they were few in number, compared to the volumes of research available on monolingual English-speaking children. The volume clearly presents the strengths and weaknesses of the available research literature. It shows us where we have been and what we have learned. The panel's comprehensiveness and inclusiveness have produced a volume that can serve as a benchmark—a major resource illustrating the state of knowledge and science at a crucial point when new research attention is focused on the education of language-minority students.

The volume is also important because it can inform ongoing and future studies, which can build on its findings and improve on the methods used in that earlier research, just as we do in other fields of science. In addition, it highlights areas where more research is needed; thus, it should serve to generate more work on this important topic.

Finally, I personally see this volume as important because, like the NRP report, but in an even broader and more comprehensive way, it should serve to demonstrate that there are new criteria being brought to bear on how we compile, analyze, and report literature surveys. The methodology published in this volume should serve as an example to the field.

Although there are many reasons that it is important, ultimately, the value of this volume is that it will contribute to an ongoing national effort, which will perhaps become more unified through this document, to more fully understand and address the educational needs of language-minority children in an informed, evidence-based, intelligent, and compassionate manner. Our nation is now aware of its own changing demographics. This volume, and the products it encourages and contributes to, should help us move beyond awareness to additional action.

REFERENCE

National Institute of Child Health and Human Development. (2000). *Report of the National Reading Panel. Teaching children to read: An evidence-based assessment of the scientific research literature on reading and its implications for instruction. Reports of the subgroup.* (NIH Publication No. 00-4754). Washington, DC: U.S. Government Printing Office. Also available online: http://www.nichd. nih.gov/publications/nrp/report.htm

Preface

In the United States, a large and growing number of students come from homes where English is not the primary language. In 1979, there were 6 million language-minority students; by 1999, this number had more than doubled to 14 million students. Language-minority students are not faring well in U.S. schools. For the 41 states reporting on both participation and success of English-language learners in English reading comprehension, only 18.7% of the students assessed scored above the state-established norm (Kindler, 2002).[1] Moreover, whereas 10% of students who spoke English at home failed to complete high school, the percentage was three times as high (31%) for language-minority students who spoke English and five times as high (51%) for language-minority students who spoke English with difficulty (National Center for Education Statistics, 2004). Rapid increases in the numbers of language-minority children and youth, as well as their low levels of literacy attainment and its consequences—high dropout rates, poor job prospects, and poverty—create an imperative to attend to the literacy development of these students.[2]

This volume is the culmination of a process that began in the spring of 2002, when the Institute of Education Sciences staff selected a panel of 13 experts in

---

[1]Twenty-five states used state-designated tests to assess English reading comprehension. Other commonly used tests include the Language Assessment Scales (LAS; 15 states) and Terra Nova (11 states). Kindler (2002) reports that the currently available state data do not offer a clear picture of English-language learners' reading achievement because the assessment tools and testing policies differ from state to state, as well as among districts within a state. Other difficulties in data interpretation result because the data are from different grades, and the grade designations were not reported to the Department of Education.

[2]An Urban Institute survey of 3,400 immigrant households conducted in 1999 to 2000 in New York City and Los Angeles brings home the value of speaking English (Fix & Capps, 2002). The survey, which was conducted in five languages, revealed that more than half of immigrant adults in the two cities were limited English proficient (LEP); roughly 60% to 70% of the LEP immigrants had low incomes (below 200% of the poverty level), but only about one third of the English-proficient immigrant adults had low incomes. The survey also revealed that limited English skills were more highly correlated with poverty, food insecurity, and other measures of hardship than even legal status—that is, being undocumented. See chapter 2 for more demographic information on language-minority students and youth.

second-language development, cognitive development, curriculum and instruction, assessment, and methodology to review the quantitative and qualitative research on the development of literacy in language-minority students. These experts formed the National Literacy Panel on Language-Minority Children and Youth.[3] The formal charge to the panel was to identify, assess, and synthesize research on the education of language-minority children and youth with respect to their attainment of literacy, and to produce a comprehensive report (this volume) evaluating and synthesizing this literature.

Through extensive discussion, the panel identified five domains to investigate: the development of literacy in language-minority children and youth, cross-linguistic relationships, sociocultural contexts and literacy development, instruction and professional development, and student assessment. Within each research domain, the panel identified a series of research questions that guided the review of that domain. To address these research questions, the panel was divided into five subcommittees. Each subcommittee was responsible for overseeing the synthesis of the research in a particular domain. Over the course of five meetings, a number of subcommittee meetings, and numerous conference calls, the substantive issues in each of these areas were outlined and discussed, and the relevant literature was reviewed. The panel also held several open meetings to gain public advice and input from educators, community members, and researchers. The first set of meetings was held in the fall of 2002 to determine what the research, policy, and practitioner communities considered important research questions. In 2003 and 2004, panelists offered presentations on the work of the panel in a variety of professional venues.

This volume has undergone two rounds of external review by anonymous reviewers selected by the U.S. Department of Education. In all, the volume has gone through seven drafts. The intended audience for this volume is researchers interested in the development of literacy in language-minority students; sections are relevant to researchers studying literacy more generally, as well as to practitioners concerned about improving the education of language-minority students.

Funding for the project was provided to SRI International and the Center for Applied Linguistics by the U.S. Department of Education's Institute of Education Sciences and the Office of English Language Acquisition. Funding was also provided by the National Institute of Child Health and Human Development (NICHD) through funds transferred to the U.S. Department of Education.

The chapters in Parts I through V review the state of knowledge on the development of literacy in language-minority children and youth. Each part begins with a synthesis chapter that states and justifies the research questions for the chapters in that part, provides background information, describes the methodology used, summarizes the empirical findings reported, addresses

---

[3]The panel was served by a principal investigator, Diane August, who managed the project; Timothy Shanahan, chairperson, who helped guide the panel's work; and two methodologists—David Francis, who provided expertise in quantitative methodology, and Frederick Erickson, who provided guidance in qualitative methodology. Catherine Snow and Donna Christian served as senior advisors to the panel. In addition, the panel was served by two senior research associates who were instrumental in preparing several of the chapters: Nonie Lesaux and Cheryl Dressler.

methodological issues, and makes recommendations for future research. The synthesis chapter is followed by review chapters that provide more detail on the individual studies reviewed for that part.

The volume begins with an introductory chapter (chap. 1) and a demographic overview (chap. 2). It concludes with a cross-cutting chapter (chap. 21) that summarizes the volume as a whole, identifies cross-cutting themes, and makes recommendations for future research. The specific themes of Parts I–V and the topics of chapters within each part are as follows:

Part I: Development of Literacy in Second-Language Learners
          Development of Literacy
          Second-Language Oral Proficiency and Second-Language Literacy

Part II: Cross-Linguistic Relationships in Second-Language Learners
          Cross-Linguistic Relationships in Working Memory, Phonological Processes, and Oral Language
          First-Language Oral Proficiency and Second-Language Literacy
          First- and Second-Language Literacy

Part III: Sociocultural Contexts and Literacy Development for Language-Minority Students
          Sociocultural Influences on the Literacy Attainment of Language-Minority Children and Youth
          Sociocultural Context in Which Children Acquire Literacy

Part IV: Educating Language-Minority Students: Instructional *Approaches and Professional Development*
          Language of Instruction
          Effective Literacy Teaching for English-Language Learners
          Qualitative Studies of Classroom and School Practices
          Literacy Instruction for Language-Minority Children in Special Education Settings
          Teacher Beliefs and Professional Development

Part V: Language and Literacy Assessment of Language-Minority Students
          Language and Literacy Assessment

ACKNOWLEDGMENTS

The panel wishes to acknowledge the ongoing support and assistance of officials from the federal agencies. Our thanks go to Gil Narro García from the Institute of Education Sciences, who served as the Contracting Officer's Representative for the project at the U.S. Department of Education and also served as an advisory committee member for the panel along with Peggy McCardle from the NICHD, National Institutes of Health; Kathleen Leos from the Office of English Language Acquisition, U.S. Department of Education; and Sandra Baxter from the National Institute for Literacy.

The panel benefited from the assistance of numerous research assistants, including Daniel Bekele, Gina Biancarosa, Amy Crosson, Jennifer Kang, Michael Kieffer, Adele LaFrance, Marjolaine Limbos, Elana Peled, Patrick Proctor, and Barbara Schuster. An editor of an earlier draft of the volume, Rona Briere, greatly improved its readability. Russell Gersten and Jill Fitzgerald reviewed sections of the volume and provided detailed comments to the panel. The panel benefited from the support of staff at the Center for Applied Linguistics and SRI International. At SRI, Marilyn Gillespie served as project manager, and Regie Stites served as a senior advisor. At the Center for Applied Linguistics, Grace Burkart managed the project, and Christina Card served as administrative assistant. Special thanks also go to SRI staff who worked on the final production of the volume: Klaus Kraus, SRI senior editor; Stacey Eaton, administrative specialist; and Bonnee Groover, technical administrator.

Most of all, thanks and acknowledgment of extraordinary effort are due to the members of the panel and the chair. In addition to participating in meetings and numerous conference calls, and reading and reviewing thousands of pages of studies and background materials, many members and staff took responsibility for preparing chapters in this volume.

—Diane August Principal Investigator
National Literacy Panel on Language-Minority Children and Youth

REFERENCES

Fix, M. E., & Capps, R. (2002). *Immigrant well-being in New York and Los Angeles* (Brief No. 1 in series *Immigrant families and workers:* Facts and perspectives). Washington, DC: Urban Institute. Retrieved September 9, 2005, from http://www.urban.org/url.cfm?ID=310566

Kindler, A. L. (2002). *Survey of the states' limited English proficient students and available educational programs and services. 2000–2001 summary report.* Washington, DC: National Clearinghouse for English Language Acquisition.

National Center for Education Statistics. (2004). *The condition of education, 2004.* Retrieved July 16, 2004, from http://nces.ed.gov/programs/coe

1

Introduction and Methodology

Diane August and Timothy Shanahan
Charge to the Panel

The formal charge to the National Literacy Panel on Language-Minority Children and Youth was to identify, assess, and synthesize research on the education of language-minority children and youth with respect to their attainment of literacy, and to produce a comprehensive report evaluating and synthesizing this literature. The panel's review indicates that many factors influence second-language literacy development, among them the age at which skills are acquired, individual differences in second-language oral proficiency and cognitive abilities, first-language oral proficiency and literacy, some sociocultural variables, and classroom and school factors. Our review also reports on our knowledge base about assessment.

Key terms germane to the panel's charge are defined next.

Literacy skills are defined in this review as including prereading skills, such as concepts of print and alphabetic knowledge; word-level skills, including decoding, word reading, pseudoword reading, and spelling; and text-level skills, including fluency, reading comprehension, and writing skills. For purposes of this review, *oral language proficiency* denotes knowledge or use of specific aspects of oral language, including phonology, vocabulary, morphology, grammar, and discourse domains; it encompasses skills in both comprehension and expression. We also include studies that examine phonological processes (phonological recoding, phonological memory, and phonological awareness) because it has been hypothesized that these processes mediate the development of written forms of language (Adams, 1990; Ehri, 1998; Metsala & Walley, 1998; Scarborough, 2001).

A frequently used term is *societal/national/official language*. A societal language is one, often one of several, of the languages used in a country. A language considered to be the chief language in a country is the national language. English is the national language of the United States, but it is not its *official* language (although some states have made English the official language within their boundaries). Official status is conferred on a language by national law or by the nation's constitution. An official language is mandated for use in official government transactions and communications, in courts of law, and in laws and regulations governing the nation as a whole. French is both the national and official language of France. Canada has two official languages—English and French.[1]

There are many labels for the students and programs under consideration in this report. The most commonly used term, *language minority*, refers to individuals from homes where a language other than a societal language is actively used, who therefore have had an opportunity to develop some level of proficiency in a language other than a societal language. A language-minority student may be of limited second-language proficiency, bilingual, or essentially monolingual in the second language (August & Hakuta, 1997). Individuals who come from language backgrounds other than a societal language and whose second language proficiency is not yet developed to the point where they can profit fully from instruction solely in the second language are called *second-language learners*. In instances where the students are acquiring English as a second language, they are referred to as *English-language learners*. We have elected to use this term, first proposed by Rivera (1994) and adopted by the National Research Council's Committee on Developing a Research Agenda on the Education of Limited-English-Proficient and Bilingual Students (August & Hakuta, 1997). The term *limited English proficient* (LEP) may be used, however, when we are quoting another source or citing legal requirements. Note that we have chosen to forgo the editorially convenient practice of reducing *English-language learners* to an abbreviation. Appendix 1.B includes a list of standard terms used in the report to describe study subjects and the language status of the language or literacy components they are acquiring (e.g., vocabulary in their first language, oral proficiency in their second language).

Two other terms appear frequently in this volume. The first is *bilingual students/education programs*. Some of the programs intended to serve the needs of second-language learners use the students' native language as they acquire the second language. Thus, the term *bilingual* is often used to refer to programs when they use students' first language as well as a societal language for instructional purposes. We use the term *bilingual* to refer to an individual with a language background other than the societal language who has developed proficiency in his or her primary language and some proficiency in the second language.

PURPOSE OF THE VOLUME

The main purpose of this volume is to contribute to the construction of a knowledge base on the development of literacy in language-minority students by conducting a comprehensive review of the research on this topic and generating from this review answers to the specific research questions posed in the report. A second purpose is to develop a research agenda to address key knowledge gaps. To accomplish these goals, the panel was comprehensive in its review of the research; it focused broadly on language-minority students and, as noted later in the section on the nature of the review, included a variety of study types addressing a broad array of questions deemed pertinent to the literacy education of language-minority children. As is seen, not all such questions can be classified as *what works* questions, despite their obvious relevance to literacy attainment of language-minority students.

The panel established strict criteria for the identification and selection of relevant literature. The panel incorporated into the review and reported on all studies deemed relevant to the proposed questions that also met our inclusion criteria in the expectation that the studies might, in the aggregate, shed light on our research questions, even if they failed to do so individually. These decisions were motivated by the knowledge that such a comprehensive approach to the review, evaluation, and report was crucial for benchmarking the progress we have made in developing a science of literacy education for language-minority children and for determining the future research that is needed in this endeavor.

PROCEDURES USED TO CONDUCT THE REVIEW

Panel Staff

In constituting the panel, individuals were invited only if they had deep expertise in critical components of literacy, language learning, or research methodology, and an effort was made to include language-minority researchers. Five of the panelists have non-English-language backgrounds, including Spanish/ Argentinian, Hebrew, Spanish/Mexican, and Japanese. In addition, five panelists have important cross-cutting expertise: two are methodologists, two are experts in learning disabilities, and one is an expert in the assessment of students from culturally and linguistically diverse backgrounds.

To address the research questions detailed herein, the panel was divided into five subcommittees, each of which was responsible for overseeing the synthesis of the research in a particular domain. The panel was served by a principal investigator, Diane August, who managed the project; a chairperson, Timothy Shanahan, who helped guide the panel's work; and two methodologists—David Francis, who provided expertise in quantitative methodology, and Frederick Erickson, who provided guidance in qualitative methodology. Catherine Snow and Donna Christian served as senior advisors to the panel. In addition, the panel was served by two senior research associates who were instrumental in preparing several of the chapters: Nonie Lesaux (chaps. 3, 4, and 14) and Cheryl Dressler (chap. 9). A list of the subcommittees can be found in Appendix 1.A. Biographical sketches of the panel members and other contributors can be found at the end of this volume. In addition to the reviews by Christian, Snow, Fitzgerald, and Gersten solicited by the panel, this volume also reflects the input of anonymous reviewers solicited by the funding agency. These reviewers provided detailed commentary on multiple drafts, and their unnamed contributions were an instrumental part of the process leading to this volume.

Identification of Research Questions

Through extensive discussion, the panel identified five domains to investigate: the development of literacy in language- minority children and youth (chaps. 3–5), cross-linguistic and cross-modal relationships (chaps. 6–9), sociocultural contexts and literacy development (chaps. 10–12), instruction and professional development (chaps. 13–18), and student assessment (chaps. 19–20). Within each research domain, the panel identified a series of research questions that guided the review of that domain:

- *Development of literacy in language-minority children and youth:* What are the differences and similarities between language-minority and native speakers in the development of various literacy skills in the societal language? What are the profiles of those language-minority students identified as having literacy difficulties? What factors have an impact on the literacy development of language-minority students? What is the relationship between English oral proficiency and English word-level skills? What is the relationship between English oral proficiency and English text-level skills?
- *Cross-linguistic and cross-modal relationships:* What is the relationship between language-minority children's first- and second-language oral development in domains related to literacy? What is the relationship between oral development in the first language and literacy development in the second language? What is the relationship between literacy skills acquired in the first language and literacy skills acquired in the second language?
- *Sociocultural contexts and literacy development:* What is the influence of immigration (generation status and immigration circumstances) on literacy development, defined broadly? What is the influence of differences in discourse and interaction characteristics between children's homes and classrooms? What is the influence of *other* sociocultural characteristics of students and teachers? What is the influence of parents and families? What is the influence of policies at the district, state, and federal levels? What is the influence of language status or prestige?
- *Instruction and professional development:* What impact does language of instruction have on the literacy learning of language-minority students? What can be done to improve the literacy achievement of language-minority children? What do we know about various approaches to literacy instruction with language-minority students, including language-minority students in special education settings? What does the research tell us about teacher beliefs and attitudes, the nature of professional development of teachers who will teach literacy to language-minority students, and the influence of professional development on teacher beliefs and practice?
- *Student Assessment:* What assessments do states and school districts use with language-minority students for identification, program placement, and reclassification purposes? Are the assessments used for these purposes useful and appropriate? What do we know about alternative

assessments of oral English proficiency and literacy? What first- and second-language vocabulary and wide-scale literacy assessments for language-minority students have been investigated? What does the research inform us about accommodations for language-minority students taking these assessments? Are the assessments currently used to predict the literacy performance of language-minority students (including those with reading disabilities) useful and appropriate? What research has focused on language and literacy measures or methods developed for the identification of language-minority students eligible for special education services (including speech and hearing)? What standardized (commercial) and researcher-developed oral proficiency, literacy, and literacy-related assessments have been used by the researchers whose work is reviewed throughout this volume?

Source of Publications and Current Database

The panel could not critically examine all studies on the development of literacy in language-minority children and youth because of budget and time constraints and other practical considerations, such as the lack of public availability of some studies. Thus, on the basis of the research questions listed before, we established parameters for this review to conduct as far-reaching and nonexclusive a search of the research literature as possible. For the most part, the review focused on language-minority children ages 3 to 18 acquiring literacy in a societal language. However, to answer some questions, we also reviewed research on the acquisition of literacy in a foreign language, if the foreign language were English, and studied the acquisition of French by English speakers in Canada. The review incorporated only research published in peer-reviewed journals dating back to 1980. However, to be consistent with prior reviews on this topic, the group that examined effects of language of instruction on literacy (chap. 14) accepted evaluation studies dated before 1980.

For some chapters, dissertations and technical reports were used if the research in peer-reviewed journals did not provide sufficient information to answer the research questions. Book chapters and literature reviews were used to provide context for the findings presented; these are used in the discussions, but not in establishing the research findings. Rigorous methodological standards were applied in both the selection and analysis of research studies. To be included, studies had to report data; no thought pieces were included. If language-minority students did not make up at least 50% of the sample, outcome data had to be disaggregated for those students. For experiments or quasi-experiments, the study had to include a control or comparison group and had to use either random assignment to conditions or pretesting or other matching criteria to establish the degree of comparability between groups prior to treatment. Each group sample had to have more than four subjects. We set this minimum-sample-size criterion because experts agree that sample sizes of five or more can yield valid tests of mean differences when sample sizes are equal and/or assumptions of the t test are met (see research literature on simulations involving t tests; Maxwell & Delaney, 2003). Single-subject or multiple-baseline studies were accepted for the review because, like group experiments, they examine the impact of an instructional approach and allow us to draw causal links between use of the approach and the outcomes observed. The sample size rule does not apply to these studies. The programs cited in studies in chapter 14 (language of instruction) included at least a 6-month span between the onset of instruction and posttests to ensure a program has actually been implemented; in these cases, most treatment durations were of at least 1 year. For correlational studies, samples had to consist of 20 subjects or more. These are clearly minimal standards of acceptability with regard to sample size and are not intended as an endorsement of such studies, nor did the panel necessarily view studies meeting this standard as being of uniform quality. Rather, the panel intended to establish minimum parameters for a study to have the potential to contribute to the knowledge base when considered in concert with other research in a given domain.

Our selection and acceptance procedure involved several steps. As the research associates identified new studies through comprehensive literature searches, panelists reviewed abstracts of these studies to determine whether they were relevant and made preliminary decisions on which studies should be retained in the database. The criteria at this stage were very inclusive; panelists retained all studies unless it was clear from an abstract that a study failed to meet the criteria or was not relevant to the question at hand. On the basis of these preliminary decisions, hard copies of full articles were acquired. The research associates then coded the studies according to inclusion criteria established by the panel. For those studies that met the initial inclusion criteria, panelists reviewed hard copies to determine whether the studies should be rejected or retained. These decisions were based on relevance, as well as the adequacy of the technical quality of the study. Appendix 1.C presents the criteria used to assess studies for inclusion.

The approximately 1,800 titles initially identified were gradually reduced as the panelists examined each study more carefully. The database now consists of 970 studies (293 of which were used for this report because they are relevant to the research questions posed and meet methodological criteria established by the panel). A substantial number of studies were accepted in each domain: development of literacy (79), cross-linguistic and cross-modal relationships (60), sociocultural contexts and literacy development (75), instruction and professional development (118), and assessment (37). The societal language most represented in the database is English. The majority of studies were conducted in the United States, followed by the United Kingdom, Canada, and Australia. However, studies from the Netherlands, Finland, and Israel appear as well. It should be noted that in some cases the same study is cited in multiple locations in one chapter, as well as in multiple chapters; this is the case if a study is relevant to more than one research question.

The working database is rich in detail and was constructed not only to aid the work of the panel, but to serve as a resource for readers of the report. As such, a compact disc containing a searchable database accompanies the report. The database replaces chapter tables that were too lengthy to include in the document and makes it possible for users to access information related to each study, as well as to search for information across studies. The searchable database includes many of the fields that were part of the working database, including the bibliographic citation, abstract, research domains covered, specific foci of the study, description of the research sample, the measures used, the types of analyses performed, the methods used to collect data in qualitative studies, and the authors' findings.

Search Procedures

To identify studies for use in this review, we conducted a series of literature searches. These entailed extensive searches of various electronic databases and hand searches of particular journals. The purpose of these carefully documented search procedures was to ensure the most comprehensive, unbiased search possible for all studies relevant to the questions. In addition, the intent was to use a set of search procedures that could be replicated for future reviews.

In all, seven research literature searches were conducted. The first search was conducted during June and July 2001 by a working group established to explore the feasibility of a full-panel study. A second search was conducted in response to modifications of study inclusion criteria made at the first full-panel meeting in May 2002. This search focused on obtaining formerly excluded document types, such as dissertation abstracts and technical reports, formerly excluded studies that measured teacher rather than child outcomes, and formerly excluded studies that involved language-minority children in contexts where English is not a societal language. A third search was conducted in response to changes in inclusion criteria made at the second full-panel meeting in July 2002. This search focused on obtaining technical reports that describe interventions (see chap. 15) and formerly excluded studies that involved foreign-language literacy acquisition. A fourth search in response to changes in inclusion criteria made at the third full-panel meeting, in October 2002, was conducted to ensure that we included language-minority students who are Native American and English-based Creole and pidgin speakers, studies that examined first-language literacy outcomes for language-minority children, and studies in which literacy-related components (vocabulary, metalinguistic awareness, and phonological awareness) were the dependent variables. A fifth search was conducted in response to panel requests at the fourth full-panel meeting in April 2003 to locate additional studies on assessment and instruction. A sixth search filled in gaps in the coverage of literacy studies for Native Americans. A seventh search was conducted to update the database to 2001–2002. More detailed information about these searches, including databases, search terms and strategies, and numbers of studies identified, is presented in Appendix 1.D.

Coding Instrument

Once studies had been identified, it was important that key information was abstracted from each study so that it could be combined or compared with information from other studies, and that the coding process could be used to document why some studies were not used for the various analyses. For this reason, a common coding instrument was developed for three broad functions. The first two functions were process related. The first process-related function was to ensure that each study included in the database met specific acceptance criteria related to study relevance, sample characteristics, and methodology (see Appendix 1.C for a list of these criteria). The second process-related function was to manage the review process, ensuring that all accepted studies were included in the review and that studies not accepted were excluded. The third function was to encode specific types of information for all accepted studies to provide (a) an overview of the studies cited in each part of the report, (b) a description of researcher-developed and commercial assessments used for research cited in the report, and (c) data necessary to create a searchable database. (See also the previous section on Source of Publications and Current Database.) Additional information about the development of the coding instrument and the data it was used to collect is reported in Appendix 1.E.

Public Advice and Input

To gain public advice and input from educators, community members, and researchers who were not on the panel, two sets of outreach meetings were held. Through the networks of contacts in the field of SRI International and the Center for Applied Linguistics (CAL), people at key organizations were identified to nominate interested stakeholders. In addition, federal agency personnel and personnel at school districts near the meeting sites were asked to nominate possible participants. Further, announcements were posted on CAL's Web site, and local media were contacted.

The first set of meetings was held to determine what the research, policy, and practitioner communities considered important research questions. One meeting was held at the Los Angeles County Office of Education on September 19, 2002, and a second at CAL in Washington, DC, on September 24, 2002. Approximately 100 participants attended the two meetings: educators from districts and schools, including superintendents, principals, and teachers; parents and parent–teacher representatives; researchers and members of professional organizations; representatives of advocacy groups; and government officials. Forty-one participants presented oral testimony at the two meetings.

The second set of meetings was held to obtain feedback on the draft final report. One meeting was held at the National Reading Council's annual meeting in Scottsdale, Arizona, December 3–6, 2003, and the other at the International Reading Association Meeting in Reno, Nevada, May 1, 2004. At both meetings, panelists presented preliminary findings from the draft report and answered questions from the audience. Six panelists and the principal investigator attended the National Reading Council meeting; three panelists and the principal investigator attended the International Reading Association meeting.

NATURE OF THE REVIEW

Types of Research Evidence and Breadth of Research Methods

Scientific investigation into education has required the use of a complex and varied collection of research procedures. Part of this variety is due to the complexity of the educational enterprise (Shavelson & Towne, 2002) and the wide range of disciplines that have attempted to understand education over the years (Lagemann, 2000). Accordingly, a search of the educational research literature will identify studies using many different research designs, including experiments and quasi-experiments, single-subject designs, case studies, ethnographies, and correlations, as well as many variants of these.

In the use of such a complex body of data, the panel was guided by the findings of the Committee on Scientific Principles for Education Research: "multiple methods, applied over time and tied to evidentiary standards, are essential to establishing a base of scientific knowledge" (Shavelson & Towne, 2002, p. 2). The committee goes on to indicate that one of the hallmarks of scientific inquiry is the application of appropriate methodology to the questions being asked.

Controlled experiments and quasi-experimental designs are essential if we are to evaluate the relative effectiveness of particular actions (such as the adoption of particular instructional methods, materials, and interventions) and to test the generalizability of alternative theoretical claims. The panel raised the question of effectiveness—that is, how can we best improve literacy achievement for language-minority students? To answer this question, the panel relied exclusively on experimental and quasi-experimental studies designed to evaluate causal claims (see chaps. 14 and 15).

However, the panel's charge also required review of the research literature addressing questions about the nature of literacy development, relationships among various language learning abilities, and the status of particular approaches in the education of language-minority students. These questions are better answered through descriptive, ethnographic, and correlational studies. Such studies can play an important role in theory development, including identifying potentially important variables, generating hypotheses during the early stages of investigation into new issues, and determining how something worked (as opposed to identifying what works or how well it works). As a result, the panel's efforts to review the literature extended beyond the base of experimental and quasi-experimental studies in an effort to form a comprehensive view of what is currently known about the literacy of language-minority students.

Theoretical Framework

As with all good inquiries, we have linked our research questions to a broad conceptual framework regarding the development of literacy in language-minority children and youth. Second-language literacy development must be considered within a *multidimensional, dynamic* framework.

First, the development of the components of language and literacy are influenced in significant ways by a host of individual difference factors, the most important of which are related to phonological processes, second-language oral proficiency skills, underlying cognitive abilities, general intelligence, and educational background. The nature of these relationships is complex because some of these individual difference factors influence certain components of language and literacy development, but not others.

Second, the development of literacy entails cumulative, hierarchical processes. The nature of development is dynamic; relationships among its various aspects are not static and may change as a result of the learner's age, attainment of proficiency in prerequisite skills, previous learning, instruction, motivation, and so on.

Third, language-minority students are subject to an additional set of intervening influences—those related to their language proficiency and literacy in their first language. Moreover, the nature of the first and second languages influences this relationship because, for some languages, there is a strong contrast between skills in the first and second languages, whereas for others, the contrast is not as sharp. Moreover, the extent of this contrast between skills in first and second languages varies across the component skills of the languages, further complicating the development of a comprehensive view of the factors influencing language-minority students' literacy development.

Fourth, the sociocultural context in which children are acquiring their second language influences learning. Children develop within a broad set of environments and circumstances: in families, neighborhoods, classrooms and schools, and societies. For many language-minority students, the important contextual issues include poverty, which, as noted earlier, is common among these students; attendance in underfunded schools; low social status accorded to members of certain ethnic and immigrant groups; familial stress; and incompatibility between home and school environments (e.g., language differences).

Finally, developing literacy in a second language depends to a great extent on the amount and quality of the schooling that is provided to language-minority students. Amount and quality of schooling are a function of what is taught, the instructional methods and routines that are used, the intensity or thoroughness of instruction, how well and appropriately learning is monitored, how coordinated it is, and the level of teacher preparation.

Data Analysis

Research synthesis in many scientific fields has grown markedly during the past two decades. Part of that growth is probably due to the knowledge explosion, which has required researchers, practitioners, and policymakers to make sense of much more data than previously available. Another reason for this growth has surely been the development of electronic search capacity and meta-analysis and related methods for ensuring that syntheses are unbiased and scientific in their approach to measuring effects and relations among variables and to aggregating findings across studies.

Quantitative synthesis techniques allow researchers to create an empirical portrait of the combined results of a set of studies. They allow researchers to obtain cross-study averages for the measurement of differences, relationships, and outcomes, as well as to attribute variations in these patterns to variability in participants, contexts, and research methods and to identify the amount of error or inconsistency in a set of findings. They allow for the comparison of studies on a common metric and for a systematic accounting of the sources of variance across studies, including differences in the design and quality of the original studies. These quantitative techniques include counting study outcomes (box scores), combining probabilities from inference tests, and analyzing effect sizes (meta-analysis; Cooper, 1998).

Although the concept of an effect size emerged from experimental research (an effect size is a standardized measure of the magnitude of *effect* of an experimental treatment), effect sizes are not limited to experiments. Methods for calculating effect sizes for correlations and group comparisons have been developed, and these uses are common (Lipsey & Wilson, 2001). Effect sizes are useful in nonexperimental research because they provide weighted estimates of the average differences among groups or the average correlations among measures. In such cases, effect sizes are more properly discussed as measures of group differences or strength of association rather than of effects, per se, because of the lack of experimental intervention.

When a sufficient number of quantitative studies addressed the same conceptual hypothesis relevant to a given research question and met the other criteria then meta-analytic techniques were used in this review to make sense of the results. This was the case in chapter 4, where we examined differences between language-minority students and monolingual speakers in word reading and spelling, and in chapter 14, where we examined the effectiveness of bilingual instruction compared with English-only instruction. Although we would have liked to use meta-analysis in other chapters, these were the only instances where meta-analysis was possible. See the appendixes to chapters 3, 6, and 9 for documentation.

As noted previously, we established several criteria for deciding when to employ meta-analysis in addressing any given research question. First, we required that the literature search and inclusion criteria result in a pool of at least five studies that tested the same conceptual hypothesis. This criterion was established as a minimum number of studies for computing a mean effect size because we also desired to test that the mean effect size was different from 0. This criterion is supported by research on the mean effect size and confidence intervals for the mean reported in Hedges and Olkin (1985). Second, the subjects included in the pool of studies available for meta-analysis were either all acquiring a second language or all acquiring a foreign language. That is, we did not combine studies of students acquiring a second language with studies involving students acquiring a foreign language in any given meta-analysis. Finally, for studies that examined the relationship between language or literacy components in a first and second language, we required that the study examine these relations in the same students. That is, we excluded studies that compared first-language learners and second-language learners to address the L1–L2 connection because such studies only indirectly address the relationship between the L1 and L2 language and literacy components. Thus, only studies that employed within-subject correlations were incorporated into meta-analyses that addressed these questions.

For those questions for which quantitative techniques were not appropriate, a systematic interpretive procedure (Fitzgerald, 1995a, 1995b; Glaser, 1978) was used to examine the research and summarize findings across studies. For each research question, using an iterative process, studies were categorized by major themes or foci. Studies in each group were reread and classified with regard to similarities, differences, and results to determine cross-cutting themes, as well as methodological strengths and weaknesses.

With regard to enhancing the reliability of interpretations, the processes used to analyze the research included (a) conducting a thorough review of the research to locate all relevant studies consistent with the panel's criteria, (b) incorporating all relevant information from each study in the synthesis, and (c) providing sufficient detail about each study (in the text, appendixes, and tables or in the searchable database) to enable readers to verify the evidence used to support the author's conclusions (Fitzgerald, 1995a, 1995b; Moss, 1994). It should be noted that we evaluated and reviewed individual studies according to the canons of the type of research conducted in that study. Appendix 1.F includes the quality criteria panelists used to guide their review of studies that met the inclusion criteria and thus had been incorporated into the review. Moreover, we took care not to overclaim on the basis of type of evidence. For example, correlational studies were used only to estimate strength of association and qualitative studies to examine process and context and identify hypotheses that should guide future study, but not to show causation (i.e., what works).

SCOPE OF THE VOLUME

This volume is organized partly around the traditional distinction between basic and applied research, but is also structured to reflect specific areas of concern for educational policymakers. Parts I and II address basic research questions about bilingualism, second-language acquisition, and relationships between first- and second-language oral proficiency and literacy. Part III, on sociocultural context and literacy development, addresses both basic research about the relationship between sociocultural variables and student outcomes and more applied research related to the influence of sociocultural variables on the contexts in which students acquire second-language literacy. Parts IV and V are organized around more practical issues: program evaluations that explore the influence of native-language instruction on second-language literacy, effective instruction, schooling processes and programming, professional development, and assessment. These topics were selected because they represent key areas of concern in current discussions of educational reform.

With regard to the chapters that focus on schooling and instruction, differing research traditions (program evaluation, research on effective instructional practice, and research that examines instructional and schooling processes or the context in which schooling occurs) are treated separately in individual chapters so the reader can get a sense of how the evidence from each tradition or data source is analyzed and how inferences are drawn. The chapters on language of instruction (chap. 14) and research on effective instruction (chap. 15) are based on experimental and quasi-experimental studies, whereas the chapter that examines instructional processes and contexts (chap. 16) is based on qualitative studies. Chapter 17 (Children Educated in Special Education Settings) and Chapter 18 (Teacher Beliefs and Professional Development) draw on both types of studies because the focus of these chapters is on a specific population or topic, respectively.

A final contextual parameter for this volume is a set of assumptions shared by the majority of members of this panel, which echo those of the Committee on Developing a Research Agenda on the Education of Limited-English Proficient and Bilingual Students. They are as follows: (a) all children in the United States should be able to function fully in the English language; (b) English-language learners should be held to the same expectations and have the same opportunities for achievement in academic content areas as other students; and (c) in an increasingly global economic and political world, proficiency in languages other than English and an understanding of different cultures are valuable in their own right and represent a worthwhile goal for schools.

OVERVIEW OF FINDINGS

Developmental Perspective

The studies reviewed in Part I indicate that certain components of literacy cannot fully develop until other, precursor skills are acquired. For efficient word-recognition skills to develop, for example, it is necessary to have good decoding and orthographic skills; without accurate and fast word-recognition skills, learners cannot achieve satisfactory levels of reading comprehension. However, efficient reading comprehension depends not only on efficient word-recognition skills, but also on general language proficiency.

The dynamic nature of development means that the relationships among the components of literacy are not static and may change with the learner's age, levels of second-language oral proficiency, underlying cognitive abilities, and previous learning. For example, certain aspects of language and literacy are related to general cognitive maturity. Adolescent second-language learners (schooled only in their first language) have well-developed phonological awareness skills in both languages, but a similar level of development would not be as likely for 6-year-olds, who are cognitively less advanced in this regard. Similarly, older English-language learners notice cognates common to Spanish and English, but primary-level learners are less likely to do so.

An important finding that emerges from the research reviewed in Part I is that, by and large, for language-minority children, word-level components of literacy (e.g., decoding, spelling) either are or can be (with appropriate instruction) at levels equal to those of their monolingual peers. However, this is not the case for text-level skills, like reading comprehension, which rarely approach the levels achieved by their monolingual peers. Findings from this part also suggest that oral language skills are an important dimension of literacy development.

Although the effect of second-language oral proficiency on word-level skills is limited, having well-developed second language oral proficiency is associated with well-developed reading comprehension skills. More specifically, the evidence suggests that vocabulary knowledge, listening comprehension, syntactic skills, and the ability to handle metalinguistic aspects of language (such as providing definitions of words) are associated with reading comprehension. Although the charge of the panel was to review the research on the development of literacy, clearly another crucial area of investigation is how to build second-language oral proficiency in second-language learners, alone as well as in the context of developing their literacy and content area knowledge.

The Role of First-Language Oral Proficiency and Literacy in Second-Language Literacy Development

One difference between first- and second-language literacy development is that second-language learners have an additional set of intervening influences—those related to first-language literacy and oral proficiency. Thus, second-language learners differ in some significant ways from first-language learners in literacy learning because they bring to this challenge an additional and different set of language resources and experiences.

The studies reviewed in Part II provide ample research evidence that certain aspects of second-language literacy development (e.g., word and pseudoword reading, cognate vocabulary, reading comprehension, reading strategies, spelling, and writing) are related in important ways to performance on similar constructs in the first language; that common underlying abilities play a significant role in second-language development as they do in first-language literacy development; that certain error types can be understood in terms of differences between the first and second languages; that well-developed literacy skills in the first language can facilitate second-language literacy development to some extent; and that some cross-language influences are more likely to affect certain aspects of second-language literacy development than others, and to operate during some but not all stages of literacy development. There is also evidence for cross-modality influences, although cross-modality transfer has not been observed across the board. For example, first-language oral vocabulary does not appear to predict second-language reading comprehension.

To illustrate the role that first-language oral proficiency and literacy play in second-language learning, it would be useful to consider letter name knowledge, an important precursor to first- and second-language literacy development. It is difficult to achieve reading and writing fluency without achieving automaticity in this component. If the first and second languages are typologically close to each other, as is the case when Spanish-speaking children learn to read English, we would expect that familiarity with the Spanish alphabet would contribute to the acquisition of spelling in English. At the same time, because of typological differences, Arabic- or Chinese-speaking English-language learners may have greater difficulty with the English alphabet in English. It is likely, however, that with age and instruction, typological influences on spelling will dissipate, although they may still influence syntactic components. At the same time, underlying cognitive processes cannot be ignored. Individual differences in phonological awareness, phonological recoding, or phonological memory will affect the acquisition of spelling skills in English regardless of first-language background.

The Influence of Sociocultural Variables

The six sociocultural areas examined for this review were immigration status; discourse/interactional characteristics; other sociocultural factors; parents and family influences; district, state, and federal policies; and language status or prestige. In general, and with some exceptions, the studies reviewed in Part III indicate there is surprisingly little evidence for the impact of sociocultural variables on literacy achievement or development. However, this statement should be interpreted in light of the fact that studies have tended to be descriptive rather than trying to document empirical links between sociocultural factors and student literacy outcomes. In fact, one general shortcoming in this area is that relatively few studies have examined the impact of sociocultural factors on actual student outcomes. Even when student outcomes are reported, however, study designs often do not permit making strong inferences about the influence of sociocultural factors on literacy achievement.

Studies reviewed in Part III suggest that bridging home–school differences in interaction patterns or styles can enhance students' engagement, motivation, and participation in classroom instruction. This finding is certainly not trivial, but it is not the same as finding that bridging home–school differences improves literacy achievement or development. This relationship has not yet been demonstrated. Culturally meaningful or familiar reading material does appear to facilitate student comprehension. But culturally familiar reading material is a relatively weak predictor of reading comprehension, compared with the language of the material in relationship to student proficiency in that language. Students perform better when they read or use material in the language they know better. Overall, literacy outcomes are more likely to be the result of home (and school) language and literacy learning opportunities, irrespective of sociocultural factors such as immigration circumstances or students' cultural characteristics.

The literature reviewed for this volume supports three sets of conclusions, to varying degrees, about the role of the home in language-minority children's literacy achievement. First, language-minority parents express willingness and often have the ability to help their children succeed academically. For various reasons, however, schools underestimate and underutilize parents' interest, motivation, and potential contributions. Second, more home literacy experiences and opportunities are generally associated with superior literacy outcomes, but findings in this regard are not consistent, and precise conclusions are difficult to draw. Measures of parent and family literacy often predict child literacy attainment, but two studies found that parents' reading behavior was unrelated to children's literacy outcomes. Features of family life (e.g., domestic workload, religious activities) appear to influence the value children place on reading and their concepts of themselves as readers. Parent education is associated with literacy outcomes (see chap. 3 for discussion of the effects of socioeconomic status [SES] on literacy development at the individual level).

Third, the relationship between home language use and language-minority children's literacy outcomes is unclear. Correlational studies point to language-specific effects: Home experiences with the first and second languages are positively (but modestly) correlated with children's literacy achievement in the first and second languages, respectively, and negatively (also modestly) correlated with children's literacy achievement in the other language. Four studies, however, yielded findings that tended to counter this generalization. Overall, these studies provide insufficient basis for policy and practice recommendations.

Classroom and School Factors

Unfortunately, research has failed to provide a complete answer to what constitutes high-quality literacy instruction for language-minority students. However, what is evident from the existing research is that, as is true for language-majority students, instruction that provides substantial coverage of key components of literacy has a positive influence on the literacy development of language-minority students. Focusing instruction on key components, such as phonemic awareness, decoding, oral reading fluency, reading comprehension, vocabulary, and writing, has clear benefits. Some of the instructional research shows that enhanced teaching of these various elements provided an advantage to second-language learners; the more complex programs that were studied typically tried to teach several of these elements simultaneously and were also usually successful.

Although second-language literacy instruction should focus on the same curricular components as first-language literacy instruction, the differences in the children's second-language proficiency make it important to adjust instruction to meet the needs of second-language learners. The research has provided a sketchy picture of what some of these adjustments might be. For example, particular phonemes and combinations of phonemes are not present in Spanish, which means that young Spanish-speaking students learning to read in English might need more phonemic awareness work with particular elements than would be true for first-language learners. Given the large number of shared cognates between some languages and English, it may be wise for teachers to help second language-learners transfer cognate knowledge from a first to a second language.

Another important finding with regard to instruction is that successful instructional approaches do not improve the literacy skills of second-language learners as much as they do those of first-language learners. To learn literacy with maximum success, students need to have command of the kinds of literacy skills and strategies emphasized in these studies, as well as sufficient knowledge of oral English. It is not enough to teach reading skills alone, but instruction must teach these component skills *while* fostering extensive oral English-language development. That the oral English development provided in most programs is insufficient can be seen in studies that have revealed the success of many second-language learners in developing word recognition, spelling, and decoding skills while continuing to lag behind their first-language peers in reading comprehension and vocabulary. The more promising of the complex literacy instruction routines that have been studied (such as -instructional conversations) provide instructional support of oral language development in English along with high-quality instruction in literacy skills and strategies.

The patterns of learning across these studies suggest that the basic ordering of teaching is likely to be the same between first- and second-language learners—with greater attention to decoding required early in the process and relatively more direct and ambitious attention to comprehension later on. Vocabulary and background knowledge should be targeted intensively throughout the entire sequence (at one time, we might have claimed that this emphasis distinguished second-language literacy from first-language literacy, but recent research again suggests similarity more than difference). The need to develop stronger English-language proficiency as the basis for becoming literate in English argues for an early, ongoing, and intensive effort to develop this proficiency. It also should be apparent, given the transferability of some literacy skills, that teachers should build on these skills for students who have already developed these transferable skills in their home language.

Language-minority students who are literate in their first language are likely to be advantaged in the acquisition of English literacy. Just as the studies cited in Part II of this volume highlight cross-language relationships, the studies in chapter 14 demonstrate that language-minority students instructed in their native language (primarily Spanish in this report) as well as English perform, on average, better on English reading measures than language-minority students instructed only in their second language (English in this case). This is the case at both the elementary and secondary levels. It also should be noted, that recent evaluations of beginning reading programs used to teach non-English-speaking children to read in English are showing promising results. This is an important finding, in that first-language instruction is not an option in many schools where children speak multiple languages or instructional staff is not able to provide first-language instruction.

Findings from the effective schools and professional development research suggest that systemic efforts are important; the school change research indicates that outside change agents help the process, but also that change is difficult to achieve.

Assessment

The assessments cited in the research to gauge language-minority students' language proficiency and to make placement decisions are inadequate in most respects. For example, most of these measures do not assess development over time or predict how well English-language learners perform on reading or content area assessments in English. For teaching purposes, it may be that low-cost alternative assessments can be developed to measure aspects of students' literacy performance. For example, a cloze test based on students' literacy and content area instruction might provide information on students' vocabulary, semantic, syntactic, and discourse knowledge of English.

The few studies that were reviewed on standardized and standards-based tests point to linguistic and cultural issues that should be considered when such tests are used to determine the knowledge and skills of English-language learners. For example, these students may know different vocabulary items in each of their languages, making it difficult to assess their total vocabulary knowledge with an assessment in only one of the languages, or they may understand text in a second language, but be unable to communicate this understanding in that language. The research findings reported in Part III also provide some evidence that children understand text better if it is culturally familiar.

With regard to assessments used to predict the literacy performance of language-minority students, several researchers found that letter naming and tests of phonological awareness in English were good predictors of these students' performance in English reading. Because the researchers did not control for students' oral English proficiency or examine their native-language literacy development or performance on the same measures, however, the findings have to be qualified. Although several of the researchers used criterion measures to determine low performers or students with reading disabilities, findings that some low-performing language-minority students substantially improved their reading performance with instruction suggest that additional longitudinal studies are needed that test the predictors against language-minority students' actual reading performance. The evidence regarding teacher judgment and the nomination of language-minority students who might be in danger of dropping out or needing intensive reading services was quite limited. The findings suggest, however, that teacher nomination may be more reliable when teachers are asked to respond thoughtfully to specific criteria, rather than express their opinions spontaneously. Because teacher judgment and assessment play a significant role in the education of language-minority students, additional research needs to explore teacher judgment as an assessment tool.

Almost all of the researchers who dealt with the identification of language-minority students eligible for special education, language disorder services, or learning disability instruction recommended that language-minority students should be assessed in both languages. Very little research has focused on identifying older language-minority students with learning difficulties, and this is an important area for future study.

REFERENCES

Adams, M. J. (1990). *Beginning to read: Thinking and learning about print.* Cambridge, MA: MIT Press.

August, D., & Hakuta, K. (1997). *Improving schooling for language-minority children: A research agenda.* Washington, DC: National Academy Press.

Cooper, H. (1998). *Synthesizing research: A guide for literature reviews.* London: Sage Publications

Crystal, D. (1992). *An encyclopedic dictionary of language & languages.* Oxford: Blackwell.

Demmert, W. G., Jr., & Towner, J. C. (2003). *A review of the research literature on the influences of culturally based education on the academic performance of Native American students.* Portland, OR: Northwest Regional Educational Laboratory.

Ehri, L. C. (1998). Grapheme–phoneme knowledge is essential for learning to read words in English. In J. L. Metsala & L. C. Ehri (Eds.), *Word recognition in beginning literacy* (pp. 3–40). Mahwah, NJ: Lawrence Erlbaum Associates.

Fitzgerald, J. (1995a). English-as-a-second-language learners' cognitive reading processes: A review of research in the United States. *Review of Educational Research, 65*(2), 145–190.

Fitzgerald, J. (1995b). English-as-a-second-language reading instruction in the United States: A research review. *Journal of Reading Behavior, 27*(2), 115–152.

García, G. (2000). Bilingual children's reading. In M. Kamil, P. Mosenthal, P. Pearson, & R. Barr (Eds.), *Handbook of reading research* (Vol. III, pp. 813–834). Mahwah, NJ: Lawrence Erlbaum Associates.

Gersten, R., & Baker, S. (2000a). The professional knowledge base on instructional practices that support cognitive growth for English-language learners. In R. Gersten, E. Schiller, & S. Vaughn (Eds.), *Contemporary special education research: Syntheses of the knowledge base on critical instructional issues* (pp. 31–79). Mahwah, NJ: Lawrence Erlbaum Associates.

Gersten, R., & Baker, S. (2000b). What we know about effective instructional practices for English-language learners. *Exceptional Children, 66*(4), 454–470.

Glaser, B. G. (1978). *Theoretical sensitivity: Advances in the methodology of grounded theory.* Mill Valley, CA: Sociology Press.

Greene, J. P. (1997). A meta-analysis of the Rossell and Baker review of bilingual education research. *Bilingual Research Journal, 21*(2/3), 1–22.

Hedges, L. V., & Olkin, I. (1985). *Statistical methods for meta-analysis.* San Diego: Academic Press.

Johnson, B. T. (1989). D-stat: software for the meta-analytic review of research literatures. Hillsdale, NJ: Lawrence Erlbaum Associates.

Kamil, M., Mosenthal, P., Pearson, P., & Barr, R. (Eds.). (2000). *Handbook of reading research* (Vol. III). Mahwah, NJ: Lawrence Erlbaum Associates.

Lagemann, E. C. (2000). *An elusive science: The troubling history of education research.* Chicago: University of Chicago Press.

Lipsey, M. W., & Wilson, D. B. (2001). *Practical meta-analysis.* Thousand Oaks, CA: Sage.

Maxwell, S. E., & Delaney, H. D. (2003). *Designing experiments and analyzing data: A model comparison perspective* (2nd ed.). Mahwah, NJ: Lawrence Erlbaum Associates.

Metsala, J. L., & Walley, A. C. (1998). Spoken vocabulary growth and the segmental restructuring of lexical representations: Precursors to phonemic awareness and early reading ability. In J. L. Metsala & L. C. Ehri (Eds.), *Word recognition in beginning literacy* (pp. 89–120). Mahwah, NJ: Lawrence Erlbaum Associates.

Moss, J. (1994). *Using literacy in the middle grades: A thematic approach.* Norwood, MA: Christopher-Gordon.

Office of Bilingual Education and Minority Languages Affairs. (2001). *Report of the Spanish language research on multiple language literacy.* Newark, DE: International Reading Association.

Richards, J. C., Platt, J., & Platt, H. (1992). *Dictionary of language teaching & applied linguistics.* Burnt Mill, Harlow, Essex, UK: Longman.

Rivera, C. (1994). Is it real for all kids? *Harvard Educational Review, 64*(1), 55–75.

Rossell, C. H., & Baker, K. (1996). The educational effectiveness of bilingual education. *Research in the Teaching of English, 30*(1), 7–69.

Scarborough, H. S. (2001). Connecting early language and literacy to later reading (dis)abilities: Evidence, theory, and practice. In S. Neuman & D. Dickinson (Eds.), *Handbook for research in early literacy* (pp. 97–110). New York: Guilford.

Shavelson, R. J., & Towne, L. (Eds.). (2002). *Scientific research in education.* Washington, DC: National Academy Press.

Solano-Flores, G., & Trumbull, E. (2003). Examining language in context: The need for new research and practice paradigms in the testing of English-language learners. *Educational Researcher, 32*(2), 3–13.

Willig, A. (1985). A meta-analysis of selected studies on the effectiveness of bilingual education. *Review of Educational Research, 55*(3), 269–317.

APPENDIX 1.A: NATIONAL LITERACY
PANEL SUBCOMMITTEES

Subcommittee 1: Development of Literacy in Language-Minority Children and Youth
  Esther Geva
  Keiko Koda
  Nonie Lesaux
  Linda Siegel

Subcommittee 2: Cross-Linguistic Relationships
  Cheryl Dressler
  Fred Genesee
  Esther Geva
  Michael Kamil

Subcommittee 3: Sociocultural Contexts and Literacy Development
  Diane August
  Claude Goldenberg
  Robert Rueda

Subcommittee 4: Instruction and Professional Development
  Diane August
  Isabel Beck
  Margarita Calderón
  Frederick Erickson
  David Francis
  Nonie Lesaux
  Timothy Shanahan

Subcommittee 5: Student Assessment
  Diane August
  Georgia García
  Gail McKoon

Methodologists and Advisors to the Panel
  David Francis
  Frederick Erickson
  Donna Christian
  Catherine Snow

APPENDIX 1.B: STANDARD TERMS USED
IN WRITING THE NLP REPORT

1.   The following terms are used to describe subjects

Language minority refers to individuals from homes where a language other than the societal language is actively used, who therefore have had an opportunity to develop some level of proficiency in a language other than the societal language. Thus, children in the United States who come from Spanish- or Chinese-speaking homes are referred to as *language minority*. A language-minority student may be limited proficient in their second language, bilingual, or essentially monolingual in their second language (August & Hakuta, 1997).

Individuals who come from language backgrounds other than English and whose English proficiency is not yet developed to the point where they can profit fully from English-only instruction are called *English-language learners.* We have elected to use this term, first proposed by Rivera (1994) and adopted by the National Research Council's Committee on Developing a Research Agenda on the Education of Limited-English-Proficient and Bilingual Students (August & Hakuta, 1997).

The term *limited English proficient* (LEP) may be used, however, when we are quoting another source or citing legal requirements. Note that we have chosen to forgo the editorially convenient practice of reducing *English-language learners* to an abbreviation.

Children learning an unspecified second language are called *second-language learners.*

However, a child who is learning Dutch as a second language is referred to as a *second-language learner of Dutch.*

Children who speak a language as their first language are called *native speakers.* Thus, a child who speaks English as a first language is a native English speaker, a native speaker of English, or a native-English-speaking student or child. A child who reads English as a first language is referred to as a *native-language reader of English.*

Children who speak only one language are called *monolinguals* or *monolingual children.*

2.   The following terms are used to describe literacy or language components:

First-language vocabulary refers to vocabulary in a child's first language. Thus, for a native English speaker, this would refer to vocabulary in English.

Second-language vocabulary refers to vocabulary in a child's second language. Thus, for a Spanish-speaking child learning English, this would refer to vocabulary in English.

APPENDIX 1.C: ACCEPTANCE CRITERIA

Acceptance/rejection criteria (such as age of subjects, methodological criteria, etc.) are presented in the section of the instrument labeled *Elimination Round 1*. Elimination Round 2 was added to the instrument to give panelists an opportunity to reject articles that were not relevant to their research questions or did not meet the established methodological criteria. Criteria for accepting studies are reported next.

Elimination Round 1

Year published/produced
  Published after 1979.

Language of publication
  Published in English.

Publication type
  Peer-reviewed journals (all parts).
  Technical reports (Part III, chap. 11; Part IV, chaps. 14 and 15; and Part V).
  Dissertations (Part IV, chaps. 14 and 15).

Research focus
  Literacy (all parts except Part II, chap. 7).
  Oral language related to literacy (Part II, chap. 7).

Subjects' age
  3–18 years.

Language context for study
  Subjects are language-minority students (all parts).
  Target language is English AND English is the societal language (all parts).
  Target language is a societal language other than English (Part I, chap. 4; Part II, chap. 9; and Part III).
  Target language is English, but English is NOT the societal language (Parts I and II).

Duration of Program
  The programs included at least a 6-month span between the onset of instruction and posttests (chap. 14).

Methodological Rigor
  Reports empirical data (all parts).
  Data disaggregated for key study groups, and/or target group is 50% or more of sample (all parts).

Experiments and Quasi-experiments
  Study has control group, comparison group, or normative data (all chapters that include experimental and quasi-experimental studies).
  Comparison samples include more than four subjects.

Quasi-experiments
  Pretesting of outcomes of interest or other matching criteria employed; exception is regression discontinuity design.

Correlational studies
   Sample size 20 or more.

Elimination Round 2

Studies are rejected if:
   Serious confounds exist in the design of the research that prevent effects
   from being attributed to variables of interest.
   Not relevant to research questions.
   Other criteria for rejection noted by panelists.

APPENDIX 1.D: SEARCHES

First Search

The researchers searched the ERIC, PsycInfo, LLBA, and Sociological Abstracts databases using keywords derived from each of the research questions. The exact keywords used in the different databases varied because each database has its own categorization of keywords and subject headings. In general, key-words defining the population (English as a second language, limited English proficient [LEP], non-English speaking, bilingual, linguistic minorities, and/or immigrants) were combined with keywords describing the research questions. An additional search was made of MEDLINE and the MLA Bibliography using more general keywords, and very few articles were found in those databases.

Only articles in refereed journals and relevant references from the following seven major reviews were included: August and Hakuta (1997), Fitzgerald (1995a, 1995b), García (2000), Gersten and Baker (2000a, 2000b), and Kamil, Mosenthal, Pearson, and Barr (2000). *Ulrich's Periodicals Directory* online (www.ulrichsweb. com) was used to determine whether a journal is peer reviewed. For those that did not appear in Ulrich's, additional information was obtained online or through phone calls to the journal publishers. The first search generated 857 abstracts.

Second Search

The second search focused on obtaining formerly excluded document types, such as dissertation abstracts and technical reports—formerly excluded studies that measure teacher, rather than child outcomes; and formerly excluded studies that involve language-minority children in contexts where English is not a societal language. The second search added 696 abstracts to the database.

Supplementary searches of several databases were performed. In most cases, the relevant citations and abstracts were downloaded into EndNote or Excel and then imported into a FileMaker Pro database for coding. The ERIC search, how-ever, yielded a number of citations that lacked an abstract. The procedures for obtaining the missing abstracts are described next in the context of a description of the five supplementary searches that comprised the second search.

1.   Supplementary Search of ERIC

At the first meeting, the panel modified the research questions and the criteria for types of documents to be accessed. As a consequence, a supplementary search of ERIC was conducted to retrieve the following types of documents:

- Technical reports that describe the context in which English-language learners and language-minority students are educated. The search yielded 150 citations, 128 of which contained no abstract. Citations lacking abstracts were reviewed by a researcher, who identified relevant citations and obtained the corresponding abstracts. The abstracts of eight citations were judged relevant and added to the database. The remaining 121 citations were not pursued for the following reasons: already in the database (12), not about children 3–18 (35), about deaf learners (5), thought piece (15), review (18), book (3), other (32).

- Technical reports describing assessments. The search yielded 65 citations with no abstract. Two of these citations were judged relevant, and their abstracts were located and added to the database. The remaining 63 citations were not pursued for the following reasons: already in the database (18), not about children 3-18 (22), not about English-language learners (6), thought piece (7), dissertation or master's thesis (3), and other (7).
- Journal articles involving professional development designed to promote various components of literacy in English-language learners and language-minority children (34 citations).
- Journal articles investigating the acquisition of literacy in languages other than English by language-minority children (35 citations).

The researcher performed two versions of the searches for each question, searching ERIC by way of the Dialog OnDisc search engine. Keywords defining the population were combined with literacy component keywords and then crossed with keywords related to the domains under investigation (i.e., instructional context, assessment, professional development, and the acquisition of other societal languages by language-minority students).

Keywords used to define the population: English (second language)/limited English-speaking/non-English-speaking/LEP/Spanish-speaking or Spanish American/Chicano/Chicana/Latino/Latina/Hispanic/Mexican American/ Spanish culture/Cubans/Dominicans/Puerto Ricans/bilingualism/bilingual students/multilingualism/or language dominance

Keywords used to define the literacy components: reading, reader, literacy or illiteracy or biliteracy

Keywords related to instructional context: school surveys/national surveys/ teacher surveys/state surveys/statistical surveys/statistical significance/ predictor variables/national norms/analysis of variance/comparative analysis/ educational trends meta-analysis/benchmarking/trend analysis/robustness (statistics)/correlation analysis of covariance/data collection/feasibility studies/or state of the art reviews or document type-information analyses/ literature reviews/state-of-the-art papers or document type-statistical data

Keywords related to assessment: surveys/statistical analysis/statistical data/ statistical significance/statistical studies/statistical surveys/analysis of covariance/ analysis of variance/comparative analysis/educational trends/meta-analysis/ trend analysis/data collection/feasibility studies/national norms/robustness (statistics)/state-of-the-art reviews/correlation/benchmarking/ document type-information analyses/literature reviews/state-of-the-art papers/evaluation/ research/problems/methods/utilization/criteria/formative evaluation/curriculum-based assessment/educational assessment/testing/language tests/standardized tests/measures (individuals)

Keywords related to professional development/knowledge base needed for teaching: teacher education/teacher education programs/extended teacher education

programs/knowledge base of/teaching/knowledge level/teacher competencies/
professional development/training education/teacher improvement

*Keywords related to the acquisition of a societal language by language-minority
children:* second-language learning/second-language instruction/second
languages/ L2, interference (language)/language dominance/language problems/
language research/transfer of training/skill development/generalization/
language/communication/proficiency/oracy

    *2. Supplementary Search of PsycInfo, LLBA, Sociological
       Abstracts, MLA, and ERIC*
A supplementary search of PsycInfo, LLBA, Sociological Abstracts, MLA, and
ERIC for studies related to context, professional development, and the acquisi-
tion of a societal language by language-minority children was conducted.
Because this supplementary search retrieved articles that were relevant to
research questions other than those specifically queried, but that were not yet
in the database, it was decided to conduct complete searches of PsycInfo,
LLBA, Sociological Abstracts, MLA, and ERIC, as well as the British and
Australian Education Indexes. Keywords defining the population (language
minority, second language, language learners, bilingual, ESL, ELL, non-native)
were combined with keywords describing the research questions.

Question 1: Relationship between oral language proficiency and literacy:
language/reading/speech development, oral/verbal communication, vocalization,
voice, grammar, phonological awareness, phonemic awareness, comprehension

Question 2: Transfer of literacy skills from first to second language: transfer of
training/learning/cognitive processes, skill development

Question 3: Literacy development: reading, literacy, language acquisition,
second-language learning, writing, at risk persons, spelling, decoding

Question 4: Context for literacy development: classroom environment/teacher
education/knowledge base for teaching/professional development/ classroom
culture/teacher beliefs/language status/ cooperative learning/student
motivation/teacher training/teacher education

Question 5: Strategies and professional development for promoting literacy: educational strategies/theories, teaching methods, lesson plans, instructional
design/effectiveness/improvement

Question 6: Assessment: evaluation, testing, assessment, measures

    3. Supplementary Search of References from Seven Major Reviews
A supplementary search of the references of the seven reviews (August &
Hakuta, 1997; Fitzgerald, 1995a, 1995b; Gersten & Baker, 2000a, 2000b; García,

2000; Kamil et al., 2000) was conducted. This search identified an additional 32 articles pertinent to the contexts in which language-minority students are educated, the professional development of teachers of language-minority students, or the acquisition of a societal language by language-minority students.

4.   *Supplementary Search of Dissertation Abstracts*

In response to the panel's decision to include dissertations, a supplementary search of Dissertation Abstracts was conducted using UMI ProQuest Digital Dissertations. The citations included in this search were limited to work written in English between 1990 and 2002. Dissertations not covered by searching the Dissertation Abstracts, but that were found in other database searches (ERIC, LLBA, PsycInfo, MLA, and Australian Education Index), were also added. The dissertation search produced 272 citations, 23 of which were MA theses. The MA theses were deleted, resulting in 249 dissertations. As with the search for relevant journal articles, the search for dissertations used keywords defining the population (ESL, ELL, bilingual, linguistic minority, language minority, second language, non-native speaker, etc.) and combined them with keywords describing the research questions.

Research question keywords: literacy, reading, vocabulary, spelling, writing, phonological awareness, decoding, comprehension, teacher training, professional development, transfer, assessment, evaluation, instruction, language/reading/literacy development, instruction, oracy, environment

5.   *Supplementary Search of the Tables of Contents of Frequently Cited Journals:*   Because journals may not be consistently abstracted through the databases, a review of the tables of contents of the 16 journals most frequently cited in the first review was conducted. The researcher performed the search by locating the journal's Web site. In cases where no Web site existed, the researcher searched the electronic databases by journal. Table 1.D.1 lists the journal titles, the number of citations found in CAL's first search, and the number of additional articles found through reviewing the journal tables of contents.

All abstracts retrieved in the second search were imported into FileMaker and coded. The 857 abstracts generated by the first search were reviewed in light of modifications to research questions and inclusion criteria. This review resulted in the following actions:

- All articles that had been rejected because (a) they were not about English-language learning, (b) English was not the societal language, or (c) the outcome in the study referred to the teacher were reexamined. Those that could not be rejected on the basis of other rejection criteria (e.g., age or document type) were recoded entirely.
- Articles that involved children younger than age 3 were rejected.
- Articles that did not report research results, including thought pieces and literature reviews, were rejected.

TABLE 1.D.1
Results of Supplementary Search of Frequently Cited Journals

Journal Title	Articles From First Search	Additional Articles From Table of Contents Search
Bilingual Research Journal/NABE Journal	24	21
TESOL Quarterly	21	100
Reading Teacher	19	33
Applied Psycholinguistics	9	21
Language Learning	9	43
Language Arts	8	12
Reading Improvement	8	15
Bilingual Review	7	7
Elementary School Journal	7	5
Journal of Reading, Writing and Learning Disabilities International (Reading and Writing Quarterly)	6	0
Language Testing	6	23
Modern Language Journal	6	55
Reading Research Quarterly	6	5
American Educational Research Journal	5	4
Hispanic Journal of Behavioral Sciences	5	1
Journal of Reading	5	22

Third Search

A third search was conducted in response to changes in the criteria for acceptance of an article made at the second panel meeting. The research questions that guided the second search were also used in the third search.

The third search focused on obtaining technical reports that describe interventions (i.e., technical reports that are relevant to the effective practices domain) and formerly excluded studies that involve foreign-language literacy acquisition. Such studies had to meet several criteria for inclusion, explicit connection to reading, writing, or literacy; explicit statement of subjects' age(s); and relevance to the relationship between first- and second-language literacy or to the development of literacy (for the domains that included studies of English as a foreign language). All abstracts retrieved in the third search were imported into the FileMaker Pro database and coded.

In addition, the 1,553 abstracts generated by the first and second searches were reviewed in light of modifications to inclusion criteria. Specifically, all articles that had been rejected because (a) they were not about English-language learners/language-minority students, and (b) the target language was not a societal language were reexamined. Those that could not be rejected again on the basis of other rejection criteria (e.g., document type), that were relevant to the domains including studies of English as a foreign language, that specified subjects' age(s), and that were explicitly connected to reading, writing, or literacy were coded *accepted*. Fourteen abstracts relevant to the domain of effective practices and 11 abstracts involving foreign language literacy acquisition were added in this way to the set of acceptable abstracts.

TABLE 1.D.2
Results of third search of ERIC

Keywords (Foreign Language +)	References Found	References Added to Database
Literacy	16	0
Reading	113	1
Interference (language)	129	1
Transfer of training	82	0
Spelling or invented spelling	43	0
Vocabulary/vocabulary development/vocabulary skill/basic vocabulary	630	1
Writing	100	0
Phonological awareness (phonology/beginning reading/ decoding/reading achievement)	69	0
Literacy	159	0
Totals	1,341	3

TABLE 1.D.3
Results of Third Search of LLBA

Keywords (Foreign Language +)	References Found	References Added to Database
Literacy	103	1
Reading	250	1
Interference and transfer	250	1
Writing	250	0
Spelling	67	0
Decoding	53	0
Totals	12	3

TABLE 1.D.4
Results of Third Search of PsycInfo

Keywords (Foreign Language +)	References Found	References Added to Database
Literacy	8	1
Reading (oral reading + reading achievement + reading comprehension + reading development + reading disabilities + reading skills + reading speed + remedial reading)	79	1
Writing (writing skills)	4	0
Decoding	0	0
Transfer (negative + positive + learning transfer)	17	0
Spelling	6	0
Phonology + metalinguistics + language development	106	1
Totals	220	3

TABLE 1.D.5
Results of Third Search of Sociological Abstracts

Keywords (Foreign Language +)	References Found	References Added to Database
Literacy	0	0
Reading	4	0
Interference and transfer	0	0
Writing	7	0
Spelling	1	0
Decoding	0	0
Vocabulary	0	0
Phonological awareness	0	0
Totals	973	0

TABLE 1.D.6
Results of Third Search of MLA

Keywords (Foreign Language)	References Found	References Added to Database
Literacy (+ relationship to literacy + on literacy + rhetoric & composition)	11	0
Reading	15	2
Transfer	17	0
Writing	24	0
Spelling	0	0
Decoding	0	0
Totals	67	2

The third search consisted of two phases: a search of the Web site of the National Clearinghouse for English Language Acquisition (NCELA) and a third search of the databases of ERIC, LLBA, PsycInfo, Sociological Abstracts, and MLA.

1. Search of the NCELA Web Site
A search of the NCELA Web site was conducted to retrieve technical reports involving interventions. The researcher searched both the NCELA Bibliographic Database (which has a simple search engine) and NCELA's Online Library (which has a somewhat more sophisticated search engine). Neither of the search engines allows searching according to document type; in other words, one cannot specify *technical reports* or *research reports*.

The researcher searched by using the following combinations: intervention strategies and reading, intervention and reading and minority, intervention and reading and Hispanic, intervention and reading and Spanish, intervention and reading and LEP, and intervention and reading and limited English.

TABLE 1.D.7.
Results of fourth search of ERIC

Search	Keywords (+ denotes "or" in the search process)	References Added to Database
Title III Search	[Puerto Rico + Alaska/Alaska natives + American Indian/Native American + Pacific Islanders (Hawaii/Hawaiian/Native Hawaiian, Guam/Guamanians, Samoa/Samoans, Carolinian, Fiji, Kosraean, Melanesian, Micronesian, Northern Mariana Islander, Palauan, Papua New Guinean, Ponapean, Polynesian, Solomon Islander, Tahitian, Tawrawa Islander, Tokelauan, Tongan, Trukese, and Yapese)] AND [Literacy + Reading + Writing + Vocabulary + Spelling]	4
L1 Literacy Search	[First language + Native Language] AND [Literacy + Reading + Writing + Spelling + Vocabulary + Language Acquisition + Metalinguistic awareness/Phonological awareness]	1
EFL Search	EFL/English as a Foreign Language + Literacy + Literacy education + Family literacy	0
	Phonological awareness + Phonology	0
	Oral language	0
	Vocabulary + Vocabulary development + Vocabulary skills	0
	Reading + Decoding + Basal reading + Beginning reading + Content area reading + Oral reading + Reading ability + Reading achievement + Reading readiness + Reading skills + Reading strategies	0
	Writing	0
	Spelling + Invented spelling	
	Metacognitive awareness	0
		0
Creole Search	Haitian Creole	0
	Cape Verdean Creole	0
	Acadian	0
	Total	5

The NCELA search yielded 15 citations without abstracts. Five of these citations were judged relevant to Research Question 5; the abstracts of these five citations were located and added to the database. The remaining 10 citations were not pursued for the following reasons: already in the database (1), conference paper (3), book chapter (1), bibliographies (2), and other (3). The two bibliographies that resulted from the NCELA search were also reviewed, contributing an additional nine citations to the database.

TABLE 1.D.8
Results of Fourth Search of LLBA

Search	Keywords	References Added to Database
Title III Search	[Puerto Rico + Alaska/Alaska natives + American Indian/Native American + Pacific Islanders (Hawaii/Hawaiian/Native Hawaiian, Guam/Guamanians, Samoa/Samoans, Carolinian, Fiji, Kosraean, Melanesian, Micronesian, Northern Mariana Islander, Palauan, Papua New Guinean, Ponapean, Polynesian, Solomon Islander, Tahitian, Tawrawa Islander, Tokelauan, Tongan, Trukese, and Yapese)] AND [Literacy + Reading + Writing + Vocabulary + Spelling]	9
L1 Literacy Search	[First language + Native Language] AND [Literacy + Reading + Writing + Spelling + Vocabulary + Metalinguistic Awareness/Phonological Awareness]	1
EFL Search	EFL/English as a Foreign Language + Literacy	0
	Oracy	0
	Vocabulary	3
	Phonological awareness	0
	Spelling	0
	Metacognitive awareness	2
	Reading	2
	Writing	1
Creole Search	Haitian Creole and literacy	0
	Haitian Creole and reading	0
	Haitian Creole and writing	0
	Haitian Creole and spelling	0
	Haitian Creole and vocabulary	0
	Haitian Creole and phonological awareness	0
	Cape Verdean Creole	0
	Acadian	0
	Total	27

2. *Third Search of ERIC, LLBA, PsycInfo, Sociological Abstracts, and MLA*

A third search of ERIC, LLBA, PsycInfo, Sociological Abstracts, and MLA was conducted for studies related to foreign-language acquisition. Tables 1.D.2 through 1.D.6 present the results of the foreign-language search.

TABLE 1.D.9
Results of Fourth Search of PsycInfo

Search	Keywords	References Added to Database
Title III Search	[Puerto Rico + Alaska/Alaska natives + American Indian/Native American + Pacific Islanders (Hawaii/Hawaiian/Native Hawaiian, Guam/Guamanians, Samoa/Samoans, Carolinian, Fiji, Kosraean, Melanesian, Micronesian, Northern Mariana Islander, Palauan, Papua New Guinean, Ponapean, Polynesian, Solomon Islander, Tahitian, Tawrawa Islander, Tokelauan, Tongan, Trukese, and Yapese)] AND [Literacy + Reading + Writing + Vocabulary + Spelling]	9
L1 Literacy Search	[First language + Native Language] AND [Literacy + Reading + Writing + Spelling + Vocabulary + Metalinguistic awareness/Phonological awareness + Language Development]	1
EFL Search	EFL/English as a Foreign Language + Literacy + Phonology + Spelling + Reading + Reading skills + Reading Development + Word recognition + Phonological awareness Writing + Writing skills	0
	Vocabulary	0
	Metacognitive awareness + Words (phonetic units)	0
		0
Creole Search	Haitian Creole	0
	Cape Verdean Creole	0
	Acadian	1
	Total	11

Of the 3,574 citations called up from these searches, only 11 were added to the database. The remaining abstracts were not added for the following reasons: not about children ages 3 to 18, age of subjects not specified in abstract, not relevant to Research Question 2 or 3, and opinion paper or literature review.

Fourth Search

On the basis of testimony at the two outreach meetings and suggestions from panelists at the third panel meeting, a fourth search was conducted to include studies relevant to (a) literacy development of Title III populations and non-English-based-Creole and pidgin speakers; (b) development of first-language

TABLE 1.D.10
Results of Fourth Search of Sociological Abstracts

Search	Keywords	References Added to Database
TITLE III Search	[Puerto Rico + Alaska/Alaska natives + American Indian/ Native American + Pacific Islanders (Hawaii/Hawaiian/Native Hawaiian, Guam/Guamanians, Samoa/Samoans, Carolinian, Fiji, Kosraean, Melanesian, Micronesian, Northern Mariana Islander, Palauan, Papua New Guinean, Ponapean, Polynesian, Solomon Islander, Tahitian, Tawrawa Islander, Tokelauan, Tongan, Trukese, and Yapese)] AND [Literacy + Reading + Writing + Vocabulary + Spelling]	1
L1 Literacy Search	[First language + Native Language] AND [Literacy + Reading + Writing + Spelling + Vocabulary + Metalinguistic awareness/Phonological awareness + Language Development]	0
EFL Search	EFL/English as a Foreign Language + Literacy	0
	Phonological awareness	0
	Metacognitive awareness	0
	Oracy	0
	Reading	0
	Vocabulary	0
	Spelling	0
	Writing	0
		0
Creole Search	Haitian Creole	0
	Cape Verdean Creole	0
	Acadian	0
	Total	1

literacy for language-minority children, even if not coupled with second-language outcomes; (c) acquisition of English as a foreign language (EFL) for research questions being considered by Groups 1, 2, and 3; (d) Canadian and dual-immersion programs; and (e) vocabulary, metalinguistic awareness, and phonological awareness. The fourth search added 108 new abstracts to the database.

In response to Criteria 1, 2, and 3, a researcher conducted a fourth search of ERIC, LLBA, PsycInfo, Sociological Abstracts, and MLA using keywords defining the population combined with literacy component keywords. Tables 1.D.7 through 1.D.11 present the keywords used in the fourth search and the results.

In summary, as a result of the fourth search, the following studies were added to the database:

TABLE 1.D.11
Results of Fourth Search of MLA

Search	Keywords	References Added to Database
Title III Search	[Puerto Rico + Alaska/Alaska natives + American Indian/ Native American + Pacific Islanders (Hawaii/Hawaiian/Native Hawaiian, Guam/Guamanians, Samoa/Samoans, Carolinian, Fiji, Kosraean, Melanesian, Micronesian, Northern Mariana Islander, Palauan, Papua New Guinean, Ponapean, Polynesian, Solomon Islander, Tahitian, Tawrawa Islander, Tokelauan, Tongan, Trukese, and Yapese)] AND [Literacy + Reading + Writing + Vocabulary + Spelling]	0
L1 Literacy Search	[First language + Native Language] AND [Literacy + Reading + Writing + Spelling + Vocabulary + Metalinguistic awareness/Phonological awareness + Language development]	0
EFL Search	EFL/English as a Foreign Language + Oracy + Literacy	0
	Reading	0
	Phonological awareness	0
	Writing	0
	Spelling	0
	Vocabulary	0
	Metacognitive awareness	0
Creole Search	Haitian Creole	0
	Cape Verdean Creole	0
	Acadian	0
	Total	0

TABLE 1.D.12
Results of Querying FileMaker Pro Abstract Database to Retrieve and Recode Articles Relevant to New Criteria

Linguistic Group/Language Issue	Number of Previously Rejected Studies Recoded as Accepted
Title III populations	
First-language literacy outcomes not accompanied by second-language outcomes	4
Vocabulary, metalinguistic awareness, phonological awareness	32
Canadian and dual-immersion programs	9
Total	73

TABLE 1.D.13
Results of the Fifth Search for the Effective Instruction Group

Source	Journal Articles	Reports	Dissertations
Greene (1997)	1	3	1
Rossell & Baker (1996)	4	10	1
Willig (1985)	0	1	0
August & Hakuta (1997), chapter 6	2	5	0
OBEMLA report of the Spanish Language Research on Multiple Language Literacy (2001)	0	0	0
Reading and Writing	2	0	0
The National Research and Development Centers Web site	0	10	0
World Bank	0	3	0
Totals	9	32	2

- 23 references relevant to Title III populations (10 for Native Americans, 6 for Pacific Islanders, 3 for Hawaiians, 2 for Puerto Ricans, and 1 for Alaska Natives)
- 2 references relevant to first-language literacy development
- 8 references relevant to EFL literacy development
- 2 references relevant to literacy development of French-based-Creole speakers

A second type of search conducted as a result of the outreach meetings and panelists' suggestions involved querying the existing FileMaker Pro abstract database to retrieve and recode articles relevant to Title III populations, the development of first-language literacy, the acquisition of EFL, Canadian and dual-immersion programs, and studies of vocabulary, metalinguistic awareness, and phonological awareness (Items 1–5) that had been rejected according to prior criteria. Table 1.D.12 shows the numbers of previously rejected articles that were added to the database in accordance with the revised acceptance criteria.

Fifth Search

The fifth search focused on obtaining studies that met specific needs of the effective practices and assessment domains. The fifth search added 114 abstracts to the database.

For effective practices, the search looked for studies that examine the effects of the instructional use of the native language on the literacy development of language-minority children. Acceptance criteria for this domain were revised to permit the inclusion of studies that were published before 1980. The search involved the following steps. Results are shown in Table 1.D.13.

TABLE 1.D.14
Results of the Fifth Search for the Assessment Group

Source	Number of Relevant References Found
ERIC	13
LLBA	8
PsycInfo	2
MLA	0
Sociological Abstracts	0
CRESST Web site	9
Dissertation Abstracts	17
Solano-Flores & Trumbull, 2003	22
Total	71

- Searching for studies that are in relevant references from four key review articles (August & Hakuta, 1997; Greene, 1997; Rossell & Baker, 1996; Willig, 1985).
- Searching the National Research and Development Center Web site (http://research.cse.ucla.edu) using keywords such as *language minority, literacy, reading, second language, bilingual/bilingualism,* and *writing.*
- Searching the Web site (http://www.kluweronline.com) of the journal *Reading and Writing.* All studies posted on the Web were examined to determine their relevance to the questions being considered by the effective instruction group.
- Searching the World Bank Web site (http://www-wds.worldbank.org/default.jsp?site=wds) using the following keywords: *language minority, literacy, native/first language, bilingual/bilingualism, second language, reading,* and *writing.*

Because of the scarcity of studies relevant to the assessment of language-minority children's literacy skills, the assessment group decided to expand the acceptance criteria to include dissertations and to also consider studies that are relevant to content-area assessment for language-minority children. In addition, the assessment group requested a supplementary search of the five main databases (ERIC, LLBA, PsycInfo, Sociological Abstracts, and MLA) using specific keywords that had not previously been used. The search involved the following steps. Results are shown in Table 1.D.14.

- Searching the five databases using keywords defining the population combined with the following keywords: *content area, math/mathematics, science, academic achievement, cloze, recall, think-aloud, placement, identification,* and *miscue.*
- Searching the Web site for CRESST, the National Center for Research on Evaluation, Standards, and Student Testing (http://www.cse.ucla.edu/products/reports_set.htm). All studies listed on this Web site were examined for their relevance to the research questions being considered by the assessment group.

- Searching *Dissertation Abstracts* using the keywords defining the population combined with the following keywords: *assessment, test, content area, math/mathematics, science, academic achievement, cloze, recall, think-aloud, placement,* and *identification.*
- Examining references from a key review article (Solano-Flores & Trumbull, 2003) to retrieve studies relevant to the assessment group.

Sixth Search

The sixth search involved retrieving relevant references from the bibliography of a document flagged by a panelist on the culturally based education of Native American students (Demmert & Towner, 2003).

Seventh Search

The final search focused on obtaining studies published in 2001 and 2002. The researchers searched the ERIC, PsycInfo, LLBA, and Sociological Abstracts databases using keywords and procedures employed in the previous searches.

APPENDIX 1.E: ADDITIONAL INFORMATION ABOUT THE CODING INSTRUMENT

Development

A variety of instruments were reviewed for adaptation. They include those developed by various national organizations, including the National Reading Panel, the National Center to Improve the Tools of Educators (EQI Quality Review Tool), the American Psychological Association and the Society for the Study of School Psychology (Procedural Manual for Review of Evidence-Based Interventions), and the What Works Clearinghouse (Design and Implementation Assessment Device, Version 0.3). No instrument met the needs of the panel. Thus, Drs. August and Francis, in collaboration with panelists, created a coding instrument that could be used for coding a variety of study types, including group comparisons, correlational studies, and qualitative studies. It was also adapted to be especially useful for coding studies on a specific population of interest—in this case, language-minority students. During the development process, Drs. August and Francis solicited extensive feedback from the panel and used this feedback to revise the instrument. To establish interrater reliability, the research assistants used the instrument to code 12 studies that were randomly sampled from the six research domains and that reflected the different methodologies employed by the studies. A coding manual was developed to accompany the coding instrument. It includes instructions for coding, as well as a glossary of key terms.

Components of the Coding Instrument

Cover Page: bibliographic information, review information, abstract, accept/reject decisions.

Elimination Round 1: year published, language of publication, publication type, research focus, age requirements for inclusion, research domains, language context, initial screening criteria for methodological rigor, accept/reject decisions, and reasons for rejection.

Elimination Round 2: serious confounds exist that prevent effects from being reasonably attributed to the variables of interest; study is not relevant to research question; other criteria for rejection and explanation.

Focus of Study: author's stated research questions, panelists' comments on author's stated research questions, focus of study (literacy/oracy domains examined).

Setting and Sample Information (General): location of study, population density, school setting of the study, societal and target language information, and selection processes for the districts, schools, teachers, and students.

Setting and Sample Information (Group specific): general group description; number of participants; numbers of classrooms, schools, and districts; types of school programs from which sample was selected; age and grades; gender, SES, ethnicity, birthplace; attention/retention information;

language/literacy characteristics (both first- and second-language oral language and reading proficiency level and how measured); exceptional learner characteristics (e.g., learning disabled, academically gifted, etc.); classroom context, (classroom instruction context such as ESL pull-out and transitional bilingual program); and years of first- and second-language instruction and teacher characteristics.

Measures (measures or indicators used in quantitative and qualitative studies): name of measure, year published, developer, description, and variable types (dependent and/or independent).

Analyses Reported: types of quantitative and/or qualitative analyses used in the study.

Study Results: Three different categories are designed for different types of studies (group, correlational, and qualitative). The group studies category is further divided into intervention studies, program evaluation, and intact group/no manipulation studies. For each type of study, the study description, design features, and result sections are provided separately.

Coding and Electronic Database

The Microsoft Word version of the coding instrument was converted into a FileMaker Pro format. Once the objective criteria of the studies had been coded by the research assistants and exported to six databases aligned with the research domains, panelists, through passwords, were able to access the coded studies in their domain, review and comment on the work of the research assistants, and code the quality criteria for the studies in their domain. To access the database, panelists opened FileMaker Pro 6.0 and logged on to the database remotely using their password.

APPENDIX 1.F: QUALITY CRITERIA USED TO GUIDE THE REVIEW OF STUDIES INCORPORATED IN THE SYNTHESIS

GLOBAL RATINGS FOR QUANTITATIVE STUDIES

Sample

Sample is entirely adequate for the stated purposes of this study, keeping in mind representativeness, comparability, and attrition. I have high confidence in the evidence of this study based on the sample.

There are minor concerns in one or more dimensions, but no serious concerns in any dimension. I have reasonably high confidence in the evidence based on this sample.

There are serious concerns in one dimension or many minor concerns in one or more dimensions, but no near-fatal concerns; I have some confidence in the evidence based on this sample; I am willing to make tentative decisions.

Measures

All or most of the measures used are valid, reliable, and appropriate for the purposes of the study as it relates to the question(s) of this synthesis. I have high confidence in the evidence of this study based on the measures.

There are minor concerns about one or more of the measures, but no serious concerns about any measures with regard to validity. I have reasonably high confidence in the evidence of this study based on the measures.

There are serious concerns about one or more of the measures or many minor concerns about more than one measure. I have some confidence in the evidence of this study based on the measures.

Research Design

The research design and analyses are appropriate and well suited to the purposes of the study. I have high confidence in the evidence of this study based on the design and analyses.

There are minor concerns about the design or specific analyses, but no serious concerns about the design or analysis. I have reasonably high confidence in the evidence of this study based on the design and analyses.

There are serious concerns about the design or some of the analyses, but no fatal concerns. I have some confidence in the evidence of this study based on the design and analyses.

GLOBAL RATINGS FOR QUALITATIVE STUDIES

Overall quality of data collection
  Completely lacking or substantially inappropriate/insufficient.
  Lacking to a substantial degree, but marginally appropriate/sufficient.
  Lacking to some degree, but mostly appropriate/sufficient.
  Fully appropriate/sufficient.

Data Analysis and Reporting

Author has examined alternative or competing explanations for finding(s).

Finding(s) or theme(s) is supported by specific data.

There is information about the relative frequency of event(s) or occurrences (i.e., their typicality or atypicality).

The range of variation is reported and explanation is provided or examined.

Author used multiple data sources for triangulation.

2

Demographic Overview

Diane August

STUDENTS

As noted in chapter 1, the proportion of language-minority children and youth speaking a language other than English at home has dramatically increased—from 6% in 1979 to 14% in 1999 (National Center for Education Statistics, 2004, p. 7). In 1979, 6 million children and youth were language minority. By 1999, that number had more than doubled to 14 million. In 1999, of those who spoke a language other than English at home, Spanish was the most frequent language spoken (72%), followed by Asian languages (21%), and then other European languages (10%) (National Center for Education Statistics, 2004, p. 10). Although Spanish speakers are by far the largest group of language-minority students, Spanish is not the dominant second language in several states. According to Kindler (2002), for example, in 2000–2001, states reported that Blackfoot predominated in Montana, French in Maine, Hmong in Minnesota, Ilocano in Hawaii, Lakota in South Dakota, Native American in North Dakota, Serbo-Croatian in Vermont, and Yup'ik in Alaska. Kindler also notes that during this same school year, more than 460 languages were reported to be spoken by limited-English-proficient (LEP) students in the United States.

In 1999, one third of 5- to 24-year-old language-minority children and youth reported having difficulty speaking English. Moreover, native-born children who spoke a language other than English at home were more likely than their foreign-born peers to speak English very well (78% vs. 49%). Among native-born children who spoke a language other than English at home, those with native-born parents were more likely than those with foreign-born parents to speak English very well. Among foreign-born children who spoke a language other than English at home, the more recently the child had come to the United States, the more likely that child was to report difficulty speaking English: 74% of those who came between 1996 and 1998 spoke English with difficulty, compared with 49% of those who came between 1990 and 1994. Thus, children who had been in the United States 4 to 9 years had less difficulty speaking English than those who had been in the United States 0 to 3 years.[1] Finally, it should be noted that the prevalence of limited-English proficiency declines across generations to the point where it largely disappears by the third generation, at least in terms of percentage of the population.[2]

According to data collected for the annual Survey of State Educational Agencies in the United States, conducted by the Office of English Language Acquisition (Kindler, 2002), in 2000–2001, states reported that English-language learners[3] were enrolled primarily in prekindergarten through third-grade classrooms (44%), followed by the middle grades (35%) and high school (19%). California enrolled the largest number of English-language learners in public schools (1,511,646), followed by Puerto Rico (598,063), Texas (570,022), Florida (254,517), New York (239,097), Illinois (140,528), and Arizona (135,248). The Outlying Areas, however, have the highest overall percentages of English-language learners, with the Marshall Islands, Micronesia, the Northern Mariana Islands, Palau, and Puerto Rico each reporting more than 95% of their students having limited-English proficiency.

RANGE OF INSTRUCTIONAL AND ORGANIZATIONAL CONTEXTS

Patterns of segregation of English-language learners in some instances may impede educators' and schools' capacity to meet high new standards. According to the *Schools and Staffing Survey, 1999-2000* (National Center for Education and Statistics, 2002b), nationally more than half (53%) of English-language learners attend schools where more than 30% of their fellow students are also English-language learners. In contrast, only 4% of non-English-language learner students go to schools where more than 30% of the student body is English-language learners. These patterns of segregation appear to be reproducing themselves in the 22 "new-growth" states to which many immigrants moved in the 1990s. In the new-growth states, 38% of English-language learners attend schools where more than 30% of the student body is English-language learners. In the six major immigrant destination states (California, Texas, Florida, New York, Illinois, and Arizona), the percentage is much higher—60% of English-language learners are in schools where more than 30% of the students are English-language learners. These patterns of segregation are particularly striking, given the percentages of the population represented by English-language learners. In the six major destination states, only 13% of the students are English-language learners; in the 22 new-growth states, this figure is just 4%. Schools with high concentrations of English-language learners may have more difficulty than others demonstrating annual yearly progress toward standards-based goals.

---

[1]Data come from the U.S. Department of Commerce, Census Bureau, Current Population Surveys and supplemental questions asked in 1979, 1989, 1992, 1995, and 1999.

[2]Source: Tabulations by the Urban Institute from the Census 2000 Supplementary Survey (C2SS); includes Puerto Ricans.

[3]English-language learners are a subset of language-minority students; they are language-minority students who are limited English proficient.

English-language learners are educated in a variety of settings. Survey data (Development Associates, 2003) indicate that at the time of the survey, across program types, 11.7% of English-language learners received no services, 36.4% received some special language services, and 52% received extensive services.[4] The most common service types provided to English-language learners were some services, all English (24.7%); extensive services, all English (23.2%); and extensive services, significant native-language use (17%). Since the last survey in 1993,[5] there has been a significant decrease in the number of English-language learners receiving extensive services in the native language and a significant increase in students receiving extensive services in all English. Across all service types, the percentage of English-language learners receiving all-English instruction increased from 37.2% to 59.6%, whereas the percentage of English-language learners in predominantly Spanish instruction decreased from 40.1% to 20.4%. Native-language use was more prevalent in the elementary grades.

TEACHERS

Data on the characteristics and training of instructional staff reveal that an estimated 1,273,420 public school teachers instructed English-language learners in Grades K–12 during the 2001–2002 school year. This represents a dramatic increase over the preceding decade—from 15% of all teachers in 1991–1992 who worked with at least one English-language learner to 42.6% in 2001–2002 (Development Associates, 2003). The academic background and certification of teachers who worked with English-language learners were varied. Among those who taught at least one English-language learner, 5.6% had a master's or doctoral degree in a relevant field; 23.2% had bilingual education, English as a second language (ESL), or other relevant certification; and 9.8% were working with provisional credentials (Development Associates, 2003). However, the qualifications of teachers who taught three or more English-language learners improved: An estimated 45.8% of these teachers had at least a master's degree, and 53.7% held a bachelor's degree; an estimated 97.6% held one or more relevant certifications, including 18.1% who held ESL certification, and 11.1% who held bilingual education certification. Among those teachers who described their primary responsibility as ESL, 77.4% held ESL certification. From these statistics, it is apparent that most teachers who teach at least three English-language learners are certified. However, many whose primary responsibility is not ESL have received no training in working with this population of students; an issue is how well they have been prepared through regular coursework to carry out that responsibility.

---

[4]Some services refers to instructions designed for English-language learners that supports regular instructions they are receiving. Included in these service types are pull-out English as a second language (ESL) for less than 10 hours per week or having an aide who speaks the student's native language present in the classroom. Extensive services refers to those services in which a substantial portion of the student's instructional experience is specifically designed to address his or her needs, such as 10 or more hours a week of special ESL classes in which at least one subject area is taught a specially designed curriculum and approach.

[5]The 1993 survey used a different methodology from later surveys to collect the survey data, so some degree of caution should be used in interpreting the data.

With regard to professional development, 6 of 10 teachers who worked with at least three English-language learners reported they had received inservice training specifically related to the teaching of these students in the past 5 years; overall, they had received a median of 4 hours of such training. According to *The Condition of Education, 2002* (National Center for Education Statistics, 2002a),[6] in 1999–2000, only 12.5% of teachers who taught English-language learners had received 8 or more hours of training in teaching these students during the preceding 3 years.[7] From these statistics, it is apparent that the levels of professional development of teachers who work with English-language learners fall short of what is needed. Although a majority of these teachers had received some professional development, a large proportion (40%) had not, and the amount of training specifically related to English-language learners was limited.

In California, researchers have documented the limited amount of professional development teachers of English-language learners have received. After Californians passed Proposition 227 in 1998, large numbers of bilingual programs were replaced by English-only *structured immersion* programs. Since that time, many nonbilingual teachers have experienced a sudden influx of English-language learners into their classrooms. Yet, for the most part, they lack preparation and expertise to help them teach these students, according to a study released by the Center for the Future of Teaching and Learning (Gándara, Maxwell-Jolly, & Driscoll, 2005). In a survey of 5,300 California teachers, more than half of those who had up to 50% English-language learners in their classrooms had attended only one in-service training in bilingual or ESL methods—or none at all—over the past 5 years. The survey also found that the more preparation respondents had in serving English-language learners, "the more likely they were to cite challenges involving shortcomings in instructional programs and resources for these students." Other sponsors of the study included Policy Analysis for California Education (PACE) and the University of California's Linguistic Minority Research Institute (LMRI).

LITERACY OUTCOMES

The educational reading and language arts outcomes for English-language learners are discouraging. According to the U.S. Department of Education's *State Education Indicators with a Focus on Title I,*[8] in Arizona, where 15% of students are English-language learners, 12% of all students at the fourth-grade level fall far below standards in reading and language arts, compared with 35% of

---

[6]Excepted from U.S. Department of Education National Center for Education Statistics (2002b), Table 1.19, pp. 43–44.

[7]According to the survey, the numbers include both full-time and part-time teachers in traditional public schools in the United States.

[8]One source of state data is *State Education Indicators with a Focus on Title I, 1999–2000* (U.S. Department of Education, 2002). The profiles in that report focus on the status of each indicator as of the 1999–2000 school year. States reported student achievement results for the 1999–2000 school year for mathematics and reading/language arts at three grade levels, as specified by Title requirements before the program's reauthorization in 2002: elementary—grade 3, 4, or 5; middle—grade 6, 7, 8, or 9; and high—grade 10, 11, or 12.

English-language learners; at the eighth-grade level, 30% of all students fall far below the standards, compared with 69% of English-language learners. In Florida, where 10% of students are English-language learners, 42% of all students at the fourth-grade level are partially proficient, compared with 92% of English-language learners; at the eighth-grade level, 54% of all students are partially proficient, compared with 95% of English-language learners. In Texas, where proportionately more English-language learners are meeting state standards in reading and language arts at both the fourth- and eighth-grade levels (59% and 52%, respectively), only 13% (compared with 31% overall) of these students at the fourth-grade level and 2% (compared with 27% overall) at the eighth-grade level reach advanced proficiency in reading and language arts. Likewise, the *Survey of the States' Limited English Proficient Students and Available Educational Programs and Services 2000–2001 Summary Report* (Kindler, 2002) indicates that for the 41 state education agencies (SEAs) reporting on both participation and success of English-language learners in English reading comprehension, only 18.7% of the students assessed scored above the state-established norm.[9]

According to *The Condition of Education, 2003* (National Center for Education Statistics, 2003), dropouts from high school are more likely to be unemployed and to earn less when they are employed than those who complete high school. In addition, high school dropouts are more likely to receive public assistance than high school graduates who do not attend college. As defined by National Center for Education Statistics (2004), the *dropout rate* represents the percentage of an age group that is not enrolled in school and has not earned a high school credential (i.e., diploma or equivalent, such as a General Educational Development [GED] diploma). According to this definition, in 1999, among 18- to 24-year-olds not enrolled in a secondary school, 31% of language-minority students had not completed high school, compared with 10% of students who spoke English at home. Moreover, failure to complete high school is associated with ability to speak English. Among language-minority students, about 51% of language minorities who spoke English with difficulty had not completed high school, compared with about 18% of language minorities who spoke English very well. Furthermore, the lower the level of English proficiency, the lower the probability of completing high school.

These data are particularly troublesome because a fundamental restructuring of the American economy that began in the early 1980s has made postsecondary education or training the threshold requirement for good jobs. The trend toward job creation that favors at least some postsecondary education or training is evident in industry and occupational data (Carnevale & Desrochers, 2003). Just since 1973, the share of all jobs that require at least some college has risen from 28% to more than 60%. Postsecondary requirements are most prevalent in technology

---

[9]Twenty-five states used state-designed tests to assess English reading comprehension. Other commonly used tests include the Language Assessment Scales (LAS) (15 states) and Terra Nova (11 states). It should be noted that Kindler (2002) reports that the currently available state data do not offer a clear picture of English-language learners' reading achievements because the assessment tools and testing policies differ from state to state, as well as among districts within a state. Other difficulties in data interpretation result because the data are from different grades, and the grade designations were not reported to the Department of Education.

jobs, education and health care jobs, and white-collar jobs, which now comprise 60% of all jobs. Jobs on the factory floor have been declining, but the share that requires at least some college has increased from 8% to 31%.

IMMIGRATION IN OTHER COUNTRIES

Although the bulk of the studies covered by this report were conducted in the United States, studies from six other countries are also included: the United Kingdom, Canada, Australia, the Netherlands, Finland, and Israel.[10] Among these countries, Israel stands out because 36% of its population of approximately 6.7 million are foreign born. Since 1989, nearly 1 million immigrants have come to Israel from the former Soviet Union, and in recent years up to 50,000 Ethiopian Jews (14,000 in 1991 alone) have entered the country. Although Hebrew and Arabic are the official languages of Israel, other important languages are Yiddish, Russian, English, and Amharic.

In the other five countries, the net migration rate ranges from a low of .63 migrants per 1,000 in Finland to a high of 6.01 migrants per 1,000 in Canada. (The rate for the United States is 3.52 per 1,000.) Finland has quite a homogeneous population. By far the majority (93%) are Finnish speaking, with Swedes making up 6% of the population and the remaining 1% comprising a few thousand Sami (Lapps) and others. Canada is certainly more diverse, as indicated in part by the distribution of languages: Anglophone, 28%; Francophone, 23%; other European, 15%; mixed background, 26%; Asian/Arabic/African, 6%; and indigenous Amerindian languages, 2%.

Since World War II, both the United Kingdom and the Netherlands have needed to accommodate large numbers of immigrants from non-European countries. The largest minorities in the United Kingdom (making up 2.8% of the population) have come from former Commonwealth countries such as India, Pakistan, and the West Indies. The largest minority communities in the Netherlands are the Moroccans, Turks, and Surinamese. Even so, 83% of the population is Dutch.

REFERENCES

Carnevale, A., & Desrochers, D. (2003). *Standards for what? The economic roots of K–16 reform.* Princeton, NJ: Educational Testing Service.

Development Associates. (2003). *Descriptive study of services to LEP students and LEP students with disabilities: Volume IA. Research report– Text.* Retrieved July 16, 2004, from http://www.devassoc. com/pdfs/vol_1_text.pdf

Gándara, P., Maxwell-Jolly, J., & Driscoll, A. (2005). *Listening to teachers of English language learners.* Santa Cruz, CA: Center for the Future of Teaching and Learning.

Kindler, A. L. (2002). *Survey of the states' limited English proficient students and available educational programs and services. 2000–2001 summary report.* Washington, DC: National Clearinghouse for English Language Acquisition.

Library of Congress. (n.d.). *Country studies.* Retrieved July 16, 2004, from http://lcweb2.loc.gov/frd/cs/cshome.html

---

[10]Information for these countries that is cited here is found in U.S. Department of State (n.d.) *Background notes and Library of Congress* (n.d.) *Country studies.*

National Center for Education Statistics. (2002a). *The condition of education, 2002.* Retrieved July 16, 2004, from http://nces.ed.gov/pubs2002/2002025.pdf

National Center for Education Statistics. (2002b). *Schools and Staffing Survey, 1999–2000.* Retrieved July 16, 2004, from http://nces.ed.gov/pubs2002/2002313.pdf

National Center for Education Statistics. (2003). *The condition of education, 2003.* Retrieved July 16, 2004, from http://search.nces.ed.gov/query.html?charset=iso-8859-1&qt=condition+of+education+2003

National Center for Education Statistics. (2004). *Languages minorities and their educational and labor market indicators—Recent trends.* Retrieved July 16, 2004, from http://nces.ed.gov/pubs2004/2004009.pdf

U.S. Department of Education. (2002). *State education indicators with a focus on Title I, 1999–2000.* Retrieved July 16, 2004, from http://www.ed.gov/rschstat/eval/disadv/2002indicators/edlite-titlepage.html

U.S. Department of State. (n.d.). *Background notes.* Retrieved July 16, 2004, from http://www.state.gov/r/pa/ei/bgn

I

Development of Literacy in Second-Language Learners

3

Synthesis: Development of Literacy in Language-Minority Students

Nonie Lesaux and Esther Geva

Part I of this volume reviews research focused on the development of literacy skills among language-minority students and, in particular, the course of their literacy development; the predictors of their development, including second-language oral skills; and the distinction between learning disabilities and reading difficulties associated with second-language status. The reader is referred to chapters 4 and 5 for detailed descriptions and analyses of the studies that we reviewed. Five specific questions guided our review:

1. What are the differences and similarities between language-minority and native speakers in the development of various literacy skills in the societal language? (chap. 4)
2. What are the profiles of those language-minority students identified as having literacy difficulties? (chap. 4)
3. What factors have an impact on the literacy development of language-minority students? (chap. 4)
4. What is the relationship between English oral proficiency and English word-level skills? (chap. 5)
5. What is the relationship between English oral proficiency and English text-level skills? (chap. 5)

Language-minority students enter U.S. schools needing to learn oral language and literacy in a second language, and they have to learn with enormous efficiency if they are to catch up with their monolingual English classmates. Thus, understanding the basics of these students' literacy development, including the domains where they can be expected to learn in ways like their classmates and the domains where they show unique developmental trajectories, is of the utmost importance. Furthermore, given the overrepresentation of language-minority students among struggling readers, it is important to find mechanisms for early identification of those likely to struggle, so as to provide prevention services before they fall far behind. Finally, instruction for language-minority students should focus on those competencies that are most closely related to their ultimate success in reading and writing.

We know the characteristics of code instruction that work for beginning readers of English and can be presumed to be effective with second- and first-language learners. But normal classroom instruction does not tend to emphasize oral language proficiency for monolinguals, because they already possess well-developed oral language skills. How much emphasis should be placed on developing oral proficiency among second-language learners as a route to academic and literacy success? Only if we examine the relationship between second-language oral proficiency and second-language literacy in language-minority students (research questions 4 and 5) will we know for sure.

The vast majority of research on the development of reading and writing skills—including the cognitive processes at work (e.g., Adams, 1990; Chall, 1996; Siegel, 1993) and the effects of reading difficulties on children's knowledge and vocabulary (e.g., Stanovich, 1986)—has been conducted with native English speakers. Information about the normal developmental trajectories of literacy for language-minority students, as well as the variables that influence these trajectories, would contribute to evidence-based methods of literacy instruction for language-minority students and the establishment of common expectations for their literacy achievement.

In this chapter, we first present background information that guided our review. Then, following a brief description of the methodology of the review, we present a summary of the empirical findings relevant to the research questions. The final section focuses on directions for future research.

BACKGROUND

The basic framework for understanding literacy development derives inevitably from research conducted with monolinguals. Literacy development is a process that is both cumulative and componential, influenced by individual, contextual, and instructional factors, and starts before school entry and continues into adulthood.

Early skills that are related to reading and writing typically start developing long before children enter school; these include oral language skills, familiarity with print, an understanding of the concepts of print, an understanding of text structures, and the acquisition of knowledge. Learning how speech is represented in writing requires both the capacity to analyze spoken language into smaller units and learning the rules for representing those units with graphemes. While children are learning to decode and encode with fluency and accuracy, they must also attend to the process of reconstructing the writer's meaning. Ultimately, reading and writing become tools for learning and communicating knowledge and concepts, as well as for developing vocabulary and other skills.

It is critical in reading instruction to ensure that children have the opportunity to integrate learning the code (by developing skills in phonological awareness, letter knowledge, phoneme–grapheme relationships, spelling rules, fluency) with learning all that is necessary to read for meaning (by developing skills in vocabulary, world knowledge, discourse structure, comprehension strategies, purposes for reading). However, research on reading development typically differentiates these two aspects of the system, as do we in setting up the theoretical framework here and in reviewing results related to language-minority learners later.

Oral Language Proficiency

For language-minority learners, oral language proficiency plays an important role in the acquisition of skilled reading. Oral language proficiency is a complex construct that has been conceptualized and operationalized in diverse ways in research on English-language learners. It includes both receptive and expressive skills and can also encompass knowledge or use of specific aspects of oral language, including phonology, vocabulary, morphology, grammar, discourse features, and pragmatic skills. In addition, the term can refer to general aspects of language proficiency and has been assessed globally in some studies, using self-ratings or teacher rating scales, for example.

For purposes of this review, phonology, considered part of oral language, includes the ability to recognize and produce the sounds and sound sequences that make up language. Phonology that is a part of normal oral language development is measured, for example, by speech production tasks and neither entails nor requires the explicit or conscious ability to call up knowledge of the sound system as is required by phonological processing tasks.

Phonological Processing

An important precursor to word reading ability is phonological processing, or the ability to use the sounds of the language to process oral and written language; globally, one's phonological processing abilities have an impact on reading acquisition and comprehension (e.g., Stanovich & Siegel, 1994). Findings from longitudinal, cross-sectional, and intervention studies have converged to demonstrate the crucial role of phonological processing in acquiring reading skills and are skills typically assessed in studies of reading (e.g., Wagner & Torgesen, 1987; Wagner, Torgesen, & Rashotte, 1999).

Research has identified three specific aspects of phonological processing:

- *Phonological awareness is* the ability to consciously attend to the sounds of language as distinct from its meaning. For children learning to read in their first language, phonological awareness skills have been shown to be significantly correlated with initial reading skills, especially decoding (Adams, 1990). *Phonemic awareness* is a less inclusive term than phonological awareness. It is the "insight that every spoken word can be conceived as a sequence of phonemes. Because phonemes are the units of sound that are represented by the letters of the alphabet, an awareness of phonemes is key to understanding the logic of the alphabetic principle and thus to the learning of phonics and spelling" (Snow, Burns, & Griffin, 1998, p. 52). *Phonological segmentation* and *phonemic segmentation* refer to the methods of indexing phonological and phonemic awareness. Examples include identifying words that rhyme or that have the same initial (*cat–card*), medial (*cat–bad*) or final (*ca–sit*) sound, saying what is left after the initial sound of a word has been stripped away (*cat–at*), and blending sounds.

- *Phonological recoding* refers to the processes required when a nonphonological stimulus, such as a written word or picture, is converted to phonological output. It is typically measured by such tasks as rapid naming of letters, pictures, or numbers. Naming-speed tasks (referred to as rapid automatized naming [RAN]) assess the rate at which verbal labels for high-frequency visual stimuli are produced; these tasks measure linguistic fluency and speed of cognitive processing.

- *Phonological memory* refers to coding information phonologically for temporary storage in working or short-term memory; it is often measured using digit span or pseudoword repetition tasks. In this report, some studies used phonological short-term memory tasks that require individuals to simply repeat a series of digits, letters, or pseudowords but do not require any manipulation or additional processing.

Working Memory

Some of the studies reviewed in this report focused on working memory (WM) in addition to short-term memory (STM). Both WM and STM have been shown to be independently related to word recognition and reading comprehension performance (Swanson & Siegel, 2001). However it is important to note that they are not terms to be used interchangeably, and the two types of tasks are inherently different. Although both require attention to stimuli presented for recall to occur, the crucial distinction is that WM tasks demand active manipulation of the information presented while concurrently holding the information in memory (Baddeley, 1986), whereas STM tasks require only the direct recall of information as discussed in the previous section. WM is often measured using tasks, such as repeating a string of letters or numbers in reverse order to that presented.

Specific to a complex domain like reading comprehension, WM is vital as the reader must simultaneously decode words, remember, and actively process what has been read (Swanson & Saez, 2003). In the early reading acquisition stage, WM is critical as the grapheme–phoneme conversion rules for each segment of the word are recalled and held in memory as the reader decodes each part of the word (Siegel, 1993). Implicated in WM tasks is the individual's STM ability, in that STM ability has an impact on the amount of phonological information being held in memory for recall. Thus, the common link among any verbal memory task is the ability to store and/or access the sound structure of the language, thus drawing on phonological processing skills.

Word-Level Skills

Early in the process of learning to read, skilled readers begin learning to use letter–sound relationships to decode print. Simultaneously, they build up a sight vocabulary of words encountered frequently in text. Thus, word reading involves a combination of phonological and visual skills. Decoding skills are needed if students are to be effective when they encounter complex and unfamiliar words, especially as both the demands and volume of text increase as children progress through school. Similarly, building a sight word vocabulary in long-term memory (LTM) is important for word reading and also contributes to students' fluent, automatic word reading and text comprehension.

For most readers, increased practice with reading age-appropriate materials typically results in gains in fluency of word recognition (Kame'enui & Simmons, 2001). Of course, as fluency develops, it is important that children also begin to attend to the meaning of text to acquire knowledge and develop vocabulary, as well as skills related to literacy.

Spelling development parallels the process of learning to read and is, in fact, an application of sound–symbol relationships in a written format. Research conducted with native English speakers has shown that reading and spelling draw on common cognitive-linguistic processes, as well as unique orthographic processes (Berninger, Abbott, Abbott, Graham, & Richards, 2002; Fitzgerald & Shanahan, 2000). In the initial stages of learning to read, when children are acquiring an understanding of how to apply sound–symbol relationships to decode text, they typically also develop the ability to encode words.

As previously mentioned, learning to read and spell involves mastery of the association between printed and spoken forms of language (e.g., Adams, 1990; Ehri, 1998; Foorman, Francis, Fletcher, Schatschneider, & Mehta, 1998; Mann, 1993; Moats, 1994; Stanovich & Siegel, 1994). Phonological skills in particular, have been shown to be essential for learning to read and spell, not only alphabetic orthographies (e.g., Bradley & Bryant, 1983; Liberman, Shankweiler, Fischer, & Carter, 1974; Lundberg, Olofsson, & Wall, 1980), but also nonalphabetic orthographies, such as Chinese (Perfetti, 1999).

For the majority of readers, typically by the middle elementary years, word reading skills are well developed and fluent, and the primary focus of reading instruction shifts from "learning to read" to "reading to learn" (Chall, 1996). Research on reading difficulties has clearly demonstrated the cumulative nature of reading skills. That is, without mastery of decoding, fluency is compromised; if decoding and fluency are not automatic, the reader's ability to extract and construct meaning from text effectively and efficiently is compromised (Perfetti, 1985).

Text-Level Skills

It is typically not until the middle elementary years that readers begin to acquire a significant volume of concepts and knowledge as a result of reading. If a child is experiencing reading difficulties, the result may be a knowledge base and vocabulary that are insufficient for comprehension of the increasingly complex reading material students confront in the later elementary years and high school (Stanovich, 1986).

Reading comprehension poses the challenge of translating printed words into sounds in an accurate and efficient manner while constructing meaning out of what is being read. To comprehend text, readers must draw on their lexical knowledge (vocabulary), semantic knowledge (meaning), syntactic knowledge (language structure), and background and textual knowledge (Bernhardt, 2000). However, reading comprehension can be undermined by any number of factors, including the reader's knowledge and skills (e.g., reading accuracy and speed, vocabulary, background knowledge), text presentation (e.g., discourse structure, clarity, syntactic complexity), and factors associated with the activity of reading (e.g., motivation; see RAND Reading Study Group, 2002).

Writing, like reading comprehension, is an integrated text-level process that involves word-level skills (e.g., letter production, spelling); cognitive abilities, such as WM, linguistic awareness, and attention; and higher order skills, including planning, metacognition, strategy use, and self-regulation (Berninger & Richards, 2002; Wong, 1997). Just as effective reading comprehension is dependent, in part, on fluent, automatic decoding, effective writing development depends, in part, on automatization of low-level transcription skills (Berninger et al., 1992). Specifically, such skills as letter production must be fluent so that cognitive resources, especially WM, can be devoted to integrating all the other processes involved in creating written output.

Both cognitive and metacognitive processes contribute to writing development during middle school and high school (Wong, 1997). When creating written text, particularly expository text, students must generate discourse in the absence of the social context of oral communication (Berninger & Richards, 2002). As with reading comprehension, writing is influenced by sociocultural practices (Pérez, 1998), and learning the discourse styles specific to a particular culture is part of learning to write and comprehend written texts.

Variation Among Individuals

Although these broad principles conceptualize literacy development at the word and text levels, there is considerable variation among individuals in the way in which these processes occur. Many factors, internal and external to the child, influence the speed and trajectory of literacy development. A primary external influence, of course, is instruction—both formal instruction in phonological awareness, letter–sound correspondences, vocabulary, and comprehension processes, and the incidental instruction associated with language- and literacy-rich environments. Thus, although literacy development is conceptualized as the acquisition of increasingly complex skills and strategies, the effectiveness with which any individual child, whether language minority or not, develops into a proficient reader may depend heavily on his or her schooling experience, including exposure to appropriate instruction, both formal and informal. For language-minority children and youth, the development of literacy skills in a second language is arguably even more challenging than for native speakers. The same array of word- and text-level skills must be learned, although such learning may begin at a later age, perhaps without the same level of foundation in the cognitive and linguistic precursors to literacy or with sociocultural presuppositions that differ from those of native speakers and often by children facing social, fiscal, and familial challenges (see Part III). These children are often subject to poorly prepared teachers and suboptimal teaching (see Part IV).

Child-level factors that have been shown to relate to success in literacy development among monolinguals include literacy-related skills at school entry (Snow et al., 1998); oral language skills, including vocabulary (Stahl, 2003); background knowledge (Afflerbach, 1990); demographic factors (Hart & Risley, 1995; Snow et al., 1998); motivation and engagement (Guthrie & Wigfield, 2000); and the presence of dyslexia, learning disabilities, or language impairment (Lyon, 1995; Shaywitz et al., 1999). Diagnosable disabilities that interfere with normal reading development are estimated to occur in 5% to 15% of the monolingual population. Presumably, similar percentages of the bilingual population experience such difficulties, although over- and under-identification of English-language learners with learning disabilities related to the difficulty of accurate identification and assessment have complicated efforts to arrive at reliable estimates (see Part V).

METHODOLOGY OF THE REVIEW

The studies in the database that address the development of literacy in language-minority students are varied in paradigm, methodology, and the factors hypothesized to influence literacy development. In many ways, this variation reflects the complexity of examining second-language literacy development.[1] The bulk of the studies reviewed in Part I used correlational designs to examine the relationship between precursor and outcome variables or to investigate the link between second-language oral skills and reading/writing skills in the second language. A number of studies used between-group designs in which language-minority learners and native speakers were compared on indexes of oral language proficiency and literacy. The logic of this design is analogous to that of a classic experimental design in which one seeks to determine whether between-group differences on one variable (e.g., monolingual–bilingual) are associated with comparable differences on another variable of interest (e.g., written-word recognition). Failure to find comparable differences on both variables suggests the lack of a relationship between the variables in question, whereas finding comparable differences on both variables suggests a link. However, although these studies can suggest links between the variables of interest in this chapter, and thus have been retained for review, the evidence they provide is indirect only.

The methods used to summarize findings in Part I included both narrative analysis and the calculation of effect sizes; that is, average correlations or average weighted differences between groups were calculated when five or more studies with comparable data were available. It would have been preferable to report effect sizes for all comparisons between second-language learners and monolingual speakers or all correlations of subcomponents of literacy with indexes of oral language proficiency.[2] However, there were only two instances where five or more independent studies were available to contribute data to such calculations—studies that investigated differences between language-minority students and monolingual English speakers in word reading and spelling. Even when these kinds of effect sizes could be calculated, given the

---

[1]In examining the research on the development of second-language literacy skills, as well as the factors that influence second-language literacy skills, we reviewed a broad range of studies. Given that a large number of studies focus on development, broadly speaking, many of the studies reviewed here are also examined in other chapters. In other chapters, however, there is an emphasis on and a more in-depth discussion of particular aspects of the studies, such as the relationship between oral proficiency and literacy (chaps. 5–8), cross-linguistic literacy transfer (chap. 9), and the sociocultural context of literacy development (chaps. 11 and 12).

[2]In this chapter, when more than one relevant correlation was reported, the average of the correlations was used in the analysis.

small numbers of studies included in these combinations and the lack of sampling equivalence, no effort was made to provide a thorough analysis of the sources of variation in those correlations or comparisons. It should be remembered that these are not experimental data, and it is easy to overinterpret bivariate correlations or group differences in such circumstances. Appendix 3.A provides explanations of the reasons that particular research studies were not subjected to quantitative synthesis techniques.

Because of the limited opportunity to synthesize with quantitative techniques, detailed narrative analyses are provided. These narratives rely on the entire collection of studies on a topic or issue, rather than just the subset that could provide effect size estimations. It is important, however, to bear in mind that studies that use multiple regression often provide information that is more nuanced than information provided in simple correlations. Furthermore, a thorough meta-analysis of simple correlations of such small amounts of nonexperimental data, without clear sampling equivalence, has the potential of being more misleading than informative. Caution should be exercised, therefore, in interpreting effect sizes based on a small number of studies that report simple correlations.

Chapter 4 reviews studies comparing the development of literacy skills among monolinguals and language-minority students and those that identify factors influencing that development, with a focus primarily on cognitive and linguistic factors (chaps. 11 and 12 review the findings of research on sociocultural influences on the literacy attainment of language-minority students). The chapter also reviews the few studies that have focused on language-minority students identified as having literacy difficulties (chap. 17 reviews studies that examine instructional approaches for language-minority students educated in special education settings). Some of the studies reviewed in chapter 4 also include measures of underlying cognitive processes that support literacy, such as phonemic and syntactic awareness, and some research focused on cross-linguistic relationships between first- and second-language literacy; however, we did not focus on these aspects of the studies because they are addressed in chapters 7 to 9. With respect to those studies addressing the literacy difficulties of language-minority students, the majority included only measures of second-language literacy and related skills.

Chapter 5 reviews those studies focused on the relationship between second-language oral proficiency and various second-language reading skills in language-minority students. Although conceptually we could have subsumed the content of chapter 5 in chapter 4, we have chosen to review the research reported in chapter 5 separately because of the importance of oral proficiency in the development of literacy in second-language learners. Chapters 4 and 5 are both organized by literacy outcomes (e.g., word- and text-level skills), and findings are reported within a developmental framework, beginning with research on young children in the elementary school years, continuing with middle-school students, and finally high school students.

For chapter 4, studies included in the review were studies conducted with children who were language-minority students acquiring the societal language; for chapter 5, children in the samples were language-minority students acquiring English as a societal language or as a second or foreign language. All studies provided empirical outcome measures related to the research questions (for chap. 4, these outcomes were quantitative; for chap. 5, they were qualitative or quantitative).

SUMMARY OF EMPIRICAL FINDINGS

The findings of the literature reviewed in each of the following two chapters highlight the multidimensional nature of literacy development for language-minority students with respect to both the skills involved in successful reading and writing achievement and the broad range of factors that influence this achievement. The most salient and consistent finding across these two chapters is the overall paucity of developmental research, the one exception being those studies that have been conducted to examine the literacy development of elementary school students, mostly children in the primary grades. Thus, the reading development of later elementary or secondary school language-minority students has received scant research attention. A second finding is the limited amount of research focused on text-level skills. The findings reported in Chapters 4 and 5 allow us to draw relatively firm conclusions about the word reading development of language-minority children and youth. In contrast, the conclusions to be drawn from the findings of the limited research on reading comprehension and writing development of language-minority learners as compared with native speakers—and on the factors that influence these multi-dimensional skills—are much less definitive.

In the following paragraphs, we summarize the findings of the available literature with regard to the five questions listed at the beginning of this chapter.

Differences and Similarities Between Language-Minority and Native Speakers in the Development of Literacy Skills

We reviewed studies that compared (a) the word-level skills (i.e., word reading, spelling) and (b) the text-level skills (i.e., reading comprehension, writing) of language-minority students with those of their monolingual peers.

Those studies that compared the word reading skills of language-minority students and their native-speaking peers indicate that the two groups perform at similar levels on measures of phonological processing and word reading. As presented in chapter 4, the findings from the meta-analytic work in this area confirm that, on the basis of the research, there is little or no difference between the performance of language-minority students and their native-speaking peers on measures of word reading accuracy. Meta-analysis based on the data from 10 studies indicated that the first- and second-language speakers were equivalent in word reading accuracy (effect size = −.09, not statistically significant).

It should be noted that these studies were conducted primarily with children in the elementary school years, although they were from varying home-language backgrounds. The studies were conducted in different contexts, both linguistically and demographically (i.e., Canada, England, the Netherlands, the United States) and with samples of varying ages[3] (kindergarten through eighth grade) and ability levels; some studies employed a longitudinal design, whereas others were cross-sectional. The second-language learners were native speakers of Punjabi, Urdu, Arabic, Italian, Portuguese, various Asian language

---

[3]Although, as noted, most samples consisted of elementary school-age children.

backgrounds, and mixed-language backgrounds. Two of the studies reviewed examined the word reading performance of native Turkish speakers learning to read and receiving instruction in Dutch. In most studies, the authors note that the language-minority learners had been enrolled in schools for several months (in the case of studies that began in kindergarten) or for one or more years (in the case of studies conducted with language-minority learners beyond the primary grades) before being assessed. Across all studies reviewed in this part, factors considered in the interpretation of the findings, if reported, included language(s) of instruction, socioeconomic status (SES) of the language-minority and monolingual groups, print exposure, and method(s) of literacy instruction. We also considered the extent to which findings are generalizable.

Studies examining the spelling performance of second-language learners have found it to be similar to that of monolingual children, at least for English-language learners, who represent the majority of the samples in the studies reviewed in this section. Only one study reviewed examined the spelling development of language-minority students acquiring a language other than English; the findings from that study diverged from those of the others in that the spelling ability of the language-minority students was not as advanced as that of the monolingual children. Meta-analysis based on the data from nine studies indicated that the first- and second-language speakers were equivalent in spelling ability (effect size = -.13, not statistically significant).

Findings of studies on reading comprehension paint a very different picture from the ones focused on word reading and spelling. The few available studies that compared language-minority students with their native-speaking peers, conducted primarily in the Netherlands, yielded highly consistent results, indicating that the reading comprehension performance of language-minority students falls well below that of their native-speaking peers. This finding is not surprising; reading comprehension is compromised when skills such as oral language and relevant prior knowledge are insufficient to support understanding of the text. Although such factors can also compromise reading comprehension among native speakers, language-minority students reading in a second language are more likely to have underdeveloped skills in these areas, which would explain their overall difficulties with reading comprehension.

The few studies that examined the writing ability of English-language learners are highly diverse in the tasks and assessment criteria employed. As a result, we cannot use their findings to draw substantive conclusions about the writing development of language-minority students. Additionally, because none of these studies were longitudinal, it is not possible to extract substantive findings about the factors that influence the trajectory of writing development for language-minority students.

Factors That Have an Impact on the Literacy Development of Language-Minority Children and Youth[4]

Predictors of Word-Level Performance.   Second-language predictors of second-language word-level literacy skills among language-minority students in the primary grades are similar to those identified in decades of research on early

---

[4]Oral language factors that influence literacy development are addressed in the next section.

reading development conducted with native speakers. Skills such as phonological processing and concepts of print that predict later literacy development in language-minority students are consistent with those identified in studies conducted with English monolingual children. Research has also shown that phonological processing skills, including phonemic awareness, rapid naming, and phonological memory, assessed in the first or second language, predict word identification skills in English for language- minority students.

Predictors of Text-Level Performance. The large number of studies that examined factors that influence reading comprehension demonstrated that many variables at both the individual (e.g., background knowledge, motivation) and contextual (e.g., story structure, home literacy, demographics) levels influence the second-language reading comprehension of language-minority students. Although these studies typically did not include a direct comparison between language-minority students and native speakers, these same variables have been shown in other work to relate to monolinguals' reading comprehension.

Profiles of Language-Minority Students Identified as Having Literacy Difficulties

The preliminary findings suggest that in the area of word-level skills, there are similar proportions of language-minority students and monolingual speakers classified as poor readers. In addition to the similar prevalence of reading difficulty, each of the studies found that, with the exception of oral language skills, the overall profiles of poor readers in the two groups were very similar. As with monolinguals experiencing reading difficulties, both groups demonstrated difficulties with phonological awareness and WM. Thus, findings from studies with language-minority students with word-level difficulties suggest that underlying processing deficits, as opposed to language-minority status, are primarily related to word-level difficulties.

Interestingly, in the studies conducted with middle-school students with reading difficulties, the English-language learners designated as disabled readers had better scores on phonological measures than their native-English-speaking peers designated as reading disabled. This finding should be further investigated, because it differs from the findings on younger learners.

Relationship Between English Oral Proficiency and English Literacy

Word and Pseudoword Reading. As presented in chapter 5, studies conducted with elementary and middle-school students that examined the relative contributions of English-language learners' English oral language proficiency and phonological processing skills to their English word and pseudoword reading skills, identified differential contributions of the skills. Measures of oral language proficiency in English correlated positively with word and pseudoword reading skills in English but were not strong predictors of these skills. In contrast, various aspects of phonological processing skills in English (phonological awareness, rapid letter naming, phonological memory) were much more robust predictors of word and pseudoword reading skills. This finding emerged whether oral language proficiency was assessed with global measures of proficiency, measures of discrete language skills, such as vocabulary knowledge or grammatical sensitivity, or with teachers' ratings. It emerged from studies that used cross-sectional or longitudinal designs. The conclusion that there is only a modest association between English oral language proficiency and word reading skills in English applies to elementary and middle-school English-language learners who come from different language and instructional backgrounds. Only one study was conducted with English-language learners at the high-school level; findings indicate positive correlations between oral language proficiency and performance on word reading skills, as well as between oral proficiency and phonological awareness. Although oral language proficiency may not be a key predictor of word reading skills, it is likely to be correlated to some extent with underlying processing skills (phonological awareness, rapid naming, and phonological memory) that do predict word identification skills in both English-language learners and children learning to read in their first language.

Spelling. Only a handful of studies have examined the relationships between English oral language proficiency and the English spelling skills of English-language learners in the elementary grades. Nonetheless, findings of both correlational studies and studies comparing native-English-speaking students and English-language learners reveal that measures of English oral language proficiency, such as vocabulary and syntactic sensitivity are not strongly related to English spelling skills. This conclusion is tentative, however, given the small number of studies that have addressed this relationship. Even less can be said about the relationship between English oral language proficiency and spelling among English-language learners in higher grades.

As was the case for word reading, research suggests that various aspects of phonological processing skills in English, including phonological awareness and WM, play a significant role in the spelling skills of English-language learners. The evidence also shows that native English speakers and English-language learners who are poor and good spellers have similar phonological processing and WM skills despite differences in their oral language proficiency in English. Again, little can be said about the role of phonological processing skills in the spelling ability of older English-language learners; only one study explored this question with older students—in this case, Hebrew speakers learning English as a foreign language.

Reading Comprehension. In contrast with its role in word-level skills, well-developed oral language proficiency in English is associated with well-developed reading comprehension skills in English for those students who are reading in a second language. The evidence suggests that the components of English-language proficiency that are linked to English reading proficiency are English vocabulary knowledge, listening comprehension, syntactic skills, and the ability to handle metalinguistic aspects of language, such as providing definitions of words. The crucial role of oral vocabulary knowledge in reading comprehension was documented by four studies conducted with elementary or middle-school English-language learners. Research findings suggest that limited vocabulary knowledge is associated with low levels of reading comprehension in English, and English-language learners with a large repertoire of high-frequency and academically relevant words are better able to process written texts than English-language learners without such a repertoire.

In general, for students with higher second-language proficiency, second-language reading is a function of both second-language proficiency and first-language reading ability, whereas students with lower levels of second-language proficiency are less able to apply their first-language reading skills to reading in a second-language.

Finally, as noted elsewhere in this report, differences in the reading comprehension abilities of English-language learners can be attributed not only to oral language proficiency but to individual factors, such as cognitive ability and memory, word reading skills, contextual factors, such as SES, home-language use, and literacy practices, and to differences in instructional and other educational experiences. Parts III and IV address these questions more fully.

Writing. Unfortunately, a limited number of studies have examined the relationship between English oral language proficiency and writing in English. As is the case with reading comprehension, studies of elementary and middle-school English-language learners suggest that well-developed oral language skills in English are associated with better writing skills in English. Oral language skills of English-language learners that are related to writing include listening comprehension and vocabulary knowledge. Because phonological memory also plays a role, the research suggests that the link between second-language oral and writing skills is mediated by underlying phonological processing skills.

Limited research also suggests that there are many aspects of oral language proficiency that are important for proficient writing in English as a second language, including decontextualized language skills; grammatical skills; and knowledge of cohesive devices, such as anaphora, relativization, temporal reference, and conjunctions, which enable the writer to express ideas not limited to the here and now. In addition, the acquisition of proficient writing skills entails good spelling skills, metacognitive skills, such as audience awareness, and familiarity with and opportunities to practice writing different text genres. There is scant evidence, however, for the role and development of these kinds of skills in English-language learners of any age group.

Quality of writing may also be linked to first-language writing skills. One study conducted with upper elementary age students found that Spanish-speaking English-language learners with relatively better developed writing skills in Spanish were able to use Spanish discourse-level knowledge when writing in English, although their oral language skills in English were less well developed than their skills in Spanish.

Methodological Issues

Examining and conducting research on literacy development among language-minority students is a complex undertaking. In interpreting the research, several issues arise: it is critical to consider the variables that were not included in the study but may have played a mediating or moderating role in the results obtained; it is critical to consider that apparent predictors may represent a proxy for another skill or demographic variable that in fact explains the outcome; and, finally, it is critical to consider the quality and domain of the assessments administered in these studies. Overall, there is a lack of developmentally appropriate and reliable instruments for assessing oral language, literacy, and related skills for this population of students. In the absence of assessments of background knowledge or discourse knowledge, for example, it is not possible to speak to their role in literacy performance. In general, more high-quality assessments and assessments for more domains are needed to better understand the literacy development of language- minority students.

RECOMMENDATIONS FOR FUTURE RESEARCH

Because the population of language-minority students includes a significant number of students who have poor academic achievement as compared with their majority-culture peers (National Center for Education Statistics, 1995), it is imperative that more be learned about the development of literacy skills by this population and the nature of their difficulties.

Reading Readiness Skills of Language-Minority Students

We do not know whether emergent literacy skills vary by first-language background, amount of time in the country (for immigrant populations), or other factors, such as preschool attendance. Nor is it clear how early literacy skills might relate to later literacy outcomes given that only one of the longitudinal studies that included kindergarten measures followed the sample past second grade. It is important to look longitudinally to determine long-term outcomes, particularly with respect to reading comprehension. This research would help inform models of early identification and intervention for at-risk second-language learners.

Word-Level Skills of Language-Minority Students

A careful look at the findings of this review reveals many unanswered questions about the word-level skills of language-minority students. First, although it appears that word-level skills can develop to the same extent in language-minority and monolingual children in the primary grades, the extent to which this finding may be contingent on a particular type of literacy instruction provided to children is unclear. Although some studies are explicit about the instructional context, others are not. Also unclear is the extent to which language-minority students who achieve word reading accuracy comparable to that of native speakers also achieve a comparable level of fluency. Fluent and automatic word reading is critical for reading comprehension, and only one study in our review looked at the speed and efficiency of word reading. Finally, research is also needed to examine the development of spelling in older second language learners.

Text-Level Skills of Language-Minority Students

There is a need for more research on the development of text-level skill in language-minority students and how this development compares with that of monolingual students. Only seven studies in our database compared the reading comprehension of language-minority and monolingual children; five of these were conducted in the Netherlands, one in the United States, and one in Canada.

Despite the finding of research that reading comprehension is an area of weakness for language-minority students, minimal information is available on the nature of their comprehension difficulties and the specific skills having the greatest influence on reading comprehension (e.g., vocabulary, reading fluency). For example, more research is needed on how reading fluency in English-language learners impacts reading comprehension. Research is also needed to examine precursors to reading fluency and instructional practices that can enhance reading fluency in English-language learners across the school years. Additionally, research is needed on the role of demographic and contextual variables, such as years of second-language instruction in performance in this area. The research needs to be conducted with similar measures and across various populations of language-minority students.

Finally, research is needed to examine writing development in different age groups, including the role of spelling skills, decontextualized language skills, and the use of cohesive devices (such as anaphora, relativization, temporal reference, and conjunctions) that might enable language-minority student writers to express ideas not limited to the here and now. Equally important is instructional research targeting metacognitive skills (such as audience awareness) and familiarity with and opportunities to practice writing different text genres in the acquisition of proficient writing skills by language-minority students.

Learning Difficulties

Although learning disabilities are present in all groups, regardless of age, race, language background, and SES (Lyon, Shaywitz, & Shaywitz, 2003), estimates of the prevalence range from 5% to 15 % of the population (e.g., Lyon, 1995, 1999). Given the high proportions of language-minority students who are failing in school (National Center for Education Statistics, 2003), it is likely that many of them do not have learning disabilities. By and large, the answer to the question of who is an English-language learner with a learning disability is a problem of disentangling the interactions among second-language learning difficulties and such factors as resources in schools, opportunities to learn, the sociocultural context, and the quality of psychometric issues.

For researchers, the issues related to special education and language-minority students emphasize the need to answer related questions about issues, such as component skills that influence developmental trajectories, early predictors of difficulties, appropriate intervention, and the role of early screening for literacy difficulties.

The most prevalent criterion for reading disability used in the studies we reviewed was scoring in the 25th percentile or below on a standardized reading measure. Typically, no other information was provided about these children. In addition to the need to collect data on the salient linguistic and literacy variables that influence academic achievement for these learners, there is a need to investigate the sociocultural variables that affect the achievement of English-language learners in the United States (U.S. Department of Education & National Institute of Child and Human Development, 2003). Thus, in addition to academic variables, contextual variables, including those related to home language use and SES, instructional type (bilingual, ESL support, or mainstream), and characteristics of reading instruction, such as quality and language of instruction, should be considered when possible.

The Relationship of Oral Language Proficiency to Second-Language Literacy

It would be important to determine whether the finding that phonological processing skills are better than oral language proficiency as predictors of word reading skills is true of English-language learners at all levels of English oral language development, and whether it generalizes to word reading fluency.

It is important to note that, in general, the number of studies examining the relative contributions of oral language proficiency and phonological processing skills to word recognition skills in English-language learners declines as one moves from the lower to the upper grades. More research is needed on the role of English oral language proficiency in word reading for older students. Moreover, teasing apart the potential contributions of second-language oral proficiency, particularly lexical knowledge, aspects of phonological processing, such as phonological awareness and rapid naming, and orthographic skills, in older English-language learners is crucial, because the findings of such research could have important implications for instructional and assessment practices.

More research is needed, as well, on the extent to which typological similarities or differences between English and the learner's spoken and written first language mediate the relationships among specific aspects of second language, phonological and orthographic processing skills, and word recognition skills in English.

Additional research is needed to understand the developmental foundations of spelling skills in English-language learners, and the role played in writing by accurate and fluent spelling skills. Different languages and orthographic systems have different phonological, orthographic, and morphosyntactic features; all of these factors, as well as the age at which English-language learners learn to spell in English, may affect the nature and ease with which specific spelling and orthographic skills develop in English-language learners from different native-language backgrounds.

Given the findings of research conducted with monolinguals that established the strong relationship of oral proficiency to text-level skills, questions concerning the role of language proficiency in the domains of reading fluency and comprehension are particularly pertinent in second-language contexts, but there is almost no research in this area. These domains should be studied with English-language learners of different age groups, in different educational programs, and with different first-language backgrounds. Moreover, much more research is needed to identify the specific oral language skills that are related to aspects of reading comprehension, such as familiarity with text structure and text genre conventions.

One possible implication of the findings of the review of studies that focus on the relationship of oral language proficiency to reading comprehension is that, by focusing instruction on English-language proficiency, particularly academic vocabulary development, it may be possible to enhance English-language learners' reading comprehension skills. Improved reading comprehension, in turn, may expand vocabulary and other academically relevant language skills. This is an area requiring more systematic investigation.

Finally, more research is needed to analyze and achieve consensus on the construct of oral language proficiency. A number of questions deserve more careful examination and study: (a) whether there is an underlying ability or aptitude or a single construct that predisposes the second-language learner to do better on more complex skills; (b) whether language skills are hierarchically nested; and (c) what relationship exists between these constructs and other constructs, such as phonological processing, as well as specific literacy components at different points in development.

Recommendations for Study Design and Methodology

There is a need for systematic research that carefully examines the development of literacy by language-minority students, including the individual and contextual influences involved. The majority of studies in our review were cross-sectional in nature. Although longitudinal research is the most informative method when studying development in children, longitudinal research is particularly important for studying the development of literacy in language-minority students. In those students, language and literacy skills are undergoing rapid change, development of second-language skills may go hand in hand with decline of first-language skills, growth is likely to be nonlinear, and many of our questions can be answered only by tracking development and response to instruction over time.

In the following, we provide additional recommendations for designing studies that contribute maximally to our understanding of the development of literacy skills in language-minority students.

Groups Included in the Study. The majority of research on language-minority students has been conducted with children in elementary schools and predominantly in the primary grades. Studies of language-minority students in the middle-school and secondary school years are needed. For example, as noted previously, teasing apart the potential contributions of second-language oral proficiency and aspects of phonological processing, such as phonological awareness and orthographic skills, in older English-language learners is crucial. The findings of such research would have important implications for instructional and assessment practices, as well as for policy decisions pertaining to the education of these students. Likewise, research with older learners that carefully identifies the components involved in the reading comprehension process would also have important implications for practice and policy decisions.

For certain questions, it is crucial to include samples of both English-language learners and native speakers. As noted, many of the studies we reviewed would have been more informative had they included a sample of native speakers and examined whether certain factors have a differential impact on word- and/or text-level skills for the two groups. As an example, we do not know whether the impact of vocabulary or metacognitive skills on reading comprehension differs for these two groups and, if so, how it might differ. This knowledge would be particularly useful for planning effective instruction and interventions for language-minority students.

Further, language-minority students are a heterogeneous population. More research is needed to examine individual differences in the acquisition of literacy skills in this population. Specifically, research in this area should be designed to examine those factors most related to positive outcomes for these students and those most related to the achievement of children experiencing literacy difficulties.

Demographic Context of the Study.   Given what we know about the demographics of literacy achievement, it is also crucial that studies be explicit about the SES of the participants or at least the schools and neighborhoods in which the research was conducted. Further, if possible, studies comparing the achievement of language-minority students and native speakers should attempt to match the groups on SES; otherwise, this factor is likely to bias the results and confound their accurate interpretation.

Language and Instructional Context.   The research has conceptualized language-minority students primarily as a single, distinct population. Future research must begin to recognize the heterogeneity of this population with respect to language use in the home, school, and community. In particular, information should be provided about the intensity of exposure to the second language for the sample being studied. Children whose native language is the dominant language spoken in their neighborhood and by many other students at school, and who therefore continue to use and develop language and perhaps literacy skills in that language, are likely to have a different trajectory of language and literacy development from that of children whose home language is not spoken in their community.

In addition, if we are to interpret findings accurately, the educational context of each study should be described in sufficient detail. As noted, the development of literacy skills is directly dependent on and reflective of instructional practices.

Assessment.   Studies in this area have used a number of standardized and researcher-developed measures (see chap. 20 for a summary). With regard to the assessment of oral language proficiency among English-language learners, our review of the research indicated that two approaches have been used:

(a) a global approach based on general indexes of proficiency, teacher ratings, self-ratings, indexes of language use at home, and reports of language preferences; (b) an approach assessing specific aspects of oral language proficiency, including grammatical knowledge, syntactic awareness, vocabulary knowledge, quality of formal definitions provided to nouns, and listening comprehension of sentences or narratives. These two approaches were used in a wide variety of studies, including those that employed different measures of oral language proficiency, involved learners at different ages and with different first languages, and were conducted in different learning settings. Clearly, more research is needed to systematically examine the predictive and construct validity of global and specific aspects of oral language proficiency measures with respect to literacy.

To the extent possible, future research should employ measures that have proved reliable and yielded results related to the questions of interest. It is also important to design studies with the intent of replicating current findings and generating a cohesive body of research; doing so involves employing measures to which other researchers have access. Finally, assessing a range of skills within the language-minority population is essential, so we can know whether the difficulties of language-minority students are due to a learning disability, language background, SES, or instructional factors.

Analyses.   Some studies in our review examined the literacy achievement of groups of language-minority students spanning several grade levels in school. This may be a feasible and logical design, but when the study results are reported, performance should be disaggregated by grade level. Moreover, studies focused on literacy difficulties usually compare language-minority students with typical native speakers, when a comparison with struggling native speakers would be more important and informative. Most of the studies reviewed made the former comparison.

Much research in this area has been conducted with a quantitative approach and analytic techniques that have yielded findings *on the average*, thus not addressing individual variability. This is a particular problem in light of the heterogeneity of the language-minority population. To better understand developmental trajectories and individual differences, there is a need for studies that lend themselves to individual growth modeling with samples large enough to identify subgroups of students showing differentiated growth patterns. Further, a multifactorial approach would enable us to disentangle learner, textual, contextual, and instructional factors that may contribute to the development of reading comprehension in language-minority students.

Finally, we need to analyze systematically and reliably the errors that language-minority students coming from different language backgrounds make in reading, spelling, and other literacy skills. It is also important to compare these error patterns with those of errors made by native speakers. These error analyses may provide a clue to the specific areas in which language-minority students are having difficulty—errors that reflect more general developmental trajectories, as well as errors that reflect important information about first-language influence.

APPENDIX 3.A: STUDIES EXCLUDED
FROM META-ANALYSIS

Chapter 4: Development of Literacy

Phonological awareness skills of language-minority students
Only two studies (Cisero & Royer, 1995; Jackson, Holm, & Dodd, 1998) were identified.

Phonological awareness skills of language-minority students with literacy difficulties
Only four studies (Chiappe & Siegel, 1999; Chiappe, Siegel, & Wade-Woolley, 2002; Everatt, Smythe, Adams, & Ocampo, 2000; Wade-Woolley & Siegel, 1997) were identified.

Phonological recoding in lexical access of language-minority students with literacy difficulties
Only three studies (Chiappe et al., 2002; Everatt, Smythe, Adams, & Ocampo, 2000; Wade-Woolley & Siegel, 1997) were identified.

Print awareness skills of language-minority students
Only one study (Bialystok, 1997) was identified.

Word reading skills of language-minority students with literacy difficulties
Meta-analyses were not conducted on this topic, because of the seven identified studies, five (Abu-Rabia & Siegel, 2002; Chiappe, Siegel, & Wade-Woolley, 2002; Da Fontoura & Siegel, 1995; D'Angiulli et al., 2001; Wade-Woolley & Siegel, 1997) did not use quantitative techniques to specifically examine students with learning disabilities.

Spelling development of language-minority students with literacy difficulties
Meta-analyses were not conducted on this topic, because the identified studies (Abu-Rabia & Siegel, 2002; Chiappe, Siegel, & Wade-Woolley, 2002; Da Fontoura & Siegel, 1995; D'Angiulli et al., 2001; Wade-Woolley & Siegel, 1997) did not use quantitative techniques to specifically examine students with learning disabilities.

Factors that influence second-language spelling
Of the nine studies that investigated factors that influence the spelling development of language-minority students, one study reported no correlations (Chiappe & Siegel, 1999); in one study, the SEM model contains the full sample of language-minority and monolingual speakers (Verhoeven, 2000); in one study, correlations have partialed out (D'Angiulli, Siegel, & Serra, 2001); in one study, the correlation table does not disaggregate language-minority students and monolingual speakers (Wade-Woolley & Siegel, 1997); and in one study, the data reported (frequency of error types in writing) is not appropriate for meta-analysis (Cronnell, 1985).

First-language influence on second-language spelling
Only two studies (Cronnell, 1985; Fashola et al., 1996) report on this topic. It is more fully treated in chapter 9.

Development of reading comprehension skills of language-minority students
Of the five identified studies, one (Verhoeven, 1990) was not appropriate for
meta-analysis, because it does not report means and standard deviations for the
first- and second-language speakers.

Readiness and word-level skills related to reading comprehension
Five studies investigated readiness and word-level skills related to reading
comprehension: in one study, the SEM model contains the full sample (language-minority students and monolingual speakers; Verhoeven, 2000); in two
studies, outcomes are reported for an assessment that measures more than
comprehension (McEvoy & Johnson, 1989; Reese et al., 2000).

Understanding of literacy related to reading comprehension
Only one study (Aarts & Verhoeven, 1999) was identified.

Language use and first-language literacy related to reading comprehension
Five studies were briefly mentioned in this chapter (Hansen, 1989; Kennedy & Park,
1994; Nagy et al., 1993; Nagy, McClure, & Mir, 1997; Okamura-Bichard, 1985) but are
reported in more depth in other chapters. Studies designed to examine the relationship between first-language oral language proficiency and second-language literacy
are reviewed in more depth in chapter 8; those designed to examine the relationship
between first- and second-language literacy are reviewed in more depth in chapter
9, and those examining the impact of language use in the home on reading development are reviewed in more depth in chapter 11.

Meta-linguistic awareness related to reading comprehension
Only one study (Carlisle, Beeman, & Shah, 1996) was identified.

Reader strategies related to reading comprehension
Only two studies (Padrón, Knight, & Waxman, 1986; Padrón & Waxman, 1988)
were identified.

Background knowledge, cultural background, and motivation related to reading comprehension
Four studies (Droop & Verhoeven, 1998; García, 1991; Hacquebord, 1994;
Hannon & McNally, 1986) examined the influence of background knowledge,
whereas four studies (Abu-Rabia, 1995, 1996, 1998a, 1998b) examined the influence of motivation. Thus, no five studies examined the same construct and its
relationship to reading comprehension.

Educational context related to reading comprehension
Only three studies (Abu-Rabia, 1996, 1998a, 1998b) were identified.

Acculturation related to reading comprehension
Only one study (García-Vázquez, 1995) was identified.

Text factors related to reading comprehension
Only one study (Bean, 1982) was identified.

Demographic factors related to reading comprehension
Of the six identified studies, at least three do not report correlations (Buriel &
Cardoza, 1988; Collier, 1987; Ima & Rumbaut, 1989).

Multiple factors related to reading comprehension
Only one study (Connor, 1983) was identified.

The development of writing skills for second-language learners
Only four studies (Bermúdez & Prater, 1994; Davis, Carlisle, & Beeman, 1999;
Ferris & Politzer, 1981; Lanauze & Snow, 1989) were identified.

Chapter 5: Relationship Between Second-Language Oral Proficiency and Second-Language Literacy

L2 oral proficiency and L2 word and pseudo-word reading
Of the 11 studies investigating the relationship between L2 oral proficiency and
L2 word and pseudo-word reading, 2 investigate the acquisition of English as
a foreign language (Abu-Rabia, 1997; Muter & Diethelm, 2001), in 3 studies age
is partialed out (Gholamain & Geva, 1999; Gottardo, 2002; Gottardo, Yan,
Siegel, & Wade-Woolley, 2001), and in 2 studies no correlations are reported
(Geva, Yaghoub-Zadeh, & Schuster, 2000; Jackson & Lu, 1992).

L2 oral proficiency and L2 spelling
Of the six identified studies, two (Everatt, Smythe, Adams, & Ocampo, 2000;
Wade-Woolley & Siegel, 1997) compare outcomes in spelling for English-
language learners and native English-speaking children; they do not examine
relationships between second-language oral proficiency and spelling within
a sample of English-language learners. One study does not assess second-
language oral proficiency (Stuart-Smith & Martin, 1997); rather it examines the
relationship between phonological processes and spelling.

L2 oral proficiency and L2 fluency
Only one study (Jackson & Lu, 1992) was identified.

L2 oral proficiency and L2 reading comprehension
Of the nine identified studies, two (Beech & Keys, 1997; Peregoy & Boyle, 1991)
are quantitative studies but do not report correlations; one study is qualitative
(Jiménez et al., 1996); and two examine students acquiring English as a foreign
language (Dufva & Voeten, 1999; Lee & Schallert, 1997).

L2 oral proficiency and L2 general measures of reading performance
Only three studies (Pérez, 1981; Saville-Troike, 1984; Wilkinson, Milosky, &
Genishi, 1986) were identified.

L2 oral proficiency and L2 writing
Of the five identified studies, one (Yau & Belanger, 1985) is quantitative but
does not report correlations.

4

Development of Literacy

Nonie Lesaux with Keiko Koda, Linda Siegel, and Timothy Shanahan

This chapter focuses on the development of reading readiness, word-level, and text-level skills in language-minority students. In each of the sections, we first review those studies that compared language-minority students with their native-speaking peers. Where possible, within each of these sections, we also report on studies that compared language-minority students who had literacy difficulties with their native-speaking peers who were also experiencing literacy difficulties. Given the complexity of studying literacy development, as well as the significant individual differences in the acquisition of reading skills and the heterogeneity inherent among language-minority children and youth, we also report on studies that examine the skills and factors involved in the development of literacy in language-minority students. We consider factors such as age, instructional context, socioeconomic status (SES), and length of exposure to language and literacy in both the native and target languages as potential mediating factors in the development of literacy skills for this population. Although these factors are described more fully in other parts of this volume, they are referenced here as well to provide a more comprehensive account of development. (See Table 4.1 for a list of the other chapters in which these studies appear.)

The following research questions are addressed in this chapter:

1. What are the differences and similarities between language-minority and native speakers in the development of various literacy skills in the social language?
2. What are the profiles of those language-minority students identified as having literacy difficulties? Of those studies that compared language-minority students with difficulties and native speakers with difficulties, are there differences in prevalence by language group?
3. What factors have an impact on the literacy development of language-minority students?

TABLE 4.1
Cross-Reference: Factors That Influence Literacy Development

Appears in Chapter 4	Appears in Other Chapters
Factors Related to Word Reading Skills	
Arab-Morghaddam & Sénéchal, 2001	5,8,9
Chiappe, Siegel, & Gottardo, 2002	5,20
Chiappe, Siegel, & Wade-Woolley, 2002	5
Da Fontoura & Siegel, 1995	5,7,8,9
Gholamain & Geva, 1999	5,7,8,9
Gottardo, 2002	5,7,
Quiroga, Lemos-Britton, Mostafapour, Abbott, & Berninger, 2002	5,7,8
Verhoeven, 1990	No other
Verhoeven, 2000	No other
Factors Related to Spelling Skills	
Abu-Rabia & Siegel, 2002	No other
Arab-Morghaddam & Sénéchal, 2001	5,8,9
Chiappe & Siegel, 1999	No other
Chiappe, Siegel, & Gottardo, 2002	5,20
Cronnell, 1985	8
Da Fontoura & Siegel, 1995	5,7,8,9
D'Angiulli, Siegel, & Serra, 2001	No other
Verhoeven, 2000	No other
Wade-Woolley & Siegel, 1997	5
Factors Related to Reading Comprehension Precursor and Word-Level Skills	
Aarts & Verhoeven, 1999	11
McEvoy & Johnson, 1989	No other
Reese, Garnier, Gallimore, & Goldenberg, 2000	9,11
Verhoeven, 1990	No other
Verhoeven, 2000	No other
Understanding of Literacy	
Aarts & Verhoeven, 1999	11
Language Use and First-Language Literacy	
Nagy, McClure, & Mir, 1997	9
Kennedy & Park, 1994	11
Hansen, 1989	11
Okamura-Bichard, 1985	8
Metalinguistic Awareness	
Carlisle, Beeman & Shah, 1996	5
Reading Strategies	
Padrón & Waxman, 1988	No other
Padrón, Knight, & Waxman, 1986	No other
Background Knowledge, Cultural Background, and Motivation	
Droop & Verhoeven, 1998	No other
García, 1991	9,11,20

(Continued)

TABLE 4.1
(Continued)

Hacquebord, 1994	No other
Hannon & McNally, 1986	11,20
Abu-Rabia, 1995	11
Abu-Rabia, 1996	11
Abu-Rabia, 1998a	11
Abu-Rabia, 1988b	11
Acculturation	
García-Vázquez, 1995	11
Demographic Factors	
Buriel & Cardoza, 1988	8,11
Cahill, 1987	11
Fernández & Nielsen, 1986	No other
Ima & Rumbaut, 1989	11
Rosenthal, Baker, & Ginsburg, 1983	No other
Multiple Factors	
Connor, 1983	11

THE DEVELOPMENT OF LITERACY-RELATED SKILLS

Literacy development is a process that begins early in childhood, long before children attend school, and involves many different skills and experiences. Before formal reading instruction, the process of becoming literate includes, but is not limited to, the development of oral language skills (e.g., vocabulary, phonological awareness), experience with print, an understanding of the concepts of print, and the acquisition of knowledge. Many of these skills begin developing before reading acquisition and continue to develop once children learn how to read; thus, they have been shown to be related to reading both longitudinally and concurrently (for reviews, see Adams, 1990; Snow, Burns, & Griffin, 1998). Many of the skills do not necessarily involve print or formal instruction, but have nevertheless been identified as related to young children's reading ability (see Adams, 1990; Snow, Burns, & Griffin, 1998). The majority of studies that examined literacy-related skills of young children were focused on phonological processing; however, we also reviewed one study that focused on print awareness. It is important to note that few studies in our database were longitudinal in nature, which is a crucial design for better understanding development over time; it was decades of longitudinal research that identified those early skills related to later reading ability. Thus, in this section, we report on the results of studies conducted with young children that examined concurrent relationships among such skills as oral language, print awareness, and reading ability. Given the lack of longitudinal designs, the findings we report are based on cross-sectional research, examining skills concurrently.

Phonological Processing

As noted in chapter 3, an important oral language precursor to word reading ability is phonological processing, or the ability to use the sounds of the language to process oral and written language. Globally, one's phonological processing abilities have an impact on reading acquisition and comprehension (e.g., Stanovich & Siegel, 1994). Several reviews of research on phonological awareness have converged to demonstrate a strong relationship between monolingual children's phonological awareness and their eventual success in reading (e.g., Adams, 1990; Snow, Burns, & Griffin, 1998). For a small number of children (15%–20%), phonological awareness does not develop or improve with time (Fletcher et al., 1994; Francis, Shaywitz, Stuebing, Shaywitz, & Fletcher, 1996). Longitudinal studies with monolinguals have confirmed the persistence of deficits in phonological skills (e.g., Fletcher et al., 1994) for children with reading disabilities. Studies on adults with reading disabilities have also found that the difficulties associated with reading reflect a persistent deficit in phonological skills (e.g., Bruck, 1990, 1992; Wilson & Lesaux, 2001).

As noted in chapter 3, another aspect of phonological processing is phonological recoding in lexical access. Rapid naming, the predominant task in this category, has emerged as a predictor of early word reading ability (e.g., Bowers, 1995; Felton & Wood, 1989; Torgesen, Wagner, & Rashotte, 1994; Wolf, 1997). Much research has also focused on whether rapid naming, like phonological awareness, is an independent core deficit for some individuals with a reading disability (e.g., Lovett, Steinbach, & Frijters, 2000; Wolf & Bowers, 1999). Although rapid naming is a low-level discrete skill, the relevant reading skill that is related to rapid naming is word identification. Fluent oral reading of printed words is required so that resources can be devoted to the comprehension process. Previous research has identified rapid naming as an ability that is related to fluent, automatic decoding in monolingual English speakers (e.g., see Wolf & Bowers, 1999). For this reason, a measure of rapid naming is typically included among batteries of early reading-related tasks; in this report, some studies conducted with young children included a measure of rapid naming.

Given the linguistic nature of phonological skills, it is of interest whether these skills play a similar role in the reading acquisition for both monolingual and language-minority students. In particular, we were interested in whether, across studies, there is a group of language-minority students who appear to have significant difficulties in phonological processing, similar to the proportion and profile of monolinguals who experience such difficulties.

Phonological Awareness Skills of Language-Minority Students.   Given the available evidence, it is not possible to conclude how bilingualism relates to phonological awareness skills. Although most studies indicate that second-language learners tend to perform as well as or better than monolinguals on phonological tasks (see chap. 7), two studies found differences in favor of monolinguals (Cisero & Royer, 1995; Jackson, Holm, & Dodd, 1998). On the basis of the findings of the review in chapter 7, it would appear that this relationship is not simple; it depends on a variety of factors, including the age or stage of second-language development of the second-language learner, the child's relative proficiency in each language, the specific combination of languages the child is learning, and other mitigating factors, such as early language and literacy experiences. The variation among studies with respect to these kinds of factors may account for their divergent results regarding the relationship between bilingualism and phonological awareness. Nevertheless, studies that have examined the relationship between phonological awareness skills in either the first or second language and later reading ability have found that indexes of reading readiness, including measures of phonological skills, predicted aspects of language-minority students' later second-language reading development regardless of whether the measures were in the student's first or second language (see chap. 8).

Phonological Awareness Skills of Language-Minority Students With Literacy Difficulties. In addition to the studies that examined phonological awareness skills in heterogeneous samples of language-minority students (see chap. 7), four studies in our database examined the phonological processing skills of language-minority students in the primary grades who were classified as having literacy difficulties. The studies were conducted in Canada (Chiappe & Siegel, 1999; Chiappe, Siegel, & Wade-Woolley, 2002; Wade-Woolley & Siegel, 1997) and the United Kingdom (Everatt, Smythe, Adams, & Ocampo, 2000); in each, the language-minority students were acquiring English. Two of these studies (Chiappe et al., 2002; Wade-Woolley & Siegel, 1997) included mixed samples from diverse linguistic backgrounds: one (Everatt et al., 2000) focused on language-minority students who were Sylheti first-language speakers; one (Chiappe & Siegel, 1999) focused on language-minority students who were Punjabi first-language speakers. In each of these studies, as is the case for the majority of the studies reviewed in this chapter, only measures of second-language literacy and related skills were included; no information is provided about native language and literacy proficiency.

In each of the four studies, those language-minority students who were classified as having difficulties in spelling (Everatt et al., 2000) or word reading (Chiappe & Siegel, 1999; Chiappe et al., 2002; Wade-Woolley & Siegel, 1997) also demonstrated difficulties in phonological awareness, and these difficulties were very comparable to those of their monolingual peers who were similarly classified.

For example, Chiappe, Siegel, and Wade-Woolley (2002) found that first-grade English-language learners who were designated as reading disabled had scores on phonological awareness tasks (i.e., pseudoword repetition, phoneme recognition, and phoneme deletion and substitution) that were significantly lower than those of English-language learners from the same classrooms who were classified as average readers. In addition, the English-language learners who were disabled readers had scores similar to those of native English-speaking children who were also classified as disabled readers.

Likewise, Chiappe and Siegel (1999) found that English-language learners from Punjabi-speaking backgrounds who were classified as disabled readers had lower scores on tasks involving pseudoword repetition, phoneme recognition, and phoneme deletion and substitution compared with their English-language learner peers who were classified as average readers. In addition, the phonological awareness scores of the English-language learners who were having difficulty were similar to those of the native English-speaking children who were demonstrating significant reading difficulties. Individual reading skills, rather than language-minority status, were a significant correlate of phonological awareness skills.

Wade-Woolley and Siegel (1997) found that children designated as reading disabled had significantly lower scores than English-language learners who were average readers on a test that required them to imitate pseudowords and on a phoneme deletion test that required them to say a word without the first phoneme (e.g., pink without the /p/). Further, the English-language learners who were designated as reading disabled showed difficulties similar to those native English speakers designated as reading disabled.

Consistent with the findings of the three Canadian studies, Everatt et al. (2000), studying 7- and 8-year-old English-language learners from Sylheti-speaking homes in the United Kingdom, found that children who had low scores on a spelling dictation test had deficits in phonological skills, including the detection of rhymes and the repetition of nonwords, compared with their English-language learner peers matched on a nonverbal ability task who did not have literacy difficulties. On phonological tasks involving the repetition of words, the discrimination of sounds, or the recognition of which words started with the same sound, there were no group differences between the English-language learners and native English-speaking children who were identified as poor spellers.

These studies show that there is significant variation in phonological awareness skills among language-minority students. It is important to note that in each of the studies, the majority of the language-minority students studied had no difficulties in this area; moreover, in these four studies, there was a population of non-language-minority children similar in presentation and prevalence of phonological awareness difficulties to the English-language learners. On the basis of previous research with native English speakers (for reviews, see Adams, 1990; Snow et al., 1998), this group of students with phonological and reading difficulties in the primary grades is at significant risk for school failure.

Phonological Recoding in Lexical Access of Language-Minority Students With Literacy Difficulties. Some studies also examined the rapid-naming skills of language-minority students with literacy difficulties. Rapid naming of letters, numbers, or objects is one of a number of tasks that assess phonological recoding in lexical access. Given the emphasis on speed, this skill has been linked to reading fluency.

Three of the four studies discussed earlier included measures of rapid naming. In their study of English-language learners from diverse linguistic backgrounds, Chiappe, Siegel, and Wade-Woolley (2002) found that within their sample of first-grade English-language learners, children designated as reading disabled made significantly more errors and were slower than average readers who were also English-language learners on a measure of rapid naming of pictures. In their study with a similar design, Wade-Woolley and Siegel (1997) found that within their sample of second-grade English-language learners, poor readers made significantly more errors and were slower than average readers on a measure of rapid naming of numbers.

Similarly, in their study of 7- and 8-year-old Sylheti first-language-speaking children, Everatt et al. (2000) found that on a measure of rapid naming of pictures, the children in the low spelling group had lower scores than the children who were average spellers. It should be noted that among the average spellers, the English-language learners had significantly better scores on rapid naming than did the native English speakers.

These three studies included native English speakers and English-language learners who demonstrated significant difficulties in reading and spelling. Despite their differing linguistic backgrounds, the children did not differ in their rapid-naming ability. These preliminary findings suggest there is a group of English-language learners with literacy difficulties who, like native English speakers, also demonstrate poor performance on rapid-naming tasks.

Print Awareness

Another skill related to reading development is awareness of print. Research with monolingual English-speaking children has shown that having an under-standing of the symbolic function of print is important for reading acquisition. Research examining children's concepts of print focuses on children at the preschool age who are not yet literate, but may have prereading skills, such as alphabet knowledge and the ability to print and recognize the written form of their name (Snow et al., 1998).

Print Awareness Skills of Language-Minority Students.   One study in our database (Bialystok, 1997) examined children's understanding of print awareness and found that bilingual learners were better than monolingual children on their understanding of the general symbolic properties of written English. More specifically, Bialystok studied bilingual (French-English and Chinese-English) 4- and 5-year-olds and compared them with monolingual English speakers of the same age on their understanding of how print relates to language. For all bilingual children, both first and second languages were spoken in the home and the proficiency in the two languages was equivalent; in addition, the stories were available in both languages. All the children in the study had a similar level of understanding of the formal concepts of print (i.e., knowledge of the alphabet, letter identification, ability to print or recognize their name), and their general language proficiency as assessed by vocabulary was about the same. Despite these similarities, the monolingual and bilingual children showed different degrees of understanding of the general symbolic properties of written English. The bilingual children understood the general symbolic rep-resentation of print better than the English monolinguals—specifically, the invariance with which a print label represents an object, and the fact that the meaning of the print label does not change with the context. The 5-year-old Chinese–English bilingual children also showed a more advanced understand-ing of the symbolic representation of English print relative to the English mono-linguals. It should be noted that the samples of bilingual students were just as proficient in English as the monolingual sample of students. No information is reported on the SES of children in the sample.

The Development of Precursor Literacy Skills: Summary

It is difficult to draw strong conclusions about the nature of precursor skills that predict later literacy development in language-minority students from these studies, but we note that the findings are consistent with those of studies conducted with monolingual English-speaking children (for a review, see National Institute of Child Health and Human Development, 2000; Snow et al., 1998). In the aggregate, it is possible to conclude that, as with monolingual English-speaking children, word awareness, letter knowledge, and phonemic awareness are predictors of the word identification and reading fluency skills of language-minority students.

THE DEVELOPMENT OF SECOND-LANGUAGE WORD-LEVEL SKILLS

Word Reading

Research with monolingual readers has revealed that skilled word reading involves a combination of visual and phonological processes (Seidenberg & McClelland, 1989). Visual processes initiate word identification and trigger other processes—most important, decoding processes that require the reader to identify the correct sound–symbol correspondence (i.e., the correspondence between the sounds of the language and the printed letters). The greatest variance in reading comprehension performance is accounted for by the accuracy and speed of single-word reading (Perfetti, 1985). If a child has difficulty with word reading, these problems will have a negative impact on reading comprehension. To gain meaning from a text to the same extent as normally achieving peers, it is important that children's word reading is characterized by automaticity (Kame'enui & Simmons, 2001). Children with highly automatized word recognition abilities are able to allocate more resources to text comprehension (e.g., Adams, 1990).

When examining word reading development for all learners, it is also important to consider their ability to read pseudowords (combinations of letters that can be pronounced, but are not real words in the language in question). This provides insight into basic decoding skills in the absence of meaningful context or memory for words; readers need to be able to develop this ability because, although using context can be helpful and necessary in some cases, relying on context is frequently misleading (Share, 1995). Those studies that have examined the word reading skills of native speakers and language-minority students have used measures of word and pseudoword reading that typically involve a list of words of increasing difficulty that the child reads aloud. Context-free word recognition is a process that clearly differentiates good and poor readers (Stanovich, 1980), and for the majority of individuals with a reading disability, their difficulties stem from deficits in basic word-level skills, which ultimately impede effective reading comprehension and vocabulary development (e.g., Shankweiler, 1989). Despite the importance of word reading for reading comprehension, even if a child is able to read or pronounce words in the text, he or she may not necessarily know what they mean. Thus, word reading is considered a necessary but not sufficient skill for reading comprehension.

For this review, we identified studies that focused on the development of word reading for second-language learners. Whereas some studies were designed to compare the reading skills of second-language learners with those of their monolingual peers, others focused strictly on the reading achievement of second-language learners and the variables that had an influence on that ability. Some studies in our database compared the word reading skills of English-language learners who had word reading difficulties and their monolingual English-speaking peers with similar difficulties.

Overview of Findings: Word Reading Skills of Language-Minority Students. Intensity and length of exposure to the second language appear to be important for the development of word reading skills. Yet even after some minimal exposure to second-language reading, word reading skills appear to be equivalent in monolingual and language-minority students. This is the case despite the fact that, in the majority of studies that identified similar word reading skills in native speakers and language-minority students, the latter children performed more poorly on measures of oral language proficiency, such as syntactic awareness and vocabulary.

It appears that having an alphabetically transparent language as a first language and acquiring some reading skills in that language may facilitate the acquisition of second-language decoding skills (see chap. 9 for a review of these studies). Instruction that emphasizes the development of phonological awareness and stresses systematic phonics instruction in the second language may also help develop word reading skills, but the relevant studies reviewed in this chapter (Chiappe, Siegel, & Gottardo, 2002; Chiappe, Siegel, & Wade-Woolley, 2002) do not provide a direct test of this hypothesis (see chap. 15 for a review of intervention studies). In general, available evidence indicates that word recognition and pseudoword reading may be equivalent skills for language-minority children and native speakers.

This generalization is supported by the fact that the studies were conducted in different contexts (i.e., Canada, England, the Netherlands, the United States), with samples of varying ages (kindergarten through eighth grade) and ability levels; some studies employed a longitudinal design, whereas others were cross-sectional. The studies included samples of English-language learners who were native speakers of Punjabi (Chiappe & Siegel, 1999), Urdu (Mumtaz & Humphreys, 2001), Arabic (Abu-Rabia & Siegel, 2002), Italian (D'Angiulli, Siegel, & Serra, 2001), and Portuguese (Da Fontoura & Siegel, 1995); who were from various Asian-language backgrounds (Geva, Yaghoub-Zadeh, & Schuster, 2000); and who came from mixed-language backgrounds (Chiappe, Siegel, & Wade-Woolley, 2002; Wade-Woolley & Siegel, 1997). Two of the studies reviewed examined the word reading development of Turkish first-language speakers learning to read and receiving instruction in Dutch (Verhoeven, 1990, 2000). Factors considered in the interpretation of the findings, if reported, included language(s) of instruction, SES of the language-minority and monolingual groups, print exposure, and method(s) of literacy instruction.

It is important to specify that the finding that language-minority students are comparable to native speakers in word reading across languages, locations, and age groups was robust over a variety of measures of accuracy of word identification; however, none of the studies reviewed included a measure of speed of word identification.

Given that language-minority students in today's classrooms are learning to read in a language in which they are not yet proficient, it is also important to examine the prevalence and nature of word reading and spelling difficulties for this group. Several studies in our database demonstrated that within samples of English-language learners, there is a group of children who experience difficulties with word reading and spelling in a very similar manner to native speakers. Together, the studies that support this finding included English-language learners in Canada (Abu-Rabia & Siegel, 2002; Chiappe & Siegel, 1999; Chiappe, Siegel, & Wade-Wooley, 2002; D'Angiulli et al., 2001; Da Fontoura & Siegel, 1995; Wade-Woolley & Siegel, 1997), the United States (Miramontes, 1987), and the United Kingdom (Everatt et al., 2000). These studies included samples of primary-grade students (Chiappe & Siegel, 1999; Chiappe, Siegel, & Wade-Woolley, 2002; Wade-Woolley & Siegel, 1997) and students in the middle elementary school years (Abu-Rabia & Siegel, 2002; D'Angiulli et al., 2001; Da Fontoura & Siegel, 1995; Miramontes, 1987). None of the studies in our database that examined the word-level skills of second-language learners experiencing difficulties included a sample of students of secondary school age. Among the English-language learners across the studies, there were first-language speakers of Arabic (Abu-Rabia & Siegel, 2002), Italian (D'Angiulli et al., 2001), Portuguese (Da Fontoura & Siegel, 1995), Punjabi (Chiappe & Siegel, 1999), and Spanish (Miramontes, 1987). Two of the studies (Chiappe, Siegel, & Wade-Woolley, 2002; Wade-Woolley & Siegel, 1997) included mixed samples of children from diverse linguistic backgrounds.

Word Reading Skills of Language-Minority Students. Eight studies examined the word reading ability of English-language learners in the primary grades (Chiappe, Siegel, & Gottardo, 2002; Chiappe, Siegel, & Wade-Woolley, 2002; Geva et al., 2000; Jackson & Lu, 1992; Limbos & Geva, 2001; Verhoeven, 1990, 2000; Wade-Woolley & Siegel, 1997). All but one of the studies (Jackson & Lu, 1992) involved students enrolled in schools in Canada, where all English-language learners receive English instruction in mainstream classrooms from school entry. In each of the studies, the English-language learners and the monolingual English speakers in the same classrooms demonstrated equivalent word and pseudoword reading abilities.

Two of the studies reviewed (Chiappe, Siegel, & Gottardo, 2002; Chiappe, Siegel, & Wade-Woolley, 2002) compared the development of literacy skills in a group of English-language learners and their monolingual English classmates in a school district in Canada. Most of the English-language learners were immigrants to Canada who spoke a language other than English at home with their parents, siblings, and extended families. Chiappe, Siegel, and Gottardo (2002) found that in kindergarten, English-language learners performed similarly to English monolinguals on a letter identification task and a simple word reading task, but more poorly on measures of oral proficiency; furthermore, between the fall and spring of kindergarten, the English-language learners showed greater growth in literacy skills than their monolingual English-speaking classmates. This latter pattern, despite lower oral proficiency for the English-language learners, was also evident in performance improvement from kindergarten to the spring of first grade (Chiappe, Siegel, & Wade-Woolley, 2002). The longitudinal findings also indicate that by first grade, there were no differences between the English-language learners and the monolingual English speakers on measures of word and pseudoword reading.

Three other studies also revealed the similarity between the word and pseudoword reading ability of English-language learners and monolingual

English- speaking children (Geva et al., 2000; Limbos & Geva, 2001; Wade-Woolley & Siegel, 1997). In a study comparing English monolinguals with English-language learners from two Asian backgrounds (South Asian, Chinese), Geva et al. (2000) found no differences between English-language learners and monolingual English- speaking children on a task of word recognition in first and second grades. The children in the study received instruction in English as a second language for 30 to 40 minutes daily in groups of three to five, with a focus on the development of skills in English (oral and written) or readiness for literacy.

Limbos and Geva (2001) conducted a study of a sample of English monolinguals and English-language learners in Canada. In this study, many of the English-language learners were born in Canada, although they did not speak English until they began attending school. The most common first language of the English-language learner group was Punjabi. The children were administered oral language and reading measures in first grade. The results indicate that in first grade, although the English-language learners as a group performed more poorly than the English monolinguals on measures of expressive and receptive vocabulary and sentence repetition, there were no group differences on measures of word and nonword reading.

Wade-Woolley and Siegel (1997) examined the phonological awareness, word reading, and pseudoword reading skills of a group of English-language learners as compared with their monolingual English-speaking peers. The primary languages spoken by the English-language learners in this study were Cantonese, Mandarin, Gujarati, Urdu, and Punjabi. Most of the English-language learners in the study were immigrants to Canada who spoke a language other than English at home with their parents, siblings, and extended families, and they were reported to attend middle-class schools. In second grade, there were no differences between the groups on measures of word and pseudoword reading.

One study (Jackson & Lu, 1992) was designed to examine the reading performance of a group of 12 kindergarten English-language learners considered precocious readers, recruited by teacher nomination and review of kindergarten screening records from the gifted-program application process. None of the children came from families with incomes low enough to qualify for free or reduced-price lunches. The findings from this study corroborate those of the Canadian studies discussed earlier, albeit with a much less rigorous design and a small sample. Compared with a large sample of monolingual English precocious readers, the performance of the English-language precocious readers was similar on all reading tasks.

In a U.K. study, Mumtaz and Humphreys (2001) found that their sample of 7- and 8-year-old Urdu first-language speakers learning English had higher scores on regular word reading and pseudoword reading tasks than monolingual children of the same age. This finding may reflect that the children had learned to read Urdu, a language with a predictable relationship between letters and sounds. Although the English-language learners had higher scores than their monolingual English-speaking peers on tasks of regular word reading and pseudoword reading, they had lower scores on an irregular word reading task. It may be that they were relying on a strategy that was successful in Urdu, in which each letter has only one pronunciation, but not in English. Further evidence of the use of this ineffective strategy for English reading is that the children made errors on these irregular words that could be categorized as regularizations (e.g., *island* read as /*izland*/). The monolingual English-speaking students in the study made fewer of these regularization errors.

In addition to the studies discussed previously, other longitudinal studies conducted in the Netherlands provide some evidence that initial differences in word reading abilities between language-minority and monolingual students disappear over time. In each school, 20% to 50% of the children in the class were members of ethnic minority groups, and in both studies, the language-minority students were from working-class backgrounds. Specifically, research on the word reading ability of language-minority students, predominantly Turkish monolinguals, acquiring Dutch in the Netherlands revealed that any differences between their word reading ability and that of monolingual Dutch children generally disappeared after 2 years of formal literacy instruction (Verhoeven, 1990, 2000). In the first year of school for all these learners, reading instruction was in Dutch; in the second year of school, some additional reading instruction was offered in the children's native language.

The method of Dutch reading instruction for all children in these studies combined whole-word and decoding principles. The author reported that in the first 4 months, short texts were presented with sight words, in combination with analytic phonics teaching. Along with word decoding, spelling exercises were given with the same word patterns. Following the short text and simple spelling exercises, more complex and varied texts were introduced to increase the children's reading and spelling fluency. Beyond word spelling, there was no other writing instruction during the first 2 years of school.

One of the studies (Verhoeven, 1990), with Dutch second-language learners from Turkish-speaking backgrounds, found that in their first year of reading instruction, the second-language learners lagged behind their Dutch monolingual peers in decoding ability. After almost 2 years (20 months) of literacy instruction, however, this group difference had disappeared. The children in the study came from working-class families and had had only minimal exposure to print on entry to school.

In another longitudinal study with a larger, more diverse sample that included third- and fourth-grade Dutch second-language learners from Turkish, Moroccan, Surinamese, and Antillean language backgrounds, Verhoeven (2000) found that monolingual Dutch and Dutch second-language learners did not differ in word reading and decoding skills and had equivalent sound-blending skills. However, the language-minority children had significantly lower scores on tasks measuring grapheme knowledge (i.e., the ability to produce the sound of the letters) and phonemic segmentation skills. These tasks require a more sophisticated production of isolated phonemes than do simpler decoding tasks. In addition, the differences in the metalinguistic skills became more pronounced the longer the children were in school, although their word reading was equivalent to that of native speakers, suggesting that these difficulties with metalinguistic skills may not have had a significant influence on initial acquisition of reading and decoding skills.

A much smaller number of studies focused on word-level skills of children beyond the early elementary grades. Three studies comparing the word reading ability of English-language learners and monolingual English-speaking students were conducted with samples of older elementary and middle-school learners in Toronto, Canada. One of the studies found an advantage in favor of the English-language learners (D'Angiulli et al., 2001), whereas the others found equivalent word reading skills for English first- and second-language learners (Abu-Rabia & Siegel, 2002; Da Fontoura & Siegel, 1995).

Abu-Rabia and Siegel (2002) studied the word reading ability of a group of fourth- to eighth-grade bilingual Arabic–English children. The children were being educated in English; however, they spoke Arabic at home and attended classes for 3 hours a week, where they were taught to read, write, and speak in Arabic. There were no significant differences between the normally achieving Arabic first-language children and English monolinguals on word and pseudoword reading tasks and on a visual task in which they had to recognize the correct spelling of a word in contrast to a pseudohomophone (e.g., *brain–brane*). However, the English monolinguals had higher scores on an orthographic awareness task in which they had to recognize which of two pronounceable letter strings could be an English word (e.g., *filv–filk*). Performance on this task was probably influenced by amount of exposure to English print. The authors provide no information about exposure to print; yet given that the home language was Arabic, the English-language learners probably had had significantly less exposure to print in English than their monolingual English-speaking classmates.

Similar findings are reported by Da Fontoura and Siegel (1995), who examined literacy development among a group of Portuguese–English bilingual and monolingual English-speaking fourth through sixth graders. Although the majority of instruction for the English-language learners was in mainstream English classrooms, these students also attended Portuguese classes for 30 minutes each day as part of a heritage language program. The English-language learners were from low socioeconomic backgrounds; the English monolinguals had slightly higher and more heterogeneous socioeconomic levels. Oral proficiency scores, as measured by a grammatical sensitivity task (oral cloze), were significantly lower for the bilingual group; however, the two groups were similar on measures of word recognition, phonological awareness, and verbal working memory skills in English.

Whereas Abu-Rabia and Siegel (2002) and Da Fontoura and Siegel (1995) found similar levels of word reading achievement in English monolinguals and English-language learners, D'Angiulli et al. (2001) report an advantage in favor of the bilinguals. In their study, tasks of word and pseudoword reading were administered to a group of Italian–English bilinguals and a group of monolingual English-speaking fourth through eighth graders. As in the Da Fontoura and Siegel (1995) study, the majority of the bilinguals' instruction was in mainstream English classrooms, and these students also attended Italian classes in school each day for 30 minutes as part of a heritage language program. All children in this study were of middle-class backgrounds.

Word Reading Skills of Language-Minority Students With Literacy Difficulties. In addition to examining the word reading ability of samples of first- and second-language learners with a range of abilities in the elementary grades, three studies (Chiappe & Siegel, 1999; Chiappe, Siegel, & Wade-Woolley, 2002; Wade-Woolley & Siegel, 1997) conducted further analyses after classifying the first- and second-language samples on the basis of their performance on measures of language or literacy. A fourth study (Everatt et al., 2000), discussed earlier, examined the reading performance of children identified as poor spellers by teacher nomination and performance on a spelling measure.

In the studies with first (Chiappe & Siegel, 1999) and second graders (Wade-Woolley & Siegel, 1997), children with reading disability were defined as those with scores at or below the 25th percentile on standardized measures of word reading. In another study of kindergarten children (Chiappe, Siegel, & Wade-Woolley, 2002), the children were classified as at risk or not at risk on the basis of their performance on a rhyme-detection measure of phonological processing.

In the study that classified children in kindergarten, approximately 25% of English-language learners were identified as at risk, compared with about 15% of native English speakers. In first grade, the not-at-risk group performed better than the at-risk group on all measures of literacy, including two measures of word reading and a measure of nonword reading.

In the studies that classified children in first and second grade (Chiappe & Siegel, 1999; Wade-Woolley & Siegel, 1997), by definition, the children identified as average readers in each of the first- and second-language groups scored higher on tests of word reading than those identified as poor readers. More interesting, and more important for the issue of disentangling language proficiency problems from reading difficulties, similar proportions of English-language learners and native English speakers were classified as poor readers in first and second grade, which is in contrast to the study with kindergarteners. In addition to the comparable prevalence of reading difficulty, each of the studies found that the overall profiles of English-language learners and native English speakers who were poor readers were similar on all tasks administered. Individual phonological skills, rather than language-minority status, were a significant correlate of reading skills in the overall sample of students. Further, in both studies, there was no interaction between reader (i.e., poor, average) and language groups (i.e., language-minority, native English speakers). If, in fact, language-minority students are predisposed to low achievement, we would expect to see such an interaction effect, such that more language-minority students would be classified as poor readers.

In their U.K. study of English-language learners from Sylheti-speaking backgrounds, Everatt et al. (2000) found that the children who had low spelling achievement also had deficits in word and pseudoword reading, compared with their English-language learner peers whose spelling and reading scores were in the average range.

As with the studies of elementary learners, the three studies conducted with learners in the middle-school years also examined the performance of students with reading difficulties. Each of these studies used a classification system based on a standardized measure of word reading. Two (Abu-Rabia & Siegel, 2002; Da Fontoura & Siegel, 1995) classified children as poor readers if they had scores at or below the 25th percentile and as average if they had scores at or above the 30th percentile. The third (D'Angiulli et al., 2001) classified children as poor readers if they had a score below the 30th percentile and as average if their scores were at or above the 30th percentile. Similar proportions of English-language learners and native English speakers were classified as poor readers. In addition to the similar prevalence of reading difficulty, each of the studies found that the overall profiles of native and second-language poor readers were very similar on all tasks administered.

In addition to the prior global findings, which were also observed in the studies of primary-grade learners, two findings are specific to one of the studies with middle-school learners classified as poor readers. Da Fontoura and Siegel (1995) found that English-language learners who were poor readers had significantly higher scores on a measure of pseudoword reading and spelling than native English speakers also classified as poor readers.

Another approach to studying individual differences in oral language proficiency and second-language reading is to examine the nature of oral reading miscues. Miramontes (1987) analyzed the oral reading miscues of fourth-, fifth-, and sixth-grade Mexican American students in Spanish (first language) and English (second language). Half of the students received initial literacy instruction solely in English, whereas the other half received literacy instruction in Spanish until transitioning into English in third grade. Each group was further divided into successful and poor readers on the basis of teacher referral and performance on a standardized measure; poor readers were reading at least 1.5 years below grade level. Half of the English-instructed group and half of the Spanish-instructed group were designated as reading disabled. The authors report that oral reading miscues by students whose initial literacy instruction was in Spanish—regardless of whether they were classified as successful or poor readers—demonstrated greater use of both phonetic and contextual information than was the case for students who received English instruction only. The finding that children instructed bilingually demonstrated stronger reading skills must be interpreted with caution, however, because miscue analysis was the only outcome, and the characteristics of instruction were not thoroughly described.

Word Reading Skills: Meta-Analytic Findings and Summary. As described in chapter 3, average weighted differences of native speakers and second-language learners were calculated when there were five or more studies with comparable data that provided sufficient statistical information. Average differences between each sample on each measure were combined within studies and then weighted by sample size to correct for bias (d statistic). Examination of word reading differences between these two groups, as measured in 10 studies, revealed a small average difference between groups (–.09). (See Table 4.2; a positive difference indicates that the native speakers did best, and a negative difference indicates that the second-language learners did best.) Although this result suggests that the second-language learners could read words better than the native speakers, this difference was not statistically significant (i.e., it did not differ from zero). This means these groups were equal in word reading ability. The homogeneity test indicated that all the variation in this sample of mean differences would be expected from sampling error alone (Q = 8.13, df = 9, p > .05).

Findings from the narrative review also suggest that in comparisons of the word reading skills of English-language learners and native English speakers, it was found that after some instruction in a second language, the word reading skills of English-language learners often matched those of native English speakers. From this research, it is impossible to determine how much instruction is necessary for this level of achievement to occur. Although the word reading skills often reached levels of equivalence, English-language learners tended to perform more poorly on measures of syntactic awareness (Abu-Rabia & Siegel, 2002; Chiappe & Siegel, 1999; Chiappe, Siegel, & Gottardo, 2002; Chiappe,

TABLE 4.2
Comparisons of Word and Pseudoword Reading Skills of First- and
Second-Language Students

Study	Weighted Mean Difference	Number of Second- Language Students	Number of First- Language Students
Abu-Rabia & Siegel, 2002	.05	56	65
Chiappe, Siegel, & Wade-Woolley, 2002	−.09	131	727
Chiappe, Siegel, & Gottardo, 2002	.05	59	540
Chiappe & Siegel, 1999	−.22	38	51
D'Angiulli, Siegel, & Serra 2001	−.79*	81	210
Da Fontoura & Siegel, 1995	−.12	37	106
Geva, Yaghoub-Zadeh, & Schuster, 2000	−.02	248	100
Limbos & Geva, 2001	−.04	258	124
Verhoeven, 2000	.05	331	1812
Wade-Woolley & Siegel, 1997	.23	40	33
Total	−.09	1,279	3,768

*Correlation significantly different from 0.

Siegel, & Wade-Woolley, 2002; D'Angiulli et al., 2001; Da Fontoura & Siegel, 1995; Wade-Woolley & Siegel, 1997) and vocabulary (Geva et al., 2000; Limbos & Geva, 2001).

In each of the studies reviewed, the English-language learners showed a range of abilities similar to that of the native English speakers. Furthermore, each of the studies identified a group of English-language learners whose performance was well below average on word and pseudoword reading and related skills, similar to that of a native English-speaking group designated as reading disabled. Interestingly, in all three of the studies with middle-school learners (Abu-Rabia & Siegel, 2002; Da Fontoura & Siegel, 1995; D'Angiulli et al., 2001), the English-language learners who were reading disabled had better scores on phonological measures than their reading-disabled, native English-speaking peers. This finding may reflect heightened metalinguistic awareness skills among the bilingual students. This finding should be investigated in future studies.

The similar prevalence and profile of disabled readers in English first- and second-language groups suggest that, at least at the word reading level, it is possible to reliably identify disabled readers. For example, Limbos and Geva (2001) examined the relationship between teacher ratings of at-risk children and children's performance on reading measures; for the native English speakers, there was a match between children's word identification and teachers' nominations. In the case of the English-language learners, however, teachers identified poor word identification skills but attributed them to the children's second-language status, although the correlations between oral comprehension and the reading scores were low to moderate. In general, overreliance on oral language proficiency may hamper the identification of second-language children who may be at risk for reading disability. Indeed, the research suggests that for elementary school learners of all grade levels and reading abilities, phonological skills are more closely related to word reading ability than is language-minority status.

Factors That Influence Second-Language Word Reading Skills

Research with native speakers has identified various processes and skills that influence the development of word reading skills in young children. These include cognitive skills, such as working memory; phonological processing skills, such as rapid naming and phonological awareness; language skills, such as vocabulary; and skills and knowledge that reflect children's experience with print and literacy, such as letter identification. Research focused on identifying children at risk of reading difficulties has identified a combination of cognitive measures and measures that are a proxy for children's experience with print that is effective for identifying these children (Lyon et al., 2001; Snow et al., 1998).

Nine studies in our database examined those factors that influenced word reading development among children learning to read in their second language (Arab-Moghaddam & Sénéchal, 2001; Chiappe, Siegel, & Gottardo, 2002; Chiappe, Siegel, & Wade-Woolley, 2002; Da Fontoura & Siegel, 1995; Gholamain & Geva, 1999; Gottardo, 2002; Quiroga, Lemos-Britton, Mostafapour, Abbott, & Berninger, 2002; Verhoeven, 1990, 2000). Collectively, these studies identify a cluster of competencies underlying initial word reading development among language-minority students: second-language phonological awareness, knowledge of second-language sound–symbol correspondence rules, second-language letter knowledge, and working memory measured in the second language. These factors are essentially identical to the known requisites for reading acquisition among monolingual native English-speaking children (e.g., Adams, 1990; Foorman, Francis, Fletcher, & Lynn, 1996; Olson, Wise, Johnson, & Ring, 1997; Scanlon & Vellutino, 1997; Snow et al., 1998). In view of the converging evidence from these studies, it appears reasonable to conclude that the development of second-language decoding skill depends on the underlying competencies in the second language, similar to those promoting first-language decoding development. The extent and manner in which second-language oral proficiency influences readiness skills and subsequent word reading skills is explored in chapter 5.

Depending on the study design, the second-language learners involved in the study, and the measures available to researchers, it is possible to examine factors that influence reading development from a cross-linguistic or a strictly second-language perspective. In studies examining literacy development from a cross-linguistic perspective, similar measures are administered to children in their first and second languages, and the relationship between them is examined (see chap. 9). In contrast, when development of reading is examined strictly from a second-language perspective, whereby language-minority students are administered tasks only in their second language, the analyses typically focus on comparing those factors that influenced reading development for the second-language learners and an equivalent group of native speakers. Some of the studies reviewed for this chapter used measures in both the first and second languages to examine the influence of native skills on second-language word reading (Arab-Moghaddam & Sénéchal, 2001; Da Fontoura & Siegel, 1995; Gholamain & Geva, 1999; Gottardo, 2002; Quiroga et al., 2002), whereas others included only second-language measures and examined their influence on second-language word reading (Chiappe, Siegel, & Gottardo, 2002; Chiappe, Siegel, & Wade-Woolley, 2002; Verhoeven, 2000).

Those studies that examined the influence of first-language skills on the development of reading in the second language found that certain skills in the first language did indeed have a significant influence on children's reading in the second language. This was the case in studies with second-language learners from Spanish-speaking (Gottardo, 2002; Quiroga et al., 2002), Portuguese-speaking (Da Fontoura & Siegel, 1995), and Persian-speaking (Arab–Moghaddam & Sénéchal, 2001; Gholamain & Geva, 1999) backgrounds. The findings from these studies are discussed in greater detail in Part II, which focuses on cross-linguistic relationships in oral language and literacy skills.

In another study with English-language learners from Spanish-speaking backgrounds, Gottardo (2002) investigated the relationship between first- and second-language oral language proficiency and reading skills in first grade. The Spanish speakers were children of low socioeconomic backgrounds whose parents were migrant workers from Mexico. The children were administered vocabulary, word reading, syntactic knowledge, and phonological tasks. The results demonstrate that second-language word reading ability was correlated with second-language phonological processing skills, second-language vocabulary knowledge, and first-language word reading ability. Similarly, in their study of English-language learners from Portuguese-speaking backgrounds, Da Fontoura and Siegel (1995) found that pseudoword reading in English and Portuguese correlated highly with word recognition skills in both English (the second language) and Portuguese (the first language). This finding suggests that for these English-language learners, first- and second-language phonological and reading skills were related. Findings from both of these studies are discussed further in chapters 5 and 9.

In related work, Gholamain and Geva (1999) found that for their sample of English-language learners from Persian-speaking backgrounds, letter-naming speed and working memory assessed in Persian and English had a significant association with word reading development both within and across languages. This sample included first- through fifth-grade children learning to read in English and Persian concurrently; the authors report that children attending the schools where the research was conducted typically came from middle-class, well-educated immigrant families. It is important to note, however, that the findings of this study may not be generalizable to all Persian-speaking language-minority youth, because the authors selected only those children whose language in the home was Persian but who reported on a questionnaire that English was their dominant language. For a more in-depth discussion of the cross-linguistic nature of the findings of this study, see Part II of this volume.

Similarly, Arab-Moghaddam and Sénéchal (2001) studied a group of English-language learners in second and third grades in Canada to investigate the concurrent development of reading and spelling in English (the second language) and Persian (the first language). The children had received their formal instruction at school in English; however, they also attended private Persian classes for approximately 6 hours a week. An examination of the relationship between performance on English and Persian measures of reading and related cognitive processes demonstrated that English orthographic and phonological skills predicted unique variance in decoding performance in English, whereas Persian orthographic and phonological skills predicted unique variance in decoding performance in Persian.

Studies comparing those factors that influence second-language reading for second-language learners, without measures of first language, have yielded relatively consistent findings, suggesting that similar processes influence reading development for both first- and second-language learners.

Chiappe, Siegel, and Gottardo (2002) found that for English-language students and monolingual English children, performance in the fall of kindergarten on English measures of letter identification, phonological awareness, and rapid picture naming predicted English literacy performance at the end of kindergarten. Specifically, performance in the fall on two English measures of phonological awareness, sound mimicry, and rhyme detection were predictive of children's performance on an English measure of simple spelling administered in the spring.

With the same cohort in first grade (Chiappe, Siegel, & Wade-Woolley, 2002), patterns of correlations among the variables used in the study were comparable among English-language learners and monolingual English speakers. For both groups, letter identification, spelling, phoneme deletion, and syntactic awareness measured in English were strongly associated with English word reading ability. For both the monolingual and second-language learners in the study, kindergarten letter identification was the strongest predictor of first-grade word recognition skills.

Two of the previously described studies of language-minority learners acquiring Dutch in the Netherlands found that for second graders from diverse linguistic backgrounds (Verhoeven, 2000), performance on a Dutch grapheme knowledge measure and first-grade decoding ability in Dutch were significant predictors of second-grade word reading ability in Dutch. For a group of Turkish-speaking second graders (Verhoeven, 1990), Dutch oral proficiency had the strongest influence on word reading.

Finally, in one study focused on the strategies children used while reading English words, a miscue analysis of the word reading of English-language learners in elementary school was conducted. O'Toole, Aubeeluck, Cozens, and Cline (2001) compared the reading errors of a group of English-language learners from Sylheti first-language backgrounds with those of a group of monolingual English-speaking students. The children in the study ranged in age from 5 to 11 years, and all were typical readers. The authors hypothesized that children from this language-minority group would use fewer semantic cues than their monolingual peers when reading narrative, graded passages selected so the children would be able to read with understanding, but also be likely to make a significant number of errors. Errors the children made while reading aloud were coded and classified; no significant differences were found between the monolingual and second-language groups for some types of reading errors, such as inserted words, omissions, self-corrections, and words reversed. Furthermore, no significant differences were found in the number of semantic cues used by monolingual and bilingual children when making substitution errors. As a group, the children in the study made significantly more graphophonic than syntactic or semantic substitutions. This finding may be more indicative of novice rather than skilled reading.

Taken together, the studies reviewed here provide evidence that language-minority students can develop word reading skills comparable to those of their native-speaking peers. The findings from these studies indicate that indexes of reading readiness, including measures of language-related skills, phonological processing, and general cognitive ability, have an influence on second-language word reading development for second-language learners. This pattern of findings suggests that the process of learning to read in a second language for language-minority students is influenced by the same skills that influence reading for native speakers. This overall finding is evident whether the measures are administered in the first or second language. It is also possible that the similarity in factors that influence first- and second-language reading stems from the universality of the requisites for reading acquisition across languages, a notion akin to the universal grammar of reading proposed by Perfetti (2003). At the same time, we cannot make claims about whether there is a differential relationship for these variables for the two populations because the majority of studies examining those factors that influence word reading development for language-minority students did not include a comparison group composed of native speakers.

Spelling Development

Learning to read and learning to spell are related and make use of similar skills; a combination of phonological processing and orthographic processing skills, as well as visual memory, is needed to learn to spell in English. Spelling requires the application of phoneme–grapheme correspondences in a written format (Juel, 1991). Phonological skills enable spellers to segment the sounds in words and try to represent those sounds with corresponding letters, whereas orthographic skills in spelling provide the ability to spell from memory. Children store and access the orthographic representations of words, which involve knowledge of the letters and their sequence in the words to be spelled. In the case of deep orthographies, such as English, it is particularly important that children rely on both phonological and orthographic skills for accurate word spelling. Developing successful spelling skills may be an additional challenge for language-minority students, who are likely to have had less exposure to the language and literacy in the second language than their native-speaking peers.

Studies examining the spelling development of second-language learners have found it to be similar to that of monolingual children, at least for English-language learners, who represent the majority of the samples in the studies reviewed in this section (Abu-Rabia & Siegel, 2002; D'Angiulli et al., 2001; Da Fontoura & Siegel, 1995; Fashola, Drum, Mayer, & Kang, 1996; Limbos & Geva, 2001; Tompkins, Abramson, & Pritchard, 1999; Wade-Woolley & Siegel, 1997). Only one study reviewed examined the spelling development of language-minority students acquiring a language other than English (Verhoeven, 2000); the findings from that study diverged from those of the others in that the spelling ability of the language-minority children was not as advanced as that of the monolingual children.

Spelling Development of Language-Minority Students.   Four studies (Limbos & Geva, 2001; Wade-Woolley & Siegel, 1997; Tompkins et al., 1999; Verhoeven, 2000) examined the spelling ability of language-minority students in the primary grades. In their previously described study, Wade-Woolley and Siegel

(1997) found that second-grade English-language learners and native speakers did not differ significantly on a real-word and pseudoword spelling task, nor did the groups differ when required to represent lax vowels (represented with a single grapheme) or tense vowels (represented with multiple graphemes) through explicit spelling conventions. The results were similar for words with and without consonant clusters. The second-language learners who were considered average readers made spelling errors similar to those of their monolingual English speaking peers; the spelling performance of the groups was similar. Likewise, Limbos and Geva (2001) found no differences between monolingual English speakers and English-language learners on a measure of word spelling administered in first grade.

In contrast to the studies reviewed previously, one study of young children yielded findings suggesting that second-language spelling may not be as well developed for second-language learners as for their monolingual, language-majority peers. Despite the similar word reading skills of Dutch monolingual and second-language learners in the first 2 years of school, Verhoeven (2000) found that the groups differed in spelling ability: The spelling skills of the language-minority children were not as advanced or efficient as those of the language-majority children. Given that the language-minority children in this study were from four different language backgrounds—Turkish, Moroccan, Surinamese, and Antillean—and results were not disaggregated by native background, it is not possible to examine how their lower spelling skills, reported for the whole group on the average, may have varied as a function of language background.

Four studies have examined the spelling abilities of older learners in elementary school. The three studies discussed earlier that examined the literacy development of older elementary school children in Toronto, Canada, found that English-language learners and monolingual English speakers who were typical readers had similar spelling ability (Abu-Rabia & Siegel, 2002; Da Fontoura & Siegel, 1995; D'Angiulli et al., 2001). Together, the studies identified this pattern with fourth- to sixth-grade English-language learners from Portuguese, Italian, and Arabic backgrounds. In each study, the test of word spelling was an English spelling dictation.

In contrast to these findings, a cross-sectional study of native Spanish speakers learning English (Fashola et al., 1996) found that they made more errors than monolingual English speakers. Perhaps more interesting, from a developmental perspective, was that the group of fifth and sixth graders made fewer errors than the group of third and fourth graders. This finding suggests that for language-minority students, spelling skills may improve with time and exposure to instruction, albeit perhaps more slowly than is the case for their native-speaking peers.

Spelling Development of Language-Minority Students With Literacy Difficulties. Each of the five studies discussed previously that examined the word reading skills of English-language learners designated as reading disabled also included measures of spelling in English. These children had lower scores on word and pseudoword spelling tasks than their classmates who were English-language learners and were designated as average readers (Chiappe, Siegel, & Wade-Woolley, 2002; Da Fontoura & Siegel, 1995; Wade-Woolley & Siegel, 1997). In addition, and similar to the word reading findings, the scores on measures of

TABLE 4.3
Comparison of Spelling Skills of First- and Second-Language Students

Study	Mean Weighted Effect Size	Number of Language Minority Participants	Number of Monolingual Participants
Chiappe, Siegel, & Gottardo, 2002	0.25	59	540
Abu-Rabia & Siegel, 2002	−0.66	56	65
Chiappe, Siegel, & Wade-Woolley, 2002	0.25	131	727
Da Fontoura & Siegel, 1995	−0.68*	37	106
D'Angiulli, Siegel, & Serra, 2001	−1.45*	45	64
Limbos & Geva, 2001	−0.04	258	124
Tompkins, 1999	−0.07	40	40
Verhoeven, 2000	0.15	331	1812
Wade-Woolley & Siegel, 1997	0.39	40	33
Total	−.13	1,022	3,447

*Significantly different from 0.

spelling for the native English speakers and the English-language learners designated as poor readers were very similar. In one study, the spelling patterns of these two groups that were designated as reading disabled were strikingly similar (Wade-Woolley & Siegel, 1997). For example, the reading-disabled groups had more difficulty spelling words with than without consonant clusters, whereas average readers spelled both sets of words with equal success.

Consistent with the trend of higher performance among the second-language learners designated as reading disabled, compared with the monolinguals designated as poor readers, the three studies with learners in the middle years (Abu-Rabia & Siegel, 2002; Da Fontoura & Siegel, 1995; D'Angiulli et al., 2001) found that English-language learners designated as poor readers had higher scores on an English spelling test than native English speakers designated as poor readers. This pattern is consistent with the former group's higher scores on measures of phonological awareness and again suggests the possibility of positive transfer from Portuguese or heightened metalinguistic awareness as a result of being bilingual.

Taken together, these findings suggest that underlying processing deficits, as opposed to language-minority status, are related to reading and spelling difficulties. Furthermore, in two of the studies (Chiappe, Siegel, & Wade-Woolley, 2002; Wade-Woolley & Siegel, 1997), there was no interaction effect for language group (first or second language) or reader group (average vs. poor or disabled reader).

Spelling Development: Meta-Analytic Findings and Summary. Effect sizes were used to estimate the weighted average differences between groups, and these results guided the analysis of spelling development of second-language learners. Examination of spelling differences between native speakers and second-language learners in nine studies (Table 4.3) revealed a small average difference between groups (effect size: −.05). Although this finding suggests that second-language learners spelled a bit better than the native speakers, this difference was not statistically significant (i.e., it did not differ from zero). A test of homogeneity showed that there was significant variance in these spelling studies ($Q = 313.141$, $df = 8$, $p > .05$).

In summary, findings from the meta-analysis and narrative review suggest that, over time, English-language learners can accomplish a level of English spelling proficiency equivalent to those of native-language speakers, although in two studies (Fashola et al., 1996; Verhoeven, 2000) the second-language learners (English and Dutch) demonstrated relatively greater difficulties with spelling.

Factors That Influence Second-Language Spelling

Nine studies in our database investigated second-language factors that influence the spelling development of language-minority students (Abu-Rabia & Siegel, 2002; Arab-Morghaddam & Sénéchal, 2001; Chiappe & Siegel, 1999; Chiappe, Siegel, & Gottardo, 2002; Cronnell, 1985; Da Fontoura & Siegel, 1995; D'Angiulli, Siegel, & Serra, 2001; Verhoeven, 2000; Wade-Woolley & Siegel, 1997). Five studies (Abu-Rabia & Siegel, 2002; Arab-Moghaddam & Sénéchal, 2001; Chiappe & Siegel, 1999; Chiappe, Siegel, & Gottardo, 2002; Da Fontoura & Siegel 1995) focused on second-language basic literacy skills as predictors of spelling development. Taken together, their findings suggest that factors associated with spelling performance in a second language are similar to factors that influence word reading (i.e., phonological awareness skills, letter knowledge, and orthographic knowledge) and that word reading and spelling skills are, in fact, highly correlated.

In addition to the studies examining the second-language factors that influence second-language spelling for language-minority students, two studies (Cronnell, 1985; Fashola et al., 1996) report that spelling errors in English among Spanish–English bilingual children (second to sixth grades) reflected their use of Spanish (first language) sound–symbol correspondence rules. These two studies are discussed in chapter 9.

In the previously discussed study of kindergarten language-minority students from diverse linguistic backgrounds learning English, Chiappe, Siegel, and Gottardo (2002) found that scores on a simple spelling task administered in English in the spring of kindergarten were influenced by letter identification, pseudoword repetition, rhyme detection, and spelling tasks administered in English in November of kindergarten. Similarly, in a study previously described, Wade-Woolley and Siegel (1997) found that for second graders from diverse linguistic backgrounds, the accuracy of real-word spelling in English was predicted by English pseudoword decoding and phoneme deletion for both monolingual English speakers and second-language learners.

In their study of English-language learners from Persian-speaking backgrounds, Arab-Moghaddam and Sénéchal (2001) demonstrated that, although spelling in English was predicted by both phonological skills (ability to discriminate a pseudohomophone from a nonword but pronounceable letter string) and orthographic skills (ability to discriminate a correctly spelled word from its pseudohomophone), differences in Persian spelling performance were explained solely by orthographic skill. The discrepant results for English and Persian may be explained by differences in first- and second-language orthographic properties; these findings are also addressed in Part II of this volume.

Two studies of children in the middle years of elementary school demonstrated the significant role of phonological processing in word spelling. Abu-Rabia and Siegel (2002) found that for English-language learners, spelling performance in English was strongly related to English word and pseudoword reading abilities, as well as English phonological and orthographic skills. For these native Arabic speakers between the ages of 9 and 14, working memory was also a strong correlate of spelling. English (second-language) spelling was also significantly correlated with the same set of skills in Arabic (the first language). Da Fontoura and Siegel (1995) examined English spelling skills among poor and typical readers of Portuguese-speaking backgrounds. These English-language learners were in mainstream English classes in the fourth through sixth grades. The English spelling scores of the two groups were found to be highly correlated with English word and pseudoword reading performance.

In a cross-sectional study involving native Spanish speakers, Cronnell (1985) compared spelling errors made by third and sixth graders. The analysis indicated that 27% of errors committed by third graders were induced by the application of first-language rules; for sixth graders, this was the case for 33% of errors. Roughly 30% of errors were identified as developmental, however, because they resulted from the omission of grammatical inflections. (See Part II of this volume for a more in-depth discussion of the cross-linguistic nature of the findings of this study.) These omission errors are often observed among monolingual children as the result of a normal developmental process in spelling (Treiman, 1993; Treiman & Bourassa, 2000).

Fashola et al. (1996) found that Spanish–English bilingual students in second through sixth grades made significantly more spelling errors than did monolingual English-speaking children. The errors were consistent with Spanish phonological and orthographic rules, and younger bilingual children (second and third graders) made considerably more first-language-influenced errors than older students (fifth and sixth graders). However, bilingual and monolingual children across grades did not differ in the number of errors not influenced by the first language. Given the cross-linguistic nature of this study, the results are discussed further in chapter 9.

Finally, in a study of language-minority students acquiring Dutch as a second language, Verhoeven (2000) found that the early development of Dutch word spelling was explained by knowledge of phoneme–grapheme correspondence and phonemic segmentation, but that these factors appeared to have only a moderate impact on spelling ability over time. In that study, as discussed, the Dutch second-language learners did not perform as well as their monolingual Dutch peers on a measure of word spelling.

The Development of Word-Level Skills: Summary

Studies examining the development of word reading and spelling among language-minority students have demonstrated that, in the majority of cases, the development of these skills is very similar to that of native speakers in the same context. These similarities are evident not only in the findings of those studies examining the word reading and spelling achievement of second-language learners as compared with their monolingual peers, but also in the findings of those studies examining the variables that influence word spelling and reading. For both native speakers and second-language learners, factors, such as phonological awareness and orthographic skills, were found to influence word reading and word spelling. The studies in this area focused primarily on elementary school-age children who were receiving almost all of their instruction in their second language.

The spelling difficulties experienced by some English-language learners appear similar to those experienced by some native English speakers. As well, on the basis of some studies, it appears that exposure to a first language that is a more regular, predictable language than English may actually result in a positive transfer of first-language spelling skills to a second language, especially if the language-minority students have spelling difficulties. This possibility is further discussed in Part II of this volume.

The studies reviewed vary significantly in the extent to which the demographic context of the study is reported. Some report the SES of either the children or the school(s) where the research was conducted (Abu-Rabia & Siegel, 2002; Chiappe & Siegel, 1999; Cronnell, 1985; D'Angiulli et al., 2001; Da Fontoura & Siegel, 1995; Gholamain & Geva, 1999; Gottardo, 2002; Jackson & Lu, 1992; Mumtaz & Humphreys, 2001; Tompkins et al., 1999; Verhoeven, 1990, 2000; Wade-Woolley & Siegel, 1997). Others provide some information about the demographics of the sample (e.g., children in the two language groups lived in the same neighborhoods), but no specifics on the SES of the language-minority students (Arab-Moghaddam & Sénéchal, 2001; Chiappe, Siegel, & Gottardo, 2002; Chiappe, Siegel, & Wade-Woolley, 2002; O'Toole et al., 2001). Still others report no socioeconomic information (Bialystok, 1997; Fashola et al., 1996; Geva et al., 2000; Limbos & Geva, 2001; Quiroga et al., 2002).

Finally, although many of the studies reviewed report the language of instruction and whether children were receiving any instruction in their native language, none describes the overall intensity of exposure to the native language. Because there is likely to be significant variability in the study samples and settings, specific details about the ratio of language-minority students to native speakers in the classroom and the language environment of the schools and communities would add considerable depth to the interpretation of the results of studies addressing the development of literacy skills among language-minority students. Moreover, especially in studies with language-minority students in the middle and secondary school years, studies should examine and report the length of schooling in the second language experienced by the learners.

THE DEVELOPMENT OF SECOND-LANGUAGE TEXT-LEVEL SKILLS

Although readiness skills (e.g., phonological awareness, concepts of print) and word-level skills (e.g., word reading and spelling) are important in the early stages of literacy acquisition and indeed are requisite for reading comprehension, they are not sufficient as effective text-level skills. At a higher level are reading comprehension and writing of connected text—complex text-level skills that require conceptual processing, such as drawing on prior knowledge, making inferences, and resolving structural and semantic ambiguities. This higher level processing also involves the integration of many linguistic and cognitive skills (e.g., vocabulary, syntax, working memory) with word-level skills, as well as with background knowledge. For any learner, especially for language-minority children and youth, reading comprehension and writing are complex, multifaceted tasks.

There is a lack of research examining the reading comprehension development of language-minority students, and the studies that do exist are characterized by significant variability in methodology, particularly the way in which reading comprehension is assessed. More research is needed to provide a better understanding of the development of text-level skills in language-minority students.

Development of Reading Comprehension Skills for Language-Minority Students

Five studies conducted in the Netherlands have examined the reading comprehension performance in Dutch of language-minority students as compared with their monolingual, native-speaking peers. Four of the studies (Aarts & Verhoeven, 1999; Droop & Verhoeven, 1998; Verhoeven, 1990, 2000) included samples of children of elementary and middle school age, spanning first through eighth grades, whereas only one (Hacquebord, 1994) examined the reading comprehension skills of language-minority youth in secondary school.

An overall finding based on a review of this limited number of studies is that the second-language reading comprehension skills of language-minority children and youth did not appear to develop to the same extent as those of their language-majority peers; most of the studies demonstrated that the former children performed at lower levels than their monolingual peers (Aarts & Verhoeven, 1999; Droop & Verhoeven, 1998; Hacquebord, 1994; Verhoeven, 1990, 2000). The development of reading comprehension, like that of word-level skills, is highly dependent on effective instruction, and we know little about the quality of curriculum and instruction in these studies. Existing large-scale data sets on the school achievement of language-minority students in the United States and abroad suggest that comprehension is a significant area of difficulty for these learners, and the findings on reading comprehension presented in this report certainly suggest this is the case.

Reading Comprehension Skills of Language-Minority Students. Four studies (Aarts & Verhoeven, 1999; Droop & Verhoeven, 1998; Verhoeven, 1990, 2000) that examined the development of reading comprehension among language-minority students and their monolingual counterparts included samples of children of elementary school age, spanning first through eighth grades. Two of these studies were conducted with language-minority students during their first 2 years of schooling in the Netherlands (Verhoeven, 1990, 2000). The results indicate that, despite comparable performance on word reading at the end of their second year of school, the Dutch second-language learners performed more poorly than their Dutch monolingual peers on a measure of reading comprehension focused on students' performance on text coherence, anaphoric reference, and inferencing tasks. In one of the studies (Verhoeven, 1990), the language-minority students were exclusively Turkish first-language speakers from working-class backgrounds. Verhoeven reports that these students showed measurable improvement in Dutch reading comprehension subskills, including the ability to draw inferences and the understanding of anaphora.

Because the Dutch monolinguals also made similar gains in their comprehension subskills, however, the comprehension gap between the two groups of learners remained throughout the study period.

In the other study (Verhoeven, 2000), the language-minority students included children from working-class families with Turkish, Moroccan, Surinamese, and Antillean language backgrounds. As in the previous study (Verhoeven, 1990), the language-minority students performed more poorly than their Dutch monolingual peers on all reading comprehension tasks. Also as in the previous study, the performance gap on the comprehension subskill of understanding anaphoric relations remained stable over the course of the 2-year study, with the Dutch monolinguals consistently outperforming the Dutch second-language learners. In contrast to the previous study, however, the performance gap on the subcomponent of inferencing decreased over time probably because the Dutch monolingual group reached a ceiling score on the measure.

It is important to note that the previous studies followed students through only the first 2 years of schooling. Thus, the studies do little to inform our understanding of how proficient language-minority students become in comprehending text written in their second language with more exposure to that language.

Another study of young readers in the Netherlands was designed to examine the influence of culturally relevant background knowledge and the linguistic complexity of text on reading comprehension performance (Droop & Verhoeven, 1998). Reading culturally familiar text improved comprehension and reading performance for third-grade native Turkish and Moroccan speakers receiving their instruction in Dutch. All children in this study were from working-class families. The Turkish and Moroccan language-minority students and a group of Dutch monolinguals with comparable decoding skills were provided with texts to read in Dutch that consisted of topics either culturally familiar to the language-minority students or drawn from Dutch culture. In addition, some texts were considered linguistically simple and others linguistically complex; linguistic complexity was analyzed by counting the mean length of sentences, words, and syllables and by examining complexity of verbal groups and noun compounds. A facilitating effect of cultural familiarity was found for both reading comprehension and reading efficiency for the Dutch monolinguals and the language-minority children. For the latter children, this finding was limited to those texts that were linguistically simple presumably because of limited knowledge of the target language. These findings are consistent with findings reported in chapter 11.

In a study designed to examine the literacy attainment of Turkish children in the Netherlands by the end of primary school, Aarts and Verhoeven (1999) compared the literacy attainment of Turkish children acquiring Dutch and that of Dutch monolinguals in the Netherlands. The second-language learners of Dutch were generally of low SES, and those in the monolingual Dutch-speaking group were matched on SES, age, and gender. Although the students were matched for mean age, however, it is important to note that, within the Dutch second-language group, the students had an age range of 11 to 14 years. Thus, some students in that group had been retained at least one grade or, on entry into school, had been placed in a lower grade than would be age appropriate. The students were administered tests of both school literacy and functional literacy in Dutch: The former, administered to all students annually in the

Netherlands, was composed of multiple-choice questions designed to test vocabulary, spelling, and syntax ability; the latter included multiple-choice questions that tapped the ability to make sense of the written features of such items as a newspaper article. The performance of the native speakers of Turkish on the school literacy test was compared with that of the overall Dutch population of students, as opposed to the matched comparison group of monolingual Dutch students. The functional literacy test was administered to the native speakers of Turkish and a group of monolingual Dutch students.

On the school literacy test, the Turkish language-minority students got about 50% of the items correct, compared with an average of 70% for the Dutch population. Group differences were significant for both grammatical abilities and discourse skills. On all but one of the Dutch functional literacy items, the Dutch monolingual students performed significantly better than the Turkish language-minority students. Overall, the Turkish children did not achieve nativelike literacy proficiency in Dutch as measured by these tests. After at least 8 years of schooling, the students from Turkish-speaking backgrounds were significantly behind monolingual Dutch children on measures of both functional and school literacy.

Only one of these studies conducted in the Netherlands (Hacquebord, 1994) examined the development of reading comprehension among language-minority students as compared with their monolingual counterparts at the secondary level. Hacquebord (1994) compared comprehension performance as related to linguistic and conceptual knowledge among Dutch monolingual and Turkish–Dutch bilingual secondary school students. The native Turkish speakers had immigrated to Holland at least 3 years before the study and were enrolled in either lower general education or vocational training classes together with their Dutch monolingual peers. The groups did not differ, however, in domain-specific background knowledge and nonverbal IQ. These Turkish language-minority youths had significantly lower scores on comprehension than their Dutch monolingual classmates. The measure of comprehension consisted of passages of text with true–false questions at three different discourse levels (micro and macro). Analyses revealed that the Dutch monolinguals performed significantly better on the questions probing microlevel information (words and clauses), but the groups were relatively equal in dealing with the questions about macrolevel information (e.g., a text's main idea, the author's intent). It may be that the language-minority students were using top–down strategies and concentrating on the conceptual aspects of the text—and/or that they understood the gist of the story, but lacked specific word knowledge to respond to the microlevel questions. Although both groups improved during the 3 years of secondary schooling examined, the rates of growth were similar, and thus the differences between the two groups remained relatively constant.

Reading Comprehension: Summary.   All studies showed language-minority students performing less well than their native-speaking peers on measures of reading comprehension. Unfortunately, these studies provide little or no information about the reading comprehension instruction that these students were receiving.

Factors That Influence Second-Language Reading Comprehension

In considering variables that influence successful text comprehension, it is essential that the specific demands imposed by the text and task be taken into account (RAND Reading Study Group, 2002). In many studies in our database, however, the measure used is not described or represents a global construct of comprehension, and there is no analysis of the different components measured. Moreover, in many cases, the text type is not specified. More specifically, only three comprehension studies reviewed here provide information on specific comprehension subskills measured: coherence building, anaphora resolution, and inference (Verhoeven, 1990); anaphora resolution and explicit/implicit meaning relations (Verhoeven, 2000); and macro- and microlevel text information detection (Hacquebord, 1994). Only two provide specific information about the text type employed (Hacquebord, 1994; Nagy, García, Durgunoglu, & Hancin-Bhatt, 1993).

According to the studies reviewed, factors that influence second-language reading comprehension tend to fall into one of two categories: individual or contextual. Individual factors include such variables as readiness skills, word-level skills, background knowledge, and motivation; contextual factors include such variables as SES and text attributes. Although length of time in the country and instruction are likely to have an influence on reading comprehension for language-minority students, there is little evidence available to examine their influence.

What follows is a summary of the research on factors that influence second-language reading comprehension.

Precursor and Word-Level Skills. Studies of monolinguals have revealed the role of readiness skills, particularly phonological awareness and word-level skills (primarily word reading), for reading comprehension (e.g., Adams, 1990; Cunningham & Stanovich, 1998; Perfetti, 1997). Five studies (Aarts & Verhoeven, 1999; McEvoy & Johnson, 1989; Reese, Garnier, Gallimore, & Goldenberg, 2000; Verhoeven, 1990, 2000) examined the influence of readiness and word-level skills on the development of reading comprehension among language-minority youth.

Four longitudinal studies in our database demonstrated that second-language word-level skills, including letter knowledge, print concepts, and word reading, were predictors of second-language reading comprehension in the later grades (McEvoy & Johnson, 1989; Reese et al., 2000; Verhoeven, 1990, 2000). Together these studies included language-minority students from Spanish- and Punjabi-speaking backgrounds learning to read English, as well as Turkish-speaking children learning Dutch.

In a longitudinal study involving native Spanish-speaking children from low socioeconomic backgrounds, Reese et al. (2000) found that aspects of language ability assessed in English (the second language) in kindergarten, including having higher levels of oral proficiency in English, were related to earlier transition to English reading once these children began to attend school, and that early English proficiency was predictive of level of English reading proficiency in middle school. Additionally, measures of Spanish early literacy skills (letter knowledge, decoding, and print concepts) administered in kindergarten predicted English reading comprehension ability in seventh grade. Reading comprehension measures were subtests from standardized assessments, but little information about the specific tasks was reported.

In another study with native Spanish speakers, McEvoy and Johnson (1989) investigated the reading achievement of low-income, Mexican-American first through fourth graders as predicted by their performance at age 5 on two English kindergarten batteries. One of the batteries of measures focused primarily on cognitive and verbal skills, whereas the other focused on school readiness skills, such as letter identification. The children's families had participated in a parent–child development support program when the children were between the ages of 1 and 3. In 64% of the families, Spanish was the preferred language. The reading achievement data were based on children's scores on a global, standardized measure of reading administered annually within the school district (Iowa Test of Basic Skills [ITBS]). Analyses demonstrated that, in isolation, each battery administered in kindergarten predicted later reading achievement. When results from the two batteries were combined, however, prediction of later reading achievement was even stronger. In interpreting the findings of this study, it is important to note that the batteries were able to predict reading achievement, based on a composite measure, for a group of children who differed both linguistically and demographically from the children in the normative sample for the kindergarten batteries.

Both of Verhoeven's (1990, 2000) studies with second-language learners of Dutch in their first 2 years of school demonstrated the importance of word reading skills and oral proficiency for reading comprehension performance. Verhoeven (1990) found that, in first grade, Dutch word reading efficiency and oral proficiency were related to Dutch reading comprehension for native Turkish speakers learning to read in Dutch. By the end of second grade, however, the explanatory power of word reading efficiency had decreased, and the influence of oral proficiency (vocabulary and syntax knowledge) had increased. Similarly, in another study with Dutch second-language learners, Verhoeven (2000) found that, for native Turkish speakers in first grade in the Netherlands, word reading efficiency and vocabulary accounted for significant variance in Dutch reading comprehension. Both of these studies used a series of tasks to assess components of reading comprehension, including students' understanding of coherence and anaphoric reference. In addition, students' inferencing abilities were assessed with comprehension questions probing explicit and implicit meaning relations between the sentences read.

Together the prior findings demonstrate the strong interrelationships among language and literacy skills and the cumulative effect of reading skill development on effective text comprehension.

Understanding of Literacy.   In a cross-sectional study of older Turkish second-language learners of Dutch and native Dutch speakers in the Netherlands, Aarts and Verhoeven (1999) found that for the Turkish second-language learners of Dutch, performance on Turkish and Dutch school literacy tasks and on a Turkish functional literacy task was moderately correlated with performance on a Dutch functional literacy task. For this same group of second-language learners of Dutch, performance on the Turkish and Dutch functional literacy tasks was moderately related to performance on the Dutch school literacy task. The latter task, administered to all students annually in the Netherlands, comprised multiple-choice questions designed to test ability in vocabulary, spelling, and syntax, whereas the functional literacy task included multiple-choice questions that tapped the ability to make sense of the written features of such items as a newspaper article. The findings address the relationship of first-language to second-language comprehension ability, whether functional or academic, as well as the relationship of comprehension across genres. Studies examining such cross-linguistic relationships are reviewed in chapter 9.

Language Use and First-Language Literacy.   Some studies of language-minority students have examined the influence of language and literacy skills in the first language on second-language reading comprehension. The findings of these studies are briefly presented here; studies designed to examine the relationship between first-language oral language proficiency and second-language literacy are reviewed in more depth in chapter 8, those designed to examine the relationship between first- and second-language literacy in chapter 9, and those examining the impact of language use in the home on reading development in chapter 11. Several studies have examined the influence of first-language literacy skills and language use in the home on second-language reading comprehension performance. Given that language-minority students come from linguistically diverse backgrounds, how their first-language oral and written knowledge may affect their reading in a second language is of interest to the field of education.[1]

Studying a group of fourth-, fifth-, and sixth-grade native Spanish speakers from two predominantly Hispanic urban elementary schools, Nagy et al. (1993) found that cognate recognition ability was closely related to English reading comprehension performance. In another study of native Spanish speakers and English monolinguals, Nagy, McClure, and Mir (1997) examined the relationship between cross-linguistic errors on a task of lexical inferencing and reading comprehension performance. In the lexical inferencing task, the students had to select among four choices the most appropriate meaning for a nonword that was embedded in one to three sentences of English text. The native Spanish sample was composed of students enrolled in bilingual education (Spanish–English) classes and students in an English-only instructional setting in the same urban school district; the monolingual English students were from a small town.

The errors the students made on the lexical inferencing task were classified as (a) transfer errors, those consistent with Spanish but not English syntax; and (b) nontransfer errors, those not consistent with the syntax of either language. Overall, the native Spanish speakers made significantly more transfer and nontransfer errors than the monolingual English students. Nontransfer errors were significantly negatively correlated with reading comprehension in Spanish and English,

---

[1] Chapters 8 and 9 provide a comprehensive review of those studies conducted with language-minority students that were designed to examine cross-linguistic transfer in the areas of oral and writtten language.

whereas transfer errors were positively correlated with Spanish reading comprehension and unrelated to reading comprehension in English. Within the native Spanish group, the English-only-instructed students made fewer nontransfer errors than the bilingually instructed students but slightly more transfer errors.

Two studies in our database provide insight into language use and the influence of contextual variables on reading achievement. To investigate the impact of home language and other contextual variables on the academic achievement of a national sample of middle-school students in the United States, Kennedy and Park (1994) studied two groups of eighth-grade students—one ($n = 1,131$) of Asian origin (including Chinese, Filipino, Japanese, Korean, Vietnamese, Laotian, and Cambodian) and the other ($n = 1,952$) of Mexican origin. Variables in the study included indicators of the students' home background, SES, social-psychological variables, and indicators of school effort. The reading achievement measure was a standardized measure used as part of a battery of achievement tests not described in any detail. For the Asian-American students, home language was significantly related to performance in reading; students not speaking English in the home achieved a significantly lower score than those who did. For Mexican American students, much of the association of home language with achievement could be accounted for by socioeconomic and social-psychological factors.

In a study of native Spanish speakers, Hansen (1989) focused on the relationship between English-language gains in reading comprehension and auditory vocabulary throughout the school year and summer. The sample consisted of second and fifth graders from low socioeconomic backgrounds. The assumption was made that, during the summer, the children would be exposed more fully to family and community contexts—in this case, Mexican. However, the author provides no specific information about the children's summer activities. During the summer months, the children in the sample continued to increase in auditory vocabulary skills at about the same rate as they did during the school year. By contrast, the rate of growth in comprehension skills dropped dramatically in the absence of schooling. Further, the changes in rates of gain were far less uniform for comprehension than for auditory vocabulary; most of the students appeared to increase their auditory vocabulary over the summer at about the same pace as they had during the school year. Whereas language use (Spanish or English) in informal settings, such as leisure time with peers, was significantly associated with language gains, it was not significantly related to comprehension gains, but language use with peers during collaborative projects in the classroom was. According to the authors, the study findings suggest that, although the acquisition of simpler second-language skills (such as basic auditory vocabulary) may be facilitated by casual and relaxed use of language, the acquisition of a more complex and demanding skill (such as reading comprehension) in a second language requires experience with context-independent or formal use of language. However, future research must address this hypothesis using a study design that includes assessment of language use and related activities during the summer months.

Finally, in a study of sixth-grade Japanese students temporarily residing in the United States, Okamura-Bichard (1985) found that a composite measure of students' self-reports of their English listening, speaking, vocabulary, reading, and writing skills correlated highly with their performance on a global measure of reading that included vocabulary and comprehension components. The test employed was designed for third graders, but was used out of level with these sixth graders on the rationale that students in the study had been in the United States for 1 to 5 years. English reading test scores were also found to be related to years of English schooling. It should be noted that this study was focused primarily on the relationship between Japanese-language maintenance and English- language proficiency and the factors that influence success in bilingual development. It is discussed in further detail in chapter 5.

Metalinguistic Awareness. Awareness of language structures, including syntactic and pragmatic awareness, has been identified as having a significant influence on reading comprehension (e.g., Vellutino, Scanlon, Small, & Tanzman, 1991). Some research on bilingual children has focused on their metalinguistic awareness. This research has often been guided by the hypothesis that, especially at a young age, bilingual children may have a metalinguistic advantage because developing two languages draws children's attention to the structural aspects of the languages and gives them the opportunity to analyze and contrast the features of the two languages (Bruck & Genesee, 1995).

One study in our database demonstrated that abilities to reflect on and analyze language forms and functions were related to second-language reading comprehension performance. Carlisle, Beeman, and Shah (1996) examined the extent to which students' performance on an English reading comprehension task could be predicted by their performance on an English listening task and a word definition task in Spanish, considered to be an index of metalinguistic capabilities in the native language because the quality of definitions derives from reflection on the properties and uses of the language. The study was conducted with a sample of native-Spanish-speaking high school students from rural areas in Mexico receiving bilingual education services who had insufficient proficiency for mainstream English classrooms. The authors describe the city where the study was conducted as being ethnically diverse and working class. The English comprehension measure consisted of passages adapted from textbooks at the third-, fourth-, and fifth-grade levels. Comprehension was assessed with the sentence verification technique, whereby students had to judge whether ideas in the sentence did or did not appear in the passage. The students' word definitions were transcribed, analyzed, and scored for formal and informal definitional quality. The results indicate that quality of formal word definition (metalinguistic awareness) and English listening skills both contributed significantly to English reading comprehension performance. This study also contained measures and analyses related to Spanish-language proficiency and reading ability, and thus is reviewed in Part II of this volume.

Reader Strategies. Research on reading comprehension has consistently demonstrated that skilled readers use a variety of cognitive and metacognitive strategies to comprehend effectively and to use reading as a tool for learning (e.g., Palincsar & Brown, 1984; Pressley, 2000). Two studies in our database examined English-language learners' reported strategies while reading as compared with those of their monolingual English-speaking peers. The results of these studies indicate that English-language learners from Spanish-speaking backgrounds in elementary school used strategies both qualitatively and quantitatively different from those of their monolingual peers.

Padrón, Knight, and Waxman (1986) conducted a study to determine the comparability of the strategies that bilingual and monolingual students reported using to comprehend text. The students in the study were third and fifth graders who were either English monolinguals or native Spanish speakers reading in English. Students were asked to read silently a short passage that was within their reading level; they were stopped at regular intervals and asked to describe the strategies they were using to comprehend the passage. The strategies reported were classified into 14 categories (e.g., rereading, concentrating, predicting outcomes), and the results were examined by language group. For monolinguals, the most frequently cited strategy was concentrating on the story (e.g., thinking about the story, keeping it in mind, remembering it). No student cited the strategy of reading to answer questions that a teacher might be likely to ask. In contrast, this was the most frequently cited strategy for the group of language-minority students. Also in contrast to the monolingual children, no language-minority students reported using imaging strategies (i.e., making a picture in their mind), noting/searching for salient details, or predicting outcomes. Although it is known that strategy use is a significant aspect of skilled comprehension (e.g., Pressley, 2000), this study did not link reported strategy use to reading comprehension outcomes; thus, it is unclear which of these strategies may have been most effective for comprehension. In addition to the differences in strategy use by language group, the monolingual students reported using significantly more strategies than the language-minority students. It is important to note, however, that the number of times the students were stopped was unclear, especially given that the passage was only 120 words, as was whether the passages administered to the children were controlled in organization, type, and structure. This poses a problem for interpreting the findings, in that differences in such factors may have resulted in differences in reported strategies.

In another study designed to provide insight into students' strategies while reading, Padrón and Waxman (1988) studied the effects of second-language learners' reported strategies on gains in reading comprehension between January and April of a given school year. In January, Spanish-speaking English-language learners in the third, fourth, and fifth grades responded to questionnaire items on the extent to which they used particular strategies, and they were also administered a standardized test of reading comprehension comprising passages and multiple-choice questions. In April, the students were again administered the test of reading comprehension. The authors examined whether reported strategies were related to gains in reading comprehension over the 3 months of the study. As expected, two of the strategies included on the questionnaire that students reported using (thinking about something else while reading and saying the main idea over and over) were negatively related to students' gains in reading comprehension. These two variables, together with students' pretest reading comprehension performance, accounted for the majority of variance in reading comprehension performance in April. According to the authors, the results of the study indicate that students' perceptions of the cognitive strategies they use have predictive validity for their reading comprehension and lend support to the use of self-report measures in assessing strategy use. It is important to note, however, that 12 other strategies on the questionnaire expected to be related to reading comprehension did not make a significant contribution to reading comprehension performance. Further, *self-report* may be a misnomer, because the children had to choose from a predetermined list of strategies. Finally, although the study identified two ineffective strategies as reported by language-minority students reading English, it did not identify strategies that were positively related to reading comprehension.

Background Knowledge, Cultural Background, and Motivation. Given the importance of background knowledge for successful reading comprehension, as demonstrated by research with monolingual students (e.g., Anderson & Pearson, 1984), several studies have investigated the impact of such knowledge on text comprehension for second-language learners (Droop & Verhoeven, 1998; García, 1991; Hacquebord, 1994; Hannon & McNally, 1986). Studies that examined the relationship between cultural background knowledge and literacy are also described in chapter 11.

García (1991) examined the reading comprehension ability of fifth- and sixth-grade native-Spanish-speaking students and English monolinguals from two schools of middle to low SES in the United States. The reading comprehension measure administered to the children consisted of six expository passages at various levels of difficulty. The results of the study demonstrate that the performance of the native Spanish speakers was significantly lower than that of the native English speakers on an English reading comprehension measure. When native Spanish speakers' score on a test of prior knowledge related to the passages was controlled for, however, the group differences disappeared. Further, when the effect of question type was examined, even with prior knowledge controlled for, there were group differences on textually implicit questions. The author reports that the native-Spanish-speaking students had a tendency to interpret these questions literally. These results suggest that the English-language learners had underdeveloped background knowledge for the test administered and were not inclined to draw inferences from the text when it was appropriate to do so.

Similarly, Droop and Verhoeven (1998) found that the comprehension performance of Turkish and Moroccan third-grade children in the Netherlands was considerably better when they read culturally familiar text (describing students' own first-language culture), as opposed to text describing their second-language (Dutch) culture, which was considered culturally unfamiliar to the second-language learners of Dutch. To assess this skill, children were asked to respond to 5 questions constructed to assess prior knowledge and 12 *wh-* questions designed to assess their comprehension of the text.

In a study of second-language secondary school learners of Dutch in the Netherlands, Hacquebord (1994) demonstrated that linguistic and conceptual knowledge may have had differential impacts on text comprehension performance among Turkish–Dutch bilingual secondary school students. Whereas second-language linguistic knowledge of Dutch appeared to enhance micro-level text analysis, background knowledge that was relevant to the text being read facilitated global text understanding. The fact that the second-language learners' restricted linguistic knowledge did not impede their global text understanding implies that relevant background knowledge among second-language learners may compensate for their limited linguistic knowledge during comprehension. This finding probably reflects the age and experience of this sample of older second-language learners. Although the authors do not provide specific details, it is likely that many of these students had schooling experience and literacy skills in their native language and thus relevant background knowledge on which to draw. The role of prior literacy and schooling experience in second-language reading comprehension is an underdeveloped area of research that would yield valuable information for second-language instruction and policy.

To examine the relationship of reading comprehension performance to background knowledge and cultural background, Hannon and McNally (1986) conducted a study of 7- and 8-year-olds from various demographic and linguistic backgrounds in the United Kingdom. The sample included native-English-speaking children from working-class homes, native-English-speaking children from middle-class homes, and children from homes where English was a second language. The reading measure was a multiple-choice sentence completion test. The test was administered as a group reading test, but also as an individual oral test 1 week later; this was done to gain insight into children's understanding of test items as distinct from their ability to read the items.

In addition to making mistakes on the reading test, many children made mistakes on the oral test, which made no demands on their reading ability. The children's understanding of test items and overall performance was found to vary considerably according to cultural background: The English speakers from working-class backgrounds and the language-minority children showed significantly poorer performance than those English speakers from middle-class backgrounds on both the oral and reading tests. Further, there was a high correlation between errors on each form of the test. These findings, along with the results of analyses demonstrating that oral test performance predicted the majority of variance in reading test performance, and even more of the variance when taken together with social class, provide clear evidence that low socioeconomic and/or language-minority status, independent of reading ability, has a significant influence on English reading comprehension performance. (SES is discussed further later in the section on contextual factors.) These results also have important implications for reading comprehension assessment and instruction. Specifically, they highlight the fact that word reading skills are a necessary but not sufficient condition for effective comprehension. They suggest that the difficulties for some groups of children may lie strictly in their lack of the background knowledge or oral proficiency necessary for the demands of the test. These findings are consistent with research on monolinguals revealing that background knowledge is a strong predictor of text comprehension among first-language readers (e.g., Anderson & Pearson, 1984; Moravcsik & Kintsch, 1993).

In a series of studies of Arabic students, Abu-Rabia (1995, 1996, 1998a, 1998b) studied the impact of two types of motivation—instrumental (e.g., learning the language to get a job or pursue higher education) and integrative (e.g., learning the language to make Jewish friends)—on language-minority students' reading comprehension performance, as well as the impact of cultural familiarity with the text at hand.

In one study, Abu-Rabia (1995) examined the factors that influence English reading comprehension performance for a group of eighth-grade Arab-Canadian English-language learners who had been living in Toronto, Canada, for 2 or 3 years. The home language of the students was Arabic, and they attended Arabic heritage language programs for 2 hours a week. The factors examined included students' cultural background, first-language proficiency, second-language proficiency, instrumental motivation, and integrative motivation, as well as the language of the text. The reading comprehension measures (Arabic and English) included six passages with 10 multiple-choice questions per passage. Of the 10 questions, 5 were literal and referred to explicit material from the passage, whereas the other 5 were inferential. The Arabic passages included Arabic cultural content so the influence of culturally relevant content on reading comprehension performance could be examined. Abu-Rabia found that instrumental and integrative motivation contributed equally to variance in reading comprehension. However, the main finding of interest is that an Arabic cultural background did not facilitate students' reading comprehension in stories with Arabic cultural content even when this content was presented in the first language. Overall, comprehension was better in English than in Arabic. These findings are interesting and perhaps counterintuitive, and they are inconsistent with the results of Abu-Rabia's (1996, 1998a, 1998b) other studies of Arabic-Hebrew bilinguals in Israel. It is important to note, however, that the context was quite different: These children were language-minority students who had lived in Canada for at least 2 years and were receiving their instruction predominantly in English.

In a study of 15- and 16-year-old native-Arabic-speaking Druze students living in Israel and acquiring Hebrew and English as additional languages, Abu-Rabia (1996) examined the role of the students' interest in reading comprehension performance in Hebrew and the influence their cultural background had on their comprehension of culturally familiar and unfamiliar stories in Hebrew. The study was also designed to investigate the influence of students' attitudes toward Hebrew learning on reading comprehension performance in Hebrew. The Druze minority students possessed positive instrumental and integrative motivation toward the Hebrew language and its speakers; however, the culturally familiar content of the text facilitated reading comprehension, and the students were more interested in reading the culturally familiar texts. Level of cultural familiarity and students' reports of a tendency toward assimilation explained a significant amount of variance in Hebrew reading comprehension performance.

Abu-Rabia (1998a) conducted a related study with 15- and 16-year-old native Arab speakers residing in Israel and learning Hebrew and English as their additional languages. Abu-Rabia found that familiar content of text facilitated reading comprehension for the Arab language-minority students. The results also indicate that the Arab language-minority students in Israel who participated in the study possessed instrumental attitudes and external integrativeness (i.e., no identification with the target language and its culture) toward the Hebrew language and speakers, but did not possess internal integrativeness (i.e., identification with the target language and culture). Finally, cultural familiarity of text, individual interest in the text, and instrumental motivation were powerful predictors of Hebrew reading comprehension for the native Arabic speakers.

In another similar study, Abu-Rabia (1998b) examined the cultural background of eighth-grade native Arabic speakers learning Hebrew in Israel and their attitudes as factors potentially influencing reading comprehension performance. The majority of students were of low SES. The 74 students were assigned randomly to four experimental groups, each of which received four stories: (a) Jewish stories in Hebrew, (b) Jewish stories in Arabic, (c) Arab stories in Arabic, and (d) Arab stories in Hebrew. Each story was accompanied by 10 multiple-choice questions (5 explicit and 5 implicit), and students were able to refer back to the text while they worked through the questions. Participants were also administered a questionnaire designed to examine Arab students' attitudes toward learning Hebrew. They were asked to rate, on a scale of 1 to 5, their agreement with particular statements, each with a focus on one of the two types of motivation. Instrumental motivation was conceptualized by agreement with statements that reflected learning Hebrew for reasons such as getting a job or pursuing higher education, and integrative motivation by agreement with statements focused on learning Hebrew for reasons such as meeting Jewish friends.

The results of the attitude questionnaire showed that the motivation of the Arab students in learning Hebrew was primarily instrumental rather than integrative. Arab students achieved higher scores on stories with Arab cultural content than on stories with Jewish cultural content, whether in Arabic or Hebrew. On the explicit information questions, instrumental motivation of Arab students in Israel toward learning Hebrew was the strongest predictor, followed by content familiarity and the language of the text. On the implicit inference questions, instrumental motivation was the strongest predictor of performance, followed by text content, language of text, and finally integrative motivation. The significant predictors of total reading scores (combination of explicit and implicit questions) were instrumental motivation and content of text, not integrative motivation or language of text.

In three of these studies conducted by Abu-Rabia and colleagues (1996, 1998a, 1998b), the impact of educational context on second-language reading comprehension of minority students in Israel was examined. In Israel, the Israeli Arab population learns the societal language, Hebrew, as a second language, and there is little social interaction between Jews and Arabs. Further, the Arab school system receives 30% to 50% fewer resources than the Jewish school system, and the Arab schools have a severe lack of services for pedagogical development and children with learning/reading disabilities. Hebrew instruction typically takes place 5 hours a week beginning in Grade 4, and a final matriculation exam in Hebrew must be passed in Grade 12 to enroll in higher education in Israel. Abu-Rabia suggests that the combination of unfamiliar Jewish text content and a problematic social context may have negatively influenced the Arab students' second-language learning process. Given their focus on the social context of literacy development, the findings of these studies are also discussed in chapter 11.

Acculturation.   One study in our database examined the influence of acculturation on reading achievement. Acculturation is defined as the process of learning new cultural rules and interpersonal expectations as a direct result of contact with another distinct cultural group (Berry, Poortinga, & Pandey, 1997; Roysircar-Sodowsky & Maestas, 2000). Participation in two cultures often results in changes in attitudes and behaviors toward both the minority and dominant groups (Berry et al., 1997; Phinney, Romero, Nava, & Huang, 2001). For immigrant children and adults, acculturation takes place in varying degrees and along multiple pathways (Portes, 2000). In the research on development, acculturation is typically operationalized by measuring language use and preference, attitudes toward the first and second languages, and peer group preferences (Roysircar-Sodowsky & Maestas, 2000). For language-minority students, especially recent immigrants, schools may be the primary source of contact with the majority culture and thus play an important contextual role in acculturation (Phinney et al., 2001; Suárez-Orozco & Suárez-Orozco, 2001).

García-Vázquez (1995) conducted a study to examine the influence of acculturation to the school environment and to the student's own culture on the reading achievement of Mexican American youth. The English-language learners were in seventh through ninth grades in a rural Midwestern town; no information about the SES of the participants is provided. One of the acculturation measures administered to the children was a scale developed to measure their adaptation to the school environment; it consists of items that address the number of years in the United States, in the school district, and in English-as-a-second-language (ESL) or bilingual education classrooms, as well as degree of first- and second-language proficiency and ethnicity or nation of origin. No information on the reliability or validity of the scale is provided. The second acculturation measure used was one designed for Mexican-American students—a 10-item scale that assesses such factors as English proficiency, parents' occupations, language preference and language spoken at home, and identification preference. The information for each student was drawn from student folders, as was their score on a standardized, global measure of reading that is administered to all children in the school. Both scales yield a total score that falls along a single continuum of less to more acculturated. There were no statistically significant correlations between any measure of acculturation and reading achievement, suggesting that for the students studied, maintaining identification with their Mexican ethnicity did not have a significant effect on their English reading achievement. More research with validated instruments is needed to draw conclusions about the influence of acculturation on reading achievement.

Text Factors. A number of text attributes, including plot structure, pronoun reference, text content and difficulty, organization, vocabulary density, syntactic complexity, discourse style, and genre, influence reading comprehension (Kintsch & Van Dijk, 1978; for a discussion, see RAND, 2002). See also chapter 11 for a discussion of the influence of culturally familiar text and text language on literacy. One study in our database was designed to examine the influence of text attributes on the reading comprehension of second-language learners.

Bean (1982) conducted a study to examine the effects of story structure on the English reading comprehension of fourth- and fifth-grade native Spanish speakers. The children attended a suburban school, but no specific demographic information is provided. Students were assigned to one of three story conditions. After reading a passage silently, they were asked to retell the story in their own words and then respond orally to questions designed to assess their understanding of the gist of the story. In the first condition, students read a portion of a text that had not been manipulated in any way. In the second condition, the same portion of text had been rewritten to make obscure pronoun referents more explicit without modifying the story structure. In the third condition, the story structure had been modified to delete trivial events that detracted from a predictable problem-solving pattern. The results indicate that students were able to comprehend the gist of the story significantly better when it had been restructured to conform to a predictable problem-solving scenario.

Demographic Factors.   Research examining the influence of demographic factors (e.g., SES) and other contextual variables not discussed earlier (e.g., schooling experiences) on reading comprehension performance has been conducted primarily with monolingual students. This research has shown these factors to have an influence on reading achievement (e.g., National Center for Education Statistics, 1995). In addition, several studies in our database examined the influence of such factors on the development of second-language reading comprehension skills. The measure of reading employed in these studies is usually described in general terms as reading comprehension or a composite measure of reading typically comprising several skills related to comprehension, including vocabulary.

Although SES and length of second-language schooling were found to be strongly correlated with second-language reading performance, based on large data sets with aggregated group data, the studies provide little information, beyond correlations, explaining why and how these factors influence second-language literacy development. See Part III for further discussion of the role of demographic factors on literacy development.

In a study of a sample of 12th graders, Buriel and Cardoza (1988) examined the influence of language status and SES on achievement for first-, second-, and third-generation Mexican American high school seniors. The standardized reading achievement measure (no specific details provided) was administered to students as part of a U.S. national survey, with a particular focus on collecting data on language-minority students. The results indicate that there were no differences in reading achievement among first-, second-, and third-generation Mexican American students. For the first- and second-generation students, their aspirations were the only variable having a significant influence on reading achievement. In addition to their aspirations, the third-generation students were influenced in their English (second-language) reading achievement by Spanish oral proficiency and Spanish literacy.

Cahill (1987) conducted a study of Italian 10-year-old English-language learners to identify the personal, familial, and schooling factors critical to the development of bilingual competence (i.e., listening, speaking, reading, and writing in two languages). The author reports that the students were living in an area generally classified as working- and lower middle-class with middle- and upper middle-class pockets. The English reading measure is described as a 20-item reading test; no specific details about the test are provided. Factors found to be significantly correlated with English reading included performance on measures of nonverbal intelligence, cognitive style, modern-language aptitude, and self-concept. Also significantly correlated with children's English (second-language) reading ability were their scores on a questionnaire assessing their liking for school and, based on parent interviews, parents' support for academic achievement and Italian language development.

Three large-scale studies (Fernández & Nielsen, 1986; Ima & Rumbaut, 1989; Rosenthal, Baker, & Ginsburg, 1983) examined the reading performance of language-minority youth. Within a sample of U.S. high school students, Fernández and Nielsen (1986) identified four distinct groups: monolingual English-speaking Hispanics ($n = 474$), bilingual Hispanics ($n = 1,876$), monolingual English-speaking Whites ($n = 13,436$), and bilingual Whites (non-Hispanic) from diverse linguistic backgrounds ($n = 1,260$). The study was designed to examine the effects of language proficiency, SES, and length of U.S. residency on academic achievement. The attributes of the reading assessment are not described. The analyses demonstrated that for the bilinguals, self-assessed proficiency in the first and second languages was correlated with scores on standardized reading tests. For each of the four groups, SES was a significant predictor of performance on reading; for the Hispanic English monolinguals, it was the only significant predictor. For the White bilinguals, gender, English proficiency, and use of their other language were predictors of reading performance, in addition to SES. For the Hispanic bilinguals, gender, English proficiency, Spanish use, and being of Cuban ethnicity were significant predictors.

In another large-scale survey study involving 12,322 students in first through sixth grades, Rosenthal et al. (1983) compared the relative impact of home background variables (SES and ethnicity) and pattern of home language use on a global measure of reading achievement. Their results indicate that home background variables were related more strongly than home language use to academic achievement among Hispanic children in U.S. schools. However, greater use of the first language (Spanish) had a negative impact on academic achievement in English. Students whose parents reported the exclusive use of Spanish in helping with homework scored significantly lower than those whose parents reported using both English and Spanish or English alone. It is important to consider third or mediating variables in interpreting these findings; for example, it may be that strictly Spanish-speaking homes are of lower SES than homes where both English and Spanish are spoken. Other mediating variables may include language used for instruction as well as quality of instruction.

Ima and Rumbaut (1989) conducted a study of a large sample ($n = 5,472$) of refugee language-minority youth to examine the English proficiency and academic achievement of this population. Within the larger sample, the authors also examined the academic achievement of a random sample of Southeast Asian students ($n = 239$) that encompassed five linguistic groups (Khmer, Lao, Hmong, Chinese, and Vietnamese). The analyses were conducted by using home survey data and school records of the participants, including their scores on a global reading achievement measure that included vocabulary and comprehension subtests. A comparison of the academic performance of the subsample of Southeast Asian students and the other language-minority students showed that the former were most likely to be classified as limited English proficient and, among all the ethnic groups, had the lowest scores on the reading achievement measure. A comparison of the educational attainment of the five Southeast Asian subgroups demonstrated that the Vietnamese students had the highest reading scores, followed by the Chinese, the Vietnamese, the Khmer, the Lao, and, finally, the Hmong. Because the sample of 239 was divided into five subgroups, the cell sizes were too small to permit examination of predictors of reading achievement for each subgroup. As preliminary, relatively unstable findings, the authors report that the higher the parents' level of education, the more time the students had spent in the United States, and the younger they were, the higher their scores were on the composite reading measure.

Finally, Collier (1987) conducted a study of 1,548 language-minority students in kindergarten through 11th grade who came from more than 100 different countries and spoke more than 75 different languages; Spanish, Korean, and Vietnamese speakers represented the largest language groups within the sample. The students were of lower to middle-class socioeconomic backgrounds (65% qualified for free or reduced-price lunches) by U.S. economic standards, but the author reports that they had strong middle-class backgrounds in their home countries. The students had little or no proficiency in English, and they were close to grade level in academic skills in their first language. The sample included all language-minority children who had been placed in beginning-level classes in English as a second language on entry to U.S. schools and had remained in the school system for several years. Those who tested below grade level in their first-language skills and older students with little or no formal schooling in their first language were excluded from the study. In the district where the study was conducted, students were in mainstream English classrooms and received some ESL instruction daily until staff members believed they could function full time in the mainstream; this usually happened within 2 to 3 years of entry into the school system.

Collier investigated whether age at entry into U.S. schools affected the rate of development of academic language skills among the 11 language groups, examined by grade, within the sample. The majority of comparisons by length of residence in the United States demonstrated that, within the language-minority groups, by grade, the more years of English schooling they had, the higher were their scores on a global measure of English reading achievement. In reading and other content areas examined, the language-minority students who arrived in the United States between the ages of 8 and 11 were the fastest achievers, requiring 2 to 5 years to reach the 50th percentile on the standardized measure. Students who entered the program between the ages of 5 and 7 were still 1 to 3 years behind in academic achievement (as assessed with normed instruments), compared with the 8- to 11-year-olds when both groups had the same length of residence. Further, students who arrived between the ages of 12 and 15 experienced the greatest difficulties and were projected by the author to require 6 to 8 years to reach average levels on the standardized measures of academic achievement.

Multiple Factors.   Research on the factors that influence reading comprehension performance has identified many factors, both individual and contextual, as having an impact on comprehension (see RAND, 2002, for a discussion). One study (Connor, 1983) in our database, conducted with English-language learners, examined the influence of a large number of variables ($n = 21$) on students' reading comprehension performance. This study is also discussed in chapter 11.

This study was designed to identify individual, sociocultural, and language factors that influenced the reading skills of a sample of English-language learners in the United States. The sample consisted of 91 students in Grades 2 through 12 (55% elementary school, 15% middle school, and 30% high school) from 21 different language backgrounds. A standardized measure of reading comprehension was used; the test form selected for each student depended on his or her grade level and the teacher's estimate of the student's reading ability. Socioeconomic information collected included parental level of education and the child's SES.

Variables that had a positive effect on reading scores included grade level in school, Vietnamese language background, percentage of English spoken at home, higher level paternal occupation, and number of students in the ESL classroom. Although grade level and class size had a positive effect on reading scores, it is important to consider the nature of these relationships. The larger the class size, the stronger the relationship with achievement; given that the class sizes increased with grade level, up to 12, a likely third variable in this relationship is oral language proficiency, which is likely to be developing with increasing years of ESL classes, such that older children with more English are likely to in be larger classes.

Surprisingly, intensity of instruction in ESL showed a statistically significant negative effect on reading score. The author suggests that this finding reflects that teachers were correctly allocating more hours to the children who were in need of this instruction. However, it is also important to consider that the methods of instruction for these learners may not have been effective or suited to the difficulties the language-minority students were experiencing.

Predictors that did not have a significant effect on reading performance included gender, number of siblings and birth order, hours of TV watching, number of public library visits, length of parents' stay in the United States and parents' levels of education and social status.

For several reasons, this study provides minimal opportunity to draw substantive conclusions about the factors that influence the reading comprehension performance of language-minority students. The sample included 91 students from 2nd through 12th grades, and the findings were not disaggregated by grade or reading ability. Moreover, the study addressed the influence of 21 variables on reading achievement. The sheer number of variables and corresponding sample size, as well as the limited theoretical basis for the model, are problematic for interpretation of the results.

Factors That Influence Second-Language Reading Comprehension: Summary. The studies reviewed in this section demonstrate that many variables at both the individual (e.g., literacy skills, motivation) and contextual (e.g., home literacy, demographics) levels influence the second-language reading comprehension of language-minority students. Many of these studies included only a sample of language-minority students, with no comparative sample of native speakers. Thus, it is not possible to determine whether the impact of these factors may vary as a function of language status.

The Development of Writing Skills for Second-Language Learners

Like reading comprehension, writing is a multidimensional process. It involves word-level skills (e.g., letter production, spelling), cognitive abilities (e.g., working memory, attention), and higher order skills (e.g., planning, metacognition, strategy use, and self-regulation). Just as effective reading comprehension is dependent, in part, on fluent, automatic decoding, effective writing development depends, in part, on automatization of low-level transcription skills (Berninger, Yates, Cartwright, Rutberg, Remy, & Abbott, 1992). Specifically, such skills as letter production must be fluent so that cognitive resources, especially working memory, can be devoted to integrating all the other skills involved in creating written output. Both cognitive and metacognitive skills contribute to writing development during middle and high school (Wong, 1997). With respect to language-minority students, it is important to note that their writing skills do not simply mirror their oral language proficiency. When creating written text, particularly expository text, students must generate discourse in the absence of the social context of oral communication (Berninger, 1994). As with reading comprehension, writing is influenced by sociocultural practices (Pérez, 1998); discourse styles that are specific to particular cultures may differ from those of the language-minority student (Schierloh, 1991).

Four studies in our database that examined the writing performance of language-minority students focused on English-language learners. In all four studies, the language-minority students were native Spanish speakers. Three of the studies focused on late elementary and middle-school students (Bermúdez & Prater, 1994; Ferris & Politzer, 1981; Lanauze & Snow, 1989), whereas one focused on children in elementary school (Davis, Carlisle, & Beeman, 1999).

The four studies varied in the way writing was assessed and examined. Students were asked to compose a genre-specific piece based on a short prompt (Bermúdez & Prater, 1994; Davis et al., 1999) or to write in response to a picture (Lanauze & Snow, 1989) or short film (Ferris & Politzer, 1981). All the studies scored the students' writing on multiple dimensions, including overall quality, linguistic and syntactic complexity, lexical variety, genre-specific features, semantics, productivity, and spelling.

The samples in all four studies were limited to language-minority students, without a comparison group of monolinguals. Two studies examined writing performance in both the first and second languages (Davis et al., 1999; Lanauze & Snow, 1989), whereas the other two studies (Bermúdez & Prater, 1994; Ferris & Politzer, 1981) examined writing performance in the second language only.

In the only study that examined language-minority students' writing in the early elementary grades, Davis et al. (1999) examined the Spanish and English writing of Spanish-speaking children in first, second, and third grades. The children were in a mainstream English program and were receiving instruction in a literature-based program. For approximately 20% of the day, however, they received Spanish oral language instruction. The students wrote on the topic "The funniest thing that happened to me" in both English and Spanish, with a one-week interval between the two. The compositions were scored on productivity, linguistic complexity, spelling, long words, and discourse. In addition to the writing task, the authors designed a reading comprehension measure for both languages based on grade-level-appropriate books in Spanish and English written by the same author. The students answered multiple-choice questions assessing their comprehension of a segment of each book. Analyses revealed that there was a significant effect of grade on writing proficiency; significant development in English writing took place from first through third grades, with the most dramatic development taking place between first and second grades. There was no significant effect for language of the assessment (English or Spanish). The study revealed that productivity and spelling in English were significantly related to all five aspects of Spanish writing measured in this study, whereas English linguistic complexity was significantly related to all Spanish measures except discourse. Additionally, there was a significant relationship between all measures of English writing and English reading comprehension.

In their study of fourth and fifth graders, Lanauze and Snow (1989) compared the English and Spanish composition ability of children from Puerto Rican working-class families whose primary home language was Spanish. The children were enrolled in a Spanish–English bilingual program. The sample included three groups of English-language learners with differing levels of proficiency in English and Spanish based on teacher ratings: One group of students had high proficiency in both languages, another had high proficiency in Spanish with limited proficiency in English, and the third had limited proficiency in both languages. The children were given a writing task, in both Spanish (first language) and English, in which they had to describe a picture. The writing samples were scored for language complexity and sophistication, language variety, and how much and what kind of information was provided about the picture. The authors found that first-language proficiency was a better predictor of writing performance than second-language proficiency. The children who were rated *good* in both languages (GG) and those rated *poor* in English, but *good* in Spanish (PG), scored better in Spanish and English than the children rated poor in both languages (PP). The PG children made more spelling errors and more language interference errors in English than did the GG children. English writing was equivalent. In addition, the PG group wrote longer, syntactically more complex, and semantically more complete essays than the PP group in both English and Spanish. The authors suggest that the PG children were transferring academic and literacy skills from the first to the second language before their second-language oral–aural skills had sufficiently developed, so that the poorer performance of the PP group in English may have reflected their lack of academic and literacy skills in their first language. The findings of this study show that there is significant variation within the English-language learner population. These individual differences and the low scores of some of the students may indicate a possible learning disability, and they may highlight the importance of the examination of individual differences in writing skills. This study is also reviewed in chapter 9.

In another study of fourth graders, Bermúdez and Prater (1994) examined the persuasive writing of native-Spanish-speaking students from two inner-city schools. The sample of language-minority students included a group of children identified as being in the process of acquiring English proficiency, who thus attended ESL classes, as well as a group of English-language learners who had already been mainstreamed into regular English classrooms. The children were asked to write an essay in response to a standard prompt designed to elicit persuasive writing. Writing samples were then assessed according to a holistic score of the overall quality of persuasive discourse, as well as the number and category of appeals made in the writing sample. The results indicate that there was no significant effect for group (instruction in ESL vs. mainstream) on any of the persuasive essay criteria. On the basis of this lack of group differences, the authors concluded that students may have been exiting ESL classes without having achieved a high level of expertise in persuasive writing. An effect of gender was also detected: Female English-language learners ($n = 18$) performed better than their male counterparts ($n = 19$). One caution related to this study is that the authors provided no reliability statistics on their procedure for scoring the essays.

The fourth study of writing conducted with middle-school students (Ferris & Politzer, 1981) compared the composition skills of two groups of seventh- and eighth-grade native Spanish speakers. One group had been born and educated in Mexico until the third or fourth grade and then in English in the United States through middle school, whereas the other had been born in the United States and educated in English from kindergarten. Students were asked to write on a short film that had been prerated for its level of interest and motivation to Spanish speakers; they were asked to write at least 100 words as they viewed the film, after which they were given 40 minutes to complete the writing sample. English composition skills were assessed by using holistic evaluation for clarity and coherence and a frequency count evaluation of grammar errors; the writing was also assessed for structural complexity. Despite their differences in language and context of instruction, there were no significant differences between the two groups on the English composition measures.

The two studies that examined writing ability in both the students' first and second languages (Davis et al., 1999; Lanauze & Snow, 1989) found that performance in the first language reflected aspects of performance in the second language and vice versa. Given the small number of studies, coupled with the heterogeneity of those studies in task, assessment, and grade levels, it is not possible to draw substantive conclusions about the writing development of language-minority youth. Additionally, because none of these studies was longitudinal, it is not possible to determine the factors that influence writing development in language-minority children.

Text-Level Skills: Summary

In general, there has been a dearth of research on the development of text-level skills, specifically reading comprehension and writing, among language-minority students that informs our understanding of how these skills may develop differently for this population, compared with monolingual speakers. Only seven studies in our database compared the reading comprehension of language-minority youths and their monolingual peers. Of those seven studies, five were conducted in the Netherlands, one in the United States, and one in Canada. Overall, the results of these studies suggest that reading comprehension is an area of difficulty for language-minority students as early as the second grade and through to high school. This finding is not surprising given the multidimensional nature of reading comprehension and the influence of such factors as vocabulary and prior knowledge on comprehension performance.

Studies examining the factors that influence reading comprehension confirmed that, as for monolingual speakers, factors related to the individual (e.g., word-level skills, motivation), the text (e.g., story structure), and the social context (e.g., home literacy practices, demographics) have an influence on the reading comprehension performance of second-language learners. Some studies demonstrated that indeed second-language learners' comprehension is adversely affected by a lack of appropriate prior knowledge (e.g., García, 1991) or of cultural familiarity with the text (e.g., Abu-Rabia, 1998a, 1998b).

It is also of note that most studies examining the factors that influence reading comprehension included only a language-minority student sample without a comparison group of monolingual speakers. Thus, it is not possible to determine whether the impact of those factors varies as a function of language background.

Similarly, each of the writing studies reviewed analyzed the writing abilities of a single group of language-minority students without a comparison with native speakers. Findings from two of these studies (Davis et al., 1999; Lanauze & Snow, 1989) suggest that cross-linguistic transfer may play an important role in second-language writing.

Studies reviewed in this section vary significantly in the extent to which the demographic context of the study is reported. Some studies report the SES of either the children or the school(s) where the research was conducted (Aarts & Verhoeven, 1999; Abu-Rabia, 1998b; Bermúdez & Prater, 1994; Buriel & Cardoza, 1988; Collier, 1987; Droop & Verhoeven, 1998; García, 1991; Hansen, 1989; Ima & Rumbaut, 1989; Lanauze & Snow, 1989; McEvoy & Johnson, 1989; Padrón et al., 1986; Reese et al., 2000; Verhoeven, 1990, 2000). Others provide some such information but not the specific SES of the language-minority students (Abu-Rabia, 1998a; Cahill, 1987; Carlisle et al., 1996; Padrón & Waxman, 1988). Still others provide no socioeconomic information (Abu-Rabia, 1995, 1996; Bean, 1982; Davis et al., 1999; Ferris & Politzer, 1981; García-Vázquez, 1995; Hacquebord, 1994; Nagy et al., 1993, 1997; Okamura-Bichard, 1985). In other studies, demographic factors are included as variables in the analyses (Connor, 1983; Fernández & Nielsen, 1986; Hannon & McNally, 1986; Kennedy & Park, 1994; Rosenthal et al., 1983).

The importance of reporting SES in these studies stems from the fact that SES at the aggregate (i.e., neighborhood or school) level has a stronger relationship to school achievement (White, 1982) than that at the individual level. Although there are several possible explanations for this finding, and results are inconclusive about which specific characteristics have the strongest impact, it is important to note that children from low-income neighborhoods attend schools that have limited resources and perhaps less educational opportunity as a result. The implications of this observation are important in considering the role of SES in the academic achievement and opportunities to learn of language-minority students, given that many of these children reside in low-income areas (August & Hakuta, 1997; Snow et al., 1998).

Taken together, the findings from these studies indicate that language-minority children and youth are a heterogeneous group, and attention must be paid to the range of individual differences among them. It is clear that on measures of word reading and spelling, many language-minority children are performing at levels similar to those of their native-speaking peers. It also appears that a similar proportion of language-minority students have difficulties in their second languages that resemble the reading disabilities of native English speakers. With regard to reading comprehension, unlike the findings of studies that focus on language-minority students' performance on word-level tasks, these students experience difficulties as compared with their native-speaking peers. Such difficulties may be related to limited oral language proficiency, lack of exposure to print, limited opportunities to learn and poor quality of literacy instruction, and inability to navigate complex text and draw inferences from prior knowledge. Thus, the difficulties of language-minority children should not necessarily be attributed to a learning disability. Instead, research should focus on optimal educational interventions for these children that consider both contextual and child-level factors.

5

Second-Language Oral Proficiency and Second-Language Literacy

Esther Geva

In this chapter, we examine studies pertaining to the relationship between English oral language proficiency (vocabulary, grammar, and listening comprehension) and various English reading skills among English-language learners. Although oral language proficiency is one of the many components that influence the development of literacy, it is reported on separately in this chapter, rather than as part of chapter 4, because of the important role it is presumed to play in the development of literacy in language-minority students. The chapter is organized according to literacy outcomes. We begin by reviewing studies that examine the relationship between diverse aspects of English oral proficiency and word-level reading skills in English, including word and pseudoword reading and spelling. This is followed by an examination of research on the relationships between various aspects of oral language proficiency in English and text- or discourse-level skills (i.e., reading comprehension and writing). Each of these skill sets is addressed within a developmental framework.

Quantitative studies often measure one or two aspects of oral language proficiency (e.g., vocabulary, grammatical skills). The use of such measures enables researchers to compare performance among groups in a systematic way. Qualitative studies often use elicitation techniques to obtain speech samples from a relatively small number of participants. Some researchers believe that where oral language proficiency is concerned, the whole is bigger than the sum of the parts, and that naturalistic, authentic language samples provide more valid assessments of language proficiency. Both types of studies are included in this chapter.

The following research questions are addressed in this chapter:

1. What is the relationship between English oral proficiency and English word-level skills?

2. What is the relationship between English oral proficiency and English text-level skills?

WORD-LEVEL SKILLS

Relationship Between English Oral Proficiency and English Word and Pseudoword Reading

This section focuses on research on the relationship between English oral language proficiency and second-language word and pseudoword reading. Examining this relationship in English-language learners is important so that we can examine whether English-language learners are at a disadvantage relative to their monolingual, native-speaking peers in the development of word and pseudoword reading skills because of their limited English proficiency (Geva & Wade-Woolley, 2004).

The largest number of studies examining the relative contribution of English oral proficiency in English to the development of word-level and pseudoword reading skills in English, the students' second language, involved elementary school-age children. Some of these studies found that oral language proficiency in English (typically conceptualized in terms of vocabulary or grammatical knowledge) is not a unique or, for that matter, robust predictor of word-level reading skills in English. Some studies that used a regression approach found that, although English oral language proficiency may correlate positively and significantly with word and pseudoword reading skills in English and may explain some unique variance in these reading skills, certain aspects of phonological processing (e.g., phoneme deletion and rapid automatized naming [RAN]) in English are more robust and consistent predictors of English word and pseudoword reading.

A study by Jackson and Lu (1992) provides indirect evidence for a lack of association between oral language proficiency in English and English word reading skills. This study involved a group of English-language learners from a variety of first-language backgrounds who demonstrated advanced reading comprehension skills in English before beginning Grade 1. These precocious English-language learners scored more than 1 standard deviation below the native-speaking comparison group on two measures of oral language proficiency—oral cloze and sentence memory. Yet they were just as fluent as the monolingual group on word reading. Thus, these precocious readers were able to read better than might be expected on the basis of their oral language skills in English.

Three studies involved Latino children. In the first study, Durgunoglu, Nagy, and Hancin-Bhatt (1993) found that English oral proficiency was not a significant predictor of English word and pseudoword reading skills, whereas Spanish phonological awareness was significant in a group of beginning (first-grade) readers of low socioeconomic status (SES). English oral proficiency was measured with the Pre-Language Assessment Scales (Pre-LAS), in particular, subtests that examine expressive and receptive language skills in three domains of oral language—morphology, syntax, and semantics.

A recent study (Quiroga, Lemos-Britten, Mostafapour, Abbott, & Berninger, 2002) also examined predictors of word reading skills in Spanish–English bilingual students in Grade 1. This study found that English oral language proficiency (measured with the Pre-LAS) did correlate moderately with word reading and pseudoword decoding in English. In addition, the correlation of phonological awareness (a phoneme-deletion task) with English word reading and pseudoword decoding skills was high. However, regression analyses showed that phonological awareness explained significant and unique proportions of the variance in the students' English word reading and pseudoword reading scores, but scores on the Pre-LAS test did not explain unique variance in these reading skills when they were entered into the regression after phonological awareness and letter knowledge in English.

In another study involving Spanish-speaking children, Gottardo (2002) also reports a significant but small correlation between English oral language proficiency measures and word reading measures in English. More specifically, she examined the relationship between a number of language skills (semantic and syntactic processing), phonological awareness, and word reading skills in primary-level, Mexican American, English-language learners of low SES. The children were being taught in English. Correlational analyses showed that English oral proficiency measures of vocabulary and syntactic processing correlated significantly with the children's performance on an English word reading test. Regression analysis revealed further that performance on a word reading task in English was related most strongly to performance on a pheneme deletion task, but that knowledge of English vocabulary maintained a significant relationship with reading and explained a unique proportion of the variance (3%) even after the effects of phonological processing were taken into account. One possible explanation for the difference between the Durgunoglu et al. (1993) study and the Gottardo (2002) study with regard to the role of vocabulary and syntactic processing in word and pseudoword reading skills is this: In the latter study the children were being taught in English so that their English language skills were more developed, whereas in the former study the children were in a transitional bilingual education program and presumably had had less exposure to English and fewer opportunities to develop their English-language proficiency at the time of the study.

The other studies reviewed here involved children from a range of linguistic, ethnic, and educational backgrounds. Muter and Diethelm (2001) examined the association between various aspects of phonological awareness and vocabulary knowledge in English, on the one hand, and early reading development in English, on the other hand, in a group of middle-class children from multilingual backgrounds at the International School in Geneva. Students were administered measures of English phonological awareness, letter knowledge, vocabulary, and single-word reading. Vocabulary knowledge measured at age 5 did not predict word reading skills a year later when the children were 6 years old. Two aspects of phonological awareness measured when the children were 5 years old, rhyming and phonemic segmentation, significantly predicted word reading skills a year later, as did letter knowledge. Multiple-regression analyses conducted with data from the first-grade students showed that, after general cognitive ability had been partialed out, the two skills that contributed most significantly to word reading ability were English letter knowledge followed by phonological segmentation in English;

English vocabulary, entered last, was also significant and explained 4% of the unique variance.

A longitudinal study conducted by Geva, Yaghoub-Zadeh, and Schuster (2000) also suggests that there is a weak relationship between English oral language proficiency and word reading in English-language learners coming from various first-language backgrounds, and a relatively strong association between phonological processing skills measured in the second language and second-language word reading. Regression analyses revealed that English oral language proficiency, assessed with a vocabulary test (Peabody Picture Vocabulary Test–Revised [PPVT–R]) at the end of Grade 1 and the beginning of Grade 2, did not predict English word recognition and pseudoword decoding skills at the end of Grade 2. At the same time, two aspects of phonological processing (phonemic awareness and rapid automatized naming of letters), which were assessed in English at the end of Grade 1 and the beginning of Grade 2 and were entered after the vocabulary measure, were significant predictors of word and pseudoword reading at the end of Grade 2. This study also reports analyses that examined the shared variance among the predictor variables. The results indicate that phonemic awareness and RAN shared variance with each other, but also that each explained unique variance on word reading skills. However, vocabulary knowledge did not explain any unique variance and did not share variance with phonemic awareness and RAN.

Gottardo, Yan, Siegel, and Wade-Woolley (2001) conducted a study in Canada with Grade 1 to 8 English-language learners whose home language was Chinese and who were attending schools where English was the language of instruction. The authors used a statistical control—covarying age—to handle the large age range in the sample. The authors found that the correlations of English oral proficiency, as measured by a grammatical sensitivity cloze task, and English word or pseudoword reading skills did not reach significance. At the same time, the correlations of an English phoneme-deletion task with word reading tasks were all positive and significant. Of relevance to the discussion of the relative contributions of various aspects of English oral language skills to word reading skills in English is the fact that the correlation between the English cloze task (the measure of oral English proficiency) and the English phoneme-deletion task was positive and significant. However, because the English cloze measure did not correlate with the word reading skills, it was not entered into the regression analyses. The regression analyses indicated that English phoneme deletion was a unique and significant predictor of word reading in English even when the effects of Chinese phonological processing skills (measured with a rhyme recognition task) were statistically controlled.

Other studies have found a significant but relatively small association between oral vocabulary knowledge in English and English word reading in primary-grade students. For example, Arab-Moghaddam and Sénéchal (2001) studied Grades 2 and 3 Farsi–English speakers living in Canada. These children's schooling was in English, and they also attended heritage language programs in Farsi. Their English vocabulary scores correlated significantly with their English word reading scores. However, the correlation between vocabulary knowledge in English and word reading skills was in the moderate range, whereas the correlation between phonological processing skills (assessed with pseudoword decoding)[1] and English word reading skills was high. Regression analysis showed further that, even after vocabulary knowledge in English was taken into account, explaining 15% of the variance, phonological processing skills in English, entered next, explained an additional 43% of the variance in word recognition in English.

Essentially the same conclusion was reached by Da Fontoura and Siegel (1995) in a study involving slightly older children. The authors examined the relationships between English oral language proficiency (as assessed by an oral grammatical sensitivity cloze task) and English word reading skills in Grades 4 to 6 Portuguese–English bilingual children of low SES attending a Portuguese heritage language program in Canada. The correlation between the students' oral language scores in English and their word reading scores in English was positive but moderate. However, the correlation between their pseudoword decoding scores in English (and Portuguese) and their word reading scores in English was positive and high. That is, children who had good command of phoneme–grapheme correspondence rules in English (as measured by the pseudoword decoding task) also had good word reading skills in English.

Only one study in our database examined the relationship between English oral language proficiency and English word reading skills in high school students. This study, conducted by Abu-Rabia (1997), involved 60 tenth-grade students of English as a foreign language whose first language was Hebrew. Abu-Rabia reports that English oral language proficiency, measured with a grammatical sensitivity cloze task, correlated significantly with performance on word reading skills in English. Although Abu-Rabia's findings could be taken as evidence that oral language proficiency in English is related to word reading skills in high school students of English as a foreign language, the picture may be more complex: In a number of studies reviewed in this chapter, the oral cloze task used to assess oral language proficiency also correlated significantly with working memory (e.g., Abu-Rabia, 1997; Da Fontoura & Siegel, 1995) and, in the case of the Abu-Rabia study, with arithmetic skills. The results of these studies suggest that the oral cloze task may be tapping into grammatical sensitivity as well as more general, underlying cognitive abilities.

In summary, studies that used regression techniques and examined the relative contributions of English oral language proficiency and phonological processing skills to English word and pseudoword reading skills have found that the measures of oral language proficiency in English explained a significant, although modest, proportion of unique variance (usually 3%–4%) in students' English word and pseudoword reading scores. At the same time, phonological processing skills (including phonemic awareness and rapid automatized naming) and measures of working memory in English tend to be more robust and consistent predictors of English word and pseudoword reading skills, and they

---

[1] According to the authors (Arab-Moghaddam & Senechal, 2001), "pseudoword reading tasks can be a valid indicator of children's use of phonological skills because it measures children's ability to decode nonsense words for which they presumably have no lexical knowledge (p. 143)" Typically, researchers do not use pseudoword reading to assess phonological awareness; however, findings from studies that use this measure to assess phonological awareness are in line with findings from studies that assess phonological awareness with orally presented tasks. Moreover, in order to decode psedowords, students must already have developed phonological awarness.

explain a larger proportion of unique variance than do measures of English oral language proficiency. These conclusions emerged from studies that assessed a variety of oral language proficiency skills (e.g., vocabulary knowledge or grammatical sensitivity); used cross-sectional and longitudinal correlational designs or between-group designs; and involved elementary, middle school, and high school English-language learners who came from different language and instructional backgrounds. It is important to note, however, that the number of studies examining the relative contributions of oral proficiency and phonological processing skills to word-level reading skills in English-language learners declines considerably as one moves from the lower to the upper grades.

Therefore, these conclusions can be drawn with more certainty for younger than for older English-language learners. However, the relationship between English oral proficiency and word reading skills (both real words and pseudowords) has been found to be variable, due, at least in part, to factors related to the assessment of oral proficiency. Some measures of oral language proficiency like the oral cloze tests may be assessing other skills such as working memory and general mental ability, not only oral language proficiency. Furthermore, not all measures of English proficiency are sensitive to the full range of proficiency levels, such as measures of grammatical sensitivity. Thus, in some studies, the lack of relationship between English oral language proficiency and word reading skills may be due, in part, to a restriction in range in the measure of oral language proficiency; this is less likely to be the case for older learners who started their schooling in English at an earlier age and thus display a wider range of proficiency levels. Finally, some oral language skills may be more related to word and pseudoword reading than others. For example, lexical knowledge is more predictive of word reading than is syntactic knowledge. Thus, we must be cautious not to overgeneralize when discussing the relationship between oral proficiency and word-level reading skills.

In addition, in assessing the results of correlational studies, it is also important to distinguish between the bivariate relation between predictors and outcomes and the unique relations among these same measures. For example, a positive correlation often exists between measures of phonological awareness and measures of oral language proficiency, both of which are also positively related to measures of word-level reading skill. In such cases, some portion of the relation between each of the predictors (i.e., phonological awareness and oral language proficiency) and the outcome (i.e., word-level reading skill) is shared with the other predictor, and some portion of the relation is unshared with the other predictor. The latter represents a unique relation between the predictor and the outcome. If the pair of predictors is used in a regression model to predict outcomes in word-level reading skill, care must be taken not to misinterpret the meaning of the respective regression coefficients, which are measures of the predictors' unique associations with the outcome. To base conclusions on regression coefficients without taking into account bivariate correlations can lead to invalid inferences about the relations among predictors and outcomes. In addition, one must be extremely cautious in considering the order in which variables are added to prediction models when such orderings are based on the data rather than theory. Because data-based orders of entry of variables in regression equations are greatly affected by individual sample statistics, such orderings often do not replicate from one sample to another unless sample sizes are large and representative.

Relationship Between English Oral Proficiency and English Spelling

Despite the demonstrated importance of foundational skills such as phonological skills (e.g., Bradley & Bryant, 1983; Liberman, Shankweiler, Fischer, & Carter, 1974; Lundberg, Olofsson, & Wall, 1980; Perfetti, 1999), mastery of the association between printed and spoken forms of language (e.g., Adams, 1990; Ehri, 1998; Foorman, Francis, Fletcher, Schatschneider, & Mehta, 1998; Mann, 1993; Moats, 1994; Stanovich & Siegel, 1994), and knowledge of letter names (Treiman & Cassar, 1997), little research is available on the developmental foundations of spelling in English-language learners in general, and on the role of oral language proficiency and phonological processing in the spelling performance of English-language learners in particular.

A handful of studies have addressed the relationship between oral language proficiency in English and the development of spelling skills in English among English-language learners. Overall, the findings of these studies indicate that phonological awareness assessed in English correlates significantly with the English spelling skills of English-language learners. There is little evidence that aspects of English oral language proficiency such as vocabulary or grammatical skills play a crucial role in the development of English spelling skills in English-language learners.

Studies providing indirect assessments of the role of English oral language proficiency in spelling in English are documented by Wade-Woolley and Siegel (1997) and Everatt, Smythe, Adams, and Ocampo (2000). The former study (discussed previously) compared the spelling performance of young native English speakers and English-language learners as a function of their first- and second-language status and their English reading skills. Grade 2 children classified as average or poor readers, based on their performance on a word recognition task, were given a battery of word and pseudoword spelling and reading tests in English, along with a host of phonological processing tasks (phonological awareness, phonological memory, and rapid naming). Their oral language proficiency in English was assessed by using a grammatical sensitivity cloze task. The native-English-speaking children significantly outperformed their English-language learner counterparts on the cloze task, as well as on two tests of phonological processing skills—sound mimicry and phoneme deletion. However, there was no difference between the two groups on the spelling tasks, suggesting that there is no direct link between oral proficiency (assessed with a grammatical sensitivity cloze task) and spelling accuracy in English for English-language learners. Regression analyses further revealed similar processing profiles for the two groups: In both groups, real-word spelling was significantly correlated with both phoneme deletion and pseudoword decoding, and pseudoword spelling was correlated significantly with pseudoword decoding.

Similar results are reported by Everatt et al. (2000), who also compared the performance of primary-level native-English-speaking children and English-language learners who were either good or poor spellers. Average spellers in each language group exhibited similar profiles, as did poor spellers in each group. Compared with the good spellers, poor spellers in each group performed significantly less well on measures of word recognition and pseudoword reading, as well as on phonological processing measures (rhyme detection, rhythm sequencing, and reverse memory span). One group was English proficient and one was not, yet both groups had similar profiles with regard to spelling and phonological processing skills. This implies that language proficiency was less relevant to spelling performance than phonological processing.

In a study reviewed previously, Jackson and Lu (1992) also examined the orthographic skills of a small sample of children from a variety of linguistic backgrounds who, before beginning first grade, had demonstrated an advanced ability to comprehend written English. The English-language learners had lower scores than the native-English-speaking comparison group on the oral proficiency tests, but were just as accurate and, in fact, faster than the monolingual group on an orthographic matching task. More specifically, the bilingual group outperformed the monolingual group in the speed with which they were able to access orthographic knowledge and distinguish between real words and sound-alike pseudowords, suggesting again that there may be little association between oral language proficiency and orthographic skills in English among English-language learners.

Only one study focused on spelling skills in high school English-language learners. This study, by Abu-Rabia (1997) (discussed previously), involved 60 tenth-grade students of English as a foreign language whose first language was Hebrew. The study found that oral language proficiency in English, measured with a grammatical sensitivity cloze task, did not correlate with performance on an assessment of orthographic conventions in English. However, oral proficiency in English did correlate positively and significantly with a task that measured spelling recognition of real words in English. More specifically, the orthographic conventions task required the students to judge which word in each pair of pseudowords was a legitimate spelling pattern in English. The spelling recognition task assessed students' ability to recognize the correct spelling of real words. The findings of this study may be taken to suggest that oral English proficiency measured with a grammatical sensitivity cloze task is not related to knowledge of the orthographic conventions of English spelling while it is related to spelling recognition of real words. However, there may have been measurement problems with the latter measure. In particular, unlike consistent differences between skilled and less skilled readers on all other language and reading tasks in both English and Hebrew, there were no differences between the reading groups on this assessment of orthographic conventions, and the performance in both groups was rather low, suggesting chance performance. In contrast, performance on the grammatical sensitivity cloze task is significantly related to high school students' spelling recognition. As noted earlier, the grammatical sensitivity cloze task appears to capture more than grammatical knowledge.

Finally, one study (Arab-Moghaddam and Sénéchal, 2001) examined the relative contribution of phonological processing skills and vocabulary knowledge to English spelling skills. In this study (discussed previously), the authors studied Grades 2 and 3 Farsi–English speakers living in Canada. The correlation between children's English vocabulary scores and English spelling scores was positive and moderate. At the same time, the correlation between spelling and phonological skills assessed with a pseudoword reading task (i.e., reading pronounceable letter strings) was very high. Regression analysis showed further that vocabulary knowledge in English explained 17% of the variance, and phonological processing skills in English, entered into the equation in a subsequent step, explained an additional 40% of the variance in spelling English words.

In summary, with one exception, the review indicates that grammatical skills in English are not strongly related to spelling skills in English-language learners in elementary and middle school. However, this conclusion must be regarded as tentative given the small number of studies that addressed this issue. Moreover, little can be said about the relationship between English oral language proficiency and English spelling in higher grades. One study of high school students did find a correlation between grammatical skills and spelling recognition. However, the task used to measure oral language proficiency may have been capturing more than oral language proficiency because it was highly and significantly correlated with a measure of memory and math performance. There is some evidence that, unlike grammatical knowledge, vocabulary knowledge in English may be correlated with spelling skills in English, but this possibility, based on one study, requires replication. Finally, the existing evidence indicates that phonological processing skills play a significant role in the spelling skills of English-language learners; furthermore the evidence suggests that native English speakers and English-language learners who are poor spellers have similar cognitive profiles despite differences in their vocabulary and grammatical proficiency in English.

Word-Level Skills: Overall Summary

A number of conclusions emerged from our review with regard to word-level skills:

- English oral language proficiency skills explain a modest proportion of unique variance (usually 3%–4%) in students' word reading scores.
- Phonological processing skills (including phonemic awareness and rapid automatized naming) and working memory in English are more robust and consistent predictors of accurate English word reading skills and explain a larger proportion of unique variance than do aspects of English oral language proficiency such as vocabulary and grammatical skills. This may be especially true when aspects of oral language proficiency, such as vocabulary knowledge, grammatical sensitivity, and discourse knowledge, are not developed sufficiently because of restriction of range issues.
- The review of studies on the relationship between second-language oral proficiency and spelling suggests that there is not a strong relationship between grammatical sensitivity in English and the English spelling skills of elementary-level English-language learners, but that vocabulary skills in English may be related to spelling skills in English.
- The review also appears to indicate that spelling accuracy among English-language learners is predicted by various phonological processing skills (such as phoneme deletion, rapid naming, phonological memory) and pseudoword decoding.

TEXT-LEVEL SKILLS

Relationship Between English Oral Proficiency and English Reading Fluency

Recent research on monolingual English-speaking children emphasizes the dynamic, developmental nature of the acquisition of reading fluency (Fuchs, Fuchs, Hosp, & Jenkins, 2001; National Institute of Child Health and Human Development, 2000; Wolf & Katzir-Cohen, 2001). According to recent research, reading fluency in the early stages entails gradual acquisition of the ability to execute accurately and automatically relatively low-level skills involved in reading (e.g., decoding). Once readers have achieved fluency with these skills so that they are effortless, further development of fluency entails a shift to prosodic features of language and the allocation of attention to comprehension. *Dysfluent* reading can be the result of impairment in any of these component processes (Wolf, Bowers, & Biddle, 2000; Wolf & Katzir-Cohen, 2001). The rate at which children decode affects their reading comprehension. Thus, poor reading fluency can reflect decoding skills that are not automatized, limited knowledge of text structure, and/or a limited repertoire of text processing strategies, such as use of context clues. Dysfluent reading also can be the result of inadequate oral proficiency with which to map written language. Questions about the role of oral language proficiency in reading fluency are particularly pertinent in second-language contexts. Because of the first-language focus of the theories on fluency, less attention has been given to the potential role of oral English proficiency in facilitating reading fluency.

We identified only one relevant study involving elementary school English-language learners. Jackson and Lu (1992) studied children from a variety of first-language backgrounds who demonstrated an advanced ability to comprehend text in English (assessed with the Peabody Individual Achievement Test [PIAT]) before beginning Grade 1. The authors report that these precocious readers had lower scores than native-English-speaking comparison students on English oral language tests, but were just as fluent as that group on oral text reading and as proficient on word recognition and orthographic tasks. Thus, these advanced English-language learners were able to read more fluently than might have been expected given their oral language skills in English.[2] We identified no relevant research on the relationship between English oral language proficiency and reading fluency in middle or high school English-language learners.

Relationship Between Oral English Proficiency and English Reading Comprehension

Overall, studies of English-language learners in elementary school have found consistently that oral language proficiency in English and English reading

---

[2] A study of native-English-speaking children who attended a bilingual English–Hebrew program (Geva, Wade-Woolley, & Shany, 1997) showed that, although language proficiency in Hebrew (the second language) did not explain variance in word reading fluency in Hebrew, it played a significant role in explaining variance in Hebrew text reading fluency.

comprehension are positively correlated. Dufva and Voeten (1999) assessed the language and literacy development of native-Finnish-speaking students learning English as a foreign language from Grades 1 to 3. They report that third-grade English reading comprehension skills and oral vocabulary were highly correlated.

Beech and Keys (1997) examined the reading comprehension, oral vocabulary, and decoding skills of 7- and 8-year-old bilingual, poor, inner-city Asian children living in the United Kingdom. The authors report that the English-language learners scored significantly lower than the native English speakers on tests of English oral vocabulary and on a cloze-type test of reading comprehension (whereas the differences on word reading were not significant). This finding provides indirect evidence that reading comprehension is related to oral language proficiency. Because the researchers did not include oral vocabulary scores in their regression analyses, however, this study fails to inform us about the relative contributions of oral vocabulary and docoding skills to reading comprehension in these students.

Carlisle, Beeman, Davis, and Spharim (1999) examined the link between oral vocabulary skills and reading comprehension in a group of language-minority elementary school students whose English reading achievement was below average. The authors report that the ability to provide formal and informal definitions for nouns in English (and Spanish) was related to vocabulary knowledge in English and, in accord with the findings of the other studies reviewed in this section, that vocabulary knowledge in English (and Spanish) contributed significantly to reading comprehension in English.

Peregoy and Boyle (1991) examined the relationship between a variety of English oral language skills and reading comprehension in six Mexican-American third-grade children who were English-language learners. Using a simulated science lesson about seashells (Wong Fillmore's Shell Game), the children's oral language proficiency was evaluated with respect to grammatical complexity, well-formedness, informativeness, and listening comprehension. The authors explored the relationship between these oral proficiency skills and reading comprehension evaluated on the basis of responses to multiple-choice questions presented after each of four short passages. Nonparametric analyses revealed that those English-language learners with better developed reading comprehension skills significantly outperformed *low comprehenders* on all oral language measures. Moreover, the *high comprehenders* performed significantly better than *intermediate comprehenders* on well-formedness and informativeness. There was no statistically significant difference on any of the measures between low and intermediate readers. Stated differently, English-language learners who were better comprehenders had more sophisticated oral language skills than did students with less well-developed reading comprehension skills. The results of this study suggest that oral language proficiency in young English-language learners in the elementary grades is positively linked to reading comprehension.

Peregoy (1989) conducted a study at the middle-grades level to examine the relationship between oral language proficiency and reading comprehension of six Mexican-American, bilingual fifth-grade children who attended a Spanish–English bilingual program. The oral production measure required children to tell a story about a four-frame picture sequence; it was scored in terms of fluency (number of words produced), total number of propositions produced, grammatical complexity, and well-formedness. The reading comprehension assessment was based on three passages taken from the Stanford Diagnostic Reading Test, followed by multiple-choice comprehension questions. One of these passages was administered in Spanish. In general, there was a correspondence between language proficiency in English and reading comprehension in English; those children whose scores on the oral language proficiency indexes were high also had better scores on reading comprehension.

Evidence for a positive relationship between oral language proficiency measured by a listening comprehension task and reading comprehension in middle-grades students is provided by a study conducted by Royer and Carlo (1991). These authors examined the relationship between the English listening comprehension and reading comprehension skills of Spanish–English English-language learners who were attending transitional bilingual programs. The researchers tracked the students' performance from Grade 5 to Grade 6 and used two versions of the Sentence Verification Technique to evaluate listening comprehension (i.e., oral language proficiency) and reading comprehension. The results reveal that listening comprehension skills in English, the second language, assessed in Grade 5 were one of the best predictors of English reading comprehension a year later.

Also at the middle-grades level, one study (Jiménez, García, & Pearson, 1996) examined the influence of Spanish-speaking English-language learners' understanding of cognate relationships on their reading comprehension. Jiménez et al. (1996) report that bilingual students in Grades 6 and 7 who had a better awareness of the relationships between English and Spanish cognates used more successful strategies to infer word meanings, which in turn enabled them to comprehend texts better. This study illustrates the importance of considering individual differences among English-language learners from the same language backgrounds in explaining variances in reading comprehension. Further, it illustrates that language background may influence reading performance; children from first-language backgrounds that do not share cognates with English would not have the possibility of being advantaged in this way.

Carlisle, Beeman, and Shah (1996) examined the relationship between English oral language proficiency and English reading comprehension in Mexican American students who ranged in age from 14 to 20. Their primary measures of oral language proficiency were (a) tests of listening comprehension, grammatical knowledge, and vocabulary; and (b) a "definitions" test, in which students were asked to provide definitions for high-frequency words. Reading comprehension was assessed in English and Spanish by using a sentence verification technique. Of particular relevance to the present discussion was the finding that performance on two different aspects of oral language proficiency—English listening comprehension and quality of vocabulary definitions—jointly explained 50% of the variance in English reading comprehension scores.

In a test of Cummins' (1979, 1990) threshold hypothesis, Lee and Schallert (1997) examined the relationship of two aspects of English oral language proficiency (vocabulary knowledge and grammaticality judgments) and first-language reading ability to English reading comprehension in 9th- and 10th-grade Korean students of English as a foreign language. Both oral language proficiency in English and first-language reading comprehension skills correlated with reading comprehension in English. However, English oral language proficiency made the greater contribution. Moreover, the correlations between first- and second-language reading rose with higher second-language oral proficiency scores.

Finally, one study explored the relationship between oral storytelling skills and comprehension. Oral storytelling skills can be viewed as an advanced aspect of oral language proficiency.[3] Goldstein et al. (1993) investigated the oral storytelling skills of Mexican American students in Grades 7 to 9 and the relationships between those skills and reading comprehension in English; they found a significant correlation. Specifically, the students' ability to present the goals of the protagonist (which may include planning and consequences, as well as other story elements), as opposed to simply offering descriptions of the characters and their actions without indicating causal relationships, was associated with superior performance on a standardized reading comprehension test.

In summary, the findings from the available research on second-language learners suggest that having well-developed oral language proficiency in English is associated with well-developed reading comprehension skills in English. More specifically, the available research suggests that comprehension is related to diverse components of English-language proficiency, including oral vocabulary knowledge, awareness of cognates, listening comprehension, oral storytelling skills, and syntactic skills. In addition, the study by Carlisle, Beeman, and Shah (1996) indicates that the ability to handle decontextualized aspects of language (such as providing definitions of words) appears to be related to enhanced reading comprehension. It should be noted that the majority of studies we reviewed focused on relatively young school-age children, and not much is known about older school-age students.

These findings, however, need to be put into perspective. As noted in chapter 4, to be capable comprehenders, children also need to acquire the precursor literacy skills in either the first or second language, such as the skills underlying accurate and effortless recognition of printed words. Differences in the reading comprehension abilities of English-language learners can also be attributed to cognitive ability and memory. Finally, findings of the few multivariate studies that are available suggest that the relationship between English oral language proficiency and English reading comprehension is also mediated by contextual factors, such as home language use and literacy practices and SES, as well as by differences in instructional and other educational experiences (see chaps. 10–12 for a discussion of the former and chaps. 13–18 for a discussion of the latter).

Relationship Between English Oral Proficiency and General Measures of English Reading Performance

Three studies examined the relationship between English oral proficiency and general measures of reading performance. Wilkinson, Milosky, and Genishi (1986) examined English oral language proficiency by assessing the ability of Hispanic English-language learners in Grade 3 to make requests and receive

---

[3]At the same time, it is important to acknowledge that oral storytelling captures not only the language skills necessary to tell a story but also cultural knowledge and opportunities to become familiar with story genres.

adequate responses during interactions in all-student instructional groups. Their results show positive correlations between the ability to make successful requests and reading achievement scores as measured by total scores on the Metropolitan Achievement Test (i.e., decoding, spelling, and reading comprehension subtests).

In another study, Pérez (1981) demonstrated that systematic daily instruction in receptive and expressive vocabulary skills improved reading comprehension skills in third-grade, Mexican American English-language learners. The vocabulary instruction that focused on synonyms, antonyms, multiple-meaning words, and idiomatic expressions enhanced the students' reading skills as assessed by the Prescriptive Reading Inventory, a test that includes decoding, word recognition, written vocabulary, and reading comprehension subtests (see chap. 15 for a description of this study).

That oral vocabulary knowledge is crucial for reading comprehension was documented two decades ago by Saville-Troike (1984). She conducted a retrospective analysis to ascertain why a group of children matched for English proficiency at the beginning of the school year differed in their academic achievement at the end of the year. Children in Grades 2 to 6 were given a series of oral language tests (covering syntactic knowledge and vocabulary knowledge) and the reading subtest of the Comprehensive Test of Basic Skills (CTBS).[4] The correlation between the students' syntactic knowledge and reading test scores was nonsignificant; however, there was a significant correlation between their vocabulary knowledge and performance on the reading test. Because the author failed to specify the components of the reading test (CTBS) that were included in the analysis, it is not possible to determine the exact nature of students' general reading performance.

Relationship Between English Oral Proficiency and English Writing

As mentioned in chapter 4, writing is a multidimensional process. It involves word-level skills (e.g., letter production, spelling), cognitive abilities (e.g., working memory, attention), and higher order skills (e.g., planning, metacognition, strategy use, and self-regulation). Developing and orchestrating the various writing skills present many challenges to first-language learners (Berninger & Swanson, 1994; Graham & Harris, 2000; Scott, 1989; Snelling & Van Gelderen, 2004; Whitaker, Berninger, Johnston, & Swanson, 1994; Wong, Wong, & Blenkinsop, 1989). Few studies of English-language learners have examined the relationship between English oral language proficiency and writing in general or with specific skills involved in the writing process. Nevertheless, the available research suggests that well-developed oral language skills in English are associated with better writing skills in English.

In one of two studies at the elementary level, Davis, Carlisle, and Beeman (1999) investigated individual differences in the English and Spanish writing development of young Hispanic English-language learners in Grades 1 to 3 who were receiving instruction in both English and Spanish. The students were

---

[4]The CTBS includes a number of reading-related subtests—reading comprehension, language, punctuation, and writing.

given listening and reading comprehension tests and were also asked to write two compositions, one in English and one in Spanish. Their writing samples were analyzed with respect to productivity, linguistic complexity (as assessed by number of *t* units), spelling, word length (including variety and sophistication of vocabulary), and level of discourse. Significant correlations were found between the students' English listening comprehension scores and their writing scores (specifically, productivity, spelling, use of long words, and discourse), but correlations between these listening scores and an index of linguistic complexity (*t* units) in writing were not significant. Lack of linguistic complexity is related to the fact that, on the whole, these Hispanic children did not produce very long texts. The researchers attributed this reluctance to lack of experience and motivation.

A study conducted by Dufva and Voeten (1999), reviewed previously, also examined the relationship between a more restricted writing task and two aspects of oral language proficiency: listening comprehension and vocabulary knowledge. Writing was assessed with a cloze procedure, in which students were asked to fill in missing sentences or words pertaining to a story that was initially presented to them orally. Both tasks were administered in English to a sample of native-Finnish-speaking students in Finland when the children were in Grade 3. Correlational analyses revealed that vocabulary knowledge and listening comprehension in English (concurrent predictors) and phonological memory (longitudinal predictor) were all significant predictors of writing in English.

Only two studies in our database examined the relationship between oral language proficiency and writing in middle-school English-language learners. A consistent and alarming observation emerging from these studies is the generally poor quality of these students' writing. The two studies attempted to trace the source of these difficulties. Indirect evidence of a lack of association between oral language skills and certain aspects of writing comes from a study by Lanauze and Snow (1989). In particular, these authors conclude that discourse-level indexes of quality of writing may not be linked directly to oral language proficiency. They studied the development of these writing skills in a group of Grades 4 and 5 Spanish–English bilingual children from working-class backgrounds. On the basis of teacher ratings of oral language proficiency, the children, who were attending a bilingual program, were classified as good in English and Spanish (GG), poor in English and Spanish (PP), or poor in English but good in Spanish (PG). As would be expected, the students in the PP group, whose language skills were poor in both the first and second languages, were writing poorly in both languages. Interestingly, however, the performance of students in the GG and PG groups was highly similar on the English quality-of-writing indexes. The authors conclude that students who had relatively better developed writing skills in Spanish were able to use that knowledge in English, although their oral language skills in English were less well developed than those in Spanish.

Additional information about the role of oral language proficiency in second-language writing comes from a correlational study conducted by Lumme and Lehto (2002). These authors administered a variety of expressive and receptive oral language proficiency tasks in English (auditory discrimination, vocabulary, listening comprehension, conversational skills) and phonological awareness to Grade 6 native-Finnish-speaking students who were learning English as a foreign language in a school in Finland. Of primary interest is the finding that students' scores on the writing subtest of the Finnish National Test of English correlated with those on other subtests assessing vocabulary and grammar skills. Moreover, the writing scores correlated positively with basic phonological–orthographic skills in Finnish and with academic achievement in Finnish. The latter results suggest that the link between second-language oral proficiency and second-language writing skills may be mediated by underlying phonological processing skills. It is not possible to disentangle the precise role of each factor, however, because only simple correlations are reported. It should also be noted that the students were learning English as a foreign language rather than English as a second language. The results must be interpreted within this context.

We identified one relevant study at the high school level (Yau & Belanger, 1985) that examined the relationship between oral language proficiency in English and writing skills in students learning English as a foreign language. This study provides indirect evidence that English oral proficiency is related to writing quality. Cross-sectional groups of Cantonese high school students in Grades 9, 11, and 13 wrote narrative and expository texts in English that were then analyzed with respect to the presence and frequency of syntactic structures of varying complexity. The authors report that the participants performed less well than English native speakers in Grade 9, but comparably by the time they reached Grade 13. The performance level of English native speakers was established from previous research. Unfortunately, the authors do not report students' proficiency in English or attrition rates by grade level, nor did they include a control group of first-language students. The findings suggest that as these English-as-a-foreign language students reached a more advanced level of second-language proficiency (e.g., in the case of the Grade 13 students), they were better able to combine sentences (as can be seen by their increased t-unit length, clause length, and number of clauses per t unit). However, one cannot assume that the older students were more proficient in oral English. Moreover, if they were more English proficient, it cannot be assumed that this improvement in writing was related to oral proficiency; it may also have been related to cognitive maturation.

In general, research on the role of oral English proficiency in the development of English writing skills in English-language learners is limited. It suggests that well-developed oral language skills, including vocabulary and grammatical knowledge, as well as phonological awareness, are related to various indexes of writing quality. We know from the first-language literature that developing and orchestrating the various writing components presents many challenges to first-language learners because writing is a complex activity. Writing may present a special challenge to English-language learners, and having well-developed language skills may be necessary but not sufficient for ensuring writing proficiency in English as a second language. The acquisition of proficient writing skills probably also entails good spelling skills; decontextualized language skills; the use of cohesive devices, such as anaphora, relativization, temporal reference, and conjunctions that enable the writer to express ideas not limited to the here and now;

metacognitive skills, such as audience awareness; and familiarity with and opportunities to practice writing different text genres. At present, however, there is scant evidence of the role and development of these kinds of skills in English-language learners of any age group.

Text-Level Skills: Summary

The following conclusion emerged from our review with regard to text-level skills:

- The available research suggests that English oral language proficiency is consistently implicated when larger chunks of text are involved, whether in reading comprehension or writing.

Database References for Part I

Aarts, R., & Verhoeven, L. (1999). Literacy attainment in a second language submersion context. *Applied Psycholinguistics, 20*(3), 377–393.

Abu-Rabia, S. (1995). Attitudes and cultural background and their relationship to English in a multicultural social context: The case of male and female Arab immigrants in Canada. *Educational Psychology, 15*(3), 323–336.

Abu-Rabia, S. (1996). Druze minority students learning Hebrew in Israel: The relationship of attitudes, cultural background, and interest of material to reading comprehension in a second language. *Journal of Multilingual & Multicultural Development, 17*(6), 415–426.

Abu-Rabia, S. (1997). Verbal and working-memory skills of bilingual Hebrew–English speaking children. *International Journal of Psycholinguistics, 13*(1), 25–40.

Abu-Rabia, S. (1998a). Attitudes and culture in second language learning among Israeli– Arab students. *Curriculum and Teaching, 13*(1), 13–30.

Abu-Rabia, S. (1998b). Social and cognitive factors influencing the reading comprehension of Arab students learning Hebrew as a second language in Israel. *Journal of Research in Reading, 21*(3), 201–212.

Abu-Rabia, S., & Siegel, L. S. (2002). Reading, syntactic, orthographic, and working memory skills of bilingual Arabic–English speaking Canadian children. *Journal of Psycholinguistic Research, 31*(6), 661–678.

Arab-Moghaddam, N., & Sénéchal, M. (2001). Orthographic and phonological processing skills in reading and spelling in Persian/English bilinguals. *International Journal of Behavioral Development, 25*(2), 140–147.

Bean, T. W., Levine, M. G., & Graham, R. C. (1981). Beginning ESL readers' attention to the graphemic features of print. *Reading Improvement, 18*(4), 346–349.

Beech, J. R., & Keys, A. (1997). Reading, vocabulary and language preference in 7- to 8-year-old bilingual Asian children. *British Journal of Educational Psychology, 67*(4), 405–414.

Bermúdez, A. B., & Prater, D. L. (1994). Examining the effects of gender and second language proficiency on Hispanic writers' persuasive discourse. *Bilingual Research Journal, 18*(3/4), 47–62.

Bialystok, E. (1997). Effects of bilingualism and biliteracy on children's emerging concepts of print. *Developmental Psychology, 33*(3), 429–440.

Bruck, M., & Genesee, F. (1995). Phonological awareness in young second language learners. *Journal of Child Language, 22*, 307–324.

Buriel, R., & Cardoza, D. (1988). Sociocultural correlates of achievement among three generations of Mexican American high school seniors. *American Educational Research Journal, 25*(2), 177–192.

Cahill, D. P. (1987). Bilingual development of Italo-Australian children. *Australian Review of Applied Linguistics, 4*, 101–127.

Carlisle, J. F., Beeman, M. M., Davis, L.-H., & Spharim, G. (1999). Relationship of metalinguistic capabilities and reading achievement for children who are becoming bilingual. *Applied Psycholinguistics, 20*(4), 459–478.

Carlisle, J. F, Beeman, M. B., & Shah, P. P. (1996). The metalinguistic capabilities and English literacy of Hispanic high school students: An exploratory study. *Yearbook of the National Reading Conference, 45*, 306–316.

Chiappe, P., & Siegel, L. S. (1999). Phonological awareness and reading acquisition in English- and Punjabi-speaking Canadian children. *Journal of Educational Psychology, 91*(1), 20–28.

Chiappe, P., Siegel, L. S., & Gottardo, A. (2002). Reading-related skills of kindergartners from diverse linguistic backgrounds. *Applied Psycholinguistics, 23*(1), 95–116.

Chiappe, P., Siegel, L. S., & Wade-Woolley, L. (2002). Linguistic diversity and the development of reading skills: A longitudinal study. *Scientific Studies of Reading, 6*(4), 369–400.

Cisero, C. A., & Royer, J. M. (1995). The development and cross-language transfer of phonological awareness. *Contemporary Educational Psychology, 20*(3), 275–303.

Collier, V. P. (1987). Age and rate of acquisition of second language for academic purposes. *TESOL Quarterly, 21*(4), 617–641.

Connor, U. (1983). Predictors of second-language reading performance. *Journal of Multilingual & Multicultural Development, 4*(4), 271–288.

Cronnell, B. (1985). Language influences in the English writing of third- and sixth-grade Mexican American students. *Journal of Educational Research, 78*(3), 168–173.

Da Fontoura, H. A., & Siegel, L. S. (1995). Reading, syntactic, and working memory skills of bilingual Portuguese–English Canadian children. *Reading and Writing, 7*(1), 139–153.

D'Angiulli, A., Siegel, L. S., & Serra, E. (2001). The development of reading in English and Italian in bilingual children. *Applied Psycholinguistics, 22*, 479–507.

Davis, L. H., Carlisle, J. F., & Beeman, M. (1999). Hispanic children's writing in English and Spanish when English is the language of instruction. *Yearbook of the National Reading Conference, 48*, 238–248.

Droop, M., & Verhoeven, L. T. (1998). Background knowledge, linguistic complexity, and second-language reading comprehension. *Journal of Literacy Research, 30*(2), 253–271.

Dufva, M., & Voeten, M. J. M. (1999). Native language literacy and phonological memory as prerequisites for learning English as a foreign language. *Applied Psycholinguistics, 20*(3), 329–348.

Durgunoglu, A. Y., Nagy, W. E., & Hancin-Bhatt, B. J. (1993). Cross-language transfer of phonological awareness. *Journal of Educational Psychology, 85*(3), 453–465.

Everatt, J., Smythe, I., Adams, E., & Ocampo, D. (2000). Dyslexia screening measures and bilingualism. *Dyslexia, 6*(1), 42–56.

Fashola, O. S., Drum, P. A., Mayer, R. E., & Kang, S.-J. (1996). A cognitive theory of orthographic transitioning: Predictable errors in how Spanish-speaking children spell English words. *American Educational Research Journal, 33*(4), 825–843.

Fernández, R. M., & Nielsen, F. (1986). Bilingualism and Hispanic scholastic achievement: Some baseline results. *Social Science Research, 15*(1), 43–70.

Ferris, M. R., & Politzer, R. L. (1981). Effects of early and delayed second language acquisition: English composition skills of Spanish-speaking junior high school students. *TESOL Quarterly, 15*(3), 263–274.

Fitzgerald, J., & Shanahan, T. (2000). Reading and writing relations and their development. *Educational Psychologist, 35*, 39–50.

García, G. E. (1991). Factors influencing the English reading test performance of Spanish-speaking Hispanic children. *Reading Research Quarterly, 26*(4), 371–392.

García-Vázquez, E. (1995). Acculturation and academics: Effects of acculturation on reading achievement among Mexican American students. *Bilingual Research Journal, 19*(2), 304–315.

Geva, E., Yaghoub-Zadeh, Z., & Schuster, B. (2000). Part IV: Reading and foreign language learning: Understanding individual differences in word recognition skills of ESL children. *Annals of Dyslexia, 50*, 121–154.

Gholamain, M., & Geva, E. (1999). Orthographic and cognitive factors in the concurrent development of basic reading skills in English and Persian. *Language Learning, 49*(2), 183–217.

Goldstein, B. C., Harris, K. C., & Klein, M. D. (1993). Assessment of oral storytelling abilities of Latino junior high school students with learning handicaps. *Journal of Learning Disabilities, 26*(2), 138–132.

Gottardo, A. (2002). The relationship between language and reading skills in bilingual Spanish–English speakers. *Topics in Language Disorders, 22*(5), 46–70.

Gottardo, A., Yan, B., Siegel, L. S., & Wade-Woolley, L. (2001). Factors related to English reading performance in children with Chinese as a first language: More evidence of cross-language transfer of phonological processing. *Journal of Educational Psychology, 93*(3), 530–542.

Hacquebord, H. (1994). L2-reading in the content areas: Text comprehension in secondary education in the Netherlands. *Journal of Research in Reading, 17*(2), 83–98.

Hannon, P., & McNally, J. (1986). Children's understanding and cultural factors in reading test performance. *Educational Review, 38*(3), 237–246.

Hansen, D. A. (1989). Locating learning: Second language gains and language use in family, peer and classroom contexts. *NABE: The Journal for the National Association for Bilingual Education, 13*(2), 161–180.

Ima, K., & Rumbaut, R. G. (1989). Southeast Asian refugees in American schools: A comparison of fluent-English-proficient and limited-English-proficient students. *Topics in Language Disorders, 9*(3), 54–75.

Jackson, N., Holm, A., & Dodd, B. (1998). Phonological awareness and spelling abilities of Cantonese–English bilingual children. *Asia Pacific Journal of Speech, Language, and Hearing, 3*(2), 79–96.

Jackson, N. E., & Lu, W.- H. (1992). Bilingual precocious readers of English. *Roeper Review, 14*(3), 115–119.

Jiménez, R. T., García, G. E., & Pearson, D. P. (1996). The reading strategies of bilingual Latina/o students who are successful English readers: Opportunities and obstacles. *Reading Research Quarterly, 31*(1), 90–112.

Kennedy, E., & Park, H.- S. (1994). Home language as a predictor of academic achievement: A comparative study of Mexican and Asian American youth. *Journal of Research and Development in Education, 27*(3), 188–194.

Lanauze, M., & Snow, C. E. (1989). The relation between first- and second-language writing skills: Evidence from Puerto Rican elementary school children in bilingual programs. *Linguistics and Education, 1*(4), 323–339.

Lee, J. W., & Schallert, D. L. (1997). The relative contribution of L2 language proficiency and L1 reading ability to L2 reading performance: A test of the threshold hypothesis in an EFL context. *TESOL Quarterly, 31*(4), 713–739.

Limbos, M., & Geva, E. (2001). Accuracy of teacher assessments of second-language students at risk for reading disability. *Journal of Learning Disabilities, 34*(2), 136–151.

Lumme, K., & Lehto, J. E. (2002). Sixth grade pupils' phonological processing and school achievement in a second and the native language. *Scandinavian Journal of Educational Research, 46*(2), 207–217.

McEvoy, R. E., & Johnson, D. L. (1989). Comparison of an intelligence test and a screening battery as predictors of reading ability in low income, Mexican American children. *Hispanic Journal of Behavioral Sciences, 11*(3), 274–282.

Miramontes, O. B. (1987). Oral reading miscues of Hispanic students: Implications for assessment of learning disabilities. *Journal of Learning Disabilities, 20*(10), 627–632.

Mumtaz, S., & Humphreys, G. W. (2001). The effects of bilingualism on learning to read English: Evidence from the contrast between Urdu–English bilingual and English monolingual children. *Journal of Research in Reading, 24*(2), 113–134.

Muter, V., & Diethelm, K. (2001). The contribution of phonological skills and letter knowledge to early reading development in a multilingual population. *Language Learning, 51*(2), 187–219.

Nagy, W. E., García, G. E., Durgunoglu, A. Y., & Hancin-Bhatt, B. (1993). Spanish–English bilingual students' use of cognates in English reading. *Journal of Reading Behavior, 25*(3), 241–259.

Nagy, W., McClure, E., & Mir, M. (1997). Linguistic transfer and the use of context by Spanish–English bilinguals. *Applied Psycholinguistics, 18*, 431–452.

Okamura-Bichard, F. (1985). Mother tongue maintenance and second language learning: A case of Japanese children. *Language Learning, 35*(1), 63–89.

O'Toole, S., Aubeeluck, A., Cozens, B., & Cline, T. (2001). Development of reading proficiency in English by bilingual children and their monolingual peers. *Psychological Reports, 89*(2), 279–282.

Padrón, Y. N., Knight, S. L., & Waxman, H. C. (1986). Analyzing bilingual and monolingual students' perceptions of their reading strategies. *Reading Teacher, 39*(5), 430–433.

Padrón, Y. N., & Waxman, H. C. (1988). The effect of ESL students' perceptions of their cognitive strategies on reading achievement. *TESOL Quarterly, 22*(1), 146–150.

Peregoy, S. F. (1989). Relationships between second language oral proficiency and reading comprehension of bilingual fifth grade students. *NABE: The Journal of the National Association for Bilingual Education, 13*(3), 217–234.

Peregoy, S. F., & Boyle, O. F. (1991). Second language oral proficiency characteristics of low, intermediate and high second language readers. *Hispanic Journal of Behavioral Sciences, 13*(1), 35–47.

Pérez, E. (1981). Oral language competence improves reading skills of Mexican American third graders. *Reading Teacher*, *35*(1), 24–27.

Quiroga, T., Lemos-Britton, Z., Mostafapour, E., Abbott, R. D., & Berninger, V. W. (2002). Phonological awareness and beginning reading in Spanish-speaking ESL first graders: Research into practice. *Journal of School Psychology*, *40*(1), 85–111.

Reese, L., Garnier, H., Gallimore, R., & Goldenberg, C. (2000). Longitudinal analysis of the antecedents of emergent Spanish literacy and middle-school English reading achievement of Spanish-speaking students. *American Educational Research Journal*, *37*(3), 633–662.

Rosenthal, A. S., Baker, K., & Ginsburg, A. (1983). The effect of language background on achievement level and learning among elementary school students. *Sociology of Education*, *56*(4), 157–169.

Royer, J. M., & Carlo, M. S. (1991). Transfer of comprehension skills from native to second language. *Journal of Reading*, *34*(6), 450–455.

Saville-Troike, M. (1984). What really matters in second language learning for academic achievement? *TESOL Quarterly*, *18*(2), 199–219.

Tompkins, G. E., Abramson, S., & Pritchard, R. H. (1999). A multilingual perspective on spelling development in third and fourth grades. *Multicultural Education*, *6*(3), 12–18.

Verhoeven, L. T. (1990). Acquisition of reading in a second language. *Reading Research Quarterly*, *25*(2), 90–114.

Verhoeven, L. T. (2000). Components in early second language reading and spelling. *Scientific Studies of Reading*, *4*(4), 313–330.

Wade-Woolley, L., & Siegel, L. S. (1997). The spelling performance of ESL and native speakers of English as a function of reading skill. *Reading & Writing: An Interdisciplinary Journal*, *9*(506), 387–406.

Wilkinson, L. C., Milosky, L. M., & Genishi, C. (1986). Second language learners' use of requests and responses in elementary classrooms. *Topics in Language Disorders*, *6*(2), 57–70.

Yau, M. S. S., & Belanger, J. (1985). Syntactic development in the writing of EFL students. *English Quarterly*, *18*(2), 107–118.

Background References
for Part I

Adams, M. J. (1990). *Beginning to read: Thinking and learning about print*. Cambridge, MA: MIT Press.

Afflerbach, P. P. (1990). The influence of prior knowledge on expert readers' main idea construction strategies. *Reading Research Quarterly, 25*(1), 31–46.

Anderson, R. C., & Pearson, P. D. (2002). A schema-theoretic view of basic processes in reading comprehension. In P. D. Pearson (Ed.), *Handbook of reading research* (pp.255–292). Mahwah, NJ: Lawrence Erlbaum Associates.

August, D. L., & Hakuta, K. (1997). *Improving schooling for language-minority learners*. Washington, DC: National Academy Press.

Baddeley, A. D. (1986). *Working memory*. Oxford: Oxford University Press.

Bernhardt, E. B. (2000). Second language reading as a case study of reading scholarship in the twentieth century. In M. L. Kamil, P. B. Mosenthal, P. D. Pearson, & R. Barr (Eds.), *Handbook of reading research* (Vol. 3, pp. 791–811). Mahwah, NJ: Lawrence Erlbaum Associates.

Berninger, V. (1994). Intraindividual differences in levels of language in comprehension of written sentences. *Learning and Individual Differences, 6*, 433–457.

Berninger, V. W., Abbot, R. D., Abbot, S. P., Graham, S., & Richards, T. (2002). Writing and reading: Connections between language by hand and language by eye. *Journal of Learning Disabilities, 35*, 39–56.

Berninger, V., & Richards, T. (2002). *Brain literacy for educators and psychologists*. San Diego, CA: Academic Press.

Berninger, V. W., & Swanson, H. L. (1994). Modifying Hayes & Flowers' model of skilled writing to explain beginning and developing writing. In E. Butterfield (Ed.), *Children's writing: Toward a process theory of development of skilled writing* (pp. 57–81). Greenwich, CT: JAI.

Berninger, V. W., Yates, C., Cartwright, A., Rutberg, J., Remy, E., & Abbott, R. (1992). Lower-level developmental skills in beginning writing. *Reading and Writing: An Interdisciplinary Journal, 4*, 257–280.

Berry, J. W., Poortinga, Y. H., & Pandey, J. (Eds.). (1997). *Handbook of cross-cultural psychology: Theory and method*. Boston: Allyn & Bacon.

Bowers, P. G. (1995).Tracing symbol naming speed's unique contributions to reading disabilities over time. *Reading and Writing: An Interdisciplinary Journal, 7*, 1–28.

Bradley, L., & Bryant, P. (1983). Categorizing sounds and learning to read: A causal connection. *Nature, 301*, 419–421.

Bruck, M. (1990). Word-recognition skills of adults with childhood diagnoses of dyslexia. *Developmental Psychology, 28*, 439–454.

Bruck, M. (1992). Persistence of dyslexics' phonological awareness deficits. *Developmental Psychology, 28*, 874–886.

Bruck, M., & Genesee, F. (1995). Phonological awareness in young second language learners. *Journal of Child Language, 22*, 307–324.

Buriel, R., & Cardoza, D. (1988). Sociocultural correlates of achievement among three generations of Mexican American high school seniors. *American Educational Research Journal, 25*(2), 177–192.

Chall, J. S. (1983). *Learning to read: The great debate.* New York: McGraw-Hill.

Chall, J. S. (1996). *Stages of reading development* (2nd ed.). Fort Worth, TX: Harcourt Brace College Publishers.

Cummins, J. (1979). Linguistic interdependence and the educational development of bilingual children. *Review of Educational Research, 49*(2), 221–251.

Cummins, J. (1984). *Bilingualism and special education: Issues in assessment and pedagogy.* Clevedon, UK: Multilingual Matters.

Cunningham, A. E., & Stanovich, K. E. (1998). The impact of print exposure on word recognition. In J. Metsala & L. Ehri (Eds.), *Word recognition in beginning literacy* (pp. 235–262). Mahwah, NJ: Lawrence Erlbaum Associates.

Ehri, L. C. (1998). Grapheme–phoneme knowledge is essential for learning to read words in English. In J. Metsala & L. Ehri (Eds.), *Word recognition in beginning reading* (pp. 3–40). Hillsdale, NJ: Lawrence Erlbaum Associates.

Felton, R. H., & Wood, F. B. (1989). Cognitive deficits in reading disability and attention deficit disorder. *Journal of Learning Disabilities, 22,* 3–13.

Fitzgerald, J., & Shanahan, T. (2000). Reading and writing relations and their development. *Educational Psychologist, 35,* 39–50.

Fletcher, J., Shaywitz, S., Shankweiler, D., Katz, L., Liberman, I., Stuebing, K., et al. (1994). Cognitive profiles of reading disability: Comparisons of discrepancy and low achievement definitions. *Journal of Educational Psychology, 86,* 6–23.

Fletcher, J. M., Francis, D. J, Shaywitz, S. E., Lyon, G. R., Foorman, B. R., Stuebing, K. K., & Shaywitz, B. A. (1998). Intelligent testing and the discrepancy model for children with learning disabilities. *Learning Disabilities Research and Practice, 13,* 186–203.

Foorman, B. R., Francis, D. J., Fletcher, J. M., & Lynn, A. (1996). Relation of phonological and orthographic processing to early reading: Comparing two approaches to regression-based, reading-level-match designs. *Journal of Educational Psychology, 88,* 639–652.

Foorman, B. R., Francis, D. J., Fletcher, J. M., Schatschneider, C., & Mehta, P. (1998). The role of instruction in learning to read: Preventing reading failure in at-risk children. *Journal of Educational Psychology, 90,* 37–55.

Francis, D., Shaywitz, S., Stuebing, K., Shaywitz, B., & Fletcher, J. (1996). Developmental lag versus deficit models of reading disability: A longitudinal, individual growth curve analysis. *Journal of Educational Psychology, 88,* 3–17.

Fuchs, L. S., Fuchs, D., Hosp, M. K., & Jenkins, J. R. (2001). Oral reading fluency as an indicator of reading competence: A theoretical, empirical, and historical analysis. *Scientific Studies of Reading, 5,* 239–256.

Geva, E., & Wade-Woolley, W. (2004). Issues in the assessment of reading disability in second language children. In I. Smythe, J. Everatt, & R. Salter (Eds.), *International book of dyslexia: A cross-language comparison and practice guide* (pp.195–206). Chichester, England: Wiley.

Graham, S., & Harris, K. (2000). Helping children who experience reading difficulties: Prevention and intervention. In L. Baker, J. Dreher, & J. Guthrie (Eds.), *Engaging young readers: Promoting achievement and motivation* (pp. 43–67). New York: Guilford.

Guthrie, J., & Wigfield, A. (2000). Engagement and motivation in reading. In M. Kamil, P. B. Mosenthal, P. D. Pearson, & R. Barr (Eds.), *Handbook of reading research* (Vol. 3, pp. 403–422). Mahwah, NJ: Lawrence Erlbaum Associates.

Hart, B., & Risley, T. (1995). *Meaningful differences in the everyday experience of young American children.* Baltimore, MD: Paul H. Brooks.

Juel, C. (1991). Beginning reading. In R. Barr, M. L. Kamil, P. B. Mosenthal, & P. D. Pearson (Eds.), *Handbook of reading research* (Vol. 2, pp. 759–788). New York: Longman.

Kame'enui, E., & Simmons, D. (2001) Introduction to this special issue: The DNA of reading fluency. *Scientific Studies of Reading, 5*(3), 203–210.

Liberman, I., Shankweiler, D., Fischer, F., & Carter, B. (1974). Explicit syllable and phoneme segmentation in the young child. *Journal of Experimental Psychology, 18,* 201–212.

Lovett, M. W., Steinbach, K. A., & Frijters, J. C. (2000). Remediating the core deficits of developmental reading disability: A double-deficit perspective. *Journal of Learning Disabilities, 33,* 334–358.

Lundberg, I., Olofsson, A., & Wall, S. (1980). Reading and spelling skills in the first school years predicted from phonemic awareness skills in kindergarten. *Scandinavian Journal of Psychology, 21,* 159–173.

Lyon, G. R. (1995). Research initiatives in learning disabilities: Contributions from scientists supported by the National Institute of Child Health and Human Development. *Journal of Child Neurology, 10,* 120–126.

Lyon, G. R. (1999). In celebration of science in the study of reading development, reading difficulties, and reading instruction: The NICHD perspective. *Issues in Education: Contributions from Educational Psychology, 5,* 85–115.

Lyon, G. R., Fletcher, J. M., Shaywitz, S. E., Shaywitz, B. A., Torgesen, J. K., Wood, F. B., et al. (2001). Rethinking learning disabilities. In C. E. Finn, A. J. Rotherham, & C. R. Hokanson (Eds.), *Rethinking special education for a new century* (pp. 259–287). Washington, DC: Fordham Foundation.

Lyon, G. R., Shaywitz, S. E., & Shaywitz, B. A. (2003). A definition of dyslexia. *Annals of Dyslexia, 53,* 1–14.

Mann, V. A. (1993). Phonemic awareness and future reading ability. *Journal of Learning Disabilities, 26,* 259–269.

Moats, L. C. (1994). The missing foundation in teacher education: Knowledge of the structure of spoken and written language. *Annals of Dyslexia, 44,* 81–104.

Moats, L. C. (2001). *Speech to print.* Baltimore, MD: Paul H. Brooks.

Moravcsik, J. E., & Kintsch, W. (1993). Writing quality, reading skills, and domain knowledge as factors in text comprehension. *Canadian Journal of Experimental Psychology, 47,* 360–374.

National Center for Education Statistics. (1995). *Approaching kindergarten: A look at preschoolers in the United States. National household education survey.* Washington, DC: U.S. Department of Education, Office of Educational Research and Improvement.

National Center for Education Statistics. (2003). *National Assessment of Educational Progress, 2003, reading assessments.* Washington, DC: U.S. Department of Education, Institute of Education Sciences.

National Institute of Child Health and Human Development. (2000). *Report of the National Reading Panel. Teaching children to read: An evidence-based assessment of the scientific research literature on reading and its implications for reading instruction* (NIH Publication No. 00-4769). Washington, DC: U.S. Department of Health and Human Services.

Olson, R. K., Wise, B., Johnson, M. C., & Ring, J. (1997). The etiology and remediation of phonologically based word recognition and spelling disabilities: Are phonological deficits the "hole" story? In B. Blachman (Ed.), *Foundations of reading acquisition and dyslexia: Implications for early intervention* (pp. 305–326). Mahwah, NJ: Lawrence Erlbaum Associates.

Palincsar, A. S., & Brown, A. L. (1984). Reciprocal teaching of comprehension-fostering and comprehension-monitoring activities. *Cognition and Instruction, 1*(2), 117–175.

Pérez, B. (Ed.). (1998). *Sociocultural contexts of language and literacy.* Mahwah, NJ: Lawrence Erlbaum Associates.

Perfetti, C. A. (1985). Reading ability. In B. Hutson (Ed.), *Advances in reading/language research* (pp. 231–256). London: Oxford University Press.

Perfetti, C. A. (1997). Sentences, individual differences, and multiple texts: Three issues in text comprehension. *Discourse Processes, 23,* 337–355.

Perfetti, C. A. (1999). Comprehending written language: A blueprint of the reader. In C. Brown & P. Hagoot (Eds.), *The neurocognition of language* (pp. 167–208). New York: Oxford University Press.

Perfetti, C. A. (2003). The universal grammar of reading. *Scientific Studies of Reading, 7*(1), 3–24.

Phinney, J., Romero, I., Nava, M., & Huang, D. (2001). The role of language, parents, and peers in ethnic identity among adolescents in immigrant families. *Journal of Youth and Adolescence, 30,* 135–153.

Portes, A. (2000). An enduring vision: The melting pot that did not happen. *International Migration Review, 34*(1), 243–248.

Pressley, M. (2000). What should comprehension instruction be the instruction of? In M. L. Kamil, P. B. Mosenthal, P. D. Pearson, & R. Barr (Eds.), *Handbook of reading research* (Vol. 3, pp. 545–559). Mahwah, NJ: Lawrence Erlbaum Associates.

RAND Reading Study Group. (2002). *Reading for understanding: Toward an R&D program in reading comprehension.* Washington, DC: Author.

Roysircar-Sodowsky, G. R., & Maestas, M. V. (2000). Acculturation, ethnic identity, and acculturative stress: Evidence and measurement. In R. H. Dana (Ed.), *Handbook of cross-cultural and multicultural assessment* (pp. 131–172). Mahwah, NJ: Lawrence Erlbaum Associates.

Scanlon, D. M., & Vallutino, F. R. (1997). A comparison of the instructional backgrounds and cognitive profiles of poor, average, and good readers who were initially identified as at risk for reading failure. *Scientific Studies of Reading, 1*(3), 191–215.

Scott, C. (1989). Problem writers: Nature, assessment, and intervention. In A. Kamhi & H. Catts (Eds.), *Reading disabilities: A developmental language perspective* (pp. 303–344). Boston: Allyn & Bacon.

Seidenberg, M. S., & McClelland, J. L. (1989). A distributed, developmental model of word recognition and naming. *Psychological Review, 96*(4), 523–568.

Shankweiler, D. (1989). How problems of comprehension are related to difficulties in decoding. In D. Shankweiler & I. Liberman (Eds.), *Phonology and reading disability: Solving the reading puzzle* (pp. 35–68). Ann Arbor, MI: University of Michigan Press.

Share, D. L. (1995). Phonological recoding and self-teaching: Sine qua non of reading acquisition. *Cognition, 55*, 151–218.

Shaywitz, S. E., Fletcher, J. M., Holahan, J. M., Schneider, A. E., Marchione, K. E., Stuebing, K. K., Francis, D. J., Pugh, K. R., & Shaywitz, B. A. (1999). Persistence of dyslexia: The Connecticut Longitudinal Study at adolescence. *Pediatrics, 104*(6), 1351–1359.

Siegel, L. S. (1993). The development of reading. In H. W. Reese (Ed.), *Advances in child development and behavior* (pp. 63–97). San Diego: Academic Press.

Snelling, P., & Van Gelderen, A. (2004). The effect of enhanced lexical retrieval on second language writing: A classroom experiment. *Applied Linguistics, 25*, 172–200.

Snow, C. E., Burns, M. S., & Griffin, P. (Eds.). (1998). *Preventing reading difficulties in young children.* Washington, DC: National Academy Press.

Stahl, S. S. (2003). Vocabulary and readability: How knowing word meanings affects comprehension. *Topics in Language Disorders, 23*(3), 241–247.

Stanovich, K. E. (1986). Matthew effects in reading: Some consequences of individual differences in the acquisition of literacy. *Reading Research Quarterly, 21*, 360–407.

Stanovich, K. E., & Siegel, L. S. (1994). The phenotype performance profile of reading disabled children: A regression-based test of the phonological-core variable-difference model. *Journal of Educational Psychology, 86*, 24–53.

Suarez-Orozco, C., & Suarez-Orozco, M. (2001). *Children of immigration.* Cambridge, MA: Harvard University Press.

Swanson, H. L., & Saez, L. (2003). Memory difficulties in children and adults with learning disabilities. In H. L. Swanson, K. Harris, & S. Graham (Eds.), *Handbook of learning disabilities* (pp. 182–198). New York: Guilford.

Swanson, H. L., & Siegel, L. S. (2001). Learning disabilities as a working memory deficit. *Issues in Education: Contributions From Educational Psychology, 7*(1), 1–48.

Torgesen, J. K., Wagner, R. K., & Rashotte, C. A. (1994). Longitudinal studies of phonological processing and reading. *Journal of Learning Disabilities, 27*(10), 276–286.

Treiman, R. (1993). *Beginning to spell: A study of first-grade children.* New York: Oxford University Press.

Treiman, R., & Bourassa, D. (2000). Children's written and oral spelling. *Applied Psycholinguistics, 21*, 183–204.

Treiman, R., & Cassar, M. (1997). Spelling acquisition in English. In C. Perfetti, L. Rieben, & M. Fayol (Eds.), *Learning to spell* (pp. 61–80). Hillsdale, NJ: Lawrence Erlbaum Associates.

U.S. Department of Education & National Institute of Child Health and Human Development. (2003). *Symposium summary. National Symposium on Learning Disabilities and English Language Learners.* Washington, DC: Author.

Vellutino, F. R., Scanlon, D. M., Small, S. G., & Tanzman, M. S. (1991). The linguistic basis of reading ability: Converting written to oral language. *Text, 11*, 99–133.

Wagner, R. K., & Torgesen, J. K. (1987). The nature of phonological processing and its causal role in the acquisition of reading skills. *Psychological Bulletin, 101*(2), 192–212.

Wagner, R. K., Torgesen, J. K., & Rashotte, C. A. (1999). *Comprehensive test of phonological processing.* Austin, TX: Pro-Ed.

Whitaker, D., Berninger, V., Johnston, J., & Swanson, L. (1994). Intraindividual differences in levels of language in intermediate grade writers: Implications for the translating process. *Learning and Individual Differences, 6*, 107–130

White, K. R. (1982). The relation between socioeconomic status and academic achievement. *Psychological Bulletin, 91*, 461–481.

Wilkinson, L. C., Milosky, L. M., & Genishi, C. (1986). Second language learners' use of requests and responses in elementary classrooms. *Topics in Language Disorders, 6*(2), 57–70.

Wilson, A. M., & Lesaux, N. K. (2001). Persistence of phonological processing disorders in college students with dyslexia with age-appropriate reading skills. *Journal of Learning Disabilities, 34*(5), 394–400.

Wolf, M. (1997). A provisional integrative account of phonological and naming-speed deficits in dyslexia: Implications for diagnosis and intervention. In B. Blachman (Ed.), *Foundations of reading acquisition and dyslexia* (pp. 67–92). Hillsdale, NJ: Lawrence Erlbaum Associates.

Wolf, M., & Bowers, P. G. (1999). The double-deficit hypothesis for the developmental dyslexias. *Journal of Educational Psychology, 91*, 415–438.

Wolf, M., Bowers, P., & Biddle, K. (2000). Naming-speed processes, timing, and reading: A conceptual review. *Journal of Learning Disabilities, 33*, 387–407.

Wolf, M., & Katzir-Cohen, T. (2001). Reading fluency and its intervention. *Scientific Studies of Reading, 5*, 211–239.

Wong, B. Y. L. (1997). Research on genre-specific strategies in enhancing writing in adolescents with learning disabilities. *Learning Disability Quarterly, 20*(2), 140–159.

Wong, B., Wong, R., & Blenkinsop, J. (1989). Cognitive and metacognitive aspects of learning disabled adolescents' composing problems. *Learning Disability Quarterly, 12*, 310–323.

II

Cross-Linguistic Relationships in Second-Language Learners

6

Synthesis: Cross-Linguistic Relationships

Fred Genesee, Esther Geva, Cheryl Dressler, and Michael Kamil

Part II focuses on research that addresses relationships across languages in the development of literacy skills in children and adolescents who are learning to read and write English as a second language. Three general questions guided our review of these studies:

1. What is the relationship between language-minority children's first- and second-language oral development in domains related to literacy? (chap. 7)
2. What is the relationship between oral development in the first language and literacy development in the second language? (chap. 8)
3. What is the relationship between literacy skills acquired in the first language and literacy skills acquired in the second language? (chap. 9)

The scope of these questions is broadened in chapter 8 to include the acquisition of English as a foreign language and in chapter 9 to include not only English as a foreign language, but societal languages that are not English. The studies in chapters 7 and 9 focus on the effects within one modality—oral language in chapter 7 and literacy in chapter 9—whereas the studies reviewed in chapter 8 examine cross-modal effects (i.e., the influence of first-language oral language skills on the acquisition of reading and writing in English as a second language).

Answers to these questions are important for theoretical as well as practical reasons. Theoretically speaking, understanding the nature and extent of cross-language effects in the acquisition of literacy skills in English as a second language (ESL) is critical for developing a comprehensive theory of second-language literacy development. In contrast to monolingual English-speaking students, language-minority students bring an additional set of resources or abilities and face an additional set of challenges when learning to read and write in ESL. Relevant to our purposes, they bring additional resources or abilities that are linked to their first language—both its oral and written forms. In a broader sense,

153

they also often bring cultural knowledge and experiences linked to their first language and culture that can influence the development and use of reading and writing skills in English. See Part III for a discussion of research pertinent to these sociocultural issues. Studies on cross-language/modal effects are important to understand whether and in what ways the additional linguistic resources of language-minority students influence their literacy development in English and, more specifically, whether the course of acquisition of literacy in ESL is different from that of native-English-speaking children as a result of these effects.

Practically speaking, understanding the nature of these cross-language and cross-modal influences and the conditions that affect their expression is important for designing pedagogical interventions that facilitate the successful acquisition of reading and writing skills in ESL. Taking first-language influences into account does not necessarily mean teaching in the first language. Rather, it means, among other things, taking into account first-language influences when trying to understand the progress of language-minority students in school, when seeking to identify the sources of difficulty individual students may have in mastering ESL, and when devising educational curricula that are relevant and appropriate to language-minority students even if their education is entirely through the medium of English.

We begin this synthesis by presenting pertinent background information. We then describe the methodology of our review. Next, we summarize the findings of the literature on the three research questions addressed by our review. After identifying methodological issues, we recommend directions for future research.

BACKGROUND

A number of theories related to language and literacy development underlie the research that was reviewed, and we have used these theoretical perspectives to discuss the results of these studies, where appropriate, in the review chapters that follow. Some of these theories are concerned exclusively with issues relevant to monolingual learners and some with issues relevant to second-language learners. The most salient theoretical frameworks emanating from investigations of second-language learning that figure in our discussion of cross-language issues include transfer, underlying cognitive abilities, target language influences, and interlanguage theories. We also refer to theories of transfer emanating from cognitive psychology (Bransford & Schwartz, 1998).

Transfer

The majority of studies reviewed in this chapter have investigated cross-language relationships with reference to one of two theoretical orientations: the contrastive analysis hypothesis (Lado, 1964) and the interdependence hypothesis (Cummins, 1978, 1979).[1] Contrastive analysis involves analyzing a

---

[1]In the case of the interdependence hypothesis, the authors explicitly state that they were testing Cummins' theories. However, Researchers investigating specific first- and second-language linguistic contrasts (such as spelling or cognate studies) based on analyses of two particular languages did not explicitly situate their studies within the framework of the contrastive analysis hypothesis.

learner's first and second languages to identify structural (i.e., grammatical) similarities and differences (see Lado, 1964, for an early version of this theory of transfer). According to the contrastive analysis hypothesis, second-language errors will be made (interference) when learners encounter structures in the second language that differ from or are unfamiliar to them in their first language. This hypothesis has undergone considerable refinement since it was first introduced. Contemporary versions of this theory include the possibility that transfer from the first language can facilitate second-language learning when the two languages share features (e.g., phonological forms or cognate vocabulary). In this case, second-language acquisition would be accelerated. Typological similarity is fundamental to the contrastive analysis hypothesis insofar as languages that are typologically similar (e.g., English and Spanish or German) share more structural features than languages that are typologically distant (e.g., English and Chinese or Korean).

Although contrastive analysis theory continues to focus on the comparison of structural features of languages, more recent work in this paradigm has identified nonstructural factors (i.e., those not related to grammar) that influence (i.e., promote or inhibit) transfer. One such factor is psychotypology—learners' perception of the similarity between their first and second languages. It has been argued that transfer is more likely to occur if learners do not view the two languages as significantly different from each other (Kellerman, 1977). For example, the existence of cognates in two languages may not be a sufficient condition for transfer of cognate knowledge to occur; a belief on the part of the learner that the two languages are similar may be necessary (but probably not sufficient) as well. An additional factor that is thought to constrain transfer derives from the notion of markedness. Linguistically *unmarked* features are those that are universal or present in most of the world's languages, and these are thought to be more susceptible to transfer than typologically unusual features (Eckman, 1977, 1985; Hyltenstam, 1984). In most languages, for example, final consonants are devoiced; thus, the devoicing of final consonants is an unmarked feature. In English, final consonants may be voiced or voiceless. When a learner whose first language is unmarked with respect to this feature (e.g., German) learns English, first-language transfer is predicted when the learner is pronouncing a final consonant in the second language that is voiced. Thus, both *back* and *bag* would be pronounced bæk. It is not predicted, however, that the English speaker will voice final consonants in German because this feature is more marked, or unnatural, in the first language (English), but not in the second (German). More contemporary conceptualizations of the contrastive analysis hypothesis also acknowledge that transfer interacts with a host of additional factors, such as developmental processes and language/literacy proficiency (Ellis, 1994; Odlin, 1989).

The contrastive analysis hypothesis was originally formulated to explain the influence of the first language on the acquisition of subsystems of the second-language *grammar* (e.g., phonological, lexical, morphological, syntactic). Within the current discussion of cross-language relationships in the acquisition of literacy, the hypothesis is most relevant to studies investigating structural domains tied to literacy, such as phonology (e.g., in studies of spelling) and lexical knowledge (e.g., in studies of cognate relationships). However, the contrastive analysis hypothesis cannot account for the existence of cross-language relationships in literacy constructs that are more psychological in nature, such as metacognitive strategies that are used in the first and second languages.

In the second theoretical orientation, the interdependence hypothesis, Cummins (1981, 2000) has postulated that acquisition of first and second languages is developmentally interdependent; that is, development of the first language can influence and, in particular, facilitate development of the second. However, not all aspects of first-language development are postulated to be equally facilitative of second-language development. In this regard, Cummins distinguishes between language for academic and higher order cognitive purposes and language for day-to-day interpersonal communication—commonly referred to as cognitive academic language proficiency (CALP) and basic interpersonal communicative skills (BICS), respectively (see Cummins, 2000, for a full explication of these constructs). These language constructs are characterized by the extent of contextual support during language use and the cognitive demands implicated during verbal communication. Context-embedded communication, such as talking about a movie with someone who has also seen it, is characteristic of day-to-day social language use. The meanings participants seek to convey are supported by shared context or common experiences, and the participants are able to negotiate meaning actively and directly. For *context-reduced communication*, such as discussing a movie with someone who has not seen it, careful use of language is required to provide information that will ensure clear communication because the participants cannot draw on immediate contextual cues or shared experiences. This form of communication is especially important in school.

The other continuum in Cummins' framework refers to the cognitive demands required of communication. *Cognitively undemanding communication* requires language skills that have been overlearned and, thus, call for little cognitive involvement on the part of the participants. An example is talking about a favorite sport while watching it. *Cognitively demanding communication*, in contrast, calls for language skills that have not been fully automatized. Examples are explication of the methods and results of a scientific experiment, as well as arguments for and against nuclear disarmament. It is language for higher order cognitive purposes—that is, those that are context reduced and cognitively demanding (e.g., literacy-related language skills)—that are developmentally interdependent. More specifically, Cummins (2000) posits that, "academic proficiency transfers across languages such that students who have developed literacy in their first language will tend to make stronger progress in acquiring literacy in their second language" (p. 173), and this is hypothesized to be true because first- and second-language academic language skills are developmentally linked to common underlying proficiencies.

An additional hypothesis formulated by Cummins associated with the interdependence hypothesis is the threshold hypothesis; this hypothesis is also related to transfer, albeit indirectly. The threshold hypothesis implicates transfer insofar as there are positive linguistic effects that result from attaining sufficient levels of competence in both languages. Whatever the precise mechanism, this hypothesis raises important questions regarding cross-language relationships in second-language literacy development—namely, are there relative levels of oral proficiency in the two languages of English-language learners that are necessary to facilitate cross-language relationships and, if so, what are these requisite levels?

It has proved difficult to define with any precision the constructs and developmental relationships proposed in Cummins' hypotheses, and, indeed, they have been the subject of considerable controversy (see e.g., Edelsky, Hudelson, Flores, Barkin, Altweger, et al., 1983; MacSwan & Rolstad, 2003). In particular, it is not entirely clear what Cummins means by his construct of *common underlying proficiency*. We take it to refer to procedural knowledge that underlies language use for academic or higher order cognitive purposes and entails for example, the skills involved in defining words or elaborating ideas verbally as is often required when language is used for academic purposes. We differentiate Cummins' notion of common underlying proficiency from underlying cognitive abilities, which we discuss next. We also assume that it does not refer to structural features of the type that figure in the contrastive analysis framework. Despite some uncertainty about the constructs involved, this framework warrants consideration here because of its prevalence in current research on second-language literacy development, especially in research reviewed in chapter 9.

Both of these theoretical frameworks assume what Bransford and Schwartz (1998) call a "direct application"approach, which "characterizes transfer as the ability to directly apply one's previous learning to a new setting or problem" (p. 68). This is evident in the emphasis on transfer of structures in the contrastive analysis hypothesis and in the emphasis on transfer of language proficiencies in the interdependence hypothesis of Cummins. Empirical tests of transfer using these theoretical frameworks have tended to examine transfer of specific knowledge or skills in isolation from other processes or strategies—what Bransford and Schwartz refer to as "sequestered problem solving." In essence, current frameworks for studying cross-linguistic relationships in second-language learning have circumscribed the nature of transfer and methods used to study it in specific ways. We return later to Bransford and Schwartz's "preparedness for future learning" proposal, which offers a broader framework, to illustrate that alternative frameworks are available for studying cross-linguistic transfer.

Throughout this review, the term *transfer* is used to describe cross-language relationships found in structures that belong exclusively to the linguistic domain (e.g., phonology), as well as skills that involve cognitive and language abilities (e.g., reading comprehension).

Target Language Influences

In contrast to theories based on notions of first-language transfer, some theories include the premise that second-language acquisition, including literacy, can be accounted for primarily by reference to features of the target language being learned (Dulay & Burt, 1974). Such influences result in developmental patterns, including errors, that resemble those made by first-language learners of the same language and thus are often referred to as *developmental influences*. Target language effects of this sort may be influenced by the nature of the target language. For example, English is considered to have a deep orthographic structure, in that the relationship between the orthographic and phonological systems is complex and often obscure. For example, take the sound "f": it can be represented in English by each of the following graphemes: "f" as in *fur*, "ph" as in *phenomenon*, and "gh" as in *enough*. In the case of English spelling, then, target language (English) influences are expected to emerge relatively late in development owing to the depth or opaqueness of some sound–letter correspondences. In this case, knowledge of first-language phonology might be expected to play a role in early stages of learning to spell, especially if the learner has a first language with a shallow orthographic system, such as Spanish.[2] However, although knowing how to spell in Spanish may enable children to spell with relative ease certain phonemes that are common to Spanish and English, learning to spell phonemes in the target language (English) that have multiple spellings will result in developmental patterns or errors that reflect the challenges of the target language. For example, like their English-as-a-first-language counterparts, English-language learners will take longer to learn to spell inconsistent exemplars (e.g., "ph" and "gh"). In other words, target language influences would be expected to emerge relatively early in development for certain spelling elements because of the nature of the spelling system of the target language. In contrast to transfer, target language or developmental influences are not cross-linguistic in nature. Yet as was just illustrated, the emergence of developmental errors can be influenced by characteristics of the target language, and this effect, in turn, can indirectly influence the role of first- language transfer.

Interlanguage Theories

Interlanguage theories, developed by researchers working on second-language acquisition in adults, acknowledge the importance of both first- and second-language sources of influence on second-language development. Most notably, Selinker (1972) and Nemser (1971) argue that the mental representations or abstract system of rules of the target language constructed by second-language learners can best be described as an interlanguage—that is, "a grammatical system with its own internal organizing principles which may or may not be related to the [first and second languages]…" (Towell & Hawkins, 1994, p. 23). Interlanguage theories move theories of second-language acquisition away from an exclusive reliance on first- or second-language influences and postulate that aspects of the internal organization and developmental trajectory of second-language acquisition may be unique.

Underlying Cognitive Abilities

Relationships between first- and second-language acquisition have also been attributed to *underlying cognitive abilities* (Geva & Ryan, 1993). Working memory, phonological short-term memory (e.g., pseudoword repetition), phonological awareness, and phonological recoding (e.g., RAN) are commonly identified in the research literature as such abilities. Phonological short-term memory is a

---

[2]Spanish has a shallow orthography, in that there is a relatively consistent and clear relationship between letters and sounds.

good example of a common underlying ability that has been investigated in research on learning to read in a second language. Like other common underlying abilities, it is thought to be part of one's general cognitive endowment and to be largely independent of specific language experiences or other experiential factors. This does not mean that experience does not influence the development of phonological short-term memory or other abilities in this category, but the abilities apply to the acquisition of any language. These underlying abilities are thought to account for individual differences in the rate and success of language learning for a first, second, or any other language. Phonological awareness, although thought to influence the acquisition of reading in any language, is probably influenced in subtle ways by one's early language and literacy experiences. Nevertheless, awareness that language comprises sounds and sounds have different structural and functional properties is at the core of phonological awareness, and individual differences in such awareness account for differences in learners' success in literacy in the first or second language. The aspects of phonological awareness that are language specific account for relatively little cross-language variance.

It is important to distinguish working memory and phonological processing from Cummins' notion of common underlying proficiency. Cummins' notion is clearly language dependent and developmental in nature. In contrast, underlying cognitive abilities are thought to be fundamentally cognitive and nonlinguistic in nature and are part of one's innate endowment—they are not learned. More specifically, Cummins' notion of language for academic purposes is clearly an acquired proficiency that is intimately linked to language experience, in contrast with phonological processing and working memory.

Moderator Variables

Finally, cross-language and cross-modal influences on the development of literacy in a second language can be moderated by a broad range of variables, as noted earlier in the case of transfer. Moderator variables include such factors as level of proficiency in the first and second languages (see Cummins' threshold hypothesis), the extent to which and the ways in which the first language is used in the home, socioeconomic and generational status, instruction, and even personality. The influence of moderator variables is discussed in chapters 7 to 9, as appropriate, whereas the influence of moderator variables related to sociocultural factors is discussed in detail in chapters 10 to 12, and instruction is discussed in chapters 13 to 18.

METHODOLOGY OF THE REVIEW

Detailed analyses and summaries of findings for the three questions identified at the outset of this chapter are presented in chapters 7 to 9. The review of research was conducted as described in the introduction to this report. The findings are summarized with respect to language learning outcomes that are relevant to the main question addressed in each chapter. For example, in chapter 7 (the link between first- and second-language oral proficiency), the results are reviewed in terms of working memory, phonological processes, and oral language abilities (i.e., phonology, vocabulary, grammar, and discourse); see chapter 3 for definitions of these constructs. These variables are adjusted in chapters 8 and 9 to better reflect the literacy outcomes addressed in the research reviewed in those chapters; moreover, not all domains are discussed for each question. Word-level outcomes are described first and are followed by descriptions of text-level outcomes. The findings are organized according to grade-level categories—elementary, middle, and high school—when possible. This is a narrative review of evidence. Appendix 6.A describes why particular research studies that tested the same hypothesis were not subjected to quantitative synthesis techniques.

Many of the studies reviewed in these chapters used correlational designs to examine the links between first-language oral and literacy skills and reading/writing skills in English. A number of studies used between-group designs. In some cases the groups consist of English-language learners, on the one hand, and monolingual English-speakers, on the other. Students in each group are compared on indices of English; e.g., spelling errors. The logic of this design is analogous to that of a classic experimental design in which one seeks to determine whether between-group differences on one variable (e.g., ELL vs English speaker group) are associated with diferences on the outcome measure of interest (e.g., errors in English spelling). Failure to find differences between the groups on spelling suggests the lack of a relationship with the group variable in question, whereas finding differences on spelling suggests a link (e.g., spelling patterns of ELLs is due to LI phonology). However, although these studies can suggest links between the variables of interest in this chapter and thus have been retained for review, the evidence they provide is indirect only.

In other cases, ELLS were divided into subgroups based on one variable; e.g., L1 vocabulary skills, and their performance on a second variable is then examined; e.g., English-L2 reading skills. If ELLs who are good English readers are also found to have relatively good L1 vocabulary skills whereas the poor English readers have relatively poor L1 vocabulary skills, it can be inferred that the difference in English reading scores is related to differences in L1 vocabulary knowledge. Failre to find differences between the ELL subgroups in L2 spelling would suggest a lack of relationship between L1 vocabulary and English reading. These studies can provide descriptive evidence that the variables of interest are related to one another, but do not provide evidence of causal connections. Thus, it is important to emphasize that studies of this type are essentially also correlational in nature and, thus, they provide only descriptive evidence of the associations among the variables of interest.

SUMMARY OF EMPIRICAL FINDINGS

Although the studies reviewed for Part II vary in many important respects, including their research designs and the language and literacy constructs assessed, they all sought to understand how first- and second-language literacy development may be interrelated. As discussed earlier, transfer theory is one of the most powerful and most frequently cited frameworks used to discuss and examine literacy development of English-language learners. The studies reviewed here provide ample evidence for transfer with regard to specific linguistic structure/properties and psycholinguistic processes, although the evidence is not consistently robust in all cases and varies as a function of the construct under study (e.g., comparing phonological awareness with syntactic knowledge). As noted earlier, however, the empirical evidence for transfer uncovered by extant research is probably circumscribed by the researchers' particular conceptualizations of transfer. Research carried out within contrastive analysis and interdependence theories indicates that certain aspects of second-language oral proficiency and literacy are related in some important ways to performance on similar (or identical) constructs in the first language. There is also evidence for cross-modality influences, although cross-modality transfer has not been observed across the board. For example, first-language vocabulary does not appear to predict second-language reading comprehension.

Despite current evidence for transfer and its strong appeal, a cross-language framework, especially one that focuses on transfer as the primary influence, is not sufficient for understanding the full complexity of second-language literacy development among the diverse English-language learners who are being schooled in ESL. As discussed in a previous section, transfer is not the sole source of influence in second-language oral proficiency and literacy development. Common underlying abilities (e.g., working memory) also play a significant role in second-language development as they do in first-language development; certain error types can be understood in terms of typological differences between the first and second languages; features of the target language mediate development, especially in advanced stages; and well-developed oral language and literacy skills in the first language can facilitate second-language literacy development to some extent.

Our review indicates that it may be time to move thinking about and research on second-language literacy development beyond simple frameworks that do not accommodate the complex processes that interact dynamically across grade levels as English-language learners acquire literacy in ESL. As an example, a conceptualization of transfer as "preparedness for future learning" might broaden the notion of transfer, as well as research paradigms for studying it, and thus expand our understanding of what constitutes cross-linguistic transfer in second-language learning. The concept of preparedness for future learning emanates from current theories of transfer (e.g., Bransford & Schwartz, 1998) that view the learner's use of knowledge from the first language as evidence of resourcefulness; that is, the learner's ability to generalize knowledge and abilities in the first language to second-language literacy tasks is seen as a type of cross-language bootstrapping. Viewed from this perspective, transfer could entail not only corresponding or analogous skills, but also meta-linguistic or meta-cognitive skills that emerge from competence in the first language. An example would be English-language learners who transfer comprehension monitoring skills from the first to the second language. Discussion of the complex and interrelated factors that impinge on second-language literacy development is presented in chapter 21.

The Relationship Between Language-Minority Children's First- and Second-Language Oral Development in Domains Related to Literacy

The studies reviewed in chapter 7 examine cross-language relationships in (a) working memory; (b) phonological processes; and (c) oral language, including phonology, vocabulary, grammar, and discourse-level skills. Definitions of working memory and of each type of phonological process are provided in chapter 3.

With respect to working memory, there were only three studies, but all three provided statistically significant evidence for significant relationships between working memory in English-language learners' (ELL) first language and English. With respect to phonological processing, there was consistent evidence of significant cross-language effects for phonological awareness, such that English-language learners with high levels of phonological awareness in the first language also had relatively high levels of phonological awareness when assessed in the second language. The evidence from studies of phonological recoding and phonological short-term memory, although suggesting that cross-language effects exist, was inconsistent. This inconsistency may be due to the limited research in each of these domains. More specifically, there were two studies on phonological short-term memory and three on phonological recoding. Thus, additional research is needed to examine these domains further.

With respect to oral language, there was evidence of cross-language effects with respect to phonological development. More specifically, English-language learners were found to exhibit developmental patterns in the second language in speech discrimination, speech production, and intraword segmentation that differed from those of native English speakers, but reflected characteristics of the first language. In other words, differences between the first and second languages resulted in second-language patterns that differed from target-language forms. In another study, first-language influences resulted in second-language patterns of phonological development that resembled those of children with speech impairment, underlining the importance of this line of research to ensure that English-language learners are not inappropriately judged to be impaired based on what are normal development patterns in their second language. In general, however, it is impossible to know at this time how robust these effects are because these studies varied considerably with respect to both the ages of the students and the specific language domains examined. Moreover, there are only one or two studies in each domain.

There was also evidence of first-language effects on second-language vocabulary development. Studies on the acquisition of ESL vocabulary revealed that cross-language lexical effects are most likely to occur in what might be regarded as higher order vocabulary skills, such as interpretation of metaphors, paradigmatic associations, and quality of formal definitions. Studies showing that English-language learners are able to take advantage of cognate relationships also indicated cross-language effects. Clearly, cross-language cognate effects are relevant only when English-language learners have a first language that shares cognate vocabulary with English. It remains to be shown whether these cross-language lexical effects represent transfer of knowledge from one language to another or the influence of language-independent cognitive capacities that make some children better language learners—whether of the first or second language. It is also possible that both influences are at work. In fact, a number of the studies of lexical development suggest that correlations between first and second languages are due to such general language-independent influences—metalinguistic abilities that are reflected in quality of formal word definition and conceptual-attentional capacity.

Studies of the development of grammar and discourse-level skills in English among English-language learners are inconclusive with respect to cross-language effects because there is little overlap in focus among studies on grammar and there have been no studies on discourse-level skills.

The Relationship Between Oral Development in the First Language and Literacy Development in the Second Language

A narrative summary of findings from studies of elementary, middle, and high school students indicates that measures of first-language oral proficiency (e.g., vocabulary tests, grammatical sensitivity tasks, teacher ratings) either do not correlate with English word reading skills or do not explain unique variance in English word reading skills. However, a consistent pattern emerged with regard to the relationship between phonological processing in the first language and word-level reading and spelling skills in English. Phonological skills developed in processing the first language have the potential to exert a strong positive impact on English word reading. In line with this conclusion, the review of studies of school-age children from different first-language back-grounds and educational settings (e.g., various heritage language programs in Canada, Mexican American children in bilingual programs in the United States, English-language learners residing in the United Kingdom who speak Urdu at home, Hebrew-speaking Israeli high school students learning English as a foreign language) suggests that different aspects of phonological processing skills measured in students' first language (e.g., rhyme detection; phonological awareness involving segmentation, blending, and matching; phonological memory; and rapid automatized naming) and working memory correlate significantly and consistently with word-level reading skills in English. The findings also suggest that second-language processing skills that are linked to literacy may be better developed than the parallel first-language skills, possibly as a result of exposure to systematic literacy instruction in the second language. There is some evidence, however, that the relationship may be conditioned by similarities and differences between the first language and English.

Studies of spelling errors that either used between-group designs or focused on spelling development suggest that students' spelling errors could be traced to differences between Spanish (the first language) and English (the target language) phonology, such as /b/–/v/ misspellings, the spelling of /d/ for /th/, and the simplification of final consonant clusters (e.g., *han* for *hand*). In contrast, studies of spelling that used correlational designs failed to find significant rela-tionships between first-language oral proficiency and English spelling skills possibly because the first-language oral proficiency measures used in the latter studies are less related to spelling than the measures used in the former studies.

As for text-level aspects of literacy (i.e., reading comprehension and writ-ing), global measures of oral language proficiency in the first language (such as self-ratings or measures of listening comprehension in the first language) do not appear to be related to the development of reading comprehension or writ-ing skills in English. Although overall, first-language oral proficiency does not appear to constrain or enhance English-language learners' reading comprehen-sion in English, first-language reading comprehension is directly related to second-language reading comprehension (see chap. 9). There is also limited evidence that specific aspects of first-language competence, such as knowledge of first- and second-language cognates, are associated with the development of reading comprehension in English.

This relationship may be mediated by the association between first- and second-language phonological processing skills (see chap. 7) and the role of first-language phonological processing in second-language word recognition skills (see chap. 8). Cross-language effects are not invariant and may be influenced by typological, sociocultural, and instructional factors.[3]

Finally, it is difficult to generalize from the available studies about the relationship between first-language oral proficiency and English writing skills in English-language learners because the studies differ in many respects. Nevertheless, they provide suggestive evidence that cross-language/cross-modal effects on the development of second-language writing skills are more likely to occur when discrete rather than general aspects of first-language oral proficiency (e.g., range of vocabulary, rather than overall proficiency) are examined.

The Role of Cross-Linguistic Transfer in Second-Language Literacy Acquisition for Children Who Are Learning English as a Second or Foreign Language

The studies reviewed in this section examined cross-language influences of literacy knowledge, processes, and strategies in students who are learning a second language. These studies differ from those reviewed for the previous two questions, in that they include only students who are literate in their first language, and they employ *written* measures of the constructs investigated. The general approach within these studies was to isolate specific components that underlie the reading process (vocabulary, word recognition, reading comprehension, spelling, etc.) and test the nature of their relationships across languages. Some studies were guided by the contrastive analysis hypothesis, but the majority of studies looked at the transfer of universal/conceptual proficiencies that underlie literacy. As a result of the review, it appears that the contrastive analysis hypothesis works with both structural factors (e.g., constructs of language distance and markedness) and nonstructural factors (e.g., perceived linguistic distance, first-language proficiency, and development) to account for transfer in the domains of spelling, vocabulary, and word recognition. Transfer of higher order literacy skills (such as reading comprehension and strategy use), in contrast, is explained more adequately within Cummins' interdependence hypothesis. These two theories appear to mark the boundaries between purely linguistic and conceptual knowledge.

The studies measuring word reading demonstrate cross-language relationships in word and pseudoword reading. These studies also suggest that this relationship holds across a wide range of ages, from beginning readers in early elementary school to advanced learners in high school; across normally developing and disabled readers; across language pairs that are structurally close and distant; and across varying levels of second-language proficiency.

---

[3]For a more extensive discussion of sociocultural factors, see chapters 11 and 12; for further discussion of instructional issues, see chapters 15 and 16.

At the same time, several studies provided evidence that the phonological processes underlying word recognition are influenced by the orthography of the first language and are thus language specific. In considering facilitation versus interference, the strong correlations found between first- and second-language word reading performance across studies show that students who are better at word reading in one language are also better at it in the other. This relationship could be a result of factors specific to reading in the first and second languages, but there is some evidence of influence of nonlinguistic skills related to general cognition.

Studies of spelling point to differing influences of first-language phonological and orthographic knowledge at different levels of second-language proficiency; students who are at higher levels in the second language produce errors similar to those observed in first-language acquisition. This reflects within-language developmental pathways, rather than cross-language processes. Most of the studies viewed the acquisition of second-language spelling as a stage in which reliance on the first language early in the process is facilitative because many of the phoneme–grapheme mappings applied in both the first language and English. However, the small number of studies available does not allow for conclusive statements.

With respect to vocabulary, most studies show that various aspects of word knowledge appear to transfer across languages. Positive transfer of vocabulary knowledge was shown to occur in cognate recognition. These effects were mediated by developmental factors, proficiency level, and the actual or perceived typological distance between the languages. In the process of inferring meaning for unknown words, transfer may also be negative, as when meaning is erroneously assigned to words on the basis of influence of first-language syntax. Such cases of negative transfer are thought to be language dependent and may be resolved through exposure to the second language, but may persist even as students become more proficient in the target language.

For reading comprehension, which requires the ability to understand complex written language beyond the word level, most studies looked at older students (above Grade 3). Reading comprehension ability in the first language was found to correlate significantly with reading comprehension in the second language under most conditions (typological distance, language status, direction of transfer, age of learner, and tasks). The evidence also suggests a facilitative effect, in that processes underlying reading comprehension, when developed in one language, are predictive of reading comprehension in the other (and no evidence of interference was found).

A similar relationship was found for reading strategies, again investigated primarily with older students. Most studies that addressed this component found that bilingual students who read strategically in one language also read strategically in their other language (subject to proficiency level and other influences). The effects tended to be facilitative, with no evidence of interference found (e.g., in strategies related to accessing cognate knowledge). In general, strategic reading skills do not need to be relearned as second-language acquisition proceeds because they are not language specific.

For writing, most studies showed that aspects of writing skills that have been developed in one language can be accessed for writing in the other. The skills assessed included emergent skills associated with the writing process, but also skills related to higher order processes, including discourse elements in beginning writers and sense of story structure in older elementary students.

As for the question of facilitation versus interference, as in other domains, skills associated with the writing process developed in one language appear to be available for application to the other and thus demonstrate facilitation.

METHODOLOGICAL ISSUES

The studies reviewed in Part II employed a variety of methodologies, the most frequent being error analyses, correlational/regression analyses, and between- and within-group comparisons. Despite these varied methodologies, all of the studies shared a common goal: to identify associations among features, skills, or levels of competence in learners' first and second languages. Our discussion of methodological issues pertaining to the studies revolves around this common goal and focuses on the logic of research designed to elucidate cross-language relationships.

Correlational techniques were used by many of the studies because, obviously, correlations can be used to identify associations between the first and second language in the same or related domains of language development. However, simple correlational analyses between single first- and second-language measures are limited in their ability to elucidate the precise nature of the association between first- and second-language and literacy development because they do not consider alternative theoretically plausible possibilities. For example, evidence for transfer of the type represented in Cummins' developmental interdependence theory often consists of significant positive correlations between academic skills in the first and second languages, such as reading comprehension. Although significant positive correlations between first- and second-language reading comprehension may be suggestive of transfer of reading skills, they are not sufficient because other factors may also be at work. Pursuing our reading comprehension example, a plausible alternative would be that individual differences in overall cognitive ability underlie, and may even explain, the significant correlation between first- and second-language reading comprehension insofar as English-language learners with superior levels of cognitive ability may also have superior first- and second-language reading skills. Alternatively, cognitive ability along with first-language reading ability may be at work. If research is to provide precise descriptions of first- and second-language relationships, multivariate analyses will be necessary. Alternative conceptualizations of transfer that also include multivariate approaches, such as that proposed by Bransford and Schwartz (1998), will provide more comprehensive conceptualizations of transfer because they consider a broader range of influences in the transfer phenomenon.

Simple correlational techniques are further limited in that they can only reveal an association between the first and second language (or between oral and written language skills), not the precise causal nature of the relationship. The clearest evidence for the causal role of transfer from the first language to second-language development would come from intervention studies designed to promote acquisition of a particular subcomponent of literacy in the first language, with subsequent testing of the same component in the second language. For example, to establish that knowledge of sound–letter correspondencies in the L1 facilitates L2 spelling would require research that provides training of sound–grapheme correspondencies in the first language of an experimental group of English-language learners and no such training for a control English-language learner group. Evidence from subsequent assessment of experimental and control group students' knowledge of sound–grapheme correspondence in the second language that the former outperformed the latter would constitute evidence for transfer. However, no such studies emerged from our search.

Many of the studies conducted within the contrastive analysis framework were based on analyses of how the first- and second-language systems of the learners differed with respect to particular features; analysis of student errors was then undertaken to determine the extent of influence of the first language. This was typically the case with studies of spelling, for example, in which second-language spelling errors could be explained on the basis of differences between first- and second-language phonology and orthography. Although such studies did not necessarily involve formal correlational analyses, they were intended to reveal associations between second-language errors and features of the first language. For example, when attempting to spell words such as *bump*, Spanish-speaking English-language learners might produce *bup*. This could be interpreted as negative transfer from Spanish because words in Spanish do not end in consonant clusters—arguably, *bup* is a simplification of the English form in accordance with Spanish phonological rules. However, such an interpretation would be premature because this particular transfer error is not distinguishable from developmental errors made by native-English-speaking learners. In fact, in initial spelling, children learning English as their first language are unable to spell preconsonantal nasals correctly, and in spelling a word such as *bump*, they may omit the *m*.

Moreover, findings based on a sample of only second-language learners coming from a single first-language background do not allow one to attribute the presence of a first-language feature in the second language unambiguously to transfer from the first language because other explanations could account for the same results. Stronger evidence for transfer would come from comparisons with the error patterns of native English speakers, if known, as well as from results for English-language learners with different language backgrounds— some speaking a first language that does not have the target feature and some speaking one that does (double dissociations). If both groups of students made the error predicted on the basis of a contrastive analysis, a source other than transfer, such as developmental factors, might be implicated. Finally, conclusions of cross-language studies on second-language literacy acquisition can be misleading if they do not provide longitudinal results for learners across age/grade levels. In particular, studies that report significant associations between English-language learners' first and second languages in specific domains at one point in development give the impression that these effects are either permanent or characteristic of learners at all ages. Longitudinal data are called for if we are to distinguish negative transfer from the first language that inhibits learning in the second language in the long run from negative transfer that reflects a short-term strategy used by novice learners to bootstrap into the second language system. Indeed, the latter possibility enjoys some empirical support from evidence reported earlier that first-language effects on second-language development tended to occur more frequently in novice second-language learners and in the early stages of second-language learning in some domains. In any case, the implications of these alternative interpretations of transfer are theoretically and practically significant. Theoretically, evidence of short-term negative transfer would argue for the bootstrapping hypothesis, whereas evidence of long-term negative transfer would argue for fossilization; that is, acquisition of a target-deviant form that is a part of the learner's stable language system. Practically speaking, short-term transfer would be cause for minimal concern Indeed, it could be taken as evidence for acquisition. In contrast, evidence of long-term negative transfer would be cause for educational concern.

Strong evidence of relationships and influences between English language learners' first and second languages in second-language literacy development is provided by the studies reviewed here. At the same time, more complex research designs are called for if we are to better understand the precise nature of these relationships, the causal mechanisms they entail, and their long-term developmental impact on second-language learning. In particular, there is a need for more longitudinal intervention studies with multivariate designs that examine learners with different language backgrounds (including native English speakers) across grade levels and take into account the multiple factors that may influence relationships between first and second oral language proficiency and literacy.

DIRECTIONS FOR FUTURE RESEARCH

Reading Readiness

The foundations for literacy development are established during the preschool years, both at home and, in some cases, in preschool. Research on the development of reading readiness skills in English-language learners during the preschool years is sparse at present, particularly with respect to cross-language and cross-modal relationships. A variety of issues concerning reading readiness in English-language learners' first language and how this facilitates the acquisition of literacy in ESL require empirical investigation, including (a) types of readiness skills that develop in English-language learners in different home environments, (b) factors that influence their development, (c) differences in readiness development among English-language learners who speak typologically diverse languages, (d) interventions that can promote their development in the home and the preschool, and (e) how these factors influence the development of English literacy in school.

Despite the importance that has been attached to phonological awareness for early literacy development among researchers and policymakers alike, additional research is still needed to better understand cross-linguistic aspects of phonological awareness and, in particular, the specific phonological awareness skills in the first language that promote early second-language literacy development and under what circumstances such cross-linguistic facilitation is evident. In a related vein, we need research that examines the influence of phonological awareness in the first language on English second-language literacy development at different grade levels, including for those students who begin schooling in English in the primary grades and those who begin in upper elementary, middle, or high school. Research on phonological awareness training in the first language for English-language learners who are at risk for reading difficulty in English as a second language would also be beneficial.

Relationship Between First-Language Literacy and Second-Language Literacy for Academic Achievement

Although the development of reading and writing skills is a goal in itself, reading and writing in school are intimately linked to academic development. Yet cross-language relationships between reading and writing development in specific academic domains (e.g., science) have received scant empirical attention. More specifically, at present, we have virtually no empirical evidence for whether specific first-language reading and writing skills that are linked to particular academic domains, such as mathematics, science, and social studies, influence acquisition of the corresponding reading and writing skills in ESL; how these relationships might change over grade levels; and how they are mitigated by typological similarities in discourse styles of the English language learners' first and second languages.

Writing

Research on the development of writing skills in English-language learners is extremely sparse, and research on cross-linguistic influences in the acquisition of writing skills by English language learners is even more sparse. Thus, much more research that focuses on the relationship between English language learners' first- and second-language skills in the context of learning to write for academic purposes in English is necessary. This should entail studies that investigate the influence of first-language oral as well as first-language reading and writing skills on English second-language writing development. The small set of studies that examined the relationship between first-language oral proficiency and English writing serves to identify gaps in the extant research base, including studies on the potential role of specific aspects of first-language linguistic knowledge (e.g., cohesion, syntactic complexity, decontextualized oral language skills, range and type of vocabulary, familiarity with various discourse genres); typological similarities and differences among the target language, English, and different first languages; the development of writing skills across grade levels; and the impact of systematic and sustained practice in writing in the first language on second-language writing development.

The acquisition of proficient writing skills probably requires good spelling skills; decontexualized language skills that enable the writer to express abstract, complex ideas; the acquisition of meta-cognitive strategies such as audience awareness; and familiarity with and opportunities to practice writing different text genres. Research that examines cross-linguistic aspects of all of these issues is needed if we are to advance our understanding of English second-language writing.

Other Groups of Second-Language Learners

Two characteristics of English-language learners are deserving of special attention: (a) students with different first languages and sociocultural backgrounds, and (b) students at different grade levels. There is little research on English-language learners whose first language is not Spanish—for example, students who speak Vietnamese, Hmong, Cantonese, and Korean, which are common languages among English-language learners in certain U.S. locations (Kindler, 2002). Research is especially needed that examines cross-linguistic relationships among component skills that underlie literacy in relation to typological similarity with and difference from English. There is also little research at present on middle- and high school English-language learners, both those who begin schooling in English at the middle- or high school levels and those who have been in schools where English is the language of instruction since primary school and are continuing into middle and high school. Research on most aspects of cross-linguistic influences in the literacy development of middle- and high school students is needed.

Similarly, research on cross-linguistic relationships in the literacy development of English-language learners with language delays or impairments is called for if we are to meet the learning needs of all language-minority students, especially in light of the rigorous accountability standards that have been mandated by the No Child Left Behind (NCLB) legislation.

Recommendations for Study Design and Methodology

Longitudinal, Multivariate Research Designs.   The issues under research in this section are complex and dynamic—complex because there are multiple variables that influence literacy development, multiple components to literacy development (e.g., phonology, vocabulary, grammar), and alternative theoretical frameworks that have influenced the way in which research in the field has been operationalized; and dynamic because the causal relationships that underlie the development of reading and writing and their influence on academic achievement change as English-language learners progress through school. The most common research designs uncovered in our review were correlational and between-group designs.

Greater use of longitudinal designs in the study of cross-linguistic relationships would lead to a clearer understanding of literacy development and its many determinants. In addition, the use of multilevel, longitudinal designs would allow for clearer explication of the student, teacher, family, school, and societal factors that influence students' literacy development and the precise ways in which these factors operate and interact.

Intervention Studies.   To advance our understanding of the role of cross-linguistic relationships in literacy development, research is needed that examines the transfer of literacy-related language subskills, as identified earlier, using intervention studies. In such studies, students would be randomized to receive either first-language training or not. Subsequently, both groups would receive second-language training in the task to which transfer was expected to occur. The first component of the test would be to show that the group that received first-language training developed the first-language skill to a higher level than the group that did not receive first-language training. Next, to test for transfer, the group that received first-language training would be examined to determine whether they learned the second-language skill at a more rapid pace (i.e., acquired new knowledge in the second language more quickly) or otherwise outperformed the group that did not receive the training. Either of these outcomes would be considered evidence of transfer from the first to the second language because the students' acquisition of a second-language skill was enhanced by their acquisition of a first-language skill. Students' differential acquisition of the first-language skill was a result of random assignment, this would allow for a reasonably strong inference that transfer had taken place. To make the study stronger, the group that did not receive the first-language training could receive training in something that is not expected to enhance the first-language skill that transfers to the second language, but instead enhances an unrelated first-language skill that is not expected to transfer.

Such research not only would advance our understanding of cross-language relationships in the development of literacy skills in ESL, but also would provide critical information for the development of home- and school-based interventions.

Standardized Assessment Tools. Synthesizing and generalizing results from the extensive and varied research that has been conducted on cross-linguistic aspects of literacy development in English-language learners is complicated by measurement issues. In particular, at present, different tests are used to assess the same underlying construct. In some cases, a problem arises because different tasks are used to assess the same construct without ascertaining how the assessments relate to one another. For example, Abu-Rabia (1997) and Da Fontoura and Siegel (1995) assessed working memory by using a sentence-completion task, while Gholamain and Geva (1999) used an opposites task (see chap. 7 for details). In other cases, such as in studies of phonological awareness, complications arise because a construct may actually be composed of different components (such as phoneme-deletion ability vs. rhyme-detection ability) and thus warrant the use of different tests, but only one test is used and the author generalizes to the construct as a whole; this is problematic in that there is insufficient research on the distinctiveness of each component and their developmental relationship to one another. More research on the validity of tests/tasks that are used to assess key constructs in this domain is required. As well, standardization of test instruments used to assess important constructs that have been used in cross-linguistic literacy research (e.g., phonological awareness, working memory, oral language proficiency) would be useful so that it would be possible to compare across studies the cross-linguistic influences in literacy development for learner groups with different first languages (e.g., Spanish vs. Chinese), at different ages/grades (5–17 years of age), and with different sociocultural backgrounds.

Careful Description of the Learner Group. Our understanding of literacy development in English-language learners could also be enhanced considerably if greater care were taken in the description of study samples. At present, descriptions of learner groups are often sketchy, leaving many unanswered questions about significant characteristics of the learners. To provide better and more detailed descriptions of student samples, researchers would need to agree on what characteristics to describe and what standards to follow when reporting information about these characteristics—that is, what kind of information (and in what detail) is needed about the socioeconomic status (SES), schooling opportunities, language skills, and language and literacy background of English-language learners at the time of testing.

New Conceptual Paradigms

Understanding of cross-linguistic influences in second-language literacy development could be enhanced if additional conceptualizations of transfer were explored. As noted previously, Bransford and Schwartz (1998) have argued that thinking about transfer should be broadened to include the notion of *preparedness for future learning*. Bransford and Schwartz's framework shifts attention away from a search for direct transfer of knowledge and skills to include the ability to learn new language and literacy skills by drawing on all of the learner's resources.

In a similar vein, Riches and Genesee (2006) have argued that when it comes to literacy development, English-language learners are best conceptualized as having a reservoir of knowledge, skills, and abilities that serve second-language learning and use. Some of these will be the same skills and knowledge possessed by monolinguals, and others will be unique to bilinguals and encompass discrete language skills, related to, for example, phonology and grammar, as well as knowledge and experience acquired through the medium of the first language and first-language learning.

In studying transfer, the relationship among a host of variables, some linked directly to language structures and strategies of the type emphasized by contrastive analysis and interdependence theories and others involving cognitive and other problem-solving skills of an entirely different nature from those that have been considered to date would be explored. Both of these conceptualizations would broaden our understanding of cross-linguistic effects in second-language learning and improve the way these effects are studied.

APPENDIX 6.A: STUDIES EXCLUDED FROM META-ANLYSIS

Chapter 7: Cross-Linguistic Relationships in Working Memory, Phonological Processes, and Oral Language

L1–L2 working memory
Only three studies (Abu-Rabia, 1997; DaFontoura & Siegel, 1995; Gholamain & Geva, 1999) were identified.

L1–L2 phonological awareness
Of the eight identified studies, one examined English as a foreign language (Abu-Rabia, 1997); in two studies, age is partialed out in the correlations (Gottardo, 2002; Gottardo Yan, Siegel, & Wade-Woolley, 2001); two studies use a between-groups design that does not allow for directly examining the relationship between first- and second-language phonological awareness (Hsia, 1992; Liow & Poon, 1998); and in one study, phonological processing is assessed in English only (Mumtaz & Humphreys, 2001).

L1–L2 RAN
Only three studies (Gholamain & Geva, 1999; Gottardo, 2002; Gottardo, Yan, Siegel, & Wade-Woolley, 2001) were identified.

L1–L2 phonological short-term memory
Only two studies (Gottardo, Yan, Siegel, & Wade-Woolley, 2001; Mumtaz & Humphreys, 2001) were identified.

L1–L2 phonology
Only four studies (Holm et al., 1999; Hsia, 1992; Kramer & Schell, 1982; Kramer et al., 1983) were identified.

L1–L2 oral vocabulary
Only three studies (Carlisle, Beeman, Davis, & Spharim, 1999; Johnson, 1989; Ordóez, Carlo, Snow, & McLaughlin, 2002) were identified.

L1–L2 Grammar
Of the six identified studies, three (Quinn, 2001; Shin & Milroy, 1999; Spada & Lightbown, 1999) do not report correlations.

Chapter 8: First-Language Oral Proficiency and Second-Language Literacy

L1 oral proficiency and L2 word reading
Of the nine identified studies, in two studies age is partialed out in the correlations (Gholamain & Geva, 1999; Gottardo, Yan, Siegel, & Wade-Woolley, 2001); one studies English as a foreign language (Abu-Rabia, 1997); one study uses a between-groups design that does not allow for directly examining the relationship between first-language oral proficiency and second-language word reading (Mumtaz & Humphreys, 2002); and in one study, there are no measures of first- language proficiency, but only of second-language dialect pronunciation (Ahern, Dixon, Kimura, Okuna, & Gibson, 1980).

L1 oral proficiency and L2 spelling
Of the seven identified studies, one study examines students acquiring a foreign language (Abu-Rabia, 1997); in one study, age is partialed out (Gottardo et al., 2001); and three studies use a between-group design that does not directly allow for studying the relationship between L1 oral proficiency and L2 literacy (Cronnell, 1985; Ferroli & Shanahan, 1993; Jackson, Holm, & Dodd, 1998).

L1 oral proficiency and L2 text-level skills
Of the six identified studies, one study does not report correlations (Buriel & Cardoza, 1988), and one study examines students acquiring a foreign language (Dufva & Voeten, 1999).

L1 oral proficiency and L2 writing
Only two studies were identified (Cronnell, 1985; Okamura-Bichard, 1985).

Chapter 9: First- and Second-Language Literacy

L1–L2 word recognition
Of the five identified studies, two examine students acquiring a foreign language (Abu-Rabia, 1997; Chitiri & Willows, 1997), and in one study (Gholamain & Geva, 1999), age is partialed out in the correlations.

L1–L2 reading comprehension

Of the eight identified studies, one presents information in a way that does not allow the computation of effect sizes that are comparable (Verhoeven, 1994); in one study, correlations are not reported (Nagy, McClure, & Mir, 1997); and two study English as a foreign language (Lee & Schallert, 1997; Schoonen, Hulstijn, & Bossers, 1998).

L1–L2 spelling

Of the five identified studies, two study English as a foreign language (James & Klein 1994; Nathenson-Mejía , 1989); one is qualitative (Edelsky, 1982); two only provide measures of first- language phonology (Fashola, Drum, Mayer, & Kang, 1996; Zutell & Allen, 1988); and in one study a first-language spelling test is administered, but no correlations were reported (Ferroli & Shanahan, 1993).

L1–L2 vocabulary

Of the seven studies that measure the extent to which students recognize structural and semantic overlap in first- and second-language cognates, one study does not provide Spanish measures (García, 1991); two studies are qualitative (Garcia, 1998; Jiménez, García, & Pearson, 1996); one study does not report correlations between L1 and L2 vocabulary (Hancin-Bhatt & Nagy, 1994); one study provides no first-language measures (Saville-Troike, 1984); and one study examines English as a foreign language (James & Klein 1994).

Of the three studies that compare the nature of the vocabulary produced by students in their first and second languages on a number of indexes of lexical sophistication and complexity, one study does not report correlations (Francis, 2000).

Only one study examines the effect of first-language syntactic knowledge on the guesses students make about the meanings of new words encountered in the second language, but does not report correlations (Nagy, McClure, & Mir, 1997).

LI–L2 strategy use

Of the six identified studies, three are qualitative (García, 1998; Jiménez, García, & Pearson, 1996; Langer, Bartolome, Vÿasquez, & Lucas, 1990), and one studies students who are acquiring English as a foreign language (Schoonen et al., 1998).

L1–L2 writing

Only four studies are reported (Davis et al., 1999; Edelsky, 1982; Francis, 2000; Lanauze & Snow, 1989).

7

Cross-Linguistic Relationships in Working Memory, Phonological Processes, and Oral Language

Fred Genesee and Esther Geva

The studies reviewed in this chapter examine cross-linguistic relationships in first- and second-language working memory, phonological processes, and oral language, all domains of development thought to be related to literacy. More specifically, the research on phonological processes includes phonological awareness, phonological recoding, and phonological short-term memory, and the research on oral language includes phonological skills (including auditory discrimination, intraword segmentation, and speech production), vocabulary, grammar, and discourse-level skills. Each is defined in chapter 3. The following review is organized around each of these domains and subdomains. In principle, it would be desirable to review cross-linguistic studies systematically by age (grade) or stage of second-language development because one might expect more first-language influence in the early stages of second-language development and less later, when learners have acquired more competence in the target language. However, there were not enough studies per age group (elementary, middle, and high school), nor was there sufficient comparability in dependent measures within age/grade levels to discuss the studies by developmental level. Nevertheless, age is considered in the following review as a potential mediating factor.

The following research question is addressed in this chapter: What is the relationship between language-minority children's first- and second-language oral development in domains related to literacy?

WORKING MEMORY

As explained in chapter 3, working memory tasks demand *active manipulation* of the information presented while concurrently holding the information in memory (Baddeley, 1986). Three studies examined correlations between working memory in English and students' first language (Abu-Rabia, 1997; Da Fontoura & Siegel, 1995; Gholamain & Geva, 1999). Abu-Rabia as well as Da Fontoura and Siegel assessed working memory by using a sentence-completion task in which students had to provide a missing word in each of a set of sentences that increased in number of words over the course of the experiment, and then to repeat all the missing words. Gholmain and Geva used an opposites task, in which basic, frequent adjectives and nouns were presented in combination with other words; students had to present the opposite of each word in correct order of presentation at the end of each trial. Abu-Rabia examined Grade 10 Hebrew–English bilinguals, DaFontoura and Siegel examined Portuguese–English bilinguals who were in Grades 4 to 6 in Canada, and Gholmain and Geva examined Persian–English bilingual students in Grades 1 to 5 of a heritage language program in Canada. All three studies report significant correlations between working memory in the students' first and second languages.

PHONOLOGICAL PROCESSES

Phonological processes reflect underlying processes related to phonological aspects of language. As described in chapter 3, phonological processes include phonological awareness, phonological recoding, and phonological short-term memory (Lumme & Lehto, 2002).

Phonological Awareness

The largest number of studies in the domain of phonological processing analyzed the relationship between first- and second-language phonological awareness, and most, but not all, used correlational analyses comparing language-minority students' phonological awareness in their first and second languages (Abu-Rabia, 1997; Cisero & Royer, 1995; Gottardo, 2002; Gottardo, Yan, Siegel, & Wade-Woolley, 2001; Hsia, 1992; Mumtaz & Humphreys, 2001; Quiroga, Lemos-Britten, Mostafapour, Abbott, & Berninger, 2002; see also Hsia, 1992, in the phonology section). With the exception of Abu-Rabia, all studies in this group report significant correlations or relationships between specific components of first-language phonological awareness and the corresponding or different measures of second-language phonological awareness. A variety of indices of phonological awareness were examined: initial/final phoneme detection and deletion (Cisero & Royer, 1995; Gottardo, 2002; Gottardo et al., 2002), rhyme detection (Cisero & Royer, 1995; Gottardo et al., 2002; Mumtaz & Humphreys, 2001), phoneme (and word) segmentation (Hsia, 1992), and phoneme blending, segmenting, and matching (Quiroga et al., 2002). Abu-Rabia's discrepant findings may be due to the task he used. Students were given pairs of words in English or Hebrew and asked to identify which sounded like a real word. This is not a conventional phonological awareness task in that the students did not have to manipulate the sound segments that make up these words; they simply had to say which words in each pair sounded more like a real word in English or Hebrew. Moreover, his students were in Grade 10, whereas students in the other studies were in primary school—preschool, kindergarten, or Grade 1. Arguably, the link between first- and second-language phonological awareness may diminish with age as learners acquire more complex second-language skills, although this possibility has not been well studied. It is also possible that the discrepancies are due to the typological differences between Hebrew and English.

Using a between-group rather than a correlational design, Liow and Poon (1998) carried out an interesting study with multilingual students (English–Bahasa Indonesian–Mandarin Chinese), ages 9 to 10 years, to examine the impact of exposure to different types of script on phonological awareness. They found that students whose dominant language was English or Bahasa Indonesian exhibited higher levels of phonological awareness than the Mandarin Chinese group, whose primary exposure to written language was in Chinese. English and Bahasa Indonesian use alphabetic scripts, whereas Chinese uses a nonalphabetic logographic script. Thus, the link between graphemes and phonemes was easier for the former than for the latter students. This study suggests that language-minority students who have had exposure to written forms of the first language are likely to have better phonological awareness in English if their first language uses an alphabetic script rather than if it uses another type of script.

Phonological Recoding

The three studies that examined phonological recoding used rapid automatized naming tasks (RAN) and yielded inconsistent results (Gholamain & Geva, 1999; Gottardo, 2002; Gottardo et al., 2001). On the one hand, Gholamain and Geva report a significant correlation between first- and second-language RAN, using a letter naming task, in Grades 1 to 5 Persian–English, English-language learners, but no significant correlation between second-language oral language proficiency and second-language RAN. However, in two separate studies, one using a continuous number naming task with Grade 1 Mexican-American, English-language learners (Gottardo, 2002) and one using continuous number and letter naming tasks with Grades 1 to 8 Chinese–English, English-language learners (Gottardo et al., 2001), Gottardo et al. failed to find significant correlations between first- and second-language RAN. The reason for the discrepancy in results in these studies is not clear, but it could be due to the broad age range examined by these researchers.

Phonological Short-Term Memory

Two studies examined phonological short-term memory in students' first and second languages by using a pseudoword repetition task (Gottardo et al., 2001; Mumtaz & Humphreys, 2001). Mumtaz and Humphreys report a significant correlation between word repetition scores in Urdu and English among a group of Urdu–English bilinguals with a mean age of 7.8 years. Gottardo et al. (2001), however, found no significant correlations between first- and second-language phonological short-term memory. One explanation for the discrepancy between these results and those reported by Mumtaz and Humphreys is that Gottardo and colleagues examined Chinese–English bilingual students in Grades 1 to 8, and aggregating data across grades in a single correlation may have obscured age-specific correlations.

Phonological Processes: Summary

In summary, there is evidence for cross-linguistic effects in phonological processes. This evidence is reported in studies of phonological awareness and, to some extent but not consistently, in studies of phonological short-term memory and phonological recoding. More research in the latter domains is needed to determine how extensive the relationship between first- and second-language phonological processing really is because the number of studies in each domain is limited at present. There is some evidence, although it is limited, that cross-language effects in phonological awareness are more likely among younger learners or during early stages of second-language development than later because once students have acquired higher levels of second-language proficiency, phonological awareness is probably less important. In contrast, studies of phonological short-term memory report significant cross-linguistic relationships for students at a wide range of ages. Much more research is needed that systematically examines how age influences the relationships between first- and second- language ability in these three domains.

ORAL LANGUAGE

Phonology

For purposes of this review, phonology, considered part of oral language, includes the ability to recognize and produce the sounds and sound sequences that make up language. A number of studies examined cross-language relationships in phonology: Holm et al. (1999) examined speech production, Hsia (1992) examined intraword segmentation, and Kramer and Schell (1982) and Kramer et al. (1983) examined phonological (sound) discrimination. These studies are reviewed here because the oral language relationships they examined may be related to second-language reading and writing. For example, Kramer and colleagues examined English-language learners' difficulty in discriminating phonological contrasts in English (the second language) that do not exist in the first language, and Holm and colleagues studied speech production patterns of language-minority students in Britain for evidence of first-language influences. There are only one or two studies for each outcome measure. Therefore, these studies are not considered in separate subsections. Moreover, this small research base limits the generalizability of the conclusions that can be drawn.

Holm and colleagues examined the phonological productions of typically developing English-language learners in Britain; the children ranged in age from 4.8 to 7.5 years and spoke either Mirpuri, Punjabi,[1] or Urdu as their first language. Analyses of these children's phonological development indicated

---

[1]Some authors use the alternative spelling *Panjabi*, but we have adopted the single spelling *Punjabi* for consistency.

that they were acquiring separate first- and second-language phonological systems, but they were not acquiring English phonology in the same way that native English speakers do. In particular, they exhibited production patterns in English that could be construed as symptomatic of language impairment if first-language influences were not considered: "For example, the number of voicing and aspiration errors in the bilingual children's speech would be considered unusual for a monolingual child. Many of the bilingual children were not releasing their final consonants and were replacing them with glottal stops" (Holm et al., 1999, p. 284). However, these second-language production patterns should not be considered a sign of impairment, but a consequence of transfer from their first language.

Additional evidence for first-language influences comes from Hsia's (1992) finding that preschool Mandarin Chinese–English bilingual children demonstrated patterns of intraword segmentation in English that differed from those of monolingual English speakers—patterns that could be linked to the stress patterns of Chinese, their first language. Hsia also reports that the segmentation patterns of Mandarin Chinese bilinguals in English resembled those of native English speakers by Grade 1, suggesting that first-language influences are more likely in the early stages of second-language acquisition, but are replaced by second-language target patterns as acquisition progresses. Additional, albeit inferential, support for early first-language influences on second-language development comes from Abu-Rabia's finding that, as noted earlier, there were no significant correlations between the performance of Hebrew–English bilinguals on a Hebrew language task and the corresponding English version of the task (i.e., phonological memory) presumably because, as the children became more proficient in the second language, there was less influence from the first language.

Finally, Kramer and Schell (1982) examined cross-linguistic effects in the auditory discrimination of Grades 1 to 3 Spanish–English bilinguals. They found that these children had difficulty discriminating contrasts in English that are not used in Spanish (e.g., *v–b*, *ch–sh*, *s–sp*). In a follow-up study, Kramer et al. (1983) found that training over 4 weeks targeting difficult-to-discriminate contrasts in English improved student discrimination performance in comparison with that of students who did not receive such training.

In summary, studies of cross-language effects in the domain of phonology provide evidence for first-language influences on second-language acquisition. More specifically, English-language learners were found to exhibit developmental patterns in sound discrimination and production that were not like those of the target language, but reflected characteristics of the first language. It is impossible to ascertain the generalizability of these effects, however, because these studies varied considerably with respect to both the ages of the students and the specific language domains examined. Moreover, the number of studies in each domain was limited. In all cases, the first-language influences resulted from differences between the first and second languages that resulted in nontargetlike forms (Hsia, 1992; Kramer & Schell, 1982; although see Liow & Poon, 1998, for an example of facilitation with respect to phonological awareness).

Nontargetlike forms (or errors) in second-language development as a result of first-language influences are probably reported more often than facilitation of first language on second-language development because the former are easier to document than the latter. To document errors in second-language development that may be due to interference from the first language, researchers simply have to show that English-language learners are producing nontargetlike forms that can be linked to first-language forms. Finding evidence of facilitation would require researchers to show that English-language learners with first languages that are similar to English acquire specific features of English faster than English-language learners with first languages that differ significantly from English. In any case, even examples of so-called first-language interference or errors in the second language should be interpreted as evidence of English-language learners' proactive use of existing first-language skills to bootstrap into English in the absence of the corresponding second-language skills; in other words, these effects are evidence of positive learning (see Bransford & Schwartz, 1989, for a similar argument).

The importance of examining cross-linguistic effects is illustrated by the Holm et al. (1999) study, in which first-language influences resulted in second-language patterns of phonological development that resembled those of children with speech impairment. Documenting the influence of the first language on the second is important if we are to assist speech and language professionals and educators in properly identifying students with disabilities.

Vocabulary

Three studies of cross-language effects on vocabulary development were identified (Carlisle, Beeman, Davis, & Spharim, 1999; Johnson, 1989; Ordóñez, Carlo, Snow, & McLaughlin, 2002). The learners included in these studies were drawn from a wide range of grade levels: from primary grades (Carlisle et al., 1999) to the upper elementary grades (Johnson, 1989; Ordóñez et al., 2002). At issue is whether second-language vocabulary knowledge or skills are influenced by first-language vocabulary knowledge or skills.

In Johnson's (1989) study, Grades 2, 4, and 6 English-language learners were asked to interpret the meaning of English and Spanish metaphors that were constructed by inserting topic words (e.g., *my sister* and *rock*) into the sentence frame "____ was a ___," producing metaphors such as "my sister was a rock." The students were asked to interpret the resulting metaphors. There was a significant correlation between the cognitive complexity of their interpretations in Spanish and English. Multiple-regression analyses using complexity of metaphor interpretation in English and Spanish as outcome measures and a variety of predictor variables (including conceptual–attentional capacity) revealed that conceptual capacity was significantly related to complexity of metaphor interpretation in both languages, suggesting that more general, language-independent abilities, not language-specific transfer, may have been at work.

Ordóñez et al. (2002) report that cross-language correlations in vocabulary knowledge are more likely to occur for higher order than for lower order vocabulary knowledge. Higher order vocabulary knowledge (which the authors refer to as *paradigmatic*) is exemplified by definitions that define words in higher order or superordinate terms—for example, "a boat is a means of transportation." Lower order vocabulary knowledge (or what the authors refer to as *syntagmatic*) is exemplified by definitions of a nonhierarchical nature, such as defining a word in physical or functional terms—for example, "an envelope is made of paper and is used to send letters." The authors found that cross-language correlations were moderately high and significant for paradigmatic vocabulary knowledge, but low and nonsignificant for syntagmatic knowledge. Their subjects were Grades 4 and 5 bilingual Spanish–English children.

In a similar vein, Carlisle et al. (1999) found nonsignificant correlations between the quality of first- and second-language informal definitions for Spanish–English bilinguals in Grades 1 to 3, whereas there was a significant correlation between languages ($r = .36$, $p < .05$) when the quality of formal definitions was examined. Formal definitions may exemplify both higher order language skills and what is often referred to as *academic language* skills. In both studies, these cross-language correlations for quality of formal definitions may be due to more general, underlying cognitive factors, rather than direct transfer of lexical knowledge from one language to another.

In summary, three studies of vocabulary knowledge among English-language learners (whose first language was Spanish) suggest that there are significant and positive cross-language effects on lexical knowledge. Because all three studies report some first-language influences, age or stage of development may not be important to cross-language effects on vocabulary development, but more research is needed given the small number of studies reviewed. Moreover, these effects appear to be more pronounced for higher order than for lower order knowledge (Carlisle et al., 1999; Ordóñez et al., 2002). All three of these studies involved tasks that called on learners' explicit understanding of the meaning of words and their ability to articulate those meanings clearly. Thus, one could argue that these tasks reflect metalinguistic abilities that exceed the kind of implicit knowledge underlying day-to-day communication. At the same time, the correlation between first- and second-language lexical knowledge reported in these studies may be due to language-independent influences of a general cognitive nature (Johnson, 1989). Multivariate studies that include alternative predictor measures, some language specific and some language independent, are called for to disentangle these possibilities.

To the extent that future research continues to provide evidence in support of cross-language effects in vocabulary development, it would follow that oral language support for English-language learners' literacy development could be provided in either the first or second language and that this support should focus on language skills that are linked to higher order cognitive or academic tasks—that is, language for categorizing, reasoning, and abstract thought. At the same time, studies on learners of typologically distinct languages (e.g., Turkish and Dutch) that have few structural and functional similarities were not reviewed in this chapter. Thus, we do not know the extent to which current findings would obtain for learners with other first-language backgrounds. Although one would expect less pronounced cross-language effects in typologically different languages, further research on learners acquiring typologically distinct second languages is needed to examine this issue empirically.

Discourse and Grammar

No studies were identified that examined the relationship between first- and second-language discourse-level skills as, for example, the narration of stories.

Six studies were identified that examined cross-language effects in the grammatical development of English-language learners. The basic question is whether the acquisition of oral English grammar by English-language learners is the same as that for monolingual native English speakers and/or whether there is evidence of influences from first-language grammar on second-language grammatical development. Two of the six studies involved students in the early elementary grades: Duncan and Gibbs (1987) examined Punjabi–English bilinguals, ages 6½ to 8½, in Britain, whereas Shin and Milroy (1999) examined Grade 1 Korean–English bilingual children in Britain. Two studies involved students in upper elementary grades: Morsbach (1981) examined German–English and Japanese–English bilingual students, ages 11 to 13, in London, whereas Spada and Lightbown (1999) examined Grade 6 French–English bilingual students in Quebec. The final two studies involved learners from a wide range of grade levels. Quinn (2001) examined students from kindergarten to Grade 6 in England; the first languages of these learners were not specified. Flanigan (1995) examined understanding of anaphora and relativization in English-language learners, ages 6½ to 11, with a variety of first languages. Age of learners is a potentially important variable in this research because one might expect to find more first-language influences when learners are young and in the early stages of second-language acquisition. However, this issue is not addressed explicitly in any of the studies, even that of Quinn (2001), which included learners from a broad age range.

There is no consistent pattern in the results of these studies, either when they are subdivided by age or when they are considered together. Thus, whereas Duncan and Gibbs (1987) found that the grammatical development of young Punjabi–English bilinguals (as assessed by the acquisition of morphemes of the types examined by Brown [1973] in his classic early acquisition studies) resembled that of native English speakers, Shin and Milroy (1999) found that the order of morpheme acquisition of their Korean–English students differed from that reported for native English speakers. A similar discrepancy is evident in the studies on learners in the upper elementary grades. Morsbach (1981) found that the comprehension of English morphosyntax by German–English and Japanese–English students resembled that of native English speakers. However, Spada and Lightbown (1999) report that native-French-speaking students acquired the ability to formulate questions in English differently from native English speakers, reflecting influences from their first language (French). The differences between these two studies may be due to differences between comprehension and production; that is, learners may be more likely to exhibit targetlike abilities in comprehension tasks, whereas their performance in production may be more subject to first-language influences. Finally, Flanigan (1995) found little evidence of first-language influences in the acquisition of anaphora or relativization by English-language learners with a variety of first languages—some that were typologically similar to and some that were typologically different from English (e.g., English–German vs. English– Chinese). Flanigan's results could be said to argue for targetlike acquisition patterns. In contrast, Quinn (2001) reports that her learners' receptive and expressive abilities with respect to English grammar did not resemble those of native English speakers. The utility of this study is limited, however, because the comparison with native English speakers was based on test norms, and Quinn did not disaggregate the learners by grade level. The lack of consistency in these studies cannot be attributed to language typology because studies examining the acquisition of typologically similar languages (French–English in Spada & Lightbown, 1999) differ as much as studies examining the acquisition of typologically different languages (Japanese–English in Morsbach, 1981; Korean–English in Shin & Milroy, 1999).

In summary, no clear trends can be discerned in this small group of studies, whether they are considered as a group or separated by age. Clearly, more research is needed in this domain of language development. Typological similarity of the learners' languages must be considered carefully in future research because typologically similar languages might be expected to yield evidence of less first-language influence than typologically dissimilar languages (although transfer may actually be occurring). Typologically dissimilar languages would be expected to show evidence of first-language influences. For, example English and Spanish are typologically different with regard to certain aspects of grammar; Spanish permits null subjects (i.e., the subject of the sentence can be omitted), but this is not the case in English. Thus, Spanish-speaking children who are acquiring English might drop the subject in oral and written English. Systematic examination of English-language learners with typologically different languages is important to pinpoint areas of grammar and discourse that are most likely to exhibit cross-linguistic effects.

8

First-Language Oral Proficiency and Second-Language Literacy

Esther Geva and Fred Genesee

This chapter reviews research on the extent to which first-language oral proficiency is related to the development of literacy skills in English. Research on children learning to read in their first language has shown that word-level reading skills are linked to phonological processing, but only marginally related to oral proficiency skills. In contrast, both phonological processing and oral proficiency skills have been implicated in reading comprehension. It is important to examine whether the same relationships hold between first-language oral proficiency skills and second-language literacy development.

Two overarching questions underlie the research discussed in this chapter:

1. What is the relationship between first-language oral proficiency and second-language word-level literacy skills?
2. What is the relationship between first-language oral proficiency and second-language text-level literacy skills?

The chapter is organized according to literacy outcomes. We begin by looking at word-level skills (word reading, pseudoword reading, and spelling) and then turn to text-level skills (reading comprehension and writing). Each of these skill sets is addressed within a developmental framework. Various theoretical issues are addressed briefly, including the extent to which the relationships between specific first-language oral proficiency skills and English literacy skills in English-language learners mirror those noted for native speakers of English, and whether typological similarities between learners' first and second languages influence these relationships.

RELATIONSHIPS BETWEEN FIRST-LANGUAGE ORAL PROFICIENCY AND WORD AND PSEUDOWORD READING SKILLS IN ENGLISH

In this section, we review research on the relationship between English-language learners' oral language proficiency skills in their first language and their word and pseudoword reading skills in their second language—in this case, English.

Two studies conducted in the United States with English–Spanish bilingual children in elementary school have yielded rather similar results. In one study, Durgunoglu, Nagy, and Hancin-Bhatt (1993) examined the English word and pseudoword reading skills of first-grade bilingual beginning readers whose dominant language was Spanish. They found that first-language oral proficiency measured by the Pre-Language Assessment Scales (Pre-LAS), with subtests that examine expressive and receptive language skills in three domains of oral language (e.g., morphology, syntax, and semantics), did not predict performance on the English word reading and pseudoword decoding tasks. However, children's level of phonological awareness in their first language, Spanish, predicted their English word reading and pseudoword decoding skills.

A study by Quiroga, Lemos-Britten, Mostafapour, Abbott, and Berninger (2002) yielded similar results. The participants in this study were first-grade Spanish–English bilinguals who had not had systematic instruction in Spanish. The researchers found that Spanish oral language proficiency as measured by the Pre-LAS was not related to English word or pseudoword reading, whereas phonological awareness in Spanish (and in English) was highly correlated with word and pseudoword reading in English. When all predictors were examined together, using regression analysis, the authors found that first-language oral proficiency did not explain any unique variance in word or pseudoword reading in English. However, English phonological awareness explained unique variance in word and pseudoword reading in English, whereas Spanish phonological awareness, entered after English phonological awareness, did not explain additional unique variance. The latter finding may reflect a suppressor effect related to the positive and significant correlation of phonological awareness measured in Spanish with phonological awareness measured in English. Given the strength of the correlation between phonological awareness in Spanish and English, it is likely that, had phonological awareness in Spanish been entered first, it would have been a significant predictor of word-recognition skills in English as well. The strong correlations between first- and second-language phonological awareness suggest that phonological awareness is a common underlying proficiency.

Findings from five other studies involving elementary and middle-grade English-language learners with different first languages (Farsi, Cantonese, and Urdu) suggest that the results reported earlier are not limited to English-Spanish bilinguals. In a study of native-Farsi-speaking English-language learners in Grades 1 to 5, Gholamain and Geva (1999) found that verbal working memory and RAN, assessed in the first language (Farsi), accounted for significant variance in the students' word and pseudoword reading scores in English. In contrast to previous studies that failed to find a significant correlation between oral language proficiency and word-level reading skills, teacher ratings of Farsi oral language proficiency in this study correlated positively and significantly with the children's word and pseudoword reading skills in English. The correlations were in the moderate to low range. Moreover, unlike the two studies discussed previously, results of regression analysis reveal that, once the effects of Farsi working memory and Farsi letter naming speed (RAN) had been accounted for, oral proficiency in Farsi explained an additional 4% of the variance. Arguably, teacher ratings of language proficiency may not be a valid measure of oral proficiency because it may be difficult to rate oral language proficiency independently of academic achievement in general and reading achievement in particular. Support for this caution comes from the results of another study involving a similar group of participants. In this study of Farsi–English bilingual children in second and third grades, Arab-Moghaddam and Sénéchal (2001) found that first-language vocabulary knowledge (Farsi) did not correlate with word reading scores in English. In contrast, oral vocabulary knowledge in English correlated significantly with word reading skills in English.

Essentially the same conclusion was reached by Da Fontoura and Siegel (1995) in a study of the relationships between first-language grammatical sensitivity (assessed with an oral cloze task that tapped into students' knowledge of grammar) and second-language reading in fourth- to sixth-grade, low-socioeconomic status (SES) Portuguese–English bilingual students attending a Portuguese heritage language program. The oral cloze scores in students' first language (Portuguese) did not correlate with word or pseudoword reading in English. However, the authors also note that the bilingual readers who had good word-level reading skills in their second language had similar profiles with respect to phonological processing, word-level reading skills, and spelling in their first language. Likewise, the students who had poor word-level reading skills in the second language had similar profiles in both languages. These findings argue that not only are first- and second-language word-level reading skills interrelated, but so, too, are phonological processing skills necessary for word reading. That students who had poor phonological skills in their first language also had poor phonological skills in their second language also suggests that phonological processing captures an underlying proficiency that is related to word reading performance in the first and second languages.

In a cross-sectional study spanning Gades 1 to 8, Gottardo, Yan, Siegel, and Wade-Woolley (2001) administered parallel measures of phonological processing and word reading in English and Cantonese to Cantonese–English bilingual students. Oral language proficiency skills were assessed in both languages using a grammatical sensitivity task (oral cloze). As in the Da Fontoura and Siegel (1995) study, there were no significant correlations between grammatical sensitivity in Cantonese (the first language) and word and pseudoword reading skills in English. However, phonemic awareness in Cantonese, assessed by a rhyme-detection task, correlated significantly with word and pseudoword reading skills in English.

Mumtaz and Humphreys (2002) examined the relationship between 7- and 9-year-old Urdu–English bilingual students' phonological processing (including digit span, nonword repetition, and rhyme detection), oral proficiency skills in Urdu, and word and pseudoword reading skills in English, their second language. Mumtaż and Humphreys used a between-group design in which students were divided into high- and low-vocabulary groups based on their performance on a vocabulary task in their first language (Urdu). Whether they had to read English words in isolation or in sentence contexts, the students with relatively strong Urdu oral vocabulary performed significantly better on English regular word and pseudoword reading than on English irregular word reading, compared with the group of children with low Urdu vocabulary knowledge. However, error analysis showed that the group with high Urdu oral vocabulary, in comparison with the low-vocabulary group, made significantly more errors in reading irregular words in English than in reading regular words—they pronounced irregular words as if they conformed to general spelling-to-sound patterns (i.e., regularization errors in English). These results may indicate that children with high oral language proficiency in the first language (Urdu) may be better at applying Urdu decoding skills to English word reading of irregular words, resulting in relatively more errors in English irregular word reading. Of particular relevance to the question of cross-language influences, correlational analyses showed that two aspects of phonological processing measured in Urdu (rhyme detection and phonological memory) correlated positively and significantly with word-level reading skills in English. However, once the influence of phonological awareness in Urdu had been removed, using analysis of covariance (ANOVA), the interaction between word-level reading skills and command of Urdu oral vocabulary was not significant. This latter result suggests that the better English word and pseudoword reading skills in the group of children who had high vocabulary knowledge in Urdu was due to better phonological awareness skills in English and Urdu.

Results of a study by Ahern, Dixon, Kimura, Okuna, and Gibson (1980) of fourth-grade speakers of the Hawaiian Creole dialect of English (HCE) indicate that links between first-language oral skills and word-level reading skills in English are not invariant. Hawaiian students' word reading skills in English were assessed by their ability to perceive minimal pairs in standard English containing phonological contrasts that do not exist in HCE (e.g., distinguishing the long and short vowel sounds in *leak–lick*). First-language oral proficiency (measured by an index of HCE) was negatively correlated with English word reading. Students who were dominant in HCE were less able to discriminate words in standard English that contained English-specific phonological contrasts. At the same time, students who were aware of the phonological differences between HCE and standard English overcorrected to take those differences into account and had significantly fewer English word reading errors. The authors conclude that instruction can enhance language-minority students' ability to identify differences between the first and second languages and thereby compensate for interference from first-language oral proficiency.

Only one relevant study (Abu-Rabia, 1997) examined the relationship between first-language oral proficiency and word-level reading skills in high school English-language learners. In a study of 10th-grade students learning English as a foreign language in Israel, Abu-Rabia found that first-language (Hebrew) oral language proficiency, as measured by a grammatical sensitivity task (oral cloze), did not correlate with the students' performance on English word reading tasks, including word attack and word recognition. However, the correlations between measures of phonemic awareness and working memory in Hebrew and word-level reading skills in English were positive and moderately high.

The overall paucity of research on high school students may be due to a number of factors, including the assumption that high school English-language learners have already acquired basic word-level reading skills in English or their first language, and thus at this level text-level reading and writing should be the target of instruction and research. The extent to which these assumptions are valid, especially in English-language learners who immigrate to English-speaking communities when they are older, is open to question.

Taken together, findings from studies of elementary and middle-school students and one study involving high school children indicate rather consistently that measures of first-language oral proficiency do not correlate with English word reading skills (Abu-Rabia, 1997; Arab-Moghaddam & Sénéchal, 2001; Da Fontoura & Siegel, 1995; Durgunoglu et al., 1993; Gottardo et al., 2001; Quiroga et al., 2002) and do not explain unique variance in English word reading skills. This was true for a wide variety of first languages, including Farsi, Cantonese, Urdu, Hebrew, and Spanish. The only exception is the study by Gholamain and Geva (1999), in which teacher ratings of oral proficiency skills correlated with word-level skills.

The picture is quite different, however, when relationships between first-language phonological processing skills and English word reading skills are examined. The results of several studies of children from different first-language backgrounds and educational settings, conducted in the United States, the United Kingdom, Canada, and Israel, suggest that first-language phonological processing skills are closely related to the development of word reading skills in English. This finding appears across a variety of phonological processing measures, including rhyme detection in Chinese (Gottardo et al., 2001) and Urdu (Mumtaz & Humphreys, 2002); awareness of grapheme–phoneme correspondences as measured by pseudoword reading (Abu-Rabia, 1997; Arab-Moghaddam & Sénéchal, 2001); phonological awareness involving segmentation, blending, and matching (Durgunoglu et al., 1993; Quiroga et al., 2002); rapid naming of discrete items such as letters or digits (RAN); and working memory (Abu-Rabia, 1997; Da Fontoura & Siegel, 1995; Gholamain & Geva, 1999; Mumtaz & Humphreys, 2002).

Studies cited in this section indicate that the relationship between first-language oral proficiency and English word-level skills can also vary somewhat as a function of the measures used to assess phonological awareness in each language. For example, it may be that the grammatical sensitivity measures used to assess first-language oral proficiency by Abu-Rabia (1997), Da Fontoura and Siegel (1995), and Gottardo et al. (2001) are not precise enough to capture the aspects of the first-language oral proficiency that are linked to second-language word reading.

In addition, first- and second-language typological factors appeared to be related to differences in linguistic constructs, such as syllable structure and stress patterns. The Ahern et al. (1980) study of Hawaiian children and Mumtaz and Humphreys' (2002) study of Urdu–English English-language learners suggest the need for caution to avoid adopting a simplistic view of the relationships between phonological processing skills in children's first language and word reading skills in English. The studies indicate that the effects may vary depending on the similarity and differences between the first- and second-language orthography. It may be prudent to adopt a more refined framework in which certain relationships are universal, but conditional on similarities and differences between the first language and English. Age may also be a factor that influences the relationship between first-language oral proficiency and second-language word reading skills. Students' level of first-language oral proficiency and literacy is likely to influence the relationship.

RELATIONSHIP BETWEEN FIRST-LANGUAGE ORAL PROFICIENCY AND SPELLING IN ENGLISH

In this section, we review studies that examine the relationship between first-language oral proficiency and spelling in English. Extensive research on the early development of spelling skills in native-English-speaking children learning to read and write in English has shown that knowledge of letter names is essential for beginning writing, that young native-English-speaking children develop knowledge of the orthographic patterns of their language by progressing from small to large units, and that morphological strategies also guide their spelling (Treiman, Tincoff, Rodriguez, Mouzaki, & Francis, 1998). By comparison, less research is available on the developmental foundations of spelling for language-minority students (see chap. 4) and on the role of first-language oral proficiency in the English spelling performance of English-language learners.

Three correlational studies at the elementary and middle-grade levels examined the role of first-language oral proficiency in the acquisition of English spelling skills (Arab-Moghaddam & Sénéchal, 2001; Da Fontoura & Siegel, 1995; Gottardo et al., 2001). In a study of second- and third-grade Farsi–English bilingual children living in Canada, Arab-Moghaddam and Sénéchal (2001) found that vocabulary knowledge in Farsi, the students' first language, did not correlate with their spelling performance in English, although vocabulary knowledge in English did. Similar findings are reported by Gottardo et al. (2001) in a study of Chinese–English bilingual students in Grades 1 to 8. They found that oral proficiency in students' first language, Chinese (as measured by a cloze task of grammatical sensitivity), did not correlate with performance on an orthographic-recognition task in English, in which students were asked to judge which member in each pair of pseudowords was a possible English spelling. However, phonological awareness in Chinese (measured by rhyme detection) correlated significantly with scores on the English spelling task. Of additional interest, scores on a tone-detection task in Chinese did not correlate significantly with scores on the English spelling task, arguably because tones are irrelevant to English orthography and spelling.

Da Fontoura and Siegel (1995), reviewed earlier, examined the relationship between oral language proficiency (as measured by a grammatical sensitivity cloze task) and spelling in a group of fourth- to sixth-grade, low-SES Portuguese–English bilingual children who were attending a Portuguese heritage language program. First-language oral proficiency did not correlate with spelling scores in English (although English oral proficiency did). However, pseudoword decoding in Portuguese (i.e., a measure of the ability to match orthographic patterns to phonemes) correlated significantly with spelling in English. This study again illustrates the lack of a relationship between grammatical sensitivity in first- and second-language spelling skills. At the same time, it illustrates the relevance of phonological and orthographic skills, measured in the first language, to spelling in the second language.

Only one study (Abu-Rabia, 1997) examined the English spelling skills of high school students. This study (mentioned previously) involved native-Hebrew-speaking students learning English as a foreign language in Israel. Abu-Rabia administered a battery of parallel tests of syntactic skills, decoding skills, orthographic knowledge, and working memory in English and Hebrew to 60 tenth graders. Although Abu-Rabia found significant positive correlations between Hebrew and English within a number of domains (i.e., working memory, grammatical sensitivity, and orthographic skills), he found no significant correlations between performance on a grammatical sensitivity cloze task in Hebrew (participants had to judge for each pair of pseudowords which item sounded like a real work in Hebrew) and performance on a test of English orthographic conventions (participants had to select in each pair of pseudowords the one that could be the spelling of a real word in English). Nor did Abu-Rabia find a correlation between performance on a phonological choice task in Hebrew and the English orthographic conventions task. The phonological choice task required participants to select in each pair of printed pseudowords the one that sounded like a real word in Hebrew. These findings differ from those of the studies reviewed earlier possibly because of methodological factors associated with the dependent measure (the English orthographic conventions task). In particular, unlike consistent differences between skilled and less-skilled readers on all other language and reading tasks, both in English and in Hebrew, there were no differences between these reading groups on the orthographic conventions task (administered in English or in Hebrew), and the performance in both groups was rather low, suggesting chance performance. However, performance on the syntactic sensitivity cloze test in Hebrew did correlate with performance on another task that focused on spelling skills in English. In this spelling-recognition task, students were required to select the correct spelling of real words in English. The conclusion that there is a relationship between first-language oral proficiency and second-language spelling needs to be qualified, however, because the task demands of the grammatical sensitivity cloze task capture not only oral proficiency, but various aspects of cognitive ability; the test correlates positively and significantly with memory assessed in Hebrew, as well as with performance on an arithmetic test.

In addition to the correlational studies that examined the relationship between first-language oral proficiency and spelling skills in English, some studies examined this question within a contrastive analysis framework. Two studies (Cronnell, 1985; Ferroli & Shanahan, 1993) found that features of first-language (Spanish) phonological awareness had an effect on spelling in English. Cronnell (1985) examined the nature and frequency of English spelling errors in writing samples of Mexican American English-language learners of low SES in Grades 3 and 6. He reports that many of the students' spelling errors could be traced to differences between Spanish and English phonology (e.g., *b*—*v* misspellings, the spelling of *d* for *th*, and the simplification of final consonant clusters—*han* for *hand*). In a similar study, Ferroli and Shanahan (1993) studied the effects of first-language phonology (voicing) on invented spelling in English in second- and third-grade bilingual Latino children attending a transitional bilingual program in the United States. These students were prone to using spelling patterns in English that were appropriate for voiceless sounds (derived from Spanish) when letters that correspond to voiced sounds (derived from English) were called for (e.g., /p/ vs. /b/).

In summary, correlational designs failed to find significant relationships between measures of first-language oral proficiency and English spelling skills. As with word reading skills, it may be that the grammatical sensitivity measures used to assess first-language oral proficiency by Abu-Rabia (1997), Da Fontoura and Siegel (1995), and Gottardo et al. (2001) are not precise enough to capture the aspects of first-language oral proficiency that may be linked to second-language spelling. However, measures of first-language phonological processing (e.g., phonological awareness) and English spelling skills correlate with each other rather consistently. Given the small group of studies that examined this relationship, the conclusion that there is a positive relationship between phonological processing in the first language and spelling in English is rather tentative at this point; it needs to be examined in additional studies involving English-language learners coming from different first-language backgrounds and different age groups.

Quasi-experimental studies focusing on error analysis (Cronnell, 1985; Ferroli & Shanahan, 1993) suggest that typological differences between the phonology of the first and second languages are reflected in patterns of second-language spelling acquisition. Specifically, the evidence suggests that phonological differences between English-language learners' first language and English can hinder or facilitate the acquisition of specific English spelling patterns (e.g., voicing contrasts; see Cronnell, 1985; Ferroli & Shanahan, 1993).[1] Caution is clearly called for in interpreting these results because of the limited number and scope of these studies and because of methodological flaws (e.g., the absence of comparison groups composed of students from a variety of first-language backgrounds) and the possibility that the spelling errors reflect developmental patterns, including errors that resemble those made by first-language learners of the same language (see chap. 6).

Studies reported on in this chapter suggest that the link among first-language oral language proficiency, phonological processes, and spelling achievement in English is not invariant. It is important to consider the measures used and typological similarity between the first and second languages. Thus, multivariate studies are needed to disentangle the relationships between these factors and spelling development in English-language learners. Finally, the virtual absence of relevant studies on high school students is of concern.

RELATIONSHIP BETWEEN FIRST-LANGUAGE ORAL PROFICIENCY AND READING COMPREHENSION IN ENGLISH

Research has shown that the development of reading comprehension skills in monolingual English-speaking students is complex (Spiro & Myers, 1984), and

---

[1]For a more comprehensive treatment of the transfer issue in first- and second-language learning, see chapters 7 and 11.

that one factor that influences reading comprehension is oral language proficiency (Carver, 2000). Unfortunately, in contrast to the wealth of research on the development of reading comprehension in native English speakers, there is little research on the development of second-language reading comprehension skills in language-minority students at all grade levels, from elementary to high school (see chap. 4 for a review of this research) and even less research on the role of first-language oral proficiency in the development of second-language comprehension.

Only one study examined the relationship between first-language oral proficiency and reading comprehension in English in elementary school English-language learners. Using structural equation modeling (SEM), Dufva and Voeten (1999) examined the reading comprehension skills of third-grade Finnish-speaking students who were learning English as a foreign language in school. Among other findings, they report that students' listening comprehension skills in Finnish, assessed in Grade 1, had an indirect effect on English reading comprehension scores in Grade 3. However, the link between Grade 1 Finnish listening comprehension skills and Grade 3 English reading comprehension skills was mediated by the students' reading comprehension skills in Finnish in Grade 2 (direct effect). That is to say, Grade 1 listening comprehension in Finnish correlated with Grade 2 reading comprehension in Finnish, which in turn correlated with English reading comprehension in Grade 3. These researchers also report that the students' phonological memory, assessed in Finnish in Grade 2, correlated significantly with Grade 3 reading comprehension in English (direct effect). The findings from this single study underscore the multidimensional nature of the development of reading comprehension in a nonnative language.

Research on English-language learners in middle school has not found a relationship between first-language oral proficiency and English reading comprehension. In a longitudinal study of fifth- and sixth-grade Spanish-speaking English-language learners in a transitional bilingual education program, Royer and Carlo (1991) found no significant correlation between the students' Spanish listening comprehension skills assessed in Grade 5 and their reading comprehension skills in English in Grade 6. A similar lack of association between first-language proficiency and reading comprehension in English was found in one study that used self-report measures. Okamura-Bichard (1985) found that self-ratings of first-language proficiency did not correlate with reading comprehension in English in a group of sixth-grade bilingual Japanese–English students.

Finally, one study (Nguyen, Shin, & Krashen, 2001) that examined the relationship between first-language oral proficiency and reading outcomes, more broadly defined (combined reading and language subtests on the Stanford Achievement Test), found no significant relationship. The study examined Vietnamese English-language learners in Grades 5 to 8, and the measure of first-language oral proficiency was self-reported ratings. Because these authors do not report correlations for the reading comprehension subtest alone, the precise nature of this association is difficult to interpret. Nevertheless, this study also points to a lack of relationship between first-language proficiency and general second-language reading achievement.

Only one study in the database examined the relationship between first-language oral proficiency and English reading comprehension in high school

English-language learners. Buriel and Cardoza (1988) examined the relationship between self-reports of first-language (Spanish) proficiency and English reading comprehension in ninth-grade Spanish–English bilingual students. Reading tests that had been standardized on the High School and Beyond senior sample were used to assess reading outcomes (Heyns & Hilton, 1982). Students were first-, second-, or third-generation Mexican Americans living in the southwestern United States. Findings suggest that the relationship between first-language proficiency and English reading comprehension is more complex than that reported in studies of younger English-language learners. These researchers did not find significant relationships between first-language proficiency and English reading comprehension for first- and second-generation Mexican-American high school English-language learners. However, they report significant negative relationships between first-language proficiency and/or use and English reading for third-generation Mexican-American students (see chap. 11 for further discussion of the relationship of home language use to English reading outcomes).

In summary, across the different levels of schooling, the findings from this limited group of studies are complex. On the one hand, most found no relationship between reading comprehension in English and first-language oral proficiency measured through self-ratings of first-language proficiency or language use (Kennedy & Park, 1994; Nguyen et al., 2001; Okamura-Bichard, 1985) and through listening comprehension (Royer & Carlo, 1991). However, in the case of students learning English as a foreign language, one study found that listening comprehension in the first language related indirectly to reading comprehension in English. In this study, first-language listening comprehension was more directly related to first-language reading comprehension; first language reading comprehension was directly related to second-language reading comprehension. There is also some evidence from research reported in this and other chapters that intervening factors may influence this relationship—more specifically, that phonological memory (Dufva & Voeten, 1999) and sociocultural context (Buriel & Cardoza, 1988) are associated with the development of reading comprehension in English.

RELATIONSHIP BETWEEN FIRST-LANGUAGE ORAL PROFICIENCY AND WRITING IN ENGLISH

Few studies systematically examined the relationship between first-language oral proficiency and the acquisition of English writing skills. No studies examined the relationship between first-language oral proficiency and emerging writing/composing skills in English in elementary or high school English-language learners.

Two studies (discussed earlier) examined the relationship between first-language oral language skills and English writing development in middle-school English-language learners (Cronnell, 1985; Okamura-Bichard, 1985). As noted earlier, first-language influences on second-language development provide a useful, albeit indirect, method for studying factors that affect the development of English writing skills. Using this framework, Cronnell (1985) examined the nature of the errors found in the English writing samples of Mexican-American students from low-SES backgrounds in Grades 3 and 6. Cronnell reports that the students made syntactic errors in English that reflected nonstandard grammatical usage (e.g., word order problems, use of double negatives) that could be attributed to influences from the students' first language. Cronnell also notes that the overall quality of the students' writing was not necessarily related to the frequency of spelling or syntactic errors; some students were able to write well-constructed stories despite numerous such errors. Okamura-Bichard (1985) studied sixth-grade Japanese–English bilingual students whose families resided temporarily in the United States. These bilingual learners attended a public school during the week and a Japanese school on the weekend. Okamura-Bichard found that measures of listening comprehension in Japanese did not correlate with self-report measures of writing ability in English. The question arises whether the failure to find cross-language effects is due to the fact that most first-language oral proficiency skills are less important than phonological awareness in predicting the development of text-level second-language competence; to the typological dissimilarity between Japanese and English, especially in their writing systems; or self-report measures of writing that were invalid. Overall, too little research has been done in this area to conclude anything about the relationship between first-language oral proficiency and second-language writing ability.

9

First- and Second-Language Literacy

Cheryl Dressler with Michael Kamil

The focus of this chapter is on the cross-linguistic influences of literacy knowledge, processes, and strategies in children who are learning a second language. As is the case with all chapters in this volume, the majority of studies reviewed here concern language-minority children who are learning English as a second language (ESL). Because the study of cross-language transfer in educational psychology has its origins and a lengthy and productive tradition in Europe (see e.g., Ringbom, 1978; Skutnabb-Kangas & Toukomaa, 1976), we also include investigations of literacy transfer in foreign-language learning contexts where English is the foreign language.[1] In addition, at least one influential conceptualization of literacy transfer hypothesizes it to occur at the level of underlying proficiency, involving cognitive accomplishments that may be relatively independent of the linguistic domain. Therefore, we consider findings of those studies addressing first- to second-language transfer in language-minority children learning societal languages other than English that are relevant to the topic of transfer in the acquisition of first- and second-language literacy.

This chapter differs from chapters 7 and 8, which also address cross-linguistic transfer extensively in discussing the relationships between oral language proficiency and literacy, in that it (a) includes only those studies whose subjects possess some degree of literacy in their first and second languages, (b) examines transfer exclusively in studies employing *written* measures of the constructs investigated, and (c) includes only studies that investigate first- to second-language transfer within subjects and studies of group comparisons that also

---

[1]The corpus contains five such studies. Studies of the acquisition of English as a foreign language are included because the vast majority of foreign-language studies that address our research questions have investigated the learning of English in this context.

examined transfer within subjects.[2] Further, although chapters 7 and 8 examine relationships between the same construct in the first and second languages (e.g., first-language word reading and second- language word reading), they also look at the relationships between constructs that are different in each language (e.g., first-language word reading and second-language comprehension). In contrast, within the corpus of studies reviewed here, the general practice has been to examine the relationship between the same construct in each language.

Thus, the chapter is organized according to the subcomponents of literacy investigated in this manner: word reading, spelling, vocabulary, [3] reading comprehension, strategy use, and writing. The studies reviewed have examined outcomes in either the reading or writing modality and employed both quantitative and qualitative methods. They have typically aimed either to (a) analyze second-language outcomes with the goal of identifying influences from what is known about the first-language grammar and lexicon[4], or (b) examine correlations between a construct in the first language and the corresponding construct in the second language.

The following research questions are addressed in this chapter:

1. For what components of literacy is there a relationship between first- and second-language literacy?

   • Under what circumstances is there evidence for cross-language influences that facilitate literacy acquisition in the second language?
   • Under what circumstances does literacy in the first language interfere with second-language literacy?

2. What evidence does this body of studies provide to support or contradict theoretical accounts of transfer?

WORD READING

Word-level skills, such as word reading and spelling, have been shown to affect reading comprehension, such that difficulties at the word level in either meaning association or pronunciation impede reading comprehension (for a review, see Adams, 1990). Spelling and word reading are closely related skills in that both depend on phonological and orthographic processing skills [5] (Gough,

---

[2]This criterion excludes, for example, studies that compare the second-language achievement of students educated through the first language with that of comparable students receiving education in a second language. Although superior performance by the first group is often cited as evidence for the transfer of academic skills, conclusions drawn from such a design do not correspond to the aspects of transfer addressed by our research questions.

[3]As noted in chapter 6, the construct of vocabulary knowledge is complex. It may be viewed in literacy research as an indicator of oral language proficiency (as in chap. 8). However, both the conceptual nature of word knowledge and its reciprocal relationship with reading (vocabulary knowledge influences reading comprehension, reading influences vocabulary growth; Anderson & Freebody, 1981) render it an important literacy component in the current discussion as well.

[4]Or vice versa because a few of the studies reviewed examined transfer from the second to the first language.

[5]Orthographic processing refers to translating written symbols to a visual code and activating the meaning of that visual code" (Durgunoglu & Hancin-Bhatt, 1992, p. 394).

Juel, & Griffith, 1992; Gough & Tunner, 1986; Juel et al., 1986). Further, word reading ability has been shown to be related to the cognitive constructs of phonological memory and speed of lexical access (Gholamain & Geva, 1999).

With respect to the transfer of word reading skills, three studies in this category tested the relative explanatory power of the script-dependent hypothesis and the central processing/central deficit hypotheses. Briefly, the script-dependent hypothesis emphasizes the importance of the nature of orthography in reading acquisition and suggests that the process of converting graphemic representations to phonological representations in word reading is easier and more efficient within orthographic systems that are relatively transparent and characterized by regular sound–symbol associations. Proponents of this hypothesis argue further that the incidence and patterns of reading disability across languages may be a function of the orthographic complexity of a language (Gholamain & Geva, 1999). In contrast, central processing/central deficit hypotheses highlight the role of underlying cognitive factors (such as verbal ability and phonological memory) in word reading. Within these models, children who are good readers in the first language are likely to be good readers in the second language, and children who are reading disabled in one language are likely to experience reading disability in the other as a result of deficiencies in the mental processes underlying reading. In two of the three studies that tested these competing hypotheses, the central deficit hypothesis is described as a corollary to Cummins' interdependence hypothesis (Abu-Rabia, 1997; Da Fontoura & Siegel, 1995); in the third, no explicit reference to Cummins is made (Gholamain & Geva, 1999).[6] All three studies in this set explored word reading skills in children exposed to first-language orthographies that are more transparent and regular than that of English, the second language.

Five studies have looked at transfer in word reading. In contrast to studies on other components of reading, only one of these studies involved native Spanish speakers learning English. Students in these studies ranged from 1st graders (Durgunoglu, Nagy, & Hancin-Bhatt, 1993) to 5th graders (Gholamain & Geva, 1999) to children ages 9 to 12 (Da Fontoura & Siegel, 1995) to 10th graders (Abu-Rabia, 1997; Chitiri & Willows, 1997).

Da Fontoura and Siegel (1995) assessed the reading, language, and memory skills of 37 Canadian children ages 9 to 12. The children spoke Portuguese at home, received school instruction in English, and attended a heritage language program at school, where they were taught to read and write in Portuguese. The researchers tested two contrasting hypotheses: (a) reading difficulties would be more apparent in English than in Portuguese because, relative to English, Portuguese has a predictable relationship between phonemes and graphemes with few irregularities (the script-dependent hypothesis); and (b) reading difficulties would be manifested in both languages because they are related to an underlying proficiency (central deficit hypothesis). The authors found significant cross-language relationships on measures of word and pseudoword reading, working memory, and syntactic awareness. The correlations

---

[6] In personal correspondence, Esther Geva, one of the authors of this study, explained that the central processing hypothesis is related to Cummins' interdependence hypothesis, but underscores underlying cognitive processes, such as memory and phonological processing, so that the focus is on universals or what is common across languages.

between English and Portuguese word and pseudoword reading were .52 ($p < .001$) and .64 ($p < .0001$), respectively.

Because the first- and second-language measures of reading, language, and memory were all highly correlated, students with reading problems in English were likely to show reading problems in Portuguese, indicating general language deficits. The study further examined the performance of reading-disabled children in the bilingual sample with that of a comparison group of monolingual students that also included normally achieving and disabled readers.[7] The reading-disabled bilingual children had significantly higher scores than the reading-disabled monolingual children on the English pseudoword reading test and the English spelling test (although they had significantly lower scores on tests of syntactic awareness). The authors suggest that the bilingual reading-disabled students may have been transferring skills developed through experience with a more transparent and regular orthography to English decoding.

In another test of the interdependence hypothesis, Abu-Rabia (1997) investigated whether similar difficulties appear in students who are learning languages with different orthographic systems. Specifically, he studied the relationship among reading, syntactic, orthographic, and working-memory skills in 60 Hebrew–English bilingual 10th graders in Israel. The subjects were administered tests of working memory, oral cloze, orthographic knowledge (i.e., identifying which of two pseudowords could be a spelling of a word), word attack, and word identification in Hebrew and English. Abu-Rabia found statistically positive and significant correlations among all Hebrew and English tests except the phonological and orthographic tasks. He attributes the lack of significant relationships on these two tasks to the divergent natures of the orthographies being investigated. However, cross-language correlations for word (.58) and pseudoword (.65) tasks were strong. To further test the interdependence hypothesis, the sample was divided into a group of skilled and less-skilled readers based on their performance on the Hebrew word identification task. The *t* tests revealed significant group differences on all English and Hebrew tests except the orthographic tasks, suggesting that, in general, bilingual children who experience reading difficulty in one language are likely to have similar problems in their other language. The author speculates that lower than expected orthographic scores in Hebrew may have been a result of the use of vocalized Hebrew in the orthographic measure, a version of Hebrew text used in initial literacy instruction, but with which subjects in this study had had no recent experience and thus reportedly found difficult to read. No explanation of the virtually identical group scores for the English version of the orthographic task is given. However, because the ability to differentiate among learners contributes to the reliability of a measure, it is possible that the psychometric properties of this measure are problematic. In summary, the author reports that, overall, the data support Cummins' interdependence hypothesis with respect to all reading, language, and memory skills measured. However, as with Da Fontoura and Siegel (1995), Abu-Rabia claims that orthographic skills are language specific and thus not subject to transfer. The finding that orthographic skills are language specific is questionable,

---

[7]Reading-disabled children were those who earned a score of $<= 25$ on the Wide Range Achievement Test–Revised (WRAT–R).

however, given the characteristics of the particular orthographic task used as the basis for this claim.

In a sample of 70 Canadian children in Grades 1 to 5, Gholamain and Geva (1999) examined the extent to which parallel basic reading skills in English and Persian could be understood by considering common underlying cognitive processes and the unique orthographic characteristics of these two alphabetic systems. Persian is a modified form of an Arabic script, with sound–symbol correspondences that are more regular than is the case in English. The children were enrolled in schools where English was the language of instruction and in a Persian heritage language program, through which they received 3 hours of instruction per week in reading and writing. The students were administered measures of working memory, letter naming speed, and word and pseudoword reading. The authors found that students who performed better on measures of reading and cognitive skills in English, their language of formal schooling, were more likely to perform better in Persian, their home language. This pattern of intercorrelations, the authors suggest, provides support for the central processing hypothesis. The authors also found, however, that orthographic differences between Persian and English influenced the development of decoding skills in each language. Specifically, once children had mastered the Persian phoneme–grapheme conversion rules at the end of Grade 2, they were able to apply them accurately to complex and unfamiliar words in Persian so that their performance in Persian, the language in which they had received minimal instruction, approximated their performance in English.

Chitiri and Willows (1997) found that word reading in bilinguals depended on language-specific operations. They investigated the processing patterns of bilingual 10th-grade native Greek speakers with advanced proficiency in English as a foreign language, compared with those of monolingual Greek and English speakers. To test the hypothesis that the greater transparency of the Greek orthography would result in students' heavier reliance on the phonological code than the visual in word reading, they examined the role of syllabic and stress effects in the students' performance. A second research question investigated the impact of a salient difference between Greek and English syntax: Because Greek uses inflections to express relationships that are expressed in word order in English, native Greek speakers pay more attention to function words (which are also inflected in Greek) and noun endings that carry affixes than do native English speakers, who focus more on the beginning parts of content words.

Subjects were administered a letter cancellation task in which they were required to cross out each instance of a specific target letter within a text. This task is informative in that when subjects cross a letter out, they indicate that letter identification is proceeding in a conscious manner, whereas if the letter occurs in a word but is not crossed out, letter identification is not conscious and subjects are thought to be forming units larger than a letter as they read. The subjects were instructed to read for comprehension and were given comprehension questions subsequent to the reading.

Findings from this study indicate an effect of differences in orthographic systems, in that the bilingual students' patterns of letter cancellation in two- and three-syllable words approximated those of monolingual Greek students, but were different from those of monolingual English students. With respect to syntax, bilingual students processed inflected function words and noun endings that carried inflected affixes to a greater extent than did English mono- linguals, but to a slightly lesser extent than did monolingual Greek students. The authors attribute this finding to an interlanguage effect. The bilingual students, although highly proficient readers of English, read more slowly and made more errors in English than in Greek, possibly as a consequence of pro- cessing patterns transferred from the first language. Thus, this study provides evidence that even at advanced levels of language proficiency, typological dis- similarity may result in interference in second-language reading processes.

Durgunoglu et al. (1993) conducted a study to investigate factors influencing the English word reading performance of 27 first-grade Spanish-speaking students characterized as limited English proficient (LEP). The students were enrolled in a transitional bilingual education (TBE) program and had received most of their instruction in Spanish. They were administered tests of letter naming, Spanish phonological awareness, Spanish and English word reading, English word and pseudoword reading, and Spanish and English oral profi- ciency. Multiple regression analyses revealed that Spanish word reading signif- icantly predicted performance on the English word and pseudoword reading tasks and, further, that Spanish phonological awareness predicted English word reading. These results indicate cross-language transfer of word and pseu- doword reading abilities in students with limited second-language proficiency.

In summary, findings from four of the five studies reviewed previously yielded results that support the interdependence hypothesis (Abu-Rabia, 1997; Chitiri & Willows, 1997; Da Fontoura & Siegel, 1995; Gholamain & Geva, 1999), suggesting that across a wide range of ages, word reading skills acquired in one language transfer to the other. At the same time, differences in orthographic complexity between English and the students' first languages were found to influence the transfer of word reading skills, revealing a heavier reliance on the phonological than the visual strategy in processing the second language when the first-language orthography is transparent. This finding suggests that processing strategies applied in word reading are language specific. The Chitiri and Willows study further demonstrates that students with a high level of proficiency in two languages that have significantly different orthographies may develop interlanguages—systems of processing patterns that are different from those used by monolingual students in either language.

SPELLING

All studies discussed in this section have examined transfer from first language to English orthography; thus, a few words are in order about the nature of English orthography and the challenges it poses for spellers and readers. Knowledge of the spelling–sound correspondences in the English orthographic system has been shown to be an important determinant of reading ability (Bear, 1982; Ehri & Wilce, 1987; Juel, Griffith, & Gough, 1986; Morris & Perney, 1984). In early spelling acquisition, children learn to spell structurally simple words for which sounds map onto letters in a straightforward manner (e.g., BED for [bɛd]). As reading ability develops, however, children frequently encounter words whose spellings cannot be derived reliably from the sounds that form them. For example, *steak, leak, head,* and *area* (Juel et al., 1986) contain an identical letter sequence, *ea,* that corresponds to four different sounds. At yet more advanced levels of reading—Grade 5 and beyond—students are exposed to myriad pairs of etymologically related words whose connections are not readily perceived on an auditory basis, such as *sign/signature, local/locality, molecule/molecular,* and *serene/serenity.* The ability to spell such pairs of words correctly demonstrates an understanding of morphological relatedness in English words, knowledge considered critical in vocabulary acquisition (Nagy & Anderson, 1984). Thus, whereas phonology informs the early acquisition of spelling skills, the inverse appears to be true at advanced stages of spelling development: Exposure to the English orthographic system influences how speakers conceptualize the sound structure of words, and higher order word knowledge is necessary for the correct spelling of words. Finally, a series of spelling studies have demonstrated that, through their interactions with print, children learning their first language proceed through sequential stages of orthographic knowledge (Henderson, 1981) that are influenced by exposure to written material and level of cognitive development (Zutell, 1992).

In this section, we review a number of studies that have examined transfer through the analysis of spelling errors in the second language. These studies have been conducted largely within a contrastive analysis framework, with the assumption that differences in the phonological systems of the first and second languages will result in errors that reflect first-language phonology and thus constitute interference. Because the spelling system of a language is closely linked to its phonemic system, the question arises whether to attribute negative transfer in spelling to differences in phonology or in phoneme–grapheme mappings between the first and second languages. As James and Klein (1994) explain, "If L1 [first language] pronunciation influences L1 spelling and L2 [second language] pronunciation, and L2 pronunciation affects L2 spelling, then L1 phonology may be said to affect L2 spelling indirectly via L2 phonology, or directly … so that [while] for the native speaker there is only one factor related to spelling at this level, namely the pronunciation, for the [L2 speller] there are three factors: L1 phonology, L1 spelling and L2 phonology" (pp. 34–35). This description of influences on second-language spelling can help guide our interpretation of the results of the studies discussed here. Other studies have measured correlations between first- and second-language spelling knowledge; still others have aimed to ascertain the effect of the differences between first- and second-language orthography on the spelling of English-language learners.

Eight studies have investigated first-language influences on spelling in English among students in Grades 1 to 6. Six of these studies involved native speakers of Spanish, one of German, and one of Persian. All of the first languages reported on in this group of studies are relatively more transparent, regular, and consistent with respect to sound–letter correspondences than is English. As mentioned earlier, one factor affecting transfer is linguistic complexity: When students are acquiring a second language with features that are more complex than the corresponding features in the first language, negative transfer is predicted. Thus, the studies described here have largely aimed to account for students' performance in English with reference to differences in orthographic depth between the first and second languages.

Four studies have examined the influence of the first language on second-language spelling at the level of the grapheme (Fashola, Drum, Mayer, & Kang, 1996; Ferroli & Shanahan, 1993; James & Klein, 1994; Zutell & Allen, 1988).

These studies typically have employed a combination of correlational and error analyses.

Zutell and Allen (1988) investigated the spelling errors of Spanish-speaking children in Grades 2, 3, and 4 in four categories of features with which students were predicted to have difficulty, based on contrasts in Spanish–English phonology/orthography: long vowel *e*, long vowel *a*, initial blend *s*, and initial consonant *y* (as assessed through a spelling test). The aim of the study was to discover what effect Spanish pronunciation and spelling have on children's English spelling strategies. They found significant differences in the difficulty of the four categories. Long *vowel e* and initial *blend s* were the most difficult, with students making more total (but not specifically predicted) errors in these categories than in the others. More predicted errors were made with long vowel *a*, long vowel *e*, and initial *consonant y* than with the other categories. Further, Zutell and Allen found that these errors were fairly evenly distributed across grade levels; when children were grouped according to their overall performance on the test instead of grade, however, those who were less successful made significantly more of the predicted errors, whereas those who were more successful were more likely to make *legal* (intralingual) errors on vowels. Finally, in post hoc analyses, Zutell and Allen noted that the final [z] (represented by *s*) in *please* presented an additional source of difficulty for the students in their sample, as it was occasionally represented, even by the better spellers, with a *c* or *cs*. In English, *c* is almost never used for [z], and the fact that it was by these spellers suggests, according to the authors, that the students may not have perceived the articulatory feature that distinguishes [s] and [z]—voicing. The authors speculate that Spanish influence may lead to a pronunciation in which word-final [z] is pronounced more like a soft *c*.[8]

One characteristic of English phonology is that most consonants are paired with another that differs only in voicedness—for example (/p/–/b/, /f/–/v/, /t/–/d/, [s]–[z], /k/–/g/)[9]. Because voicing is phonemic in English, this feature distinguishes word meanings (e.g., *pin–bin, fat–vat*). In Spanish, in contrast, voicedness does not generally distinguish words (Ching, 1976). Ferroli and Shanahan (1993) looked at consonant voicedness as a contrastive dimension and concluded that children who are transitioning from Spanish to English orthography must "come to terms with voicing before arriving at correct English spellings" (p. 5). Their sample included 47 second- and third-grade Spanish-speaking students in a transitional bilingual education program who had been receiving reading and writing instruction in Spanish and were beginning in English. The authors administered 18–50-word developmental English spelling tests over a period of 20 weeks to determine how the children changed

[8]This phonological source of difficulty may not be distinguishable from the influence of first-language orthography. For example, in Latin American Spanish, the letters <c>, <s>, and <z> can all be pronounced identically, leading to Spanish spelling errors such as COCER for COSER (C. Snow, personal communication, June 2004).

[9]The second phoneme in each case is voiced.

in their renderings of various spelling features. In addition to regular spelling words that the children could study and practice, five new words incorporating key spelling features were added to the weekly spelling tests. The authors found that consonant knowledge often transferred, so that what the children knew in Spanish helped with spelling in English. Additionally, they noted that some of the errors the children produced in English could be attributed to Spanish–English differences in voicing, and they identified a hierarchical sequence of four spelling strategies through which native Spanish speakers may progress as they become increasingly proficient spellers in English. For example, a sound that does not occur in Spanish, [ ] (as in *pleasure* and *measure*), elicited the following misspellings: J, SH, CH, and H. The researchers describe the hierarchy of strategies with reference to voicing and place of articulation, so that the most sophisticated representation (Strategy 4), J, is voiced and produced in the same place of articulation as the target sound [ ]; SH (Strategy 3) is voiceless, but has the same place of articulation; CH (Strategy 2) is voiceless and articulated near the target sound; and H (Strategy 1) is presumed to have been chosen because the name of the letter H includes the sound represented by CH ([č]).[10]

Although they focused on errors predicted on the basis of a contrastive analysis, both Zutell and Allen (1988) and Ferroli and Shanahan (1993) conducted their studies within a developmental framework. That is, they implicitly acknowledged that there are both inter- and intralinguistic influences on children's spelling (i.e., that, like native speakers of English, second-language spellers progress through stages of spelling development), although they did not specifically identify errors made by English-language learners that resemble first-language developmental errors.

Fashola et al. (1996), in contrast, did not consider any possible intralingual influences on their subjects' spelling, and this is a limitation of their study. The authors investigated errors on eight English spelling features for which errors could be predicted for children who were correctly applying Spanish phonological and orthographic rules for English words: the /k/, /h/, /b/, /e/, /u/, /U/, and /i/ phonemes, and the "all cluster" (as in *handball*). They administered a spelling test to second- and third-grade, and to fifth- and sixth-grade Spanish-speaking students classified as limited English proficient. The test was also given to same-age monolingual peers as a control. Fashola and colleagues found that Spanish-speaking students made significantly more predicted, but not nonpredicted, errors than the control groups. In other words, the students transferred their knowledge of first-language phonological and orthographic rules to the second language in an early stage of English literacy acquisition. The authors further found that error frequency declined with age, presumably as a result of greater cognitive ability among the older students.

Several issues arising from the design of the study need to be considered, however. First, as noted earlier, the selection of items for the spelling test was based entirely on Spanish–English contrasts in letter–sound relationships; no

---

[10]This strategy is analogous to the letter-name strategy employed by beginning spellers, who match individual sounds in words with the names of letters in the alphabet. Using this strategy, the word *train* is spelled TRAN and *lady* is written as LADE.

intralingual factors were considered. Thus, although each item contained specific contrastive phonemes, from an intralingual perspective, the items presented a broad range of achievements that first-language learners must negotiate as they progress in English spelling (e.g., *vase*—long vowel marking; *happy*—consonant doubling).

Second, although items on the spelling list administered are referred to as *common* English words, they varied enormously in frequency of use (e.g., *happy* vs. *treble*). Finally, the spelling words were presented in an isolated fashion, rather than in context, so that nonphonetic information that students typically use when they spell could not be accessed. For example, the word *seam* was included, and its homophone *seem* counted as correct. Supplying a context for this target word would have provided information on students' ability to distinguish between this homophonic pair, which would require invoking knowledge of the syntactic function of the words (i.e., choosing either the verb [*seem*] or the noun [*seam*]). As Henderson (1985) explains: "Homophones are the key to learning how to spell English. They exemplify the basic meaning principle: things that mean alike are spelled alike; things that mean differently are spelled differently" (p. 63). Finally, little information is provided about the sample. The students are said to have been *transitioning* from Spanish to English, but we are given no information about their instructional context or levels of first- and second-language literacy proficiency. The fact that the students characterized as limited English proficient made significantly more predicted errors (predicted, i.e., based on the assumption that they were using their knowledge of Spanish phoneme–grapheme correspondences in their English spelling) relative to the monolingual control group certainly indicates that they did apply Spanish grapheme–phoneme mapping rules to English. Yet with no information about students' English literacy proficiency or history of exposure to English, the contribution of these findings is limited; we cannot interpret them in terms of the interlanguage the students were constructing, which necessarily has features of both the native and target languages.

James and Klein (1994) acknowledged at the outset of their study of the spelling strategies used by German students of English as a foreign language that, "due to the characteristics of English spelling the influence of the native language is not the sole error source in the English spelling of foreign learners" (p. 32). The authors describe the spelling and proofreading strategies of 185 students, ages 12 to 13, who had received instruction in English for 6 months. They were administered a dictation task containing 145 words. Results of the spelling analyses suggest that German-speaking students of English are influenced in their spelling by two language systems and that transfer takes place in spelling. Specifically, the authors found that there was a large number of intralingual errors (such as confusing homophonic forms, as in *to, too,* and *two*), but that most errors were caused by phonological interference from German. Although they do not describe interference with reference to specific phonemes, the authors report that there was more evidence of negative transfer from first-language phonology with vowels than with consonants.

Two studies looked at the correlations between spelling knowledge in the first and second languages. Davis and colleagues (1999) examined the extent to which English-language instruction was transferred to native Spanish by first, second, and third graders enrolled at a parochial school in Chicago. The subjects were not yet orally proficient in English. The authors administered a narrative writing assignment to the students and scored them on several aspects of writing development, including the number of words spelled correctly. The cross-language correlation on this index was moderately significant: .35 ($p < .05$). The authors interpret this finding as evidence of transfer of spelling achievement from the second language (English, the language of instruction) to the first, Spanish. In the case of transfer of spelling ability, the children in this sample were confronted first with an opaque orthography and could apparently apply grapheme–phoneme conversion rules to Spanish without instruction in that language.

In contrast to Davis and colleagues, Arab-Moghaddam and Sénéchal (2001) found that the first- and second-language spelling performance of Iranian children in Grades 2 and 3 who were learning literacy in Persian and English concurrently did not correlate significantly. Persian is alphabetic, adapted from Arabic script, and written from right to left, but it is visually different from Roman alphabetic systems. In this study, spelling knowledge was assessed by a 38-word spelling test with items ranging in frequency and orthographic complexity; spelling accuracy was measured by counting the total number of words spelled correctly. According to the authors, the low correlation between Persian and English spelling scores (.25, controlling for grade level) suggests that the simultaneous acquisition of spelling skills in two such typologically distant languages may occur independently. The discrepancy between these findings and those of Davis et al. (1999) cannot be attributed to the ages of the subjects because they were the same age. Rather, it is possible that the nature of the task (analysis of spelling in a writing task vs. a spelling test) influenced the results. Another strong possibility relates to the differences between the Persian and English orthographies relative to the Spanish and English orthographies: It is possible that transfer in the domain of spelling is more likely to occur in languages that are typologically related.

Finally, two studies involved qualitative analyses of spelling strategies employed in the emergent writing of Spanish–English bilinguals. Nathenson-Mejía (1989) studied the writing produced by 12 native-Spanish-speaking first graders enrolled in an American school in Mexico who were acquiring literacy in their first language and learning English as a foreign language. The author spent 90 minutes a week for 9 weeks reading and discussing English trade books, conducting a shared rereading, and eliciting writing samples from the children (captions for pictures they drew related to the story that was read). She analyzed more than 200 pieces of writing and concluded that these students used their knowledge of orthography in both English and Spanish to produce written work in English. Some of the English–Spanish contrasts investigated were [s]/[es] (*stop* written as ESTOP), [t] or [ð] versus [d] (*the* written as DE), [š] versus [č] (*short* written as CHORT), and vowel sounds. Nathenson-Mejía found that the students relied heavily on Spanish pronunciation and orthography—specifically, that Spanish rules for spelling dominated when the children were working on new words, words for which the English and Spanish pronunciations were close, or words for which the English letter or sound did not exist in Spanish.

Further, although many invented spellings did occur, much of the students' writing used conventional English spellings. Some developmental changes were noted over the period of the study: The words *the* and *happy* began to be written accurately by the students. The author attributes this change to the frequency with which the children saw these words in print in class. These results suggest that in initial stages of acquisition, children rely heavily on first-language graphophonic rules (similar to the children in the Fashola et al. [1996] study who were transitioning to English), but that strategies are altered as the students gain exposure to the English writing system.

Edelsky (1982) hypothesizes that the relationship between first- and second-language writing is not one of interference, but rather one of the application of first- to second-language writing. She looked at writing samples in both Spanish and English from nine native-Spanish-speaking children in Grades 1, 2, and 3 of a bilingual program that emphasized writing and a whole-language approach to literacy. The children had either acquired English concurrently with Spanish or were acquiring it as a second language in school. Exposure to English print in the classroom was minimal, although some children read primarily English books during free reading time. Literacy instruction was provided in the first language exclusively through Grade 2, although the children had some experience with English in print. Four hundred and seventy-seven Spanish and 49 English writing samples were collected at four times during a single school year. These samples were analyzed according to a number of features (discussed in more detail later), including spelling. Like Nathansen-Mejía (1989), Edelsky (1982) found that when the children spelled in English, they made use of Spanish orthography—for example, BA LLANA UMEN (bionic woman) and AI JOUP LLU GOU AGIEN TU SCU (I hope you go again to school). These spellings reveal a great deal of interdependence between the subjects' Spanish and English spelling systems, but there was differentiation with respect to some features: <k> was reserved almost exclusively for English, and tildes and accents for Spanish. Further, the children's production of forms such as MSR (for *Mrs.*), WALKIN (for *walking*), and THE (alternating with DA) shows that they were not only applying Spanish grapho–phoneme conversion rules in English spelling, but they were also using a visual strategy (which is necessarily intralingual). Edelsky suggests that transfer in this case can be explained by the application of a general language-acquisition strategy she terms *use of the input*, interacting with specific features of the language in which the children were writing, so that they were continually creating hypotheses about spelling based on linguistic input in the first and second languages.

A limitation of this study is that it does not describe differences among children in the different grades. For example, one would expect to see relatively less reliance on Spanish orthography in the English spelling of the third graders, who were (a) reported to be receiving English instruction, and (b) in a more advanced stage of literacy development than first graders. In no instance is movement toward more accurate target forms attributed to development or even to input. Input is described only as preferences by some children for English reading materials during free reading time.

In summary, findings from error analyses and studies of emergent writing indicate that, in the early stages of second-language spelling development, there is an effect both of first-language phonology and first-language graphophonic rules on students' spelling of English words (Edelsky, 1982; Fashola et al., 1996; James & Klein, 1994; Nathansen-Mejía, 1989; Zutell & Allen, 1988).

With the exception of the work of James and Klein, all spelling studies reviewed here interpreted the first-language influence from a general problem-solving perspective, viewing reliance on first-language phonology and orthography early in second-language acquisition as facilitative—an application of analytic skills and comparable to the phenomenon of invented spelling for emergent first-language spellers. Indeed, the use of first-language knowledge in the absence of second-language knowledge, as in the case of these learners in the initial stages of second-language acquisition, is not considered to represent transfer, but rather a *falling back* on the native language (Odlin, 1989).[11]

Several studies demonstrated that, with increased exposure to English print, students progress from heavy reliance on the phonological strategy in spelling (spelling by ear) to use of the visual strategy as well. Such developments point to the dynamic quality of interlanguages (Selinker, 1972), whereby learners may exhibit a mix of linguistic patterns—some typical of the first language (interlingual) and some of the second (intralingual) language.

Six of the seven studies reviewed here investigated transfer from the first to the second language; the single study that looked at reverse transfer (Davis et al., 1999) found it to occur from English to Spanish spelling, despite the fact that students had received no instruction in Spanish literacy. This finding may reflect the markedness factor: Perhaps when students are confronted with a more complex system initially, they are able to apply initial graphophonic strategies learned widely and successfully to a less complex language.

The two correlational studies reviewed yielded contrasting findings for the transfer of spelling knowledge across languages. The discrepancy between the findings of Arab-Moghaddam and Sénéchal (2001) and those of Davis et al. (1999) cannot be attributed to the students' ages, which did not differ. Rather, it is possible that the nature of the task (analysis of spelling in a writing task vs. a spelling test) influenced the results. Another possibility lies in the differences between Persian and English relative to Spanish and English orthographies; it is possible, therefore, that spelling knowledge gained in one language will transfer to another only when the two languages are closely related.

VOCABULARY

Vocabulary knowledge has long been linked to performance on reading comprehension measures in research involving monolingual speakers of English (Freebody & Anderson, 1981). One goal of vocabulary research has been to estimate vocabulary size and growth during the school years. It is estimated that, on average, children learn 3,000 new words per year (Nagy & Herman, 1987). A second goal of vocabulary research has been to identify characteristics of words that render them difficult to learn. Chall (1987) explains that at about Grade 4 or 5, students transition from *learning to read* (decoding) to *reading to learn* and encounter in textbooks, for example, vocabulary that is increasingly

---

[11]Code switching and translating are further examples of falling back that do not constitute cross-language transfer.

specialized, abstract, and literary. This shift presents a particular challenge to students for whom English is a second language.

Studies of cross-language relationships in vocabulary knowledge have employed both quantitative and qualitative methodology and fall into three categories. Several studies have focused on measuring the extent to which students recognize structural and semantic overlap in first- and second-language cognates (i.e., words with common etymological roots and similar forms and meanings). These studies (García, 1991, 1998; Hancin-Bhatt & Nagy, 1994; James & Klein, 1994; Jiménez, García, & Pearson, 1996; Nagy, García, Durgunoglu, & Hancin-Bhatt, 1993; Saville-Troike, 1984) are discussed in the first subsection. A second group of studies have compared the nature of the vocabulary produced by students in their first and second languages on a number of indexes of lexical sophistication and complexity, a focus typically found in studies with writing outcomes. These studies (Davis, Carlisle, & Beeman, 1999; Francis, 2000; Lanauze & Snow, 1989) are reviewed in the second subsection. Finally, one study (Nagy, McClure, & Mir, 1997), reviewed in the final subsection, examined the effects of first-language syntactic knowledge on the guesses students make about the meanings of new words encountered in the second language.

Cognate Vocabulary

Seven studies have explored the influence of cognate relationships on students' first- and second-language vocabulary knowledge. Five of the seven involved English-language learners who were first-language speakers of Spanish, ranging in age from Grade 4 to 8; one study looked at English-language learners who spoke a variety of first languages (in Grades 2–6), some of which were non-Indo-European; one considered English–German cognates for students ages 12 and 13 studying English as a foreign language. The question addressed in these studies is: What is the role of first- and second-language cognates in the reading/writing performance of students learning English as a second or foreign language?

In a study that examined the role of English–German cognates in the spelling errors of German 12- to 13-year-old beginning learners of English as a foreign language on a dictation task, James and Klein (1994) found that the students were influenced by cognate relationships. Specifically, the authors describe the frequent use of German spelling conventions in the spelling of English words that are similar in meaning and structure to their German counterparts (e.g., *familie*/family, *habe*/have, *bruder*/brother, *vater*/father, *haus*/house) as an instance of *real word transfer* from German to English. Further, although transfer of this kind apparently facilitated vocabulary comprehension (although this was not the focus of the study) in some cases, in others it resulted in the production of homophonous forms that were not etymologically related (so-called *false friends*), so that, for example, students wrote *fahr* (drive) for English *far* and *ei* (egg) for *I*. The authors speculate that subjects were relying too heavily on similarities in phonological structure between first- and second-language vocabulary terms and not sufficiently on other aspects of words, such as syntactic function, in their representations. This reliance was probably a reflection of the status of these subjects as beginning learners of English.

Interestingly, although English has Germanic roots, historical events such as the Norman Conquest influenced the lexicon to such an extent that 40% of contemporary English vocabulary is estimated to be of Romance origin. In a fascinating instance of ontogeny recapitulating phylogeny, the words associated with more concrete, basic vocabulary are largely Germanic in origin, whereas those associated with more abstract, literary concepts are Latinate. Thus, the cognates recognized by the German-speaking subjects in the James and Klein study are basic terms (simple verbs, kinship terms).

Because Latinate–English cognates are associated with higher level, academic English vocabulary and because such terms are typically used in everyday speech by speakers of Romance languages, it has been hypothesized that the meanings of words that are rarely spoken in English, but are necessary for higher levels of reading comprehension, may be accessible to Spanish speakers through their first language (Hancin-Bhatt & Nagy, 1994). Accordingly, a number of studies have examined cognate knowledge in native-Spanish-speaking English-language learners.

In one such study, Jiménez et al. (1996) used think-aloud protocols to (a) examine the first- and second-language strategic reading processes of eight Latino sixth and seventh graders who had been identified as successful English readers, and (b) compare these processes with those of three Latino students who were less successful readers and three monolingual English-speaking students who were successful readers. All of the Latino students were orally bilingual and biliterate in English and Spanish; 8 of the 11 had received 2 to 4 years of bilingual schooling, but by sixth grade all had transitioned to English-only instruction. The major objective of the study was to explore the question of how biliteracy and bilingualism affect metacognition (this study is examined in more detail in the discussion of strategy use below). With respect to vocabulary, the authors found that the major obstacle to comprehension for both the successful and less successful Latino readers was unknown vocabulary. In contrast, the monolingual English readers did not experience notable difficulty with the vocabulary used in the target texts. More important, the successful Latino readers openly accessed cognate vocabulary when they read, especially in Spanish, their less dominant language. For example, one student inferred the meaning of the Spanish word *cantidades* as follows: "*Cantidades*, that means a lot or like in English…quantities" (p. 103). The less successful readers, in contrast, did not "know how to use their knowledge of Spanish to enhance their comprehension of English text and vice versa" (p. 106).

García (1991) also found vocabulary knowledge to be more of a deterrent to reading comprehension for Spanish-speaking English-language learners than for their monolingual English-speaking counterparts. With a sample of 127 fifth- and sixth-grade students, 51 of whom were bilingual Latino children and 53 monolingual English speakers, she employed quantitative and qualitative methodology to examine factors that influence Spanish-speaking Latino children's reading test performance. Her qualitative analysis of responses given by a subsample of children (12 bilingual, biliterate Latino and 6 monolingual English) to questions asking how they determined their answers to vocabulary questions shed some light on the extent to which children's knowledge of a word in the first language transfers to the second language. She found that the Latino students' comprehension of certain words was adversely affected by the way the word was used in their first language. For example, the English word *advantage* was related by most Latino students to a Spanish word that means "take advantage of" (*aprovecharse de*) and so was not seen as something helpful in the context. Failure to assign meaning accurately to the English form based on its Spanish cognate in this case may have had to do with differences in the structure of the meanings (i.e., the core meaning and its associations) of the word across the two languages. Such knowledge is probably language specific and requires experience and familiarity with the cultural context in which the word is used (Schwanenflugel, Blount, & Lin, 1991). García further found that some readers showed no awareness of cognates, even cognate pairs that have obvious structural parallels in their Spanish and English forms, and so could not exploit this source of information.

García (1998) investigated the cross-language transfer of reading strategies (discussed in more detail later) of four fourth-grade students, all Spanish–English bilinguals who were also literate in both languages. Each student read two expository and two narrative passages in both English and Spanish. Students were free to use English, Spanish, code switch, or code mix during the think-aloud and interview. With respect to the transfer of vocabulary knowledge, García reports that none of the students accessed cognates while reading the expository texts, and only a few with the narrative texts. She suggests that the ability to use cognates may be subject to developmental constraints and/or that explicit instruction in cognate identification is required.

Saville-Troike (1984) conducted a retrospective analysis to explain why a group of children who began their school year with an equal lack of proficiency in English were at different levels of achievement in English-medium instruction by the end of 1 year. The sample included 19 children in Grades 2 through 6 who were native speakers of one of seven languages: Japanese, Korean, Hebrew, Arabic, Spanish, Icelandic, or Polish. Criteria for subject selection were (a) very little or no prior exposure to English, (b) coming from a well-educated family, and (3) initial literacy in the native language. The principal finding from this study is relevant to the question of the relationship between the level of second-language oral language proficiency (including vocabulary knowledge) and reading comprehension (addressed in previous chapters in Part I). With respect to the influence of first-language vocabulary knowledge on second-language vocabulary, Saville-Troike identified transfer in the strategies the students used to determine the meanings of unknown words. Specifically, in an analysis of different types of errors made on multiple-choice vocabulary tests, she observed that speakers of Western European languages selected alternatives with a stem similar to that of the target word. In other words, they searched for cognates. In contrast, Japanese children were more likely to choose an alternative that had the same sequence of two or more letters in any position within the word, including the end of a syllable or a suffix. The author speculates that the Japanese first-language students employed "a strategy which may be similar to conducting a visual search for a common 'radical' in a Chinese character" (p. 214). Because letter sequences in these positions do not provide the same kind of clue to the meaning of a word as is found in the stem, these findings suggest that speakers of closely related languages have a tool at their disposal not available to students whose first language is typologically distant from the target language.

Cognate awareness and its relationship to reading comprehension was the focus of an important study by Nagy et al. (1993). Within a sample of 74 Spanish–English bilingual, biliterate fourth, fifth, and sixth graders from two predominantly Hispanic urban elementary schools, the authors sought to determine (a) whether there was any relationship between students' knowledge of words and concepts in Spanish and their understanding of vocabulary in an English text, and (b) whether lexical transfer (if it occurred) was mediated by students' ability to recognize cognates.

Students read four expository texts at the Grade 4 level that contained numerous clear Spanish–English cognates. Comprehension of the passages was assessed through a multiple-choice test, which included 34 target cognates from the passages. Students demonstrated their level of cognate awareness through a cognate-circling task in which they were given a copy of the four experimental passages and asked (after being given a brief explanation of what a cognate is) to circle all the cognates they found.

Students' performance on the English multiple-choice test was found to be significantly related to reported knowledge of the word in Spanish, when reported English word knowledge was controlled for. The authors interpret this finding as a reflection of transfer of Spanish lexical knowledge to reading in English. Moreover, analyses revealed an interaction between Spanish vocabulary knowledge and recognition of cognates, such that performance on the English multiple-choice items was highest in those cases where the student both knew the word in Spanish and recognized the English cognate. They found further that there was considerable variability in cognate usage, with few students using all possible cognates in the texts. The data also revealed that cognate recognition depended on the degree of orthographic overlap between cognate pairs, with greater congruence being associated with higher recognition.

One aspect of word knowledge involves knowing a word's derivational possibilities or, more generally, its morphological structure. Indeed, for first-language speakers of English, the rapid vocabulary growth observed in elementary school children may result from an ability to analyze the structural components of words, so that, for example, "students who have learned the meaning of 'observe' may be able to understand 'observable,' 'unobservable' and 'observation' by analyzing constituent morphemes and combining them in a generative process" (White, Power, & White, 1989, p. 285). Further, the ability to perform such analyses, or engage in *morphological problem solving*, is thought to increase with age (Anglin, 1993).

Only one study in this corpus investigated cross-language morphological knowledge.[12] Hancin-Bhatt and Nagy (1994) hypothesized that, because there exist systematic relationships between Spanish and English derivational and inflectional suffixes—as in, for example, the regular correspondences between the English {ity}, {ing}, and {ly} and Spanish {idad}, {a/endo}, and {mente}, respectively—students' knowledge of these parallels can facilitate vocabulary development. They investigated the development of Latino children's knowledge of morphology between Grades 4 and 8, as well as the extent to which they used morphological knowledge in cognate recognition. All subjects were bilingual

---

[12]Saville-Troike (1984) did investigate transfer at the level of morphology, but through oral language measures.

and biliterate in Spanish and English. To determine whether the students were aware of the systematic relationships between Spanish and English suffixes, they were asked to provide the Spanish translation of a list of English words. The list contained English cognates and noncognates and included words of both types that had derivational and inflectional suffixes, including stems and derivatives (*facile–facility*) and stems plus inflected forms (*short–shortly*). The students were better at recognizing cognate stems in suffixed words (e.g., *amicable–amicably*) than noncognate stems in suffixed words (e.g., *short–shortly*), "suggesting that, in closely related languages such as Spanish and English, cross-language transfer may play a role, not just in recognizing individual words, but also in the learning of derivational morphology" (p. 289). Further, controlling for Spanish and English vocabulary knowledge, the authors found that the ability to recognize cognates compared with noncognates increased dramatically between the fourth and eighth grades, indicating a developmental trend.

The findings from these studies suggest that transfer of cognate vocabulary from English-language learners' first language to English:

- Can enhance word reading and comprehension of text.
- Is mediated by typological similarity between the first language and English.
- Is influenced by the degree of orthographic overlap between cognate pairs.
- Is influenced by students' ability to discern systematic relationships among suffixes.
- Is mediated by reading proficiency such that it appears to occur at higher but not lower levels of such proficiency.
- Can occur as reverse transfer in that vocabulary concepts and labels acquired in the language of instruction (English) can transfer to the first language.
- May impede comprehension in cases in which meaning associations that exist in one language are erroneously applied to the cognate in the other language.
- Is influenced by learners' cognate awareness, which appears to develop with age.

Without exception, these studies provide evidence for cross-language transfer of cognate vocabulary. At the same time, the studies highlight a number of constraints on the process of accessing and using cognate knowledge. For example, it appears that certain aspects of word knowledge are understood only through experience with English, the second language (García, 1991; James & Klein, 1994), and in conjunction with other sources of information about a word's meaning (James & Klein, 1994). Further, positive transfer of vocabulary knowledge is most likely to occur when it involves languages that are typologically similar (Saville-Troike, 1984). However, even when the first language and English are closely related, vocabulary transfer may not occur if the learners perceive the languages to be distant (Ellis, 1994; García, 1991, 1998; Jiménez et al., 1996; Kellerman, 1977; Nagy et al., 1993). An important criterion for the occurrence of transfer is learners' metalinguistic awareness of cognate relationships (between whole words or parts of words), an awareness that appears to be developmentally mediated (Hancin-Bhatt & Nagy, 1994; Nagy et al., 1993). Finally, cognate transfer appears to be influenced by the degree of orthographic overlap between cognate pairs. In summary, transfer between cognates occurs optimally with closely related first and second languages and in learners possessing high levels of reading proficiency, cognitive flexibility, and metalinguistic awareness.

Complex Vocabulary

In contrast to the cognate studies reviewed earlier, the objective of the studies discussed in this section was not primarily to investigate students' awareness/ use of vocabulary items in the first and second languages that shared cognate status. Rather, the focus of these studies was on measuring the extent to which students' first- and second-language vocabulary use was parallel with respect to measures of lexical complexity and sophistication. Lanauze and Snow (1989) administered a writing task in the first and second languages to students enrolled in Grades 4 and 5 of a bilingual program; the students came from working-class Puerto Rican families and used Spanish as the primary home language. The children were rated by their teachers as good or poor in terms of language proficiency (including oral fluency, aural comprehension, and reading skills) in both languages, resulting in the formation of three groups: children rated as good in both English and Spanish (GG), poor in English but good in Spanish (PG), and poor in both languages (PP). Writing was analyzed with respect to linguistic complexity, semantic content, and linguistic variety. The first two indicators of writing quality are discussed later; it is the measures of linguistic variety—measures of the degree to which children used an enriched vocabulary in their writing samples—that are relevant here.

Measures of linguistic variety included counts of the number of different words/total words, number of different verbs/total words, and number of different colors/total words. Color term frequencies were measured simply because the children used them often, but verb use was analyzed because, as the authors explain, they "are linguistically more complex than nouns and thus better indicators of language sophistication" (p. 327). Cross-linguistic correlations for indexes of linguistic variety were significant only for the PG group. Correlations were positive but low for the GG group and often negative for the PP group. According to the authors, these findings suggest that cross-language transfer of enriched vocabulary in writing occurs with students who are in an early stage of second-language acquisition and have well-developed first-language skills—the PG group. It does not occur for students whose first-language skills are poor (PP) or for those whose first- and second-language skills are both relatively well developed (GG). In the latter, the authors hypothesize, the two systems have become independent of one another.

Francis (2000) analyzed narrative writing samples from 69 third- and fifth-grade students in Mexico. The children were proficient in both Náhuatl, an indigenous language, and Spanish. Because the students received instruction only in Spanish, this study investigated transfer from an official school language to the first language (reverse transfer). With respect to vocabulary, students' use of cognitive verbs in writing samples in both languages was analyzed. As noted previously, verbs are linguistically more complex than nouns, and their use is believed to provide a window into students' application of higher order thought processes. Francis argues further that the use of cognitive verbs (e.g., verbs that indicate internal psychological states, represent counterfactual conditions, and reveal characters' intentions) requires high levels of abstraction and is thus indicative of students' ability to use decontextualized language. In both languages (Náhuatl and Spanish) and at both grade levels, the author found significantly more students using at least one cognitive verb than using no cognitive verbs. Francis also found differences between the two ages groups, with significantly more fifth graders using more cognitive verbs than third graders; this indicates that the use of cognitive verbs in writing is related to cognitive development. According to the author, these results reflect cross-language influences of decontextualized language in the realm of vocabulary.

Reporting on the results of another study that investigated reverse transfer, Davis et al. (1999) argue that when the language of instruction is the second language and students have not yet acquired proficiency in that language, writing skills show significant development first in the second language and later in the first language. The students in this study were first-language Spanish speakers in Grades 1 to 3 receiving literacy instruction in English. Their proficiency levels in both languages are described as "below average in relation to developmental expectations in Spanish and English" (p. 242). The students were asked to write English and Spanish compositions on the topic "The funniest thing that happened to me...." The compositions were scored on a number of aspects of writing development (productivity, spelling, and linguistic complexity). With respect to vocabulary, the number of different words containing seven letters or more was counted, serving as an index of variety and sophistication. In contrast to findings for most aspects of writing development investigated, the authors did not find a cross-language relationship in the use of long words, which they suggest is evidence that vocabulary learning is language specific.

The three studies discussed previously yielded conflicting findings. Whereas Francis (2000) found reverse transfer in the use of verbs of cognition, such that students who used such verbs in the language of instruction also used them in the first language, Lanauze and Snow (1989) found transfer of complex vocabulary use to occur only in students with high first-language and low second-language proficiency. Davis et al. (1999) found no relationship between first- and second-language vocabulary knowledge as measured by long words used.

It is likely that a difference in age among the students accounts for the lack of significant findings in the Davis et al. (1999) study. Lanauze and Snow (1989) and Francis (2000) studied students in Grades 3 to 6, whereas Davis et al. looked at students in Grades 1 to 3. It is possible that the nature of word knowledge in subjects in the latter age group is more basic and concrete, so that the students in the Davis et al. study were not cognitively mature enough to demonstrate the kind of higher order vocabulary knowledge that may transfer across languages.

The discrepant findings of Lanauze and Snow (1989) and Francis (2000), however, cannot be accounted for by age differences among the subjects and have important implications for transfer on a theoretical level. If, as hypothesized by Cummins (1978, 1979), positive transfer implicates common underlying abilities assessed through tasks that measure the use of decontextualized language, then the finding of Lanauze and Snow—that there was no relationship between enriched vocabulary use in the first and second languages—challenges this theory.

Syntactic Aspects of Vocabulary Knowledge

In a study designed to shed light on the process of second-language vocabulary acquisition in English-language learners, Nagy, McClure, and Mir (1997) explored the effects of Spanish–English bilinguals' first-language knowledge of syntax on their ability to guess the meanings of new words in English (the second language). Specifically, the researchers investigated the possibility that hypotheses formed about the meaning of verbs in the second language may be influenced by the relationships between the lexical meanings of verbs and their syntactic behavior in the first language. The subjects in this study were 134 seventh and eighth graders, 41 Spanish–English speakers receiving bilingual instruction in an urban school district, 45 Spanish–English speakers receiving English-only instruction in an urban school, and 48 monolingual seventh graders. Two types of errors (transfer and nontransfer) were compared on a task in which bilinguals and monolinguals used brief English contexts to choose among possible meanings for unfamiliar verbs. Transfer errors, which were answers consistent with Spanish verb argument structure, were positively correlated with reading proficiency in Spanish and unrelated to reading proficiency in English, whereas nontransfer errors, which were inconsistent with the syntax of both languages, were found to be negatively correlated with reading proficiency in both Spanish and English. First-language syntactic knowledge was thus found to influence guesses about the meanings of unfamiliar words in a second-language context. Further, the rate of transfer errors remained constant across levels of English reading proficiency, suggesting that this specific type of transfer may persist even at high levels of second-language proficiency.

Summary

In the aggregate, the results of studies on the transfer of vocabulary knowledge (with the exception of Davis et al., 1999) suggest that aspects of word knowledge transfer across languages. In the process of inferring meaning for unknown words, transfer may be negative, as when meaning is erroneously assigned to words based on the influence of first-language syntax (Nagy et al., 1997) or the meaning associations of cognates are not differentiated in the two languages (García, 1991). Such cases of negative transfer are thought to be language dependent and may be resolved through exposure to the second language, but may persist even as students become more proficient in the second language (Nagy et al., 1997). Positive transfer has also been shown to occur at the word level in cognate recognition, mediated by developmental factors and the typological or perceived distance between the first and second languages.

READING COMPREHENSION

Current views of reading conceptualize literacy as a process in which reader and text interact to construct meaning (Adams, 1990; Perfetti, 1985).

Accordingly, effective reading involves the coordination of both lower level processes (such as word identification, discussed earlier) and higher level cognitive processes, including concept activation, encoding of meaning into propositions, activation of prior knowledge,[13] and comprehension monitoring (Frederiksen, 1980; Perfetti, 1988). A key consideration in the study of transfer in bilingual reading comprehension in children is the first-language literacy proficiency of the students. Whereas investigations of transfer in oral domains of language proficiency can generally assume that students have acquired competence in the first language, the acquisition of reading requires considerably more effort and instruction. As a result, the first-language reading proficiency of language-minority students has been found to vary widely in studies that investigate literacy (Hornberger, 1989). A second important consideration in the study of bilingual reading acquisition is the oral proficiency of the students in the second language. In monolingual readers literacy is typically built on a strong oral language base, whereas this is often not the case for students studying English as a second/foreign language.

Thus, two central questions have been addressed by studies in this category. The first is whether the level of reading comprehension ability in the first language is correlated with or predicts reading comprehension ability in the second language (or vice versa). All studies in this set tested this hypothesis; three of them were conducted within the framework of Cummins' interdependence hypothesis. The second question is the mediating role of oral proficiency in the second language, with the assumption that insufficient second-language oral proficiency may prevent a student from effectively employing processes and strategies associated with accurate reading comprehension (Cummins' threshold hypothesis). Of the eight studies reviewed here, two tested the threshold hypothesis among middle- and high school students of English as a foreign language (Lee & Schallert, 1997; Schoonen, Hulstijn, & Bossers, 1998), and three longitudinal studies investigated the validity of the interdependence hypothesis among language-minority students in elementary school (Royer & Carlo, 1991; Verhoeven, 1994) and elementary and middle school (Reese, Garnier, Gallimore, & Goldenberg, 2000). One study examined cross-lingual transfer in third and fifth graders speaking an indigenous first language (Francis, 2000), and one study investigated relationships between first- and second-language reading comprehension ability in Spanish-speaking English-language learners at the middle-school level (Nagy, McClure, & Mir, 1997). Finally, one study examined children's understanding of narrative fables in Spanish and English (Goldman, Reyes, & Varnhagen, 1984).

Lee and Schallert (1997) examined the contribution of second-language proficiency and first-language reading ability to second-language comprehension in a study based on the threshold hypothesis of language proficiency (Cummins, 1979). They administered tests of English oral language proficiency (assessed through vocabulary knowledge and grammaticality judgments) and

---

[13]The important role of prior knowledge in reading comprehension is well established. One relevant aspect of prior knowledge for bilingual children is the extent to which cultural knowledge influences reading comprehension. No study meeting the acceptance criteria of our group has investigated this question. See chapter 11 for a discussion of cultural factors influencing reading comprehension.

English and Korean reading comprehension to a sample of 809 Korean 9th- and 10th-grade students learning English as a foreign language. The results of this study indicate that English language proficiency was a stronger predictor of English reading comprehension than was Korean reading comprehension. Consistent with the threshold hypothesis, the authors found a weak relationship between first- and second-language reading comprehension performance for students at low levels of second-language proficiency and a positive relationship for students whose oral English was more proficient. Thus, for students with high levels of second-language oral proficiency, reading ability in the second language appeared to be a function of both second-language proficiency and first-language reading ability, whereas for students with lower proficiency, transfer of first-language literacy skills was short-circuited by limited second-language proficiency.

Schoonen et al. (1998) obtained similar results in their study of the transfer of reading skills among students studying English as a foreign language. The subjects in this case were 274 native-Dutch-speaking students in Grades 8 and 10 who were in their third and fifth year of learning English as a foreign language, respectively.[14] The authors sought to determine the relative predictive power of (a) a language-specific factor (as assessed by second-language vocabulary knowledge), and (b) a language-independent factor representing an underlying reading ability (as assessed by metacognitive strategy use) in second-language reading comprehension performance. Further, the study included subjects at varying levels of second-language proficiency to test for interactions in the relationship between first- and second-language reading and second-language vocabulary knowledge/second-language reading.

Vocabulary knowledge was assessed by means of a Dutch–English translation task. Metacognition was assessed in the first language by using a questionnaire. Reading comprehension was measured in Dutch and English by means of standardized, multiple-choice tests. Results of analyses of covariance (ANCOVA) showed that first- and second-language reading comprehension performance correlated significantly for both Grade 8 students (.61) and Grade 10 students (.62). These correlations dropped substantially when first- and second-language vocabulary knowledge was partialed out (to .07 and .21, respectively) and when metacognitve knowledge was controlled for (.10 and .07, respectively). Thus, the correlation between first- and second-language reading comprehension ability was explained by both vocabulary and metacognitive knowledge, but second-language vocabulary knowledge was much more important in predicting second-language reading comprehension in Grade 8 than in Grade 10, whereas metacognition made a greater contribution in Grade 10 than in Grade 8. The students in Grade 8, having had 2 years of instruction in English as a foreign language, were apparently below the threshold that would have permitted a greater transfer of metacognitive reading strategies.

In another test of Cummins' interdependence hypothesis, Royer and Carlo (1991) assessed the listening and reading comprehension skills of students

---

[14]The sample included students in Grade 6 as well, but they were not considered in addressing the research question related to transfer and were not administered all the assessments of interest in the present discussion.

enrolled in a transitional bilingual education program in which the majority of language instruction was delivered in Spanish, the students' first language. Specifically, oral and written versions of the sentence verification technique (SVT) were administered on three occasions (Times 1, 2, and 3) over a 17-month period. Analyses of these data involved examining which Time 1 scores—those for reading or listening comprehension—predicted Time 3 English reading comprehension scores. Results indicate that Time 1 Spanish reading comprehension scores were the best predictor of English Time 3 scores. The authors argue that because reading skills but not listening skills were correlated across languages, this study provides evidence that transfer occurs at the level of cognitive academic language proficiency (i.e., the transfer of educational skills or strategies) and not at the level of general language ability. A second significant predictor of second-language reading comprehension was second-language listening skills.

In a similar vein, Reese et al. (2000) conducted a longitudinal study of emergent literacy factors and the extent to which they predict later reading proficiency among bilingual populations. They followed 66 Spanish-speaking kindergartners through Grade 7. Most of the children were enrolled in transitional bilingual programs and transitioned at varying rates, depending on their English-language proficiency, during the 8 years. By seventh grade, all were enrolled in English instruction. In kindergarten, the children were administered measures of early literacy development in Spanish, including tests of letter identification, word reading, writing, and concepts about print. Shortly after entering school, they were also administered tests of English oral proficiency—either the Bilingual Syntax Measure (BSM) or the IDEA Proficiency Test. English reading achievement in Grade 7 was predicted by both English-language proficiency (.48, $p < .01$) and kindergarten literacy scores (.47, $p < .01$). The data reveal the following pattern: The children who performed better on the Spanish literacy measures in kindergarten were also better at maintaining grade-level Spanish reading (as assessed by yearly tests), were the earliest to transition to English reading instruction, and achieved a higher level of English reading in middle school. The authors suggest that these findings highlight the interdependence of first- and second-language oral language proficiencies, and that the early first-language literacy–later second-language literacy relationship, in particular, provides support for theories that underpin bilingual education (Cummins, 1981).

Verhoeven (1994) also aimed to find empirical evidence for the linguistic interdependence hypothesis in a longitudinal study of the language and literacy skill development of 6-year-old Turkish children learning Dutch as a second language. The sample included Turkish first-language students who were receiving initial literacy instruction in Turkish and Turkish first-language students who were first learning to read in Dutch, so that the possibility of bidirectional transfer could be explored. The degree of interdependence between first- and second-language skills varied according to linguistic level. There was limited transfer at the level of vocabulary and syntax, whereas there was strong transfer for reading efficiency (as measured by a word reading task) and reading comprehension abilities (as assessed by tasks measuring coherence comprehension, anaphora comprehension, reading comprehension in Dutch, and coherence comprehension in Turkish). Further, the transfer relationship was bidirectional, so that reading efficiency and comprehension skills initially acquired in Turkish transferred to Dutch and vice versa. According to the author, the interdependence of decontextualized, highly abstract literacy skills is in accordance with Cummins' theoretical framework.

Francis (2000) investigated the reading and writing performances of bilingual children in Mexico who were equally proficient speakers of an indigenous language, Náhuatl, and Spanish. The children were third and fifth graders receiving reading and writing instruction almost exclusively in Spanish. Although the focus of this study was writing, the author did administer a cloze comprehension assessment in each language as well. A significant correlation was found between performance on the Spanish and Náhuatl versions of the tests ($r = .45$, $p < .001$). Thus, in general, children who performed better on the Spanish cloze test also performed better on the Náhuatl cloze test.

Nagy et al. (1997) obtained similar results in their study of syntactic transfer in Spanish–English English-language learners. The correlation between reading proficiency measures in Spanish (the first language) and English (the second language) among a sample of bilingual seventh and eighth graders was .69 ($p < .01$). This strong relationship provides evidence, the authors argue, for the view that some components of reading are language independent, so that knowledge gained in a first language transfers to reading in the second language.

Finally, one study examined cross-language reading comprehension within a specific genre: narrative fables. Goldman, Reyes, and Varnhagen (1984) studied 32 Spanish–English bilingual subjects in Grades 4 to 6 who had begun reading in Spanish and most of whom were at grade level in Spanish, their first language.[15] The 12 fourth graders were orally proficient in both languages and had been reading in English for 1 year. Eight of the 20 sixth graders were classified as limited English proficient and had been reading in English for 1 year; the remaining 12 sixth graders were reading at grade level in English. The students read four fables—two in Spanish and two in English. Outcomes were quality of recall (an index of the literal level of comprehension), answering "why questions" (an index of the inferential level of comprehension), and answering a "lesson question" or providing the moral of the fable (an index of the ability to think abstractly and generalize).

Students were able to respond to both the Spanish and English texts in whichever language they chose. The researchers found that for the students who were orally proficient in English and Spanish, comprehension performance levels in the first language were positively correlated with performance in the second language, although for the recall measure, the correlation did not reach significance. For the group of students classified as limited English proficient, it was hypothesized that if no transfer from the first to the second language occurred, these students' English performance would mirror that of bilingual children in Grades 1 and 2[16] (who had had a comparable amount of

---

[15]This study included four separate experiments involving children in Grades K to 6 who either listened to or read the fables, depending on age and proficiency in the target language. Because we required written language outcomes for studies reviewed in this section, only those students who read the fables are discussed.

English instruction), and that if transfer did occur, the students' comprehension of English fables would be consistent with the level of comprehension they displayed in Spanish. The authors found the second hypothesis to be true, demonstrating, they argue, first- to second-language transfer of knowledge of content and structure despite limited second-language proficiency. More specifically, once basic orthographic parsing and coding skills were in place, the children were able to demonstrate comprehension of fables in the second language. Similar trends were reported for the why and lesson questions.

In summary, all these studies provide evidence for the cross-language transfer of reading comprehension ability in bilinguals. This relationship holds (a) across typologically different languages (Korean and English; Lee & Schallert, 1997; and Dutch and Turkish; Verhoeven, 1994); (b) for children in elementary, middle, and high school; (c) for learners of English as a foreign language and English as a second language; (d) over time (Reese et al., 2000; Royer & Carlo, 1991; Verhoeven, 1994); (e) from both first to second language and second to first language (Francis, 2000; Verhoeven, 1994); and (f) within a specific genre (Goldman et al., 1984).

With respect to the influence of level of second-language proficiency, these studies present conflicting findings. The two studies involving students of English as a foreign language demonstrated that transfer of reading comprehension is mediated by proficiency in the second language, such that students with insufficient proficiency in the second language do not demonstrate transfer of first-language literacy comprehension skills (Lee & Schallert, 1997) or exhibit a pattern of transfer in which the power of first-language reading ability to predict second-language reading performance increases with proficiency in the second language (Schoonen et al., 1998). However, the English-language learners in the Goldman et al. (1984) study demonstrated comprehension of English text that was comparable to their understanding of first-language texts despite limited English proficiency. The difference in these findings can probably be attributed to differences in tasks: Unlike the students of English as a foreign language, those in the Goldman et al. (1984) study could demonstrate understanding of second-language texts through their first language. A second reason for the conflicting findings may have to do with text genre. It has been established that recall of story content is facilitated by an awareness of text structure (National Institute of Child Health and Human Development, 2000), so that familiarity with the fable genre may account for important variance in the second-language comprehension displayed by the subjects.

Finally, the Royer and Carlo (1991) finding that reading skills, but not listening skills (a measure of general language ability), correlate across the first and second languages provides some evidence countering the notion that a positive correlation between first- and second-language reading comprehension can be accounted for by language-independent capacities that make some children better language learners, demonstrating that transfer occurs at the level of academic proficiency. Further, although not specifically examining the threshold hypothesis, Royer and Carlo also found proficiency in the second language (as measured by listening comprehension) to be a significant predictor of second-language reading comprehension. These findings were corroborated by Reese et al. (2000).

---

[16]See Note 15 regarding the inclusion in this study of children in Grades K to 6.

READING STRATEGIES

There is a substantial body of evidence from studies of monolinguals suggesting that reading comprehension is enhanced by the use of comprehension strategies (National Institute of Child Health and Human Development, 2000). According to Baker and Brown (1984), skilled readers possess an enhanced awareness of the reading process and knowledge of themselves as learners and thinkers. Strategy use may be cognitive (i.e., strategies that help solve a problem directly) or metacognitive (strategies that monitor the effectiveness of the selected cognitive strategy; Schoonen et al., 1998). An alternative way of conceptualizing metacognition stems from the information-processing model of cognition proposed by Paris, Lipson, and Wixson (1983), in which a distinction is made between two types of knowledge used in reading: declarative and procedural. *Declarative knowledge* can be described as "knowing that" and includes knowledge of facts, rules, theories, passages, and so on, whereas *procedural knowledge* is "knowing how" and is demonstrated during the performance of a task.

The central question addressed in the studies reviewed here is whether the use of cognitive and metacognitive strategies in one language is also observed in the other language. Consistent with studies of transfer in several of the literacy components discussed in this chapter, some studies on strategy use have also aimed to determine whether strategic reading in the second language depends crucially on students' level of proficiency in that language or whether higher level strategies acquired in the first language are available to support second-language reading, regardless of proficiency in the second language.

Strategic reading has been investigated in six studies. Five of these studies looked at transfer between Spanish and English in Grades 3 through 7. One study examined transfer in native-Dutch-speaking 6th, 7th, and 10th graders learning English as a foreign language. Strategy use was generally assessed by the use of (a) checklists or surveys in which students indicated or reported strategies they used while reading in their two languages (Calero-Breckheimer & Goetz, 1993; Schoonen et al., 1998), or (b) think-aloud protocols (García, 1998; Jiménez et al., 1996). It should be noted at the outset that both of these methods of measuring strategy use have been criticized. Self-report data collected in first-language reading studies have revealed inconsistencies between what children—especially younger (Carrell, 1989) but also older children (Phifer & Glover, 1982)—say they do while reading and what they actually do. Think-alouds, in contrast, permit a more direct investigation of the strategic reasoning processes employed in reading and are designed to reveal the extent to which students' declarative and procedural knowledge converge. However, some researchers have expressed concerns about subjects' (particularly younger children's) ability to describe the processes they perform, as well as the possibility that reporting disrupts the comprehension process (Afflerbach & Johnston, 1984; Jacobs & Paris, 1987).

Calero-Breckheimer and Goetz (1993) found transfer of strategies across Spanish and English. Their sample consisted of 26 Hispanic third and fourth graders. The students were bilingual and biliterate in English and Spanish and had participated in a bilingual program for at least 2 years. The students read English and Spanish versions of two stories, one each at the second- and third-grade levels. Strategy use was assessed through an interview (the experimenter asked the children what kinds of strategies they had used to comprehend the text) and the completion of a strategy-use checklist. The authors found that students tended to report the same number and type of strategies whether reading in Spanish or English: The correlations among the frequencies of different strategies reported in the two languages were .85 and .89 for the interview and checklist, respectively.

At the middle-school level, Jiménez et al. (1996) found that more successful Spanish–English bilingual students used a range of reading strategies, of which a few were identified as unique to bilinguals. The researchers employed think-aloud protocols and retellings to describe and compare the strategic reading processes of 11 bilingual (comprising both successful and less successful readers of English and all orally fluent in English) and 3 successful monolingual sixth and seventh graders. All students read both expository and narrative passages. The researchers found that the successful bilingual readers did not differ substantially from the successful monolingual readers in that both groups invoked prior knowledge, made inferences, and monitored comprehension. In contrast, the strategy use of the less successful bilingual readers was both less varied and less sophisticated. In comparison with the less successful bilingual group, the successful bilingual readers possessed a greater awareness of the relationship between Spanish and English, as revealed through (a) the use of strategies that were uniquely bilingual (searching for cognates, translating), and (b) comments made by the students revealing their explicit awareness that strategies such as questioning, rereading, evaluation, and "the notion that reading must make sense" (p. 103) applied to both languages. Further, in contrast to the less successful bilingual group, the more successful bilingual readers saw reading in English and Spanish as essentially the same activity; they had a unitary view of reading. In declarative terms, the less successful Latino readers (a) viewed bilingualism as more damaging than did the successful group, (b) saw their knowledge of the first language as a source of confusion in reading English, and (c) believed that the two languages were dissimilar, so that knowledge of one was not helpful in reading the other. In procedural terms, they did not practice the bilingual strategies.

García (1998) used think-aloud protocols to investigate the cross-language transfer of metacognitive reading strategies and the influence of genre on the reading performance of four Spanish–English bilingual students in Grade 4. All students had been educated from kindergarten through at least Grade 3 in a transitional bilingual education program and were stronger readers in Spanish than in English. The students' oral proficiency scores on the English Language Assessment scales were between 5 and 4. Each student read an expository and a narrative passage in each language. Students were free to use English, Spanish, code switch, or code mix during the think-aloud and interview. García found the cross-language transfer of strategy use difficult to discern because it was affected by text genre, text difficulty, and the students' language dominance and reading ability. Nevertheless, she found that students who exhibited better reading comprehension in Spanish were also better at comprehending English text and that the better readers used more varied strategies, providing evidence for the transfer of reading expertise across languages. Finally, like Jiménez et al.

(1996), García identified a number of bilingual strategies that involve the use of both languages simultaneously: code switching, code mixing, and translation. Translation was of particular interest because its effectiveness depended on the form it took. Whereas direct or word-for-word translation was not an effective aid to comprehension, paraphrased translating, in which students put the translation in their own words, was.

In a study of the transfer of decontextualized language skills, Langer, Bartolome, Vásquez, and Lucas (1990) investigated the meaning-making strategies of 12 fifth-grade students of Mexican heritage. The students were bilingual in English and Spanish and had at least a minimal amount of literacy in both languages. Meaning-making ability was operationalized by Langer and colleagues as comprising the following: (a) envisionment building (the ability to create a representation of the text and modify it as new information is encountered), (b) the ability to hypothesize (e.g., predict), (c) understanding of text language (Spanish or English), and (d) familiarity with the characteristics of genres (i.e., narrative vs. report). The students read four passages at the fourth-grade level (two in English, two in Spanish) in two genres—story and report. For each text, students answered questions to tap envisionment, addressing (a) and decontextualized[17] probing questions designed to gather information about students' knowledge and strategies beyond what was learned from the envisionment questions, addressing (b) to (d). In addition, students participated in oral and written recall tasks designed for each passage. Finally, the students' oral responses provided a basis for English-language proficiency ratings: Students were rated on a scale from 1 (*can speak almost no English*) to 5 (*can speak English fluently*).

Several levels of inquiry in this study provided the opportunity for students to demonstrate meta-abilities in their responses to questions (about text content or vocabulary items) that were relatively more decontextualized. The ability to answer the more decontextualized questions was characteristic of high envisionment scores for students across languages, independent of proficiency in the language. In other words, even for students with limited second-language linguistic knowledge, the use of good meaning-making strategies was the strongest predictor of how well they understood and remembered texts in both languages. The use of good meaning-making strategies also correlated positively with performance on English standardized reading tests ($r = .79, p < .01$). The authors conclude: "These findings support Cummins' (1984) interdependence principle that a 'common underlying proficiency' makes the transfer of literacy skills possible across languages" (p. 463).

Hernández (1991) measured the comprehension of seventh-grade students with both English and Spanish texts. The sample included seven Spanish-speaking, non-English-proficient students attending summer school prior to seventh grade. All the students had resided in the United States for less than 19 months. They were at grade level in their Spanish reading, but could not decode in English. The students received comprehension strategy instruction in Spanish through a modified reciprocal teaching approach. Specifically, they were

---

[17]These questions "required students to objectify and discuss the texts, past experiences, and their knowledge of language" (Langer et al., 1990, p. 437).

reminded of the purpose of reading and taught the strategies of question generating, summarizing, and predicting. Through pre- and posttest designs (using identical pre- and posttest measures, a potential flaw in the design), the author found that the use of the taught strategies significantly improved the students' comprehension of Spanish texts. In addition to the pre- and postmeasures, students were prompted to demonstrate the use of comprehension strategies by the researcher-teacher. Students' verbalizations during these strategy-use sessions were transcribed, and the data were analyzed to identify the application of particular strategies in each language.

With respect to transfer, Hernández reports that the students demonstrated the use of all strategies taught in their efforts to comprehend English first-grade-level texts: "There was basically no difference in the way the students demonstrated use of the strategies during this session and during the daily instructional sessions that occurred with Spanish text" (p. 102). This statement is contradicted by the finding that, although the students' understanding of a Grade 4-level Spanish text improved with strategy instruction, the strategies were applied in English in the absence of text comprehension. Further, students' verbal protocols revealed that they relied heavily on illustrations accompanying the second-language text instead of the text. Thus, according to the author, the students displayed "text-independent" strategy use and "strategy use without comprehension" (p. 103). One might question whether the application of strategies learned in the first language to pictures rather than to second-language text, which has little effect on story comprehension, constitutes a genuine transfer of strategy use. These results may illustrate that high-level skills, such as metacognitive strategy use, are not language bound. However, transfer from a first to a second language has a pragmatic component as well (facilitation or interference), so that a demonstration of positive transfer would imply a transfer of comprehension ability. Thus, this study does not demonstrate transfer in strategy use.

In stark contrast to the Hernández study, Schoonen et al. (1998) found that a threshold second-language linguistic knowledge was necessary for the cross-language transfer of metacognitive skills to occur. Within a sample of 488 native-Dutch-speaking students in Grades 6, 8, and 10, the researchers sought to determine the relative role of vocabulary knowledge and metacognitive ability in first- and second-language (English) reading comprehension.[18] Metacognition was assessed in the first language by using a questionnaire in which students rated themselves on a 4-point scale with respect to (a) assessment of themselves as readers, (b) knowledge of reading goals and comprehension criteria, (c) knowledge of text characteristics, and (d) knowledge of reading strategies. Findings indicate that, compared with vocabulary knowledge, metacognitive knowledge was not a significant predictor of first-language reading ability for students in Grade 6, whereas for students in Grades 8 and 10, both metacognition and vocabulary were important predictors. The authors conclude that the Grade 6 students had not yet acquired metacognitive knowledge of reading, suggesting that such skills are developmental. In

---

[18]Only students in Grades 8 and 10 were included in cross-lingual analyses.

foreign-language reading, both vocabulary knowledge and metacognition predicted performance, although the influence of metacognition increased in Grade 10. These results suggest that (a) the ability to read strategically may follow a developmental trajectory, and (b) transfer of this ability is mediated by vocabulary knowledge in the second language.

In summary, with the exception of Hernández (1991), all the studies reviewed previously provide evidence supporting the notion that bilingual children who read strategically in one language also do so in their other language. Further, the extent of strategy use in students' reading correlates positively with reading performance. The two studies that investigated first- and second-language strategic reading processes in students not proficient in the second language yielded conflicting findings. Langer et al. (1990) found that it was the use of good meaning-making strategies, and not the degree of second-language proficiency, that distinguished better from poorer readers. In contrast, Schoonen et al. (1998) found a greater influence of metacognition on second-language reading performance at higher levels of second-language proficiency and a language proficiency threshold below which no application of strategy use occurred.

Studies employing think-aloud protocols provide valuable insights into the cross-language functioning of reading strategies. Indeed, findings from Jiménez et al. (1996) and García (1998) offer a window into the interrelated lexical systems operating in bilinguals. The identification of uniquely bilingual strategies (such as cognate recognition) in these two studies illustrates ways in which the interaction of two languages in a bilingual can give rise to strategies that are available in neither the first nor the second language, but are part of an autonomous system with its own internal organizing principles.

Interestingly, none of Calero-Breckheimer and Goetz's (1993) subjects identified strategies that can be described as unique to bilinguals. This is perhaps a result of the younger ages of their subjects (Grades 3 and 4) or the manner in which strategy use was assessed. The subjects in the Jiménez et al. (1996) and García (1998) studies demonstrated strategy use in both procedural and declarative terms through think-alouds, whereas those in the Calero-Breckheimer and Goetz study were given an opportunity to demonstrate only declarative or conscious knowledge of strategies they used in reading. It is possible that explicit knowledge about oneself as a reader is influenced by development (as Schoonen et al. [1998] found for sixth-grade students of English as a foreign language).

Alternatively, it may be that an individual's development of bilingual strategies requires a minimal level of metalinguistic knowledge—an awareness of the structural and lexical similarities and differences between the two languages. Increased metalinguistic awareness distinguished better from poorer readers in the Jiménez et al. (1996) study, such that the better readers recognized and exploited similarities between English and Spanish; the poorer readers, in contrast, viewed their two languages as more dissimilar than alike. This result again suggests that it is not just typological similarity as defined by linguists that predicts transfer of literacy components, but also the psychological or perceived distance on the part of the learners.

WRITING SKILLS

Current models of literacy view reading and writing as two facets of a single process that emerge simultaneously in literacy development. In general, writing involves generating products with attention to (a) mechanics (e.g., the use of capitalization and punctuation), (b) purpose and audience, and (c) genre (narrative or expository). Narrative writing elements include story structure (setting, characters, and plot), whereas in expository writing more attention is paid to the central purpose and organization of the piece (Lipson & Wixson, 1991).

Like reading, writing is often, although not always, a decontextualized language activity and thus a potentially fruitful medium for the investigation of cross-language relationships within academically mediated language skills. The development of competence in discourse, for example, involves mastering grammatical structures (e.g., knowing how to use discourse connectors to establish coherence in a text), which are not required in contextualized language activities.

Four studies have focused on the relationship between writing ability in the first and second languages. All involved language-minority children acquiring a societally dominant language. In three of the studies, the second language was English; in one, it was Spanish. The studies investigated writing performance in children across Grades 1 to 6.

In a qualitative study of emergent writing, Edelsky (1982) analyzed the writing samples of nine native-Spanish-speaking children in Grades 1 to 3 who were in a bilingual program and had varying levels of proficiency in English. Edelsky characterizes the process of writing as "the orchestration of multiple cuing systems (graphic, graphophonic, syntactic, semantic, pragmatic)" (p. 214) and argues that a learner's ability to coordinate these systems in the first language can help the second-language learner to manipulate and make sense of the second-language's writing system. General principles found to apply across languages include directionality of print, the strategies used to end a composition or increase its length, and the knowledge that text is contextually constrained (e.g., code switching occurred much more frequently in oral discourse than in the children's compositions). Instances of what might be called *interference* (see the discussion of the same study in the prior section on spelling) are attributed to an interaction between the second-language proficiency of the writer and language-specific characteristics of the two writing systems involved.

In a study by Lanauze and Snow (1989), limited second-language proficiency did not limit the ability of writers proficient in the first language to transfer those abilities to the second language. The authors analyzed the narrative writing samples of Spanish-speaking fourth- and fifth-grade English-language learners in a bilingual program. They found that of three categories of features—(a) linguistic complexity (as assessed by number of words, number of *t* units, mean length of *t* units, etc.), (b) linguistic variety (as assessed by variety and frequency of use of verbs and color terms, discussed earlier), and (c) semantic content (reflected in the number of color words used and the distribution of *t* units into general description, specific description, positional statement, and action statement)—only the linguistic variety scores showed significant cross-language correlations, and only for students whose Spanish proficiency was good and English proficiency poor (according to teachers' ratings). Students rated either poor or good in both languages did not transfer first-language discourse skills to second-language writing.

This finding, according to the authors, suggests that first-language proficiency is the major determinant of second-language academic writing skills, and therefore challenges Cummins' (1979) prediction of the rapid development of basic interpersonal communicative skills (BICS) relative to cognitive academic language proficiency (CALP) in the second language: "The children in this study who had high levels of performance on academic tasks in Spanish performed relatively well in an assessment of English [cognitive academic language proficiency] while still performing quite poorly in assessments of English [basic interpersonal communicative skills]" (p. 338).

Francis (2000) studied a group of 69 third- and fifth-grade students from four classes enrolled in a bilingual primary school. The majority of the students had age-appropriate conversational proficiency in both Spanish and Náhuatl (the principal indigenous language of the region), as assessed by teacher ratings. Virtually all literacy teaching was conducted in Spanish, so researchers were able to examine the application of literacy skills learned through one language to literacy tasks in another language that children understood, but in which they had not had opportunities to read and write. The students were administered cloze reading tests and a narrative writing task in Náhuatl and Spanish.[19] Scoring of the writing tasks emphasized elements that contributed to overall coherence in story structure (inclusion of reference to problem/theme, sequence, events/details, ending). An analysis of variance (ANOVA) revealed significant group differences in "sense of story structure" in favor of the fifth graders, showing a developmental trend. With respect to cross-lingual relationships, the correlation between sense of story structure scores in Náhuatl and Spanish was significant ($r = .57$, $p < .001$). Although the author concludes that all the study results point to interdependence in literacy competencies—specifically "that bilingual students avail themselves of access to literacy-related [cognitive academic language proficiency] skills when presented with academic language tasks in either language" (p. 184)—he does not invoke the notion of transfer as an explanation. Rather, he reserves the term *transfer* for describing the mechanism responsible for first- and second-language correlations among skills that are language specific. The interrelationships observed in the writing samples of his bilingual subjects, Francis argues, are better accounted for by access to "core competencies tied to text and discourse processing [that] are not stored in either [the first or second language]" (p.189).

Like Francis (2000), Davis et al. (1999) looked at the influence of instruction in the second language on first-language skills in which students had no liter-

---

[19]The students in this study are distinct from others in this corpus with regard to the sociolinguistic context in which they are learning: Náhuatl is an indigenous language that has not been standardized. However, the authors argue that because Spanish and Náhuatl have congruent phonological inventories, the students could effectively use the phoneme–grapheme correspondences they were familiar with through Spanish orthography.

acy experience. Specifically, they examined writing development in Spanish speakers in Grades 1 to 3 receiving literacy instruction in English. The students were asked to write a narrative essay in English and Spanish. Compositions were scored on multiple aspects of writing development (spelling and vocabulary were discussed previously). Discourse elements were evaluated by using a 6-point scale, with a score of 0 given to compositions with no comprehensible text and a score of 6 given to narratives that included elaboration of one or more of character, action, and setting. The authors found that discourse level in English was significantly related to discourse level in Spanish. They further observed significant growth in discourse elements in both Spanish and English between first and second grades. Because comparable growth on most other indexes of writing development (i.e., productivity, linguistic complexity, long words, and spelling) were apparent in the English texts between Grades 1 and 2, but in the Spanish texts between Grades 2 and 3, the lag was interpreted as a transfer of academic skills acquired earlier in the second language to the first language a year later. The simultaneous growth in the first and second languages in the case of discourse suggests, according to the authors, that factors other than school instruction may influence this aspect of writing (e.g., listening to books read in the classroom or being exposed to storytelling at home). This study provides evidence for the transfer of story structure knowledge across languages, although the acquisition of a sense of story structure here is not attributed to instruction (as it is in Francis, 2000).

In summary, the studies reviewed here suggest a number of possibilities about first- and second-language writing relationships. First, for beginning writers, what is known about writing in the first language provides the basis for hypotheses formed in second-language writing (Edelsky, 1982; again, this is not transfer per se, but a falling back on the first language in the absence of second-language knowledge). Second, for young children receiving instruction in the second language exclusively, writing skills may develop first in the second language and subsequently in the first. Third, for older children with varying proficiency in the first and second languages, aspects of writing ability may correlate only for students proficient in the first but not in the second language, suggesting that early in second-language acquisition these children draw on resources available to them in their first language. For older elementary students who are proficient in both languages, these studies present conflicting findings. Lanauze and Snow (1989) found that such students showed no relationship between first- and second-language writing, suggesting that the linguistic systems become independent at more advanced stages of development, whereas Francis (2000) found that writing sophistication and complexity were related in the first and second languages.

Finally, Lanauze and Snow (1989) found that cognitive academic language proficiency in English exceeded basic interpersonal communicative skills in English for the group of children proficient in Spanish but not in English. This may be related to the fact that the children in this study had been in an instructional setting with a significant first-language component, so that the development of academic language proficiency was supported, and they could benefit from instruction that promotes cognitive academic language proficiency skills.

SUMMARY AND CONCLUSIONS

The results of the studies reviewed in this chapter are discussed here with respect to the following research questions. Findings from studies relevant to all six literacy components are discussed with respect to the first and then the second research questions:

1. For what components of literacy is there a relationship between first- and second-language literacy?

   - Under what circumstances is there evidence for cross-language influences that facilitate literacy acquisition in the second language?
   - Under what circumstances does literacy in the first language interfere with second-language literacy?

2. What evidence does this body of studies provide to support or contradict theoretical accounts of transfer?

Question 1

Research question 1 has been addressed across all literacy components; a variety of first languages, ages, and language-status conditions; and in both cross-sectional and longitudinal studies.

Word Reading.   Without exception, the studies measuring word reading outcomes demonstrated that a relationship exists between performance in word and pseudoword reading in one language and performance in the other. This relationship holds across a wide range of ages, from beginning readers in early elementary school (Durgunoglu et al., 1993) to advanced learners in high school (Abu-Rabia, 1997); across normally developing and disabled readers (Abu-Rabia, 1997; Da Fontoura & Siegel, 1995); across language pairs that are structurally close and distant; and across varying levels of second-language proficiency. At the same time, several studies provided evidence that the phonological and visual processes underlying word reading are influenced by the orthography of the first language (Abu-Rabia, 1997; Da Fontoura & Siegel, 1995; Gholamain & Geva, 1999) and thus are language specific.

As for facilitation versus interference, the strong correlations found between first- and second-language word reading performance across studies show that students who are better at word reading in one language are also better at it in the other language. This relationship could be a result of factors specific to reading in the first and second languages, but it could also be attributable to nonlinguistic skills related to general cognition. Indeed, both Gholamain and Geva (1999) and Abu-Rabia (1997) found that cognitive factors (e.g., working memory skills) accounted for significant variance in the first- and second-language reading measures.

With respect to processes used in word reading, positive transfer would imply, from a pragmatic perspective, enhanced second-language development as manifested, for example, by more rapid acquisition of the construct or skill in question than generally occurs in development. Because the relevant studies in this set considered transparent orthographies that promoted a greater reliance on phonological as opposed to visual processing strategies, the question is whether well-developed phonological awareness in the first language speeds up the acquisition of English word reading. Although it is well established that deficits in phonological processing hinder English reading acquisition, English word reading requires both phonological and visual memory skills, the former throughout development and the latter increasingly as development progresses. Thus, to determine whether heavy reliance on the phonological route to processing constitutes facilitation or interference in the long run would require longitudinal studies investigating students at different stages of reading development.

Interference was found at the level of processing in a study designed to compare the processing strategies employed by highly proficient native-Greek-speaking students of English as a foreign language with those used by native speakers of Greek and English. Findings reveal that second-language processing was slower and contained more errors than was the case for the native English readers, attributed by the authors to the transfer of features of first-language processing to the second language. Specifically, the bilingual students processed inflected function words and noun endings that carried inflected affixes to a greater extent than did English monolinguals (but to a lesser extent than monolingual Greek students), revealing, according to the authors, an interlanguage effect at the level of word processing.

Spelling. The two studies that aimed to establish whether spelling knowledge in one language of bilinguals correlates with spelling knowledge in the other yielded discrepant results (Arab-Moghaddam & Sénéchal, 2001; Davis et al., 1999). These discrepant findings may be due to (a) the different nature of the tasks, (b) the direction of transfer investigated (first to second language or the reverse), or (c) differences in the typological distance between the pairs of languages investigated. Most of the remaining studies in this category employed qualitative analyses to identify first-language phonological or orthographic influences on the second-language spelling performance of students at various levels of second-language proficiency. All five of these studies identified first-language influences on second-language spelling and found them to be particularly pronounced at lower levels of second-language proficiency. Thus, the influence of first-language phonological and orthographic knowledge differed at different levels of second-language proficiency, with higher level students producing errors similar to those observed in first-language acquisition, reflecting intralingual rather than interlingual processes.

Regarding facilitation versus interference, although the presence of first-language features in second-language spelling was widely documented across these studies, the authors did not interpret these errors primarily as instances of first- and second-language interference. Most of these studies viewed the acquisition of second-language spelling as a stage in which reliance on the first language early in the process is facilitative because many of the phoneme–grapheme mappings applied in both the first language and English. As mentioned, whether such reliance on the first-language system constitutes transfer or a falling back on first-language knowledge is an open question: Is the speller who makes use of the first language very early in second-language acquisition transferring first-language knowledge in the same way as a speller who persists in making a first-language error after considerable exposure to the second language? The small body of studies reviewed here does not provide conclusive information about the extent to which early second-language confusion arising from first-language phonology/orthography is resolved among learners because no study investigated cross-language influences on the spelling of more advanced learners. The study of transfer in this domain would clearly benefit from longitudinal studies that could disentangle the falling back phenomenon from transfer and clarify the interactions between transfer and second-language staged development.

Vocabulary. The single investigation of lexical development in the first years of elementary school found that, in early vocabulary development, the first- and second-language lexical systems of a child may be independent of each other (Davis et al., 1999).

In samples of older children, relationships were found to exist between languages that are typologically similar (Spanish–English), but among pairs of typologically dissimilar languages, the findings were mixed: The use of verbs of cognition was correlated in speakers of Spanish and Náhuatl, two dissimilar languages (Francis, 2000), but speakers of non-Indo-European languages learning English had more difficulty inferring the meaning of unknown English vocabulary than did speakers of languages closely related to English (Saville-Troike, 1984). Psychotypology, or perceived distance, also played an interesting role in constraining transfer in these studies: Among students with Spanish as their first language, those who did not perceive Spanish and English as being related to one another did not exploit the lexical similarities (cognate relationships) between the two languages. In contrast, the nature of the errors made by those with German as their first language who were beginning students of English as a foreign language suggests that they may have started out assuming that English is closer to German than it is (e.g., *far/fahr*).

Finally, it is possible that the relationship between first- and second-language vocabulary knowledge differs at different levels of first- and second-language proficiency (Lanauze & Snow, 1989). With regard to this question of facilitation versus interference, the series of cognate studies involving students with Spanish as their first language demonstrated that knowledge of Spanish (and presumably other Romance languages) can have a facilitating effect on learning English lexical items that are cognates to Spanish terms. Although several studies revealed that children's ability to discover cognate relationships independently is also mediated by the development of metalinguistic awareness, it is possible that explicit instruction in cognate awareness would allow children to exploit this potentially rich source of knowledge at younger ages— a possibility no study has yet investigated.

Interestingly, the same set of studies demonstrated a minor potential for interference between cognate pairs that overlap only partially or whose meaning associations are different in each language (García, 1991). The study that looked at the role of cognates in native German speakers (James & Klein, 1994) also found facilitation in cases in which students drew on sources of information other than phonological similarities, and found interference in instances of English–German homophones. Another occurrence of lexical interference involved the transfer of Spanish first-language verb argument structure in the process of assigning meaning to English second-language verbs. More important, transfer of this nature occurred at all levels of proficiency.

Reading Comprehension.   Word reading is a discrete language skill typically learned through direct instruction at early stages of second-language acquisition, whereas reading comprehension requires the ability to understand complex written language. Transfer in this domain was conceptualized most frequently as the transfer from one language to the other of higher order competencies learned through decontextualized language use.

Reading comprehension ability in one language was found to correlate significantly with reading comprehension in the other language under most conditions (typological distance, language status, direction of transfer, age of learner, tasks). The single condition for which the studies reviewed yielded conflicting findings concerned the role of second-language proficiency: For high school students of English as a second language, it appears that reading comprehension ability does not transfer below a certain threshold of proficiency in the second language (Lee & Schallert, 1997; Schoonen et al., 1998). However, Goldman et al. (1984) found that for Spanish English-language learners, second-language comprehension of fables mirrored that of the first language regardless of level of second-language proficiency.

On the issue of facilitation versus interference, these studies suggest that reading ability when developed in one language is predictive of reading ability in the other. With the exception of the English-as-a-foreign-language studies, Verhoeven (1994) (a subsample of his students) and Francis (2000), all studies (five) investigated the transfer of reading comprehension abilities in language-minority students whose reading ability had developed through instruction in the first language. Cross-language correlations such as those found in these studies for this population of learners have been widely interpreted as representing the transfer of higher level skills from the first language and language of instruction to the second language, providing support for bilingual education. What cannot be concluded from studies with correlational designs, however, is the extent to which factors unrelated to reading proficiency, such as ability factors, account for the cross-language relationships observed. With the exception of Royer and Carlo (1991), no study controlled for learner variables that make some children better literacy learners than others. Interestingly, no studies investigated transfer for this literacy component in children younger than Grade 3, and all but one study (Francis, 2000) looked at children in Grades 5 through high school. This fact may reflect the notion that the competencies involved in reading comprehension that are subject to transfer are linked to development, and, more specifically, that transfer of lexical skills/knowledge may precede transfer of comprehension skills.

No instances of interference were documented in this domain. That is, in no case was reading ability in one language found to result in the presence of errors or developmental delay in reading performance in the other language.

Reading Strategies.   This is a domain for which the nature of the evidence on transfer differs from that for most other components: The object of investigation—cognitive and metacognitive strategies—is not readily measurable through paper-and-pencil tests. Rather, what children do to aid their comprehension while reading (procedural knowledge) and what children know about the process of reading (declarative knowledge) were assessed across studies through either think-aloud protocols or student self-reports. Findings include both the use of linguistic transfer (as when student verbalizations indicated that a student relied on first- and second-language vocabulary knowledge in cognate recognition) and the extent to which strategic reading was practiced across languages.

As was the case with reading comprehension, most students in this category of study were older elementary or high school students, reflecting the assumption that the capacity for the meta-level abilities involved in strategy use is developmental (Schoonen et al., 1998). With the exception of the Hernández (1991) study, which did not demonstrate that the application of strategies in the second language resulted in comprehension of text, all studies revealed that students who practice strategic reading in their first language do so in their second. Whether the effective application of such strategies in the second language is mediated by second-language proficiency cannot be determined because the two studies investigating cross-language strategy use in students with limited second-language proficiency yielded conflicting results (Langer et al., 1990; Schoonen et al., 1998).

With regard to facilitation versus interference, these studies demonstrated that, all things being equal, skills associated with strategic reading ability developed in one language can be applied in the other. In other words, the skills do not need to be relearned as second-language acquisition proceeds because they are not language specific. This finding suggests, from a pragmatic point of view, that students whose first-language instruction has enabled them to develop strategies that facilitate learning the academic language required for strategic reading will apply them to the second language in a way that may accelerate second-language reading ability (see especially Langer et al., 1990).

A clear instance of facilitation was demonstrated by students' use of bilingual strategies that involved accessing cognate knowledge (García, 1998; Jiménez et al., 1996). No case of interference has been documented.

Writing. As for the question of facilitation versus interference, as in the domain of reading strategies, skills associated with the writing process that are developed in one language appear to be available for application to the other. To that extent, the general results of these studies demonstrate facilitation.[20]

Question 2

The studies reviewed in this chapter were guided by different definitions of transfer: Cross-language transfer of specific linguistic features was investigated within the framework of the contrastive analysis hypothesis in some studies; the majority of studies, however, looked at the transfer of universal/conceptual proficiencies that underlie literacy (Cummins, 1978, 1979, 1984). We summarize the evidence from our review of the literature with respect to both approaches to transfer.

---

[20]However, stronger evidence of facilitation would come from studies having a control group (see the section on methodological issues in chap. 6).

Contrastive Analysis Hypothesis. Studies in the domains of vocabulary, spelling, and word reading were conducted within the framework of the contrastive analysis hypothesis. These studies demonstrated that transfer is mediated by both structural and nonstructural factors. Structural factors that can affect the likelihood of transfer include the following:

- Language distance

  - Cross-language similarities in word forms and meanings (cognate vocabulary) were shown to be facilitative (García, 1991, 1998; Hancin-Bhatt & Nagy, 1994; Jiménez et al., 1996; Nagy et al., 1993).
  - Cross-language differences negatively affected students' ability to infer the meaning of unknown vocabulary words (Saville-Troike, 1984).
  - There was no cross-language relationship in spelling knowledge in cases in which the languages and orthographies are distant (Arab-Moghaddam & Sénéchal, 2001).
  - Processes underlying reading showed different patterns in languages that are unrelated (Abu-Rabia, 1997; Chitiri & Willows, 1997; Gholamain & Geva, 1999).

- Markedness

  - Markedness was shown to be operating in a study that looked at transfer in spelling. English is marked with respect to consonant voicedness; that is, whereas in most languages a voiced–voiceless contrast does not distinguish word meanings, in English it does. Students with a first language that is unmarked with respect to voicing (Spanish) encountered difficulty in acquiring this feature in English (Ferroli & Shanahan, 1993).
  - Two spelling studies showed that students experienced difficulty transitioning from a transparent (unmarked) to an opaque (marked) orthography (Fashola et al., 1996; James & Klein, 1994).

Nonstructural factors that can affect the likelihood of transfer include the following:

- Perceived linguistic distance (psychotypology)

  - Perceptions of the distance between the first and second languages were shown to inhibit the transfer of cognate knowledge among students who did not perceive these languages as close (García, 1991; Jiménez et al., 1996).
  - Negative transfer occurred among students who may have perceived their languages as being closer than they are (James & Klein, 1994).

- First- and second-language proficiency

  - First-language spelling features appeared early in second-language acquisition (Edelsky, 1982; James & Klein, 1994; Nathenson-Mejía, 1989).

- Development

  - Transfer of cognate knowledge depended on the learner's level of metalinguistic awareness, which is developmentally determined (Hancin-Bhatt & Nagy, 1994; Nagy et al., 1993).

In addition, the evidence from this review suggests that subcomponents of language and literacy interact to influence transfer. Within the studies of cognates, for example, the finding that cognate recognition was greater with cognate pairs that shared significant orthographic overlap implies that knowledge of first- and second-language spelling patterns influences the recognition of cognate vocabulary, providing clues to a relationship that may not be perceived on the basis of sound alone. Second, first- and second-language morphological knowledge was also shown to interact with transfer of cognate recognition. Because both orthographic and morphological knowledge are acquired over the course of the elementary and into the intermediate years, first- and second-language proficiency are additional factors that mediate the transfer of cognate vocabulary.

Threshold/Interdependence Hypotheses.
As mentioned in chapter 6, most studies with a focus on theory in this corpus were conducted within the theoretical frameworks proposed by Cummins. Because the studies were conducted across a variety of learner types, literacy subcomponents, and (most important) tasks, one cannot determine conclusively whether the hypotheses are upheld or refuted. Rather, we present this summary in recognition of the quantity of research generated by Cummins' hypotheses and as material that may suggest future research directions.

Of the five[21] studies that examined the threshold hypothesis, two found evidence consistent with the hypothesis (Lee & Schallert, 1997; Schoonen et al., 1998)—both in the domain of reading comprehension in older learners of English as a foreign language. Three studies found significant cross-language relationships in the domains of reading comprehension, strategy use, and writing despite limited second-language proficiency (Goldman et al., 1984; Langer et al., 1990; Lanauze & Snow, 1989, respectively). Langer and colleagues and Lanauze and Snow found transfer to occur in children whose first-language proficiency was high and second-language proficiency low.

A number of studies measuring word outcomes explicitly tested the interdependence hypothesis. However, Cummins (1999) considers skills such as word reading to be discrete language skills. These skills, he argues, are acquired by English-language learners simultaneously with the acquisition of conversational fluency and do not automatically generalize to academic language proficiency. It follows that, within the interdependence framework, efficient word reading is not subject to transfer because it is not seen as reflecting cognitive academic language proficiency.

In contrast, Cummins (1999) describes vocabulary knowledge as a core component of academic language proficiency. One vocabulary study found evidence in support of the transfer of cognitive language proficiencies (Francis, 2000), whereas two did not. One of the latter two, Davis et al. (1999) studied children in Grades 1 to 3 whose developmental levels possibly precluded demonstration of the type of higher level vocabulary associated with cognitive

---

[21]Durgunoglu et al. (1993) also found that word reading performance in the first and second language correlated significantly despite limited proficiency, but Cummins (1999) considers word reading a discrete language skill that is not subject to the transfer of cognitive academic language proficiency. Therefore, it is not included here.

academic language proficiency. On the other hand, the Lanauze and Snow (1989) study found no relationship between first- and second-language vocabulary use in writing among students with high levels of proficiency in the first and second languages.

Reading comprehension and strategy use are literacy domains that involve the type of academically related language skills that are hypothesized to transfer across languages. Within these domains, five studies of reading comprehension (Francis, 2000; Goldman et al., 1984; Reese et al., 2000; Royer & Carlo, 1991; Verhoeven, 1994) and five studies of strategy use (Calero-Breckheimer & Goetz, 1993; García, 1998; Jiménez et al., 1996; Langer et al., 1990; Schoonen et al., 1998) yielded findings in support of the interdependence hypothesis. Thus, support is relatively weak for the threshold hypothesis, but strong for the interdependence hypothesis. This is the case particularly within reading comprehension and strategy use, constructs measured among cognitively more mature subjects.

Cummins further hypothesizes that the transfer of academically mediated skills is bidirectional. Although most of the studies looked at first- to second-language transfer, all four studies that investigated transfer from the second to the first language found it to occur: Davis et al. (1999) and Francis (2000), writing; Verhoeven (1994), reading comprehension; and Jiménez et al. (1996), strategy use, vocabulary.

CONCLUSION

In conclusion, the contrastive analysis hypothesis and the constructs of language distance and markedness appear to work in tandem with nonstructural factors (psychotypology, first-language proficiency, and development) to account for transfer in the domains of spelling, vocabulary, and word reading; transfer of higher order literacy skills, in contrast, is explained more adequately within Cummins' interdependence hypothesis. These two theories appear to mark the boundaries between purely linguistic and conceptual knowledge.

Database References
for Part II

Abu–Rabia, S. (1997). Verbal and working-memory skills of bilingual Hebrew-English speaking children. *International Journal of Psycholinguistics, 13*(1), 25–40.

Ahern, E. H., Dixon, P. W., Kimura, T., Okuna, J. S., & Gibson, V. L. (1980). Phoneme use and the perception of meaning of written stimuli. *Psychologia: An International Journal of Psychology in the Orient, 23*(4), 206–218.

Arab-Moghaddam, N., & Sénéchal, M. (2001). Orthographic and phonological processing skills in reading and spelling in Persian/English bilinguals. *International Journal of Behavioral Development, 25*(2), 140–147.

Bernhardt, E. B., & Kamil, M. L. (1995). Interpreting relationships between L1 and L2 reading: Consolidating the linguistic threshold and the linguistic dependence hypothesis. *Applied Linguistics, 16*(1), 15–34.

Buriel, R., & Cardoza, D. (1988). Sociocultural correlates of achievement among three generations of Mexican American high school seniors. *American Educational Research Journal, 25*(2), 177–192.

Calero-Breckheimer, A., & Goetz, E. T. (1993). Reading strategies of biliterate children for English and Spanish texts. *Reading Psychology, 14*(3), 177–204.

Campbell, R., & Sais, E. (1995). Accelerated metalinguistic (phonological) awareness in bilingual children. *British Journal of Developmental Psychology, 13*(1), 61–68.

Carlisle, J. F., Beeman, M. M., Davis, L.- H., & Spharim, G. (1999). Relationship of metalinguistic capabilities and reading achievement for children who are becoming bilingual. *Applied Psycholinguistics, 20*(4), 459–478.

Carrell, P. L. (1989). Metacognitive awareness and second language reading. *Modern Language Journal, 73*, 121–133.

Chitiri, H. F., & Willows, D. M. (1997). Bilingual word recognition in English and Greek. *Applied Psycholinguistics, 18*(2), 139–156.

Cisero, C. A., & Royer, J. M. (1995). The development and cross-language transfer of phonological awareness. *Contemporary Educational Psychology, 20*(3), 275–303.

Cronnell, B. (1985). Language influences in the English writing of third- and sixth-grade Mexican-American students. *Journal of Educational Research, 78*(3), 168–173.

Cummins, J. (1981). The role of primary language development in promoting educational success for language minority students. In California State Department of Education (Ed.), *Schooling and language minority students: A theoretical framework*. Los Angeles, CA: National Dissemination and Assessment Center.

Da Fontoura, H. A., & Siegel, L. S. (1995). Reading, syntactic, and working memory skills of bilingual Portuguese–English Canadian children. *Reading and Writing, 7*(1), 139–153.

Davis, L. H., Carlisle, J. F., & Beeman, M. (1999). Hispanic children's writing in English and Spanish when English is the language of instruction. *Yearbook of the National Reading Conference, 48*, 238–248.

Dufva, M., & Voeten, M. J. M. (1999). Native language literacy and phonological memory as prerequisites for learning English as a foreign language. *Applied Psycholinguistics*, *20*(3), 329–348.

Duncan, D. M., & Gibbs, D. A. (1987). Acquisition of Panjabi and English. *British Journal of Disorders of Communication*, *22*, 129–144.

Durgunoglu, A. Y., Nagy, W. E., & Hancin-Bhatt, B. J. (1993). Cross-language transfer of phonological awareness. *Journal of Educational Psychology*, *85*(3), 453–465.

Eckman, F. R. (1985). Some theoretical and pedagogical implications of the markedness differential hypothesis. *Studies in Second Language Acquisition*, *7*, 289–307.

Edelsky, C. (1982). Writing in a bilingual program: The relation of L1 and L2 texts. *TESOL Quarterly*, *16*(2), 211–228.

Edelsky, C. (1983). Segmentation and punctuation: Developmental data from young writers in a bilingual program. *Research in the Teaching of English*, *17*(2), 135–156.

Fashola, O. S., Drum, P. A., Mayer, R. E., & Kang, S.- J. (1996). A cognitive theory of orthographic transitioning: Predictable errors in how Spanish-speaking children spell English words. *American Educational Research Journal*, *33*(4), 825–843.

Ferroli, L., & Shanahan, T. (1993). Voicing in Spanish to English knowledge transfer. *Yearbook of the National Reading Conference*, *42*, 413–418.

Flanigan, B. O. (1995). Anaphora and relativation in child second language acquisition. *Studies in Second Language Acquisition*, *17*(3), 331–351.

Francis, N. (2000). The shared conceptual system and language processing in bilingual children: Findings from literacy assessment in Spanish and Náhuatl. *Applied Linguistics*, *21*(2), 170–204.

García, G. E. (1991). Factors influencing the English reading test performance of Spanish-speaking Hispanic children. *Reading Research Quarterly*, *26*(4), 371–392.

García, G. E. (1998). Mexican-American bilingual students' metacognitive reading strategies: What's transferred, unique, problematic? *National Reading Conference Yearbook*, *47*, 253–263.

Gholamain, M., & Geva, E. (1999). Orthographic and cognitive factors in the concurrent development of basic reading skills in English and Persian. *Language Learning*, *49*(2), 183–217.

Goldman, S. R., Reyes, M., & Varnhagen, C. K. (1984). Understanding fables in first and second languages. *NABE Journal*, *8*, 835–866.

Gottardo, A. (2002). The relationship between language and reading skills in bilingual Spanish–English speakers. *Topics in Language Disorders*, *22*(5), 46–70.

Gottardo, A., Yan, B., Siegel, L. S., & Wade-Woolley, L. (2001). Factors related to English reading performance in children with Chinese as a first language: More evidence of cross-language transfer of phonological processing. *Journal of Educational Psychology*, *93*(3), 530–542.

Hancin-Bhatt, B., & Nagy, W. E. (1994). Lexical transfer and second language morphological development. *Applied Psycholinguistics*, *15*(3), 289–310.

Hernández, J. S. (1991). Assisted performance in reading comprehension strategies with non-English proficient students. *Journal of Educational Issues of Language Minority Students*, *8*, 91–112.

Holm, A., Dodd, B., Stow, C., & Pert, S. (1999). Identification and differential diagnosis of phonological disorder in bilingual children. *Language Testing*, *16*(3), 271–292.

Hsia, S. (1992). Developmental knowledge of inter- and intraword boundaries: Evidence from American and Mandarin Chinese speaking beginning readers. *Applied Psycholinguistics*, *13*(3), 341–372.

James, C., & Klein, K. (1994). Foreign language learners' spelling and proof-reading strategies. *Papers and Studies in Contrastive Linguistics*, *29*, 31–46.

Jiménez, R. T., García, G. E., & Pearson, D. P. (1996). The reading strategies of bilingual Latina/o students who are successful English readers: Opportunities and obstacles. *Reading Research Quarterly*, *31*(1), 90–112.

Johnson, J. (1989). Factors related to cross-language transfer and metaphor interpretation of bilingual children. *Applied Psycholinguistics*, *10*(2), 157–177.

Kellerman, E. (1977). Toward a characterization of the strategies of transfer in second language learning. *Interlanguage Studies Bulletin*, *2*, 58–145.

Kennedy, E., & Park, H.- S. (1994). Home language as a predictor of academic achievement: A comparative study of Mexican- and Asian-American youth. *Journal of Research and Development in Education*, *27*(3), 188–194.

Kramer, V. R., & Schell, L. M. (1982). English auditory discrimination skills of Spanish-speaking children. *Alberta Journal of Educational Research*, *28*(1), 1–8.

Kramer, V. R., Schell, L. M., & Rubison, R. M. (1983). Auditory discrimination training in English of Spanish-speaking children. *Reading Improvement*, *20*(3), 162–168.

Lanauze, M., & Snow, C. E. (1989). The relation between first- and second-language writing skills: Evidence from Puerto Rican elementary school children in bilingual programs. *Linguistics and Education, 1*(4), 323–339.

Langer, J. A., Bartolome, L., Vásquez, O., & Lucas, T. (1990). Meaning construction in school literacy tasks: A study of bilingual students. *American Educational Research Journal, 27*(3), 427–471.

Lee, J.- W., & Schallert, D. L. (1997). The relative contribution of L2 language proficiency and L1 reading ability to L2 reading performance: A test of the threshold hypothesis in an EFL context. *TESOL Quarterly, 31*(4), 713–739.

Liow, S. J. R., & Poon, K. K. L. (1998). Phonological awareness in multilingual Chinese children. *Applied Psycholinguistics, 19*(3), 339–362.

Lumme, K., & Lehto, J. E. (2002). Sixth grade pupils' phonological processing and school achievement in a second and the native language. *Scandinavian Journal of Educational Research, 46*(2), 207–217.

Morsbach, G. (1981). Cross-cultural comparison of second language learning: The development of comprehension of English structures by Japanese and German children. *TESOL Quarterly, 15*(2), 183–188.

Mumtaz, S., & Humphreys, G. W. (2001). The effects of bilingualism on learning to read English: Evidence from the contrast between Urdu–English bilingual and English monolingual children. *Journal of Research in Reading, 24*(2), 113–134.

Mumtaz, S. H., & Humphreys, G. W. (2002). The effect of Urdu vocabulary size on the acquisition of single word reading in English. *Educational Psychology, 22*(2), 165–190.

Nagy, W. E., García, G. E., Durgunoglu, A. Y., & Hancin-Bhatt, B. (1993). Spanish–English bilingual students' use of cognates in English reading. *Journal of Reading Behavior, 25*(3), 241–259.

Nagy, W. E., McClure, E. F., & Mir, M. (1997). Linguistic transfer and the use of context by Spanish–English bilinguals. *Applied Psycholinguistics, 18*(4), 431–452.

Nathenson-Mejía, S. (1989). Writing in a second language: Negotiating meaning through invented spelling. *Language Arts, 66*(5), 516–526.

Nguyen, A., Shin, F., & Krashen, S. (2001). Development of the first language is not a barrier to second-language acquisition: Evidence from Vietnamese immigrants to the United States. *International Journal of Bilingual Education and Bilingualism, 4*(3), 159–164.

Okamura-Bichard, F. (1985). Mother tongue maintenance and second language learning: A case of Japanese children. *Language Learning, 35*(1), 63–89.

Ordóñez, C. L., Carlo, M. S., Snow, C. E., & McLaughlin, B. (2002). Depth and breadth of vocabulary in two languages: Which vocabulary skills transfer? *Journal of Educational Psychology, 94*(4), 719–728.

Quinn, C. (2001). The developmental acquisition of English grammar as an additional language. *International Journal of Language & Communication Disorders, 36*(Suppl.), 309–314.

Quiroga, T., Lemos-Britten, Z., Mostafapour, E., Abbott, R. D., & Berninger, V. W. (2002). Phonological awareness and beginning reading in Spanish-speaking ESL first graders: Research into practice. *Journal of School Psychology, 40*(1), 85–111.

Reese, L., Garnier, H., Gallimore, R., & Goldenberg, C. (2000). Longitudinal analysis of the antecedents of emergent Spanish literacy and middle-school English reading achievement of Spanish-speaking students. *American Educational Research Journal, 37*(3), 633–662.

Rodrigues, R. J. (1981). A longitudinal study of bilingual English syntax. *Aztlan, 12*(1), 75–87.

Royer, J. M., & Carlo, M. S. (1991). Transfer of comprehension skills from native to second language. *Journal of Reading, 34*(6), 450–455.

Saville-Troike, M. (1984). What really matters in second language learning for academic achievement? *TESOL Quarterly, 18*(2), 199–219.

Schoonen, R., Hulstijn, J., & Bossers, B. (1998). Metacognitive and language-specific knowledge in native and foreign language reading comprehension: An empirical study among Dutch students in grades 6, 8 and 10. *Language Learning, 48*(1), 71–106.

Shin, S. J., & Milroy, L. (1999). Bilingual language acquisition by Korean schoolchildren in New York City. *Bilingualism, 2*(2), 147–167.

Spada, N., & Lightbown, P. M. (1999). Instruction, first language influence, and developmental readiness in second language acquisition. *Modern Language Journal, 83*(1), 1–22.

Verhoeven, L. T. (1994). Transfer in bilingual development: The linguistic interdependence hypothesis revisited. *Language Learning, 44*(3), 381–415.

Wang, M., & Geva, E. (2003). Spelling acquisition of novel English phonemes in Chinese children. *Reading and Writing: An Interdisciplinary Journal, 16*, 325–348.

Zutell, J., & Allen, V. (1988). The English spelling strategies of Spanish-speaking bilingual children. *TESOL Quarterly, 22*(2), 333–340.

Background References
for Part II

Adams, M. J. (1990). *Beginning to read: Thinking and learning about print*. Cambridge, MA: MIT Press.

Afflerbach, P., & Johnston, P. (1984). On the use of verbal reports in reading research. *Journal of Reading Behavior, 16*(4), 307–322.

Alderson, J. C. (1984). Reading in a foreign language: A reading problem or a language problem? In J. C. Alderson & A. H. Urquhart (Eds.), *Reading in a foreign language* (pp. 1–24). New York: Longman.

Anderson. R. C., & Freebody, P. (1981). Vocabulary knowledge. In J. T. Guthrie (Ed.), *Comprehension and teaching: Research reviews* (pp. 77–117). Newark, DE: International Reading Association.

Anderson, R. C., & Pearson, P. D. (2002). A schema theoretic view of basic processes in reading comprehension. In P. D. Pearson (Ed.), *Handbook of reading research* (pp. 255–292). Mahwah, NJ: Lawrence Erlbaum Associates.

Anglin, J. (1993). Vocabulary development: A morphological analysis. *Monographs of the Society for Research in Child Development, 58*(10), 1–166.

Asher, R. S., & Wigfield, A. (2002). Social and motivational influences on reading. In P. D. Pearson (Ed.), *Handbook of reading research* (pp. 423–452). Mahwah, NJ: Lawrence Erlbaum Associates.

Baker, C. (1996). *Foundations of bilingual education and bilingualism*. Clevedon, UK: Multilingual Matters.

Baker, L., & Brown, A. L. (1984). Metacognitive skills and reading. In P. D. Pearson (Ed.), *Handbook of reading research* (Vol. 1, pp. 353–394). New York: Longman.

Baker, L., & Brown, A. L. (2002). Metacognitive skills and reading. In P. D. Pearson (Ed.), *Handbook of reading research* (pp. 353–394). Mahwah, NJ: Lawrence Erlbaum Associates.

Bear, D. (1982). *Patterns of oral reading across stages of word knowledge*. Unpublished doctoral thesis, University of Virginia, Charlottesville.

Bernhardt, E. B., & Kamil, M. L. (1995). Interpreting relationships between L1 and L2 reading: Consolidating the linguistic threshold and the linguistic dependence hypothesis. *Applied Linguistics, 16*(1), 15–34.

Berninger, V. W., Abbott, R. D., Billingsley, F., & Nagy, W. (2001). Processes underlying timing and fluency of reading: Efficiency, automaticity, coordination, and morphological awareness. In M. Wolf (Ed.), *Dyslexia, fluency, and the brain*. Timonium, MD: York Press.

Bloome, D., & Green, J. (2002). Metacognitive skills and reading. In P. D. Pearson (Ed.), *Handbook of reading research* (pp. 395–422). Mahwah, NJ: Lawrence Erlbaum Associates.

Bransford, J. D., & Schwartz, D. L. (1998). Rethinking transfer: A simple proposal with multiple implications. *Review of Research in Education, 24*, 61–100.

Brown, R. (1973). *A first language: The early stages*. Cambridge, MA: Harvard University Press.

Carrell, P. L. (1989). Metacognitive awareness and second language reading. *Modern Language Journal, 73*, 121–133.

Carver, R. P. (2000). *The causes of high and low reading achievement*. Mahwah, NJ: Lawrence Erlbaum Associates.

Chall, J. S. (1987). Two vocabularies for reading: Recognition and meaning. In M. G. McKeown & M. E. Curtis (Eds.), *The nature of vocabulary acquisition* (pp. 7–17). Hillside, NJ: Lawrence Erlbaum Associates.

Ching, D. C. (1976). *Reading and the bilingual child*. Newark, DE: International Reading Association.

Cummins, J. (1978). Educational implications of mother tongue maintenance in minority-language groups. *The Canadian Modern Language Review, 35*, 395–416.

Cummins, J. (1979). Linguistic interdependence and the educational development of bilingual children. *Review of Educational Research, 49*(2), 221–251.

Cummins, J. (1980). The cross-lingual dimensions of language proficiency: Implications for bilingual education and the optimal age issue. *TESOL Quarterly, 14*(2), 175–187.

Cummins, J. (1984). *Bilingualism and special education: Issues in assessment and pedagogy*. San Diego, CA: College Hill Press.

Cummins, J. (1999, March). *Research, ethics, and public discourse: The debate on bilingual education*. Paper presented at the meeting of the American Association of Higher Education, Washington, DC.

Cummins, J. (2000). *Language, power and pedagogy: Bilingual children in the crossfire*. Clevedon, England: Multilingual Matters.

Dulay, H., & Burt, M. (1974). Natural sequences in child second language acquisition. *Language Learning, 24*, 37–53.

Durgunoglu, A. Y., & Hancin-Bhatt, B. (1992). An overview of cross-language transfer in bilingual reading. In R. J. Harris (Ed.), *Cognitive processing in bilinguals* (pp. 391–412). Amsterdam: North Holland.

Eckman, F. R. (1977). Markedness and the contrastive analysis hypothesis. *Language Learning, 27*, 315–330.

Eckman, F. R. (1985). Some theoretical and pedagogical implications of the markedness differential hypothesis. *Studies in Second Language Acquisition, 7*, 289–307.

Edelsky, C., Hudelson, S., Flores, B., Barkin, F., Altweger, J., & Jilbert, K. (1983). Semilingualism and language deficit. *Applied Linguistics, 4*, 1–22.

Ehri, L. C., & Wilce, L. S. (1987). Cipher versus cue reading: An experiment in decoding acquisition. *Journal of Educational Psychology, 79*, 3–13.

Ellis, R. (1994). *The study of second language acquisition*. New York: Oxford University Press.

Fitzgerald, J., & Shanahan, T. (2000). Reading and writing relations and their development. *Educational Psychologist, 35*, 39–50.

Frederiksen, J. R. (1980). Component skills in reading: Measurement of individual differences through chronometric analysis. In R. E. Snow, P. A. Federico, & W. E. Montague (Eds.), *Aptitude learning and instruction: Vol. I. Cognitive process analysis of learning and problem solving*. Hillsdale, NJ: Lawrence Erlbaum Associates.

Gough, P. B., Juel, C., & Griffith, P. L. (1992). Reading, spelling and the orthographic cipher. In P. B. Gough, L. C. Ehri, & R. Treiman (Eds.), *Reading acquisition* (pp. 35–48). Hillsdale, NJ: Lawrence Erlbaum Associates.

Gough, P. B., & Tunner, W. E. (1986). Decoding, reading, and reading disability. *Remedial and Special Education, 7*, 6–10.

Henderson, E. H. (1981). *Learning to read and spell: The child's knowledge of words*. DeKalb, IL: Northern Illinois University Press.

Henderson, E. H. (1985). *Teaching spelling*. Boston, MA: Houghton-Mifflin.

Heyns, B., & Hilton, T. L. (1982). The cognitive tests for high school and beyond: An assessment. *Sociology of Education, 55*, 89–102.

Hornberger, N. (1989). Continua of biliteracy. *Review of Educational Research, 59*, 271–296.

Hyltenstam, K. (1984). The use of typological markedness conditions as predictors in second language acquisition: The case of pronominal copies in relative clauses. In R. W. Anderson (Ed.), *Second languages: A crosslinguistic perspective*. Rowley, MA: Newbury House.

Jacobs, J. E., & Paris, S. G. (1987). Children's metacognition about reading: Issues in definition, measurement, and instruction. *Educational Psychologist, 22*(3/4), 255–278.

Juel, C., Griffith, P. L., & Gough, P. B. (1986). Acquisition of literacy: A longitudinal study of children in first and second grade. *Journal of Educational Psychology, 78*(4), 243–255.

Kellerman, E. (1977). Toward a characterization of the strategies of transfer in second language learning. *Interlanguage Studies Bulletin, 2*, 58–145.

Kindler, A. L. (2002). *Summary of the states' limited English proficient students and available educational programs and services. 1999–2000 summary report.* Washington, DC: National Clearinghouse for English Language Acquisition.

Lado, R. (1964). *Language teaching: A scientific approach.* New York: McGraw-Hill.

Lipson, M. Y., & Wixson, K. K. (1991). *Assessment and instruction of reading disability: An interactive approach.* New York: HarperCollins.

MacSwan, J., & Rolstad, K. (2003). Linguistic diversity, schooling, and social class: Rethinking our conception of language proficiency in language minority education. In C. B. Paulston & G. R. Tucker (Eds.), *Sociolinguistics: The essential readings* (pp. 329–340). Malden, MA: Blackwell.

Morris, D., & Perney, J. (1984). Developmental spelling as a predictor of first-grade reading achievement. *The Elementary School Journal, 84,* 441–457.

Nagy, W. E., & Anderson, R. C. (1984). How many words are there in printed English? *Reading Research Quarterly, 19,* 304–330.

Nagy, W. E., & Herman, P. A. (1987). Breadth and depth of vocabulary knowledge: Implications for acquisition and instruction. In M. McKeown & M. Curtis (Eds.), *The nature of vocabulary acquisition* (pp.19–35). Hillsdale, NJ: Lawrence Erlbaum Associates.

National Institute of Child Health and Human Development. (2000). *Report of the National Reading Panel. Teaching children to read: An evidence-based assessment of the scientific research literature on reading and its implications for reading instruction* (NIH Publication No. 00-4769). Washington, DC: U.S. Government Printing Office.

Nemser, W. (1971). Approximative systems of foreign language learners. *International Review of Applied Linguistics, 9,* 115–23.

Odlin, T. (1989). *Language of transfer: Cross-linguistic influence in language learning.* Cambridge, England: Cambridge University Press.

Paris, S. G., Lipson, M. Y., & Wixson, K. K. (1983). Becoming a strategic reader. *Contemporary Educational Psychology, 8,* 293–316.

Perfetti, C. A. (1985). *Reading ability.* New York: Oxford University Press.

Perfetti, C. A. (1988). Verbal efficiency in reading ability. In M. Daneman, G. E. Mackinnon, & T. G. Waller (Eds.), *Reading research: Advances in theory and practice* (Vol. 6, pp. 109–143). New York: Academic Press.

Phifer, S. S., & Glover, J. A. (1982). Don't take students' word for what they do while reading. *Bulletin of the Psychonomic Society, 19,* 194–196.

Riches, C., & Genesee, F. (in press). Crosslanguage and crossmodal influences. In F. Genesee, K. Lindholm-Leary, W. Saunders, & D. Christian (Eds.), *Educating English language learners: A synthesis of research evidence.* New York: Cambridge University Press.

Ringbom, H. (1978). The influence of the mother tongue on the translation of lexical items. *Interlanguage Studies Bulletin, 3,* 80–101.

Rubin, H., & Turner, A. (1989). Linguistic awareness skills in grade one children in a French immersion setting. *Reading and Writing: An Interdisciplinary Journal, 1,* 73–86.

Schwanenflugel, P. J., Blount, K., & Lin, P.- J. (1991). Cross-cultural aspects of word meanings. In P. J. Schwanenflugel (Ed.), *The psychology of word meanings* (pp. 71–90). Hillsdale, NJ: Lawrence Erlbaum Associates.

Selinker, L. (1972). Interlanguage. *International Review of Applied Linguistics, 10*(3), 209–231.

Sharwood-Smith, M. (1994). *Second language learning: Theoretical foundations.* New York: Longman.

Skutnabb-Kangas, T., & Toukomaa, P. (1976). *Teaching migrant children's mother tongue and learning the language of the host country in the context of the sociocultural situation of the migrant family.* Helsinki: The Finnish National Commission for UNESCO.

Snow, C. E., Burns, S. M., & Griffin, P. (Eds.). (1998). *Preventing reading difficulties in young children.* Washington, DC: National Academy Press.

Spiro, R. S., & Meyers, A. (1984). Individual differences on underlying cognitive processes in reading. In P. D. Pearson (Ed.), *Handbook of reading research* (Vol. I, pp. 471–501). New York: Longman.

Towell, R., & Hawkins, R. (1994). *Approaches to second language acquisition.* Clevedon, England: Multilingual Matters.

Treiman, R., Tincoff, R., Rodriguez, K., Mouzaki, A., & Francis, D. J. (1998). The foundations of literacy: Learning the sounds of letters. *Child Development, 69*(6), 1524–1540.

Wang, M., & Geva, E. (2003). Spelling acquisition of novel English phonemes in Chinese children. *Reading and Writing: An Interdisciplinary Journal, 16,* 325–348.

White, T. G., Power, M. A., & White, S. (1989). Morphological analysis: Implications for teaching and understanding vocabulary growth. *Reading Research Quarterly, 24*, 283–303.

Williams, J., & Snipper, G. (1990). *Literacy and bilingualism.* New York: Longman.

Zutell, J. (1992). An integrated view of word knowledge: Correlational studies of the relationships among spelling, reading, and conceptual development. In S. Templeton & D. Bear (Eds.), *Development of orthographic knowledge and the foundations of literacy.* Hillsdale, NJ: Lawrence Erlbaum Associates.

III

Sociocultural Contexts and Literacy Development

10

Synthesis: Sociocultural Contexts and Literacy Development

Claude Goldenberg, Robert S. Rueda, and Diane August

Part III (chaps. 10–12) discusses factors that go beyond the focus on individuals in the previous chapters of this volume; these factors fall under the broad heading of *sociocultural influences*. The goal of Part III is to review and evaluate the empirical evidence on the role of these sociocultural factors in the literacy development of language-minority children and youth. The studies included in this part address the following questions:

1. What is the influence of immigration (generation status and immigration circumstances) on literacy development, defined broadly?
2. What is the influence of differences in discourse and interaction characteristics between children's homes and classrooms?
3. What is the influence of other sociocultural characteristics of students and teachers?
4. What is the influence of parents and families?
5. What is the influence of policies at the district, state, and federal levels?
6. What is the influence of language status or prestige?

In chapter 11, we address the influence of each of these sets of factors on first- and/or second-language literacy outcomes, defined broadly. In chapter 12, we examine these factors in settings where language-minority children are acquiring literacy. The principal difference between chapters 11 and 12 is that the studies reviewed in the former report data on some aspect of student literacy outcomes, such as measured achievement, behavioral, or attitudinal indicators. Studies in chapter 12 report no such outcome data, although they typically make claims about the effects of sociocultural factors on literacy outcomes.

The justification for addressing sociocultural factors in this volume is straightforward, even if the topic is not: There are well-documented differences between the literacy attainment of language-minority and language-majority students (see chap. 2 for further discussion of educational outcomes). There are also differences in the literacy attainment of language-minority students from different backgrounds. Because language-minority students typically come from different sociocultural backgrounds than do mainstream English-speaking students, with variation within and across language-minority groups as well, various sociocultural characteristics might be expected to influence language-minority students' literacy outcomes.

We begin this synthesis by presenting pertinent background information. We then describe the methodology of our review. Next, we summarize the findings of the literature on the six research questions addressed by our review. After identifying methodological issues found in the studies reviewed, we recommend directions for future research.

BACKGROUND

There are many ways to characterize or define the factors addressed in this chapter; a number of publications have attempted to do so (e.g., California State Department of Education, 1986; Cole, 1995; Durán, 1983; Forman, Minick, & Stone, 1993; Jacob & Jordan, 1987; Tharp, 1989). Generally, we define *sociocultural influences* as factors that make up the broad social context in which children and youth live and go to school. These factors include a wide range of possible influences related to beliefs, attitudes, behaviors, routine practices, social and political relations, and material resources associated with groups of people sharing some nominal characteristics, such as economic or educational status; cultural, ethnic, or national origin; and linguistic group. The various and complex contexts created by these factors might directly influence learning outcomes by providing more/better or fewer/worse opportunities or motivation to learn, or by providing different types of opportunities that are somehow incongruent with expectations in the school context. These factors can also indirectly affect learning through their role in psychological and linguistic processes, such as transfer (addressed in Part II), or classroom processes, such as teaching and learning (reviewed in Part IV).

Classification of Students Into Sociocultural Groups

Why should sociocultural factors matter for explaining differences among language-minority children's literacy outcomes? The fundamental premise in this literature is that membership in one or another socially defined group influences behaviors, cognitions, motivational attributes, values, beliefs, and assumptions that then influence the learning process and, ultimately, learning outcomes. Children and youth from different sociocultural groups bring with them different experiences that might shape their classroom experiences. Although sociocultural factors can be conceived as individual-difference variables, the emphasis in the studies reviewed here tends to be on characteristics of children and youth as members of particular sociocultural groups. A key assumption is that educational outcomes for language-minority students can be enhanced if educators better understand these groups and how to design optimal learning environments for them.

There are numerous ways to classify how students from various sociocultural groups differ, and how (and whether) these differences are associated with differences in literacy or other cognitive/academic outcomes. The major classifications are by socioeconomic status (SES), race, ethnicity, and culture.

SES, a cluster of variables having to do with a person's or family's material (economic) circumstances, level of formal schooling, and occupational status, has consistently been shown to predict cognitive and academic outcomes (see e.g., Lara-Cinisomoet al., 2004). These effects are strongest when measured in the aggregate rather than at the individual level. In other words, there is a much stronger relationship to student outcomes when we consider the schools students attend or the neighborhoods in which they live, rather than the status of the students or families themselves (Sirin, 2005; White, 1982). Many studies in this area confound language-minority status, race, or ethnicity with SES. It is usually impossible to determine whether the findings (e.g., low reading achievement or an association between language-minority status and reading achievement) are actually a result of language-minority status or SES.

Geographic origin, race, and ethnicity are different but complexly related categories for differentiating students. Voluntary and involuntary immigrants have had distinct experiences in this country as a result of dramatically different immigration circumstances (Ogbu & Matute-Bianchi, 1986); Africans, Asians, and Europeans have all arrived as newcomers, but under different circumstances in different historical periods. Their experiences in this country can also vary because of different racial or ethnic group membership. There are also indigenous populations that cannot be considered newcomers—Native Americans and U.S.-born Latinos—but, if they speak a language other than English in the home, are considered part of the language-minority population. Mexicans and other Latin Americans not of European descent (primarily from Central America) are now seen as part of the large U.S. immigrant population, although many were born in this country. Their experiences can be influenced by both immigration status and ethnocultural factors.

A third way to distinguish among students is with reference to culture, perhaps the most complex of the variables. Many definitions of culture exist, but they all generally have to do with the behaviors, beliefs, attitudes, and practices of a group of people. Although cultures vary along many dimensions, Tharp (1989) suggests four classes of psychocultural variables that influence how students respond to classroom experiences:

- Social organization—how people organize themselves in groups or as individuals; for example, whether they have an individualistic or group-oriented approach to accomplishing tasks.
- Sociolinguistics—the conventions of interpersonal communication, such as wait time, proximity, rhythm and flow of conversation, and how turn taking is organized.
- Cognition—patterns of thought that can influence the learning of new skills and knowledge, such as specific cognitive abilities or cognitive styles.

- Motivation—values, beliefs, expectations, and aspirations that influence how, whether, and why individuals approach and persist in specific goals or tasks.

Tharp also identifies two constants—conditions that do not vary across cultures and are required for optimal educational outcomes regardless of culture: (a) a focus on language development, and (b) contextualized instruction. Tharp's thesis is that classrooms are productive teaching and learning environments to the extent that they follow the *prescriptions* (Tharp's term) of the constants and are compatible with home cultures as characterized by the four psychocultural variables. For some groups of students—those who are currently reasonably successful in U.S. schools—such compatibility presumably already exists. But for others, compatibility must be created for these students to receive equitable educational opportunities.

Although research in the field has not necessarily adopted Tharp's analytical scheme, the cultural compatibility framework is a common feature in this literature. Regardless of how researchers have conceptualized sociocultural factors (and, as the following chapters demonstrate, they generally have not been explicit about their conceptions), there appears to be consensus that students' sociocultural characteristics play an important role in their literacy (and general academic) development. Schools, therefore, should tailor curriculum and instruction to make children's school experiences more compatible with their natal cultures. This notion sometimes leads to observations such as the following:

> Competition will probably not motivate a class composed primarily of Native American children, for example, because their culture values cooperation. (ASCD Advisory Panel on Improving Student Achievement, 1995, p. 14)

More generally, the idea that classroom instruction and students' sociocultural characteristics should be brought into close alignment—and that doing so improves student learning—has become a prominent theme in this literature, as shown by the following example:

> Research has shown that students learn more when their classrooms are compatible with their own cultural and linguistic experience .... [Students' learning is disrupted] when the norms of interaction and communication in a classroom are very different from those to which the student has been accustomed .... The aspects of culture that influence classroom life most powerfully are those that affect the social organization of learning and the social expectations concerning communication. (Saravia-Shore & García, 1995, p. 57)

This perspective has had an impact at the policy level as well. Sociocultural factors are thought to be important enough to the education of English-language learners that the subject is a required part of some portions of the teacher certification process. In California, for example, the Commission on Teacher Credentialing certifies teachers who work with language minority students in either Cross-Cultural Language and Academic Development (CLAD) or Bilingual Cross-Cultural Language and Academic Development (BCLAD). One of the three modules that teachers must master in the CLAD certification is "culture and cultural diversity." In the BCLAD certification, teachers must master a module on "culture of emphasis."

The review that follows in this and the next two chapters might appear to reflect skepticism about the influence of sociocultural factors on educational outcomes for language-minority students. This skepticism is in reality aimed at claims that are made but not yet justified by existing research. We argue later in this chapter that better designed studies are critical for examining the relationships between sociocultural factors and student outcomes, as well as for providing robust portraits of how these factors play out in educational settings. We wish to make clear, however, that we consider sociocultural awareness on the part of educators and students alike to be a desirable end in and of itself, just as are high levels of literacy, numeracy, critical thinking, general knowledge, prosocial behavior, and other educational goals. Indeed, such awareness is part of what it means to be educated.

School Achievement Among Diverse Ethnolinguistic Groups

As discussed in chapter 2, there are differences between language-minority children and language-majority children with respect to literacy outcomes, with language-minority children often, although not always, achieving at lower levels than majority-language speakers. In addition, there are clearly differences in the literacy achievement of various sociocultural groups of students. Kennedy and Park (1994), for example, found that Asian Americans (Chinese, Filipino, Japanese, Korean, Vietnamese, Cambodian, and others) had higher reading scores than Mexican Americans in a nationally representative sample of eighth graders (Kauffman, Chávez, & Laven, 1998), despite that both groups of students were equally likely to report speaking a language other than English at·home. Ima and Rumbaut (1989) found differences in reading achievement among different subgroups of language-minority Asian students. Similar patterns of achievement differences among diverse ethnolinguistic groups exist in other countries. Leseman and de Jong (1998), for example, found large differences in Dutch vocabulary at ages 4 and 7, and more modest differences in reading achievement at the end of first grade, between Dutch children and language-minority Surinamese and Turkish children in the Netherlands. The Dutch children were the highest performing, followed by the Surinamese and then the Turkish children.

Explanations for such outcome differences among diverse language-minority groups are largely elusive. The reason is that these differences are confounded with SES and other dimensions of family life. Ima and Rumbaut's (1989) report on the reading achievement of diverse language-minority groups provides a case in point. The relatively high scores among East Asians are attributable at least partly to family SES, particularly with respect to parent education. Ima and Rumbaut report that the East Asian group "frequently includes children from 'brain drain' immigrant families (such as those headed by a Taiwanese engineer)" (p. 64). Thus, the high grade point average (GPA) of East Asian children and children in the *other immigrants* category might reflect the selective migration pattern of families with highly educated parents. Within their Southeast Asian group, for which Ima and Rumbaut had the most complete data and could do more detailed analysis by subgroup (e.g., Khmer, Vietnamese), there were differences among the subgroups: Vietnamese were the highest achieving, followed by Khmer, Laotian, Chinese-Vietnamese, and finally Hmong. Once again, SES and ethnolinguistic background were confounded. Once parent education, time in the United States, and age of student were taken into account, there was no difference in standardized reading achievement scores across the Southeast Asian subgroups.

METHODOLOGY OF THE REVIEW

The studies included in Part III are correlational, experimental, comparative, ethnographic, observational, or case study, and they use quantitative or qualitative methods. To be eligible for inclusion in the analysis in chapter 11, a study had to report data on (a) factors in one or more of the six research questions identified earlier, and (b) student outcomes (cognitive, affective, or behavioral) presumably influenced by one or more of these factors (see the following definition of *student outcomes*). Studies reviewed in chapter 12 report data on the nature of the sociocultural factors in one or more of the six areas, but there was no requirement that a study report data pertaining to student outcomes.

Student outcomes are defined in Part III as changes in students' literacy-related cognitive or affective characteristics or behaviors that are (or plausibly could be) explained by one or more sociocultural factors. We purposely chose a broad definition of outcomes not limited to literacy achievement measured through standardized tests alone. Studies reviewed here used standardized and researcher-constructed achievement tests, but they also used many other outcome indicators, including engagement and participation during instruction, analysis of writing, and story retelling. Outcomes could be gauged in the first language, second language, or both. They could also consist of qualitative data, such as detailed reports of student behavior or engagement or analysis of work products. However, in the absence of corroborating data, author claims alone about the impact of one or more sociocultural factors did not meet the criterion of outcome as defined here. Statements such as "reading improved over the course of the study" or "students more engaged in setting X as opposed to setting Y" were not considered sufficient evidence of an outcome.

We wish to emphasize, and do so again in chapter 11, that most of the studies we reviewed for this part of the volume make either explicit or implicit claims about sociocultural factors and how they affect student learning opportunities and learning outcomes. A large part of our task, therefore, was to evaluate the empirical basis for these claims. To do so comprehensively, we do not limit ourselves to outcomes as defined by test scores. As described in the preceding paragraph, to the contrary, we have taken a broad definition of *outcomes* to include observational indicators, ethnographic descriptions, examples/analyses of student products, motivational measures, participation or engagement measures, and self- or teacher reports, in addition to conventional or standardized measures. Readers should be aware that many of the studies reviewed here did not set out to study effectiveness, certainly not in outcomes measured as test scores. Instead, many investigators have sought to understand how sociocultural factors shape the contexts for students' literacy development in school, home, and community. In addition, the reader should be aware that our focus was not to look at the general effects of bilingualism or bilingual education. Rather, our focus was specifically on reading and literacy outcomes. Nevertheless, it is still reasonable to ask whether sociocultural factors influence literacy outcomes—broadly defined—for language-minority children and youth.

The criteria identified previously yielded a corpus of 50 studies for inclusion in chapter 11. In addition, a body of descriptive work related to sociocultural issues has accumulated. The most relevant of these studies are included in chapter 12, which discusses an additional 25 studies. The work reported in chapter 12 could help form the foundation for more systematic research linking sociocultural factors to student outcomes, thereby informing policy and practice decisions.

Only narrative review methods were used in this part of the volume because there were insufficient studies addressing the same conceptual hypothesis relevant to a given research question. Appendix 10.A describes why particular groups of research studies were not subjected to quantitative synthesis techniques.

SUMMARY OF EMPIRICAL FINDINGS

The Influence of Immigration Circumstances

Studies addressing this question generally focus on either generation status or circumstances of immigration. With respect to generation status, we found only one study that compared literacy outcomes among successive generations of language-minority students. Although this study found a shift from Spanish to English use across three generations of Mexican American high school seniors who reported at least some Spanish use in the home, generation status did not appear to influence English reading and vocabulary skills. Studies addressing circumstances of immigration likewise failed to uncover strong influences on literacy outcomes. Clearly, immigration and refugee experiences can create traumatic situations for children and families; however, there is no evidence that these experiences impede literacy achievement. Literacy outcomes are more likely to relate to home (and school) language and literacy learning opportunities, irrespective of immigration circumstances.

The Influence of Differences in Discourse and Interaction Characteristics Between Children's Homes and Classrooms

Many educators have suggested that minority children are socialized to interact with others at home and in their community in ways that may be at variance with expectations for interaction in school. These interaction or discourse differences may interfere with school achievement, as children are required to interact with other children and the teacher in ways that are strange or difficult for them. By extension, minimizing the interaction differences between home and school could help promote higher levels of literacy attainment by making the classroom more familiar and comfortable, and thus removing obstacles to interaction.

The available literature suggests two conclusions. First, descriptive studies (see chap. 12) provide good evidence that there are differences in norms and expectations for social interaction between the home and school environments of some language-minority students. Second, the consequences of these differences for students' literacy attainment and the effects of attempts to address or accommodate these differences in the classroom are not clear (see chap. 11). One highly influential study found that culturally compatible instruction had positive effects on native Hawaiian speakers' level of engagement and participation during reading lessons. But this study did not measure literacy achievement or comprehension of the stories being discussed, so we do not know whether the higher engagement and participation led to higher achievement or greater learning. Other studies with Navajo- and Spanish-speaking students also make claims about the effects on literacy-related student outcomes of different discourse or interaction patterns between the home and school or of instruction that accommodates student discourse or interaction characteristics. In each case, however, data or design problems preclude straightforward interpretation.

Thus, the most we can say given the available research is that bridging home–school differences in interaction can enhance students' engagement and level of participation in classroom instruction. This outcome is certainly not trivial, but it is not the same as enhancing student achievement or other types of learning outcomes—effects the existing data cannot confirm.

The Influence of Other Sociocultural Characteristics of Students and Teachers

In general, there is weak evidence that sociocultural characteristics of students and teachers have an impact on reading and literacy outcomes. One fairly consistent finding across a number of studies is that language-minority students' reading comprehension performance improves when they read culturally familiar materials. However, the language of the text appears to be a stronger influence on reading performance: Students perform better when they read or use material in the language they know better. The influence of cultural content is not as robust.

Several descriptive accounts in the literature document the many ways and different contexts in which teachers provide students with opportunities to read and write about relevant or interesting topics, either informally or in a more structured curriculum, to build on home–school connections. At the middle and secondary levels, there are similar descriptions for both writing and reading. However, we are left to speculate whether these contexts succeeded in enhancing students' literacy development.

The general hypothesis that this set of factors influences literacy outcomes remains highly plausible. However, interpretation of the research that exists is hampered because it lacks adequate designs and research methods, consistent definitions, a focus on measured literacy outcomes, and a larger theoretically driven organizing framework. Moreover, students' cultural affiliations are frequently confounded with SES—for which, as discussed earlier, there is strong evidence of an impact on literacy outcomes—rendering interpretation even more problematic.

The Influence of Parents and Families

The role of parents and families in children's academic achievement has been a topic of inquiry for more than 40 years. These studies found that language-minority families influence their children's literacy development. Three major findings emerged from our review of this literature.

First, language-minority parents express willingness and often have the ability to help their children succeed academically. There is evidence that these parents value their children's formal schooling and are responsive to attempts to involve them in supporting their children's school success. For various reasons, however, schools underestimate parents' interest, motivation, and potential contributions. School personnel do not take full advantage of home resources that could enhance outcomes for children. Although there may be differences in views about literacy and literacy practices at home and school, literacy activities are not absent in home settings, and parents consistently report valuing literacy and other academic outcomes for their children.

Second, more home literacy experiences/opportunities are generally associated with superior literacy outcomes, but findings in this regard are not consistent, and precise conclusions are difficult to find. Measures of parent and family literacy often predict child literacy attainment, but two studies found that parents' reading behavior was unrelated to children's literacy outcomes. Features of family life (e.g., domestic workload, religious activities) appear to influence the value that children place on reading and their concepts of themselves as readers. Parent education is also associated with literacy outcomes (see chap. 4 for a discussion of the effects of SES on literacy development at the individual level).

Third, the relationship between home language use and language-minority children's literacy outcomes is unclear. Correlational studies point to language-specific effects: Home experiences with the first and second languages are positively (but modestly) correlated with children's literacy achievement in the first and second languages, respectively, and negatively (also modestly) correlated with children's literacy achievement in the other language. However, there are some important exceptions. Most important are two experimental studies. One showed that promoting Spanish home literacy activities produced a positive effect on English preliteracy achievement in kindergarten, whereas the other found that promoting English home literacy activities had no effect on English literacy achievement in first grade. Two correlational studies also yielded findings counter to the language-specific effects generalization. Overall, these studies provide an insufficient basis for policy and practice recommendations. This is an area that clearly needs additional investigation.

The Influence of Policies at the District, State, and Federal Levels

Only two available studies addressing the question of policy influences included student outcomes, so the research base does not permit firm conclusions. These two studies examined the influence of policies and included literacy outcomes, but they provide only indirect tests of the hypothesis that government policies influence language-minority children's literacy outcomes. One study examined how the implicit (unofficial) U.S. language policy that privileges English affected language-minority learners and how a classroom teacher countered this effect with practices that appeared to have a positive influence on students' literacy development. A study of Swedish speakers in Finland yielded data that could be interpreted as consistent with the hypothesis that language policies and practices recognizing the value of more than one language can minimize the negative effects of language-minority status on student literacy outcomes. Both studies, however, are open to alternative interpretations.

Studies that did not examine student outcomes also point to the potential impact of government policies on language-minority children's literacy attainment. One of the few studies to have directly examined the impact of a specific policy—legislation banning bilingual education (California's Proposition 227)— found a great deal of variation in how the legislation was implemented, noting that implementation was influenced by three factors: local school context, teachers' personal ideologies, and their pedagogical reactions to the new policy.

The Influence of Language Status or Prestige

As with the research on policy, one can hypothesize that the status of a language would influence the achievement of speakers of that language. Being a member of a low-status language group may have negative effects on self-concept, motivation, and/or learning opportunities, all of which can depress literacy attainment. Spanish, for example, is generally assumed to be a low-status language in the United States (Carreira, 2000), and disproportionate numbers of Spanish speakers achieve at low levels in U.S. schools. Two studies again provide suggestive evidence in support of this hypothesis. Differences in achievement between language-minority (Swedish-speaking) and language-majority children in Finland—where both languages are of equal status—are modest compared with differences between some language-minority (e.g., Spanish-speaking) and language-majority children in the United States, where English is considered the high-status language. Yet other explanations are possible. For example, Scandinavian countries have among the highest literacy levels in the world, and students are consistently at or near the top in international comparisons. Highly literate contexts, rather than equal language status, could explain the fact that there are relatively minor differences in the achievement of majority and minority speakers in Scandinavian countries. Moreover, SES differences in general are less extreme in Scandinavian countries than in the United States, where there are enormous differences between the well-off and the less well-off economically (Smeeding, 2002). The relative parity among different ethnic groups in Scandinavian societies might explain more equitable achievement outcomes across these groups.

Several descriptive studies reviewed in chapter 12 suggest that the common perception of English as a high-prestige language in the United States may have consequences for maintenance of the first language. Other studies have examined the positive and negative impacts that language prestige in classroom and community settings can have. The findings of one study suggest that the lower prestige of Spanish may affect teachers' assessment of student competence, and thus result in low-level instructional practices.

METHODOLOGICAL ISSUES

The studies reviewed in this part are extremely diverse methodologically and draw more heavily than studies in other parts of the report from a qualitative research tradition. There are few experiments among the studies reviewed here. The scarcity of experimental designs is understandable, to some extent, because sociocultural processes are difficult to define and generally have not been studied with such designs. The field has been influenced more by anthropology and linguistics—disciplines that traditionally have not employed experimental designs—than by educational psychology and related fields. More often than not, the emphasis in this body of research has been on describing sociocultural factors in specific contexts and their potential impact on achievement and other literacy-related outcomes, rather than on empirically demonstrating a link between sociocultural factors and student learning or other outcomes of interest. Although experimental designs offer the strongest basis for causal inferences about the efficacy of specific interventions, carefully documented qualitative and other nonexperimental studies can be used to enhance our understanding of the context in which students acquire literacy. Moreover, qualitative studies can also support causal arguments when they are carefully documented and reveal specific "mechanisms"—linkages and processes—that demonstrate the influence of one factor on another. As is true of quantitative research, findings from qualitative studies are especially compelling when the results are replicated in a variety of settings and conditions. Quantitative studies (experimental or non experimental), however, are better for establishing generalizablity since they typically involve far more subjects than do qualitative studies. Of course, there will always be validity threats and alternative explanations, even with strong experimental designs and particularly in social science research. There is no "perfect" method (Shadish, 1994). As we point out below, a mixed methods approach would seem to offer great promise for future research in this area.

A methodological issue of concern in a number of the studies reviewed here (and many that were eliminated), however, is not that they are not experimental or even that they are not quantitative. Rather, the most common methodological problem is unsubstantiated claims. For example, some authors argue that culturally sensitive or culturally accommodated instruction helps promote student literacy achievement, but they fail to provide evidence that the instruction or approach had any culturally sensitive or accommodating features. Moreover, there is often some question as to whether the approach under study had any true effects. Authors might claim effects, but in fact the validity of these claims is difficult to determine because insufficient data are reported. In our analysis of a study, then, we evaluate the claims made about sociocultural factors and their relationship to students' literacy development.

In some cases, unwarranted assertion is not necessarily a shortcoming of a particular article. Rather, it is a shortcoming of the broader literature in this area, which tends to be based on propositions assumed to be true, but with inadequate empirical grounding. The most common example is the study of Au and Mason (1981), often cited to demonstrate that culturally accommodating instruction leads to superior measured reading outcomes. In fact, reading outcomes were not measured in that study; rather, the researchers measured student engagement and participation during reading lessons. Engagement and participation are certainly important, but they are not the same as measured reading achievement or measured improvement in student comprehension. Another example of faulty citation in the literature is citing the study of Rogers-Zegarra and Singer (1980) to support the proposition that stories closely paralleling students' cultural experiences promote good comprehension. This claim is at best a misinterpretation and at worst simply wrong. Rogers-Zegarra and Singer found no significant effect of ethnic content (Chicano vs. Anglo) on students' literal or inferential comprehension. At most, there was a nonsignificant interaction between reading ability and ethnic content on *scriptal* questions—questions about the story that required cultural knowledge to be answered correctly (e.g., knowledge about *Las Posadas* and *El Día de los Muertos*).

It is important to note that space constraints of journal publications make it difficult for ethnographic research and narrative reporting to be shown at their best. These methods require more space than is typically allowed by journals to document methods and analysis techniques appropriately. The absence of comprehensive methodological detail in many of the studies included here might have been a consequence of these constraints, rather than the quality of the study. Indeed, we had difficulty distinguishing between high-quality studies that had been squeezed into too little space and poor studies. Rather than risk eliminating potentially high-quality work with some conclusions worth thinking about, we erred on the side of inclusiveness. At the same time, although some of the included studies have shortcomings, others managed in a small amount of space to report findings with adequate empirical grounding.

The following are among the methodological issues we noted in our review of studies. Many, but not all, refer to the qualitative studies:

- Insufficient specification about investigator time spent in the research setting.
- Insufficient specification of data-collection techniques, data analysis techniques, number of subjects, and number of observations.
- Data not presented to confirm/disconfirm author's point of view explicitly.
- No information about how representative examples were selected.
- No information about the frequency or typicality of reported key occurrences.
- No information about whether competing interpretations were considered and evaluated.
- Insufficient triangulation across several data sources.
- Making inferences and drawing conclusions not warranted by the data reported.

As already discussed, many of the studies reviewed are descriptive and do not address directly and empirically whether the sociocultural dimension(s) they target have an impact on student outcomes. We discuss these studies separately (in chap. 12) because (a) many of these studies provide a rich source of descriptive material, as well as theory, hypotheses, and questions to be explored in future research; and (b) we use this opportunity to point out that many of the studies in this area are silent on the question of how sociocultural factors influence student outcomes. In this context, we call attention to a recent commentary by Sleeter (2004):

> Ethnographic work may be ignored in policy debates when ethnographers do not speak to the language of power. Currently that language is achievement test scores. In order to insert our work more directly into discussions of school

reform, we need to link findings, where relevant, to achievement data.... I am concerned that those who subscribe to decontextualized ways of understanding school reform will simply ignore insights of ethnography when achievement data are not included. (p. 135)

Although we disagree with Sleeter in her overemphasis on achievement test scores, her basic point is indisputable: We must connect dimensions of interest (such as sociocultural factors in student learning) with valid data about important student outcomes.

RECOMMENDATIONS FOR FUTURE RESEARCH

Specific Features of the Immigrant Experience

Given the numbers of language-minority students who are immigrants, research should systematically examine specific features of the immigrant experience that might have an impact on language-minority students' literacy development and try to disentangle these features from other, related factors, such as SES or home literacy experiences. Although some studies exist, many confounds limit the knowledge base in this area. The following questions require further study: What are the independent and combined effects of immigration status, SES, and home literacy experiences on literacy outcomes? How specifically does immigration status influence opportunity to learn (e.g., access to high-quality schooling) apart from SES? What specific behaviors, beliefs, and attitudes of immigrant parents mediate the acquisition of literacy for English-language learners? Are these different for different immigrant groups? How do these factors change with more time in the host country?

Accommodations to Home and School Discourse

Research should investigate more carefully and systematically the relationship between home and school discourse, focusing in particular on potential mismatches and the effects on student outcomes when mismatches are attenuated or eliminated. Many descriptive studies of home and community discourse and interaction patterns suggest that there are significant differences between home and school environments. But the current state of the literature does not allow us to draw strong conclusions regarding the effects of these differences on literacy outcomes, or the effects when these differences are eliminated or minimized by altering the instructional environment. Such differences may indeed be important in literacy development, so there is a need for detailed and well-designed studies that address this issue straightforwardly.

Particularly useful would be well-designed experiments comparing instruction designed to eliminate/minimize discourse mismatches for a particular language-minority group (e.g., students of Mexican descent) with effective generic instruction that does not include such a component. An additional useful control would be to include in the study another sociocultural group (e.g., English-speaking, of European descent) that would receive the identical set of contrasting instructional treatments. The null hypothesis would be either that (a) the instruction designed to minimize discourse differences between home and school would be no more effective than generic effective instruction, or (b) it would be more effective than the generic instruction for both sociocultural groups. However, if instruction designed to be accommodating to home discourse styles were more effective than the generic instruction for the students of Mexican descent, but not for those of European descent, this would provide strong evidence for the hypothesis that minimizing differences in home–school discourse promotes language-minority students' literacy development. In such a study, it would be important to design the control condition carefully so that the discourse-accommodating instruction would be compared with effective instruction. It would be useless and misleading to compare it with instruction already known to be poor. Ideally, the two instructional conditions would be as similar as possible, differentiated only by key discourse features employed by the teacher and designed to be accommodating to students' home discourse style.

Qualitative or ethnographic studies could also shed useful light on this hypothesis by using essentially the same design as that described earlier—that is, comparing students who receive culturally accommodated instruction with students who do not—but collecting detailed, fine-grained data on the nature of the classroom interactions and students' and teachers' responses to instruction. The important elements of any design would be (a) language-minority students in contrasting instructional environments—discourse-accommodating and not discourse-accommodating, and (b) some measure of student literacy outcomes expected to be influenced by the instruction. Inclusion of another ethnolinguistic group, as discussed previously, would add an informative dimension to the study.

Questions for further exploration also include the following: What specific home- and community-based discourse features need to be accommodated in classroom instruction to improve student outcomes? For example, if children come from cultures where turn-taking and wait-time rules are significantly different from those of the classroom, what is the effect on student outcomes if teachers alter these rules in their classrooms so they match the rules of the children's cultures? Do the effects of these accommodations vary depending on specific types of classroom settings and activities, for example, during interactive reading instruction? In addition, do these accommodations affect different types of literacy outcomes (e.g., measured achievement, motivation, interest, and reading behaviors)?

Other Sociocultural Accommodations to Instruction

Research needs to systematically examine other hypotheses—that is, in addition to the discourse factors discussed earlier, sociocultural accommodations and their effects on English-language learners' literacy outcomes. Although a significant amount of work has been done on sociocultural factors involved in teaching and learning, much of it is plagued by methodological and theoretical problems. Often this research is descriptive only, such that outcomes are implied or assumed, but not directly examined. Relevant variables often are not well specified; there are frequently confounds among independent variables; and a lack of differentiation among culture, SES, race/ethnicity, prior experience, and language is common. Hypotheses about sociocultural accommodations need to be investigated more explicitly, more systematically, and in relation to student literacy outcomes. Many of these hypotheses overlap substantially with the discourse-based hypotheses discussed earlier.

The overarching question in this domain is: To what extent does accommodating instructional features (e.g., social organization of the classroom) or curriculum (e.g., academic content) to English-language learners' sociocultural characteristics result in improved student cognitive, affective, and ultimately academic outcomes? If such a result can be demonstrated, is it attributable to operationalizing existing learning principles, or are different principles involved? For example, does more relevant material increase motivation and thus achievement, or does it focus attention so that instructional time is more productive? Are there universal effective teaching strategies or some that are differentially effective? Are there interactions between generic instructional strategies (e.g., direct teaching, cooperative learning) and English-language learners' sociocultural characteristics? Do particular instructional approaches result in better or worse cognitive, affective, and/or academic outcomes for certain sociocultural groups, or are effective strategies equally effective for all groups?

The recommended research designs are analogous to those proposed earlier. The prior questions can be pursued effectively with experimental design procedures or more qualitative/ethnographic methods. What is critical are (a) a comparative design, whereby students in a culturally accommodated condition are compared with similar students in an effective, but not culturally accommodated condition; and (b) a measure or gauge of student literacy (or literacy-related) outcomes. Again, inclusion of another ethnolinguistic group would add to the study's informative value.

Characteristics of Effective Parental Involvement Strategies

Are parental involvement strategies/programs effective in helping improve academic achievement for English-language learners? If so, what are the characteristics of effective programs that involve parents? The existing research suggests that parent/family factors have an impact on the literacy (and general academic) development of language-minority students, and parents are often willing to help their children succeed academically. More information is needed on how specific parental behaviors and attitudes are related to enhanced literacy development. Do the salient parental factors influencing children's literacy outcomes change over time? In what ways can schools foster and take better advantage of parent/home resources at different ages and grades? What developmental differences may suggest that different parental factors are at work in the early stages of literacy acquisition as opposed to later? Are some parents more or less responsive to being involved in their children's educational attainment? What differentiates these parents? What means can be used to engage less responsive parents? There is a great need to develop, implement, and evaluate (in terms of student outcomes) techniques and programs that can promote parent involvement to enhance student literacy development.

Observational, naturalistic, interview, and possibly survey studies could help find answers to these questions. As discussed before, experimental designs offer fundamental advantages, in that they permit systematic comparison of parents' and students' responses/outcomes under different and documented conditions. Adding a qualitative component would increase the probability of producing detailed and valid understanding about how such interventions and programs influence—or fail to influence—participants.

The effect of language use in the home is an important additional area for study. All of the correlational studies reviewed found positive within-language correlations, such that home experiences in one language positively correlate with at least some literacy outcomes in that language. Moreover, with two exceptions, there are negative across-language correlations, such that home experience in one language is negatively correlated with literacy outcomes in the other language for at least some measures. Because causality cannot be inferred from correlations, we need to understand what explains these correlations. One possibility is simply that more time spent in one language promotes greater competence in that language and detracts from competence in another language.

However, this explanation runs counter to the two experimental studies reviewed here. One study found that promoting Spanish home literacy activities produced a positive effect on English preliteracy achievement in kindergarten, whereas the other study found that promoting English home literacy activities had no effect on English literacy achievement in first grade. The time-on-task explanation also runs counter to findings reported in chapter 9 suggesting positive transfer in literacy domains across languages.

Other explanations must be explored—for example, the quality and content of parent–child interactions. It might be the case that home language that is more academically oriented has a different relationship with student outcomes than home language that is more conversational or informal. The experiment demonstrating the effects of promoting Spanish literacy in the home on English preliteracy development suggests just this possibility. Two other aspects of parents' home language use need to be studied: the relationship between parents' language use and their language competence, and parents' explanations for why they use one language or the other or a combination of the two. Different answers would have different implications for policy and practice recommendations.

Beyond such studies, it would be extremely useful to conduct additional experimental interventions wherein families would be randomly assigned to conditions that varied the balance of first- and second-language use in the home. Such a study, admittedly, would be controversial and difficult to carry out. If done successfully, however, it would yield extremely useful data about (a) how alterable home language patterns are among language-minority families, and (b) what effects can be expected from attempts to alter home language use.

The Effects of School, District, State, and Federal Policies on Language-Minority Students' Literacy Development

There is a great need for policy studies linking school, district, state, and federal policies to language-minority students' literacy development. One highly visible policy initiative, which began in California and is now drawing attention throughout the country, is designed to end primary-language instruction in schools. What is the effect of this policy shift on student literacy outcomes? Beyond such dramatic and highly publicized shifts, various states have different policy frameworks for educating language-minority students. Can we discern their effects on English-language learners' achievement?

A shift in federal policy has occurred with regard to language of instruction. Whereas Title VII of the Improving America's Schools Act (P.L. 103-382, 1994) promoted "multilingual skills" and provided funding for many two-way bilingual programs throughout the United States, Title III of the No Child Left Behind Act of 2001 (P.L. 107-110, 2002) makes no mention of the benefits of maintaining and promoting multiple language skills. Moreover, NCLB has created a high-stakes accountability environment that is unprecedented at the federal level (see ch. 20) yet limits how many years ELLs can be tested in their native language (3 in most cases with up to 2 more on a case by case basis) for language arts accountability purposes (for updated 2004 regulations, see http://www.ed.gov/legislation/FedRegister/proprule/2004-2/062404a.html; retrieved 12/13/05). How, if at all, have these changes in federal policy affected learning opportunities and literacy development among English-language learners?

At the district and school levels, myriad policies are in place for identifying, placing, instructing, and exiting from special services English-language learners. What are the effects of those policies on learning opportunities and literacy attainment?

Finally, policies with respect to the education of language-minority children vary internationally. Can we gauge the effects of these policies on language-minority populations in different countries and assess how they compare with policies in the United States?

The Role of Language Status/Prestige in Students' Literacy Development

There is a need to investigate more systematically, and in different language-use, community, and national contexts, the hypothesis that language status or prestige influences student literacy development. Is language status related to or does it influence language-minority students' cognitive, affective, and/or academic outcomes? Does this vary by different language status context or across different nation/language groups? Will enhancing the status of the home language (in the school setting and/or community) help improve language-minority students' cognitive, affective, and/or academic outcomes? If enhancing the status of students' home language is effective in promoting literacy development, what are the most promising ways to accomplish this?

There is some suggestion that technology could play a role in moderating language status issues (e.g., Lam, 2000). Given the rapidly increasing importance of technology in educational practice, a related question is whether technology (such as the Internet) as a medium of communication or instruction can attenuate the deleterious effects of a low-status language (if there are such effects) or, alternatively, help promote a higher status for a language. If technology can promote higher language status, what is the effect on student literacy development? Some of these questions would be amenable to experimental manipulations and evaluation.

Recommendations for Study Design and Methodology

Greater Attention to Assessing and Reporting Student Literacy Outcomes. Many studies in this area describe particular contexts (e.g., home, school, community) and then draw inferences about their effects on student literacy development. But there is a surprising absence of outcome data. The inferences are often reasonable, but they do not substitute for data. The lack of achievement data is particularly characteristic of studies that address the issue of culturally compatible or culturally accommodating instruction. Despite a belief among many in the field that instruction tailored to different cultural groups is superior to instruction based on general principles of teaching and learning, there is a paucity of data to support this claim. The best studies suggest that student engagement and participation, which are not the same as achievement, can be enhanced through the use of culturally compatible instruction, but even these studies are open to numerous alternative explanations.

The Application of Quality Criteria to Ethnographic Research. Because a large portion of the research in this area is qualitative or ethnographic, certain criteria should apply if the findings from this type of research are to contribute to our understanding of the field. First, researchers should document having collected observations from multiple sources and employed multiple techniques for uncovering or cross-checking varying perspectives on complex issues and events. Second, they should provide information about the relative frequency of certain events or occurrences (typicality or atypicality). Third, they should examine competing or alternative explanations. Fourth, they should make an effort to explain the range of variation in the data. Finally, their generalizations should be based on the data collected.

The Use of Mixed Research Designs. There is a need for mixed research designs that combine the best of quantitative and qualitative research methods. Quantitative methods allow for large numbers of subjects and data that are relatively easy to process. They also permit a degree of generalization, depending on how subjects are selected, as well as the calculation of effect sizes. Qualitative data permit more in-depth study of behavior and its links to other aspects of settings and contexts. When combined, these two approaches to social research have a much greater probability of shedding light on complex topics than has either one individually (Green, Camilli, & Elmore, in press; Weisner, 2005).

APPENDIX 10.A: STUDIES EXCLUDED FROM META-ANALYSIS IN CHAPTER 11

Chapter 11: Sociocultural Influences on the Literacy Attainment of Language-Minority Children and Youth

Influence of immigration status on L1 and L2 literacy outcomes
Of the five identified studies, two (Goldenberg, 1987; Monzó & Rueda, 2001) are qualitative and report no correlations.

Influence of discourse and interaction differences on L1 and L2 literacy outcomes
Of the six identified studies, three (Au & Mason, 1981; Huerta-Macías & Quintero, 1992; McCarty et al., 1991) are qualitative or report no correlations.

Influence of culturally relevant/meaningful reading material on literacy outcomes
Of the nine studies, four are qualitative (Kenner 1999, 2000; McCarty, 1993; Jiménez, 1997); two use qualitative methods to compare culturally sensitive text with standard text (García, 1991; Hannon & McNally, 1986); and in one study, the focus is on professional development (rather than reading material) geared toward helping teachers create culturally sensitive text (Schon, Hopkins, & Vojir, 1984)

Influence of culturally relevant/meaningful reading material and text language on L1 and L2 literacy achievement
Of the five studies, four were appropriate in the area of culturally meaningful reading material (Abu-Rabia, 1995, 1998a, 1998b; Lasisi et al., 1988). One study was not included because it was a qualitative analysis of the extent to which culturally accommodated text enhances comprehension (Davies, 1991).

Influence of other socioculturally related factors on L1 and L2 literacy achievement
In the 12 identified studies, the socioculturally related factors are too different to be combined in a meta-analysis.

Relationship between parent motivation, expectations, values, and beliefs and L1 and L2 literacy achievement
Of the eight identified studies, five (Brooker, 2002; Carter & Chatfield, 1986; Goldenberg, 1987; Goldenberg & Gallimore, 1991; Shannon, 1995) are qualitative and report no correlations.

Relationship between home literacy experiences and other family factors and L1 and L2 literacy achievement
Of the seven identified studies, three (Arzubiaga et al., 2002; Goldenberg et al., 1992; Pucci & Ulanoff, 1998) are qualitative and report no correlations.

Relationship between home language experiences and language-minority children's literacy development

Of the 12 identified studies, 1 was appropriate (Hancock, 2002); in 6 studies simple correlations are not reported (Brunell & Linnakylä, 1994; Brunell & Saretsalo, 1999; Buriel & Cardoza, 1988; Connor, 1983; Dolson, 1985; Hansen, 1989); 1 study is qualitative (Monzó & Rueda, 2001); and in 1 study there are no first-language measures for students who participated in the study (Koskinen et al., 2000).

Influence of policies at the district, state, and federal levels
Only two studies were identified (Shannon, 1995; Brunell & Linnakylä, 1994).

Influence of language status or prestige
Only four studies were identified (Brunell & Linnakylä, 1994; Brunell & Saretsalo, 1999; Lam, 2000; Shannon, 1995).

11

Sociocultural Influences on the Literacy Attainment of Language-Minority Children and Youth

Claude Goldenberg, Robert S. Rueda, and Diane August

This chapter reviews research on the influences of sociocultural factors on language-minority children's literacy outcomes in either the first or second language. As discussed in chapter 10, *sociocultural* comprises a broad and difficult-to-define set of constructs. Indeed, the imprecision of the terms used in this literature makes reviewing the research and drawing conclusions difficult. Another complication is that sociocultural influences (children's homes, communities, cultures, backgrounds, etc.) are typically analyzed in relation to the cultural characteristics and demands (i.e., the behavioral, affective, or cognitive expectations) of the schools children attend. Much of the research reviewed here posits that sociocultural influences on literacy attainment must be understood as the product of interactions between children's home culture and the culture of the school and classroom. One of the most prevalent assumptions (or hypotheses) in this field is that home cultures are not intrinsically positive or negative influences on children's academic attainment. What matters, rather, is the degree of fit between home and school.

According to this view, if certain cultural groups (e.g., middle-class Whites and many Asian groups) do well in U.S. schools, it is because the behavioral, affective, and cognitive norms and expectations for children are sufficiently similar at home and at school that they do not clash in ways that confuse, demotivate, or create other obstacles to children's learning. Conversely, if certain groups (e.g., African Americans, Latinos, Native Americans) do poorly in U.S. schools, it is because incompatibilities between their home cultures and the demands and expectations of the school create obstacles to student learning. Poor academic performance, in other words, is not the result of an adverse influence of children's cultural characteristics on their learning, but of schools' failure—perhaps inability—to accommodate instruction to aspects of children's home cultures.

As discussed in chapter 10, we purposefully use a broad conception of *student outcomes*, which we define as changes in students' literacy-related cognitive or affective characteristics or behaviors that are (or plausibly could be) explained by one or more sociocultural factors. Outcomes are not limited to achievement measured through standardized tests.

The chapter is organized according to the six research questions set forth in chapter 10 that examine sociocultural influences on literacy development defined broadly:

1. What is the influence of *immigration* (generation status and immigration circumstances)?
2. What is the influence of differences in *discourse and interaction characteristics* between children's homes and classrooms?
3. What is the influence of *other sociocultural characteristics* of students and teachers?
4. What is the influence of *parents and families*?
5. What is the influence of policies at the *district, state, and federal levels*?
6. What is the influence of *language status or prestige*?

THE INFLUENCE OF IMMIGRATION CIRCUMSTANCES

Language-minority children differ with respect to both how long they and their families have been in the host country and their generation status. They may be immigrants themselves, near-descendants of immigrants (first to third generation in the host country), or descendants of peoples who lived within the current borders of a country, but whose natal language is not the societal language (e.g., Native Americans and Mexicans in the United States). Some scholars have suggested that generation status has an impact on language-minority children's academic achievement, in that the immigrant generation arrives with high hopes and expectations for success (with respect to school as well as socioeconomic attainment), but certain ethnocultural groups (e.g., Latinos in the United States) subsequently become disillusioned and disappointed as they confront discrimination and limited opportunities. Ogbu and Matute-Bianchi (1986), Rumbaut (1995), and Suárez-Orozco and Suárez-Orozco (1996), for example, have argued that Latino immigrant parents may come to the United States with high regard for the value of education, but the longer they are exposed to U.S. society, the more they display a pattern of lowered expectations and the less successful their children are in school. The achievement expectations and patterns of the children of immigrants thus become similar to those of nonimmigrant involuntary minorities (e.g., African Americans in the United States). This analysis of the poor achievement outcomes of many language-minority youth has appeared in the popular press: "Immigrants arrive with tremendous positive energy. But the more exposed they are [to American life], the more their dreams fade" (Woo, 1996, p. A19).

Educators have also speculated that the persistent underachievement of many language-minority groups around the world (e.g., Latinos in the United States, Turks in Holland) may be the result of immigration circumstances that work against literacy attainment. Parents' (and children's) undocumented immigration status can adversely influence children's literacy opportunities, experiences, and development. For example, parents may be more reluctant to communicate with teachers or actually go to the school; undocumented status may indicate less certainty about remaining in the host country, and therefore less motivation to help children succeed in the country's schools; and the general precariousness of undocumented status may adversely affect the literacy (or general learning) environment in the home. With an exception noted next, however, there is no evidence that undocumented immigration status actually has a discernible impact on literacy outcomes.

Monzó and Rueda (2001) report on five case studies of Mexican-origin first- and second-grade children. The parents of two children were undocumented; the parents of two were either U.S. citizens or permanent residents; and the mother of the fifth child was undocumented, whereas the father was a permanent resident. Parents whose immigrant status was undocumented were reluctant to do anything that might reveal their status, so they did not obtain library cards. According to Monzó and Rueda, however, two children came from families who were "more successful at producing intrinsic motivation to read in a conventional sense" (p. 15), and the parents of one of these more successful children were undocumented. Despite their differing immigration status, these two children received nearly identical ratings—the highest or near highest in the group—on their valuing reading and on teacher measures of their reading achievement, engaged reading, and reading autonomy. Corroborating the finding from this case study that immigration status appears unrelated to literacy outcomes, Arzubiaga, Rueda, and Monzó (2002) report that immigration processes associated with the family becoming integrated into a new country, such as parents' satisfaction with the adaptation process, were unrelated to children's reading motivation—their valuing reading and their reading self-concept. (Details about immigration constructs and measures are reported in Rueda, MacGillivray, Monzó, & Arzubiaga, 2001, which is a chapter in an edited volume and therefore not eligible for inclusion in this review.)

Goldenberg (1987) reports on an undocumented immigrant mother, who, despite great uncertainty about her and her family's future, had a direct and positive effect on her first-grade daughter's literacy development. The mother regularly talked to the teacher to find out how her daughter was doing and what she needed to work on, she obtained a library card (although used it rarely), and she regularly worked with her daughter at home, teaching her how to read. There was unmistakable evidence that this mother was responsible for her daughter's far better than expected success in first-grade reading (the child was in a transitional bilingual education program and learning to read in Spanish). As was found in the Monzó and Rueda (2001) case studies, it appears that undocumented status is not necessarily an obstacle to creating conditions in the home that promote at least early literacy development for language-minority children.

The only evidence from the studies we reviewed that undocumented status was associated with lower reading outcomes is based on an affective measure used by Monzó and Rueda (2001). The two high-achieving girls described earlier differed on one measure: their reading self-concept. On this measure, the child of undocumented workers scored substantially below the mean of the group, whereas the child of the legal residents scored substantially above. In fact, the two children whose parents were legal U.S. residents scored far above the other three children on the reading self-concept as measured by the Student Motivation to Read Profile (Gambrell, Palmer, Codling, & Mazzoni, 1996). The significance of this finding, even if replicated, is difficult to determine, however, because self-concept has been found to be at best weakly related to measures of reading achievement. The correlation between self-concept and achievement measures has been found to be particularly weak for minority groups and those of low socioeconomic status (SES; Hansford & Hattie, 1982).

Refugee status is a potentially important variation on the immigration status theme. Ima and Rumbaut (1989) point out that "what typically distinguishes refugees from other immigrants are their motives for leaving and their persistent memories of the past, especially the acute sense of loss and trauma...." (p. 57). In a two-stage study of Southeast Asian refugee students in Grades 7 to 12, however, Ima and Rumbaut obtained few data to indicate that refugee status or experiences leading up to being a refugee influenced literacy attainment. Indeed, variability in literacy attainment across immigrant groups in general and Southeast Asian groups in particular, could be explained by differences in parents' education, years in the United States, and age of student when he or she arrived, not immigration circumstances as elaborated in the following sections (see chap. 4 for a discussion of the influence of student-level factors, such as parent education, other SES indicators, time in new country, and age of arrival, on literacy development).

In the first stage of the study (as reported earlier), Ima and Rumbaut compared the achievement of high school juniors and seniors from six ethnic groups (the authors' term)—East Asians, Southeast Asians, Filipinos, Hispanics, Pacific Islanders, and "other" immigrants. The Southeast Asians scored the lowest of all. These students had experienced the most disrupted schooling because of political strife in their native countries, but they had also been in the United States the least amount of time, and they came from less advantaged educational backgrounds than the "other Asian and other immigrant groups." Ima and Rumbaut report that "a substantial number [of the Southeast Asian immigrant students] are the children of illiterate peasants and fishermen" (p. 64).

In the second stage of the study, which involved only 7th- through 12th-grade students from five ethnic groups of Southeast Asian refugees (Vietnamese, Chinese–Vietnamese, Hmong, Khmer, and Laotian), Ima and Rumbaut found that time in the United States, age at arrival, and parent education predicted reading achievement (see chap. 4), but ethnicity (operationalized as national origin) did not. Ima and Rumbaut report that the different national groups of Southeast Asian refugees had different refugee experiences. For example, Cambodians experienced more trauma (e.g., disrupted schooling, traumatic dislocation, and extremely harsh conditions) than did Laotians. Nevertheless, none of the data suggests that these experiences influenced literacy outcomes. Southeast Asians had the highest percentage of limited-English-proficient students in the school district (San Diego), but the second highest grade point average (GPA) among ethnic groups. Despite the trauma associated with their immigration circumstances, the Southeast Asian refugees were successful in school and received high test scores in areas requiring minimal language and cultural familiarity. Their low reading scores were attributable to their relatively recent arrival and associated linguistic challenges, which the students eventually overcame. Ima and Rumbaut contend that the influence of refugee/immigrant experiences is important within a few years of immigration and then gradually dissipates.

One study in our database examined the effect of generation status on student literacy attainment.[1] Buriel and Cardoza (1988) studied a subsample of high school seniors who had participated in the High School and Beyond longitudinal study. Students who identified themselves as Mexican, Chicano, or Mexican American were selected for this study and divided into three groups based on the information they provided: (a) first-generation students—not born in the United States; (b) second-generation students—born in the United States, but with at least one parent who was not; and (c) third-generation students—who themselves, as well as both parents, were born in the United States. The students resided in different regions of the United States. There were no differences among the three groups with respect to reading and vocabulary achievement or students' and mothers' school aspirations.[2] Socioeconomically, the third-generation students had more highly educated parents and higher family incomes than the first- and second-generation students. Reading scores went up slightly, but not reliably, across the three generations; vocabulary scores fluctuated slightly, but again not reliably. In short, this study's findings do not support the proposition that generation status has an impact on students' English literacy achievement. All three generations scored somewhat below the High School and Beyond national sample.

Aside from the possible exception of some of the undocumented immigrants discussed previously, no study in our database included Spanish-speaking refugees. Some of these individuals were leaving oppressive situations in their home countries, but there is no indication in the publications that they had refugee status.

---

[1]One other study provides background information for understanding the role of generation status on literacy attainment. It addressed generational effects on literacy achievement, motivation, and expectations/aspirations among a language-minority population (Mexican American high school students). Anderson and Johnson (1971) was not part of our database because it was published before the years selected for inclusion in this review (1980–2002). We make a note of it here for background purposes. The authors found a mixed and complex picture but concluded that there is little or no difference in the amount of parental emphasis on obtaining good grades in school, completing high school, and ultimately attending college among three generations of Mexican-American families" (p. 305). They also found little or no difference in the high school English grades of immigrant, first-, and second-generation students; however, third-generation Latino students-whether they spoke English or Spanish at home-had lower English grades than the other generational groups.

[2]Although the researchers call this variable "aspirations," they actually studied "expectations" since respondents were asked how far they *thought* the student would go in his or her education. Aspirations refer to what someone hopes will happen or wants to happen; expectations refer to what someone thinks will happen or is likely to happen (Goldenberg et al., 2001).

In summary, studies addressing issues of immigration's effects on students' literacy development can generally be grouped into two categories: those focusing on circumstances of immigration, and those focusing on generation status. With respect to immigration circumstances, the studies did not reveal strong influences on literacy outcomes (Goldenberg, 1987; Ima & Rumbaut, 1989; Monzó & Rueda, 2001). Although undocumented immigration and refugee experiences can create traumatic situations for children and families, there is no evidence that these experiences impede literacy achievement specifically. Given the currently available research, it is plausible to hypothesize that literacy outcomes are more likely to be the result of home (and school) language and literacy learning opportunities, irrespective of immigration circumstances. Buriel and Cardoza (1988) is the only study located for this review that examined generation status; it compared literacy outcomes among successive generations of language-minority students. Although Buriel and Cardoza found a shift from Spanish to English use across three generations of Mexican American high school seniors who reported at least some Spanish use in the home, generation status did not appear to influence English reading and vocabulary skills.

THE INFLUENCE OF DISCOURSE AND INTERACTIONAL CHARACTERISTICS

The most well-known and influential study in this group is that of Au and Mason (1981), based on research and development conducted at the Kamehameha Early Education Project (KEEP) in Hawaii (see Tharp, 1982, for an additional description of KEEP). Au and Mason found that when classroom instructional interaction was compatible with interaction patterns in Hawaiian children's native culture, the students demonstrated "much higher levels of achievement-related...behaviors" than when instructional patterns conformed to typical U.S. classroom patterns, whereby, for example, students wait for the teacher to call on them. Au and Mason call this construct *balance of rights*—the extent to which instructional interactions permit self-selected turns by students, overlapping speech, and the absence of the teacher's explicit and overt control of the interaction. Their study found that when the balance of rights in the KEEP classrooms was such that students could speak freely and spontaneously without waiting for teacher permission—an interaction pattern similar to that at home—students' *achievement-related behaviors* (defined as academic engagement, topical and correct responses, number of idea units expressed, and logical inferences) all increased during the reading lesson.

These are potentially important outcomes, particularly to the extent that the achievement-related behaviors documented by Au and Mason actually promote higher levels of student achievement. There is in fact a literature suggesting that academic engagement and other achievement-related behaviors are associated with measured achievement (see e.g., the reviews in Wang & Walberg, 1983; Fredericks, Blumenfeld, & Parks, 2004). However, researchers also have shown that the effects of participation and engagement on actual learning are inconsistent (Karweit, 1989). The critical point with respect to this study is that achievement-related behaviors (which Au and Mason measured) and student achievement (which they did not) are not the same thing. Achievement-related behaviors can be influenced by a particular intervention (e.g., culturally accommodating instructional patterns), but we simply do not know the relationship between these behaviors and actual measured achievement in any aspect of reading.

Whereas Au and Mason examined the instructional interaction features of the KEEP program and its effects on student participation during reading lessons, Tharp (1982) evaluated the overall program in terms of its effects on measured student reading achievement. Tharp found that the KEEP program did produce positive, if modest, effects on student reading achievement (see chap. 15 for an analysis of this study's design and interpretation of its results from a different perspective). In addition to instruction accommodating the children's interactional styles, however, the KEEP program comprised a number of other elements, such as small-group format, emphasis on comprehension, active direct instruction by teachers, systematic instructional objectives, frequent monitoring of teaching, and criterion-referenced assessment of student learning. As Tharp acknowledges, "it is probably impossible to evaluate the separate program elements individually, because they always occur in interaction with others" (p. 521). What we can conclude from Au and Mason (1981) and Tharp (1982), taken together, is that (a) instructional interactions that were part of the KEEP program contributed to higher levels (quantitatively and qualitatively) of student academic engagement, and (b) the program overall contributed to somewhat higher levels of measured student reading achievement. However, we do not know the degree to which instruction that accommodated children's native interaction styles made a direct, or even indirect, contribution to their literacy attainment. This positive effect of accommodative instruction on literacy attainment therefore remains a highly plausible hypothesis.

It is also plausible, however, that the KEEP program is more effective in general, and that children will respond more enthusiastically to the give-and-take nature of its reading comprehension lessons regardless of their cultural interaction patterns. Hard evidence is lacking, but the generality of the effectiveness of the KEEP reading lessons—as opposed to culture-specific effects—is suggested by other studies with different populations of students in which the lessons pioneered at KEEP (also known as instructional conversations) were apparently employed successfully (see the analysis of Saunders, 1999; Saunders & Goldenberg, 1999, in chaps. 15 and 16 for the application of instructional conversations with Latino and mixed cultural/ethnic groups). What is lacking is a study examining culturally accommodative instructional interactions with regard to their effects on distinct groups of students—those whose culture aligns with the intervention and others whose culture does not.

Four other studies examined discourse characteristics among second-language learners. In each case, the authors make claims about the implications of differences in home and school discourse patterns for children's school success. However, important gaps in the data reported or the study designs make these claims difficult to sustain. It is highly plausible that there are interaction differences among different language/ethnic groups, but it is not at all clear what these mean for children's literacy attainment or how schools and teachers should accommodate these differences.

In a study that focused on four Spanish-speaking children in a family literacy program, Huerta-Macías and Quintero (1992) report that code switching (using both Spanish and English within the same sentence or utterance, a common feature of Latino discourse in the United States) facilitated children's writing (regardless of whether children wrote or dictated to the teacher) in English or Spanish or both in an intergenerational family literacy project involving 4- to 6-year-olds and their parents. The authors report that participating parents had above-average educational attainment compared with other parents in the project. Further, the authors report on the children's writing and give numerous examples of texts they generated. The study findings show that code switching was used by children, parents, and teachers (depending on the addressee), but occurred far less often in children's writing than in their speaking. Thus, it cannot be argued that their writing somehow reflected the linguistic environment. In fact, it is impossible to determine whether the oral language environment had any influence at all on students' writing because the authors present no data on such a connection. Further, because this was a case study of a single program in which code switching was allowed, and even encouraged, we cannot know what the children's writing development would have been like without code switching or determine its effects on emergent biliterate writing. Moreover, we do not know the extent of code switching in the children's homes and, therefore, the degree to which its use in class actually constituted a bridging of discourse practices between school and home.

Wilkinson, Milosky, and Genishi (1986) found that reading achievement among Spanish-speaking students was positively related to obtaining appropriate responses to requests in cooperative student work groups, a finding reported elsewhere in the cooperative learning literature (e.g., Webb, 1989). Comparison of these findings with the authors' previous research on native-English-speaking students reveals that the Hispanic children in cooperative groups less frequently designated an intended respondent and revised requests for a second try—two features of *effective speakers* in cooperative groups (defined as participants whose requests are met). More specifically, the authors report that Hispanic students made requests that were verbally less direct than those used by monolingual students who had participated in their previous studies. During group interactions, Spanish-speaking students spoke with their heads down and did not focus their requests on specific persons. In contrast to monolingual English students, who addressed their requests to specific individuals 83% of the time, the Latino students did so only 20% of the time.

These findings point to potentially important interaction differences between Spanish- and native-English-speaking students that could attenuate the former students' achievement in cooperative learning situations. Indeed, to the extent that particular interaction strategies (in this case, direct requests) promote higher achievement in cooperative groups, these findings suggest that cooperative learning might be a less effective learning context for Hispanic students. But this implication, which the authors do not explicitly draw but would appear to follow from their findings, appears to contradict the findings of research on cooperative learning that have shown its effectiveness for Latino students (Calderón, Hertz-Lazarowitz, & Slavin, 1998). Moreover, this was a one-group study, so there was no direct comparison with English-only students. The comparison was between the Latino students in this study and English-speaking populations in previous studies. In at least one of the latter studies (Wilkinson & Calculator, 1982), all students were from middle-class backgrounds, so there is also a likely confound of SES and language background in the comparison. Nonetheless, if the finding of consequential interaction differences between native Spanish speakers and native English speakers in cooperative groups is corroborated, it suggests that some sort of accommodation may be needed so that English-language learners will not be disadvantaged in these learning contexts.

In a study that examined the efficacy of inductive (in contrast to direct) teaching, Kucer and Silva (1999) posed the question of whether a discourse gap between home and school for many language-minority children of low SES makes inductive approaches to teaching literacy forms and conventions less effective. Delpit (1986) argues that, because of discourse socialization in the home, many children of low SES are used to a more direct and transparent form of communication. Instructional patterns involving inquiry or guided discovery that are characteristic of constructivist instructional methods may be inconsistent with the interaction patterns these children experience at home. Kucer and Silva challenge the proposition that low-income Spanish-speaking children must receive direct instruction if they are to learn the forms and conventions of English literacy. They report that transition students in a whole-language classroom made progress in some areas of literacy learning (e.g., producing syntactically and semantically more acceptable story readings, spelling), but not others (writing, writing conventions). Kucer and Silva conclude that there may be a need for direct instruction in those areas that children do not learn through inductive means.

There are a number of problems with this study, however. The authors conclude that inductive methods work well for some literacy outcomes, but that direct teaching (e.g., in the form of mini-lessons) may be necessary for others. However, no control or comparison group was used to permit strong inferences about the effects of different types of instruction. In addition, we do not know whether the significant growth that did occur in some areas was adequate. English-language learners and low-income students can make year-to-year progress yet be woefully below grade/age norms and expectations. Significant growth over time with no comparative frame is a poor criterion for judging the efficacy of programs and approaches.

McCarty, Wallace, Lynch, and Benally (1991) report on the implementation of an inquiry curriculum for Navajo students that they argue is more compatible with the inductive-inquiry learning pattern children experience in their natal settings. The curriculum was developed around the concept of "k'é, meaning kinship, clanship, and 'right and respectful relations with others and with nature'" (p. 46). The curriculum sequence was organized around concepts relevant to k'é, which expand in spiraling fashion to higher levels of abstraction, generality, and complexity. For example, the concept of interaction appears in the lower primary levels in terms of the interaction of self with family members and clan relatives.... At higher levels, students have opportunities to develop an increasingly sophisticated and critical understanding of the concept in light of interactions of groups of people, nations, and governments (p. 46). The curriculum was implemented for part of one school year in four upper elementary classrooms. In all but one classroom, instruction was conducted in Navajo.

This study is similar to that of Au and Mason, in that the authors hypothesize that when teachers use culturally familiar interaction styles with students, students are engaged more productively in lessons. But McCarty and colleagues are far less thorough than Au and Mason in reporting the instructional interaction that occurred and its effects on student participation. They present a general description of an instructional approach whereby students are encouraged to talk and generate hypotheses, using artifacts, pictures, and concepts familiar to them, contrasting this with "basic skills methods emphasizing cue-response scripted drills" (p. 48), described later in the article as "communicative interaction [in] the form of face-to-face assault" (p. 52). McCarty et al. set out to examine the effects of a teaching/learning style to which the children were accustomed "in natural situations *outside* the classroom" (p. 50; italics original). They report that the Native American students in the study responded eagerly and verbally to questioning during the highly interactive lessons, even in their second language (English). Unlike Au and Mason, however, who demonstrated through a comparative analysis with a contrasting reading lesson that students responded more positively to a culturally familiar interaction style with the teacher, McCarty and colleagues simply assert that students became more engaged when the inquiry curriculum was used. The only data offered consist of a brief report that an outspoken critic of the inquiry approach (a staff member at the school) "admitt[ed] that Navajo students will indeed respond, eagerly and enthusiastically, to classroom questioning" (p. 49) and other reports from teachers that students were willing participants in the learning activities. Moreover, no data are reported on any achievement outcomes (but see the following discussion of McCarty, 1993, for achievement data from this project).

We found no studies of the influence of discourse and interaction differences on first- and second-language literacy outcomes at the secondary level.

In summary, many educators have suggested that minority children are socialized to interact with others at home and in their community in ways that might be at variance with expectations regarding interaction at school. These interactional or discourse differences might interfere with school achievement because children are required to interact with other children and the teacher in ways that are strange or difficult for them. By extension, minimizing the interaction gap between home and school might help promote higher levels of literacy attainment by removing obstacles to interaction and making the classroom more familiar and comfortable.

The available literature suggests two conclusions. First, descriptive studies discussed in chapter 12 (Au, 1980; Gregory, 1998; Schmidt, 1995; Xu, 1999) provide good evidence that norms and expectations for social interaction differ between the home and school environments of some language-minority students. Second, however, the consequences of these differences for students' literacy attainment and the effects of attempts to address or accommodate these differences in the classroom are not clear. One highly influential study (Au & Mason, 1981) found that culturally compatible instruction had positive effects on native Hawaiian speakers' level of engagement and participation during reading lessons. But this study did not measure literacy achievement or comprehension of the stories being discussed, so we do not know whether the higher levels of engagement and participation led to greater achievement or learning. Authors of other studies involving Navajo- and Spanish-speaking students also make claims about the effects of different discourse or interaction patterns on literacy-related student outcomes or of instruction that accommodates students' discourse or interaction characteristics. In each case, however, data or design problems preclude straightforward interpretation.

THE INFLUENCE OF OTHER SOCIOCULTURALLY ROOTED FACTORS LINKED TO SOCIOCULTURAL CHARACTERISTICS OF STUDENTS AND TEACHERS

In this section, we move beyond specific issues of discourse and interaction to examine the role of other noninstructional sociocultural factors. These include such factors as student and family beliefs, attitudes, learning styles, motivation, behaviors, specific or general knowledge, and interests that are rooted in cultural or social group membership; the teacher–student cultural, ethnic, and linguistic match; teacher beliefs; classroom organization; and the degree of teacher versus student control of learning activities and content. A particular emphasis here is on the impact of culturally familiar instructional materials, meaning their content is rooted in culturally specific experiences or events.

We first examine studies that address the role of culturally relevant materials in literacy outcomes. We then consider studies examining the impact of cultural relevance in comparison with that of text language. As we see, there is some evidence for an impact of culturally familiar materials on learning outcomes such as reading comprehension; however, there is stronger evidence for the effects of text language (i.e., more familiar text language produces better comprehension). The impact of language of instruction, which often determines the language of textual materials, is covered in chapter 14. We then review studies that address a variety of other sociocultural factors, such as attitudes and family practices.

Impact of Culturally Relevant/Meaningful Reading Material on Literacy Outcomes

Although all the studies on this topic have design and possible interpretive flaws, as a group they make a modest case for the proposition that language-minority students' literacy achievement improves when they read or otherwise use culturally familiar materials. Even within this group of studies, however, at least two yielded findings that challenge the importance of culturally familiar material in facilitating or improving reading development (Abu-Rabia, 1995; Schon, Hopkins, & Vojir, 1984). Moreover, *cultural content* is usually not defined in these studies, so it is difficult to draw precise conclusions about the implications of their findings.

In two related participant observation studies, Kenner (1999, 2000) examined the biliteracy development of a Gujarati (from northwest India) child who attended a London multilingual/multicultural preschool and then an all-English primary school. This case provides one of the few examples in the body of ethnographic work that link children's socioculturally rooted experiences to indicators of literacy or literacy-related outcomes. The study demonstrates that, even within an ethnographic methodological frame, it is possible to collect and present data that have a bearing on literacy outcomes. For this reason, we discuss the study in some detail.

Parents and children in the multilingual preschool Kenner (1999) first studied were invited to bring literacy materials from home in the home language. These materials were placed in a home corner and a writing area. Parents and children were invited to write in the classroom in different languages and genres—cards, letters to relatives, posters, and travel brochures. Kenner illustrates connections children made between their areas of home interest/experience and their classroom activities, particularly around literacy. For example, the mother of one child reported he loved to watch cooking programs on TV and could relate to her how to prepare a dish he had just seen demonstrated. In the classroom, Kenner reports this child "produced a recipe involving 'one apple, two oranges, cake with jelly'" (p. 6). Children also drew on their knowledge and experience, made accessible in their home languages, to explore and produce different genres of writing, such as letters, lists, greeting cards, and recipes. Kenner describes numerous instances of his target child (Meera) making these connections and using them to read and write (e.g., letters, cards, posters, signs).

Kenner reports that letter writing at home, together with letter-writing opportunities in preschool, probably contributed to Meera's knowledge about this writing genre and to her knowledge of written conventions in both English and Gujarati. Meera's mother reported that her daughter sat next to her at home, with pen and paper, saying "I am writing a letter" as the mother wrote letters to India. At preschool, Meera learned to write her name in English; her mother, who volunteered in the classroom, showed her how to write her name in Gujarati and provided additional opportunities for learning written Gujarati (this was observed directly). When writing in the classroom, Meera used Gujarati and English script and demonstrated knowledge of appropriate formats (e.g., writing in straight lines across the page) and content (e.g., news about the family's shop and family members).

However, the examples Kenner provides show that home-based interests and experiences are not necessarily rooted in natal culture. The recipe illustration was not specific to the family's particular culture. Other children used a "Lion King" poster (produced by one of the parents in Spanish) to write out "El Rey León"; one child wrote out and built a dramatic play routine around lottery tickets. In other words, the connections children made were with their lived experiences, rather than elements of their ethnic culture per se. Nonetheless, and regardless of the cultural origin of texts and activities made available to the children, Kenner provides evidence that children drew on resources provided at school, in both English and their native language and across a range of genres, to engage in numerous literacy activities and develop literacy skills in their first and second languages.

In a successor study, Kenner (2000) followed Meera into early elementary school and found that the multicultural classroom context that had actively promoted her biliteracy development had largely disappeared. Although "the school as an institution...provided some openings for multilingual literacy," Kenner reports, it "was not structured in such a way as to allow its full development within high status curriculum activity" (p. 27). One obstacle was high-stakes national accountability exams, which tended to displace anything in the curriculum that did not directly relate to what was being tested. Despite

Meera's attempts to maintain a bilingual/biliterate focus in her schoolwork—an example, Kenner writes, of "individual agency in resisting the dominant discourse" (p. 27)—she had fewer opportunities than she did in preschool to develop language and literacy skills in her first language. Moreover, there was evidence that her first-language skills were stagnating. Whereas she had been a confident Gujarati speaker and had been developing Gujarati literacy skills at age 4, at age 7, Meera told the author she now talked to adults in English "because I don't know yet how to say in Gujarati yet…I'll speak to everyone in English" (p. 27).

Kenner followed Meera for 3 years, documenting her classroom literacy opportunities, activities, attitudes, and language/literacy development. Her bilingual/biliterate development probably benefited from the nursery school she attended, as suggested by the examples given earlier and further examples, including illustrations of Meera's emergent writing in Gujarati and English that Kenner provides. Although it is difficult to know with certainty, Meera's bilingual/biliterate development probably suffered when she moved to early primary school, where there was no systematic support for primary-language development, either oral or literate, and far less support for multicultural experiences in general. To the extent that home languages are valuable resources to be nurtured, the failure of Meera's elementary school to continue supporting her bilingual/literate development is a disappointment. However, we cannot tell what impact the second-language emphasis—along with an absence of multicultural emphasis—in early primary school had on her language and literacy development in English. Moreover, as compelling as Meera's story is as a case study, we do not know how representative her experiences and achievement in her preschool and early primary years are. Nonetheless, Kenner's work suggests important and intricate sociocultural dynamics that may influence the literacy development of language-minority children in their first or second language.

Hannon and McNally (1986) investigated the relationship between understanding of test items and performance on a reading comprehension measure (a multiple-choice sentence-completion reading test) in a sample of 72 students comprising three groups of 24 students (12 boys and 12 girls), ages approximately 8 to 9 years, from (a) working-class homes, (b) middle-class homes, and (c) homes where English was a second language (from unspecified Asian countries). The researchers found that both middle- and working-class children outperformed the children with English as a second language (and the middle-class children outperformed the working-class children). There were large discrepancies in performance among the three groups, even when the test was administered orally, suggesting that the differences among the groups were not entirely, or even mostly, due to *reading skill* per se (which the authors define as decoding/word recognition). Instead, Hannon and McNally argue, the differences in reading achievement scores were largely a function of comprehending the test content, which in turn was based on children's possessing pertinent cultural knowledge. (Hannon and McNally also found a discrepancy between oral and reading scores for both the working-class and non-native-English-speaking children, but not for the middle-class children. This finding suggests that, in addition to lacking relevant cultural knowledge, the former two groups were also less proficient in basic word reading skills, further depressing their performance.)

The findings with respect to differences in the scores on the orally administered test do suggest that the reading passages contained material that was less
understandable to the non-native-English-speaking students (and to the working-
class students, in comparison with the middle-class students), but this is about
all we can conclude from the study. On the basis of a selective post hoc analysis of several test items, the authors suggest elements that may have been less
accessible to these students. For example, one item identified for discussion
was the following:

> Jimmy … tea, because he was our guest (choices, with correct one underlined:
> 1. washed the dishes after; 2. was late for; 3. got the best cake at; 4. could not
> eat his) (p. 238)

Hannon and McNally report that 22 out of 24 middle-class students answered
this item correctly in the oral administration of the test, whereas only 9 out of
24 in each of the working-class and English-language learner groups answered
correctly. The authors' conclusion that test performance was based on possessing
relevant background knowledge is entirely reasonable. However, it appears
that the working-class students and the English as a second language (ESL)
students—the latter drawn from an inner-city school and probably largely
working class—were equally disadvantaged. In other words, language-minority
status per se was not isolated as a risk factor for poor test performance. This
design flaw once again limits what we can learn from this study about sociocultural factors related to language-minority children's literacy performance.
Student group was completely confounded with school in that students were
drawn from schools with predominantly middle-class, working-class, and
non-native-English-speaking populations, respectively. No information is provided about the non-native-English-speaking students' social class (although
judging from the fact that they attended an inner-city school, they were probably
disproportionately working class), leaving us with the finding that middle-class
children outperformed working-class children on a reading comprehension test
(administered orally or in writing) and that both groups outperformed a language-minority group on these measures. But we have no information about the
reasons for this differential performance or about the relative contributions of
social class, cultural background, and English proficiency.

García (1991) similarly found that lack of relevant background knowledge
impeded Spanish-background students on reading comprehension tests, but
her study was free of the confounds in the Hannon and McNally study. In fact,
García's study is compelling because she shows that when prior knowledge
is controlled performance differences between Hispanic and monolingual
English-speaking students essentially disappear. A qualitative component of
this study delved into the specific obstacles to comprehension the students
faced. However, little of what we mean by *familiar* had to do with students' culture as the term is typically defined, and it is difficult to conclude that culturally specific knowledge played a role in the students' test performance. The
language-minority students had difficulties with words and concepts such
as *chimpanzee, handicap,* and *advantage.* They also were more literal in their reading and did not use the vocabulary they had to draw correct inferences. There

were two topics about which the Latino students had greater or equal background knowledge compared to the non-Latinos—piñata and polar bear. The groups' scores on these passages were nearly equivalent.

McCarty (1993) describes a program, whose origins were in collaboration with the KEEP program (see Vogt, Jordan, & Tharp, 1987), "that was designed to tap the language and literacy strengths of Navajo bilingual learners" (p. 183). The classrooms used pedagogy and curriculum associated with whole-language literacy approaches (e.g., children's literature, authentic reading and writing experiences, cooperative learning, language experience). To this extent, there was nothing unique to Navajo culture about the program. The primary cultural accommodation, in addition to use of the Navajo language in the class-room, was the content selected for the thematic units studied (e.g., wind, sheep, and corn), all of which are prominent in Navajo daily life. Students engaged in academically challenging tasks and learned basic and advanced literacy skills by studying such topics, about which they had considerable background knowledge. McCarty claims that providing the Navajo children with culturally relevant experiences and topics produced more favorable learning environments and enhanced literacy outcomes.

McCarty reports rising scores on both locally developed and nationally stan-dardized tests at the school, although it is difficult to link the curricular and instructional changes she describes with those changes in scores. The KEEP col-laboration began in 1983 and lasted 5 years. Thereafter, a Title VII grant sup-ported continued development and adaptation of the KEEP model with the Navajo children. The achievement data McCarty reports are for spring 1990 to spring 1991, when the Grades K–3 children in the Navajo language arts pro-gram achieved gains of 12 percentage points on locally developed literacy mea-sures. During the same period, McCarty reports, Comprehensive Test of Basic Skills (CTBS) percentile scores "more than doubled in reading vocabulary" (p. 191). McCarty also presents examples of children's writing, indicating the sorts of written work they were producing in the language arts program. McCarty's claims of program effects are plausible, but the absence of a strong evaluation design, primarily a comparison group, attenuates her claims. The study's design makes it difficult to determine whether the language arts pro-gram had an effect on children's literacy outcomes, leaving moot the question of whether culturally accommodating curriculum materials had the hypothe-sized effect on literacy achievement.

Jiménez (1997) used culturally familiar reading materials for a strategic read-ing intervention with five very low-achieving middle-school Latino students. He reports qualitative evidence that the students became more interested in reading, that reading made more sense to them, and that they used strategic reading pro-cedures following training in strategic reading. Strictly speaking, the effect of the culturally familiar text per se is unknown because only one type of text was used in the intervention and follow-up study. But quoted comments from students indicate that they made connections with the text based on their experiences with the culturally relevant topics (e.g., making tamales, certain family events with which the students identified). Jiménez provides compelling qualitative evidence that students were employing the strategic reading processes he taught them in the intervention, but this outcome is more likely to be a result of the cognitive strategy instruction provided than of the culturally relevant readings. The impact of the culturally relevant materials is unknown, although it is possible that they played a facilitating or motivating role.

Lasisi et al. (1988) report on two experiments. In Experiment 1, seventh-grade students in Nigeria who read a culturally familiar story written in English (their second language) performed better on a literal comprehension test than did seventh graders who read culturally unfamiliar material (also in English). The effect of the culturally familiar text was only on literal comprehension; no effect was found for interpretive comprehension. *Culturally familiar* was defined as stories with characters and situations that would be known to the students—in this case, traditional Nigerian tales. Although the authors' interpretation of the study results is plausible, a number of design issues must be noted. First, only one story was used for each condition and comprehension outcome: One culturally familiar and one culturally unfamiliar story were used to compare students' literal comprehension, and one culturally familiar and one culturally unfamiliar story were used to compare students' interpretive comprehension. There was no control for story or question difficulty (the authors report only that passages and questions were verified by university and high school faculty), so there is no way to know whether passages and questions were at comparable reading levels. Moreover, the authors report that "answers to the multiple-choice questions were based on the reader's background knowledge of culture whether foreign or Nigerian," so it may be that the comprehension tests were largely tests of cultural knowledge, in which case they would not be valid assessments of reading comprehension. However, insufficient information is provided about the content of the measure to make this determination.

Abu-Rabia (1996) also examined the relationship between culturally familiar reading material and student reading comprehension. Abu-Rabia found that reading comprehension was higher when 15- to 16-year-old Druze (Arab) students read a story with Arabic content versus Jewish content; the Druze students also rated stories with Arab content higher in interest value. Both stories were presented in Hebrew. A team of 10 Hebrew teachers judged the stories to be equal in length and academic difficulty. Unfortunately, there was only one story for each condition—one with Jewish content, one with Arab content—so the results could be confounded by the particular stories used. As with the Lasisi et al. (1988) study, it is impossible to tell whether cultural familiarity or some other feature of the stories (e.g., writing quality, higher interest for reasons other than cultural content) or the questions asked explains the difference in student comprehension.

Finally, in contrast to the previously cited studies, the results of two studies conducted by Schon et al. (1984) challenge the proposition that culturally relevant reading material improves reading achievement. However, the lack of specification of the reading materials used makes interpretation of these results difficult. Schon and colleagues conducted two experiments, lasting 4 and 7 months, respectively, in which high-interest reading materials in Spanish were provided to low-achieving high school students. Unfortunately, the authors provide no detail about these materials other than to say they comprised "a wide variety of newspapers, magazines, and paperback or hardback books in Spanish, as described by Schon (1978)" (p. 33). Each experiment involved approximately 170 Hispanic high school students of low SES in a midsize southwestern U.S. city. Spanish reading, English reading, and affective (reading attitude/academic self-concept) measures were used as pre- and posttests. In one experiment, participating students' Spanish reading comprehension was superior to their English reading comprehension; in the other, English was superior to Spanish. In both experiments, however, the high-interest Spanish reading materials had no effect on Spanish or English reading comprehension or on attitudes toward reading and reading self-concept. Although analyses of covariance (ANCOVA) failed to detect any significant difference in the experimental and control means, some method-by-teacher interactions were evident on both the Spanish reading and affective measures. Classroom observation and teacher interviews revealed that U.S-born Hispanics had little interest in and rarely made use of the Spanish materials, but that recent Hispanic immigrants to the United States enjoyed the materials and used them extensively. It should be pointed out that Schon and colleagues do not specifically invoke the term *culturally relevant*. Therefore, these two studies may not be a meaningful test of this hypothesis, except to the extent that high-interest Spanish-language material can be viewed as culturally relevant or meaningful.

Overall, the studies reviewed in this section provide some, although weak, support for the proposition that culturally relevant reading or curriculum materials promote reading comprehension or literacy development more generally, and, conversely, that culturally unfamiliar materials can interfere with comprehension and literacy growth. Various design issues limit what we can conclude from the studies. The familiarity of text content certainly influences comprehension, as has been known for years. But it is not clear what role is played by cultural familiarity per se.

Comparative Impact of Culturally Meaningful Material and the Language Used in the Text

Studies discussed here examine the effects of culturally meaningful materials in comparison with those of text language (i.e., the native tongue or the second language). As with the preceding group of studies reviewed, these studies also provide some support for the impact of culturally relevant materials on reading performance, but they indicate that text language is a stronger influence: Students perform better when they read or use materials in the language they know better and/or when the text language is most clearly written and accessible.

Several studies permit some degree of comparison of the importance of text language and cultural content in influencing language-minority children's literacy development. Although Davies (1991) analyzes the content of and performance on a mathematics test, so much reading was involved that the test must be considered partly a literacy assessment. Davies concludes that English-language learners' lack of local knowledge made certain terms and pictures (e.g., skateboard, Chinese checkers, swap cards) less comprehensible. These students also faced linguistic challenges that had nothing to do with their lack of familiarity with item content. The wording of instructions (e.g., use of indefinite articles and ambiguous auxiliary verbs) and lexical density (lexical items per clause) appeared to pose perhaps greater potential difficulties for these students. Davies concludes that inadequate English proficiency is a more serious challenge than a lack of cultural familiarity with content for English-language learners, but he presents no data that would permit a direct comparison. Nonetheless, both factors are likely to interfere with reading comprehension and task performance.

Lasisi et al. (1988) conducted an experiment in which they found that the language of textual material had a stronger effect on reading comprehension than was found for cultural content in an earlier experiment. Culturally unfamiliar passages used in the first experiment (described earlier) were translated into Yoruba, the students' first language. Students did much better on both literal and higher level comprehension when passages were presented in Yoruba. Although direct comparisons of the effects of cultural content and text language on reading comprehension are not possible (neither the design nor the reported data permit such comparisons), it appears that text language had a more pronounced effect than cultural content. First, text language affected both literal and interpretive comprehension, whereas cultural content affected only literal comprehension. Second, the magnitude of differences between experimental conditions was greater when language conditions were compared than when cultural content conditions were compared. On the interpretive test, for example, group means for students who received culturally familiar and culturally unfamiliar material (both presented in English, the second language) were 3.79 and 2.43 out of 10, respectively. In contrast, group means for students who received Yoruba and English (culturally unfamiliar) materials were 5.62 and 3.00, respectively. Standard deviations are not reported, so effect sizes cannot be determined. However, the magnitude of the differences appears greater when language conditions are compared than when cultural content conditions are compared.

Abu-Rabia (1995) draws a similar conclusion about the impact of cultural content on reading comprehension. This study of Arab Canadian eighth graders in Canada found that culturally familiar reading materials made no difference in student reading comprehension. Text language, however, had a strong effect on comprehension, with students scoring higher on English than on Arabic texts. The simple explanation appears to be that the students' reading skills were stronger in English (their second language) than in Arabic (their first language), as demonstrated by a cloze test in each language administered as part of the study. Students were immigrants who had been in Canada for 2 to 3 years. Although exposed to Arabic at home and through heritage language programs, they studied in a regular English program at school. Abu-Rabia suggests that the students' multicultural background and Canada's strong multicultural climate explain the finding that cultural content did not influence reading comprehension. This may be a plausible explanation for why these results contrast so sharply with those of Abu-Rabia's studies in Israel (reviewed next), where the cultural and sociopolitical dynamics are so different. But it is also the case that this sample of Arab students was more proficient in second-language reading than in first-language reading, and these effects cannot be separated from the multicultural explanation offered by Abu-Rabia.

In one study in Israel, Abu-Rabia (1998a) used multiple texts for each cultural condition, thus eliminating the design flaw of cultural condition confounded by story. In addition, students in each experimental condition read only one type of material (Arab or Jewish) in only one language (Arabic or

Hebrew), so order of presentation was not a confound either. Eighth-grade Arab students were randomly assigned to one of four conditions—reading Jewish stories in Hebrew, reading Jewish stories in Arabic, reading Arab stories in Arabic, or reading Arab stories in Hebrew. Students read the stories and then answered comprehension questions. They received higher comprehension scores in the stories with Arabic cultural content regardless of the text language. There was also a language main effect, indicating that the students comprehended better when reading text in Arabic (regardless of cultural content). This study reveals that both cultural content and language of text can influence reading comprehension. Unfortunately, the author did not include any measures of the students' reading level, so we do not know their relative reading proficiency in Arabic and Hebrew. Because their reading achievement scores were higher in Arabic, we can assume they were stronger readers in Arabic than in Hebrew.

In a second and more complex Israeli study that attempted to separate the effects of text language and cultural content, Abu-Rabia (1998b) found that 15- to 16-year-old Arab students expressed greater interest in Arab content than in Western or Jewish content when texts were presented in English, Hebrew, or Arabic. Comprehension was highest for Arab content. The text language had essentially no effect on comprehension. Abu-Rabia reports that students were trilingual (Arabic, Hebrew, English), although no data are presented on language proficiency. As with studies described previously, there are issues regarding the experimental design. Only one story representing each of the three cultures was used; each was presented in Arabic, English, and Hebrew. (The original story in each language was translated into the other two.) The Arab story was always presented first in all three conditions (Condition 1: Arab, Jewish, Western story presented in English; Condition 2: Arab, Jewish, Western story presented in Hebrew; Condition 3: Arab, Jewish, Western story presented in Arabic). Comprehension tests were administered after subjects had read all three stories. Given the failure to counterbalance the cultural content of the stories, the results that Abu-Rabia obtained may have been a consequence of primacy effects (students recalled more Arab content because it was presented first) or fatigue (students had to read three successive stories and then answer questions about each of the three, and in each sequence the Arab content was presented first).

Impact of Other Socioculturally Related Factors on Literacy Development

Thus far, we have examined dimensions that allow some comparison and synthesis across studies—discourse/interaction differences in instruction, cultural content/familiarity of reading matter, and text language. Investigators have looked at a number of other cultural dimensions plausibly implicated in the literacy development of language-minority children and youth. However, the variability of those dimensions and the lack of a unifying framework for this research make it difficult to summarize or draw general conclusions across studies. Most of these studies fall under the general rubric of *culturally compatible*, *culturally responsive*, or *culturally accommodating* instruction, but conceptually this is a murky literature. Despite useful attempts to provide an organizing conceptual framework (e.g., Tharp, 1989), there appears to be no common ground for collecting and interpreting data on how these other sociocultural factors influence language-minority students' learning. For example, as we have already seen, some authors (e.g., Lasisi et al., 1988) consider use of the home language in classroom instruction to be a cultural accommodation. Others (e.g., Kenner, 1999) implicitly include children's experiences with mainstream mass media as part of their cultural experience. Although defining *cultural experience* in this way is probably accurate (depending on one's definition of culture), it renders problematic what we mean when we say that culture influences learning or student culture must be taken into consideration when designing curriculum and instruction for students from diverse cultural or linguistic backgrounds. Do we mean culture as in children's or families' traditional culture—ways of life, customs, beliefs, behavioral norms, values, and so on, associated with a particular ethnic or national-origin group? Or do we mean culture as in the characteristics and features of children's and families' lived experiences, a different construct. In point of fact, cultures are dynamic and always evolving. The boundaries between traditional culture and children's lived culture, which may have little to do with a researcher's conception of the children's traditional culture, become increasingly blurred (see Goldenberg & Gallimore, 1995).

Chilora and Harris (2001) investigated the effect of a match between students' and teachers' home language on English and Chichewa reading and comprehension among Malawi (Africa) elementary school students. The total sample included 2,000 Grades 2, 3, and 4 students from 65 schools in two districts; 188 teachers; 65 head teachers; and at least one community group from each school. Chichewa is the national language of Malawi. However, the majority of the pupils (64%) in these two districts spoke Chiyao, 35% spoke Chichewa, and 1% spoke other languages. Virtually all of the teachers (96%) spoke Chichewa. Only 33% also spoke Chiyao, however, which is the predominant language in the study's target area. The instructional contexts in this study involved three languages: 85% of head teachers reported that Chichewa was one of the languages of instruction, 32% said that Chiyao was a language of instruction, and teachers' guides and lesson plans (except those for Chichewa) were in English. Pupil books were written in Chichewa. The authors point out that, although Chiyao is the required language of instruction in mathematics and general studies for the Chiyao-speaking children, none of the texts was in Chiyao. Thus, there is a level of complexity to this study not found in other studies, which makes it difficult to draw conclusions and implications for policy or practice.

The authors report associations between classroom instructional language and literacy outcomes (see chap. 14 for a discussion of the relationship between language of instruction and literacy outcomes). But they also found that English reading accuracy was better among Chiyao-speaking students whose teachers spoke Chiyao at home. (They found no comparable effect on Chichewa measures.) It is difficult to interpret this finding because the authors present no relevant data or analysis. It is possible that student–teacher home language matches can be explained by classroom instructional language. In other words, Chiyao-speaking teachers were more likely to use Chiyao in the classroom; therefore, the finding that a teacher–student Chiyao home language match improved student achievement may be an artifact of first-language use in the classroom, which can be associated with improved outcomes (see chap. 14). However, teachers who spoke Chiyao at home may have had a level of understanding of their Chiyao students that permitted them to connect in a way not possible for non-Chiyao-speaking teachers. Of course, both factors may have been at work, or some other explanation may exist, but it is difficult to know. One set of findings arguing against the explanation of first language in the classroom is that in only one grade (of three studied) did the Chiyao-speaking students whose teachers used Chiyao instructionally have higher English reading achievement than Chiyao-speaking students whose teachers did not use Chiyao instructionally. Moreover, students whose teachers used Chiyao scored lower on Chichewa reading and comprehension than students whose teachers used no first-language instruction. These findings suggest that teachers' speaking Chiyao in the home and using it instructionally in the classroom were largely independent, leaving more plausible the hypothesis that Chiyao-speaking teachers were able to connect in some more effective manner with Chiyao-speaking students regardless of the language of instruction used.

Garrett et al. (1994) conducted a study in Britain to examine second-language use in writing as a form of cultural accommodation. A 12-week experiment was conducted with 10- to 11-year-old students in two different settings using pre- and posttest writing tasks. During English writing lessons conducted 1 hour per week, one group of students in each setting did prewriting preparation (gathering, selecting, and focusing information in preparation for a first draft) in English and the other group in the mother tongue. The sample included 23 students who were native Punjabi speakers (12 in the English group and 11 in the mother tongue group) and 33 pupils who were native Welsh speakers (16 in the English group and 17 in the mother tongue group). Both writing performance and a variety of student attitudes were assessed, including attitudes about writing, self, ethnic identity, the host country, and school. Some of the 15 attitudes measured (self, ethnic identity, writing, school, and host country) grew more positive over the course of the study, a phenomenon the authors attribute to use of the mother tongue. There were no differences in writing performance from pretreatment levels.

Reyes (1991) compared the performance of 10 sixth-grade bilingual Latino students on two writing activities that were presumed to differ along the dimensions of *meaningfulness* and *cultural relevance* (dialogue journals and a literature log). All 10 spoke Spanish as their first language and resided in homes where Spanish was the first language. Reyes found that dialogue journals prompted longer and more meaningful written products than did literature logs because students could control the topics they wrote about: "All ten students were able to write longer, more detailed entries when the topic centered on their families or was culturally relevant" (p. 298). Journals prompted more personal writing and even affectionate interactions between individual students and the teacher. The literature log, as the teacher wrote to one student, "is not a place for cute pictures and word pictures. It is a businesslike diary of what you are reading" (p. 300). Typical entries were brief and to the point regarding a book the student was reading. Journals elicited longer, more elaborate, and more thoughtful entries. "Students showed better control of their journal writing when the topics were self-selected, culturally relevant, familiar, personal, or important to them than when topics were imposed by the teacher" (p. 301). The implied argument is that the meaningfulness and informality of the journal led to better writing outcomes. Thus, when students chose their own topics and wrote in the language of their choice, "they were more successful in communicating their ideas" (p. 304), Reyes reports. Nonetheless, despite Reyes' argument that dialogue journals are a more desirable medium for student writing, there was no evidence of impact on writing skills: "mechanical writing skills did not appear to improve" (p. 304). Reyes reports that students in her study, unlike "students in the research literature," were not successful literature log writers (however, see Saunders, 1999, in chap. 15).

García-Vázquez (1995) examined the role of acculturation in achievement. Using a sample of 23 Mexican American students in Grades 7 to 9 in a rural midwestern town, the author administered measures of acculturation to the school environment and to the student's own culture and attempted to relate these to achievement. Garcia-Vazquez found that greater familiarity with U.S. culture (acculturation) was unrelated to standardized reading scores. Student reading achievement on the Iowa Test of Basic Skills (ITBS) did not correlate with scores on either measure of acculturation, but was related to level of English-language proficiency. Correlations between acculturation and reading were positive, but low and nonsignificant (.19 and .26), perhaps because of the small sample size (23). Nonetheless, the findings fail to support any interpretation suggesting that greater familiarity with the U.S. school environment or adaptation to U.S. culture is associated with higher literacy attainment levels.

Hernández (1991) reports on a study in which seven Spanish-speaking English-language learners, in the summer before seventh grade, participated in an intervention designed to teach reading comprehension strategies in Spanish. To make the intervention culturally appropriate, these techniques were combined with discussion that activated students' prior knowledge. Hernández argues from a schema theory perspective that instruction must "consider the cultural basis of prior knowledge (culturally sensitive schema) ... to activat[e] knowledge structures the student...is familiar with" (p. 94). All students had been in the United States for less than 19 months and were at the lowest English proficiency levels on the Language Assessment Scales (LAS), and their teachers said they had minimal English decoding skills. However, their average reading level in Spanish was only somewhat below grade norm, as measured by the Spanish version of the CTBS. Students in the study used first-language texts and received first-language instruction using reciprocal teaching (Palincsar & Brown, 1984). Hernández reports that during the study, Spanish reading comprehension increased by as much as 37% according to pre– and posttesting.

Unfortunately, it is not possible to separate the effects of the strategy training from the discussion presumed to activate students' culturally based prior knowledge. Also, the absence of a control group or an alternative design, such as a multiple baseline, limits inferences about the intervention's effect. The data show a gradual improvement in Spanish reading comprehension, but extraneous factors, such as practice effects, cannot be ruled out as influences on the students' improvement. For example, the same stories and questions were used for pre- and posttests of Spanish reading comprehension.

Kennedy and Park (1994) used data from the Base Year National Education Longitudinal Survey (1988) to examine the relationship between language spoken in the home (English vs. other, where other could be Spanish or one of the Asian languages—e.g., Chinese, Filipino, Korean; see following discussion of this aspect of the study), a number of psychosocial variables (possibly rooted in students' culture), and academic achievement for Mexican American and Asian American students. The total sample comprised two groups of eighth-grade students from across the United States—one with 1,131 students of Asian origin (Chinese, Filipino, Japanese, Korean, Vietnamese, Laotian, Cambodian, and other) and one with 1,952 students of Mexican origin. Among the variables included in the study were *social-psychological variables* (including self-concept), *educational expectations*, *locus of control*, and *school effort* as indexed by the amount of homework students reported doing. Differences were found in reading achievement and English grades in favor of the Asian students. There were also differences in locus of control, self-concept, and educational expectations, although the authors say the differences "appear small and may not have many substantive implications" (p. 192). They note, however, a large difference in the amount of time spent on homework, with the Asian students spending twice as much time as the Mexican students. The authors suggest that these difference may have a cultural origin, but "they may also be a result of the SES differences between these samples" (p. 191). Their correlational analysis indicated that students with positive self-concepts and a sense of control over the environment were likely to achieve better grades and standardized test scores. (Relationships between home language and reading achievement are discussed in a later section of this chapter.)

Aarts and Verhoeven (1999) studied sociocultural orientation (a composite of items tapping behavior and attitude of the child toward the native and majority cultures and languages), among other variables, as related to the first- and second-language literacy levels of Turkish children living in the Netherlands. Both school literacy and functional literacy were assessed in Turkish and Dutch. Data on monolingual control groups were used as benchmarks. Background characteristics related to the child, family, and school were examined to explore individual variation.

Aarts and Verhoeven's total sample comprised three groups: (a) a bilingual group of Turkish speakers in the Netherlands ($n = 222$, mean age 12.7) attending eighth grade and generally of low SES; (b) a monolingual group of Dutch students from the same classrooms as the first group, matched for SES, age, and gender ($n = 140$); and (c) a monolingual Turkish-speaking group in Turkey ($n = 276$, mean age 10.6). Overall, Aarts and Verhoeven found that the Turkish children in the Netherlands attained lower levels of literacy than their Dutch monolingual peers, and that this difference was related to home stimulation, parents' motivation for schooling, and children's self-esteem. Sociocultural orientation was related only weakly to school literacy ($r = .18$), but not to functional literacy in Dutch. Sociocultural orientation was not related to either type of literacy in Turkish. The results of this study are largely consistent with those of García-Vázquez (1995). Both studies suggest that language-minority children's orientation to the majority culture is only weakly, if at all, correlated with their literacy outcomes. This finding casts further doubt on the importance of such cultural factors to language-minority children's literacy attainment.

Connor (1983), described earlier, studied reading performance among children with a Vietnamese-language background. A number of sociocultural predictors were included in the study: percentage of English spoken at home; length of parents' stay in the United States; and parents' occupation, years of education, and occupational status. In addition, other language-related variables were examined, including months of instruction in ESL in the home country and in the United States, hours of ESL instruction per week, number of ESL students in class, hours of daily TV watching, and library visits per month. The total sample for the study consisted of 91 limited-English-proficient (LEP) children in Grades K through 12 who spoke 21 different first languages.

When sociocultural variables were examined separately, only percentage of English spoken at home and father's occupation had an effect on reading levels. When all the variables were examined simultaneously, grade in school, Vietnamese-language background, percentage of English spoken at home, higher level paternal occupation, and higher number of students in the ESL classroom had positive effects on the reading skills of the subjects. Intensity of ESL instruction showed a statistically significant negative effect on the reading scores. The authors offer no explanation, but one possibility is that students having the most difficulty learning English are given additional hours of ESL instruction, thereby producing a negative association between the two measures. One weakness of this study is that it does not allow for separation of the influences of length of U.S. residence and length of ESL instruction in the United States. The authors emphasize that sociocultural variables are complex, and that multivariate approaches are needed to examine their influences on reading performance. As noted earlier, Connor hypothesizes that Vietnamese students' superior achievement may be due to their greater "motivation to acculturate in the new [second-language] environment" (p. 285), but presents no data to support this contention.

As described earlier, Ima and Rumbaut (1989) found reading achievement differences among language-minority groups in a Southern California school district. As noted, East Asians (from China, Japan, and Korea) scored higher than Southeast Asians, Filipinos, Hispanics, Pacific Islanders, and other immigrants (from Europe, India, and the Middle East). Southeast Asians (Khmer, Vietnamese, Chinese–Vietnamese, and Laotian) were among the lowest achieving, approximately equivalent with Hispanics and Pacific Islanders. Among Southeast Asians, there were also differences among subgroups: Vietnamese were the highest achieving, followed by Khmer, Laotian, Chinese–Vietnamese, and finally Hmong. Once again, however, SES and ethnolinguistic background are seriously confounded. Ima and Rumbaut say they have insufficient data to separate the various possible explanations for group differences in achievement, although they do report that "level of academic achievement corresponds roughly to the socioeconomic composition of each group, such as the proportion of parents with more schooling" (p. 65).

Among the Southeast Asian immigrant groups, Ima and Rumbaut gathered more complete data. They used a multiple-regression analysis to examine a number of sociocultural variables, including age, years in the United States, semesters in U.S. schools, parents' level of education, employment status, level of poverty, welfare dependency, household size, and household composition (single- vs. two-parent homes). Three variables were the most predictive of CTBS reading scores: Parents' education, years in the United States, and age of the student all correlated positively and accounted for more than 40% of the variance in reading scores. Once these variables were controlled, the authors found no difference in standardized reading achievement scores across ethnic groups.

A study by Trueba et al. (1984) is comparable to the KEEP study cited earlier (Au & Mason, 1981; Tharp, 1982), in that it attempted to make productive changes in classroom practice on the basis of data about children's homes and communities. The researchers did not begin with an a priori conception of culture. Rather, the goal of the project was to discover aspects of bilingual Latino junior and senior high school students' home and community experiences that could inform instruction and then work with teachers to design modules incorporating that information into the writing curriculum. Lessons, discussions, and writing assignments were built around people and events in the community, such as functional writing tasks experienced by the students (paying bills or answering school-related queries for parents), low riders, a murder that had recently occurred, and a cheating survey the students had conducted. Pre- and postanalyses of the students' writing showed that the Latino students had improved, although modestly ($SD = .25$), during the intervention, but were still below the district mastery level.

Two design problems weaken the conclusions we can draw from this study. First, there was no comparison group, so it is impossible to interpret the growth in student writing scores; student writing and other academic skills are expected to improve over the school year even without a special intervention. Second, whatever growth in writing skills occurred could very well have been due to the students simply writing more and receiving more writing instruction. The authors report that, because writing is not part of the ESL curriculum, "the modules represent the first time some of these students have been asked to write in English" (p. 139). The authors present compelling qualitative data indicating that students and teachers were engaged and enthusiastic about the writing curriculum, which is certainly positive and might have been the result of activities rooted in experiences familiar to the students. It is difficult to determine what was responsible for the observed growth in writing. The study's conclusions would have been greatly strengthened with the inclusion of a comparison generic writing condition.

Summary

In general, there is evidence that some of the sociocultural factors examined here have an impact on reading and literacy outcomes, but this evidence is weak. One area in which several studies appear to converge on a fairly consistent finding is that language-minority students' reading comprehension performance improves when they read culturally familiar materials (Abu-Rabia, 1996; Hannon & McNally, 1986; Jiménez, 1997; Kenner, 1999, 2000; Lasisi et al., 1988; McCarty, 1993). However, text language appears to be a stronger influence on reading performance: Students perform better when they read or use material in the language they know better. The influence of cultural content is not as robust (Abu-Rabia, 1995, 1998a, 1998b; Lasisi et al., 1988). Studies examining other socioculturally related factors, including sociocultural variables in home- and school-based instructional settings, knowledge and attitudes about the host country, and teachers' language, often have methodological problems—particularly the confounding influence of SES—that limit the conclusions that can be drawn.

The general thesis that such factors influence literacy outcomes remains highly plausible, but the lack of (a) consistent definitions and research methods, (b) a focus on measured literacy outcomes, and (c) a larger theoretically driven organizing framework inhibits the design, systematic investigation, and, most important, interpretation of the existing research. Moreover, students' cultural affiliations are frequently confounded with SES—for which there is strong evidence of an impact on literacy outcomes—rendering interpretations even more problematic.

The basic hypotheses of the work just reviewed is that (a) the attributes a child brings to school (knowledge, beliefs, attitudes, motivations, behaviors, experiences with specific contexts and situations) influence how he or she deals with experiences and expectations in school; and (b) the greater the distance or discrepancy between the attributes a child brings and the experiences she or he faces in school, the greater is the hindrance to learning. Therefore, effective educational practice requires narrowing this distance between home experiences and school demands. This hypothesis allows for two distinct explanations of how the effects of sociocultural factors on literacy may operate. One, an affect-based explanation, is that sociocultural compatibility creates increased motivation and interest, better mood and attitude, greater participation, and ultimately higher achievement. The second, a cognitively-based explanation, is that sociocultural compatibility produces its effects mainly by increasing familiarity with new information and activating and promoting connections to existing (cultural) knowledge. The current research base does not allow us to determine the validity of these competing explanations, but this is an area that strongly warrants systematic investigation and theoretical explication.

THE INFLUENCE OF PARENTS AND FAMILIES

Studies reviewed in this section examined parent and family influences on language-minority children's literacy attainment. Consistent with a great deal of other research (Booth & Dunn, 1996; Hess & Holloway, 1984), the research reviewed here suggests that indicators of SES and home literacy experiences are related to language-minority children's literacy development. A second key finding is that language-minority parents are willing and able to help their children succeed academically, but that schools do not always take full advantage of these home resources.

An important but complex question is the relationship between home experiences with oral or written language and language-minority children's literacy outcomes. This question is particularly critical because parents and educators face the real issue of what language parents should use when they speak to their children or engage them in writing and reading experiences. Should home language/literacy experiences be in the home (first) language or the societal (second) language? This is not an entirely empirical question because the answer depends in part on the value parents (and the society more generally) place on maintaining the home language. Moreover, some parents may be extremely limited in the second language, so that providing their children with anything more than limited experiences in that language may not even be a realistic option, except to the degree that they can draw on other resources. To the extent that language and literacy experiences in one language are found to have positive or negative effects on literacy development in the same or other language, parents' decisions and the advice educators provide them can be empirically informed.

This section first reviews findings regarding the role of parents' motivation, expectations, attitudes, values, and beliefs in children's literacy development; the next section explores the role of parent/home literacy practices on student literacy development. Finally, we turn to the more complex issues surrounding the effects of home language experiences on literacy development.

Parents' Motivation, Expectations, Attitudes, Values, and Beliefs

A number of studies have examined parents' motivation, expectations attitudes, values, and beliefs as they relate to literacy development. Two findings cut across these studies: (a) Parents of language-minority children place a high value on their children's formal schooling and appear willing to do what they can to contribute to it, and (b) schools tend to underestimate language-minority parents' interest in and ability to contribute to their children's literacy development.

As part of a larger study of school and home effects on Latino children's literacy development, Goldenberg (1987) investigated parents' role by conducting interviews and observations with the parents of nine Spanish-speaking first graders of low SES who in kindergarten had been identified as at risk for reading difficulties (based on teacher ratings). In addition, data were gathered from teachers, and students were assessed on decoding and word-recognition skills. Goldenberg found that teachers consistently underestimated the abilities and motivation of the students' parents, who were all low-income immigrant Latinos. Parents valued formal schooling and academic achievement and wanted their children to do as well as possible in school, which they saw as the key to socioeconomic mobility. They were willing and able to help their first-grade children acquire beginning literacy skills (in Spanish, the language of instruction). In one case, a mother took it on herself to teach her daughter to read because the child was a year behind in her schooling. In other cases, parents were willing and able to help, but did so only when prompted by the teacher. Some parents could have made substantial contributions to children's early reading development, but teachers failed to exploit these opportunities, mainly because they assumed parents lacked the motivation or skill to provide their children with useful help.

Brooker (2002) also suggests that teachers can underestimate language-minority parents' interest in their children's schooling, thereby failing to take advantage of home resources that could help children progress in their literacy development. Brooker reports contrasting ethnographic case studies of two children in a British kindergarten—Troy (a monolingual English-speaking

child) and Rahman (a Bengali English learner). Although the parents of both
children were highly interested in their children's school success and motivated
to support it, the social capital of Troy's family—knowledge of the school system and how to communicate with teachers, and the ability to help their child
present himself in class—translated into enhanced literacy learning opportunities and outcomes for Troy in comparison with Rahman. Troy's mother regularly communicated with the teacher, was extremely well informed about what
was going on in the class, and kept the teacher apprised of events and circumstances (e.g., birth of a baby) that could influence her son's school performance
and behavior. This excellent home–school communication translated into
higher group placement and enhanced literacy learning opportunities in class.

Rahman's mother was no less interested in or capable of helping, but she did
not know about writing long notes to the teacher or keeping her informed
about family developments. Because home–school communication was sparse,
the teacher assumed that Rahman (who was in a group of lower achieving
children) got "no support from home" (p. 305). This assumption was categorically
incorrect, as indicated by what Rahman's mother expressed during interviews—
school success, hard work, and progress are important and expected—as well
as by reported and observed instances of organized learning at home (e.g., first-
and second-language alphabets, counting, copying writing). By the end of the
year, Brooker writes, Rahman,

> together with all the Bengali boys in his class, and all but one of the girls had
> been assigned to a lowly position in the classroom hierarchy—a position jus-
> tified perhaps by the linguistic and cultural deficits he was assumed to start
> school with, but unjustified by closer examination of his background.

As a follow-up to Goldenberg's earlier (1987) study, Goldenberg and Gallimore
(1991) studied a predominantly Hispanic elementary school with a transitional
bilingual education program, where first- and second-grade children's reading
achievement (in Spanish) improved substantially over a 2- to 3-year period as
a result of several changes in the school's early literacy program. One of these
changes involved increased parent and home involvement in children's beginning literacy development. Whereas in previous years no systematic attempts
had been made to involve parents in helping their children learn to read, teachers began sending home books and other reading materials, including homework and other assignments designed to promote literacy. The authors report
that parents were willing and able to help their children progress in early reading development, but that school staff tended to underestimate their potential
contribution. The authors claim that the increased home and parent involvement helped improve early reading achievement from around the 30th national
percentile to around the 60th. As Goldenberg and Gallimore point out, however, numerous changes had been made in the early literacy program at the
school, so it is impossible to separate out the effects of any single factor.

Carter and Chatfield's (1986) case study of a successful and relatively
high-achieving school providing bilingual education reveals a set of deeper and
richer home–school–community connections than those reported by Goldenberg
and Gallimore (1991). Sixth graders at the school achieved at higher levels in

reading (and mathematics) than students at comparable schools in the state for most years from 1980 to 1985. Other test scores also suggested that the students were achieving well; there were minimal achievement discrepancies between English speakers and English learners at the school. This case study highlights both the dynamic nature of the effective school and the mutually reinforcing interaction between the school and community. Carter and Chatfield argue that ongoing contact and communication between the school and community was an important part of the school's success. Overwhelming majorities of parents and teachers felt there were good home–school relations. Volunteers from the community worked directly with the children and helped teachers develop classroom materials. Carter and Chatfield report that the school's staff tried to improve the home–school connections even further by improving the quality of homework teachers assigned.

As with Goldenberg and Gallimore (1991), Carter and Chatfield also argue that "no single program, mechanism, or process" (p. 213) can explain achievement at the school. Their study identified a number of salient features of the school's program: a positive climate for learning, staff who were focused on outcomes, and high expectations for student achievement. In both studies, multiple factors were obviously involved, so it is impossible to disentangle the effects of community involvement from those of other factors.

Shannon (1995) reports on a year-long ethnographic study of a counterhegemonic fourth-grade classroom. *Counterhegemonic* refers to practices designed to challenge the higher status associated with speaking English in the United States. In this classroom, the teacher explicitly assigned prestige to speaking, reading, and writing in Spanish and to bilingualism in general. Through her interactions with students, classroom instruction, and visual displays around the room, the teacher emphasized the virtues of bilingualism and gave a high status to speaking Spanish. Shannon's study examines how such practices might overcome the potentially negative effects of English hegemony in the United States. The class included a mix of newly arrived immigrants, bilingual children, Chicanos learning Spanish as a second language, and students from non-Spanish-speaking homes. Quotes from the students and behavioral observations indicated a high degree of interest in and enthusiasm for bilingualism. One of the features of this classroom was significant participation by parents, almost all of whom were Spanish speakers. The author suggests that the parental support, attitudes, and pride in the teacher's valuing of Spanish were important elements mediating the outcomes. Transcripts, work samples, and quotes from the students suggest their increased use of Spanish, perceptions that Spanish helped the learning process, and valuing of bilingualism. However, it is unclear how widespread these sentiments were because data from only a few children in the class are reported, or what effects the teacher's classroom practices had on children's literacy learning apart from her explicitly promoting the value of bilingualism. Shannon presents a plausible circumstantial case for the benefits of counterhegemonic practices for bilingual and biliterate development. However, more evidence is needed of children's actual literacy growth and its relationship to challenging English hegemony, as well as the role played by parental attitudes, beliefs, and support in the process.

The evidence base provided by these last three studies is not definitive; however, it should be interpreted in light of the rather long history of the conceptualization of parent, family, and community factors as deficits (Valencia, 1997). Although the five studies reviewed in this section support the conclusion that language-minority parents possess the motivation and ability to support their children's literacy development, schools generally must take the initiative to exploit this resource. One serious limitation of this group of studies is that they are all focused at the elementary level. Three studies (Brooker, 2002; Goldenberg, 1987; Goldenberg & Gallimore, 1991) deal with preschool through second grade. Thus, we do not know to what extent parental motivation and ability to help language-minority children develop literacy skills extends beyond elementary school.

Another set of studies has examined the relationships between student literacy development and parental attitudes, motivations, expectations, and beliefs. Several problems with this group of studies preclude strong generalizations or conclusions, however. First, the number of studies is small, and their designs are correlational. The latter problem is inevitable because it would be difficult to imagine a valid experiment that would manipulate values and attitudes. One option would be to use qualitative methods to delve more deeply into parents' and children's attitudes, motivations, expectations, and beliefs so as to gauge more accurately their impacts on literacy development. Correlations provide measures of association, but we are left to infer the meaning of these associations for the population we are sampling. Only one study in the following group (Goldenberg, Gallimore, Reese, & Garnier, 2001) supplemented quantitative with qualitative data. Another problem with this group of studies is that their findings are inconsistent. This inconsistency can be due to several factors: age of subjects (elementary to high school), country and ethnicity of subjects (three studies were of U.S. Latinos, one was of Turkish children in the Netherlands), instrumentation (parent data collected from teachers, students, or parents), and concept operationalization (no two studies used the same concepts, not to mention measures, of parent values or expectations).

Aarts and Verhoeven (1999) studied the first- and second-language literacy levels of a sample of 222 Turkish children (ages 11–14) living in the Netherlands and examined a variety of factors potentially related to individual variation in their performance. Measures included both school literacy and functional literacy (abilities and knowledge required to perform literacy tasks in everyday life) in Turkish and Dutch, and results were compared with those for monolingual control groups (Turkish children in Turkey, Dutch children in the Netherlands). Teachers' reports of the family's motivation for schooling predicted the children's Turkish school literacy, Dutch school literacy, and Dutch functional literacy. School support by parents (e.g., contacts with the teacher, level of interest, discussions with the child about school) predicted Turkish school literacy only. A weakness of this study is that information on family background was gathered through the teacher or student, rather than directly from the family. Thus, teachers' answers about stimulation in the students' homes may have been influenced by student performance and what teachers were able to garner from parent contacts; hence, there is a possible nonindependence and lack of validity to the measures, as

Brooker's (2002) case studies of Troy and Rahman would suggest. Student reports of parent reading are also of unknown validity.

Durán and Weffer (1992) studied the high school experience of 157 academically talented Mexican American immigrant students taken from the top 25% of their graduating classes (mean GPA = 3.8). They looked at the role of family background factors and found that parent educational values (as perceived by students) were indirectly related to 9th-grade reading and 12th-grade achievement. Achievement was measured by the reading comprehension and mathematics tests of the Tests of Achievement and Proficiency (TAP) administered in 9th grade and four subtests, including English (content undefined, although presumably measuring one or more aspects of English language and literacy) of the American College Testing (ACT) Program, administered in 12th grade. Students from families with higher educational values tended to enroll more in the math and science enrichment program; this enrollment, in turn, was related to higher achievement as measured by the ACT. A surprising result was that the math and science enrichment program produced positive effects not only on math and science achievement, but on English achievement as well.

Virtually all parents wanted their children to attend college and saw formal schooling as a means of achieving socioeconomic mobility. The only variability with regard to educational values was in students' perceptions of their parents' academic expectations and the importance the students attached to those expectations. However, any interpretation of the origins of family educational values is speculative. As Duran and Weffer acknowledge, "The process by which immigrant background related to education value was not clarified by this study" (p. 179). It remains unclear what other factors influence parents' expectations for children's school attainment.

One study does shed light on the relationship between immigrant background and educational values, although conducted with elementary (not high school) students (Goldenberg et al., 2001). Using a mix of quantitative and qualitative methods within a longitudinal design (grades K–6), this study found that immigrant Latino parents' educational expectations for their children were influenced by their perceptions of the children's school success (particularly how motivated their children were in school), rather than that those expectations influencing student school performance. School performance and parents' expectations were unrelated early in elementary schools (grades K–1), but by the end of elementary school measures of achievement predicted parents' expectations. It is therefore likely that previously reported positive correlations between expectations and achievement reflect the fact that parents have higher expectations for children who are doing well in school.

Goldenberg and colleagues also examined the relationships among parents' years in the United States, their aspirations and expectations for their children's educational attainment, and the children's literacy achievement. Parents' years in the United States were largely unrelated to their expectations or aspirations for children's college attendance; a positive correlation between the two was found only in Grade 5. According to one hypothesis, the longer immigrants are in the United States, the more they have adverse experiences (e.g., discrimination) that have a negative impact on motivation and achievement. However, Goldenberg and colleagues found a negative correlation between years in the United States and perceived discrimination against Latinos. There was no correlation between parents' years in the United States and children's reading achievement.

In summary, Durán and Weffer (1992) found only indirect effects of family educational values (including expectations) on student achievement; Goldenberg and colleagues (2001) found effects in the opposite direction: Students' school performance (including parents' perceptions of student academic motivation) influenced parents' expectations for their children's eventual school attainment. In contrast, Buriel and Cardoza (1988) found no relationship between family educational values and student achievement. They studied a sample of first- to third-generation Mexican American high school seniors and found that student reports of mother's expectations ("As things stand now, how far in school does your mother think you will get?") were not related to the students' reading achievement. (Students' own expectations, however, did predict reading achievement.) Perceived maternal expectations were associated with English vocabulary achievement, but only among the first-generation students. As previously reported, Buriel and Cardoza found that maternal expectations did not differ across the three generations. (The same was true for student expectations.) The findings of all three of these studies suggest that there is no direct effect of language-minority parents' educational values or expectations on students' literacy achievement. The studies do point in different directions; however, differences in constructs and how they are operationalized and measured make comparisons among the studies' findings difficult. Durán and Weffer's (1992) findings suggest that by influencing certain behaviors (e.g., course taking, homework), family educational values indirectly affect outcomes. Goldenberg and colleagues' (2001) findings suggest that parent expectations do not influence achievement. Rather, the opposite seems true: Students' school performance affects parents' expectations for eventual school attainment (e.g., college attendance). Buriel and Cardoza's findings point to no association between parent expectations (as perceived by students) and students' English reading achievement (although they did find a positive association between parents' expectations and first-generation students' English vocabulary).

Home Literacy Experiences and Other Family Factors

A small number of studies have focused on language-minority children's home literacy experiences and other family factors that may influence literacy outcomes. In general, home literacy experiences and opportunities are associated with superior literacy outcomes, but more precise conclusions are difficult to obtain. SES—particularly parent education—is clearly associated with literacy outcomes. Features of family life (e.g., domestic workload, religious activities) appear to influence the value children place on reading and their self-concepts as readers. One surprising finding, reported by two studies, is that parents' reading behavior is unrelated to children's literacy outcomes. Family size and one-versus two-parent families appear not to influence literacy outcomes.

Goldenberg, Reese, and Gallimore (1992) examined the effects of school-based literacy materials entering the home in a small experimental study. The total sample consisted of 10 children in two groups—5 children in an experimental group (using booklets to promote language- and communication- based, rather than code-based, instruction) and 5 in a control group (using phonics-oriented worksheets). All children were Spanish speakers and of either Mexican or Central American background, and all were of low SES. Year-long case studies of the children found that photocopied story booklets and worksheets sent home by teachers stimulated literacy experiences at home. In other words, children had more literacy activities and opportunities at home as a result of materials sent home by the teacher. However, activities prompted by both types of materials—whether booklets or phonics worksheets—emphasized repetition (of letters, words, or text) and a lack of attention to the meaning of the text. The study produced a paradoxical finding: Children in the classrooms using story-books had higher literacy test scores than children in classrooms that sent home the worksheets. However, whereas the use of booklets in the home (which was counted and timed by home observers) was not correlated with literacy achievement, use of phonics worksheets (also counted and timed by observers) was strongly and positively correlated with early literacy outcomes. The authors suggest, and provide evidence, that the explanation for this finding lies in the fact that the worksheets were more consistent with parents' own views of how children learn to read (through memorization and repetition of letters–sound combinations) and were therefore used in a way that produced greater gains in children's literacy development. The booklets, as a means to promote early literacy development, did not jibe with parents' own under-standings, and were therefore used as worksheets, for which they were not well suited. Use of the booklets at home, therefore, was not associated with children's literacy gains.

Arzubiaga et al. (2002) examined family influences on reading motivation among Spanish-speaking children. Surveys and interviews were conducted with 18 students in an urban central city setting. An Ecocultural Family Interview (EFI) was used with students' parents, and the results were related to student reading motivation (reading engagement). The EFI explores features of family resources and constraints, beliefs, and values, as well as the needs and abilities of family members as they engage in daily routines. The study found that as domestic workload increased, the value children placed on reading decreased ($r = -.58$). The time families spent together and on religious literacy activities was positively related to self-concept as a reader ($r = .49$). Family connectedness was related to value placed on reading ($r = .60$), and family values and identity were related to self-concept as a reader ($r = .50$). Features of family life, in other words, were related to children's attitudes toward reading.

Pucci and Ulanoff (1998) conducted a study with a small sample of 12 proficient readers and 11 less-than-proficient readers. All the children were fourth graders and had Spanish as their first language. Elements of home and school environments affecting second-language reading achievement were investigated. Students answered a 13-item questionnaire about reading practices and attitudes, and they were assessed for English reading comprehension by a cloze test. Variables that correlated with differences in reading proficiency were the number of books in the home, assigned books that children read, and authors and titles recognized. In addition, in comparison with nonproficient readers, proficient readers enjoyed reading more and felt that they were proficient. They also scored significantly higher on the cloze test of reading comprehension. The correlational design of the study limits causal inferences, but the findings do suggest a relationship between print access at home and literacy outcomes. Little difference between the groups was found in time spent reading, being read to, or having reading modeled by parents (e.g., children see their parents reading a newspaper); there were no differences by gender or by teacher.

Reese, Garnier, Gallimore, and Goldenberg (2000) studied 121 Spanish-speaking kindergartners, most of low SES, enrolled in bilingual education programs. The study examined factors contributing to early Spanish literacy and later English reading for students from kindergarten through Grade 7. Results suggest that early literacy experiences in the home (e.g., reading, being read to, having books and other literacy materials) supported subsequent literacy development regardless of language. Time spent in the native language, in other words, was not time lost with respect to English reading acquisition.

Aarts and Verhoeven's (1999) study of 222 eleven- and fourteen-year-old Turkish children found that the single most important variable in explaining school and functional literacy in both Turkish and Dutch was the teacher's appraisal of home stimulation—the extent to which children's homes provided a stimulating learning environment. Other family-based variables that predicted some aspect of first- or second-language literacy (in addition to the motivational and value-related variables discussed earlier) were family SES (predicted Dutch school literacy only) and *language contact*, meaning the degree of contact the family had with Dutch (predicted Dutch school literacy only). Parents' reading behaviors in Turkish (as reported by the children) were unrelated to literacy outcomes in either language. As previously pointed out, this study is weakened by its reliance on teacher and child data to measure family variables.

Brunell and Saretsalo's (1999) study of Swedish-speaking (first-language) students in Finland (with Finnish as the second language) found that the home background (a latent variable comprising an abundance of books at home [language unspecified], father's education, and mother's education) was more significant for reading literacy in both languages than was the linguistic home background. This study is discussed at greater length in the following section addressing the impact on literacy achievement of first- and second-language use at home.

Ima and Rumbaut (1989) found that variability in CTBS reading scores across Southeast Asian groups could be explained by differences in parents' education, years in the United States, and age of student at arrival. Other family factors—one- versus two-parent family, household size, and SES indicators aside from parent education—made no difference.

Home Language Experiences and Language-Minority Children's Literacy Development

The relationship between first- and second-language experiences in the home and language-minority children's literacy development is a crucial issue for parents and teachers, who often ask what language should be used when language-minority parents speak with their children. Some might argue that parents should speak the societal language even if they are limited speakers of that language, or at a minimum they should attempt to introduce as much second-language use as possible in the home. Speaking the societal language at home, so this reasoning goes, might help children acquire the language more quickly, thereby facilitating entry into the educational mainstream. This argument is based on the time-on-task hypothesis (Rossell & Baker, 1986). According to this view, more time spent on a task leads to greater proficiency in that task. Thus, for example, more time spent engaged in English rather than Spanish activities should lead to better outcomes in English, not in Spanish. Taken a step further, this position suggests a possible negative cross-language association, such that experiences in one language may be negatively correlated with outcomes in the other. This could be true for different reasons. For example, time is necessarily limited, and more time spent with one language means less time available for the other. Another explanation is that there is negative transfer in the sense that experiences provided in one language may disrupt learning in a second language. (See Part II for a discussion of relationships between first- and second-language proficiency and literacy and chap. 14 for a discussion of the effects of native language and literacy instruction on English literacy outcomes.)

The alternative perspective is that parents should maintain the native language in the home. One reason might be that parents should interact with their children in the language they know best in order to provide the best possible linguistic models and input for children. Findings reported in Part II and chapter 14, suggesting that skills learned in the child's first language transfer to a second language, seem to indicate that maintaining the first language in the home can make a positive contribution to language and literacy in general, and to second-language acquisition in particular. Another reason for first-language maintenance in the home might be that it is important for cultural, cognitive, and pragmatic reasons, so parents should not abandon its use at home. A third reason is that failure to maintain the home language can disrupt fundamental patterns of communication between parents and children, which can have negative effects on socialization and other family dynamics (Wong Fillmore, 1991). The basic premise of all three is that use of the family language, rather than abandoning it in favor of the societal language, is advantageous to children.

Unfortunately, we do not have a clear answer to the question of what language parents of English-language learners should use or attempt to encourage at home in order to promote children's literacy development. Most of the studies in this area are correlational. Although there are some important exceptions, they generally point to a positive, although modest, correlation between the home use of a language and literacy achievement in that language, and, conversely to a negative, again very modest, correlation between the home use of a language and achievement in the other language.

The practical implications of these finding are not clear because there are different possible interpretations for these correlations. The best correlational studies on this topic control for obvious confounds, such as parent education, but other confounds that make interpretation problematic include the quality of instruction and instructional language(s) used in school, parents' first- and second-language abilities, the quality and level of language used in the home, and parents' attitudes toward using first and second languages in the home. Despite a general trend for language-specific effects of home language use, we currently do not have a sufficient basis for policy and practice recommendations on this topic. The study's correlational designs preclude any strong recommendation other than that research should be carried out to address these important questions.

The results of two experimental studies, moreover, point in a different direction from most of the correlational studies. They suggest that, at least at the kindergarten and Grade 1 levels, promoting second-language literacy in the home of English learners has minimal impact on early literacy attainment, whereas promoting first-language literacy in the home does indeed have a positive effect on second-language (English) early literacy development. Koskinen et al. (2000) found that sending home and promoting the use of English books and tapes for first-grade English-language learners had no effect on measured English literacy development (see discussion of this study in chap. 15). In contrast, Hancock (2002) found that providing reading materials in Spanish for kindergarten children to take home produced higher preliteracy skills scores, in English, than did providing reading materials in English for children to take home. We should bear in mind that these studies did not manipulate the language generally used by parents and children in the home. Such an intervention, admittedly, would be difficult to implement and study. Nonetheless, the much more circumscribed manipulations suggest that enhancing home literacy experiences in the first language affects literacy development, whereas enhancing home literacy experiences in the second language does not.

Table 11.1 depicts the relationship between first- and second-language use in the home and first- and second-language literacy achievement across the 12 studies pertinent to this topic. Summaries and analyses of these studies follow.

Positive Within-Language Associations.   Of the 12 studies, 11 report a positive association between language used in the home and literacy attainment in that language, for at least some measures and for at least one of the study's subsamples.

Four of these 11 studies found a positive correlation between first-language use in the home and first-language literacy achievement (Cell 1: Brunell & Linnakylä, 1994; Brunell & Saretsalo, 1999; Cahill, 1987; Dolson, 1985). Brunell and Linnakylä (1994) compared the literacy levels of 9- and 14-year-old Swedish-speaking children who attended a Swedish-speaking school in Finland. Finland is a bilingual country, where 94% of the inhabitants consider Finnish their home language and 6% consider Swedish their home language. Parents can choose whether their child is schooled in Swedish or Finnish; many Swedish speakers opt to school their children in Swedish. These children, who spoke Swedish as their first language and Finnish as their second, were the subjects of this study. Brunell and Linnakylä found that pupils in whose homes only Swedish was spoken scored higher on measures of Swedish literacy than did pupils whose homes were either Finnish–Swedish bilingual or where Finnish was the home language. Among the 9-year-olds, children whose parents were native Swedish speakers outscored those whose parents were native Finnish speakers ($SD = .5$). Among the 14-year-olds, the differences were less pronounced, but of the same magnitude when children who always spoke Swedish at home were compared with those who never spoke Swedish at home.

TABLE 11.1

First- and Second-Language Use in the Home and First- and Second-Language Literacy Achievement*

	First-Language Literacy Achievement			Second-Language Literacy Achievement		
	Positive	Negative	None	Positive	Negative	None
First-language use in the home	• Brunell & Linnakylä (1994) • Brunell & Saretsalo (1999) • Cahill (1987) • Dolson (1985)		• Aarts & Verhoeven (1999)	• Cahill (1987) • Dolson (1985)? (nonsig, but moderate effect size) • Hancock (2002)	• Aarts & Verhoeven (1999)? (unclear variable construction) • Buriel & Cardoza, 1988 (language spoken as child & for third generation) • Connor (1983) • Hansen (1989) • Kennedy & Park (1994) (Asian students only) • Monzó & Rueda (?) (possible negative association)	• Buriel & Cardoza (1988) • Kennedy & Park (1994) (Mexican students only)
	1	2	3	4	5	6
Second-language use in the home		• Brunell & Linnakylä (1994) • Brunell & Saretsalo (1999) • Dolson (1985)	• Aarts & Verhoeven (1999) • Cahill (1987)	• Aarts & Verhoeven (1999) • Buriel & Cardoza (1988)? (language spoken as child & for third generation only) • Connor (1983) • Hansen (1989) • Kennedy & Park (1994) (Asian students) • Koskinen et al. (2000)? (teacher rating and student self-report effects) • Monzó & Rueda (2001)?	• Dolson (1985)? (non sig., but moderate effect size)	• Buriel & Cardoza (1988) • Cahill (1987) • Kennedy & Perk, (1994) (Mexican students) • Koskinen et al. (2000)
	7	8	9	10	11	12

*A question mark (?) following an entry indicate there is some ambiguity or uncertainty about the data but that the study probably goes in the indicated cell. The note in parenthesis briefly identifies the ambiguity or uncertainty, with more extensive explanation provided in the text.

305

Unfortunately, the Swedish language-minority children were not tested in Finnish, so we do not know the relationship between language use at home and second-language literacy.

In a subsequent study, Brunell and Saretsalo (1999) studied 14-year-old Swedish-speaking students in Finland. This investigation was based on data from a national study carried out in connection with the multinational International Association for the Evaluation of Educational Achievement (IEA) Reading Literacy Study in 1991 and a similar national study in 1995. Books in the home (language unspecified) and parents' education were related to Swedish reading literacy. Language spoken in the home was weakly associated with reading achievement in Swedish, with more Swedish in the home (relative to Finnish) again predicting higher scores. This finding appears to replicate that reported by Brunell and Linnakylä (1994), although the strength of the association between home language and measured literacy attainment is difficult to compare between the two studies.

Cahill (1987) and Dolson (1985) both found that first-language use at home was associated with first-language literacy achievement. In Cahill's study, press for Italian development in the homes of second- and third-generation 10-year-old Italo–Australian children predicted Italian reading and writing skills. Dolson found that fifth- and sixth-grade Latino students whose homes maintained Spanish as the main language outperformed (on a standardized Spanish reading test) students whose families went from predominantly Spanish to predominantly English use in the home. These studies are discussed in more detail later in this section because they report other findings that contrast with most of the other studies reviewed here.

Seven studies report a positive association between second-language use at home and second-language literacy achievement (Cell 10: Aarts & Verhoeven, 1999; Buriel & Cardoza, 1988; Connor, 1983; Hansen, 1989; Kennedy & Park, 1994; Monzó & Rueda, 2001). This group also includes the experiment reported by Koskinen et al. (2000), who found a positive effect only on teacher ratings of English learners rereading English books at home and student reports of how much they practiced reading. Neither of these effects was reflected in measured literacy achievement. Koskinen et al. is discussed in greater detail later.

Monzó and Rueda (2001) studied five Spanish-speaking families, each with a student in Grade 1 or 2, and documented practices that promoted achievement motivation. All the parents of the children were immigrants and spoke little or no English. Some of the parents were undocumented, and most worked in factory jobs. The three successful readers (in terms of school grades and motivational indicators) came from homes with English-speaking family members and had siblings who attended U.S. schools. The two unsuccessful readers (all children were in English classrooms) did not have comparable language and social capital on which to draw. English-language resources and social capital in the form of siblings in U.S. schools were confounded in this study, making inferences about home language and achievement problematic.

Hansen (1989) examined family, peer, and classroom influences on reading comprehension and oral vocabulary in a sample of 117 second and fifth graders from Spanish-dominant homes. The article does not state explicitly what type of program the children were in, but it is reasonable to assume they had all-English instruction, and that all student achievement measures were taken in English. Hansen found that, during the school year, increased use of English at home predicted higher reading comprehension gains in English; there was no such relationship during the summer. Increased use of English at home was also associated with greater oral vocabulary gains, both during the school year and in the summer.[3] The finding that increased English use predicts higher English achievement scores does not, in itself, signify that increased Spanish use was detrimental to English achievement. However, because the home language variable was constructed as a single dimension, from exclusively Spanish to exclusively English, the positive correlation between English use and English achievement necessarily means a negative correlation between Spanish use and English achievement. We return to this issue later (see "Negative Across-Language Associations").

As is true of many of the other studies reviewed here, Hansen (1989) controlled neither for parents' education or another index of social class nor for parents' language abilities, again making inferences difficult about the relationship between home language use and student literacy attainment.

One researcher who did control for parents' education is Connor (1983), who found that greater use of English (the second language) in the home was positively associated with English reading achievement among 91 limited-English-proficient children (Grades 2–12) from diverse language backgrounds (Spanish, Vietnamese, Indo-European, and other). Students from homes where English was used at least 50% of the time scored slightly higher (1 point) on the Metropolitan Achievement Test (MAT) reading comprehension subtest than students from families in which no English was spoken. Unfortunately, Connor does not report the measurement unit; 1 point may be a raw score, scale score, percentile, or some other unit, so the finding is difficult to interpret, other than to say that the difference in English reading comprehension attributable to English spoken in the home is statistically reliable, but probably small. Connor also does not report how language use was measured and who provided the data. Unlike many other studies in this group, however, Connor's study controlled for and found that home English use predicted reading outcomes independent of SES.

Aarts and Verhoeven (1999) studied the relationship between various family dimensions and school and functional literacy in Turkish (the first language) and Dutch (the second language) among 222 Turkish eighth graders in the Netherlands. One variable, discussed earlier, was *sociocultural orientation*. This variable comprised 13 questions, including language spoken at home and language the student preferred to speak. As already reported, sociocultural orientation was unrelated to Turkish (first-language) literacy outcomes, but an orientation toward Dutch (second language), which presumably meant that

---

[3]Careful readers of this article will find that increased first-language (i.e., Spanish) use appears to be associated with increased second-language proficiency, based on how the measures are reported in the article. However, the scale is reported incorrectly in the published article. The study indeed found a positive correlation between English use at home and the outcomes discussed above (D. Hansen, personal communication, February 2004).

more Dutch was spoken in the home and was positively related to Dutch school literacy outcomes. Another home oral-language-use variable—*language contact*—appears to have yielded an identical pattern of associations: no association between home oral language use (first or second language) and first-language (Turkish) literacy measures, but a positive association between second-language (Dutch) home oral language use and second-language school literacy only. As already discussed, however, this variable is defined vaguely ("language contact was measured through questions about the use of both languages at home and in the neighborhood and about the proficiency in Dutch of the parents" [p. 385]), so precise interpretations about variable relationships are difficult.

Two studies had complex results that varied by subgroup included in the study. Both studies found a positive association between second-language use at home and second-language literacy achievement for one subgroup, but not the entire study sample.

Kennedy and Park (1994), discussed previously, found that the relationship between home language use and English reading achievement was different for Mexican and Asian students. Whereas the correlation between English use in the home and standardized reading scores disappeared for Mexican-origin students when SES was controlled, it remained significant, although weak, for Asians.

Buriel and Cardoza (1988) report in general no association between language use at home and Mexican American high school seniors' English reading and vocabulary achievement. However, they found that, among the third-generation students only, use of the first language (Spanish) at home when the student was a child was associated with lower second-language (English) reading and vocabulary achievement as a high school senior.[4] By implication, therefore, use of English in the home when the student was a child is associated with higher reading and vocabulary achievement in high school.

Negative Across-Language Associations.   Nine studies found a negative association between language used in the home and literacy attainment in the other language, for at least some measures and for at least one of the study's subsamples. (It should be noted that the studies have all been previously discussed; as such, all design issues and limits on plausible inferences still apply.) These findings are the other side of the coin from the positive within-language associations just discussed. Because virtually all the studies measured home language use along a single continuum from (e.g., *Only/mostly English* to *Only/mostly Spanish*), a positive correlation between use of English (or a second language) and achievement in English necessarily signifies a negative association between use of Spanish (or a first language) and achievement in English. Except for Cahill, researchers have not measured first- and second-language

---

[4]Buriel and Cardoza also report a complex pattern of correlations between students' self-reported oral and literacy proficiency in Spanish on the one hand and reading and vocabulary achievement in English on the other. These correlations were not observed for the first-generation students and differed for the second and third generations. See Part II, Cross-linguistic Relationships.

use in the home separately; instead, they have measured the relative amounts of each that parents or children report speaking at home. Thus, some of the negative associations discussed here might simply be artifacts of how the home language variable was measured. If first- and second-language use were measured independently of each other, the pattern of results might be different, as Cahill's findings suggest. This is another area ripe for future investigation.

Three studies found a negative association between second-language use in the home and first-language literacy achievement (Cell 8). Brunell and Linnakylä (1994) found that children who came from homes that were Finnish–Swedish bilingual or where Finnish (the second language) was spoken scored lower on the Swedish (first-language) reading tests than pupils from Swedish-speaking homes. In other words, greater use of the second language (Finnish) was associated with a lower performance in first-language (Swedish) literacy. Brunell and Saretsalo (1999) found that Finnish spoken with parents and at home (and Finnish identity) demonstrated a weak, but still significant, negative correlation with Swedish reading literacy. Again, more second-language use in the home was associated with somewhat poorer first-language literacy outcomes. Dolson (1985) reports that students in whose homes English became the main language (thereby displacing Spanish, which had originally been the main language) scored lower on a Spanish standardized reading test than students whose families maintained Spanish as the main language.

Six studies found a negative association between first-language use in the home and second-language literacy achievement (Cell 5). In Monzó and Rueda's (2001) five early elementary case studies, students from families where exclusively Spanish was spoken were less successful readers than students with at least one English-speaking family member and a sibling who attended school in the United States. Hansen (1989) found that more Spanish in the home predicted lower English reading comprehension and English oral vocabulary growth. Connor (1983) reports that students in Grades 2 to 12 from families of diverse language backgrounds scored slightly lower on the MAT when a non-English language was used 100% of the time in their homes, in contrast to students whose native language was used no more than 50% of the time.

Aarts and Verhoeven (1999) focus their report on the positive correlation between speaking Dutch/Dutch orientation and achievement in Dutch. However, because the variable was constructed as unidimensional, with speaking Turkish/Turkish orientation on one end of the continuum and speaking Dutch/Dutch orientation on the other end, a positive association between Dutch (second-language) orientation and Dutch (second-language) literacy indicates a negative association between Turkish (first-language) orientation and Dutch (second-language) literacy.

Buriel and Cardoza (1988), as already reported, found that, among third-generation (but not among first- and second-generation) Mexican American seniors, use of Spanish at home when the student was a child was associated with lower English reading and vocabulary achievement as a high school senior. The authors suggest that, because use of Spanish diminishes across generations, third-generation students who spoke Spanish as children "probably represent an unusual group of individuals" (p. 188). More specifically, third-generation students who had

Spanish as their mother tongue may have been "students whose families have not been economically mobile [and are] likely to find themselves in low-income environments (barrios or ghettos) that are heavily Spanish-speaking" (p. 188). If this hypothesis is correct, it suggests that use of the first language in the home per se is not detrimental to second-language reading achievement; rather, it is a marker for something else that is depressing achievement. The regression analyses reported by Buriel and Cardoza show that the relationship between first-language oral language use as a child and second-language reading/vocabulary achievement persists with SES controlled, so the negative association between first-language use and reading achievement among third-generation Mexican American seniors was not due to SES per se, but to community demographic or other factors. This is clearly another topic for future research.

Finally, Kennedy and Park (1994) found that English use in Asian eighth graders' homes was positively associated with reading achievement in English. As with Aarts and Verhoeven (1999), because this variable was constructed as a single continuum (*non-English only* to *English only*), this finding also suggests that home language use is negatively correlated with English reading achievement for Asian students.[5] No such association was found for the Mexican students once parent education was controlled (see next section).

No Association Between Home Language and Achievement. Five studies report no association between language used in the home and first- and second-language literacy attainment, for at least some measures and for at least one of the study's subsamples (Cells 3, 6, 9, and 12).

Koskinen et al. (2000), who conducted one of the two experimental studies in this group, attempted to improve early literacy development in English among English-proficient and English-learner first graders by promoting rereading of English books in the home. Koskinen et al. found no treatment effects on their two achievement measures—oral reading and writing vocabulary. The study involved 162 students from 16 first-grade classrooms in seven Title I U.S. schools. All students were nonreaders or very beginning readers. English as a second language was spoken by 105 of the students. More than 17 countries and 16 different languages were represented in the sample. Participants were assigned to one of four groups: (a) book-rich classroom environment, which included small-group shared reading three to four times per week; (b) book-rich classroom environment, plus daily rereading of books at home (in English—i.e., the second language for the English-language learner children); (c) book-rich classroom environment, plus daily rereading of books at home, augmented with audiotapes of the books; and (d) unmodified reading instruction at school. Outcome measures were an oral reading assessment, a

---

[5]The negative cross-language correlations reported here contrast with the positive cross-language correlations reported in Part II. Although these findings appear contradictory, they are not. The positive correlations reported in Part II involved literacy achievement measured in the first and second languages. In this part of the report, however, we present correlations between home language *use* and second-language literacy *achievement*. It is plausible that even when achievement measures in two languages are positively correlated, environmental inputs (in this case, home language use) function differently.

writing vocabulary assessment, an oral story retelling assessment, and various student and teacher scales designed to gauge reading motivation, behavior, and attitude. The study lasted 7 months.

Daily rereading of English classroom books in the home (with or without audiotapes) had no effect on the two literacy outcomes. There was also no effect of the daily rereading in the home (with or without audiotapes) on oral story retelling, relative to the book-rich classroom condition. All three treatment conditions, each of which included the book-rich classroom component, outperformed the control, but they were not different from each other. The researchers did not do implementation checks at home, so it is impossible to determine whether there were no effects of the home conditions because there was no follow-through or implementation in the home.

The only home effects this study found were on teacher ratings. The home reading augmented with audiotape had positive effects on teacher ratings of children's positive behaviors toward books (e.g., choose to read, talk about books), and the home reading (with and without audiotape) had positive effects on teacher ratings of the intervention's impact on children's interest and achievement. In other words, the home component, which created additional second-language oral and literacy opportunities for children, was perceived by teachers as enhancing children's reading behaviors, motivation, and interest. Because these effects on teacher ratings were not reflected in the actual measures of children's literacy development, it is difficult to know how to interpret them. Teacher ratings cannot be considered unbiased assessments of the treatments' effects because teachers rated their own students and therefore knew whether they were participating in the home literacy component. The authors report that all teachers "viewed home reading as a valuable literacy activity" (p. 32), so it is likely that knowing their children were participating in the home component could influence their ratings.

Effects were the same for English-proficient and English-language-learner children. The only English-language-learner-specific effect was on children's own reports of how much they practiced reading. English-language learners who received the audiotapes at home to accompany their rereading said they practiced more than did students who did not receive the audiotapes.

Buriel and Cardoza (1988) found no association between home language use and high school seniors' reading achievement across three generations. Home English use increased from first to second to third generations, but average student literacy scores remained the same. Within generations, there was no association between home language use and literacy achievement for first- and second-generation students. Kennedy and Park (1994) also report no correlation between home language use and student literacy achievement for Mexican students when SES was controlled. The authors speculate that the absence of a correlation between home language use and reading achievement for the Mexican students (but not the Asians) might have been due to their early bilingual education experience. However, the authors offer no elaboration, data, or further explanation.

Cahill (1987) reports no correlation between press for English at home Italian or English literacy development and in 10-year-old Italo–Australian children. Aarts and Verhoeven (1999) found no correlation between Turkish language/Turkish orientation in the home and Turkish literacy achievement of Turkish eighth graders in the Netherlands.

Positive Association Between First-Language Use and Second-Language Outcomes (Cell 4). Three studies—one experiment with Spanish-speaking kindergart-ners and two correlational studies with late-elementary-age students—report findings that stand in contrast to the other nine studies discussed. Whereas most of the studies reviewed tend to support the time-on-task hypothesis or are neutral, Hancock (2002), Cahill (1987), and Dolson (1985) report findings that support Cummins' theory of common underlying proficiency (1986) or linguis-tic interdependence (2001). They all report that enhanced experiences in the home language promote literacy development in a second language. In all three studies, the second language was English.

Hancock (2002) conducted one of two experimental studies in this group (see also the discussion of this study in chap. 15). Hancock found that sending home Spanish books and promoting Spanish reading in the home improved kindergarten children's preliteracy skills (measured in English). Hancock studied 77 Spanish- and English-speaking kindergarten children (mean age 5.6 years) in 10 kindergarten classes in two middle-class suburban schools. No informa-tion was provided about the SES of study participants per se. The Spanish-speaking students ($n = 52$) were randomly assigned to treatment and control groups; the English-speaking students ($n = 25$) served as a second control group. Teachers of children in the treatment group sent home books in Spanish each day for the children and parents to read together. Children in the control groups received English versions of the same books.

Hancock found that the Spanish-speaking children who received Spanish-language books scored significantly higher (effect size = .73) on a preliteracy skills test than did their counterparts exposed to English-language books. Just as important, the Spanish-speaking children exposed to Spanish-language books scored no differently from their English-speaking classmates exposed to English-language books. The measure used was the Test of Early Reading Ability–Second Edition (TERA–2), a standardized measure of concepts of print and language. Unfortunately, Hancock reports no pretreatment data, so we cannot be certain that both Spanish-speaking groups were equivalent at the beginning of the study. Students were randomly assigned to treatment conditions, how-ever, so it is reasonable to assume equivalence and to conclude that sending the Spanish books home had a stronger effect on preliteracy development than did sending English books.

Cahill (1987) found that a wide range of family factors influenced first- and second-language (Italian and English) reading and writing development among second- and third-generation Italo–Australian 10-year-olds. A key finding was that press for first-language development (i.e., parents' emphasis on maintaining Italian in the home) was positively associated with children's measured reading and writing achievement in the second language (English). In other words, press for the first-language—and presumably additional first-language experiences at home—predicted greater second-language literacy achievement. These findings are important for two reasons. First, as indicated, they seem to support Cummins' theory of common underlying proficiency (1986) or linguistic interdependence

(2001), which the other studies do not. Cahill reports that press for English was unrelated, whereas press for Italian *was* related, to children's English achievement, suggesting that home experiences supporting first-language development are critical for skill development in the second language. Second, the study is unusual in that it appeared to measure home language use independently for the first and second languages. In other words, Cahill did not assume that there was a single continuum of language use, from *All/mostly English* to *All/mostly Italian*. Instead, the language variables could be independent of each other and not in a zero-sum relationship.

However, a number of problems limit this study's information value. The measures consist of groups of heterogeneous variables that should be disaggregated and reported separately. For example, the language press measures (Italian and English) include items that tap parents' self-reported language proficiency, use of the language at home, correction of the child's spoken language, and monitoring of the child's reading. No scale statistics are reported, nor are relationships among individual items. In addition, there is no information on the levels of home language and literacy experiences in the first and second languages (scale means), so the relative extent of Italian and English spoken in the homes is unknown. The author appears to report correlations selectively, rather than exhaustively, so it is impossible to determine the full extent to which his data support his claims. Moreover, statistical tests are not reported for the regression analysis, so it is unclear which predictors reliably explain additional variance. Nonetheless, this study presents a counterpoint to most of the studies reviewed in this section.

Dolson's (1985) study also presents an important challenge to most of the findings discussed earlier, although his findings do not reach statistical significance with respect to literacy measures. Dolson studied Hispanic families in an urban setting to determine the differences in academic achievement, language development, and psychosocial adjustment between children whose families maintained Spanish as the main home language (additive bilingual home environment) and those from homes that had switched to English as the predominant language (subtractive bilingual home environment). The sample comprised 108 fifth and sixth graders; the determination of additive or subtractive bilingual home environment was based on student reports. Independent *t* tests were used to compare the two groups on school measures of academic achievement (English reading proficiency, mathematics, Spanish reading vocabulary, and academic GPA), language development, and psychosocial adjustment (e.g., attendance, effort GPA). Students from additive bilingual homes significantly outperformed those from the subtractive group on 5 of 10 scholastic measures (including GPA and Spanish reading achievement). However, although students from additive homes had higher scores on the CTBS English reading test than those from subtractive homes (effect size approximately .5), differences between the two groups were not significant on this measure.

Summary

The role of parents and families in children's academic achievement has been a topic of inquiry for more than 40 years. Consistent with a great deal of other research, studies in this area reveal that language-minority families influence their children's literacy development. Three findings emerged from our review of this literature.

First, language-minority parents express willingness and often have the ability to help their children succeed academically. For various reasons, however, schools underestimate and do not take full advantage of parents' interest, motivation, and potential contributions. Although views about literacy and literacy practices may differ between home and school, literacy activities are not absent in home settings.

Second, more home literacy experiences/opportunities are generally associated with superior literacy outcomes, but findings in this regard are not consistent, and precise conclusions are not available. Measures of parent and family literacy often predict child literacy attainment, but two studies found that parents' reading behavior was unrelated to children's literacy outcomes (Aarts & Verhoeven, 1999; Pucci & Ulanoff, 1998). Features of family life (e.g., domestic workload, religious activities) appear to influence the value children place on reading and their self-concepts as readers. SES—particularly parent education—is clearly associated with literacy outcomes (see chap. 4).

Third, but with some important exceptions, the relationship between home language use and children's literacy outcomes tends to be language-specific. In other words, home experiences in the first and second languages are positively correlated with child literacy achievement in the first and second languages, respectively. However, home experiences in the first or second language tend to be negatively correlated, although weakly, with child literacy achievement in the other language: Greater use of the first language predicts lower achievement in second-language literacy, whereas greater use of the second language predicts lower achievement in first-language literacy. Whereas six studies report findings suggesting negative associations between first-language use in the home and second-language achievement, three studies (Cahill, 1987; Dolson, 1985; Hancock, 2002) report contrary findings—namely, that greater use of the first language in the home was associated with higher literacy achievement in the second language. The Hancock study is particularly important because it involved an experimental manipulation of the language of literacy materials sent home. Because of conflicting and inconclusive findings, no strong practice or policy recommendations are possible with respect to language use in the home. The need for additional research is obvious.

One conclusion that can be drawn from the studies reviewed here is that schools should look for ways to engage parents in children's literacy development (although, again, what language parents should be encouraged to promote at home is far from clear). There is ample evidence that language-minority parents are motivated and, in many cases, capable of actions that would lead to improved student outcomes. Moreover, studies of apparently successful school contexts suggest that parent–home–community involvement helps explain school success. Advocates of parent involvement argue that schools should actively seek ways to collaborate with parents for children's academic benefit (e.g., Epstein, 1992, 1996; Goldenberg, 1993).

Yet even aside from the language issue, the research base presents a dilemma. On the one hand, we have evidence of low-income and minority parents' willingness and ability to help their children succeed academically, but, on the other hand, the evidence for the impact of parent involvement efforts on children's achievement is surprisingly thin. Indeed, two meta-analyses that have appeared since 1990 challenge the notion that parent involvement programs have demonstrable effects on student outcomes (Mattingly et al., 2002; White et al., 1992). Mattingly et al. show that the strongest claims for effectiveness come from studies with the weakest designs (i.e., those lacking suitable control groups). The concerns raised by these authors signal that we have failed to pay sufficient attention to documenting the outcomes of parent involvement efforts and their impact on important student outcomes.

Although we do have considerable evidence that parents are positively disposed toward these sorts of activities—perhaps especially in the area of early literacy, where parents possess the attitudes and many have at least rudimentary literacy skills and knowledge to help their children—we know less about the likely effects of such efforts on children's literacy development. A potential problem that should be acknowledged is that parents who do not speak the societal language are unable to assist their children in that language and are not able to initiate or sustain communication with the school unless special personnel or programs are in place. The academic expectations of educators for students and their parents may place an undue burden on these families.

THE INFLUENCE OF POLICIES AT THE DISTRICT, STATE, AND FEDERAL LEVELS

Many authors have speculated about the impact on literacy outcomes of various policies at different organizational levels, but there have been surprisingly few empirical investigations linking hypothesized effects to student outcomes. Although policies are usually viewed as formal and officially recognized principles and regulations, in fact they can be formal or informal. Shannon (1995), for example, discusses such an informal policy—the implicit language policy in the United States that privileges English over languages of lesser status, such as Spanish. As described earlier, Shannon conducted a year-long ethnographic study of a counterhegemonic fourth-grade classroom where the teacher explicitly assigned prestige to speaking, reading, and writing in Spanish and to bilingualism in general. The idea was to examine how such practices might overcome the presumed negative effects of the implicit policy privileging English. The study findings suggest that these practices led to several positive outcomes: increased use of Spanish, student perceptions that Spanish helped the learning process, and students' valuing bilingualism. The study had weaknesses related to the main premise, however. For example, data from only a few children in the class were reported, so how representative the sentiments expressed in the quotes and revealed by the reported behaviors is unknown. Also, teaching practices were confounded with explicit promotion of the value of bilingualism. Finally, further evidence is needed regarding children's actual literacy growth and its relationship to challenging English hegemony.

A second study relevant to the issue of language policy is that of Brunell and Linnakylä (1994) in Finland, discussed earlier in connection with home language. As noted, Finland has two official languages—Finnish (the majority group language) and Swedish—and offers full-scale education in both. The general finding of this study was that the Swedish-speaking students of Finland have achieved a high literacy level, competing well with the majority-language speakers in both Finland and Sweden. As with the Shannon study, this investigation is not a direct test of the influence of language policy on student outcomes, but its findings are consistent with the hypothesis that additive language policies and practices can affect student literacy outcomes positively.

In summary, the research base in this area is inadequate to permit firm conclusions, but the few existing studies are suggestive. Shannon (1995) describes the impact on students of the implicit (unofficial) U.S. language policy that privileges English and how a classroom teacher countered this impact with practices that appeared to have positive effects on students' literacy development. Findings of Brunell and Linnakylä's (1994) study of Swedish speakers in Finland could be interpreted as consistent with the hypothesis that language policies and practices recognizing the value of more than one language can minimize the negative effects of language-minority status on student literacy outcomes. Both studies, however, are open to alternative interpretations.

THE INFLUENCE OF LANGUAGE STATUS OR PRESTIGE

Results reported by Brunell and Linnakylä (1994), taken together with those of other studies in our database, suggest that language status might be a factor in language-minority children's literacy attainment, although definitive statements are not possible. In the United States, where Spanish is perceived to have lower status than English (Carreira, 2000), achievement differences between Spanish- and English-speaking students can be substantial (see chap. 2). Brunell and Linnakylä's study of Swedish-speaking children (the language-minority group) attending Swedish-language schools in Finland, in contrast, found what they called *marginal* differences (3%–4%) in achievement between the language-minority Swedish children and the language-majority Finns. A possible explanation is that, as discussed previously, Finnish (the majority language) and Swedish (the minority language) enjoy equal status. Brunell and Saretsalo (1999) suggest that Swedish language-minority children in Finland "in a sense...have two mother tongues" (p. 175). First-language instruction is widely accepted in Finland, and parents have the option of sending their children to Finnish or Swedish schools.

Of course, there are other possible explanations for the similar literacy outcomes among Swedish language-minority and Finnish language-majority students. Perhaps the most plausible is that the Swedish and the Finnish communities in both Finland and Sweden have a high literacy culture (Brunell & Linnakylä, 1994). Books and reading are prominent in everyday life. For example, 40% of Finnish- and Swedish-speaking 9-year-olds report reading books *for fun* every day; another approximately 30% report doing so once a week. Nearly 60% report daily comic book reading, and more than 50% report reading a magazine at least once a week. Moreover, the Swedish-speaking community in Finland appears to have somewhat higher levels of education than the Finnish population and higher levels of home literacy activities, such as number of books in the home (Brunell & Linnakylä, 1994). Such differences in favor of the Swedish population might help offset any disadvantages in reading achievement due to more first- language and less second-language use at home. In addition, SES and social status differences are less extreme in Scandinavian countries than in the United States (Smeeding, 2002), where there are enormous differences between the well-off and the less-well-off economically. The relative parity of Scandinavian societies might explain more equitable achievement outcomes across social groups, such as language-majority and language-minority students.

A final problem with interpreting the Swedish–Finn achievement comparison is that it is difficult to compare directly the language-majority versus language-minority discrepancies in reading achievement in Finland and the United States. Brunell and Linnakylä claim the difference is modest in Finland, but they do not specify how they derived the 3% to 4% figure they cite. Moreover, it is not clear that 3% to 4% is a smaller differential than we see in the United States. Buriel and Cardoza (1988), for example, found what appears to be a 2% to 4% discrepancy (based on scale scores with a mean of 50) in the reading achievement of Spanish-speaking language-minority students and a national sample based on the High School and Beyond senior sample.

We found only two other empirical studies with student outcomes that could be used to address the issue of language status and its effects on literacy development. One was Shannon's (1995) ethnographic study, described in the preceding section. In this fourth-grade classroom, certain student outcomes (increased use of Spanish, student perceptions that Spanish helped the learning process, and students' valuing bilingualism) were claimed to result from a classroom environment specifically created to promote high status for students' home language. As noted earlier, although this study presents a circumstantial case for student biliteracy outcomes linked to what Shannon calls *counterhegemonic practices*, more systematic and comprehensive evidence is needed to gauge the effects on children's actual literacy growth.

Lam (2000) conducted a study that is informative with respect to the issue of language status and prestige and its role in terms of identity formation. Lam reports a case study of a Chinese immigrant teenager whose difficulties mastering conventional English writing and speaking as taught in his ESOL classes contributed to his sense of alienation and marginalization from his adopted country. This young man had been in the United States for 5 years and viewed his prospects as bleak because of his English limitations. The fact that he was having trouble acquiring the highly valued standard English caused problems for him. Although he was not able to develop an identity through his attempts to acquire standard English, entry into the world of the Internet turned things around for him. He developed Web pages in English, corresponded with people worldwide, and engaged in a wide range of electronically mediated, text-based activities centering on global youth pop culture. His ability to use a nonstandard version of English in these activities was at least partially responsible for the less-threatening view of English acquisition he developed and his ensuing progress. He told the study's author that he had made great strides in improving his written English and could now write more fluently, even in school. He was planning to take public speaking to improve his oral delivery.

The most important shortcoming of this case study, however, is that there is no independent corroboration that any of the changes reported by the subject occurred, and that the claimed changes were in fact due to his experiences on the Internet or to the role of standard versus nonstandard English.

Although the hypothesis that relative language status and prestige influences students' first- and second-language literacy outcomes is plausible, sufficient evidence is not available to draw firm conclusions. More systematic investigation of this hypothesis is needed, particularly studies that measure student outcomes and attempt to relate them empirically to language status.

In summary, as with the research on policy, we can hypothesize that language status might influence the achievement of speakers of that language. Being a member of a low-status language group might have negative effects on self-concept, motivation, and/or learning opportunities, all of which can depress literacy attainment. Brunell and Linnakylä (1994), Lam (2000), and Shannon (1995), each in different ways, provide suggestive evidence supporting this hypothesis. However, other explanations for these studies' findings are possible. In addition, there are achievement differences among different non-English-language groups in the United States, which the status hypothesis cannot fully explain. As with virtually all the hypotheses evaluated in this chapter, much more research is needed before we can draw conclusions with some confidence.

12

The Sociocultural Context in Which Children Acquire Literacy

Robert S. Rueda, Diane August, and Claude Goldenberg

The studies reviewed in this chapter are organized into broad categories that parallel those in the preceding chapter. As discussed in chapter 10, the principal difference between chapters 11 and 12 is that the studies reviewed in chapter 11 report data on some aspect of student literacy outcomes (e.g., measured achievement, behavioral or attitudinal indicators), whereas studies in chapter 12 report no such outcome data. (In addition, the studies reviewed in this chapter, unlike those discussed in the preceding chapter, do not include technical reports.) The studies reviewed here include informative descriptive data on various sociocultural factors, and they suggest certain hypotheses about the influence of these factors on student literacy outcomes.

In chapter 12, we discuss in turn the following factors related to the literacy development of language-minority students: differences in discourse and interaction characteristics; other socioculturally related factors; parents and families; policies at the district, state, and federal levels; and language status or prestige. It should be noted that, as in other chapters, the studies are organized by the age of the subjects, beginning with the youngest learners. A disproportionately large number of the studies reviewed other socioculturally related factors (10); relatively fewer focused exclusively on parents and families (5), language status and prestige (6), discourse and interaction characteristics (3), or bureaucratic and organizational policies (1).

The study of sociocultural factors in literacy development has often focused on descriptive questions and relied more on descriptive designs and methods. As we have previously pointed out, studies in this area have been less concerned than in other areas of educational research with empirically linking factors of interest to actual student outcomes. Nonetheless, many descriptive studies have made valuable contributions to our understanding of the context in which language-minority children are educated, and of the issues raised by considering sociocultural factors in students' acquisition of literacy. This body of descriptive and exploratory work has been useful in providing an informed basis on which to develop theory.

In considering this body of literature, it is important to examine whether sociocultural constructs as defined by the studies reviewed are truly sociocultural in ways that are unique to language-minority students, the focus of this chapter. In some cases, the accommodations made are clearly unique to language-minority students (e.g., the opportunity to use either their first or second language to express themselves or curriculum aligned with cultural concepts). In other cases, the accommodations are more generic (e.g., classrooms in which teachers give students the opportunity to read and write about experiences that interest or are relevant to them). In some cases, moreover, it appears that differences between home and school contexts defined by the researchers as social may be more related to individual family differences or differences inherent in most home versus school settings, the latter being much more formal than the former. Similarly, aspects of teaching regarded as culturally accommodating could easily be considered good teaching generally (flexible wait time, making an effort to understand the home experiences of the children in one's classroom), but not necessarily be culturally specific (see e.g., Jiménez & Gersten, 1999). In the end, although it is important to consider sociocultural factors, we should heed Xu (1999) when she states that, "language minority students need to be treated as unique individuals with various home literacy experiences rather than as part of an ethnic group stereotype" (p. 236).

The chapter is organized according to five of the six topics we used to organize chapter 11 (the exception is immigration circumstances; studies of immigration circumstances all included measures of student achievement, so these studies were reviewed in chap. 11):

1. Differences in discourse and interaction characteristics between children's homes and classrooms.
2. Other sociocultural characteristics of students and teachers.
3. Parents and families.
4. Policies at the district, state, and federal levels.
5. Language status or prestige.

From a practice and policy perspective, perhaps the most important hypothesis that emerges from these studies is the following: Because children's sociocultural backgrounds and experiences influence many aspects of their cognitive, affective, and social development, schools must be aware of potential discrepancies, discontinuities, or conflicts that might result from the different experiences and expectations that language-minority children face at home (and in their communities) and those they face at school. Studies on the first three topics, to one degree or another, all make this point. Further, either explicitly or implicitly, the studies also argue that students' school experiences, and especially their literacy outcomes, can be improved if schools and teachers provide ways to bridge discontinuities or otherwise accommodate to sociocultural differences. The implicit assumption disputed by these studies is that group differences in literacy outcomes are related solely to ability differences between second-language learners and their native-speaking peers. Other studies reviewed in this chapter examine the potential effects of state and federal policies and of attitudes toward native and societal languages. The authors of these studies hypothesize that student, family, community, and educator attitudes and beliefs about the value of the home language or the value of bilingualism influence learning opportunities and achievement outcomes for language-minority children and youth.

DISCOURSE AND INTERACTION CHARACTERISTICS

Three studies examined how discourse or interaction patterns vary between home and school settings. As discussed in chapter 10, these home–school discontinuities are potentially disruptive to language-minority children's school achievement because children are being expected to interact with others at school in a way that is not consistent with how they have been socialized at home. As a corollary, aligning home–school interaction patterns is expected to enhance literacy outcomes. However, one author makes an additional point. In examining home–school interaction patterns, Xu (1999) suggests that schools not only support the kind of learning that goes on in students' homes, but provide instruction that complements home literacy practices so students will receive a more well-rounded education.

Xu (1999) reports on a case study of two Chinese kindergartners; the study examined the relationship between home and school cultures in English literacy acquisition. Observations of the classroom, monthly home visits, interviews with teacher and parents, and informal in-person and telephone conversations were used to gather information on literacy environments, literacy practices at school and at home, and the teacher's and parents' views on literacy development and interaction patterns. The study documents differences between home and school cultures.

> The home culture consisted of a literate environment, knowledgeable and supportive adults, parent–child interactions, and meaningful literacy activities, However, the classroom environment, although similar to that of their homes in one aspect (i.e., print-rich) was different in many other ways. Discontinuities between home and school included no use of Cantonese at school, a school social culture that prohibited adult–child interactions, and a curricular culture that stressed isolated skill practices rather than the more meaningful and situated home literacy experiences (prevalent in one of the homes but not the other).The author maintains that while the at home the children were supported and encouraged to construct socially and actively their literary knowledge…the school failed to provide continued support. (p. 234)

Gregory (1998) studied interactions between older and younger siblings during English-language book reading sessions at home and compared these with teacher–participant literacy interactions at school. The seven focal children were native speakers of Sylheti-Bengali, lived in an urban setting near London populated largely by families of Bangladeshi origin, and attended a school where all the children were native speakers of Sylheti-Bengali. The children regularly attended Bengali and Arabic community classes. Gregory found that in the home settings, the older siblings provided firm scaffolding that was gradually removed as the younger siblings gained confidence and ability in reading. For example, older siblings provided children reading at lower levels with frequent corrections (where the young child repeated a corrected word before continuing to read) and a focus on reading the words themselves, rather than on text comprehension. Older siblings did not model for the children who read at a more advanced level, but did ask basic questions about the text. Generally, the younger children were given the freedom to read what they felt confident in attempting independently, but were not pressured to take on more than they could manage. At all levels, the rhythm of the interactions was fast-paced (similar to Qur'anic reading). Within this secure structure, Gregory saw these beginning readers progress from reliance on the older sibling toward greater independence in reading words.

In the classroom, teacher–student interactions around oral reading contrasted with the sibling dyad in several ways. The teacher did not provide words or phrases for the children to repeat, but corrected pronunciation with the expectation that the student would advance to the next word; she questioned the students about letter–sound relationships; she posed higher level comprehension questions about the text; and she required that the students relate the text to their personal lives. Gregory suggests that for these young children, the result of the discontinuity between home literacy practices and classroom instruction was that in school, "the children [were] expected to put on a complete show without the previous rehearsal" (p. 47). Based on these home–school contrasts, Gregory argues that teachers could enhance literacy instruction for these language-minority children if they were aware of the children's home reading patterns and adopted strategies used in the sibling dyads. However, although this study effectively demonstrates discontinuities between the home and school literacy experiences for this group of children, it does not present data to support the instructional recommendations made.

Finally, within the context of the Kamehameha Early Education Project (KEEP), Au (1980) analyzed the performance of four students on a 20- to 150-minute sample reading lesson from a second-grade classroom to compare the participation structures identified in the KEEP reading lesson and in *talk story* in nonclassroom environments. *Talk story*—"the local term for a rambling personal experience narrative mixed with folk materials" (p. 95)—is a major speech event in Hawaiian culture. It is characterized by cooperative production by two or more speakers, with turn taking used as a focal structural device. The teacher in Au's study was of Hawaiian origin. The four students were representative of the KEEP students, who were "part-Hawaiian, native speakers of the local dialect, from families on welfare, and lived in urban Honolulu" (p. 96), and they were in a relatively high-proficiency reading group. On the basis of careful coding of a videotape of the lesson, Au identified nine types of participation structures in the lesson. Some of these structures were typical of conventional classroom settings, but more than half were more similar to talk story; in other words, they contrasted with how children are typically expected to interact in classroom academic settings. For example, in conventional classrooms, the typical pattern of interaction involves "the asking of a question by the teacher, a response by a student, and an evaluation of the student's response by the teacher" (p. 97), whereas in KEEP classrooms, more than half of the interaction patterns were characterized by "cooperation and precise synchronization of talk among two or more children and the teacher" (p. 97). This study provides a key part of the foundation for the work of Au and Mason (1981), which was reviewed in chapter 11.

In summary, these three studies found discontinuities between home and school discourse and interaction patterns. These discontinuities included use of only the second language at school, school teacher–student discourse patterns that decreased meaningful adult–child interactions, less opportunity for student rehearsal of appropriate responses, and teaching in some classrooms that stressed isolated skill practices, rather than more meaningful literacy experiences (prevalent in some of the children's homes, but not all). There were fewer discrepancies between home and school discourse when an explicit attempt was made by teachers to match classroom instruction to children's home discourse.

OTHER SOCIOCULTURAL CHARACTERISTICS OF STUDENTS AND TEACHERS

Numerous studies have examined the role of other sociocultural characteristics of students and teachers. In some of these studies, teachers gave students the opportunity to read and write about experiences that interested or were relevant to them (the social dimension). In others, the teacher allowed students to use either their first or second language to express themselves, or attempted to craft curriculum that was aligned with cultural concepts (the cultural dimension). In addition, one study examined how sociocultural differences between home and school create difficulty for children in school settings. There is considerable overlap between the studies reviewed in this section and those reviewed elsewhere in the chapter that focused more narrowly on interaction patterns (preceding section) or language prestige (see the following sections). The studies reported here may also include these factors as one component of the sociocultural environment.

Six studies were conducted at the elementary school level. Moll, Sáez, and Dworin (2001) present two case examples: one from a kindergarten class and the other from a third-grade class. In both cases, students were attending school in bilingual Spanish–English environments where some but not all of their classmates shared their linguistic and cultural backgrounds. The authors comment that, "literacy, whether bilingual or otherwise, must be conceptualized as intricately related, not only to the children's histories, but to the dynamics of social, cultural, and institutional contexts that help define its nature" (p. 447). In the kindergarten classroom, teachers gave students the freedom to pursue writing on topics of interest to them, as well as choose the language in which to write. According to the authors, examples of texts produced by two emergent writers in the kindergarten class indicate that "the children's writing [was] semantically driven; children [knew] that oral language can be represented by 'letters'; and the writing [was] socially mediated" (p. 442). In the third-grade classroom, the authors note that, "children were given the opportunity to: develop expertise in a variety of written genres in either or both languages; use both academic and social content as subject matter for their reading and writing; and use literacy in either language, or both languages, deliberately as a tool for thinking" (pp. 444–445). The authors note the limitations of this work: "These examples do not form part of a systematic study of biliteracy per se; rather, they represent our attempts at exploring biliteracy by selecting revealing examples gathered from our previous investigations and examples that represent children in various grades and circumstances" (p. 436). Although these descriptive examples are informative, it is not clear how the performance of these focal students compares with that of other students in this or other classrooms, nor is it clear how representative they are of these students' work in general. In addition, there are several interrelated features of the classroom that may account for student behavior and/or attitudes, including self-selected topics, freedom to write in English or Spanish, the status accorded the native language, and individual teacher dynamics, making it difficult to determine exactly what factors influenced children's literacy practices.

Townsend and Fu (1998) describe the role of social supports in the literacy development of a second-grade, non-English-speaking child who attended a predominantly middle-class school, where he was the only child in his class from a nonmainstream cultural and linguistic background. Xiaodi was observed in both his regular and English-as-a-second-language (ESL) classrooms. The authors collected samples of his work and conducted periodic interviews with him, his teachers, and his mother. Xiaodi's ESL class provided explicit language and literacy instruction in sentence structure, vocabulary, reading comprehension, and phonics (using songs and music) for 45 minutes each day. In his regular classroom, however, he joined his classmates in participating "in reading and writing workshops and [making] choices about what activities to pursue" (p. 194). His social supports in this classroom included exposure to multiple genres and literacies (teacher read-alouds, writing, discussions, and individual conferences), recognition of his language and personal skills, and the ability and time to make choices (freedom to use his native language, use of invented spellings when he began to write in English, and choice of topics of interest to him for reading and writing). A major purpose of this study was to describe the regular classroom conditions facilitating this student's introduction to and proficiency in English literacy. This study raises interesting hypotheses about early literacy acquisition, but which of the classroom or other factors (such as the home environment) may have had an impact on this student's development cannot be disentangled from the case study. A short description of this student's failure to profit in the fifth grade, when he entered a new school that appeared to be organized more rigidly around specific skills and worksheets, provides an intriguing bit of evidence about the role of the classroom context in this student's attitudes toward reading. However, the description is brief and unsystematically reported, again not permitting ruling out other explanations. The study provides an interesting hypothesis about the claim that "What's apparently most helpful for all language learners—in developing both communicative and grammatical competence—is the opportunity to construct language in personally meaningful ways that serve real communication purposes" (p. 200). Additional research in this area is needed to help make a convincing case regarding these causal attributions.

Masny and Ghahremani-Ghajar (1999) examined the relationship between literacies and school and community cultures among Somalian children in a Canadian school context. They studied two Somalian siblings, one in Grade 3 and the other in Grade 4, who were refugees with no previous formal education and no knowledge of English. Data were collected through participant observations, interviews with school staff, community informants, and the children. Samples of the children's writing and their first- and second-language skills were reviewed. The author notes that, "while cultural diversity was celebrated in the classroom, the role of the family and the community in the school was marginalized. In contrast, in African society, the community as a whole takes responsibility for the socialization and education of the young" (p. 82). Moreover, one teacher was successful in bringing the cultural and linguistic experiences of the children into the classroom, whereas the other teacher was not. In contrast to the regular teachers, the observer (who became an ESL instructor for these two children) attempted to legitimize the children's cultural and religious resources (e.g., their familiarity with literacy in Qur'anic Arabic). Furthermore, parents were invited to build home–school bonds beyond the usual contacts in order to link school and community cultures. The authors argue for a "pedagogy of difference that affirms home, community, and school cultures reproduced through multiple literacies" (p. 91) and a "pedagogy of inclusion by providing an environment where children are not silenced, where they can voice through the narratives...their histories...and their ways of learning (e.g. through collaborative practices and active involvement of the community)..." (p. 90). These are certainly suggestions worth examining as a possible means of facilitating the acquisition of English literacy for some students. As with the previous study, additional research is needed to provide clear evidence of an unambiguous link from these approaches to student outcomes.

Hornberger (1990) conducted an ethnographic study of a fourth/fifth-grade two-way bilingual program for Puerto Rican students and a fourth-grade English immersion program for culturally and linguistically diverse students, such as Southeast Asians and African Americans. The objective was to document strategies employed by the teachers that were thought to go beyond generic good teaching to promote the literacy development of language-minority children. The author identifies four themes that characterize critical aspects of contexts for teaching literacy: motivation, purpose, text, and interaction. Both teachers in the study made being in the classroom context desirable through affective and experiential bonds while focusing on literacy development. They established both broadly social purposes (bilingual/bicultural maintenance or assimilation) and more narrowly task-focused purposes for their students' development of literacy skills, and they exposed the children to a variety of texts, not just the basal readers. Finally, interaction with and around text in both classes was characterized by "taking advantage of a variety of participant structures, drawing on students' prior knowledge, and developing students' strategies for signaling understanding of text, analyzing features of text, and reasoning around text" (p. 227). This study is different from the studies reviewed so far because it documents two apparently successful teachers addressing similar issues through different instructional approaches. Whereas many authors call for a specific approach to address sociocultural factors in the classroom, this study raises the possibility that different approaches might be successful depending on the context and how the teacher is able to mediate the experiences of his or her students. In this particular study, a *successful learning context* is taken to mean "the degree that it allows children to draw on the three continua of biliterate development, that is, on both oral and written, receptive and productive, and first- and second-language skills, at any point in time" (p. 214). Although this does provide some criteria for defining *successful*, it would be informative to see how these students compare with each other and their peers on one or more outcome measures.

Similarly, Jiménez and Gersten (1999) describe the different ways in which two Latina teachers in a large urban school in Southern California incorporated culturally relevant instruction into their instructional practice (see also chap.16.). The study employed observations by multiple observers for 2 years, as well as interviews and informal conversations with school and district personnel. The students were all of Mexican origin and native Spanish speakers. Both teachers were also of Mexican origin. One teacher, raised in Southern California, taught a transitional fifth-grade class in which most of the instruction was conducted in English; the other teacher, raised in Mexico, taught a fifth/sixth-grade bilingual class in which students tended to be recent arrivals and instruction was conducted mainly in Spanish. The authors note the following teaching strategies: multiple methods, use of dual-language interaction to ensure adequate communication with students, a focus on topics that were decidedly Latino, wait time, an emphasis on communication taking priority over students' language choice, and acceptance of students' cultural backgrounds as sources of strength rather than problems. The authors argue that, despite differences in the two teachers' teaching practices, their teaching strategies were influenced by their Latina identities, as evidenced by the cited examples. Unlike much qualitative work that relies on a grounded approach, these authors had a preexisting conceptual framework for effective instructional practices. However as they note, "the particular area of disappointment for us was that we could not independently confirm through more traditional measures of assessment, student academic achievement" (p. 294). Like the Hornberger (1990) study, this research raises the possibility that different approaches might be equally successful in different contexts. Yet a clearer and more systematic demonstration of student growth as a result of these studies is needed, especially one in which individual components of a larger overall strategy could be examined. Finally, one could easily argue that some of these attributes are not necessarily indicative of cultural background, but of good teaching generally.

Schmidt (1995) examined two language-minority students' social interactions in less formal class settings in a predominantly White kindergarten class. The data were collected through observations; examination of documents and schoolwork; and interviews with school personnel, parents, and the two children–Peley from Southeast Asia and Raji from India. The results reveal that the two language-minority students were frequently misunderstood, ignored, and faced with conflicts between school and home cultures. As an example, throughout the year, these two students were alienated from the rest of the class, spending most of the class time alone. The teachers attributed the problem to personal and family characteristics, such as children's shyness and lack of social skills and the parents' low proficiency in English, whereas the author provides examples indicating that some of the conflict was sociocultural in nature. For example, although one student initially made many efforts to initiate conversations with his classmates, he was often rebuffed, and the other student's culturally appropriate drawings were misunderstood. The author also notes that the teacher did not make the class aware of and value these two students' diverse, rich linguistic and cultural backgrounds, which might have helped confer more status on these children and integrate them into the classroom. One of the problems with the study is that the criteria for choosing these focal children were not made clear. Were these the only non-White students in these classrooms, for example? In addition, although all social interactions are cultural, it is not always clear whether the difficulties these students faced were based on cultural misunderstandings or cultural conflict and how much they may have been due to other factors, such as immaturity or generally poor social skills. This study is consistent with the research that focuses on cultural conflict between school and home as contributing to poor student outcomes, but it is difficult to disentangle the constellation of factors (instructional, social, cultural, developmental, academic/cognitive) that appeared to make school a negative experience for these two students. It is clear that issues of cultural difference were virtually ignored in these classrooms. Less clear are the effects of these experiences on students' literacy growth and what to do to address the issue.

Four studies were conducted at the middle- and high school levels. In the first study, Blake (2001) argues in favor of a literacy approach in which "literacy practices and behaviors are grounded in the everyday lives and experiences of people" (p. 437) and a process approach (i.e., writers' workshop) to teaching writing. She describes the writing process engaged in by adolescent girls participating in a summer school program for children of migrant farm workers. As a teacher of these students for two summers, Blake documented one student's resistance to school, which appeared in the student's writing. Blake notes that participating in small-group conversations allowed this student to extend her discourse by providing her the opportunity to include her personal knowledge and experiences. Blake argues that such opportunities allow students to extend their writing, and she provides an example from a second student, whose writing includes numerous details from her personal life. Blake uses these two examples to argue that the process approach to writing is one that allows students from nonmainstream backgrounds to draw from their local literacies (personal experience) to improve their literacy performance in school. One issue with the article is that the author does not demonstrate how typical or atypical the writing samples are of the work of these students or other students in the summer program. A second issue is the article seems to assume that student engagement is largely or entirely a function of culturally based differences among home, school, and community such that "schooled literacy simply does not 'articulate with the existing literacy practices in the community'" (p. 436). It is entirely possible that the type of student disengagement documented in the article is simply a function of low-level remedial practices that affect students from a variety of backgrounds. Although the author's call to address this problem through the use of process writing is a suggestion worth investigating, it is possible that the problem might be addressed by a variety of more active approaches (including process writing) and a more enriched curriculum that takes into account prior knowledge. In examining "the actual literacy practices of our students, and...emphasizing the social practices of literacy" (p. 440), it is important that future research attempts to disentangle universal good teaching practices from cultural accommodations.

Moll and Díaz (1987) examined writing instruction for junior high students with limited English proficiency. For this study, the researchers met with 12 teachers from three schools on a biweekly basis to discuss how the teachers could incorporate recent information on writing instruction into their teaching. The authors report that, at the outset of the study, teachers gave their students little opportunity to produce extended writing because they felt the students lacked the basic skills necessary to complete such tasks. The researchers encouraged teachers to motivate the students by allowing them to write on topics of importance to them and creating homework assignments that would support the students' abilities to develop their writing on these meaningful topics. This approach allowed teachers to create opportunities for their students to participate in demanding, intellectual activities comparable to those of their English-proficient classmates.

The authors' main concern in the study is to examine "a major problem in the schooling of working-class Latino students...the practice of reducing or ... watering down...the curriculum to match perceived or identified weaknesses in the students" (p. 301). They present two case studies: one based on a reading example and one based on a writing example. In the reading example, the authors describe a focal student who, in a brief transcript segment, appeared to produce a more complex response to a story in the student's native language than in English. The researchers also describe follow-up lessons in which students were "able, with our bilingual assistance, to answer comprehension questions required of English monolingual readers at grade level." The claim is that "reading and communicative resources can be strategically combined or mixed to provide the children with the support necessary to participate profitably in reading lessons" (pp. 306–307). They further illustrate this approach with a writing example in which students were permitted to write on an issue of significance to them or their community, and present an example of student writing as evidence for the student's participation in "comparable, demanding intellectual activities" (p. 309). The examples presented are intriguing, but they only illustrate, rather than "prove," the "contention that the strategic application of cultural resources in instruction is one important way of obtaining change in academic performance and of demonstrating that there is nothing about the children's language, culture, or intellectual capacities that should handicap their schooling" (p. 300). The examples are illustrative, but it remains unclear whether changes in student levels of engagement are related to the use of the native language, more interesting activities, self-selection of topics, or the interest and attention of the researchers. More systematic investigation would help examine the different possibilities. It should be noted that the authors do refer the reader to other previously published work (Díaz, Moll, & Mehan, 1986; Moll, 1986; Moll & Díaz, 1985, 1987; Trueba, Moll, & Díaz, 1984, discussed in chap. 11) for more detailed descriptions of the work presented here.

Love (1996) examined the scaffolding used by an English teacher to famil- iarize 20 inner-city secondary level ESL students in Australia with aspects of text and with approaches they would need to use to produce their own texts, as well as the students' response to this scaffolding. The instruction encom- passed four phases of reading-based discussion: vocabulary explanations, nar- rative comprehension, inferential comprehension, and applied comprehension. The author presents an extract from each phase to demonstrate clear variation in the pattern of talk throughout the four stages, corresponding to some trans- fer of authority from teacher to students as they became more confident about the concepts and terminology scaffolded for them. Using the extracted tran- script selections, the author highlights the importance of both teacher-directed talk during points in a reading curriculum cycle and more jointly negotiated talk between teacher and students as a means to build students' comprehen- sion. He notes that, through oral class discussion of text using both kinds of talk formats, the teacher developed a "range of literate and ethical abilities" (p. 22)—literate in that students were able to work from evidence to inference to argument, and ethical because the text selected by the teacher focused on moral issues. The teacher, the author argues, empowered the students by pro- viding and teaching mainstream cultural modes of behavior and rules for cer- tain kinds of talk and writing. The author also notes the teacher's awareness of tension in maintaining a balance between helping the students maintain their primary, home mode of discourse and helping them learn the socially accepted, privileged code. The examples of discourse from each phase are illustrative, but the article would have benefited from specific information about how typical each illustration was of the phase from which it was drawn.

Moll (1986) provides an example of writing instruction that included assign- ments aimed to produce literacy-related interactions in the home and involve parents and other community members in the development and conduct of instruction. Students were required to use their community as a source for their learning by interviewing community members on their beliefs about bilingual- ism. Teachers' journals revealed the students' enthusiasm for and investment in the project as they engaged in writing to communicate their findings.

In summary, 10 studies examined the role of various sociocultural factors. Although these factors are not explicitly instructional, they tend to be inter- twined with instruction. For example, process approaches advocated by this group of authors create opportunities for students and teachers to bring socio- cultural (and personal) elements into the classroom curriculum and instruction. The authors of these studies provide examples of the alienation some culturally different children experience if no effort is made to integrate them into the classroom (Schmidt, 1995). Numerous studies provide examples of teachers' giving legitimacy to children's personal, communal, or cultural backgrounds in the classroom by allowing them to write about topics that interest them (Blake, 2001; Moll & Díaz, 1987; Moll et al., 2001; Townsend & Fu, 1998), use their first language if it enables them to express themselves better (Hornberger, 1990; Jiménez & Gersten, 1999; Moll et al., 2001), take the time they need to develop their second-language competency (Townsend & Fu, 1998), validate cultural experiences related to literacy (Jiménez & Gersten, 1999; Masny & Ghahremani-Ghajar, 1999), and build home–community relationships (Masny & Ghahremani-Ghajar, 1999; Moll, 1986). One study (Hornberger, 1990) suggests it is possible to achieve critical characteristics, such as motivation, purpose, and interaction, in classrooms even if the native language is not used. In this study, although one teacher did not share a common cultural/linguistic background with her students, she made up for this by creating classroom-based shared experiences, such as class trips and an annual camping trip, and classroom games that focused on literacy. Such a balance may be achieved through teacher direction and student engagement (e.g., Love, 1996, who documents the importance of both teacher-directed talk and more jointly negotiated talk between teachers and students as a means of building students' comprehension).

Taken as a whole, the studies provide useful descriptions of the methods and manner in which teachers have been able to use children's personal, communal or cultural backgrounds in the classroom. The studies are overwhelmingly based on case study approaches and ethnographic or other qualitative methods. As a body, they document the nature of sociocultural differences in the classroom and continue to raise long-standing questions regarding the effects of those differences on students' learning opportunities and achievement outcomes. Unfortunately, these studies do not provide a definitive answer to the issue of whether classroom accommodations are specific examples of universal effective teaching practices or whether they represent a unique form of teaching that must be explored and developed for specific populations of students with particular sociocultural characteristics.

Moreover, although many of the authors offer suggestions to address these issues, it seems premature, based on the available research, to specify how specific classroom practices and contexts influence different students or how to address these issues effectively from an instructional perspective. Clearly, research that connects careful documentation of these strategies with student literacy outcomes, which are both closely related to the intent of the strategy and broader in nature, would begin to provide evidence that classroom sociocultural accommodations actually help children develop literacy skills. As noted earlier, in so doing, researchers must be mindful of plausible alternative explanations and threats to validity such as subject self-selection and inadequately documented claims of the relationships among different factors, dimensions, and variables under study.

PARENTS AND FAMILIES

A number of studies have described differences between home–community and school literacy beliefs and practices. Some of this work has focused on home motivation, attitudes, values, and beliefs, and some has focused on home oral language and literacy experiences.

Home Motivation, Attitudes, Values, and Beliefs

Volk and De Acosta (2001) studied literacy as a sociocultural practice in the lives—at home, in the community, and at school—of three Spanish-dominant mainland Puerto Rican children, all of whom attended a bilingual kindergarten. Observations were conducted twice a month in the classroom and once a month in the home and in church. Interviews and informal conversations with parents, teachers, and Sunday school teachers were conducted, and students' writing samples were reviewed. The authors found both similarities and differences between parents' beliefs about literacy and those of the teacher. For example, the authors found that most of the parents believed that literacy means learning the letters and how to combine them, a belief informed by the parents' previous literacy experiences in Puerto Rican schools. The parents also believed that the meaning of text is inherent and not open to negotiation. In contrast, the teacher summarized the literacy events in the classroom as holistic and constructivist, so that meaning could be interpreted and constructed in different ways. In addition, contrary to the teacher's belief, parents of the three focal students were actively engaged in various literacy activities at home. The three children's literacy development was also promoted by the support of networks beyond the nuclear family, such as extended family members and church friends in the home and the community.

Huss (1995) describes a year-long ethnographic study involving three 5- and 6-year-old Pakistani Muslim ESL students in England. Data-collection methods included interviews with children, teacher, and parents; observations; and review of student work and documents in classroom, home, and mosque school settings. In contrast with the teacher's beliefs, students were actively engaged in literacy activities in their first and second languages at home. In the classroom, observations revealed that the students were engaged in English literacy development in multiple, interactive ways, such as construction of meaning through discussions before and during writing, solicitation of help from their peers, and other independent literacy strategies. Researchers also found that students learned classical Arabic in the mosque school and at home, and they also read books and wrote in English at home.

Huss-Keeler (1997) reports on a year-long ethnographic study of a target class of fourteen 5- and 6-year-olds, 80% of whom were Pakistani Muslims in a multiethnic urban community in England. Using interviews, observations, and student documentation, the study examined how cultural and linguistic barriers created school personnel's inaccurate perception of the Pakistani ESL students and their families. School personnel believed that the parents lacked interest in their children's education, and that the Pakistani homes lacked literacy-related activities. The author argues that the teachers' inaccurate perception was due to different, culturally bound expectations among the British White middle-class teachers and the Pakistani parents. Huss-Keeler notes that the Pakistani parents tended to attend school events that were culturally relevant (e.g., a student play about a Muslim celebration) and nonthreatening (e.g., when they did not have to speak English to an authority figure), but they did not actively engage in conversations with teachers and helping around the classroom or school, in large part, because they did not speak English. Furthermore, Pakistani parents believed that good parents trust teachers for their children's education and do not go into the school, but perform their duties at home. The parents had high interest in and hopes for their children's education. The children actively participated in literacy activities in English and Urdu with siblings and literate family members at home and learned Koranic Arabic in mosque school. Thus, the different participation patterns and beliefs of the Pakistani and White middle-class parents and the language barrier and cultural differences between parents and teachers (parents' inability to speak English and a lack of school personnel available to help parents in the school setting) resulted in inaccurate perceptions of the Pakistani parents on the part of the teachers.

Gregory (1994) examined the effect of the home culture on language-minority children's understanding and definition of reading in school and how this differed from their teachers' beliefs about reading. Data were collected from six families of Bangladeshi origin with children ages 5 to 7 in London over a 2-year period. The data were analyzed by ethnographic methods (observations and interviews in the home, English class, and community settings) and ethnomethodological methods (microlevel analysis through discourse analysis). The authors suggest that the definition of reading held by the children of Bangladeshi origin differed from that held by their teachers. The teachers understood that reading was associated with pleasure and was acquired through interaction with high-quality books, and the participation structures in the early stages of reading included "experimentation, storytelling, and pretend reading" (p. 118). In contrast, the children of Bangladeshi origin learned a different meaning of reading as they studied reading and writing in Bengali and Koranic Arabic three to four times a week. For these children, reading meant belonging to their religious, cultural community, and it was acquired through rigid, formal "reading, writing and work" (p. 118).

Oral Language and Literacy Experiences at Home and in the Community

As noted previously, Volk and De Acosta (2001) studied literacy as a sociocultural practice in the lives of three Spanish-dominant mainland Puerto Rican kindergartners at home, in the community, and at school. With regard to differences, parents believed in a more skills-oriented approach to reading instruction, whereas the teacher conceptualized literacy events in the classroom as holistic and constructivist. However, more similar to school, at home and in church, many of the literacy events were social interactions involving the collaboration of at least one other person. The authors maintain that an analysis based on matches and mismatches between home and school is too simplistic; not only were there similarities and differences, but there were "complex and shifting relationships between the three homes and the bilingual classroom" (p. 220).

In a similar study, Mulhern (1997) investigated home–school links in language-minority students' literacy acquisition through a case study of a Mexican American kindergartner in a bilingual program. The author observed Ruben in the classroom and for 3 to 4 hours in his home. Ruben lived in a low-income neighborhood with a large number of Mexican immigrants. The literacy instruction at school was conducted primarily in Spanish. Ruben displayed great interest in and keen insight into literacy activities in the classroom, particularly when he was immersed in reading books and writing for an authentic audience. His desire for literacy acquisition extended to activities at home, where he was frequently engaged in reading and writing activities. The author found that adults, particularly his mother, played an important role in reinforcing his literacy development.

Two studies reported in the preceding section also demonstrate that children are engaged in literacy practices at home. As noted, Huss (1995) reports that 5- and 6-year-old Pakistani Muslim students were actively engaged in literacy activities in their first and second languages at home, and Huss-Keeler (1997) reports that children actively participated in literacy activities in English and Urdu with siblings and literate family members.

Summary

Five studies examined the potential influence of parents and families on literacy. Three of these studies looked at home values, beliefs, and attitudes, as well as language and literacy experiences at home and at school (Huss, 1995; Huss-Keeler, 1997; Volk & De Acosta, 2001); one study examined home values, beliefs, and attitudes (Gregory, 1994); and one examined language and literacy experiences at home and at school (Mulhern, 1997).

Some of these studies highlight differences between students' home–community and school in the practice and purpose of literacy. In several of the studies, for example, literacy was found to be associated with belonging to a religious community (Gregory, 1994; Huss, 1995; Volk & De Acosta, 2001). With respect to pedagogical differences, some of the literacy practices in homes tended to be more "rigid and formal" (Huss-Keeler, 1997), such that the meaning of texts was seen as inherent and not open to negotiation. Other studies document similarities between home–community and school. In one study, for example, literacy events were social interactions involving at least one other person (Volk & De Acosta, 2001) at home and, in some instances, in school.

A picture based on static and clear-cut differences between home and school is not accurate, however. For example, Volk and De Acosta (2001) suggest that a view of home–school relationships as either match or mismatch is too simplistic, in that "there are many literacies that are similar in some ways and different in others" (p. 220). Moreover, the relationships shift over time as the literacy practices in the two domains interact with each other. For example, although it was found that the purposes of reading in both home and school were to acquire information, communicate, and maintain relationships with others, there were purposes unique to each setting. In the community, literacy was viewed as a means to gain access to God's word, whereas in school it was viewed as a way to gain pleasure. With regard to shifts over time, children's experiences with literacy at home as a social event, involving the collaboration of at least one other person, may have transformed their literacy experiences at school, where they transformed classroom time set aside for reading books and writing in journals individually into social activities, whereby they communicated with each other around these events.

The studies also document the considerable misunderstanding that exists among teachers about the home and community literacy experiences of their students, as well as about parental and community expectations for achievement (Huss, 1995; Huss-Keeler, 1997). It appears from the studies that many of these misunderstandings are a result of cultural differences (e.g., parents believe they should trust teachers to do the teaching, and thus it is not the parental role to go to school, whereas teachers see parents as uninterested; Huss-Keeler, 1997). When such gaps have been bridged, the differences that exist do not result in such negative attitudes about language-minority parents and children on the part of school staff. Huss-Keeler documents how even one home visit altered teachers' perceptions of parents' interest in their children's learning despite the parents' lack of English proficiency. Thus, it is important to help teachers understand their students' culture and home experiences. Several authors propose that professional development aimed at clarifying these cultural differences and providing a forum for discussion about them should be an important component of a school's program to ameliorate such misunderstandings between home and school–community. This is an important hypothesis that should be vigorously pursued empirically.

One study (Mulhern, 1997) also documents the importance of helping parents understand the kind of instruction children are receiving in school so that misunderstandings do not arise when children work at home. For example, emergent writing may be promoted in school, but may not be part of parents' repertoire because they were not taught this way. One way of creating more consonance between home and school may be by teachers modeling an activity and involving both parents and students (Quintero & Huerta-Macías, 1990).

A final note is that the collection of studies reviewed here portrays family experiences as diverse and shaped not only by culture, but also by highly personal attributes (Gutiérrez & Rogoff, 2003). As an example, Volk and De Acosta (2001) point to discrepancies among families of similar cultural backgrounds in the way they define the kinds of literacy events relevant to teaching reading and writing. Some families emphasized more explicit instruction in letter–sound relationships as key, whereas others drew on a broader range of resources to create literacy experiences for their children. This finding once again cautions against overgeneralizing individuals' attributes on the basis of nominal group (e.g., cultured or ethnic) membership.

POLICIES AT THE DISTRICT, STATE, AND FEDERAL LEVELS

One study in this area was devoted to the consequences of major federal- and state-level policy changes, in particular, those related to English-only instruction. Stritikus (2001) examined the ways in which three teachers in two schools in the same district responded to legislation banning bilingual education. The study findings were based on data gathered in three different classrooms—one first- and second-grade English-language development (ELD), one third-grade ELD, and one second-grade bilingual—; observations of the teachers during grade-level, all-school, and district-level meetings concerning English-language learner issues; and interviews.

Because the district in which these schools were located allowed individual schools the freedom to implement the law as they saw fit, the schools' responses were quite different. In one school, bilingual classrooms were replaced with

ELD classrooms, and the Open Court series was adopted as the schoolwide language arts series; at the second school, waivers were obtained from parents that allowed the children to remain in bilingual classrooms. This latter school eventually obtained charter school status so as to be free of the restrictions imposed by this new legislation. Stritikus found that the teachers' actions in the two schools were influenced by three factors: the local school context, the teachers' personal ideologies, and their pedagogical reactions to the new policy. Differences in the teachers' approaches to literacy education were apparent even in the two ELD classrooms where the Open Court series was in place, demonstrating the difficulty inherent in the process of policy implementation.

It is notable that we could locate only one study on the influence of state and federal policies on first- and second-language literacy outcomes. The one study we found indicates that specific federal or state policies play out differently in classrooms than they were envisioned to do. As documented by Stritikus (2001), a host of other factors, including other federal and state policies, as well as "the local school context, the teachers' political and ideological views, and their educational histories, is likely' to play a large role in determining the nature of instruction" (p. 305).

LANGUAGE STATUS AND PRESTIGE

This section reviews six studies on language status or prestige in the context of literacy instruction. Three studies focused on environments supportive of the first language, and two studies focused on negative attitudes about first-language use. A sixth study examines the role that the school as well as the wide-community play in students' language use.

In a case study, Clark (1995) focused on first- and second-language development in a bilingual program whose goals were to develop high levels of both English and Spanish proficiency. Over the course of a year, she observed a kindergarten classroom where the teacher spoke Spanish for 90% of the time at the beginning of the year and gradually transitioned to Spanish for 80% of the day; for the remainder of time, English was used in "some songs, books, computer programs, TV programs and language games." During weekly visits to the classroom, Clark observed, recorded interactions, interviewed staff and students, and collected materials, including student writing samples. This article reports on snapshots of two days: one in the early spring and one 2 months later at the end of the semester. The author provides several examples from the first observation, indicating that focal children are using invented spelling in Spanish to express themselves. Several examples from the second observation indicate that some children have begun to use invented spelling to write in English, although there has not been a sustained effort on the part of the teacher to teach English writing. According to the author, the teacher "views her students as coming from rich environments, thereby recognizing their language, their culture, and their experiences as important" (p. 624).

Manyak (2001) studied hybrid language practices used in Daily News, a literacy activity in which children share personal stories that are transcribed by either the teacher or a fellow student and later bound into a *newspaper* for the class. The study took place in a first- and second-grade English immersion classroom. Over the course of a year, Manyak collected information through participant observations, interviews with students and the teacher, and 21 tape-recorded sessions of the Daily News. The teacher accepted stories in Spanish (the students' first language) or English. The author provides vignettes indicating that students worked collaboratively and supported each other in producing news written in both languages, and notes that "by celebrating linguistic flexibility, the practice [of daily news] supported children's developing identities as bilingual and biliterate people" (p. 452).

In both of the preceding articles (Clark, 1995; Manyak, 2001), it is plausible that the teachers' beliefs about the value of biliteracy and their use of both languages in the classroom helped create an additive language-learning environment where children felt comfortable communicating in two languages. However, there may have been other instructionally relevant features of these classrooms that influenced student progress. For example, in the Clark study, the classroom utilized cooperative learning techniques, a critical thinking approach, whole language, computer writing, and thematically integrated curriculum. Additional factors in this study that may have contributed to student progress in the acquisition of English language and literacy included a strong home–school collaboration and a highly experienced teacher with a high degree of proficiency in the students' native language. Both studies would benefit from information about the relative frequency of writing in English and Spanish for these students as well as others in the classroom, and how it changed over time to help make the case that conferring status on both languages helps promote biliteracy. The data presented make it difficult to determine the range of students' English and Spanish language use in the class as a whole and in relation to their peers in other programs.

Moll and Díaz (1987) document the ways in which a reading program that required students to speak only in their second language, English, prevented third- and fourth-grade language-minority students from demonstrating their understanding of what they read in English. The students received instruction in Spanish for part of the day from a bilingual Spanish-speaking Mexican American female and in English for part of the day from a monolingual Anglo American male. The students were reading three levels below grade level in English. In observing students across these two language settings, the authors found that, although students read with varying proficiency in Spanish, all exhibited some level of comprehension of text in that language. In contrast, none of the students displayed text comprehension during English reading sessions. The authors suggest that the strong instructional focus on decoding in the English class precluded opportunities for the students to demonstrate higher level comprehension skills. The implied argument here is that students' second-language oral skills in a less-valued language lead teachers to underestimate the students' intellectual and academic capabilities. The authors conducted interviews and presented data for one student who exhibited disfluency in oral English reading (and was therefore assumed to lack comprehension of the text), but who demonstrated an understanding of the English text when invited to express herself in Spanish.

This discrepancy led the authors to devise an instructional intervention that they implemented in three lessons using grade-level English texts. The intervention was characterized by a "bilingual zone of proximal development" (p. 306), in which teachers spoke Spanish as needed to clarify the meaning of the English text, and students were encouraged to express themselves in English or Spanish. By the third lesson, the authors claim, the "students were able, with our bilingual assistance, to answer comprehension questions required of English monolingual readers at grade level" (p. 306). However, they present no student-generated outcome data to support this strong conclusion. Thus, this study provides hypotheses about the proposition that "...just as academic failure is socially organized, academic success can be socially arranged" (p. 302).

Reyes, Laliberty, and Orbanosky (1993) examined a fourth-grade classroom of 27 students, 14 of whom were of Mexican origin (10 limited English proficient and 4 bilingual students). The teacher encouraged close contact among students of different first-language backgrounds by forming mixed working groups, allowed students to use the language of their choice, and respected students' first language. The mixed grouping was described by the authors as providing "assisted performance" and "scaffolding" (p. 661) in which peer students were available as experts. Spanish was frequently used in the classroom, and the author attributes this to respect for Spanish on the part of the teacher. At the end of the school year, many positive results were observed. For example, an Anglo girl from an upper middle-class background started speaking and writing in Spanish, and her writing demonstrated her rich knowledge of the culture of her native-Spanish-speaking classmates. A highly assimilated boy of Mexican origin who refused to talk in Spanish in the beginning of the year became a translator for students with limited English proficiency and became friends with many Spanish-dominant students. The other two Spanish-dominant students started writing in English, and their interactions with Anglo students increased. Overall, 44% ($n = 12$) of the students exhibited high degrees of engagement, including second-language use, awareness and sensitivity to cultural and linguistic diversity, and engagement in cross-cultural relations. Thirty-seven percent ($n = 10$) were described as having a moderate degree of engagement, and 19% ($n = 5$) were described as low. These data are hard to interpret because the percentages of students who fell in each category at the beginning of the study was not provided. Moreover, although students seemed to make advances in language use and cultural awareness, it is difficult to pin this directly or exclusively on the teacher's values and the cultural norms she tried to create in the classroom. The claim that the children's developmental progress was a function of the prestige accorded to the two languages is a possibility, but a causal link cannot be established.

McCollum (1999) investigated patterns of interaction among Hispanic middle-school students in a two-way bilingual program to determine how these students came to value English over Spanish over a span of 3 years despite their initial positive attitudes toward Spanish. The class consisted of 29 students—21 of Mexican origin and 8 of native English speakers. Classroom observations were conducted twice a week and interviews conducted with students and teachers over the 3 years. Classroom observations of a Spanish language arts class revealed that the students' vernacular Spanish was explicitly and constantly devalued by the teacher of a Spanish class, who insisted on the use of a *high* form of the language. The students responded by switching to English to avoid being corrected. This devaluation of the Spanish language was prevalent across the school context—from the choice of language in daily routines (e.g., daily announcements in which English was used first, followed by Spanish) to different degrees of preparation and different treatments of the two standardized tests, the Iowa Test of Basic Skills (ITBS) and La Prueba. It was particularly exemplified in the fact that the native English speakers' poor performance on the ITBS led to a change in the whole program from its original two-way bilingual structure to a more English-predominant design. Social factors also played a role in the domination of English over Spanish as students strove to gain status and popularity among peers. Despite the greater number of students who were proficient in Spanish, the peer group culture associated English with popularity, and therefore many bilingual students preferred English. The author concludes that,—through both structural and cultural elements in the school, the focal students learned that English, not Spanish, was the language of power" (p. 130). There is somewhat of a confound in the study, in the sense that Spanish as the language of instruction was pitted against the local Spanish vernacular. Thus, had the vernacular use of Spanish not been an issue, it is difficult to estimate whether the conditions existing in the school would have been related to the language-use patterns observed. However, it should be noted that the students' use of nonstandard English was ridiculed on occasion as well. This study points up the interrelatedness of language, culture, socioeconomic status (SES), and related variables, and it suggests that language prestige issues not be considered in isolation from these other possible correlates. These findings are especially interesting given that the program studied was a dual-language program where the stated goal was to promote first- and second-language use.

Lotherington, Ebert, Watanabe, Norng, and Ho-Dac (1998) examined the first-language use of Vietnamese and Cambodian students in Grades 9 and 10 who were bilingual and placed in a maintenance program in Australia that placed value on their first language. The specific number of students observed is not provided in the study, but the majority of the students were born in either Vietnam or Cambodia and felt more proficient in their first language. Data were collected through surveys and interviews with students, parents, and teachers, as well as field visits to a local ethnic business district. In addition, data from a week-long diary study of students' uses of literacy was used to construct a matrix showing language use by domain. The results show that, although the students were biliterate through the first-language maintenance program and family use of the first language, English was used as the main language in literacy activities, and students tended to use it more frequently than their first language with their peers. The authors conclude that, "students varied the language of literacy events according to social context and media demands" (p. 4). They tended to use more English in reading activities, for schoolwork, and on the computer and more of the home language with family members. However, English was encroaching on these domains. Communication was more likely to be in English the younger the family member was. Moreover, most literacy activities in the home were in English despite the students' school language maintenance program. The results of language-use patterns suggest that students' language use was related to the characteristics and demands of specific social contexts. Community literacies were rarely permitted to enter into school literacy practices, whereas school literacies were found to be pervasive in the home and community. The authors note that, although multilingualism is widely encouraged, the economic benefits of English and the employment-related pressures for English make language status an issue. Based on these findings, the authors recommend a link between school literacy practices and community resources so that the students' literacy in their first language will gain equal status and prestige. Overall, the methodological details of the study are sketchy, as are the descriptions of the subjects, but the study does suggest the relative influence of pressure to acquire English in second-language learning contexts.

In summary, when teachers value students' first language it tends to be accepted by students in the class (Clark, 1995; Manyak, 2001; Reyes et al., 1993), whereas when they fail to value it (McCollum, 1999) students are less likely to have a positive attitude about it. However, value placed on the first language (Lotherington et al., 1998) may not be sufficient to promote first-language and literacy development. For example, even if there is institutional support, students are influenced by the status of peers; in schools where peers with the most status speak the second language, students tend to value that language (McCollum, 1999). As noted in Shannon (1995; reported in chap. 11, this volume), it is difficult for teachers to support first-language use when it is not accepted in the larger school context or community, even when there is a positive attitude toward the first language in the classroom. Moreover, the studies suggest that any potential effects of language prestige cannot be evaluated without consideration of related sociocultural variables such as SES, ethnicity, and cultural differences. There are potential issues related to prestige with each of these variables, thus making it difficult to disentangle the effects of a single factor such as language prestige in isolation. Nevertheless, the studies do suggest the relatively strong press, for a variety of reasons, to acquire English. The impact of this factor on second language and literacy outcomes cannot be stated unequivocally at present given the state of the research. It remains a promising area of investigation.

Database References
for Part III

Aarts, R., & Verhoeven, L. (1999). Literacy attainment in a second language submersion context. *Applied Psycholinguistics, 20*(3), 377–393.

Abu-Rabia, S. (1995). Attitudes and cultural background and their relationship to English in a multicultural social context: The case of male and female Arab immigrants in Canada. *Educational Psychology, 15*(3), 323–336.

Abu-Rabia, S. (1996). Druze minority students learning Hebrew in Israel: The relationship of attitudes, cultural background, and interest of material to reading comprehension in a second language. *Journal of Multilingual and Multicultural Development, 17*(6), 415–426.

Abu-Rabia, S. (1998a). Attitudes and culture in second language learning among Israeli–Arab students. *Curriculum and Teaching, 13*(1), 13–30.

Abu-Rabia, S. (1998b). Social and cognitive factors influencing the reading comprehension of Arab students learning Hebrew as a second language in Israel. *Journal of Research in Reading, 21*(3), 201–212.

Arzubiaga, A., Rueda, R., & Monzó, L. (2002). Reading engagement of Latino children. *Journal of Latinos and Education, 1*(4), 231–43.

Au, K. H.- P. (1980). Participation structures in a reading lesson with Hawaiian children: Analysis of a culturally appropriate instructional event. *Anthropology and Education Quarterly, 11*(2), 91–115.

Au, K. H.- P., & Mason, J. M. (1981). Social organizational factors in learning to read: The balance of rights hypothesis. *Reading Research Quarterly, 17*(1), 115–152.

Blake, B. E. (2001). Fruit of the devil: Writing and English language learners. *Language Arts, 78*(5), 435–441.

Brooker, L. (2002). "Five on the first of December!" What can we learn from case studies of early childhood literacy? *Journal of Early Childhood Literacy, 2*(3), 292–313.

Brunell, V., & Linnakylä, P. (1994). Swedish speakers' literacy in the Finnish society. *Journal of Reading, 37*(5), 368–375.

Brunell, V., & Saretsalo, L. (1999). Sociocultural diversity and reading literacy in a Finland–Swedish environment. *Scandinavian Journal of Educational Research, 43*(2), 173–190.

Buriel, R., & Cardoza, D. (1988). Sociocultural correlates of achievement among three generations of Mexican American high school seniors. *American Educational Research Journal, 25*(2), 177–192.

Cahill, D. P. (1987). Bilingual development of Italo–Australian children. *Australian Review of Applied Linguistics, 4*, 101–127.

Calderón, M., Hertz-Lazarowitz, R., & Slavin, R. E. (1998). Effects of bilingual cooperative integrated reading and composition on students making the transition from Spanish to English reading. *Elementary School Journal, 99*(2), 153–165.

California State Department of Education. (1986). *Beyond language: Social and cultural factors in schooling language minority students.* Los Angeles: Evaluation, Dissemination and Assessment Center, California State University.

Carter, T., & Chatfield, M. (1986). Effective bilingual schools: Implications for policy and practice. *American Journal of Education, 95,* 200–232.

Chilora, H., & Harris, A. (2001). *Investigating the role of teacher's home language in mother tongue policy implementation: Evidence from IEQ research findings in Malawi.* Washington, DC: American Institutes for Research/USAID, Improving Educational Quality (IEQ) Project.

Clark, E. R. (1995). "How did you learn to write in English when you haven't been taught in English?": The language experience approach in a dual language program. *Bilingual Research Journal, 19*(3/4), 611–627.

Connor, U. (1983). Predictors of second-language reading performance. *Journal of Multilingual and Multicultural Development, 4*(4), 271–288.

Davies, A. (1991). Performance of children from non-English speaking background on the New South Wales Basic Skills Tests of Numeracy: Issues of test bias and language proficiency. *Language Culture and Curriculum, 4*(2), 149–161.

Delgado-Gaitán, C. (1989). Classroom literacy activity for Spanish-speaking students. *Linguistics and Education, 1*(3), 285–297.

Dolson, D. P. (1985). The effects of Spanish home language use on the scholastic performance of Hispanic pupils. *Journal of Multilingual and Multicultural Development, 6*(2), 135–155.

Durán, B. J., & Weffer, R. E. (1992). Immigrants' aspirations, high school process, and academic outcomes. *American Educational Research Journal, 29*(1), 163–181.

García, G. E. (1991). Factors influencing the English reading test performance of Spanish-speaking Hispanic children. *Reading Research Quarterly, 26*(4), 371–392.

García-Vázquez, E. (1995). Acculturation and academics: Effects of acculturation on reading achievement among Mexican-American students. *Bilingual Research Journal, 19*(2), 304–315.

Garrett, P., Griffiths, Y., James, C., & Scholfield, P. (1994). Use of the mother-tongue in second language classrooms: An experimental investigation of effects on the attitudes and writing performance of bilingual UK schoolchildren. *Journal of Multilingual and Multicultural Development, 15*(5), 371–383.

Gersten, R., & Jiménez, R. T. (1994). A delicate balance: Enhancing literature instruction for students of English as a second language. *Reading Teacher, 47*(6), 438–449.

Goldenberg, C. (1987). Low-income Hispanic parents' contributions to their first-grade children's word-recognition skills. *Anthropology and Education Quarterly, 18*(3), 149–179.

Goldenberg, C., & Gallimore, R. (1991). Local knowledge, research knowledge, and educational change: A case study of early Spanish reading improvement. *Educational Researcher, 20*(8), 2–14.

Goldenberg, C., Reese, L., & Gallimore, R. (1992). Effects of literacy materials from school on Latino children's home experiences and early reading achievement. *American Journal of Education, 100*(4), 497–536.

Gregory, E. (1994). Cultural assumptions and early years' pedagogy: The effect of the home culture on minority children's interpretation of reading in school. *Language Culture and Curriculum, 7*(2), 111–124.

Gregory, E. (1998). Siblings as mediators of literacy in linguistic minority communities. *Language and Education, 12*(1), 33–54.

Hancock, D. R. (2002). The effects of native language books on the pre-literacy skill development of language minority kindergartners. *Journal of Research in Childhood Education, 17*(1), 62–68.

Hannon, P., & McNally, J. (1986). Children's understanding and cultural factors in reading test performance. *Educational Review, 38*(3), 237–246.

Hansen, D. A. (1989). Locating learning: Second language gains and language use in family, peer and classroom contexts. *NABE: The Journal of the National Association for Bilingual Education, 13*(2), 161–180.

Hernández, J. S. (1991). Assisted performance in reading comprehension strategies with non-English proficient students. *Journal of Educational Issues of Language Minority Students, 8,* 91–112.

Hornberger, N. H. (1990). Creating successful learning contexts for bilingual literacy. *Teachers College Record, 92*(2), 212–229.

Huerta-Macías, A., & Quintero, E. (1992). Code-switching, bilingualism, and biliteracy: A case study. *Bilingual Research Journal, 16*(3/4), 69–90.

Huss, R. L. (1995). Young children becoming literate in English as a second language. *TESOL Quarterly, 29*(4), 767–774.

Huss-Keeler, R. L. (1997). Teacher perception of ethnic and linguistic minority parental involvement and its relationships to children's language and literacy learning: A case study. *Teaching and Teacher Education, 13*(2), 171–182.

Ima, K., & Rumbaut, R. G. (1989). Southeast Asian refugees in American schools: A comparison of fluent-English-proficient and limited-English-proficient students. *Topics in Language Disorders, 9*(3), 54–75.

Jiménez, R. T. (1997). The strategic reading abilities and potential of five low-literacy Latina/o readers in middle school. *Reading Research Quarterly, 32*(3), 224–243.

Jiménez, R. T., & Gersten, R. (1999). Lessons and dilemmas derived from the literacy instruction of two Latina/o teachers. *American Educational Research Journal, 36*(2), 265–301.

Kennedy, E., & Park, H.-S. (1994). Home language as a predictor of academic achievement: A comparative study of Mexican- and Asian-American youth. *Journal of Research and Development in Education, 27*(3), 188–194.

Kenner, C. (1999). Children's understandings of text in a multilingual nursery. *Language and Education, 13*(1), 1–16.

Kenner, C. (2000). Biliteracy in a monolingual school system? English and Gujarati in South London. *Language Culture and Curriculum, 13*(1), 13–30.

Koskinen, P. S., Blum, I. H., Bisson, S. A., Phillips, S. M., Creamer, T. S., & Baker, T. K. (2000). Book access, shared reading, and audio models: The effects of supporting the literacy learning of linguistically diverse students in school and at home. *Journal of Educational Psychology, 92*, 23–36.

Kucer, S. B., & Silva, C. (1999). The English literacy development of bilingual students within a transitional whole language curriculum. *Bilingual Research Journal, 23*(4), 347–371.

Lam, W. S. E. (2000). L2 literacy and the design of the self: A case study of a teenager writing on the internet. *TESOL Quarterly, 34*(3), 457–482.

Langer, J. A. (1997). Literacy acquisition through literature (Literacy Issues in Focus). *Journal of Adolescent and Adult Literacy, 40*(8), 606–614.

Lasisi, M. J., Falodun, S., & Onyehalu, A. S. (1988). The comprehension of first- and second-language prose. *Journal of Research in Reading, 11*(1), 26–35.

Lotherington, H., Ebert, S., Watanabe, T., Norng, S., & Ho-Dac, T. (1998). Biliteracy practices in suburban Melbourne. *Australian Language Matters, 6*(3), 3–4.

Love, K. (1996). Talk around text: Acquiescence or empowerment in secondary English. *Australian Review of Applied Linguistics, 19*(2), 1–25.

Manyak, P. C. (2001). Participation, hybridity, and carnival: A situated analysis of a dynamic literacy practice in a primary-grade English immersion class. *Journal of Literacy Research, 33*(3), 423–465.

Masny, D., & Ghahremani-Ghajar, S.-S. (1999). Weaving multiple literacies: Somali children and their teachers in the context of school culture. *Culture and Curriculum, 12*(1), 72–93.

McCarty, T. L. (1993). Language, literacy, and the image of the child in American Indian classrooms. *Language Arts, 70*(3), 182–192.

McCarty, T. L., Wallace, S., Lynch, R. H., & Benally, A. (1991). Classroom inquiry and Navajo learning styles: A call for reassessment. *Anthropology and Education Quarterly, 22*(1), 42–59.

McCollum, P. (1999). Learning to value English: Cultural capital in a two-way bilingual program. *Bilingual Research Journal, 23*(2/3), 133–134.

Moll, L. C. (1986). Writing as communication: Creating strategic learning environments for students. *Theory Into Practice, 25*(2), 102–108.

Moll, L. C., & Díaz, S. (1987). Change as the goal of educational research. *Anthropology and Education Quarterly, 18*(4), 300–311.

Moll, L. C., Sáez, R., & Dworin, J. (2001). Exploring biliteracy: Two student case examples of writing as a social practice. *Elementary School Journal, 101*(4), 435–449.

Monzó, L., & Rueda, R. (2001). Constructing achievement orientations toward literacy: An analysis of sociocultural activity in Latino home and community contexts (CIERA Report No. 1-011). Ann Arbor, MI: Center for the Improvement of Early Reading Achievement.

Mulhern, M. M. (1997). Doing his own thing: A Mexican-American kindergartner becomes literate at home and school. *Language Arts, 74*(6), 468–476.

Nguyen, A., Shin, F., & Krashen, S. (2001). Development of the first language is not a barrier to second-language acquisition: Evidence from Vietnamese immigrants to the United States. *International Journal of Bilingual Education and Bilingualism, 4*(3), 159–164.

Pérez, B. (1993). The bilingual teacher (Spanish/English) and literacy instruction. *Teacher Education Quarterly, 20*(3), 45–52.

Pucci, S. L., & Ulanoff, S. H. (1998). What predicts second language reading success? A study of home and school variables. *International Review of Applied Linguistics, 121–122*, 1–18.

Quintero, E., & Huerta-Macías, A. (1990). All in the family: Bilingualism and biliteracy. *Reading Teacher, 44*(4), 306–312.

Reese, L., Garnier, H., Gallimore, R., & Goldenberg, C. (2000). Longitudinal analysis of the antecedents of emergent Spanish literacy and middle-school English reading achievement of Spanish-speaking students. *American Educational Research Journal, 37*(3), 633–662.

Reyes, M. D. L. L. (1991). A process approach to literacy using dialogue journals and literature logs with second language learners. *Research in the Teaching of English, 25*(3), 292–313.

Reyes, M. D. L. L., Laliberty, E. A., & Orbanosky, J. M. (1993). Emerging biliteracy and cross-cultural sensitivity in a language arts classroom. *Language Arts, 70*(8), 659–668.

Rogers-Zegarra, N., & Singer, H. (1980). Anglo and Chicano comprehension of ethnic stories. *Yearbook of the National Reading Conference, 29*, 203–208.

Rossell, C., & Baker, K. (1996). The educational effectiveness of bilingual education. *Research in the teaching of English, 30*, 1–68.

Saunders, W. M. (1999). Improving literacy achievement for English learners in transitional bilingual programs. *Educational Research & Evaluation (An International Journal on Theory & Practice), 5*(4), 345–381.

Saunders, W. M., & Goldenberg, C. (1999). Effects of instructional conversations and literature logs on limited- and fluent-English proficient students' story comprehension and thematic understanding. *Elementary School Journal, 99*(4), 277–301.

Schmidt, P. R. (1995). Working and playing with others: Cultural conflict in a kindergarten literacy program. *The Reading Teacher, 48*(5), 404–412.

Schon, I., Hopkins, K. D., & Vojir, C. (1984). The effects of Spanish reading emphasis on the English and Spanish reading abilities of Hispanic high school students. *The Bilingual Review, 11*(1), 33–39.

Shannon, S. M. (1995). The hegemony of English: A case study of one bilingual classroom as a site of resistance. *Linguistics and Education, 7*(3), 175–200.

Smith, P. H. (2001). Community language resources in dual language schooling. *Bilingual Research Journal, 25*(3), 375–404.

Stritikus, T. T. (2001). From personal to political: Proposition 227, literacy instruction, and the individual qualities of teachers. *International Journal of Bilingual Education and Bilingualism, 4*(5), 291–309.

Tharp, R. G. (1982). The effective instruction of comprehension: Results and descriptions of the Kamehameha Early Education Program. *Reading Research Quarterly, 17*, 503–527.

Townsend, J. S., & Fu, D. (1998). A Chinese boy's joyful initiation into American literacy. *Language Arts, 75*(3), 193–201.

Trueba, H., Moll, L. C., & Díaz, S. (1984). Improving the functional writing of bilingual secondary school students (Report No. 400-81-0023). Washington, DC: National Institute of Education.

Volk, D., & DeAcosta, M. (2001). "Many differing ladders, many ways to climb…": Literacy events in the bilingual classroom, homes, and community of three Puerto Rican kindergartners. *Journal of Early Childhood Literacy, 1*(2), 193–224.

Wilkinson, L. C., Milosky, L. M., & Genishi, C. (1986). Second language learners' use of requests and responses in elementary classrooms. *Topics in Language Disorders, 6*(2), 57–70.

Xu, H. (1999). Reexamining continuities and discontinuities: Language-minority children's home and school literacy experiences. *Yearbook of the National Reading Conference, 48*, 224–237.

Background References
for Part III

Anderson, J., & Johnson, W. (1971). Stability and change among three generations of Mexican Americans: Factors affecting achievement. *American Educational Research Association Journal, 8,* 285–309.

Bradby, D. & Owings, J. (1992). *Language characteristics and academic achievement: A look at Asian and Hispanic Eighth Graders in NELS:88 (NCES 92–479).* Washington, DC: U.S. Department of Education.

Booth, A., & Dunn, J. (Eds.). (1996). *Family and school links: How do they affect educational outcomes?* Mahwah, NJ: Lawrence Erlbaum Associates.

Carbo, M. (1995). Educating everybody's children. In R. Cole (Ed.), *Educating everybody's children: Diverse teaching strategies for diverse learners* (pp. 9–18). Alexandria, VA: Association for Supervision and Curriculum Development.

Carreira, M. (2000). Validating and promoting Spanish in the United States: Lessons from linguistic science. *Bilingual Research Journal, 24,* 333–352.

Cole, R. (Ed.). (1995). *Educating everybody's children: Diverse teaching strategies for diverse learners.* Alexandria, VA: Association for Supervision and Curriculum Development.

Cummins, J. (1979). Linguistic interdependence and the educational development of bilingual childern. *Review of Educational Research, 49,* 222–251.

Cummins, J. (1986). Empowering minority students: A framework for intervention. *Harvard Educational Review, 56,* 18–36.

Cummins, J. (1994). Primary language instruction and the education of language minority students. In C. Leyba (Ed.), *Schooling and language minority students* (2nd ed.). Los Angeles: Evaluation, Dissemination and Assessment Center, California State University.

Delpit, L. (1986). Skills and other dilemmas of a progressive Black educator. *Harvard Educational Review, 56,* 379–385.

Díaz, S., Moll, L., & Mehan, H. (1986). Sociocultural resources in instruction: A context-specific approach. In California State Department of Education, *Beyond language: Social and cultural factors in schooling language minority students* (pp. 299–343). Los Angeles: California State Department of Education, Bilingual Education Office.

Durán, R. (1983). *Hispanics' education and background.* New York: College Entrance Examination Board.

Epstein, J. (1992). School and family partnerships. In M. Alkin (Ed.), *Encyclopedia of educational research* (6th ed., pp. 1139–1152). New York: Macmillan.

Epstein, J. (1996). Perspectives and previews on research and policy for school, family, and community partnerships. In A. Booth & J. Dunn (Eds.), *Family and school links: How do they affect educational outcomes?* (pp. 209–246). Mahwah, NJ: Lawrence Erlbaum Associates.

Forman, E., Minick, N., & Stone, C. (1993). *Contexts for learning: Sociocultural dynamics in children's development.* Oxford: Oxford University Press.

Fredericks, J., Blumenfeld, P., & Parks, A. (2004). School engagement: Potential of the concept, state of the evidence. *Review of Educational Research, 74,* 59–109.

345

Gambrell, L. B., Palmer, B. M., Codling, R. M., & Mazzoni, S. (1996). Assessing motivation to read. *The Reading Teacher, 49,* 432–445.

Goldenberg, C. (1993). The home–school connection in bilingual education. In B. Arias & U. Casanova (Eds.), *Ninety-second yearbook of the National Society for the Study of Education. Bilingual education: Politics, research, and practice* (pp. 225–250). Chicago, IL: University of Chicago Press.

Goldenberg, C., & Gallimore, R. (1995). Immigrant Latino parents' values and beliefs about their children's education: Continuities and discontinuities across cultures and generations. In P. R. Pintrich & M. Maehr (Eds.), *Advances in motivation and achievement: Culture, ethnicity, and motivation* (Vol. 9, pp. 183–228). Greenwich, CT: JAI.

Goldenberg, C., Gallimore, R., Reese, L., & Garnier, H. (2001). Cause or effect? A longitudinal study of immigrant Latino parents' aspirations and expectations and their children's school performance. *American Educational Research Journal, 38,* 547–582.

Green, J., Camilli, G., & Elmore, P. (Eds.). (in press). *Complementary methods for research in education.* Washington, DC: American Educational Research Association.

Gutiérrez, K. D., & Rogoff, B. (2003). Cultural ways of learning: Individual styles or repertoires of practice. *Educational Researcher, 32*(5), 19–25.

Hansford, B., & Hattie, J. (1982). The relationship between self and achievement/performance measures. *Review of Educational Research, 52,* 123–142.

Hess, R. D., & Holloway, S. (1984). Family and school as educational institutions. In R. D. Parke (Ed.), *Review of child development research: 7. The family* (pp. 179–222). Chicago: University of Chicago Press.

Jacob, E., & Jordan, C. (Eds.). (1987). Explaining the school performance of minority students [Special Issue]. *Anthropology and Education Quarterly, 18*(4).

Karweit, N. (1989). Time and learning: A review. In R. Slavin (Ed.), *School and classroom organization* (pp. 69–95). Hillsdale, NJ: Lawrence Erlbaum Associates.

Lara-Cinisomo, S., Pebley, A. R., Vaiana, M. E., Maggio, E., Berends, M., & Lucas, S. R. (2004). A matter of class. *RAND Review 28*(3). Retrieved March 3, 2005, from http://www.rand.org/publications/randreview/issues/fall2004/index.html

Leseman, P. & de Jong, P. (1998). Home literacy: Opportunity, instruction, cooperation and social-emotional quality predicting early reading achievement. *Reading Research Quarterly, 33,* 294–318.

Mattingly, D., Prislin, R., McKenzie, T., Rodríguez, J., & Kayzar, B. (2002). Evaluating evaluations: The case of parent involvement programs. *Review of Educational Research, 72,* 549–576.

Moll, L. C., & Díaz, E. (1985). Ethnographic pedagogy: Promoting effective bilingual instruction. In E. E. García & R. V. Padilla (Eds.), *Advances in bilingual education research* (pp. 127–149). Tucson, AZ: University of Arizona Press.

Ogbu, J., & Matute-Bianchi, M. (1986). Understanding sociocultural factors: Knowledge, identity, and school adjustment. In California State Department of Education, *Beyond language: Social and cultural factors in schooling language minority students* (pp.73–142). Los Angeles: Evaluation, Dissemination and Assessment Center, California State University.

Palincsar, A. S., & Brown, A. L. (1984). Reciprocal teaching of comprehension-fostering and comprehension-monitoring activities. *Cognition and Instruction, 1*(2), 117–175.

Rossell, C. H., & Baker, K. (1996). The educational effectiveness of bilingual education. *Research in the Teaching of English, 30*(1), 7–74.

Rueda, R., MacGillivray, L., Monzó, L., & Arzubiaga, A. (2001). Engaged reading: A multi-level approach to considering socio-cultural features with diverse learners. In D. McInerny & S. Van Etten (Eds.), *Research on sociocultural influences on motivation and learning* (pp. 233–264). Greenwich, CT: Information Age.

Rumbaut, R. (1995). The new Californians: Comparative research findings on the educational progress of immigrant children. In R. Rumbaut & W. Cornelius (Eds.), *California's immigrant children.* San Diego: Center for U.S.–Mexican Studies.

Saravia-Shore, M., & García, E. (1995). Diverse teaching strategies for diverse learners. In R. Cole (Ed.), *Educating everybody's children: Diverse teaching strategies for diverse learners* (pp. 47–74). Alexandria, VA: Association for Supervision and Curriculum Development.

Schon, I. (1978). *Books in Spanish for children and young adults.* Metuchen, NJ: Scarecrow Press.

Shadish, W. (1994). Critical multiplism: A research strategy and its attendant tactics. In L. Sechrest & A. Figueredo (Eds.), *New directions for program evaluation* (pp. 13–57). San Francisco: Jossey-Bass.

Sirin, S. (2005). Socioeconomic status and academic achievement: A meta-analytic review of research. *Review of Educational Research, 75,* 417–453.

Sleeter, C. (2004). Context-conscious portraits and context-blind policy. *Anthropology and Education Quarterly, 35*(1), 132–136.

Smeeding, T. (2002). Globalisation, inequality, and the rich countries of the G-20: Evidence from the Luxembourg Income Study. In D. Gruen, T. O'Brien, & J. Lawson (Eds.), *Globalisation, living standards, and inequality: Recent progress and continuing challenges* (pp. 179–206). Canberra, Australia: J. S. McMillan.

Suárez-Orozco, C. M., & Suárez-Orozco, M. (1996). *Transformations: Immigration, family life, and achievement motivation among Latino adolescents.* Stanford, CA: Stanford University Press.

Tharp, R. (1989). Psychocultural variables and constants: Effects on teaching and learning in schools. *American Psychologist, 44*, 349–359.

Trueba, H., Moll, L. C., & Díaz, S. (1982). *Improving the functional writing skills of bilingual secondary school students.* Washington, DC: National Institute of Education.

Valencia, R. (1997). *The evolution of deficit thinking.* Bristol, PA: Falmer/Taylor & Francis.

Vogt, L., Jordan, C., & Tharp, R. (1987). Explaining school failure, producing school success: Two cases. *Anthropology and Education Quarterly, 18*, 276–286.

Wang, M., & Walberg, H. (1983). Adaptive instruction and classroom time. *American Educational Research Journal, 20*, 601–626.

Webb, N. M. (1989). Peer interaction and learning in small groups. *International Journal of Educational Research, 13*, 21–39.

Weisner, T. S. (Ed.). (2005). *Discovering successful pathways in children's development: Mixed methods in the study of childhood and family life.* Chicago: University of Chicago Press.

White, K. R. (1982). The relation between socioeconomic status and academic achievement. *Psychological Bulletin, 91*(3), 461–481.

White, K., Taylor, M., & Moss, V. (1992). Does research support claims about the benefits of involving parents in early intervention programs? *Review of Educational Research, 62*, 91–125.

Wilkinson, L., & Calculator, S. (1982). Requests and responses in peer-directed reading groups. *American Educational Research Journal, 19*, 107–120.

Wong Fillmore, L. (1991). When learning a second language means losing the first. *Early Childhood Research Quarterly, 6*, 323–346.

Woo, E. (1996, February 22). Immigrants, U.S. peers differ starkly on schools. *Los Angeles Times*, pp. A1, A19.

IV

Educating Language-Minority Students: Instructional Approaches and Professional Development

13

Synthesis: Instruction and Professional Development

Diane August and Timothy Shanahan

The chapters in Part IV review research on instruction and professional development related to literacy in language-minority students. The five chapters focus on the following research questions:

- What impact does language of instruction have on the literacy learning of language-minority students? Is it better to immerse students in English-language instruction, or are there benefits to first developing a firm basis in the home language? (chap. 14)
- What can be done to improve achievement in reading, writing, and spelling for language-minority children? (chap. 15)
- What do we know about classroom and school practices designed to build literacy in language-minority students? (chap. 16)
- What do we know about literacy instruction for language-minority students in special education settings? (chap. 17)
- What does the research tell us about teachers' beliefs and attitudes related to literacy development in language-minority students? What does the research tell us about the kinds of professional development that have been provided to teachers and how this professional development relates to teachers' beliefs and practices? (chap. 18)

BACKGROUND

These research questions are contextualized within a broad conceptual framework describing the development of literacy in language-minority children and youth. According to this framework, many individual student factors—age of arrival in a new country, educational history, cognitive capacity, and so on—influence literacy development. Second, literacy development is influenced by language and literacy in the native language, as well second-language oral proficiency skills (all are influences on literacy development unique to the second-language learning situation). Third, the sociocultural context in which children are acquiring their second language influences learning. Finally, particular educational settings and interventions influence the course of development (this framework is described more fully in chap. 1).

METHODOLOGY

The inclusion criteria for studies in this part are consistent with the inclusion criteria established for the volume as a whole. However, as specified in chapter 1, the criteria for chapter 14 (language of instruction) differ in several ways from those used in other chapters. For example, it was essential that chapter 14 be consistent with previous reviews of studies that compared bilingual instruction with English-only instruction, but this criterion required a longer time frame. Thus, studies reviewed in chapter 14 include studies conducted earlier than 1980. In addition, the programs cited in studies in chapter 14 included at least a 6-month span between the onset of instruction and posttests to ensure a program had actually been implemented; in these cases, most treatment durations were of at least 1 year.

Different research methods are useful for addressing different types of questions. The diversity of research questions posed in this section necessitates the review of studies that use a variety of research methods. Experiments, quasi-experiments, and single-subject designs are useful for determining what works because these methods of research allow us to causally link instructional efforts with student learning outcomes. These research methods help identify which instructional approaches confer the greatest learning advantages to language-minority students. Studies reviewed in chapters 14, 15, and 17 attempt to answer these kinds of "what works" questions, and, consequently, these chapters rely wholly (chaps. 14 and 15) or partly (chap. 17) on studies using experimental designs. Although logically the experimental paradigm allows for a determination of causal relationships, even with these designs caution is needed in interpreting results. Such studies may vary in quality—how well a study controls for alternative explanations of effects, how well its conditions match those in an actual classroom, and how well it describes the intervention and context in which the intervention occurs. Furthermore, the results of even the best studies are probabilistic; we have greater confidence in results that have been successfully replicated many times in independent studies. In the case of chapters 15 and 17, there are few studies that focused on the same outcome of interest (e.g., reading vocabulary). In chapter 14, where multiple studies address a common issue—the effectiveness of instruction using the native language when compared with English-only instruction—a full meta-analysis of results is provided. In chapter 15, which also relies on experimental data, and chapter 17, which includes experimental data, we did not conduct full-blown meta-analyses because it was rare that there were even three comparable studies on any approach to instruction. When few studies are available, as in this case, the findings of a meta-analysis can be misleading because they are likely to be confounded with the individual studies, the same thing that happens in any empirical research when there are too few degrees of freedom to support the questions being asked. Instead, we calculated effect sizes for each study and presented them along with detailed descriptions of the studies to facilitate subjective comparisons of particular approaches.

This part of the volume also includes ethnographic studies and case studies. Ethnographic studies—narrative descriptions of schools and classrooms—are useful for documenting the contexts in which language-minority students are educated. Ethnographic studies are cited in chapters 16, 17, and 18, as are case studies, which provide careful descriptions of changes in students' or teachers' cognitive or linguistic behaviors, the instructional approach used to achieve these changes, and the context in which the approach was implemented. Ethnographies and case studies, like experiments, vary in quality. In the best of these studies, attempts to draw connections between outcomes and instructional factors are based on theory and use rigorous measures aligned with the goals of the study. Ultimately, these studies can generate only hypotheses about the influence instruction may have on learning (because they make no systematic manipulation of the instruction, they have no control group), but they can help identify subtle factors that may affect learning, they can be a useful basis for establishing hypotheses for future inquiry, or, when joined with experimental studies, they can help explain why certain experimental results are obtained. When qualitative methods such as ethnographies were the sources of data, we used the systematic interpretive procedures already described in chapter 1.

SUMMARY OF EMPIRICAL FINDINGS

Influence of Educational Settings and Instructional Approaches on Learning

How children are taught obviously affects how much and how well they learn. The studies reviewed in Part IV produced findings in five areas related to this issue: (a) instructional methods and approaches for teaching literacy to language-minority children and youth, (b) the importance of developing students' English proficiency, (c) the essential role of quality teaching, (d) the need for systemic efforts to ensure that language-minority students are held to high standards and are provided with the resources needed to meet these standards, and (e) the difficulty of creating school change.

Methods and Approaches for Teaching Literacy to Language-Minority Students. Unfortunately, there simply are not enough quasi-experimental and experimental studies to provide a thorough prescriptive description of how best to teach literacy to language-minority students. We found only five studies on phonics and phonemic awareness instruction, two on oral reading fluency instruction, three on the teaching of vocabulary, three on reading comprehension instruction, and four on writing (see chap. 15). Clearly, these small numbers of studies are far from sufficient to allow any final determination of the most useful instructional methods for meeting the literacy needs of English-language learners. This dearth of research contrasts with the large numbers of studies of reading instruction involving native English speakers; the National Reading Panel (NRP) identified more than 400 studies of reading using narrower study selection criteria than were used here.

The studies reviewed in chapter 15 suggest that the focus of effective literacy instruction is much the same for native speakers and English-language learners; however, some adjustments to these common instructional routines are necessary. Although the nature of such adjustments needs to be explored more directly in future research, studies reviewed in chapter 15 suggest the importance of considering appropriate ways of using the native language within instructional routines. They also point to the advisability of altering curriculum coverage depending on the similarity between English and the native language and the students' levels of attainment of their native language (e.g., some letter–sound correspondences do not need to be retaught if already mastered in a native language that shares these correspondences with English) and of fine-tuning instructional routines.

With regard to fine-tuning instructional routines, studies examined in chapters 15 and 16 suggest several methods to accomplish this, with the goal of providing additional support and practice for students who are acquiring skills and knowledge in a second language. The adjustments include (a) identifying and clarifying difficult words and passages within texts to facilitate the development of comprehension; (b) consolidating text knowledge through summarization; and (c) giving students extra practice in reading words, sentences, and stories. Some studies also revealed the value of instructional routines that include giving attention to vocabulary, checking comprehension, presenting ideas clearly both verbally and in writing, paraphrasing students' remarks and encouraging them to expand on those remarks, providing redundancy, and using physical gestures and visual cues to clarify meaning.

A major finding across the studies reported in chapter 17 is that approaches grounded in different theoretical models were found to be promising for children educated in special education settings. Examples are behavioral approaches to developing sight word reading and vocabulary, as well as cognitive or learning strategy approaches and more holistic, interactive approaches that encourage thoughtful discussion of ideas. Given the small sample sizes and lack of controls in some of the studies, however, more research is needed to explore the effectiveness of these approaches. In addition, the studies suggest that it is important to consider student background variables in designing instruction. For students who are fluent speakers of a language other than English, using students' native language as a means of introducing vocabulary may work better than starting with English, and particular attention to English phonemes that do not exist in the native language may be beneficial for teaching word reading. Finally, Ruiz, Rueda, Figueroa, and Boothroyd (1995) raise the issue of "the view of learning abilities and disabilities as being internal to the child rather than acknowledging their powerful interaction with the situational context" (p. 500). In fact, the studies reviewed in chapter 17 reveal that, given proper instruction, some language-minority students classified as learning disabled can achieve grade-level norms.

Developing Students' English Proficiency. Several studies indicate that students are less able to take advantage of interventions geared to promote incidental learning in English if they do not have requisite levels of English proficiency. For example, one study examined the impact of using captioned TV as a way to build word knowledge for middle-grades second-language learners. Generally, captioned TV outperformed a *just reading* condition. However, the authors also found that higher levels of English proficiency were associated with more learning of vocabulary. In discussing the findings, the authors note that the more linguistic competence the students had, the more they acquired, supporting the need for substantial direct teacher intervention in building oral English proficiency for students who are below a threshold of linguistic competence in their new language.

Moreover, teaching English-language learners strategies (for decoding or comprehension) can be effective, but it should be combined with concerted efforts to build students' facility in English. The reason is that strategies of various types are unlikely to help students who do not have the requisite language proficiency to comprehend the text. Substantial instruction and support in developing English proficiency were evident in some studies, but not in others, and this difference may help explain the inconsistency in success with comprehension strategies or the smaller effect sizes for these procedures with second-language students. As an example, one study examined the effects of Collaborative Strategic Reading (CSR) on the peer group participation and vocabulary development of fifth-grade Spanish-speaking language-minority students, half of whom were limited English proficient (LEP). During CSR, students of various reading and achievement levels work in small, cooperative groups to assist one another in applying specific reading strategies to help them comprehend subject matter texts. The assessments used in the study reveal that, overall, students made statistically significant gains in vocabulary. However, when the data are broken down by subgroup (limited English proficient, high achieving, average achieving, and low achieving), it turns out that the high-achieving students made the greatest gains, whereas the LEP students made the smallest. The study suggests the importance of requisite levels of English proficiency for taking advantage of instruction in strategy use.

Quality of Teaching. Despite the importance of teaching, we only found five studies that focused on professional development. The results demonstrate that creating change in teachers is a time-consuming process that requires considerable investment on the part of the change agents, as well as the teachers. The five professional development efforts studied took place over extended periods (1–3 years); all involved many meetings and workshops or an intensive summer program and, in some cases, follow-up in classrooms. In addition, outside collaborators with expertise (university researchers) assisted. The studies indicate that, consistent with previous findings, teachers found professional development to be most helpful when it provided opportunities for hands-on practice, with teaching techniques readily applicable to their classroom, in-class demonstrations with their own or a colleague's students or more personalized coaching. Other means to improve the quality of teaching included the collaboration between special education teachers and resource specialists.

Systemic Efforts and Overall School Success. Findings from studies of effective classrooms and schools identify attributes related to positive student outcomes. To a great extent, the attributes overlap with those of effective schools for native English speakers, such as implicit and explicit challenging of students, active involvement of all students, providing activities that students can complete successfully, and scaffolding instruction for students through such techniques as building and clarifying student input and using visual organizers, teacher mediation/feedback to students, and classroom use of collaborative/cooperative learning. In many cases, however, there are techniques related to second-language acquisition such as sheltered English and respect for cultural diversity. There is a need for experimental investigation into the ultimate effectiveness of these approaches.

Difficulty of Creating School Change.   Several studies we reviewed show the progress schools can achieve by having staff work together to address specific school issues. For example, one study reports on the efforts school personnel made to educate two new language-minority students whose needs were markedly different from those of the majority student population. The school personnel learned about approaches for addressing the needs of these students and worked together to make instructional decisions informed by ongoing assessments of the students' progress. Another study reports on how the dynamic interplay between local and research knowledge led to improvements in students' Spanish literacy attainment. These studies highlight the importance of mobilizing staff to focus on the needs of language-minority students, even when the students are few in number, and provide evidence that a concerted school effort involving outside agents (researchers and specialists) and school personnel (principals, specialists, and classroom teachers) can make a difference in student outcomes. In these studies, all of the schools sought assistance from local universities, which assisted with staff development and school change efforts and documented the process of change. Another study highlights the importance of supporting teacher change and the need for support systems that are intensive, elaborate, and enduring to accomplish this goal. Two critical tools in supporting teacher change were a classroom implementation checklist and grade-appropriate benchmarks used to assess student progress.

Importance of Individual Differences

Students' development of literacy is influenced by a range of individual factors, including age of arrival in a new country, educational history, socioeconomic status (SES), and cognitive capacity. This point is highlighted by the differential effects of instruction on students of different ages, with differing degrees of English proficiency and varied cognitive capacity. Children's interests and concerns can also play a role. It is critical to keep in mind that language-minority students are a highly heterogeneous group, and that instruction must be designed to take such differences into account.

The studies reviewed also demonstrate the benefits of attending to the individual needs of students. For example, one study documents how a teacher successfully addressed the individual needs of her students. She provided a variety of reading activities, adjusted instruction on the basis of reading achievement level, provided a classroom library, and gave each child individual attention during writing instruction. Most pertinent for second-language learners, the teacher altered her instruction by incorporating such tactics as speaking more slowly and using simpler vocabulary, while not lowering her expectations or changing the language of instruction for these students.

Developmental Nature of Literacy Acquisition

Literacy development requires the acquisition of word-level or initial skills (those involved in word reading, pseudo-word reading, and spelling) and text-level (those involved in the interpretation and communication of meaning). Young English-language learners follow a developmental trajectory—similar to that of native speakers—in the acquisition of literacy, and this trajectory appears to be similar for children regardless of their language background (see chap. 4, this volume). Although their developmental trajectories appear to be similar, there are differences between language-minority students and their native-English-speaking peers in the acquisition of literacy. English-language learners can build on their first-language skills in acquiring their second language (see Part II, this volume). However, in some cases and for some skills, the rate is slower for English-language learners. For example, when native speakers and English-language learners are taught together, both make gains in vocabulary learning, but the vocabulary knowledge of the English-language learners tends to remain below that of their native-speaking peers. These differences result, in part, from lower levels of oral English proficiency.

It should be noted that, in the development of second-language literacy, the nature of the native and second languages matters as well as the experience students have had in developing first-language literacy. For example, Spanish-speaking children instructed in Spanish mastered graphophonics more easily than did English-speaking children instructed in English. Moreover, instruction for students who are literate in their first language could be more targeted, emphasizing those skills not yet obtained through the first language while paying less attention to easily transferable skills already mastered.

In successful instructional programs, children learn precursor skills and use them as building blocks for acquiring later, more complex skills. In learning to decode, for example, children first learn to decode simple spelling patterns for single-syllable words and then apply their knowledge of these patterns to help decode multisyllable words. Likewise, in the case of instruction targeting a specific skill, researchers have made an obvious, although often unstated, assumption about the appropriate developmental level for their subjects. Thus, for example, most programs that have successfully developed phonological awareness or phonics skills have been implemented with kindergarten and first-grade children. However, some language-minority students may begin acquiring literacy for the first time in the upper grades because of poor and interrupted schooling in their home country; others who immigrate when they are older may have acquired first-language literacy in their home country, but begin acquiring second-language literacy skills in the upper grades. Unfortunately, because of the dearth of longitudinal studies examining the instruction of language-minority students, there is little information about how best to craft instruction in early precursor skills that develop concurrently with the skills subsequent to them.

Influence of Native-Language Literacy and Second-Language Oral Proficiency on Second-Language Literacy Development

Language-minority students who are literate in their first language are likely to be advantaged in the acquisition of English literacy. Just as the studies cited in Part II highlight cross-language relationships, the studies in chapter 14 demonstrate that language-minority students instructed in their native language (primarily Spanish) as well as English perform, on average, better on English reading measures than language-minority students instructed only in their second language (English). This is the case at both the elementary and secondary levels. The strongest evidence supporting this claim comes from the randomized studies, which indicate a moderate effect in favor of bilingual instruction. However, recent evaluations of scientifically based beginning reading programs used to teach non-English-speaking children to read in English are showing promising results, suggesting that if children receive good instruction with appropriate scaffolding, they are able to master early reading skills in English. This is an important finding in that first-language instruction is not an option in many schools where children speak multiple languages or staff are not capable of providing first-language instruction.

Chapter 15 also presents findings relevant to this issue. Less evident, but no less important, is the benefit of instructional routines that, although focused on the teaching of English, exploit students' native language—for example, by using Spanish words as synonyms in vocabulary instruction or conducting instructional conversations that permit some interpretation to take place in the home language. Conversely, no immediate benefit was found to English comprehension in having students engage solely in extensive amounts of Spanish reading

As noted earlier, the results of several studies indicate that children with lower levels of English oral proficiency gain less advantage from instruction relative to more-English-proficient students. In addition, studies reviewed in chapter 15 found lower effect sizes for instructional approaches when used with English-language learners; oral proficiency in English appeared to be necessary for students to obtain maximum benefit.

The Role of Sociocultural Context in Literacy Development

As noted previously, use of language-minority students' native language is one important element of the sociocultural context in which these students are educated. Two studies found that programs incorporating culturally appropriate curriculum resulted in positive literacy and literacy-related gains for Native American children in these programs. The culturally appropriate curriculum used instructional strategies such as "informal participation structures containing overlapping speech, mutual participation of students and teacher, co-narration, volunteered speech, instant feedback and lack of penalty for wrong answers" (Tharp, 1982, p. 519). However, these programs combine many elements, and it is difficult to determine exactly what it is about the programs that made them effective. It may be that improved methods of teaching reading and writing, as well as culturally appropriate curriculum, enhanced students' literacy. Future reserve is clearly needed. Three studies examined classroom instructional activities that gave students the opportunity to share their own ideas and perspectives (social) or use their native language (cultural) and noted increased participation in classroom discourse. However, additional research is necessary to determine whether increased interaction in the second language leads to higher levels of proficiency and literacy in that language.

METHODOLOGICAL ISSUES

Strengths of the Studies

There was considerable variation in the quality of research across all study types, including experimental, quasi-experimental, case study, and ethnographic designs. We found excellent studies in each category. Some of the experimental and quasi-experimental studies reviewed in chapters 14, 15, and 17 were well designed, with reliable pre- and posttest measurements, checks on fidelity, and equivalency of control and experimental groups. These studies examined the effectiveness of various instructional approaches that could be used in schools if found to be effective. The qualitative research reviewed in chapters 16, 17, and 18 employed a wide variety of methods to collect data about the classroom context, student behavior, and instructional approaches for literacy development. Examples of methods used include teacher and student interviews; weekly videotapes; field notes; teacher journals; and observations to document the instruction that occurred, patterns of classroom interaction, the classroom and school context, and students' progress. Additional information about students' performance was obtained from reading, writing, and oral language assessments; samples of student work; and school documents. The detailed descriptions of an approach or context, of students' work or behavior, and of the criteria used to assess them enhance our understanding of the dynamic and complex nature of schooling.

Shortcomings of the Studies

Although the studies reviewed met the inclusion criteria for these chapters, they contained shortcomings. Of most concern, the quasi-experimental studies rarely provided a clear description of the adjustments that were made to various instructional routines used with English-only students to meet the needs of English-language learners. As useful as it is to know that a particular program or language approach results in a benefit to students, it is important to understand exactly how this approach was used with English-language learners. In addition, few of these studies used randomized control experiments; our confidence in these results would be greater if such approaches were used. Given that the effect sizes tended to be smaller with English-language learners than with native speakers, it would have been helpful to have English-language proficiency measures to help understand whether outcomes were mediated by language proficiency, and which students within the group succeeded most as a result of the approach. There is also a need for more descriptive data on the students and their context within these experimental efforts to discern the circumstances under which instruction works best. Also, few of the studies in chapter 15 went as long as an entire school year, and it is important to examine the effectiveness of instructional procedures over longer periods.

With regard to the qualitative studies, a first set of issues revolves around the quantity and quality of the data collected to document an approach, the context in which the approach was implemented, or the impact it had on students. In some cases, for example, insufficient detail about the approach is given, and in many cases, there is scant description of the level of implementation of the approach. When assessing the impact of an approach, many of the researchers employed measures they developed that have not been validated, or they fail to report interrater reliability in the use of these measures. In some cases, researchers use only researcher-developed assessments on a particular sample to gauge student progress. Without a standardized measure or additional information about how other samples of students perform on the researcher-developed measures, it is impossible to know how the study participants compare with other students, making it difficult to determine whether their progress was exceptional, adequate, or poor. Another assessment issue arises when authors use rubrics to score assessments that have a narrow focus or only assess what is important to them (e.g., coherence and organization in writing, but not spelling or grammar), which results in an incomplete picture of student competence in a multifaceted ability, such as writing or oral language proficiency. Finally, some authors do not describe the methods used to synthesize or analyze the data they collected, which is particularly problematic for other researchers in the field.

A second set of issues germane to the qualitative studies revolves around how well the findings and themes reported in the study are supported by the information collected. In what follows, we raise five issues that relate to confidence in the findings reported. First, in some cases, the researchers did not collect observations from multiple sources or employ multiple techniques for identifying or cross-checking varying perspectives on complex issues and events. Second, many studies do not situate narrative vignettes and quotes from participants within a framework of evidence about the range and frequency of variation in these events. Thus, it is difficult to determine how well the reported findings relate to the greater context of the study. In some cases, for example, authors report that students responded to a certain instructional technique by producing longer and more detailed essays (measured by rubrics that are explained in the study), but they fail to indicate how many students did this or how many of the essays examined exemplified these traits. Third, some authors do not give prominence to alternative or competing explanations. For example, they attribute findings to a particular instructional technique that has occurred for a limited time each day, but fail to mention that the outcomes could have been attributed to the nature of the instructional techniques used during the rest of the day. Likewise, findings could be related to other third variables, such as individual student variables (e.g., levels of first- or second-language proficiency, SES of the students or group of students), the grade level at which an approach was implemented (e.g., kindergarten, where some approaches may be more appropriate), or the sociocultural context in which an approach was used (e.g., degree of value placed on first-language use in the program), and these factors are not discussed. Fourth, some authors fail to explain the range of variation in the data presented. For example, findings from several studies suggest that, for language-minority students as a group, level of language proficiency may have influenced study findings, but this influence is not documented or explained in a discussion of the findings. A final issue is whether the generalizations presented are supported by the data collected. In some cases, there is a tendency to overgeneralize and go beyond the scope of the study with conclusions. For example, they attribute findings to all students of a given class when the study was limited to only a few students, or assume that a proxy used to measure a construct (e.g., strategy use) is the same thing as the construct (comprehension).

In closing, it is important to note that high-quality studies of literacy development in language-minority students can be difficult to accomplish in school settings, given the paucity of funds allocated for such research. Conducting good research capable of identifying a best course of action is expensive. In the past, federal funds have been devoted largely to evaluations of federally supported programs, comparison studies aimed at evaluating the efficacy of English immersion versus some native-language use, and survey research that provides descriptions of the language-minority populations and the settings in which they are educated. However, it is also necessary to fund research with language-minority students that takes a componential approach to developing and evaluating instructional techniques and approaches that promote student achievement.

FUTURE RESEARCH

The chapters in Part IV, taken together, reveal the great need for more and better research into what schools should do to improve literacy among English-language learners. Beyond the obvious need for more studies and more replications further evaluating promising instructional innovations, there is a need for a more sophisticated approach to research than has usually been apparent. Educational outcomes may be influenced by individual, sociocultural, cross-linguistic, and developmental factors. What is needed is an ambitious research agenda that pursues a systematic analysis of the effectiveness of instructional routines and the adjustments teachers make in these routines to foster success *within the context* of these individual and contextual factors that moderate and mediate literacy learning outcomes for language-minority students.

Moreover, we need to use research findings to craft new theories and inform various paradigms that in turn can be used to inform both future research and practice. Theory plays an important role in practice because findings from one study, or even a collection of studies, will never be sufficient to address the unique circumstances of any new educational situation. Educators need to understand relevant theories if they are to respond effectively to the unique circumstances they confront in meeting the diverse needs of students in their classrooms.

Methodological Recommendations for Improving the Research Base

As noted, a fundamental problem with much of experimental research reviewed here was that the authors provided too little information about the English-language learners, their context, and the nature of the instruction being provided.

Future research should report children's level of literacy or language attainment in the native language and second language so it is possible to make sense of variations in effectiveness. Moreover, studies on the teaching of language-minority students should routinely document the similarities and differences between the approaches used with the language-minority students and these same approaches used with native speakers. With such descriptions, it would be possible to determine whether different adjustments are needed for students with different first languages or at varied levels of English proficiency. Finally, the studies need to use valid, reliable literacy measures and consider the long-term (not just the immediate) impact of the instruction.

Although prospective case studies and ethnographic reports cannot determine the efficacy of instruction, they can be valuable in providing insight into the kinds of instructional adjustment that should become the focus of experimental evaluations. As noted, such research is potentially useful (on its own and when combined with experimental designs), but quality standards are needed to ensure the reliability of the observational procedures employed and to circumscribe the interpretations and generalizations that can be drawn from such work. These standards should be employed in the training of researchers, and journal editors and grant reviewers should apply them in determining which studies to publish and which to fund.

The standards developed by this panel might help create uniform standards for qualitative research on language-minority students. In documenting an approach or context in which an approach was implemented, criteria should include the number of observations per unit of analysis,[1] duration of these observations, detail (specificity and concreteness) provided in reporting these observations, and appropriateness of the methods used for documentation. With regard to whether and how findings and themes are supported by specific data (e.g., observations, interviews, assessments), criteria should include the sufficiency of diverse sources of information (triangulation), provision of information about the relative frequency of certain events or occurrences (typicality or atypicality), examination of competing or alternative explanations, explanation of the range of variation in the data presented, and presentation of generalizations presented based on the data collected.

Given the complexity of educating language-minority students, there is a need for more sophisticated research designs making use of multiple methods of inquiry. The NRP (National Institute of Child Health and Human Development, 2000) came to a similar conclusion after reviewing research on reading instruction with native English speakers. The circumstances are even more complex and the need for mixed-method designs is even more crucial with English-language learners. Within the context of experimental and quasi-experimental studies evaluating the efficacy of particular instructional approaches with this population, there is a need for close and careful observation of the implementation of these approaches and the milieu in which they are implemented. It

---

[1]For example, if the unit of analysis is the classroom, how many times was it visited? If it was a particular kind of lesson within the classroom, how many such lessons were observed? If it was a particular kind of instructional move (including moves using the mother tongue in instruction), how many instances of that move were observed?

is not enough to know that something works in the broad sense; research must strive to determine why and how it works. Mixed-method designs employing multiple research methods are the most likely avenue for achieving this level of understanding. Research of this type requires collaboration among experts from diverse areas of interest and the availability of the funding and infrastructure necessary to collaborate in this manner.

Substantive Recommendations for Improving the Research Base

Research is needed to replicate the findings described in this volume in order to build greater confidence in the findings. Especially needed are longitudinal studies that examine the long-term benefits of the various procedures that have been tried so far.

Research should go beyond identifying specific instructional approaches that are effective to examine how these approaches can be scaled up in such a way that they remain effective across contexts and populations. It has often been noted that results of research studies can be difficult to implement on a larger scale. Thus, research that goes from hypothesis to proven effectiveness in a classroom or school to effectiveness on the school- or district-wide level is needed to identify the conditions and mechanisms that would allow a research-proven approach to be applied with broader benefit.

Research needs to address not only the development of basic language proficiency and early literacy, but also the acquisition of higher level literacy skills. Part I of this volume shows that English-language learners often match native English speakers in word recognition, phonemic awareness, and spelling without necessarily attaining comparable levels of comprehension and writing in English.. Public hearings held by the panel as well as the research reviewed revealed a strong need for information on how to facilitate the literacy learning of adolescent students. Research is needed to identify effective ways to support learning of content knowledge attained through literacy in history, science, mathematics, and other school subjects.

Finally, research on literacy instruction for language-minority students should address the learning needs of students with special needs and learners at different levels of English proficiency (including older newcomers), with different levels of content knowledge, at different ages, at different levels of language and literacy attainment in the native language, and with different native-language backgrounds. Earlier we noted the need for better reporting of these characteristics so that we can glean the maximum amount of information from these studies. Here we go beyond that point to call for explicit studies of what works with different types of learners. Direct studies of this type will help validate the correlational evidence and enhance our understanding of how to teach all language-minority students to read and write most effectively.

14

Language of Instruction

David J. Francis, Nonie Lesaux, and Diane August

For many years, discussion of effective reading programs for English-language learners has revolved around the question of whether and how children's first language should be used in an instructional program. The focus of this chapter is on studies that compare bilingual programs with programs that use only English. The first part of the chapter provides background information, the second presents the methods used for the review, the third and fourth present information on studies with language minority children and heritage language studies, the fifth presents studies of French Immersion, and the remainder provides a summary of the methodological issues and findings.

The following research questions are addressed in this chapter: What impact does language of instruction have on the literacy learning of language-minority students? Is it better to immerse students in English-language instruction, or are there benefits to developing literacy in English as well as in the native language?

BACKGROUND

Program Types

In this section, we define the types of programs reviewed in the chapter and summarize findings from prior syntheses on this topic. When a child enters school with limited proficiency in English, the school faces a serious dilemma: How can the child be expected to learn the skills and content taught at the same time as he or she is learning English? There may be many options, but two fundamental categories of solutions have predominated: programs that provide instruction only in English (English-only) and programs with some native-language instruction (often called bilingual).

English-Only Programs   In an English-only setting, English-language learners are expected to learn in English from the beginning, and their native language plays little or no role in daily reading (and other) instruction. Formal or informal support is likely to be given to help them cope in an all-English context. This support may include help from a bilingual aide who provides occasional translation or explanation; a separate class in English as a second language (ESL) to help build English skills; and/or the use of scaffolded instruction, in which teachers use specific techniques to help English-language learners understand content delivered in English. English-only instruction may involve placing English-language learners immediately in classes containing native English speakers, or it may involve a separate class composed entirely of English-language learners for some period of time until the children are ready to be mainstreamed. These variations may well be important to student outcomes, but their key common feature is the almost exclusive use of English for instruction, supported by English texts.

Many authors have drawn distinctions among different forms of English-only instruction. One term often encountered is *submersion*, most commonly used pejoratively to refer to sink-or-swim strategies in which no special provision is made for the needs of English-language learners. This approach is contrasted with *structured English immersion*, which refers to a well-planned, gradual phase-in of unmodified English instruction relying initially on special techniques to make content delivered in English accessible to English-language learners. In practice, English-only programs are rarely pure types, and in studies of bilingual education they are rarely described.

Bilingual Programs   Bilingual education differs fundamentally from English-only programs in that it provides English-language learners instruction in reading and/or other subjects in their native language. In the United States, most bilingual programs involve Spanish for two reasons: the greater likelihood of a critical mass of students who are Spanish speakers, and the greater availability of teachers who are bilingual in Spanish and English, as well as of Spanish materials, compared with other languages.

In transitional bilingual programs, children may be taught to read entirely in Spanish initially and then transitioned to English. Such programs may be early-exit models, with the transition to English being completed sometime within the first 3 years of the elementary grades, or late-exit models, in which children may continue to receive some native-language instruction throughout elementary school to ensure their mastery of reading and content before being transitioned (see Ramírez, Pasta, Yuen, Billings, & Ramey, 1991). In contrast, paired bilingual models teach children to read in both English and their native language from the beginning of their schooling. Willig (1985) calls this model *alternative immersion* because children are alternatively immersed in native-language and English instruction. Within a few years, however, the native-language reading instruction may be discontinued as children develop the skills needed to succeed in English. This approach contrasts with transitional bilingual education models, in which children are first taught to read primarily in their native language and then transitioned gradually to English-only instruction.

Finally, two-way bilingual programs, or dual-language programs, provide reading instruction in the native language (usually Spanish) and English to English-language learners in classrooms where they are integrated with English speakers who also learn both languages (Calderón & Minaya-Rowe, 2003; Howard, Sugarman, & Christian, 2003). Some two-way programs begin reading instruction for English-language learners in the native language and then add English, often in third grade (with native-language reading continuing along with English after that). Other programs provide reading instruction in both languages from the beginning. The key difference between two-way bilingual and other approaches is that students are expected to develop and maintain literacy in two languages.

Heritage Language Programs   A special case of bilingual education is those programs designed to preserve or show respect for the *heritage* language of the participating children. For example, Morgan (1971) studied a program in Louisiana for children whose parents often spoke French at home, but who themselves generally spoke English. Such heritage language programs are included in this chapter if the outcome variable in the study is an English reading measure. It should be noted, however, that these programs address a different language-related issue from that usually addressed by English-only immersion or bilingual education in that the students are already proficient in English.

French Immersion Programs.   Finally, although studies of French immersion programs are not directly relevant to the question of the effectiveness of bilingual programs for language-minority students acquiring the societal language, they are important in gaining a broader understanding of the role of the socio-cultural context in literacy development. Several Canadian studies of French immersion programs, in which native-English-speaking children are taught entirely or primarily in French in the early elementary years (e.g., Barik & Swain, 1978; Genesee, Sheiner, Tucker, & Lambert, 1976, 1977), have played an important role in debates about bilingual education.

It is important to note the striking differences between the Canadian studies and those conducted with language-minority students acquiring English as a societal language in the United States. These Canadian Anglophone children were learning a useful second language but not the language for which they would be held accountable in their later schooling. Although most of the studies took place in Montreal, the children lived in English-speaking neighborhoods and attended schools in an English system. Further, these studies all involved voluntary programs, in which children's parents wanted their children to learn French. Moreover, the children in these studies were generally upper middle class, not economically disadvantaged. Because the French immersion programs were voluntary, children who did not thrive in them could be, and were, routinely returned to English-only instruction. Thus, the children who completed the programs were self-selected, relatively high achievers.

Variability Within Program Type.   As is true in most educational research on program evaluation, although the type of program accounts for some variability in practice and student achievement, its level of implementation accounts for far more (e.g., Tivnan & Hemphill, 2005). Thus, it is not surprising that, although program type typically defines broad guidelines for the use of students' native language, the amount of instructional time in which either language is used is generally not accounted for in program evaluation studies. For example, there is evidence that use of the native language is highly variable even within a single program model, depending not only on how language education policy is interpreted at the district level, but also on teachers' beliefs, interpretations of political contexts, and language skills (Gandara et al., 2000).

In addition, there is great variability within program models in the quality of instruction. In a review of bilingual research, August and Hakuta (1997) conclude that, although research has generally favored bilingual approaches, the nature of the methods used and the populations to which they have been applied have been important. Specifically, the authors conclude that program quality has been the key to positive outcomes for English-language learners. For example, carefully designed structured immersion programs using only English may be effective, but this does not justify sink-or-swim (or submersion) English-only programs. The same holds true for the quality of bilingual programs.

Further, the context in which programs are implemented varies in ways that influence their design and effectiveness. For example, parental and community goals regarding English acquisition and the benefits of bilingualism, parents' socioeconomic status (SES) and educational background, and students' age at arrival and prior academic schooling are likely to influence academic and language acquisition outcomes (for an in-depth discussion of these issues, see Parts I, II, and III, this volume). Policy also has a significant influence on programming. In the United States, for example, some states require that English be the only language used for instruction. However, directives from higher levels may not be embraced by the educators implementing a program, again resulting in differences between the program's design and actual implementation.

Previous Reviews

Views diverge in the United States regarding the value of the use of an English-language learner's first language for instruction. Researchers cite evidence that children's reading proficiency in their native language is a strong predictor of their ultimate English reading performance (August & Hakuta, 1997; Greene, 1997; Willig, 1985), bilingualism does not interfere with academic achievement in either language (Yeung, Marsh, & Suliman, 2000), and children are able to transfer some literacy skills acquired in their native language to the societal language (studies investigating the relationship between first- and second-language literacy are reviewed in chap. 9). Proponents of bilingual education use these findings, together with the belief that teaching children to read in a language in which they are not yet proficient is an additional risk factor for reading difficulties (Snow, Burns, & Griffin, 1998), to argue for initial instruction in the native language while students are acquiring proficiency in a second language. In addition to the hypothesized academic and cognitive benefits of bilingual instruction, advocates of bilingual education argue that, without native-language instruction, English-language learners are likely to lose their native-language proficiency, an important resource in its own right.

Opponents of native-language instruction argue that it interferes with or delays English-language development, because children have less opportunity for time on task in English (Rossell, 2000). Further, programs that include instruction in the native language have been criticized for relegating children who receive such instruction to a second-class, separate status within the school and, ultimately, within society (Glenn, 2000).

Reflecting this debate, reviews and research on the educational outcomes of students receiving native-language instruction have reached conflicting conclusions. For an early review, Baker and de Kanter (1981) examined more than 300 evaluations of programs designed for second-language learners. To be included in the review, a study had to either employ random assignment of children to treatment conditions, or take measures to ensure that children in the comparison groups were equivalent; studies with no control group were rejected. Of the studies initially located, only 28 satisfied the authors' criteria. Baker and de Kanter offer the following conclusion from their review: "The case for the effectiveness of transitional bilingual education is so weak that exclusive reliance on this instruction method is clearly not justified" (p. 1). Rossell and Baker (1996) used the Baker and de Kanter review as well as the work of Baker and Pelavin (1984), as the basis for their own review, in which they considered studies that evaluated alternative second-language programs. Of the 300 program evaluations read, they found only 72 methodologically acceptable. Their review included only studies of *good quality*, which they defined as having random assignment to programs, statistical control for pre-treatment differences between groups when random assignment was not possible, and applying appropriate statistical tests to examine differences between control and treatment groups. Other criteria included results based on standardized test scores in English and comparison of students in bilingual programs with control groups of similar students. Rossell and Baker conclude that most methodologically adequate studies failed to find transitional bilingual education more effective than programs with English-only instruction: "Thus the research evidence does not support transitional bilingual education as a superior form of instruction for limited English proficient children" (p. 7). It should be noted that the authors of these two studies do not state that English-only instruction is more effective, but merely that bilingual instruction should not be the only approach mandated by law.

Willig (1985) conducted a meta-analysis of the studies reviewed by Baker and de Kanter (1981), making several changes with regard to inclusion criteria. First, she eliminated five studies conducted outside the United States (three in Canada, one in the Philippines, and one in South Africa) because of significant differences in the students, programs, and contexts in those studies. She also excluded one study in which instruction took place outside the classroom. Finally, she excluded one review, because it was not a primary study. Her overall conclusion is quite different from that of Baker and de Kanter: "positive effects for bilingual programs...for all major academic areas" (p. 297). However, it should be noted that Willig was asking a fundamentally different question from that explored by Baker and de Kanter. The latter authors addressed whether bilingual education should be mandated, whereas Willig considered a more modest question: whether bilingual education works. As she notes, she conducted a series of comparisons. One set of comparisons examined how bilingual programs with and without ESL instruction compared with sub-mersion programs or programs in which English-language learners are placed in all-English classrooms with no special instructional support. A second set of comparisons examined bilingual programs that included ESL support with immersion programs that also included ESL support. For both sets of comparisons,

Willig concludes that bilingual education works better than the English-only programs with which it was compared.

Greene (1997) performed a meta-analysis of the set of studies cited by Rossell and Baker (1996), but the analysis included only 11 of those 72 studies. In addition to the criteria used by Rossell and Baker, Greene looked at studies that measured the effects of bilingual programs after at least one academic year. If students were not assigned to treatment and control groups randomly, adequate statistical control for this nonrandom assignment was defined as requiring controls for individual previous test scores, as well as at least some of the individual demographic factors known to influence those scores, such as family income and parental education. In all, Greene rejected studies cited by Rossell and Baker, because they were duplicative of other studies in the review (15), could not be located (5), were not evaluations of bilingual programs (3), did not have appropriate control groups (14),[1] measured bilingual education after a short period of time (2), and inadequately controlled for differences between students assigned to bilingual and English-only programs (25). Among the studies that met the author's standard of methodological adequacy, including all those using random assignment to conditions, Greene found that the evidence favored programs that made use of native-language instruction (average effect size 0.21).

Finally, Slavin and Cheung (2004) conducted a best-evidence synthesis, an approach that uses a systematic literature search, quantification of outcomes and effect sizes, and extensive discussion of individual studies that meet inclusion criteria. Seventeen studies met their inclusion standards. They found that, "among 13 studies focusing on elementary reading for Spanish-dominant students, 9 favored bilingual approaches on English reading measures, and 4 found no differences, for a median effect size of +0.45. Weighted by sample size, an effect size of +0.33 was computed, which is significantly different from zero ($p < .05$)" (p. 2).

Differences in study outcomes can be attributed, in part, to differences in the questions asked, the criteria for including studies, and the methods used to synthesize findings. With regard to the research questions asked, for example, the nature of the samples differed depending on the question (e.g., Willig eliminated studies conducted outside the United States, whereas Baker and de Kanter did not). Standards for methodological rigor also differed across the reviews (e.g., Greene eliminated 61 studies that had been included by Rossell and Baker). Only two of the authors (Greene, 1997; Willig, 1985) used meta-analytic techniques and therefore took into account the program effects found in each study, even if they were not statistically significant. As Greene points out, "simply counting positive and negative effect sizes is less precise than a meta-analysis, because it does not consider the magnitude or confidence level of effects" (p. 11). In fact, simple vote-counting procedures are known to be conservatively biased, and the magnitude of the bias increases as the number of studies increases (Lipsey & Wilson, 2001).

Of note is that differences in study conclusions were not large. Many reviews that have been labeled as anti-bilingual education found not that use of the native

---

[1] Greene asserts that, in most of these cases, children in the control group also received some native-language instruction.

language was worse than English-only instruction, but merely that there were no overall differences. The two reviews favorable to bilingual instruction found differences in favor of native-language instruction, but the effect sizes were small to moderate. Of interest is Willig's (1985) conclusion that the better the technical quality of the study was (e.g., if a study used random assignment as opposed to creating post hoc comparison groups), the larger were the effects. This observation raises an interesting possibility: The effectiveness debate may really be carried on at the relatively superficial level of a study's technical quality.

Although the authors of reviews may disagree on the effectiveness of bilingual education, they do not disagree about the overall quality of the available studies. All had to eliminate large numbers of studies from their reviews A flaw in many studies is the failure to equate experimental and control groups on important variables. In some instances, for example, students in the control groups were those who had exited from bilingual programs (Stern, 1975); in other instances, students in the control groups were those who had never needed bilingual services. Willig (1985) found that in the latter cases, the mean effect sizes for the bilingual groups were among the lowest in her study and favored the English-only groups. When the comparison children did qualify for the program, but were eliminated through the process of random assignment, however, the effect sizes favored the bilingual groups. Language exposure in the neighborhood and school settings can also influence differences between the groups studied. In the studies Willig reviewed, regardless of whether the neighborhood language was English or another language, effect sizes were positive for the bilingual group when both groups (i.e., the bilingual group and the English-only comparison group) had the same neighborhood language. However, when the neighborhood language of the comparison group was English and that of the experimental group was Spanish, little or no differences were found between the two groups. Another study flaw is that, in many cases, the authors do not clearly describe the program characteristics and provide little information about the fidelity or quality of program implementation. Finally, the studies cited in prior reviews have routinely ignored the problematic issue of nesting of students within classrooms.

METHODS

Our review includes the methodologically adequate studies that have been cited in previous reviews (e.g., Greene, 1997; Rossell & Baker, 1996; Slavin & Cheung, 2004; Willig, 1985), as well as other studies located in a search of the literature as described later. It is important to note that the methods applied in this synthesis have some important limitations. First, in requiring measurable outcomes and control groups, we excluded case studies and qualitative studies. Many such descriptions exist and are valuable in suggesting programs or practices that may be effective, as well as describing the context in which programs take place (studies of this nature are reported and discussed in chaps. 12 and 16). However, these descriptions do not indicate what children would have learned had they not experienced a particular program. Thus, they are not relevant to the overarching question of program effectiveness that guided the review and meta-analytic work for this chapter. Second, it is important to note that a number of the studies reviewed took place many years ago, and that both social and political contexts, as well as bilingual and English-only immersion programs, have changed over time. Thus, we cannot assume that all outcomes described here would apply to bilingual and immersion programs today. For example, methods used to coordinate and sequence the use of the two languages are much better developed now, as are methods for scaffolding English instruction.

In this chapter, we focus primarily on research comparing English-only and bilingual reading programs used with language-minority students, with measures of English reading as the outcomes. For these studies, we employed systematic procedures and inclusion criteria and discuss the studies in narrative form, while also computing, where feasible, the effect sizes for individual studies and performing a meta-analysis (Cooper, 1998; Cooper & Hedges, 1994) to compare findings across these studies. We also provide a narrative review of the French immersion studies because, as mentioned in the introduction to this chapter, they are important in gaining a broader understanding of the role of the sociocultural context in literacy development.

Searches

As part of this review, we systematically searched electronic databases for studies that compared some use of the native language with English-only instruction (see chap. 1). In addition, we attempted to obtain every study included in the reviews conducted by Willig (1985), Rossell and Baker (1996), Greene (1997), and Slavin and Cheung (2004).

Appendix 14.A contains a list of all of the studies of reading cited by Willig (1985), Rossell and Baker (1996), Greene (1997), and Slavin and Cheung (2004); it indicates those that were disqualified from this review, because they did not meet the panel's criteria for methodological adequacy as outlined next. As is apparent from the appendix, only a few of the studies met the most minimal of methodological standards, and most violated the inclusion criteria established by Rossell and Baker (1996). This does not mean that the overall conclusions of other reviews are incorrect. However, it does mean that the effects of language of instruction on reading achievement were explored by the panel with a somewhat different set of studies from those cited by previous reviews.

Criteria for Inclusion

As described in chapter 1, the studies met the same methodological standards as other experimental and quasi-experimental studies included in the overall report. Either random assignment to conditions was used, or pretesting or other matching criteria established the degree of comparability of bilingual and immersion groups before the treatments began. In some instances, pretreatment covariates were not pretest measures of outcomes, but measures of skills related to the outcomes. That is, it was not necessary that pretest measures of outcomes were available as covariates in nonrandomized studies. Studies without control groups, such as pre- and postcomparisons and comparisons with expected scores or gains, were excluded. No studies were excluded on the basis of level of pretreatment differences.

To be consistent with other previous reviews of the research that compare programs using bilingual instruction with those using English-only instruction, we allowed for a broader time frame and venue for publication. Thus, studies included in this chapter include technical reports, dissertations, and studies predating 1980. In addition to the general inclusion criteria described in chapter 1, the studies reviewed in this chapter met other standards of relevance to the purposes of this chapter:

- The studies compared children taught reading in bilingual classes and those taught in English-only classes, as defined in the preceding section. Studies of alternative reading programs for English-language learners that held constant the language of instruction are discussed in later chapters of Part IV.
- The subjects were language-minority students in elementary or secondary schools in English-speaking countries. Studies in which samples were not composed predominantly of language-minority students or that did not allow an estimate of performance separately for language-minority students were excluded (e.g., Skoczylas, 1972). Studies of other societal languages would have been included if they were analogous to the situation of English-language learners in the United States or Canada (e.g., Turkish children learning to read in Dutch in the Netherlands), but no such studies were found that met our other inclusion criteria. Studies of children learning a foreign language were not included.
- Studies of instruction in heritage languages were also included if they met our other criteria. One such study was identified (Morgan, 1971).
- The dependent variables included quantitative measures of vocabulary and English reading performance, such as standardized tests and informal reading inventories.
- Studies included at least a 6-month span between the onset of instruction and posttests; in these cases, most treatment durations were of at least 1 year.
- Despite their variation with respect to sample and context, Canadian studies of French immersion have been widely discussed and are therefore reviewed in a separate section of this chapter. They are not included in the meta-analysis. As a group, these studies are of high methodological quality and constitute effective program evaluations.

Methods of Rating Studies for Inclusion

Once studies had been selected because they were relevant, two individuals independently reviewed them against our consistent set of standards. The coding rubric for the studies can be found in Appendix 14.B. There were two circumstances in which additional reviewers examined a study: when the primary reviewers disagreed on whether an article should be included, and when the consensus opinion of the reviewers regarding inclusion or exclusion differed from the way an article had been handled in a previously published review (Greene, 1997; Rossell & Baker, 1996; Slavin & Cheung, 2004; Willig, 1985). The final disposition of such studies was determined by consensus of the coders and two methodological experts.[2] Following these procedures, we arrived at a final set of 20 studies that diverged somewhat from those of previous reviews (see Appendix 14.C). Although many studies that appear in the present chapter also appeared in the four prior reviews, some of the studies in those reviews failed to meet our inclusion criteria (see Appendix 14.A). In addition, some studies judged to meet our criteria had been excluded from one or more of the prior reviews.

Study Characteristics

Twenty studies in our database focused on evaluating the impact of language of instruction on literacy acquisition. In addition to the majority of studies focused on the acquisition of literacy by language-minority students ($n = 16$), this chapter incorporates findings from one heritage language study and three Canadian French immersion studies. In each of the following sections, studies are organized according to grade level (elementary or secondary). Of the studies focused on language-minority students acquiring the societal language, 14 studies investigated program effectiveness with students in the elementary years and 2 with students in the secondary years. Of all studies, 5 used random assignment to the instructional conditions, and 15 used a matching procedure to compare students receiving some native-language instruction with those receiving English-only instruction.

Finally, in light of our discussions in Parts I, II, and III of the various factors other than language of instruction that influence the development of literacy skills, we provide, to the extent possible for each study, sample characteristics (e.g., age, socioeconomic status [SES], length of exposure to the native and target languages); a description of the program type(s); and, if available, the method used for enrollment in the program(s). For studies that compared program types, but did not employ random assignment to instructional conditions, we describe the matching procedures.

Studies Conducted With Language-Minority Students. Fourteen studies included in our review compared language-minority students in the elementary grades who were taught to read with bilingual or English-only instruction (Alvarez, 1975; Campeau et al., 1975; Cohen, Fathman, & Merino, 1976; Danoff, Coles, McLaughlin, & Reynolds, 1978; De la Garza & Medina, 1985; Doebler & Mardis, 1980–1981; Huzar, 1973; Lampman, 1973; J. A. Maldonado, 1994; J. R. Maldonado, 1977; Plante, 1976; Ramírez et al., 1991; Saldate, Mishra, & Medina, 1985; Valladolid, 1991). These studies were characterized methodologically by random assignment to one of the instructional conditions or by a procedure whereby students were matched on pretest variables, such as reading and oral proficiency or on pre-reading skills. Two studies (Covey, 1973; Kaufman, 1968) in our review compared language-minority students in the secondary grades who were taught to read with bilingual or English-only immersion approaches. Both studies employed random assignment to one of the instructional conditions.

---

[2] David Francis, University of Houston; and Tim Shanahan, University of Illinois at Chicago.

Heritage Language Studies.   One study we reviewed (Morgan, 1971) examined the effectiveness of a program in which language-minority children received instruction in their heritage language. In this case, the heritage language was French.

French Immersion Studies.   Three studies in our review (Barik & Swain, 1975, 1978; Barik, Swain, & Nwanunobi, 1977) evaluated French immersion programs for English-speaking children in Canada. However, because they compared French immersion for English-speaking students with monolingual English instruction or brief classes in French as a second language, these were not evaluations of bilingual education per se.

Computation of Effect Sizes and Synthesis of Findings

When possible, we computed effect size estimates for each study by using the pooled within-group standard deviation and either unadjusted or adjusted posttest treatment and control means, or both, when both adjusted and unadjusted means were available. In principle, an effect size is the experimental mean minus the control mean, divided by the standard deviation. When this information was lacking, however, we estimated effect sizes by using information provided by the studies and appropriate conversion formulas provided by Shadish, Robinson, and Lu (1999) and Lipsey and Wilson (2001).[3]

The decision to examine adjusted and/or unadjusted means in these studies merits some discussion. The meta-analysis literature lacks a strong consensus on the choice of posttreatment means for the computation of effect sizes in quasi-experimental studies. The challenge, it seems, is deriving effect size estimates that will compare favorably across the collection of studies—that is, that will allow comparison of apples to apples and oranges to oranges. Because the literature on bilingual education is anything but consistent with respect to the reporting of means and standard deviations and the use of pretreatment covariates, there is no single approach that would have allowed us to estimate effect sizes in the same way for all studies. Often studies reported unadjusted means, standard deviations, and test statistics for adjusted means without providing other information necessary to compute an effect size on the adjusted means. For studies comparing groups on adjusted means, adjustments were not always based on the same covariates across studies, and rarely was the information provided to properly estimate the effect size on the adjusted means. Thus, we settled on the approach of computing effect sizes on unadjusted and adjusted means, when possible, and looking for possible factors that explained variability in the effect sizes. Two studies only reported adjusted means, and one of those studies was a randomized trial; in all, the adjusted means constituted 14% of the reported effect sizes (see Appendix 14.E). Thus, we did not feel there was sufficient variation in the type of mean reported to provide a meaningful test of the moderator variable, and we analyzed the unadjusted means with the exception of the two studies that only provided adjusted means (Alvaree, 1975; Kaufman, 1968).

---

[3]This chapter incorporates only the effect sizes for those studies in which sufficient information is provided to calculate an effect size.

In some instances, we made assumptions to be able to estimate the effect size when information was lacking. For example, we may have had to assume that the pre- and posttest standard deviations were equivalent, because the pretest standard deviation was reported but not the posttest standard deviation, or we may have had to assume that the treatment and control standard deviations were the same when only one of the two was reported. Finally, in the case of two studies (the Alice, Texas, and Houston, Texas, evaluation studies reported in Campeau et al., 1975; Cohen et al., 1976), we estimated the standard deviations from other studies that had used the same outcome measure at the same grades. More specifically, Campeau et al. reported means and significance tests for gain scores, but did not provide the additional information necessary to derive the posttest standard deviation to be used in the denominator of the effect size. Rather than use the gain score standard deviation, which would be expected to underestimate the posttest standard deviation, we estimated the standard deviation from other studies that used the same outcome measure at the same grades by computing the square root of the average of the pooled within-group variances reported in those studies.

Finally, it must be pointed out that none of the studies reviewed in this section addressed the issue of nonindependence of students who are nested inside instructional units. That is, students who receive their instruction in the same classroom/school/district are not independent, and this lack of independence must be taken into account when computing significance tests. From a practical standpoint, the failure to address this nonindependence in individual studies means that standard errors for individual studies are likely to underestimate the true standard errors, and thus confidence intervals around effect sizes for individual studies should be assumed to be too small. Although the extent of underestimation of standard errors will vary across studies to an unknown degree, we have opted not to judge the statistical significance of individual studies because of their failure to adequately address this issue of nonindependence in their analyses and reported statistics. Because the effect size standard errors are used to weigh the effect sizes in the meta-analysis, this issue also impacts the meta-analysis in an unknown way. Consequently we also examine the effect sizes using a procedure that ignores the standard errors of the individual effect size estimates. Additional details regarding study methodology and effect size computations are provided in Appendix 14.D. We performed a meta-analysis on those studies for which effect sizes could be computed; Appendix 14.E presents the effect sizes. As noted earlier, we also described all the studies included in this chapter as part of a qualitative review. For studies not included in the meta-analysis, we report study outcomes in the narrative review.

STUDIES WITH LANGUAGE-MINORITY STUDENTS

Studies With Elementary School Learners

Three of the studies conducted with elementary school learners used random assignment (Huzar, 1973; Maldonado, 1994; Plante, 1976); the remainder employed a design involving the comparison of a group of language-minority students receiving instruction in their native language with a group of language-minority students receiving no structured support in their native language (Alvarez, 1975; Campeau et al., 1975 [five studies]); Cohen et al., 1976; Danoff et al., 1978; Dela Garza & Medina, 1985; Doebler & Mardis, 1980–1981; Lampman, 1973; Maldonado, 1977; Ramírez et al., 1991; Saldate et al., 1985; Valladolid, 1991.) In these studies, the groups were generally matched by using either pretest scores on measures of reading and oral proficiency or pre-reading skills.

Studies Using Random Assignment. Plante (1976) conducted a study with Spanish-dominant Puerto Rican children who were attending a New Haven, Connecticut, elementary school. The sample included a group of children who received bilingual education in first and second grades ($n = 15$) and a group of children who received such education in the second and third grades ($n = 16$). The control group comprised second and third graders who had received no support or instruction in their native language ($n = 10$ second graders, $n = 12$ third graders). The school is described as serving a large percentage of children from low-income families. In this study, children were randomly assigned to the experimental group (a paired bilingual model) or a control group in which no native-language support was offered for Spanish-speaking children. Prior to this 2-year study, there was no native-language support for children in New Haven.

In the paired bilingual experimental condition, the native language of one teacher was Spanish and of another was English. The children in this condition were taught all their basic skills (reading, writing, math, science, social studies) in Spanish by the native-Spanish-speaking teacher while receiving instruction in English (an aural–oral approach) from the native-English-speaking teacher. The latter instruction was designed to transition the children to English-only instruction. When an individual child's oral English vocabulary was sufficiently developed, the teacher initiated reading and writing of English.

In addition to random assignment to conditions, equivalence between the experimental and control groups prior to the onset of the bilingual instruction was established on the basis of measures of oral vocabulary in Spanish and English. Plante also conducted attrition analyses, through which it was determined that attrition ($n = 14$ from the experimental group, $n = 5$ controls) did not change the arithmetic means on pretests of reading and language, and that if a chance advantage did exist, it would favor the control group.

A similar study (Huzar, 1973) was conducted in Perth Amboy, New Jersey, in a school district where children had been randomly assigned to bilingual or English-only instructional conditions. The children in the experimental condition were second-grade ($n = 41$) and third-grade ($n = 43$) Spanish-dominant Puerto Rican children who had received bilingual instruction since first grade. These two groups were compared with control groups of second ($n = 40$) and third ($n = 36$) graders with similar backgrounds receiving English-only instruction in the same school. Despite random assignment to bilingual education, Huzar also obtained school district data and determined group equivalence on measures of IQ, SES, and initial achievement on a standardized measure of kindergarten readiness. As in the Plante (1976) study, the students in the experimental group were exposed to a paired bilingual instructional model, and thus had two teachers. One teacher taught reading in Spanish for 45 minutes daily, and the other teacher taught reading in English for the same amount of time. Students in the English-only classes received 45 minutes of English reading instruction daily. The author reports that all teaching procedures and quality of instruction were the same for both groups.

Studies With Random Assignment: Elementary Children With Learning Disabilities.
Maldonado (1994) carried out a small randomized study involving language-
minority students who were in special education classes in Houston, Texas.
Twenty second- and third-grade Spanish speakers with learning disabilities were
randomly assigned to one of two groups: a bilingual group that was taught
mainly in Spanish for a year with a 45-minute ESL period, and a control group
that received traditional special education in English. During the second year,
half of the instruction in the bilingual program was in English and half in
Spanish. In the third year, instruction was primarily in English. The students in
the two groups had similar characteristics, including age, education, experience,
learning disability, language proficiency, and SES. Children's achievement was
assessed at pre- and posttest with a standardized measure of language and reading achievement (California Test of Basic Skills [CTBS]). Information reported in
the article is inconsistent and leads to widely varying estimates of the effect of
billingual instrutic. These problems are discussed in Appendix 14.D.

Studies Using Matching   De la Garza and Medina (1985) conducted a study
comparing the reading achievement of a group of Spanish-speaking Mexican
children in a transitional bilingual education program ($n = 24$) and a group of
Spanish-speaking children receiving English-only instruction ($n = 118$). The
study was conducted in Tucson, Arizona, with children of low SES, as evidenced by the majority of the sample's qualification for a free or reduced-price
lunch program. In the transitional bilingual program, instruction was in
Spanish 75% of the time in first grade, 70% of the time in second grade, and 50%
of the time in third grade. Most children in the bilingual program transitioned
into English reading in third grade. No details are provided on the number of
classrooms per grade or on whether the bilingual and English-only classrooms
were in the same or different schools.

   The children were followed from first through third grades and assessed on
measures of reading vocabulary and comprehension at the end of each year.
The students in the sample are those who had data available for 3 years.
Students in the bilingual program were required to have data available in both
English and Spanish; students in the control sample were required to have data
available in English. There are several methodological issues related to the
study. First, there was no attempt to determine whether those in the sample at
any one grade were comparable to those missing at that grade; that is, there
was no assessment of bias due to possible differential attrition. Second, although
students in the two groups were similar in ethnicity, grade level, duration of
program participation, and SES, in fact 94% of the control group was rated as
English dominant in first grade. Thus, although both groups consisted of
language-minority students, the control and bilingual education groups were
not equivalent in English-language proficiency.[4]

   Alvarez (1975) conducted a study with 147 Mexican American children of
low SES attending two schools in Austin, Texas. Seven classrooms and teachers
were included in the total sample. The sample at each school comprised a

---

[4]This may be a problem with other studies of young learners that is undetected. Although
students may be matched on a number of variables at pretest, language dominance is important
and is generally not reported.

group of children receiving instruction in Spanish and a group receiving all instruction in English; the children were followed from first to second grade. At the time of the study, bilingual education was optional, and its aim in the primary grades was to emphasize instruction in the child's native language through oral, reading, and writing activities. Simultaneously, oral English-language development was a focus, with the goal of developing sufficient proficiency so that English reading and writing instruction would be possible. By second grade, the bilingual classrooms are described as a balanced combination of Spanish and English, with reading instruction in both languages. The bilingual program paired a native-Spanish-speaking and a native-English-speaking teacher, who shared two classrooms of children.

One of the most widely cited studies of bilingual education is a longitudinal study by Ramírez et al. (1991) that compared Spanish-dominant students in English immersion schools with students receiving two forms of bilingual education: early exit (transition to English-only instruction in Grades 2–4) and late exit (transition to English-only instruction in Grades 5–6). According to a review of the Ramírez et al. (1991) study carried out by the National Research Council (NRC; Meyer & Feinberg, 1992), "All three programs were intended for students who speak Spanish, but have limited ability to speak English. All three programs had, as one of their goals, teaching students English" (p. 67). A group or cohort was followed, beginning in kindergarten, for each of the three programs. For immersion and early-exit programs, an additional cohort was followed beginning in first grade; for late-exit programs, a cohort was followed beginning in third grade.[5]

Schools from nine districts were involved overall, with five sites providing English immersion programs, and five sites providing early-exit programs. Late-exit programs were not located in the same districts as English immersion or early-exit programs. English immersion and early-exit programs were generally in the same districts and in four instances were in the same schools. Although within-site comparisons provide for a better test of English immersion versus early exit, including sites with only one program type added 16 schools in English immersion and 12 schools in early exit. Many of these sites (2 English immersion and 7 early exit) were in the same districts as the schools with both programs. In order to maximize the use of the data that existed, we included data from both kinds of sites.

Meyer and Feinberg (1992) found that the most compelling findings were from the K–1 analyses comparing the four schools that provided both early-exit and English immersion programs. Children in the two programs were well matched on kindergarten pretests, SES, preschool experience, and other factors. These authors did not think that late-exit versus English immersion comparison

---

[5]Meyer and Feinberg (1992) found three comparisons unacceptable: those using the first-grade cohort, because no information is provided about the type of program the students attended prior to first grade; comparisons between early-exit bilingual programs and immersion programs located in different schools, because, even after including the background variables in the model, statistically significant school effects were found; and comparisons of the late-exit model with the other two models, because the districts in which the late-exit model were implemented did not have the other two kinds of models, making it impossible to compare students in the late-exit programs with those in other programs while controlling for district differences.

was warranted because of differences in sites and school-level heterogeneity that was confounded with programs. However, these factors are operating in other comparisons included in our analysis. Thus, it seems reasonable to examine the English immersion versus late-exit comparisons even when the programs are located in different districts schools. Because Grade 3 is the highest grade available for any of these comparisons, no data are reported beyond that grade.

In a small study conducted in New Mexico, Lampman (1973) examined the academic achievement of 40 Spanish-speaking second graders in bilingual classrooms ($n = 20$) and mainstream classrooms in which English was the language of instruction ($n = 20$). The children in the study were matched on age, IQ, home language practices, and demographic variables. At the end of second grade, there were no differences between the two groups using grade equivalent scores. This study was not included in the meta-analysis, because the authors reported only mean grade equivalent scores and did not provide sufficient information to compute an effect size estimate.

Saldate et al. (1985) studied 62 children in an Arizona border town who attended English-only or bilingual programs. The participants in the bilingual program were Mexican American children of low SES as indicated by the location of the school they attended. The children in the English-only program were from nearby schools in the same district serving mainly Mexican Americans (60%–90%). Spanish-speaking students in the experimental group were enrolled in a bilingual/bicultural program whose goals included development of Spanish and English literacy, improvement of cognitive functioning, enhanced knowledge of Mexican and American cultures, and development of positive self-concept and motivation for learning. In first grade, the children were individually matched on a standardized measure of vocabulary and placed into pairs of experimental and control subjects. Students were followed into third grade and assessed on English and Spanish reading achievement tests. Given the small sample size of this study, the results should be interpreted cautiously, especially because the number of pairs in the analysis dropped from 31 to 19 between second and third grades, and no attrition analyses are presented. Also, the study is designed as matched pairs, but data are analyzed as independent groups. Nesting of students within classrooms is ignored as is the case with the majority of studies in this chapter.

Valladolid (1991) conducted a study to determine whether bilingual education had an impact on Hispanic language-minority students' academic achievement compared with a group of students receiving English-only instruction. The study included 107 Hispanic students who had been enrolled in a California school district from kindergarten through Grade 5. Fifty-seven of the students had been enrolled in a bilingual program throughout their schooling and 50 in a traditional English-only program. Both experimental and control groups consisted of students with similar language proficiency and background characteristics. Before students were placed in one of the two types of classes, parents and guardians were informed of the bilingual classes, and students of parents who opposed bilingual education were placed in the traditional English-only program. The bilingual program was driven by the goal of developing proficiency in the basic skills of listening, speaking, and writing in the students' native language so that these skills would transfer to the second language. Second-language vocabulary was introduced in an ESOL program. Once children transitioned into English reading (generally in third grade), they transitioned into English-language arts, math, and other academic programs. Those bilingual children identified as having limited English proficiency who were enrolled in traditional classes received daily structured lessons in English, provided on a pull-out basis by instructional aides; they also did supplementary work with English reading teachers.

Maldonado (1977) conducted a study with Mexican American children enrolled in bilingual and English-only classes in schools in Corpus Christi, Texas. The experimental group comprised children who had been enrolled in a bilingual program for 4 consecutive years—in the first, second, third, and fourth grades. The control group comprised children who had never received bilingual instruction from first through fourth grades. The students were from families of low SES. At fifth grade, all students were in a mainstream setting. First-grade reading scores were used as a control variable.

One large-scale program evaluation study was the Impact Study of the Elementary and Secondary Education Act Title VII Spanish/English Bilingual Program (Danoff et al., 1978), designed to evaluate bilingual education projects funded by the U.S. Office of Education. The study was designed to contrast the performance of students enrolled in Spanish–English bilingual programs receiving federal Title VII funds with comparable students not enrolled in such programs. During the 1975–1976 school year, students in Grades 2 to 6 in each group were pre- and posttested, and a subsample (the Follow-On Sample) of those students in second and third grades was also tested in the fall of the following year. The following procedure was used to select the sample for the study.

> From the total pool of Title VII classrooms in each of the thirty-eight project sites, a stratified random sample was drawn which included at least one classroom for each site from every grade second through sixth; to the extent that participating sites would agree, additional classrooms were randomly chosen so that approximately 40% to 50% of the Title VII classrooms in each participating site were tested. In addition, non-Title VII classrooms were selected in 20 sites, which were able to nominate non-Title VII classrooms within or near their district whose students were comparable to Title VII students in terms of ethnicity, socio-economic status, and grade levels. (p. 3)

Only 75% of the students enrolled in the bilingual classrooms were of Hispanic origin.

In all, 5,311 treatment students and 2,460 control students participated in the Impact Study; for the Follow-on Sample, there were 191 Title VII second graders, 63 non-Title VII second graders, 201 Title VII third graders, and 81 non-Title VII third graders. As mentioned earlier, the authors state that the comparison group was selected by matching Title VII program students with mainstream students within or near the district by ethnicity, SES, and grade levels. It should be noted that the students who participated in the study were selected from 11,073 students in second through sixth grades in 150 schools from 38 school districts: 7,364 students from Spanish-speaking backgrounds who were enrolled in Title VII-funded programs and 3,709 students in non-Title VII classrooms. Because of the large scope of this study, drawing from multiple school districts, it is likely that policies for enrollment in bilingual education programs, as well as the characteristics of the programs, varied from district to district.

Pooled within-group standard deviations for unadjusted posttests were available to compute effect sizes for both the unadjusted and adjusted posttest means. Nesting of students within classrooms, schools, and sites was ignored; therefore, standard errors are underestimated.

The percentages of students in the Title VII sample who had spent their entire schooling in bilingual classrooms were 40%, 35.4%, 26.1%, 17.9%, and 8.7% in Grades 2 to 6, respectively (Danoff et al., 1978). These percentages reflect the number of students who started bilingual instruction in kindergarten (assuming no grade repeats). More than 20% of the sample at each grade had spent 1 year or less in bilingual classrooms, with a high of 31.3% (Grade 2) and a low of 20.7% (Grade 5). At the same time, the authors report that programs generally tended to keep students in the bilingual classrooms once the students could function fully in English (Danoff et al., 1978). This claim seems to be at variance with the percentage of students with consistent experience in bilingual classrooms.

Further, there was differential attrition from fall to spring across the two groups. Attrition was consistently higher in non-Title VII classes, ranging from 40% to 17%, in contrast with 11% to 22% for Title VII classrooms. In all but Grade 4, the differences are relatively substantial. Although the authors state that rates of attrition were not dramatically different, they were (12%, 7%, 3%, 16%, and 18% in Grades 2–6, respectively). Given the large sample sizes ($n = 158$–$1,370$) and the large overall attrition in the non-Title VII classrooms, the differences in attrition rates seem to warrant examination for differences between those who remained in the sample and those who did not in the two groups. Appendix 14.C reports that students missing at the follow-up tended to have lower scores at the pretest than students present at both time points. Nevertheless, despite the differential attrition in all but Grade 4, the authors conclude that this effect was not likely to bias the results of the trends reported on growth.

Cohen et al. (1976) conducted a longitudinal study with Mexican American first through fifth graders of low SES. The study included three cohorts, each followed for 3 years (Grades 3–5, Grades 2–4, and Grades 1–3). Although the bilingual program was implemented in only one school, there was extensive variability in its implementation from year to year and from grade to grade. In all grades and in all years, however, teachers and aides used both English and Spanish in math, social studies, and science lessons, even at the initial stages of instruction, so that children were learning in both languages simultaneously.[6] The treatment sample was matched with students in a nearby school in the same community also received. English-only instruction, with approximately half of the comparison group also receiving special attention through ESL or Title I instruction, as well as individual tutorials. Children were tested during each year of the study. The authors note that some of the control students were spending summers in Mexico, where they may have learned to read in Spanish.

---

[6]According to the authors, "this generally meant that Spanish and English were used interchangeably (word for word, phrase for phrase, sentence for sentence) or one after the other" (pp. 3–4).

In the study, performance trends over time are based on children who remain in the cohort. The data presented in Cohen et al. (1976) raise concerns about the effects of attrition in both the treatment and control groups. The means of the scale scores show an inconsistent trend, going up and down over time with ever-decreasing sample sizes. Unfortunately, there is no analysis of attrition effects, and thus the extent to which the patterns relate to loss of subjects rather than measurement error or to changes in subjects' ability cannot be ascertained. We also note that the overall sample sizes for each group were small, ranging from 14 to 7. Questions of both the magnitude of overall attrition and whether attrition was differential across the groups hinder interpretation of the study's findings. As in most other studies in the review, the analysis does not take into account nesting of students and effects of higher level nesting units (e.g., schools) in the analysis, limiting interpretation of reported significance tests. Finally, like many other studies in this review, Cohen et al. (1976) used the Inter-American Reading Test (IART) at different grade levels. Different levels of the test were used in each year/grade of the study and are footnoted in the text as Levels I, II, and III. The three forms of the test appear not to be equated, indicating that the trend in means over time is due to changes in ability as well as changes in the test in addition to the effects of attrition noted previously. Also as noted, the published report does not provide sufficient information to estimate effect sizes directly. Rather, we had to use estimates of the standard deviation for the IART at each grade from other studies to estimate the effect sizes for this study.

Doebler and Mardis (1980–1981) compared a bilingual program in Choctaw with English-only instruction among 63 Choctaw second graders in Mississippi. All the subjects were native Choctaw speakers, and none was fluent in English. Exposure to English occurred only in the classroom, because children spoke Choctaw at home and on the playground. It should be noted that all students had been taught in Choctaw with ESL instruction in kindergarten and first grade. Seven classrooms participated in the study—four experimental and three control. The decision to participate as a bilingual or control classroom was left to the staff at each school. The bilingual program taught mathematics, reading, and science in the Choctaw language, with supplementary ESL instruction to teach English reading and language arts and reinforce content concepts taught in Choctaw. In the control condition, children were taught solely in English by certified teachers. Controlling for performance on a standardized measure of reading in English administered in the fall, there were no differences between the groups on the same measure in the spring of second grade. The analysis reported with the study did not take into account assignment at the classroom level, but instead treated students as the unit of assignment and, like other studies in the review, did not adjust standard errors for nesting effects. Finally, the study did not report sufficient information to allow estimation of the effect size and thus had to be excluded from the meta-analysis.

Exemplary Bilingual Programs. In the mid-1970s, the American Institutes for Research (AIR) produced a report on bilingual programs around the United States (Campeau et al., 1975). The studies included in that report are of interest, with the caveat that the AIR researchers were looking for exemplary bilingual programs. They began with 175 candidates and ultimately winnowed this number down to studies of 7 programs. Four studies in the report met our criteria for this review; they are described later. Three studies were excluded for the following reasons: Maine (no control group), Philadelphia (no control group), and Kingsville (no student outcome data reported).

A study in Corpus Christi, Texas, evaluated a bilingual program in three schools. The study was conducted with Mexican American native speakers of Spanish of low SES. The kindergarten program developed both English and Spanish oral language and reading readiness skills in the students, but the emphasis was on Spanish (90% of the instruction). In first grade, about 1 hour was devoted to Spanish reading and language arts and 2 hours to English reading and language arts. During Grades 2 to 4, Spanish and English reading continued to be developed. Bilingual teachers were used exclusively in kindergarten and first grade; in Grades 2 to 4, a paired model was used. The control group consisted of students in three different schools who received all their instruction in English. The students were approximately equal to control students with regard to SES. Equal numbers of students in both groups were native Spanish speakers (74%). In the 1972–1973 cohort, experimental and control classes were matched on both English and Spanish measures. Because results of kindergarten pretests for these first graders are not given, the findings should be interpreted with caution, because attrition over 2 years could have rendered the initially equivalent samples unequal. A second kindergarten cohort (1973–1974) receiving bilingual education was also compared with a control group receiving English-only instruction.

Another study included in the Campeau et al. (1975) report was conducted in Houston, Texas. Three cohorts of students in seven bilingual[7] and two English immersion schools were followed from kindergarten through third grade. The authors reported that "control groups were selected based on their similarity to the experimental groups in language, socio-economic level, and academic achievement" (p. 157). Instruction included a block of time devoted to Spanish reading and language arts. During the remainder of the day, instruction was in English for English-dominant and bilingual students. Spanish-dominant students received additional instruction in Spanish after the lessons had been presented in English. The authors note that attrition over the 4 years of the program was significant. For example, just 75 of the 290 kindergarten pupils enrolled in the bilingual program in 1969–1970 remained in the program in third grade.

A third study in Alice, Texas, also included in the Campeau et al. (1975) report, compared children placed in bilingual programs because of "English language problems, parent approval, and sufficient space" (p. 127). One control classroom at each grade level was composed of children whose oral language eligibility test scores matched those of the bilingual sample most closely. The authors report that no control student later entered a bilingual program or vice versa. The 1972–1973 group included 397 students in bilingual programs in Grades K to 3 and 102 control students; the 1973–1974 group included 504

---

[7]In 1973–1974, there were eight bilingual schools.

treatment students in Grades K to 4 and 136 controls. The bilingual program began with a focus on Spanish literacy skills in kindergarten, with some language arts instruction in English. By January of first grade, all children participated in reading instruction in English, and through to fifth grade, instruction was in equal amounts of Spanish and English. The authors note that some teachers taught one week in Spanish and the next week in English; others alternated the two every other day.

Finally, a one-year study carried out in Santa Fe, New Mexico, also included in the Campeau et al. (1975) report, examined the reading achievement of children in Grades 1 to 4. "The bilingual program added to the regular English program, a Spanish instructional component that complemented and reinforced the instruction in all content areas. Thus, students received a bilingual presentation of all the topics of study in the normal curriculum" (p. 92). In this particular district, parents chose whether to place their children in bilingual or English-only programs. Pretest scores were higher in the bilingual program in first grade, but not in the other three grades. Within each of the grade levels, a comparison was made from fall to spring of the given year.

As noted, the programs studied by Campeau et al. (1975) are not representative of all bilingual programs, because the authors focused by design on exemplary programs. A potential confound, moreover, is that we have no information about the English-only programs. If they were of inferior quality, the positive effects found for the bilingual programs may have been due to those programs' excellent instructional methods, rather than the language of instruction. Because several of these studies did have well-matched control groups and met our review criteria, however, they were included in this review.

Studies With Secondary School Learners

Two studies qualifying for our review evaluated programs that introduced Spanish-language instruction to language-minority students in the secondary grades. Both used random assignment to conditions.

Covey (1973) randomly assigned to bilingual or English-only instructional conditions 200 Mexican American ninth graders attending an urban high school in the southwestern United States. The students were selected from a group of 379 students who had initially been identified to participate. "To be included in the study, students had to demonstrate limited ability to speak English, come from a bilingual home, manifest a reading deficiency, and possess a deficiency in English and mathematics" (p. 56). The experimental intervention (i.e., the instructional techniques used with the students) is not described in any detail. The author defines *bilingual education* as "the use of two languages, one of which is Spanish and the other English, as mediums of instruction for the same student population in an organized instructional program, consisting of English, mathematics and reading," and a *regular program* as one in which "one language is used for the medium of instruction for the same student population in a well organized program which encompasses English, mathematics and reading" (p. 14). No further information is provided about the programs. The groups' scores were nearly identical at pretest on the Stanford Diagnostic Reading Test, as expected given assignment at random to treatment and control. However, the random assignment process is not discussed, making it impossible to evaluate the assignment process independently of the observed pretest mean equivalence.

It should be noted that pretests were not used as covariates in the analysis of posttests, lowering overall power for the tests of treatment effects reported in the study. At the same time, the fact that the study failed to take into account the nesting of students for instruction would lead to underestimation of standard errors, a problem affecting all other studies reported on in this review, and one that would have the opposite effect on power. It should also be pointed out for potential future reviewers that the reported analyses of within-group pre- and postchanges are incorrect as reported, in that they do not take into account non-independence of observations on the same students over time. This problem also leads to an inflation of the Type I error rate. Although the analyses reported in Covey (1973) are incorrect, the report includes sufficient information to estimate the effect size for use in the meta-analysis. That is, the problems with the reported analyses do not affect the estimate of the standardized posttest mean difference, although the nesting problem will tend to lead to underestimation of the standard error of the effect size. Again, this problem was present in all reviewed studies.

Kaufman (1968) evaluated a program in which low-achieving Spanish-speaking seventh graders were randomly assigned to bilingual or English-only instructional conditions in two New York junior high schools. One school participated in the program for one year and one participated for 2 years. As the author notes, "at each school, students in the treatment and control groups received equivalent instruction in English" (p. 523). For 45 minutes a day (3 days a week in School B and 4 days a week in School A), however, students in the treatment group received instruction in standard Spanish, with emphasis on specific reading skills in Spanish, whereas the control group received extra periods of art, music, and health education conducted in English. Some people have criticized this study, because students in the bilingual group received additional instruction in Spanish focused on reading, whereas students in the control group received additional instruction in English but focused on music, art, and health. The criticism assumes that the appropriate control is to provide an equivalent amount of additional time in English literacy instruction. However, if the study were designed in this way, the groups would not have comparable amounts of English literacy instruction. The analyses reported in the study included adjustment of posttest means for covariates other than the pretest, including language-based IQ, nonverbal IQ, age, and capacity. The study did not report unadjusted posttreatment means, however; because of random assignment, these would be expected to equal the adjusted posttreatment means in the long run. Unfortunately, the study reported outcomes in terms of grade equivalent scores and failed to report information on clustering of students in classrooms. It should also be noted that the average grade equivalent scores for students were roughly 3 to 4 years below the current grade-level placement in both groups.

HERITAGE LANGUAGE STUDIES

As noted, our review also included one study that examined the effectiveness of programs in which children who are proficient in the societal language (English in the United States) receive instruction in their heritage language. Typically, these are children whose parents also speak the societal language in the home but would like their children to be fluent in their heritage language as well.

Morgan (1971) carried out a study with almost 200 children of French-speaking parents in rural Louisiana. Fifty-four first-grade classes made up the population. Classes were either bilingual (16) or English (38) depending on the teacher's competence in French. The bilingual group participating in the study included all the students in bilingual classes whose parents scored above the median on a questionnaire crafted to assess level of proficiency in French (93 students); the monolingual group consisted of 100 students in English-only classes randomly selected from a pool of 199 students whose parents spoke above the median level of French. The first graders were followed for one year. In the bilingual classes, children were taught in both French and English. The bilingual program was designed to teach French through the oral–aural approach, and French cultural appreciation was developed through songs, plays, and real objects. Formal, structured French-language instruction was conducted for a 30-minute period each day as part of the 2—hour period of language arts instruction; the remaining 90 minutes were devoted to English language arts. All other basic instruction was in English, but casual conversation in French was allowed and encouraged. Children in the monolingual group received all of their instruction in English, and French conversation was not encouraged. These children also received 120 minutes of language arts instruction in English. At the beginning of first grade, the two groups were virtually identical on English tests of mental abilities and readiness. At the end of first grade, students were compared on four English reading measures.

SUMMARY

To evaluate the impact of bilingual education as compared with English-only instruction, we analyzed the estimated effect sizes from the 15 studies by using the *Comprehensive Meta-Analysis (CMA) Version 2* software (Borenstein, 2005). Appendix 14.E provides a table with results for each study, sample, outcome, and grade that went into the meta-analysis. For all studies, positive effect sizes indicate a difference favoring bilingual education, whereas negative effects indicate a difference favoring English-only instruction. In estimating the average effect size, we first corrected the reported effect sizes for small-sample bias; that is, we converted the effect sizes to Hedges' g^U through the CMA software (Hedges, 1981). Each effect size was also weighted by the inverse of its variance, which is a function of both sample size in the treatment and control groups and the effect size. In averaging across effect sizes, we treated each study sample as the unit of analysis. Thus, the 15 studies yielded 71 effect sizes across 26 samples. For the sake of computing average effect sizes, we averaged across different reading outcomes and grades within the same study sample to derive a weighted average for that study sample. These weighted average effect sizes for each study sample appear in Table 14.1[8] along with their estimated standard errors and 95%

---

[8]Tables appear throughout chapter.

TABLE 14-1.
Effect size statistics for individual studies

					Statistics for Each Study				
RCT	Study Name	Subgroup Within Study	Hedges' g^u	Standard Error	Variance	Lower Limit	Upper Limit	Z Value	p Value
Yes	Maldonado, 1994	Sample 1	2.1212	0.5440	0.2959	1.0550	3.1874	3.8992	.0001
	Saldate et al., 1985	Sample 1	-0.2829	0.2521	0.0636	-0.7770	0.2112	-1.1223	.2617
	de la Garza, 1985	Sample 1	0.1910	0.2194	0.0482	-0.2391	0.6211	0.8703	.3841
	Ramírez et al., 1991	Sample 1	0.1774	0.1484	0.0220	-0.1135	0.4684	1.1953	.2320
	Ramírez et al., 1991	Sample 2	0.0947	0.0954	0.0091	-0.0923	0.2817	0.9930	.3207
	Ramírez et al., 1991	Sample 3	0.0796	0.1049	0.0110	-0.1259	0.2852	0.7591	.4478
	Valladolid, 1991	Sample 1	-0.6052	0.1968	0.0387	-0.9909	-0.2196	-3.0758	.0021
	Alvarez, 1975	Sample 1	-0.1863	0.2390	0.0571	-0.6548	0.2822	-0.7795	.4357
	Alvarez, 1975	Sample 2	-0.2541	0.2389	0.0571	-0.7224	0.2142	-1.0634	.2876
	Campeau et al.,1975	Sample 2	1.8279	0.2426	0.0589	1.3523	2.3034	7.5340	.0000
	Campeau et al., 1975	Sample 3	1.3929	0.2628	0.0691	0.8778	1.9080	5.2999	.0000
	Campeau et al., 1975	Sample 5	2.6311	0.2230	0.0497	2.1941	3.0681	11.8001	.0000
	Campeau et al., 1975	Sample 6	0.2420	0.1357	0.0184	-0.0239	0.5080	1.7837	.0745
	Campeau et al., 1975	Sample 7	0.8540	0.1585	0.0251	0.5434	1.1646	5.3889	.0000
	Campeau et al., 1975	Sample 8	0.4553	0.1716	0.0294	0.1191	0.7916	2.6540	.0080
	Cohen et al., 1976	Sample 1	-0.1741	0.3904	0.1524	-0.9392	0.5911	-0.4459	.6557
	Cohen et al., 1976	Sample 2	-1.1518	0.4591	0.2108	-2.0516	-0.2519	-2.5087	.0121
	Cohen et al., 1976	Sample 3	-1.5981	0.5539	0.3068	-2.6838	-0.5125	-2.8851	.0039
	Danoff et al., 1978	Sample 1	-0.2621	0.0690	0.0048	-0.3974	-0.1269	-3.7992	.0001
Yes	Huzar, 1973	Sample 1	0.0136	0.2201	0.0485	-0.4178	0.4451	0.0619	.9506
Yes	Kaufman, 1968	Sample 1	0.0477	0.2355	0.0555	-0.4139	0.5092	0.2025	.8396
Yes	Kaufman, 1968	Sample 2	0.4696	0.2989	0.0893	-0.1161	1.0554	1.5714	.1161

(Continued)

TABLE 14-1.
(Continued)

				Statistics for Each Study					
RCT	Study Name	Subgroup Within Study	Hedges' g^u	Standard Error	Variance	Lower Limit	Upper Limit	Z Value	p Value
	Maldonado, 1977	Sample 1	0.3580	0.1845	0.0340	- 0.0036	0.7195	1.9404	.0523
Yes	Plante, 1976	Sample 1	0.7750	0.4097	0.1679	-0.0281	1.5780	1.8915	.0586
Yes	Covey, 1973	Sample 1	0.6583	0.1555	0.0242	0.3534	0.9631	4.2323	.0000
	Morgan, 1971	Sample 1	0.2541	0.1441	0.0208	-0.0283	0.5365	1.7635	.0778

Note: STANDARD errors do not take into account potential effects of clustering within studies. Confidence intervals, z-values, and p-values should be interpreted with caution.

confidence intervals. These weighted averages were then averaged to estimate the mean effect size and its standard error under each of two models: a fixed effects model and a random effects model. The weighted average across all study samples appears in Table 14.2, along with an estimate of the standard error, the lower and upper limits of a 95% confidence interval, and a test that the mean effect size equals zero. In addition to computing the average effect size across all studies, we also computed the mean separately for the studies that used randomization. This estimate appears in Table 14.2 as well. Finally, because Maldonado (1994) produced a somewhat larger effect size than the remaining randomized controlled trials (RCTs), and because information reported in Maldonado (1994) was internally inconsistent indicating possible errors in our estimate of the effect size, we also computed the mean effect size separately for the RCTs without Maldonado to assess the overall impact of this one large effect size on the mean estimate and conclusion for the RCTs. These estimates appear in the final two rows of Table 14.2.

Scanning Table 14.1 reveals a range of effect sizes from negative to positive, with at least some statistically significant positive and negative effect sizes (i.e., effect sizes in either direction that are statistically different from 0). Overall, 16 of the 26 estimated effect sizes are positive, 8 are negative, and 2 are effectively 0 (i.e., between 0 and .05). At the same time, only 7 of the 16 positive effect sizes have confidence intervals that exclude 0, and only 4 of the 8 negative effect sizes exclude 0. These observations suggest that the effect sizes vary somewhat across the studies in this review, and, in fact, a test for heterogeneity corroborates that conclusion ($Q = 323.7$, $df = 25$, $p < .0001$). Although the weighted average of the effect sizes is significantly different from 0 (mean = .18, $SE = .033$, $p < .0001$ under the fixed effects model; mean = .33, $SE = 0.127$, $p = .011$ under the random effects model; Table 14.2), the test for heterogeneity indicates that the average effect size may not describe very well the collection of effect sizes. Thus, we separately examined those five studies that used random assignment of students to condition.

Separate examination of the five studies that involved randomization (6 samples and 12 individual effect sizes) produced a somewhat larger weighted average effect size that was also statistically different from 0 under both the fixed and random effects models (mean = 0.45, $SE = .11$, $p < .0001$ under the fixed effects model; mean = .54, $SE = 0.21$, $p = .012$ under the random effects model). In addition, the test for heterogeneity again showed that the effect sizes were not consistent across the collection of studies ($Q = 18.7$, $df = 5$, $p = .002$), although in this case four of six effect sizes are positive and two fall between 0 and 0.05. That is, all effect sizes are in the same direction, but they vary somewhat in magnitude. Although these findings suggest a moderate effect of bilingual education, examination of the effect sizes included in this subset analysis indicates one large effect size of 2.12 ($SE = .54$) associated with Maldonado (1994) that we know to be problematic. Results reported in that study are internally inconsistent, in that different results reported for the same outcome and sample give different effect sizes, as described in Appendix 14.D. The effect size used in the analysis is based on the reported means and standard deviations in the paper, but assuming the reported standard deviations were actually standard errors. That is, we multiplied the reported standard deviations by the square root of the sample size. An effect size computed on the reported standard deviations would have been slightly over 7.0 in magnitude, a highly unrealistic result and one not at all consistent with other information

TABLE 14.2
Statistics for Average Effect Sizes

Model	Studies Include	Hedges' g^{u}	Standard Error	Variance	Lower Limit	Upper Limit	Z Value	p Value
Fixed	All studies	0.1835	0.0329	0.0011	0.1191	0.2479	5.5838	.0000
Random	All studies	0.3251	0.1271	0.0162	0.0760	0.5743	2.5575	.0105
Fixed	RCTs	0.4515	0.0997	0.0099	0.2560	0.6470	4.5273	.0000
Random	RCTs	0.5380	0.2140	0.0458	0.1185	0.9574	2.5136	.0119
Fixed	RCTs except Maldonado, 1994	0.3934	0.1014	0.0103	0.1946	0.5923	3.8782	.0001
Random	RCTs except Maldonado, 1994	0.3650	0.1638	0.0268	0.0440	0.6859	2.2287	.0258

Statistics for Average Effect Size

reported in the paper. Specifically, Maldonado (1994) also reports the obtained
t-test result of the difference between the means of the treatment and control
groups, and this result could not have resulted from the means and standard deviations reported in the text, because it is substantially too small. In addition, it
appears that the pre- and posttest means for the control group have been reversed.
The effect size based on the reported *t* statistic in Maldonado (1994) is still large
($d = 1.72$, compared with $d = 2.25$ prior to correction to Hedges' $g^u = 2.12$). Insofar
as it is impossible to determine which reported numbers are in error, although it
appears that the standard deviations are too small, we reanalyzed the RCTs after
eliminating Maldonado (1994) from the collection of studies to assess the magnitude of the treatment effect in the remaining four randomized trials. Here again
the weighted average of the treatment effects indicates a statistically significant,
moderately sized, average treatment effect regardless of which statistical model is
assumed for the distribution of effect sizes (mean = .39, $SE = .10$, $p < .0001$ under
the fixed effects model; mean = .365, $SE = 0.16$, $p = .026$ under the random effects
model). In addition, there is some remaining evidence of heterogeneity in the
effect sizes ($Q = 8.964$, $df = 4$, $p = .062$). Although it would certainly be possible to
take an alternative approach to dealing with the inconsistencies in the reported
data for Maldonado (1994), eliminating the study is the most conservative.
Eliminating Maldonado from the collection of all 26 effect sizes has a minimal
effect on the fixed effect estimate of the average effect size, which drops from .180
to .176, and a slightly larger, but still relatively negligible effect on the random
effects estimate, which drops from .33 to .28. Both effects remain statistically significant. Finally, because each of these analyses involves weighting by the standard
error of the effect sizes, which we know to be in error because of the likely effects
of clustering in individual studies, we also computed one sample *t*-statistics for
each of the three collections of studies. These tests completely ignore the standard
errors of the effect sizes and rely only on the collection of effect sizes across the
studies. The computed *t*-statistics were as follows: All studies $t(25) = 1.70$; RCTs,
$t(5) = 1.97$: RCT without Maldonado, $t(4) = 2.26$.

In summary, it seems reasonably safe to conclude that bilingual education
has a positive effect on English reading outcomes that are small to moderate in
size. The best evidence supporting this conclusion is that taken from the randomized studies, either with or without Maldonado (1994) included in the collection, or included with some adjustment to the estimated effect size to address
the inconsistency across the reported results of the study. It seems equally safe
to conclude that many questions regarding how to make bilingual instruction
maximally effective for students, and the factors that moderate this effectiveness, remain unanswered by studies reviewed in this chapter. We would have
liked to conduct an exhaustive examination of potential moderator variables in
the analyses conducted here, but, because of limited resources and time, could
not do so. To the extent that the studies provided relevant information, such an
analysis could yield some benefit to understanding the research literature and
instructional effectiveness.

The majority of the studies included in our review employed a matched design,
in which students came from the same or comparable schools in the same or comparable districts or used student-level covariates to postequate students on important demographic and/or achievement characteristics. The majority of these
studies also were conducted with language-minority students of elementary

school age. Most were longitudinal, and children had transitioned out of the bilingual program by posttest. A few studies were one-year studies of bilingual education, with posttests being administered before children had transitioned from native- to English-language instruction. These studies are included in this chapter, because they shed some light on the development of literacy skills for these learners in different instructional conditions. Because the programs had not been completed by children in the study, however, they are of limited value for making claims about the overall effectiveness of bilingual education programs.

In addressing the inherent problem of selection bias, the studies of Huzar (1973) and Plante (1976) are particularly important, despite taking place a quarter of a century or more ago. Both were multiyear experiments for which, because of the use of random assignment, we can rule out selection bias as an alternative explanation for the findings. Both started with children in the early elementary grades and followed them for 2 to 3 years. It is interesting that both used a model that would be unusual today—paired bilingual reading instruction provided by different teachers in Spanish and English, with transition to all-English instruction by second or third grade. The use of both Spanish and English reading instruction each day resembles the experience of Spanish-dominant students in two-way bilingual programs (see Calderón & Minaya-Rowe, 2003) more than typical transitional bilingual models, which delay English reading instruction to second or third grade.

Finally, with respect to language-minority students experiencing reading difficulties, Maldonado's (1994) study of language-minority students with learning disabilities found dramatically higher achievement gains for children transitioned over a 3-year period from Spanish to English than for those taught only in English. Although results reported for Maldonado (1994) are not internally consistent with respect to the point estimate of the treatment effect, both sets of reported results indicate a large, positive effect.

FRENCH IMMERSION STUDIES

As discussed earlier, although the studies conducted in Canada that examined the impact of French immersion programs are not directly relevant to the effectiveness of bilingual programs for language-minority learners learning the societal language, they are of value in gaining a broader understanding of the role of context in literacy development. Several French immersion studies (e.g., Barik & Swain, 1978; Genesee et al., 1976) have played an important role in debates about bilingual education. In these studies, English-speaking children (Anglophones) were taught entirely or primarily in French in the early elementary years. Rossell and Baker (1996) emphasize that these studies are examples of structured immersion, the approach favored in their review. However, Willig (1985) and other reviewers excluded them because the Canadian context differs significantly from that of the United States, as elaborated in the background section of the chapter. Moreover, in contrast to U.S. studies, the focus of the Canadian studies was primarily on whether French immersion hinders the English-language development of native English speakers. This would be analogous to determining whether English immersion hinders the development of Spanish in Spanish-speaking language-minority students.

Three studies (Barik & Swain, 1975, 1978; Barik, Swain, & Nwanunobi, 1977) met our methodological criteria for inclusion in this chapter. Each was conducted with children in the elementary school years.

Barik and Swain (1975) studied a French immersion program in Ottawa. One cohort of students was followed from kindergarten through second grade. One group of Anglophone children was taught entirely in French in kindergarten and first grade, with 60 minutes of daily English instruction in second grade, in comparison with Anglophone children taught only in English. The children were matched with respect to age, IQ, and school readiness measures administered in kindergarten. On a measure of English reading administered at the end of second grade, there were no differences between the groups. A second cohort of students was followed from kindergarten through first grade. All were Anglophone students, some in French immersion classes and some in regular English classes. At the end of first grade, the French immersion students scored significantly lower than the comparison group on all three English-language measures (word knowledge, word discrimination, and reading). It should be noted, however, that the French immersion students had received no instruction in English at this point. A third cohort included two groups of Anglophone students at the end of kindergarten. As with the other cohorts, one group was in French immersion and the other in English-only instruction. At the end of kindergarten, there were no reliable differences on either the school readiness or achievement test. The immersion group scored much higher than the comparison group on French comprehension. The comparison group had received 20 to 30 minutes a day of French as a second language.

In another evaluation of French immersion (see Barik & Swain, 1978; Barik, Swain, & Nwanunobi, 1977), the English-language performance of three cohorts of children in a bilingual program, ranging from third through sixth grades, was evaluated for 2 consecutive years in comparison with that of a cohort who received all instruction in English. The children in the French immersion program were instructed in French in mathematics, music, science, and French language arts for half of the day and were instructed in English in English language arts, physical education, and other content areas for the other half of the day. The comparison group came from a demographically similar school located near the school from which the intervention group students were selected. The comparison students were instructed only in English. For the sample that was followed from third through fourth grade, the children in the bilingual program had higher scores at fourth grade on measures of English reading comprehension and English vocabulary. For the sample followed from fourth through fifth grade, there were no differences between groups at fifth grade on measures of English reading. Similarly, for the group followed from fifth through sixth grade, there were no differences between the groups at sixth grade on measures of English reading.

The findings from these French immersion studies paint a consistent picture: At least for the overwhelmingly middle-class students involved, French immersion had no negative effect on English reading achievement, and it gave students an opportunity to acquire facility in a second language. The relevance of these findings to the U.S. situation is in (a) suggesting that similar second-language immersion programs, as well as two-way bilingual programs, for English-proficient children are not likely to hinder English reading development; and (b) providing a better understanding of how context influences learning.

METHODOLOGICAL ISSUES

Research on language of instruction faces a number of inherent issues beyond those typical of other research on educational programs. We address these issues here, as well as briefly in chapter 13.

First, many of the studies reported on in this chapter failed to account for differences in the amount of time language-minority students instructed in a bilingual setting had to acquire English before being evaluated against children instructed only in English; the point at which students are evaluated in their second language has an impact on the study findings. For example, imagine that a bilingual program teaches Spanish-dominant English-language learners primarily in Spanish in Grades K to 2 and then gradually transitions them to English, completing the process by fourth grade. If this program is compared with an English-only program, at what grade level is it legitimate to assess the children in English? Clearly, a test in second grade may be meaningless, because the bilingual program children have not been taught to read in English. At the end of third grade, the bilingual program students have been partially transitioned, but have they had enough time to become fully proficient? As a specific example, Saldate et al. (1985) studied Spanish-dominant students in bilingual and immersion schools. At the end of second grade, the bilingual students, who had not yet transitioned to English, scored lower than the immersion group in English reading, although the differences were not statistically significant. A year later, after transition, the bilingual group scored substantially higher than the immersion group in English reading. Some would argue that even the end of fourth grade would be too soon to make such a comparison fairly, because in the bilingual program, children would need a reasonable time to transfer their Spanish reading skills to English (see e.g., Hakuta, Butler, & Witt, 2000).

A longitudinal study by Gersten and Woodward (1995), not included in this chapter, because both groups received Spanish instruction, sheds some light on this issue. This study was carried out with Spanish-dominant language-minority learners in 10 El Paso, Texas, elementary schools. Five schools used a paired bilingual model, in which all subjects were taught in English, but Spanish instruction was also provided each day—for 90 minutes in first grade, declining to 30 minutes in fourth grade. The other schools followed a transitional bilingual model, which involved mainly Spanish instruction, with one hour per day of ESOL instruction, with a gradual transition to English being completed only in fourth or fifth grade. The children were well matched demographically at entry into first grade and scored near zero on a measure of English-language proficiency. In Grades 4, 5, 6, and 7, students from the two groups were compared in English reading by using the Iowa Tests of Basic Skills (ITBS). On total reading, the paired bilingual students scored significantly higher than the transitional bilingual students in fourth grade, but the effects diminished in fifth grade and were very small in sixth and seventh grades. Similar results were seen on tests of language and vocabulary. This pattern of results is probably due to the fact that, in fourth and fifth grades, the transitional bilingual students had not completed their transition to English; when they had done so, by sixth grade, their reading performance was nearly identical to that of the paired bilingual group. The overall effect size for differences was small (.07)

Other problems that characterize this research relate to selection bias. Children end up in transitional bilingual education or English immersion by processes that could have a significant impact on the outcomes, regardless of language of instruction. For example, Spanish-dominant students may be assigned to Spanish or English instruction within a school because of parental preferences in ways that have an impact on outcomes. Parents who select English programs may differ consistently from those who select Spanish programs. A parent who selects English may be less likely to be planning to return to a Spanish-speaking country, for example, or may feel more positive about assimilation. Likewise, a parent who selects Spanish may be from a home where little English is spoken. In addition, schools may assign individual children to native-language or English programs because of their perceived or assessed competence. Native-language instruction is often seen as an easier, more appropriate placement for language-minority students who are more dominant in their first than in their second language.

Further, bilingual programs are more likely to exist in schools with high proportions of English-language learners, and this is another potential source of bias. For example, Ramírez et al. (1991) found that schools using a late-exit bilingual approach had much higher proportions of English-language learners than early-exit bilingual schools, and English immersion schools had the smallest proportion of such learners. Regardless of the language of instruction, children in schools with high proportions of language-minority students, especially those from the same language background, are probably conversing less with native English speakers both in and out of school than might be the case in an integrated school that uses English for all students, because its proportion of language-minority students is low. A related issue in some evaluations is that children in the bilingual program consist of only those who have not transitioned out of the bilingual program (and thus those who have taken longer to become proficient in English); these students are compared with those who have been instructed only in English, as well as those who have transitioned out of bilingual programs. The study by Danoff et al. (1978), for example, has been criticized for comparing children in transitional bilingual education programs with those who have transitioned out of these programs.

A source of bias not unique to studies of bilingual education, but important in this literature, is the *file drawer problem*—the fact that studies showing no differences are less likely to be published or otherwise to come to light. This is a particular problem for studies with small sample sizes, which are unlikely to be published if they show no differences. The best antidote to this problem is to search for dissertations and technical reports, which are more likely to present the data regardless of the findings obtained (see Cooper, 1998).

Finally, many studies do not provide sufficient detail about the interventions to demonstrate just what is working with these students. Moreover, no study we reviewed collected fidelity data on the bilingual program or carefully assessed the nature and quality of the instruction provided to students.

OVERALL SUMMARY

In summary, there is no indication that bilingual instruction impedes academic achievement in either the native language or English, whether for language-minority students, students receiving heritage language instruction, or those enrolled in French immersion programs. Where differences were observed, on average they favored the students in a bilingual program. The meta-analytic results clearly suggest a positive effect for bilingual instruction that is moderate in size. This conclusion held up across the entire collection of studies and within the subset of studies that used random assignment of students to conditions. Supporting the argument for high-quality studies in this area, those studies in which there was random assignment to conditions (Covey, 1973; Huzar, 1973; Kaufman, 1968; Maldonado, 1994; Plante, 1976) found significant differences in favor of the students receiving native-language instruction, with effect sizes ranging from small (.01) to large (.77), exclusive of the very large effect in Maldonado (1994), and a significant average effect size across the collection of studies, regardless of which statistical model is assumed for the distribution of effect sizes (fixed effects model or random effects model).

What is also of interest and worthy of further research is that three of the studies (Huzar, 1973; Maldonado, 1994; Plante, 1976) whose results favored bilingual programs evaluated models that are a variation on the more common models of bilingual education. Each of these studies was conducted with children in the early elementary years, and one (Maldonado, 1994) with a specific sample of Spanish speakers receiving special education services for learning disabilities. Both Huzar (1973) and Plante (1976) used paired bilingual models in which children were taught reading in both English and Spanish daily, at different times of the day. In the study by Maldonado (1994), the children receiving bilingual special education were taught to read in Spanish for the first year, in Spanish and English in the second year, and in English in the third year—a more rapid transition than is typical of some transitional bilingual programs. As a group, these studies suggest an intriguing possibility: English-language learners may learn to read best if taught in both their native language and English from early in the process of formal schooling. Rather than confusing children, as some have feared, reading instruction in a familiar language may serve as a bridge to success in English because decoding, sound blending, and generic comprehension strategies clearly transfer between languages that use phonetic orthographies, such as Spanish, French, and English (see chap. 9, this volume; August, 2002; August & Hakuta, 1997; Fitzgerald, 1995a, 1995b; García, 2000).

Only two studies of secondary programs met our inclusion criteria, but both were high-quality randomized experiments. Covey (1973) found substantial positive effects of Spanish instruction for low-achieving language-minority ninth graders, and Kaufman (1968) found mixed but slightly positive effects of a similar approach with low-achieving language-minority seventh graders.

In addition to the few randomized experiments included in this chapter, the majority of studies with language-minority students, as well as the heritage language and French immersion studies, used a matched design with experimental and control groups. Taken together, the findings from these studies suggest that there are no negative effects and, in many cases, positive effects of bilingual approaches to instruction.

As noted previously, research on language of instruction may suffer from the tendency for journals to publish only articles that find significant differences. Another form of bias is the selection of exemplary programs for research purposes (e.g., the collection of studies included in Campeau et al., 1975). Given that dissertations and technical reports are less likely to suffer from such bias, we included them in our review.

Overall, where differences between two instructional conditions were found in the studies reviewed, these differences typically favored the bilingual instruction condition. This is the case for studies conducted with students in both elementary and secondary schools, and with students possessing a range of abilities. For example, the results of the one study designed to evaluate bilingual instruction for a specific population—Spanish speakers receiving special education services—favored a bilingual approach for these learners. Moreover, children in the bilingual programs studied not only developed facility with English literacy to the same extent as their peers educated in English, but also developed literacy skills in their native language. Thus, they achieved the advantage of being bilingual and biliterate.

Because of the inherent methodological problems cited in this chapter, an adequate study comparing bilingual and monolingual approaches would randomly assign a large number of children to be taught in English or their native language; pretest them on outcomes of interest, as well as on language proficiency in their first and second languages; and follow them long enough for the latest-transitioning children in the bilingual condition to have completed their transition to English and have been taught long enough in English to permit a fair comparison. In addition, researchers would carefully document the nature and quality of the instruction being provided. Unfortunately, only a few small studies of this kind have ever been conducted. As a result, the findings of studies that have compared bilingual and English-only approaches must continue to be interpreted with great caution.[9]

---

[9]IES is currently funding three evaluation studies employing experimental or quasi-experimental methods and will compare outcomes for students instructed in English only with those instructed with some use of the native language.

APPENDIX 14.A

TABLE 14.A.1

Evaluation Studies Cited in Other Reviews, But Not Included in This Review

Citation	Reasons for Rejection From This Review	Willig, 1985	Rossell & Baker, 1996	Greene, 1997	Slavin & Cheung, 2004
American Institutes for Research, 1975	Unavailable		X		
Ames & Bicks, 1978	No appropriate experimental group	X			
Ariza, 1988	Publication type: conference paper		X		
Bacon et al., 1982	No pretest measures		X	X	X
Balasubramonian et al., 1973	4 months between pre- and posttests		X		
Barclay, 1969	Unavailable		X		
Bates, 1970	No pretest measures, no literacy outcomes		X		
Becker & Gersten, 1982	Not an evaluation of bilingual programs				
Bruck et al., 1977	No adequate pretests		X		X
Burkheimer et al., 1989	No appropriate control group		X		
Carsrud & Curtis, 1979, 1980	No appropriate control group	X	X		
Ciriza, 1990	Unavailable		X		
Clerc et al., 1987	Unavailable		X		
Cohen, 1975	Publication type: book	X	X		X
Cottrell, 1971	No appropriate control group		X		

(Continued)

TABLE 14.A.1
(Continued)

Citation	Reasons for Rejection From This Review	Willig, 1985	Rossell & Baker, 1996	Greene, 1997	Slavin & Cheung, 2004
Curiel, 1979	Redundant with Curiel, 1980; no data while students in bilingual education				
Curiel et al., 1980	No pretest measures; no data while students were in bilingual education		X		
Danoff et al., 1977a, 1977b, 1978		X			
Day & Shapson, 1988	6-week duration of bilingual instruction		X		X
Educational Operations Concepts, 1991	Unavailable		X		
El Paso ISD, 1987	No appropriate pretest measure		X		
El Paso ISD, 1990	Redundant with El Paso, 1992		X		
El Paso ISD, 1992	Comparison of two bilingual programs		X		
Elizondo de Weffer, 1972	No literacy measures		X		
Genesee, Lambert, & Tucker, 1979	No adequate pretests		X		
Genesee & Lambert, 1983	No appropriate control group		X		X

(Continued)

TABLE 14.A.1
(Continued)

Citation	Reasons for Rejection From This Review	Willig, 1985	Rossell & Baker, 1996	Greene, 1997	Slavin & Cheung, 2004
Genesee et al., 1989	No adequate pretests		X		X
Gersten, 1985	No appropriate control group		X		
Lambert & Tucker, 1972	Publication type: book		X		X
Layden, 1972	Only 10-week interval between pre- and posttests				
Legarreta, 1979	No literacy outcomes	X	X		
Lum, 1971	No literacy outcomes	X	X		
Malherbe, 1946	No appropriate control group		X		
Matthews, 1979	No specificity about native-language instruction		X		
McConnell, 1980a, 1980b	Prospective case study		X		
McSpadden, 1979	Unavailable	X	X		
McSpadden, 1980	Unavailable	X	X		
Medina & Escamilla, 1992	No literacy outcomes		X		
Meléndez, 1980	No appropriate experimental group		X		
Moore & Parr, 1978	Mixed Spanish- and English-dominant students		X		

(Continued)

TABLE 14.A.1
(Continued)

Citation	Reasons for Rejection From This Review	Willig, 1985	Rossell & Baker, 1996	Greene, 1997	Slavin & Cheung, 2004
Olesini, 1971	Unavailable	X			
Pena-Hughes & Solis, 1980	Unavailable	X	X		
Powers, 1978	No pretest measures		X	X	
Prewitt-Díaz, 1979	17-week interval between pre- and posttests		X		
Ramos et al., 1967	English as a foreign language		X		
Rossell, 1990	Book chapter		X	X	
Rothfarb et al., 1987	Both groups exposed to formal Spanish instruction		X	X	
Skoczylas, 1972	No literacy outcomes	X	X	X	
Stebbins et al., 1977	No specificity about native-language instruction	X	X		
Stern, 1975	Confounds with respect to instruction; no appropriate comparison groups	X			
Teschner, 1990	Unavailable		X		
Vásquez, 1990	No pretest controls		X		
Yap et al., 1988	No appropriate experimental groups		X		
Zirkel, 1972	No literacy outcomes	X	X		

APPENDIX 14.B: CODING SHEET FOR EVALUATION STUDIES

To determine study disposition, please answer each of the following questions:

		Yes	No
1.	The study		
	a. compared language-minority children.[10]	o	o
	b. taught literacy.[11]	o	o
	c. was in classes/programs that used some native language.	o	o
	d. was against classes/programs that were taught in English.[12]	o	o

Note that the native-language group cannot be compared against tabled normative information.

	Yes	No
2. English is the societal language (except in parts of Canada where French is the societal language).	o	o
3. If no to #1, the study is based in Canada and compared…		
a. English-dominant students acquiring literacy in French as a second language.	o	o
b. to English-dominant students learning mostly in English.	o	o
4. Random assignment to conditions was used.	o	o
5. If no to #4, a control or comparison group was used and there was some assessment of comparability prior to onset of the time interval over which the inference is being made (e.g., a pretest was used).[13]	o	o
6. The language-minority students in the sample are either at least 50% of the sample or the outcome data are disaggregated by language minority status (except for French immersion studies).	o	o
7. The interval between the pre- and posttests is at least 6 months.	o	o

Study is accepted if:

- Yes to all parts of Question 1 OR yes to all parts of Question 3 AND
- Yes for 2, AND
- Yes to 4 or 5, AND
- Yes to 6 and 7.

If study is ACCEPTED, answer Question 8

8. Serious confounds exist in the design of
   the research that prevent effects from being
   reasonably attributed to the treatment
   variables of interest.[14]

If yes, please explain:

---

[10]Language-minority students are students who come from a home where a language other than English is spoken. For the purposes of our work, we also include native Hawaiian children, Alaska natives, and American Indians even if the home language is not specified.

[11]Literacy includes reading as well as skills related to reading such as writing, vocabulary, and comprehension. Studies of oral language proficiency alone are not included.

[12]Note that some English immersion classes use small amounts of the native language to clarify concepts. This still constitutes an English-only class or program.

[13]Some studies consider tests administered at the end of the year as pretests. However, such tests are not considered as pretests for our coding purposes.

[14]For example, a study that compares two programs that both use some native language instruction (Carlisle & Beeman, 2000) would be excluded, as would a study (Curiel, 1980) that does not use random assignment or include pretest data or a description of the control group.

APPENDIX 14.C

TABLE 14.C.1
Evaluation Studies Included in the Present Review and Other Reviews

Study	Characteristics	Willig, 1985	Rossell & Baker, 1996	Greene, 1997	Slavin & Cheung, 2004
Alvarez, 1975	Elementary school; matched design		X		X
Campeau et al., 1975	Elementary school; matched design				X
Cohen et al., 1976	Elementary school; matched design		X		
Covey, 1973	Secondary school; random assignment			X	X
Danoff et al., 1978	Elementary school; matched design	X	X	X	
de La Garza & Medina, 1985	Elementary school; matched design	X	X		
Doebler & Mardis, 1980–81*	Elementary school; matched design				X
Huzar, 1973	Elementary school; random assignment	X	X	X	X

(Continued)

TABLE 14.C.1
(Continued)

Study	Characteristics	Willig, 1985	Rossell & Baker, 1996	Greene, 1997	Slavin & Cheung, 2004
Kaufman, 1968	Secondary school; random assignment	X			
Lampman, 1973*	Elementary School; Matched Design		X	X	X
Maldonado, 1977	Elementary school; matched design		X		
Maldonado, 1994	Elementary school; random assignment		X		X
Plante, 1976	Elementary school; random assignment				X
Ramirez, 1991	Elementary school; matched design				X
Saldate et al., 1985	Elementary school; matched design		X	X	X
Valladolid, 1991	Elementary school; matched design		X		

TABLE 14.C.1
(Continued)

Study	Characteristics	Willig, 1985	Rossell & Baker, 1996	Greene, 1997	Slavin & Cheung, 2004
			Heritage Language Studies		
Morgan, 1971	Elementary school; matched design		X		X
			French Immersion Studies		
Barik & Swain, 1975*	Elementary school; matched design		X		X
Barik & Swain, 1978*	Elementary school; matched design		X		
Barik et al., 1977*	Elementary school; matched design	X			X

* Not included in the meta-analysis.

407

APPENDIX 14.D: ADDITIONAL NOTES ON METHODOLOGY OF STUDIES CITED IN CHAPTER AND EFFECT SIZE CALCULATIONS

Alvarez, 1975

All students in the study were nonrepeaters and nontransfers. Information on attrition is not reported. Tabled effect sizes are on adjusted means and are not strictly comparable to effect sizes computed on unadjusted means. Also, the formula used is for analysis of variance (ANOVA) F, but the F reported is the F for groups in analysis of covariance (ANCOVA). The partial correlation is not reported for the covariate. The study reports unadjusted means and the covariate means, but no standard deviations are reported. The mean-square within is not reported for the ANOVA F, so it is not possible to estimate the standard deviation from the reported statistics. All effect sizes computed here are biased away from 0 for this reason; the standard deviation is underestimated, because the covariate effect is included in the computation of F but cannot be extracted from the effect size computation. Another concern is that the posttest scores appear to be grade equivalent scores.

Campeau et al., 1975

To obtain pretest effect sizes, standard deviations were taken from the posttest data for the same cohort, grade, and school district. If no standard deviations were reported for a grade/cohort/school, then the effect size was not estimated unless a standard deviation could be derived from reported statistics for that test measure from other studies in the pool of reviewed studies or from another source using comparable samples. Specifically, we were able to estimate the variance for the IART Reading Total (RTT) measure in Grades 1 to 4 and extrapolate based on the trend there to Grade 5, insofar as the standard deviations were increasing about 5 points per grade. No effect sizes could be estimated for Santa Fe, New Mexico, or for the VOC and Reading Comp measures. In the Corpus Christi sample, standard deviations were reported. For Alice and Houston, standard deviations were estimated based on the other studies in the pool as just described. The posttest standard deviation for the control group was assumed equal to that of the treatment group, because it was not reported.

Cohen, 1976

Although the IART was used in each year, the levels are footnoted as Levels I, II, and III. To compute effect sizes, standard deviations were taken from other studies that used the IART at the same grades. We computed the average variance estimate for all studies using the IART RTT at a given grade, and we took the square root of the mean variance. These were not weighted by sample size. Standard deviations for the IART RTT were estimated for each grade based on other studies in the pool, because Cohen did not report them (see Campeau).

Huzar, 1973

In Tables 4 and 5, the author reports results for separate bilingual classrooms that differed either by having one bilingual and one monolingual teacher or two bilingual teachers. Because there were two experimental classes at each grade, this information can be used to determine the magnitude of the intraclass correlation (ICC) within the experimental condition. Assuming this ICC is consistent across first- and second-language classrooms (a nontrivial assumption) allows us to correct standard errors and point estimates for clustering. These tables are used to estimate the magnitude of the ICC in Grades 2 and 3. Within-class sample sizes are not given in the tables, but can be inferred from the standard errors of the means, which are given. Because random assignment was used, the posttest d was not adjusted.

Kaufman, 1968

The F statistics reported are ANCOVA Fs, but information on the R^2 for covariates is not presented. Consequently, ANOVA F conversions are used to estimate the effect size, which tend to underestimate the standard deviation in the population. Thus, all reported effect sizes are biased away from 0 (i.e., are more positive or more negative than they would be if a measure of the standard deviation were available).

Maldonado, 1994

It appears that one or more errors are present in the reporting of the data. Effect sizes based on the means and standard deviations are most likely wrong ($d = 7.007$). If the standard deviations reported are actually standard errors, then the effect size is a more realistic 2.2 and compares reasonably well with an effect size based on the reported t statistic, 1.7. Values currently reported in Table 14.1 for standard deviations are those reported in the article multiplied by the square root of the sample size. The standard deviations reported seem low given the metric of the test (mean = 100, SD = 15), and it appears that the reported standard deviations could be standard errors, although they are clearly labeled as standard deviations. Computing d using the original means and taking the standard deviations to be standard errors gives an effect size of 2.2. If the pre- and postmeans have been reversed for the control group in the table, the reported t statistics are close if the standard deviations are also taken to be standard errors. They are much too small if the reported standard deviations are indeed standard deviations. Taking the posttest mean for the control group to be 69, rather than 63 as is reported in the table, the effect size is 1.70, close to that based on the reported t statistic. No adjustments completely reconcile the reported statistics with one another.

Maldonado, 1977

The analysis is for Grades 2 to 5 outcomes. Science Research Associates (SRA) forms were different in each grade. The reported regression tables use the group variable as the dependent variable and list the outcome and covariate as predictors. To obtain unadjusted effect size estimates, the regression model was solved for the bivariate correlations, and these were converted to d statistics using the r to d conversion in Lipsey and Wilson (2001). To determine the direction of the effect size, information was taken from the text.

To obtain the observed bivariate correlation between Group and the outcome, the regression models reported in the paper had to be reverse engineered. The table analyses use Group as the outcome and the covariate and outcome as the predictors. To obtain r between the desired outcome and Group, we employed the equation $R^2 = \beta_1 r_{yx1} + B_2 r_{yx2}$ from Pedhazur (1997). Because R_2 and the betas are reported in the table and R_2 for the covariate is given separately, it is possible to solve the equation for r_{y2}, which can then be converted to d using the formula in Lipsey and Wilson (2001). In the text, we are told that the negative coefficient for fourth-grade mathematics indicates a mean difference in favor of the control group. Hence, it is assumed that positive betas on the outcome indicate an effect favoring the treatment group, whereas negative betas indicate an effect favoring the control group.

Morgan, 1971

Computed d is posttest d without correction for pretest. Groups were said to be equated on the pretest Metropolitan Achievement Test (MAT), but data were not provided.

Plante, 1976

Clustering of students in classrooms was ignored, and teachers were not randomly assigned to classrooms. Although ICCs at Grade 2 are small, this is not the case at Grade 3. The investigator also compared the groups on Metropolitan Readiness Test (MRT) and IQ, and groups were not statistically different. Tables 4 and 5 provide data on individual classes in the experimental group in Grades 2 and 3, respectively. These tables can be used to estimate the magnitude of the clustering effect in the bilingual classrooms, which was small in Grade 2 (.008), but large in Grade 3 (.78) because of the large mean difference between the two classrooms. Because random assignment was used, the posttest d was not adjusted.

Saldate et al., 1985

We imputed first-language standard deviation at pretest to be equal to second-language standard deviation at pretest. No standard deviation was given for first language at pretest.

TABLE 14.E.1

Effect Sizes of Studies Included in the Meta-Analysis

Study Name	Subgroup Within Study	Outcome	Time Point	Biling-ED N	English-Only N	Std Diff in Means	Std Err	Hedges' g^u	Standard Error
Maldonado, 1994	Sample 1	Reading total	2	10	10	2.215	0.568	2.121	0.544
Saldate et al., 1985	Sample 1	Unknown	2	31	31	-0.287	0.255	-0.283	0.252
Saldate et al., 1985	Sample 1	Word reading	3	19	19	0.908	0.341	0.889	0.334
de la Garza, 1985	Sample 1	Reading comprehension	2	25	117	0.192	0.221	0.191	0.219
de la Garza, 1985	Sample 1	Reading comprehension	3	25	117	0.207	0.221	0.206	0.219
de la Garza, 1985	Sample 1	Reading vocabulary	2	24	118	0.496	0.226	0.494	0.225
de la Garza, 1985	Sample 1	Reading vocabulary	3	24	118	0.249	0.224	0.248	0.223
Ramirez et al., 1991	Sample 1	Reading total	1	67	139	0.178	0.149	0.177	0.148
Ramirez et al., 1991	Sample 1	Reading total	2	67	139	-0.258	0.149	-0.257	0.149
Ramirez et al., 1991	Sample 1	Reading total	3	67	139	0.154	0.149	0.154	0.148
Ramirez et al., 1991	Sample 2	Reading total	1	252	194	0.095	0.096	0.095	0.095
Ramirez et al., 1991	Sample 2	Reading total	2	252	194	-0.100	0.096	-0.099	0.095
Ramirez et al., 1991	Sample 2	Reading total	3	252	194	0.017	0.096	0.017	0.095
Ramirez et al., 1991	Sample 3	Reading total	1	170	194	0.080	0.105	0.080	0.105
Ramirez et al., 1991	Sample 3	Reading total	2	170	194	-0.276	0.106	-0.275	0.105
Ramirez et al., 1991	Sample 3	Reading total	3	170	194	-0.067	0.105	-0.067	0.105
Valladolid, 1991	Sample 1	Reading total	4	50	57	-0.610	0.198	-0.605	0.197
Valladolid, 1991	Sample 1	Reading total	5	50	57	-0.541	0.197	-0.538	0.196
Alvarez, 1975	Sample 1	Reading comprehension	2	51	26	-0.188	0.241	-0.186	0.239
Alvarez, 1975	Sample 1	Reading vocabulary	2	51	26	0.163	0.241	0.162	0.239

(Continued)

TABLE 14.E.1
(Continued)

Study Name	Subgroup Within Study	Outcome	Time Point	Biling-ED N	English-Only N	Std Diff in Means	Std Err	Hedges' g^u	Standard Error
Alvarez, 1975	Sample 2	Reading comprehension	2	39	31	-0.257	0.242	-0.254	0.239
Alvarez, 1975	Sample 2	Reading vocabulary	2	39	31	0.072	0.241	0.071	0.238
Campeau et al., 1975	Sample 2	Reading total	1	104	27	1.839	0.244	1.828	0.243
Campeau et al., 1975	Sample 2	Reading total	2	94	21	0.924	0.249	0.918	0.247
Campeau et al., 1975	Sample 2	Reading total	3	75	22	-0.241	0.243	-0.239	0.241
Campeau et al., 1975	Sample 3	Reading total	1	106	19	1.401	0.264	1.393	0.263
Campeau et al., 1975	Sample 3	Reading total	2	95	35	1.434	0.217	1.426	0.216
Campeau et al., 1975	Sample 3	Reading total	3	101	29	0.761	0.216	0.757	0.215
Campeau et al., 1975	Sample 3	Reading total	4	75	20	0.271	0.252	0.269	0.250
Campeau et al., 1975	Sample 5	Reading total	1	125	46	2.643	0.224	2.631	0.223
Campeau et al., 1975	Sample 5	Reading total	2	97	57	0.406	0.168	0.404	0.168
Campeau et al., 1975	Sample 5	Reading total	3	85	63	0.882	0.174	0.877	0.173
Campeau et al., 1975	Sample 6	Reading total	1	119	100	0.243	0.136	0.242	0.136
Campeau et al., 1975	Sample 6	Reading total	2	205	93	0.355	0.126	0.354	0.126
Campeau et al., 1975	Sample 6	Reading total	3	79	80	0.389	0.160	0.387	0.159
Campeau et al., 1975	Sample 7	Reading total	1	146	60	0.857	0.159	0.854	0.158
Campeau et al., 1975	Sample 7	Reading total	2	161	53	0.668	0.162	0.665	0.161
Campeau et al., 1975	Sample 7	Reading total	3	218	83	0.123	0.129	0.123	0.129
Campeau et al., 1975	Sample 7	Reading total	4	98	88	0.760	0.152	0.757	0.151
Campeau et al., 1975	Sample 8	Reading total	1	145	45	0.457	0.172	0.455	0.172
Campeau et al., 1975	Sample 8	Reading total	2	155	53	0.541	0.161	0.539	0.161
Campeau et al., 1975	Sample 8	Reading total	3	146	62	0.272	0.152	0.271	0.152
Campeau et al., 1975	Sample 8	Reading total	4	151	58	0.390	0.156	0.389	0.155
Cohen et al., 1976	Sample 1	Reading total	4	14	11	-0.180	0.404	-0.174	0.390
Cohen et al., 1976	Sample 1	Reading Total	5	7	7	-0.220	0.536	-0.206	0.502
Cohen et al., 1976	Sample 2	Reading total	3	12	9	-1.200	0.478	-1.152	0.459

(Continued)

TABLE 14.E.1
(Continued)

Study Name	Subgroup Within Study	Outcome	Time Point	Biling-ED N	English-Only N	Std Diff in Means	Std Err	Hedges' g^u	Standard Error
Cohen et al., 1976	Sample 2	Reading total	4	7	7	-1.145	0.577	-1.072	0.540
Cohen et al., 1976	Sample 3	Reading total	2	7	9	-1.690	0.586	-1.598	0.554
Cohen et al., 1976	Sample 3	Reading toial	3	7	7	-1.809	0.635	-1.694	0.594
Danoff et al., 1977	Sample 1	Reading total	2	722	297	-0.262	0.069	-0.262	0.069
Danoff et al., 1977	Sample 1	Reading total	3	905	469	-0.265	0.057	-0.265	0.057
Danoff et al., 1977	Sample 1	Reading total	4	941	515	0.097	0.055	0.097	0.055
Danoff et al., 1977	Sample 1	Reading total	5	731	144	-0.287	0.091	-0.287	0.091
Danoff et al., 1977	Sample 1	Reading total	6	341	68	-0.424	0.133	-0.423	0.133
Huzar, 1973	Sample 1	Reading total	2	41	40	0.014	0.222	0.014	0.220
Huzar, 1973	Sample 1	Reading total	3	43	36	0.313	0.227	0.310	0.225
Kaufman, 1968	Sample 1	Paragraph meaning	7	41	31	0.048	0.238	0.048	0.235
Kaufman, 1968	Sample 1	Paragraph meaning	8	31	19	0.115	0.292	0.113	0.287
Kaufman, 1968	Sample 1	Word meaning	7	41	31	0.220	0.239	0.217	0.236
Kaufman, 1968	Sample 1	Word meaning	8	31	19	0.311	0.293	0.306	0.288
Kaufman, 1968	Sample 2	Paragraph meaning	7	20	25	0.478	0.304	0.470	0.299
Kaufman, 1968	Sample 2	Word meaning	7	20	25	0.039	0.300	0.038	0.295
Maldonado, 1977	Sample 1	Reading total	2	47	79	0.360	0.186	0.358	0.184
Maldonado, 1977	Sample 1	Reading total	3	47	79	0.506	0.187	0.503	0.186
Maldonado, 1977	Sample 1	Reading total	4	47	79	0.475	0.187	0.473	0.186
Maldonado, 1977	Sample 1	Reading total	5	47	79	0.378	0.186	0.376	0.185
Plante, 1976	Sample 1	Reading total	2	15	10	0.801	0.424	0.775	0.410
Plante, 1976	Sample 1	Reading total	3	16	12	0.272	0.384	0.264	0.372
Covey, 1973	Sample 1	Reading total	9	89	84	0.661	0.156	0.658	0.156
Morgan, 1971	Sample 1	Paragraph reading	1	93	100	0.255	0.145	0.254	0.144
Morgan, 1971	Sample 1	Word reading	1	93	100	0.374	0.145	0.372	0.145

15

Effective Literacy Teaching for English-Language Learners

Timothy Shanahan and Isabel Beck

In this chapter, we focus on studies of two fundamental approaches to literacy improvement: (a) one that examines enhanced instruction in particular elements of literacy (phonemic awareness, phonics, sight vocabulary, meaning vocabulary, oral reading fluency, reading comprehension, writing, and spelling), and (b) one that examines all other interventions aimed at improving literacy among English-language learners. This chapter only includes intervention studies that employed experimental, quasi-experimental, or single-subject designs.[1] After describing the review methods that we used, we examine in turn the literature on enhanced instruction in individual elements of literacy and on more complex approaches to literacy instruction.

This chapter addresses the following research question:

What can be done to increase achievement in reading, writing, and spelling for language-minority students?

METHODS

This chapter is a qualitative, narrative review (Pan, 2004). However, to facilitate study comparisons, we calculated effect sizes for each study when the requisite

---

[1]An experiment randomly assigns students to the experimental and control groups, whereas a quasi-experiment assigns preexisting groups to conditions and uses statistical controls to account for characteristics on which the groups may differ. Single-subject designs measure baseline performance and then intervene with some type of instruction; the learning is closely monitored for each subject, and various procedures are used to increase the possibility that this learning is due to the intervention (well-designed single-subject studies can strongly suggest causation, but not with the same degree of certainty as can a comparable-quality randomized control trial). We can increase our certainty about the effectiveness of a given approach further when a study is replicated; this simply means that the study has been carried out multiple times with the same results.

statistics were available. Our review includes all methodologically adequate studies that were derived from the search of the literature, as described later. It is important to note that the methods applied in this chapter have some important limitations. First, in requiring measurable outcomes, we excluded case and qualitative studies. Many such descriptions exist and are valuable in suggesting practices that may be effective (such studies are reported and discussed in chaps. 16, 17, and 18). However, such descriptions cannot reveal what children would have learned without the intervention. Thus, they are not relevant to the overarching question of program effectiveness that guided the review work for this chapter.

Criteria for Inclusion

The studies examined in this chapter met all the basic selection criteria established by the panel. Additional criteria for this part of the volume were established by the panel because of the nature of the research question and the limited amount of research available on that question. For the review here, the following additional criteria were applied:

- Studies had to address the teaching of English or the teaching of the home language as preparation for English instruction. Although a wider array of data on language learning was useful for some of the questions addressed in other chapters of this volume, we focus here almost entirely on the teaching of English. Not all languages are alphabetic, and there are differences among languages, such as syntactic characteristics. Thus, findings drawn from studies of learning in languages other than English may not generalize to English learning. We did consider some studies with other than English-language outcomes. Because most bilingual programs delay or limit English instruction for 2 to 4 years, considering only English-language outcomes would make it impossible to evaluate the early impact of these approaches. Thus, we accepted studies in which first-language instruction was being provided in preparation for a transition to English, even if they did not measure English-language outcomes. We are careful to identify these studies in the review and to treat their outcomes separately to prevent confusion.
- Studies had to examine literacy learning within the context of English as a societal language.[2] It has been hypothesized that cultural context influences second-language literacy development. Thus, for example, the learning of French may differ if it occurs while one is living in France or studying in a U.S. high school. There are also variations in the socioeconomic value of a language and the availability of language models.
- Studies must have been documented in a journal article, doctoral dissertation, or technical report. Journal articles are refereed by independent

---

[2]With the exception of three studies (Elley, 1991; Sengupta, 2000; Tsang, 1996), students in the studies cited in this chapter are language minority. In these three studies, although the students are not language minority, their first language is not English, and they are acquiring English as one of the societal languages of the country.

scientific panels to a greater extent than dissertations or technical reports, so they tend to be of higher quality. However, given the small number of studies evident in this area, the panel believed it best to cast as wide a net as possible to identify eligible studies. To ensure that we would not be misled by poorly executed research, we took great care to identify and interpret flaws in dissertations and technical reports, and we have noted these limitations throughout.

- The studies had to examine the outcome of some attempt to teach literacy in an enhanced manner. This criterion precluded studies aimed at providing descriptions of current practice or examining correlates of effectiveness.

- As reported earlier, the effectiveness of an approach to literacy instruction had to be evaluated using experimental, quasi-experimental, or single-subject research designs. The use of experimental and quasi-experimental data allows the effectiveness of an approach to be compared with a no-treatment or an alternative-treatment control. Doing so ensures that outcomes due to the use of an approach will not be confounded with the effects of normal maturation. Single-subject or multiple-baseline studies were also accepted because, like group experiments, they examine the impact of an instructional approach and allow us to draw causal links between use of the approach and the outcomes observed. Results of studies using single-subject designs cannot be combined statistically with those of group studies, but they can provide valuable confirmation or refutation of group experimental findings.

- As with all studies included in the report, studies could not have design flaws or confounds so serious that it would be impossible to determine their results with any degree of certainty. All studies have flaws, and it would be unreasonable to set aside the results of a study because it was not perfectly designed or executed. However, some studies are so seriously flawed (e.g., no measures of pretreatment performance, lack of a control group, different measures for different groups, substantial pretreatment group differences, confounding of teacher and methodological effects) that they cannot be interpreted. In such cases, the studies were not included in the review.

Methods of Rating Studies for Inclusion

Once studies were identified for potential relevance, two individuals independently reviewed them against the set of standards noted previously. Disagreements concerning inclusion were rare, and they tended to be limited to issues of quality (i.e., whether a study was too flawed to allow inclusion). Any disagreements on inclusion were easily resolved by discussion, and none required a third reader for resolution.

Meta-Analysis and the Computation of Effect Sizes

Meta-analysis provides a useful tool for systematically synthesizing collections of studies (Cooper, 1998; Cooper & Hedges, 1994). However, the nature of the literature reviewed here precluded the sound use of meta-analysis. In this chapter, we only used meta-analysis when there were a minimum of five conceptually comparable studies. Although it is possible to statistically combine almost any set of studies, meta-analytic procedures make sense only when the studies being combined are conceptually relevant, and conceptual relevance is a theoretical decision (Cooper, 1998). First, the variety of interventions in this collection of studies was simply too great to justify combining them into a single meta-analysis. For instance, some of the experimental efforts involved practices as simple as having students spend a few minutes a day for several weeks reading or listening to someone read; and others were as involved as requiring an elaborate multiyear agenda of professional development, revision of the school reading curriculum, replacement of instructional materials, establishment of intervention support for struggling readers, and reorganization of instruction in an entire school. Second, many of the studies examined approaches to teaching essential parts of literacy such as word recognition or comprehension. The comparison of results from studies of different aspects of reading would be potentially misleading if synthesized into a single meta-analysis because the teaching of all these components is necessary, and the characteristics of successful instruction in each have been found to be quite different (National Institute of Child Health and Human Development, 2000).

When sufficient numbers of studies on a particular construct do exist, it is possible to examine correlates to the variations in the construct, which can give researchers and practitioners valuable insights into aspects of the instruction that may be leading to the differences. When few studies are available, as in this case, these correlations can be misleading because they will be confounded with the individual studies, the same thing that happens in any empirical research when there are too few degrees of freedom to support the questions being asked. As future studies accumulate on various instructional approaches with English-language learners, it will become possible and worthwhile to conduct more sophisticated analyses of the data.

Nevertheless, to facilitate the comparison of studies, effect sizes were computed for each study if sufficient data were available. When possible, we computed effect size estimates for each study from treatment and control means and the pooled within-group standard deviations. When these means and standard deviations were not available, we estimated effect sizes using t or F statistics. In a few cases, adjusted means were used as the basis of these calculations because these were the only statistics available in the original studies.

Many studies make multiple comparisons, usually because they include multiple experimental groups or multiple literacy measures to evaluate the impact of an intervention. When a single study included multiple comparisons, only a single effect size was calculated for that study—an average effect across the various comparisons. There was one exception: for a study that examined multiple independent treatments that were not variants of each other (Waxman, Walker de Felix, Martínez, Knight, & Padrón, 1994). For this study, effect sizes were obtained for each independent treatment. If both native- and English-language data were available, effect sizes were calculated only for performance in English. Effect sizes were not calculated for single-subject studies. Although it is possible to calculate a kind of effect size for studies in which subjects serve as their own controls, these results are inflated and cannot be compared with those obtained from group comparisons (see Lipsey & Wilson, 2001, for a discussion of this issue). Effect sizes for the two broad topics considered next—explicit instruction in individual literacy components and complex approaches to literacy instruction—are presented in Tables 15.1 and 15.2, respectively.

EXPLICIT INSTRUCTION IN LITERACY COMPONENTS

Literacy is complex and involves the orchestration of many different skills or abilities, including phonemic awareness, phonics, oral reading fluency, reading comprehension, vocabulary, writing, and spelling. It has been shown that special instruction aimed at improving performance in any of these components can enhance overall literacy achievement. For instance, the National Reading Panel (National Institute of Child Health and Human Development, 2000) found that explicit teaching of phonemic awareness, phonics, oral reading fluency, reading comprehension strategies, and vocabulary was beneficial. Additionally, the benefits of teaching spelling (Foorman, 1999), sight vocabulary (Ehri, 1997), and writing (Hillocks, 1986) have been demonstrated in other research reviews. Because a range of instructional approaches to teaching these components have been found to be effective, we might reasonably conclude that it is not special approaches to teaching the components that mattered in these studies, but the emphasis on the components of literacy. For example, the National Reading Panel concluded that teaching children how to use sound–letter relationships to decode words led to improved early reading achievement. Several different phonics approaches were studied, all having similar positive outcomes. The pattern is evident with the other components as well: Content of instruction was found to be more important than methodological differences.

The purpose here is to determine the extent to which explicit teaching of these components confers a learning benefit on children who are learning English. It is possible that second-language literacy development is similar for native speakers and English-language learners. If so, we would expect studies of the teaching of literacy components to be equally effective with both groups. It is also possible that linguistic context is so different for the native and second languages that English-language learners may benefit from a different regimen of instruction.

We found only 17 studies addressing effects of explicitly teaching components of literacy that met the inclusion criteria outlined earlier, and we found no studies of instruction in spelling or sight vocabulary for language-minority students. By comparison, the National Reading Panel reviewed more than 400 studies on five of these components for native English speakers (not including writing), and it did not include doctoral dissertations or technical reports. As noted above, with so few studies available, we could not perform a true meta-analysis for any of the literacy components; we never had more than three conceptually comparable studies on any of the elements.

To give readers a better sense of this collection of research, each study is briefly described. To facilitate comparison, some key characteristics of each study are listed in Table 15.1 and Appendix 15.A. The characteristics reported

TABLE 15.1

Effect Sizes for Instructional Approaches Aimed at Enhanced Teaching of Specific Literacy Elements to English-Language Learners[a]

Study	N	Grade	Home Language	Type of Study[b]	Pretest Differences[c]	Treatment Duration[d]	Effect Size	Confidence Interval	Signif
Phonemic awareness & phonics									
Gunn et al., 2000	184	K–3	Spanish	RCT	No	21 weeks	.29	.07–.52	Yes
Gunn et al., 2002	117	K–3	Spanish	RCT	No	2 weeks	.38	.22–.55	Yes
Kramer et al., 1983	15	1–3	Spanish	RCT	No	4 weeks	*	—	Yes
Larson, 1996	33	1	Spanish	RCT	No	7 weeks	2.82	1.83–3.82	Yes
Stuart, 1999	112	Pre & K	Sylheti	Quasi-Exp.	Yes	12 weeks	.46	.38–.55	Yes
Oral reading fluency									
De La Colina et al., 2001	*74*	*1–2*	*Spanish*	*Single Subject*	*No*	*12 weeks*	*	—	
Denton, 2000	93	2–5	Spanish	RCT	No	8 weeks	.05	-.10–.49	No
Vocabulary									
Carlo et al., 2004	142	5	Spanish	Quasi-Exp.	*	15 weeks	*	—	Yes
Pérez, 1981	75	3	Spanish	RCT	No	13 weeks	1.12	.78–1.47	Yes
Vaughn–Shavuo, 1990	30	1	Spanish	RCT	No	3 weeks	1.40	.59–2.18	Yes
Reading comprehension									
Bean, 1982	45	4–5	Spanish	RCT	No	1 day	*	—	No
Shames, 1998	58	9–11	Haitian Creole	Quasi-Exp.	Yes	36 weeks	.20	-.36–.75	No
Swicegood, 1990	95	3	Spanish	Quasi-Exp.	*	6 weeks	.05	-.35–.45	No

(Continued)

TABLE 15.1
(Continued)

Study	N	Grade	Home Language	Type of Study[b]	Pretest Differences[c]	Treatment Duration[d]	Effect Size	Confidence Interval	Signif
Writing									
Franken et al., 1999	20	9–12	Mixed	RCT	No	6 weeks	-.16	-46–.13	No
Gómez et al., 1996	72	5	Spanish	RCT	No	6 weeks	.32	.18–.45	Yes
Prater et al., 1993	46	4–6	Spanish	RCT	No	3 weeks	.60	.30–.90	Yes
Sengupta, 2000	100	9–12	Chinese	Quasi–Exp.	Yes	36 weeks	.81	.36–1.24	Yes

[a] If the literacy outcome measures were in the students' home language, the study is printed in italics. Only one of these studies used home-language measures.
[b] RCT = Randomized controlled trial; Quasi-Exp. = quasi-experiment; Single Subject = single-subject or multibaseline design.
[c] For quasi-experimental studies; this indicates whether some kind of statistical adjustment was necessary because of pretest differences in the sample.
[d] Treatment duration is an estimate of the number of weeks of treatment (often the original studies indicated a number of months or a starting and ending date).
*Insufficient information provided in the article to allow determination.

TABLE 15-2
Effect Sizes for Instructional Approaches Aimed at Enhanced Teaching of Multiple Literacy Elements to English-Language Learners[a]

Study	Intervention	N	Grade	Home Language	Type of Study[b]	Pretest Diff.[c]	Treatment Duration[d]	Effect Size	Confidence Interval	Signif.
Encouraging reading & writing										
Elley, 1991		535	4-5	Fijian	Quasi	Yes	72 weeks	.60	.53-.66	Yes
		459	5-6							
Schon et al., 1982		114	2-4	Spanish	Quasi	Yes	32 weeks	*	–	No
Schon et al., 1984		272	9-12	Spanish	Quasi	Yes	17-30 weeks	-.08	-.38-.21	No
Schon et al., 1985		400	7-8	Spanish	Quasi	Yes	34 weeks	-.20	-.52 to .12	No
Tudor et al., 1989		45	4-5	Panjabi	Quasi	No	13 weeks	*	–	Yes
Tsang, 1996		144	8-12	Cantonese	RCT	No	20 weeks	.27	.11-.24	Yes
Reading to children										
Hancock, 2002		77	K	Spanish	RCT	No	57 weeks	.66	.10-1.22	Yes
Hastings-Góngora, 1993		11	K	Spanish	RCT	No	5 weeks	*	*	No
Ulanoff et al., 1999		60	3	Spanish	Quasi	Yes	1 day	*	*	Yes
Tutoring & remediation										
Escamilla, 1994		*46*	*1*	*Spanish*	*Quasi*	*	*12-16 weeks*	*1.15*	*.87-1.43*	*Yes*
Syvanen, 1997		16	4-5	?	Quasi	Yes	19 weeks	.12	-.41-.67	No
Other investigations										
Calderón et al., 1998	Cooperative group.	222	2-3	Spanish	Quasi	Yes	72 weeks	.59	.14-1.03	Yes
Cohen et al., 1980	Mastery learning	150	1	Spanish	RCT	No	4 weeks	.51	.28-.74	Yes

(Continued)

TABLE 15-2
(Continued)

Study	Intervention	N	Grade	Home Language	Type of Study[b]	Pretest Diff.[c]	Treatment Duration[d]	Effect Size	Confidence Interval	Signif.
Goldenberg et al., 1992	Parents	10	K	Spanish	Quasi	No	36 weeks	.53	-.20-1.26	No
Neuman et al., 1992	Captioned TV	129	7-8	Mixed	Quasi	Yes	12 weeks	.55	.37-.72	Yes
Saunders, 1999	Multi-year bilingual transition program	125	2-5	Spanish	Quasi	No	144 weeks	.57	.04-1.10	Yes
Saunders et al., 1999	Instructional conversations and literature logs	116	4-5	Spanish	RCT	No	4 days	.55	.25-.85	Yes
Tharp, 1982	Kamehameha Early Educ Program	204	1	Hawaiian	RCT	No	36 weeks	.20	.13-.45	Yes
Waxman et al., 1994	Time use	88	1-5	Spanish	Quasi	Yes	26 weeks	.65	.36-.94	Yes
	Content ESL	52	1-5	Spanish	Quasi	No	26 weeks	.01	-.32-.34	No
Success for all										
Dianda et al., 1995		*147*	*K-1*	*Spanish*	*Quasi*	*No*	*72 weeks*	*.76*	*--*	*Yes*
Slavin et al., 1998: AZ		*138*	*1*	*Spanish*	*Quasi*	*No*	*36 weeks*	*.45*	*.27-.63*	*Yes*
Slavin et al., 1998: Fairhill		50	1-3	Spanish	Quasi	Yes	72 weeks	.20	-.12-.53	No

[a] If the literacy outcome measures were in the students' home language, the study is printed in italics. Only three of these studies used home-language measures.
[b] RCT = Randomized controlled trial; Quasi = quasi-experiment.
[c] For quasi-experimental studies; this indicates whether some kind of statistical adjustment was necessary because of pretest differences in the sample.
[d] Treatment duration is an estimate of the number of weeks of treatment (often the original studies indicated a number of months or a starting and ending date).
* Insufficient information provided in the article to allow determination.

in Table 15.1 include ages/grades of the children, type of intervention, and research design characteristics. Appendix 15.A provides additional information about the language status of the sample and the intervention, including duration, instructional practices, materials, professional development, and delivery. As noted, effect sizes were calculated when possible and reported in Table 15.1. Many of the studies were quasi-experimental in design, and various methods were used to deal with initial differences between existing groups. Some used analysis of covariance (ANCOVA) to correct for differences, but none of the authors indicates whether homogeneity violations existed. Other authors present residual differences in gains. These analyses can be problematic, so the table indicates whether there were initial differences in the samples.

Phonemic Awareness and Phonics

English text is alphabetic in nature: The letters and letter combinations in written words represent the sounds or phonemes in oral language. Early phonemic awareness (the ability to identify and manipulate the individual sounds, or phonemes, in a spoken word) and phonics (knowledge of the relationship between the sounds in spoken words and the letters that represent those sounds) have been found to be important in early reading development (National Institute of Child Health and Human Development, 2000). Does teaching phonemic awareness, phonics, or sight vocabulary confer similar advantages on English-language learners?

Positive effects for a combined program of phonemic awareness and phonics were found in Stuart's (1999) comparison of *Jolly Phonics*, a phonemic awareness and phonics intervention, with a Big Books approach. The study, which took place in England, involved 112 four- and five-year-olds, the vast majority of whom (*n* = 96) were English-language learners (most were Sylheti speakers from Bangladesh). Primary school teachers volunteered to use one of the two approaches. One class from each of three schools implemented the Big Books intervention, and three classes from two other schools implemented *Jolly Phonics*. There were no significant differences in the social, ethnic, and linguistic compositions of the schools.

The teachers who implemented the Big Books approach were experienced with the approach, whereas the *Jolly Phonics* program was relatively new for the experimental teachers. In both cases, the researcher reviewed the targeted approaches with the teachers. Books were purchased for the Big Books classrooms on the basis of teacher selections, and a set of *Jolly Phonics* materials (e.g., teacher handbook, phonics workbooks, puzzles) was provided to each *Jolly Phonics* classroom. Teachers were asked to provide 1 hour of daily instruction with the targeted approach for a 12-week period, starting with whole-class instruction and then splitting into small groups. Regular visits by a member of the research project staff ensured that all children received the appropriate instruction for the prescribed hour.

Children were pre- and posttested on measures of spoken and written language, phonological awareness, and alphabet knowledge. The researchers found significant positive effects of *Jolly Phonics* in comparison with the Big Books instruction on children's acquisition of phonological awareness and phonics and on their ability to apply these in reading and writing. A delayed posttest administered 1 year later revealed that the *Jolly Phonics* group was still significantly ahead of the Big Books group in phonological awareness and phonics, as well as on standardized and experimental tests of reading and spelling.

In a second study, this one examining the effects of various instructional approaches on English phonemic awareness and the reading and spelling of English consonant–vowel–consonant (CVC) words (e.g., *bat* or *pin*), Larson (1996) randomly assigned 33 first-grade Puerto Rican students ages 5 to 7 to one of three groups. In one group, children received instruction in segmentation of orally presented Spanish CVC words until they met an 80% or 15-trial criterion, at which point they began oral segmentation of English CVC words to the same 80% criterion. A second group received segmentation instruction only in English CVC words to the same 80% criterion. Both the Spanish–English and English-only groups then received instruction in segmentation with transfer to the letters in the words taught. In this latter phase, which was in English for both treatment groups, instruction was provided in letter–sound relationships for some consonants and all short vowels. The students in both groups were trained individually for approximately 5 weeks. A third group was a no-treatment control. The two trained groups scored significantly higher than the untrained group on the posttests and delayed tests of segmenting, decoding, and spelling, but did not perform significantly differently from one another.

Beyond the overall finding that the two trained groups scored significantly higher than the untrained group on posttests and delayed tests, there were several additional findings of interest. First, the number of trials needed to learn the tasks, whether in Spanish or English, varied widely, pointing to the diversity in students' ability to learn these phonemic awareness tasks. Thus, the need for differential instruction, at least in terms of duration, is apparent. Second, it appears that training to criterion in Spanish followed by training to criterion in English was no better than training to criterion in English alone. Although the Spanish–English group did achieve criterion on the English words more rapidly than the English-only group, it is impossible to tell whether this was merely the effect of practice in general because the Spanish–English group got twice as much training as the English-only group. Whatever the cause, it is notable that the two groups showed no significant differences in their ability to transfer their segmentation skills to letters.

However, interpretation of the study's findings should be tempered by several points. For instance, it is important to note that the intervention in Larson's study included letter–sound teaching. There is evidence that approaches to phonemic awareness that include letter–sound associations are more effective than those that are only speech based (Adams, Foorman, Lundberg, & Beeler, 1998; National Institute of Child Health and Human Development, 2000; Oudeans, 2003). Instruction in phonemic awareness, accompanied by the teaching of written letters (such as using letters as counters during segmenting activities), may be considered part of phonics instruction because phonics involves knowledge of the relationship between phonemes and their written representations. In addition, the sample size was small for three comparison groups, limiting statistical power such that it was only possible to detect large effects. A larger sample may have revealed additional training effects and significant differences between the two intervention groups.

Two other studies—an original intervention (Gunn, Biglan, Smolkowski, & Ary, 2000) and a subsequent follow-up (Gunn, Smolkowski, Biglan, & Black, 2002)—found positive effects for supplemental code-emphasis instruction. All K–3 students from nine schools in three districts who were reading below grade level— 256 students, 62% of whom were Hispanic—were identified for participation. Of the Hispanic students, 84% spoke only or mainly Spanish. These students were randomly assigned to a treatment group that received supplemental instruction or to a control group that did not receive such instruction. *Reading Mastery* (Engelmann & Bruner, 1988) was used for children whose screening scores indicated they were beginning readers. *Corrective Reading* (Engelmann, Carnine, & Johnson, 1999) was used for third-grade students who were still nonreaders or were reading below grade level. Both programs emphasize phonological decoding (both stress phoneme blending, but not segmenting). However, reading practice with decodable text is included in *Reading Mastery*, and the reading of text with comprehension questions and rate-building exercises is included in *Corrective Reading*. The supplemental instruction was provided by trained assistants to groups of two to three children. When this was not feasible (presumably because of scheduling or behavioral issues), one-to-one instruction was provided. Instruction occurred daily for about 30 minutes at times other than during regular classroom reading instruction.

Effects of the intervention were determined after 4 to 5 months of instruction for 184 children (most of the attrition was due to students' moving away from these schools). A significant effect was found for the supplemental instruction in word-attack skills on the Woodcock–Johnson test. There were no differences in oral reading fluency. At the end of the second year, after 15 months of instruction, results show significantly higher scores on word attack, reading vocabulary, and passage comprehension, and approached significance ($p < .056$) on oral reading fluency. That most measures revealed an impact of this instruction after 2 years indicates the durability of the impact of the code-emphasis supplementary instruction.

An interesting secondary analysis examined the extent to which the intervention benefited children who did not speak English at the outset of the study. Data for these 19 Hispanic children showed that they benefited from the intervention as much as the other Hispanic students. In a follow-up study, Gunn et al. (2002) found that 1 year after the intervention had been completed, these English-language learners who did not speak English at the onset of the study appeared to profit as much as the Hispanic English-speaking students. It is important to note, however, that given the inadequate statistical power of such small numbers of English-language learners (16 or 17 depending on the measure) in the two Gunn studies, the findings for these students are merely suggestive.

Although Gunn and colleagues emphasized the decoding aspects of the intervention, the commercial programs used for instruction addressed more than decoding. Further, the intervention was part of a larger investigation (Barrera et al., 2002), in which supplemental reading instruction was one facet of a social-behavioral prevention program designed to reduce aggression and antisocial behavior. A portion of the gains reported here may have been due to greater attention or increased amounts of available instruction during the school day due to the social-behavioral program. In any event, it is reasonable to conclude that additional reading instruction using programs that address decoding among other key literacy variables had a positive impact on reading performance, at least within the context of a social-behavioral intervention.

Finally, a brief study of the teaching of English auditory discrimination (a component of phonemic awareness) to Mexican American children in first, second, and third grades (Kramer, Schell, & Rubison, 1983) is of some interest. The instruction focused on helping Spanish speakers discriminate among difficult English sounds (e.g., *cheat*, *sheet*). This was a limited study: Only 15 children participated, with 8 assigned to the control group. Only four sound pairs were taught, and these were presented for an unspecified amount of time over a 4-week period. The experimental group improved in their ability to discriminate among the sounds, and the control group showed no improvement. The only measure employed was a check on the auditory discrimination of the sounds taught. Although the results suggest that it was possible to teach auditory discrimination of some English phonemes to Spanish-speaking students, this occurred over such a brief time and with such a limited set of sounds that the generalizability of these results cannot be established. Moreover, the study did not attempt to measure the impact of the treatment on literacy development.

Clearly, five small studies of phonological awareness and phonics are far from sufficient to allow a determination of the most useful instructional methods for meeting the early literacy needs of English-language learners. However, the findings of all five studies are consistent with the solid findings of first-language research. The National Reading Panel examined 52 studies of phonological awareness instruction and another 38 studies of phonics instruction. Both conferred clear benefits on children's reading development, as determined by a wide range of measures, including beginning reading comprehension. The five studies of phonological awareness and phonics with English-language learners had similar results, although only one of these studies measured reading comprehension outcomes.

Additional research is needed both to replicate these findings and to help determine whether special routines or emphases are needed in these areas in teaching English-language learners from various language backgrounds. The study of Kramer et al. (1983) did not attempt to teach general phonemic awareness, but was aimed specifically at helping students hear sounds that could be confusing for those of a particular language background. Other studies of this type might be useful in helping to design approaches to phonological awareness and phonics that would be particularly effective with specific populations of English-language learners.

Oral Reading Fluency

The importance of fluency in reading is increasingly being recognized (Kuhn & Stahl, 2003; National Institute of Child Health and Human Development, 2000; Rasinski, 2003). Fluency requires accuracy (reading the words an author has written), speed, and proper expression; it depends on automatic word recognition that is carried out simultaneously with some initial interpretation of text meaning (e.g., grouping words syntactically, using punctuation). Fluency in reading is important because human capacity for processing information is limited; without fluency, readers have to attend to too many things at once, hindering other necessary cognitive activity (Kiss & Savage, 1977). For example, research has shown that comprehension tends to be weak when texts are read too slowly—that is, without fluency (LaBerge & Samuels, 1974). If students can read text fluently (without much attention to basic information- processing demands), they will have sufficient cognitive resources to think about what they read. Perfetti and Hogaboam (1975) demonstrated that fast word recognition is correlated with better comprehension, although Levy et al. (1997) showed that fluent reading performance entails more than proficient word recognition.

When native speakers engaged in repeated oral reading of passages, their reading achievement improved (National Institute of Child Health and Human Development, 2000). This oral reading practice was most successful when the students received monitoring and guidance from peers, teachers, or parents. The National Reading Panel examined 51 studies of fluency instruction, and the use of such practices led to greater fluency and better reading comprehension.

Despite the attention devoted to fluency teaching for native speakers, we found only two studies that examined fluency instruction with English-language learners. The first of these (Denton, 2000) examined two tutoring interventions: one that taught phonics and one that taught fluency directly. Students receiving these two treatments were compared with students in the regular classroom who received no tutoring, and thus we cannot determine whether the study effects were due to the nature of the teaching or the amount of extra instruction provided to the tutoring groups.

The study was conducted over 4 months and involved 93 Spanish speakers who were English-language learners in Grades 2 to 5. Students were assigned to the treatments on the basis of their scores on the Woodcock Reading Mastery Tests–Revised (WRMT–R). Those whose scores were lower than Grade 1 were assigned to the phonics intervention, whereas those scoring at Grade 1 or above were assigned to the fluency condition. Random assignment to treatment with pairing was used to match controls, resulting in four groups. The phonics intervention (*Read Well*, a commercial program) involved explicit, systematic instruction in English phonics and word reading, along with practice reading of decodable text and incidental instruction in vocabulary and comprehension. *Read Naturally* was the fluency intervention; it included repeated reading of English text with audiotapes, vocabulary and comprehension instruction, goal setting, and monitoring of student progress.

The progress of participants was assessed with the WRMT–R and curriculum-based reading selections. Students receiving the phonics intervention made significantly more progress than comparison students in word reading, consistent with earlier studies. Students receiving the fluency intervention made more rapid gains than the comparison students in oral reading accuracy and fluency. However, they evidenced no superiority over the controls in word identification, word analysis, or comprehension. Given the differences in amounts of instructional time, however, no clear conclusions can be reached.

Additional evidence suggesting that fluency instruction may be effective for English-language learners is provided by a study (De la Colina, Parker, Hasbrouck, & Lara-Alecio, 2001) that investigated the effects of Spanish fluency training using a translated version of *Read Naturally* (Ihnot, 1997). The Spanish version of this program was created by translating the English texts from *Read Naturally* and developing Spanish audiotapes of each story. The findings from this study are limited to Spanish reading because the study did not test the impact of the instruction on English reading.

Seventy-four Spanish–English bilingual students in first and second grades participated. Their level in English as a second language (ESL) was either beginner or non-English speaker. They did, however, have some native-language reading competence. Specifically, to be included in the study, students had to be able to correctly read orally 30 to 60 words per minute of a Spanish story or know beginning sounds and be able to read at least 50 Spanish sight words. Small groups of children represented each of three baselines in this multiple-baseline study. One group began the intervention immediately and continued for 12 weeks; a second group began 3 weeks later and continued through the remainder of the study; a third group began 5 weeks after the first group and continued for the remaining weeks. The interventions occurred for 45 minutes three times a week. Treatment fidelity was monitored weekly, and additional support was provided if a teacher appeared to be straying from the instructional procedures.

This study yielded several interesting findings. One is that most children, regardless of length of study participation, improved in oral reading fluency. This was not just an increase in trend line or rate of learning, but a sudden change in performance coincident with the onset of treatment for each group. These new performance levels were maintained throughout the study. Further, students in Grades 1 and 2 who were more highly engaged in the instructional materials— as assessed by number of timed readings—showed substantial gains, as evidenced by significant mean and slope differences. In Grade 1, high-engaged students improved by an average of 32 words correct per minute (WCPM), compared with about 10 WCPM for low-engaged students. In Grade 2, the same pattern was evident: 37 WCPM gained versus 17 WCPM. These differences in achievement of high- and low-engaged students suggest the need to develop ways to support and encourage student engagement with academic tasks.

In contrast to the Denton (2000) study, improvement also was found in reading comprehension, as measured by questions asked about the passages. Some caution in interpreting these results is needed, given that they are not based on validated measures of comprehension. Nevertheless, this pattern is consistent with theory regarding the role of fluency in reading, as well as with findings for native speakers of English (National Institute of Child Health and Human Development, 2000). It should be noted that students' oral reading fluency improved more than their reading comprehension—a finding also consistent with that for native English speakers.

Thus, fluency instruction benefits native speakers and appears to similarly benefit English-language learners. There is a clear need for more research into the most effective way to teach oral reading fluency to children who are learning English as a second language.

Vocabulary

Given the fundamental importance of vocabulary to reading comprehension and the obvious limitations in the vocabulary knowledge of English-language learners (who have not had the same opportunity as native speakers for oral exposure to English words before learning to read), it is surprising that we found only three experimental studies of English vocabulary learning, one of which was brief. In contrast, the National Reading Panel was able to find 45 experimental studies of vocabulary teaching with first-language students (National Institute of Child Health and Human Development, 2000).

One vocabulary experiment with English-language learners studied procedures for presenting words to first-grade Spanish-dominant students (Vaughn-Shavuo, 1990). Children were randomly assigned to two groups, and both were taught a collection of 31 words for 30 minutes per day for 3 weeks. The first group worked on learning words that were presented in individual sentence contexts. The second group worked on words presented in meaningful narratives, dictated their own sentences using the target words, and examined picture cards that illustrated the word meanings. The second group—the one that worked on elaborated meanings—mastered a greater proportion of the vocabulary words that were taught than did the control group (21 words learned vs. 9 words).

This result is consistent with findings from studies of native speakers, which have shown that instruction leading to deeper processing of word meanings and requiring greater repetition and use of words in different formats leads to higher proficiency. Clearly, there is a need for longer term investigations of such procedures, as well as consideration of the learning of more abstract words.

Pérez (1981) reports on a study of the vocabulary learning of 75 Mexican American third graders. For approximately 3 months, the children received 20 minutes of daily oral instruction in word meanings, with a focus on compound words, synonyms, antonyms, and multiple meanings. The experimental group showed significant improvement over a control group who participated solely in their regular school program on the Prescriptive Reading Inventory, a standardized informal reading inventory in which children read text aloud and answer questions. This means the children studied word meanings, but improved in their ability to read text orally and to answer questions about what they had read.

Another study examined the effects of enhanced vocabulary teaching with fifth-grade English-language learners (Carlo et al., 2004). Although the study included both English-language learners and native speakers of English, the data were analyzed separately, making it possible to determine the effects of the intervention on the population of interest. This analysis considers only the results drawn from the English-language learners (the number of subjects in the experimental group was 94 and the number for the control group was 48), and the native- English-speaking conditions were omitted from the tables for this chapter as well. The authors do not report how students were assigned to groups, but it was not randomly. However, students underwent extensive testing in vocabulary and comprehension both before and after completion of the instruction, so any preexisting differences were accounted for in the statistical analysis.

Students in the treatment group received 15 weeks of instruction, with an introduction of 10 to 12 words per week. Vocabulary instruction lasted for 30 to 45 minutes a day for 4 days per week, with 1 additional day per week devoted to review. The vocabulary was presented thematically and included homework assignments and a weekly test. The words were presented in Spanish before being introduced in English. The lessons then involved interpretation of word meanings in context, word association tasks, synonym/antonym tasks, and semantic features analysis.

Although there were no treatment gains on the Peabody Picture Vocabulary Test (PPVT), the English-language learners improved on several other measures of vocabulary and comprehension. Students improved in their ability to generate sentences that conveyed different meanings of multimeaning words and complete cloze passages, in tests of knowledge of word meanings, and on measures of word association and morphological knowledge. Students showed significant improvement on a cloze test used to evaluate comprehension, but the impact on comprehension was much lower than that on word learning. It is clear from these results that this training led to improved knowledge of the words studied.

The three studies of vocabulary instruction for English-language learners reviewed here yielded findings consistent with those of vocabulary studies of native speakers. However, there is a great need for more investigation into what constitutes sound and effective vocabulary instruction for English-language learners. It is essential that this learning be evaluated on various reading and writing measures, and that the retention of word knowledge beyond the training be considered.

Reading Comprehension

We found only three studies that examined ways of teaching reading comprehension to English-language learners. This dearth of research is in stark contrast to the number of studies of reading comprehension with native English speakers: The National Reading Panel identified 205 studies of comprehension instruction, using narrower selection criteria (i.e., no dissertations).

Two of the reading comprehension studies of English-language learners examined learning over periods longer than 6 weeks, and one considered performance during a single lesson. A further complication is that each study examined students at different grade levels (third, fourth, and fifth grades and high school).

Swicegood (1990) examined the impact of self-questioning on reading comprehension. This study randomly assigned a native-Spanish-speaking bilingual population of third graders ($n = 95$) to one of two groups. The experimental students were trained to ask themselves questions during reading for 90 minutes per day during the Spanish period. Participating in this kind of dialogue with oneself about a text has been shown to improve the reading comprehension of native-English-speaking students (National Institute of Child Health and Human Development, 2000). At the end of 6 weeks of instruction, no significant differences were found in either Spanish or English reading. The students did not transfer the questioning strategy to English, nor did they use it in their Spanish reading. This result differs from similar studies with native English speakers (National Institute of Child Health and Human Development, 2000).

Another study examined improvement in reading comprehension over an entire school year for 58 students in Grades 9 to 11—46 Haitian Creole-speaking and 12 Spanish-speaking students (Shames, 1998). Thirty of the students had been in the United States for less than 2 months, 17 had completed less than 1 year of ESL classes, and the remaining 11 had been in the program for over a year, but still met parameters for Level 1 of an English proficiency test (i.e., minimal knowledge of English). Three sections of ESL Reading and Writing I classes were randomly assigned to the treatment groups, and the Reading and Writing II class became the control group. Although, according to the author, teachers considered the students in Reading and Writing II to be more advanced readers than those in Reading and Writing I, all students met the criteria for Level 1 ESL students. Furthermore, all of the students but one were found to be nonliterate in English, according to the Language Assessment Scales (LASs).

All students received equivalent instruction in phonics and vocabulary. Participants in one of the experimental groups—the composition–translation condition—composed their own reading materials in their native languages in small collaborative groups according to the Community Language Learning model (Curran, 1972). Students' conversations were audiotaped, listened to, written down, and read with assistance from teachers. Teachers aided students in reflecting on the translation process and on vocabulary and grammar, and these texts became part of the study materials for the classes. For each unit, students were given a theme as a prompt; and each unit took approximately 2 weeks to complete. The stories generated in this group were also used as reading materials in the control group. The second experimental group was taught to use comprehension strategies (Know–Want to Know–Learned [K–W–L], and Question– Answer Relationships [QAR]). Each strategy was mastered over the course of a semester. This group used some of the stories from the composition–translation group, but mainly used selections from an American history textbook written especially for English-language learners. The third experimental group used a combination of the composition–translation and comprehension strategies conditions, with the type of instruction alternating every 2 weeks. As a result, this group only covered the K–W–L strategy. The combination group used both student-generated stories and the same American history textbook. Results demonstrate that both the comprehension strategies group and the combination group significantly outperformed the control group, but the composition–translation group did not. Although all differences between treatment groups favored the two groups receiving strategy instruction, these differences were not significant, unlike what has usually been found with native English speakers (National Institute of Child Health and Human Development, 2000).

The final reading comprehension study (Bean, 1982) was an examination of the impact of revising an English text to make it easier for an English-language learner population to understand. In this study, the first part of one basal reader story was selected for revision. One version of the story included clarification of pronoun referents, and the other clarified pronoun referent as well as made the story conform to story grammar conventions by deleting information not relevant to the story grammar. Forty-five fourth- and fifth-grade students were then asked to read one of the three versions and retell the story, and then they were probed with 10 questions relating to key ideas in the story (such as setting, initiating event, and goal formation; e.g., "What do the twins decide to do?").

Comparison of the recall of information from the texts indicated that only the third version, that clarified pronoun-referents as well as deleted trivial events, was easier than the original version, which included many distracting trivial events to establish the relationship between the twins, but that did not relate to the main events in the story and contained obscure pronoun refrents. A major limitation of this study is that it included only one text, and the modifications resulted in substantial changes in readability, altering the original text from a third-grade level to as high as a fifth-grade level in the story grammar revision. Thus, although comprehension of this text improved under the think condition, it is unclear whether students would be advantaged in the long run by only using such texts for instruction. Learning to comprehend encompasses learning how to make sense of different sorts of difficult texts, and this study implies that readability and comprehensibility are not necessarily synonymous. The findings of this study suggest that, although the typical information load or communication complexity of grade-level text may be too difficult for English-language learners, they cannot tell us whether it is better to use easier texts, less readable but more comprehensible texts, some combination of the two, or to provide instruction in how to handle the diverse readability and comprehensibility demands of texts.

Given the small number of studies reviewed here, it is impossible to determine the best way to facilitate reading comprehension for English-language learners. In contrast to the large number of studies on reading comprehension instruction in English as the first language, these few studies did not show a consistent advantage for comprehension strategy instruction.

Writing

The importance of writing and its relationship to reading has been clearly demonstrated (Tierney & Shanahan, 1992). Summaries of writing research (Hillocks, 1986) allow us to compare the findings of studies of English-language learners with existing research on native speakers. We found four experimental studies of writing instruction with English-language learners.

The first of these studies (Gómez, Parker, Lara-Alecio, & Gómez, 1996) examined the effectiveness of two instructional approaches during a 6-week summer program for low-achieving Hispanic English-language learners. The researchers used stratified (English proficiency level) random sampling to assign 72 fifth-grade students to two alternative treatments (free or structured writing) in this carefully executed study.

In the free-writing treatment, the students wrote compositions on topics of their own choosing. The emphasis of these classes was on the writing process, as opposed to the writing products. The students' work was not graded, but students received written feedback from teachers in the form of dialogue journals and from other students during classroom conferencing. Teachers were to customize the writing process on the basis of the daily interactions around the students' writing. In the structured-writing treatment, students were assigned topics to write about, and their writing was judged for syntactic and lexical accuracy as well as content. Students received prompt feedback from the teacher on the errors they made in their writing, and they were required to fix those errors. In both groups, students were allowed to compose in English or Spanish.

Students produced standardized writings weekly to allow for comparison between the two groups, and these writing samples were examined in several different ways. For example, the accuracy of the students' spelling was noted, and it was found that the structured-writing group improved on this measure over the 6 weeks, whereas the spelling of the free writers clearly deteriorated. The two groups evidenced some improvement in analytic rating scores of their writing (topic development, organization, meaning, sentence construction, or mechanics), but there were no significant differences in these ratings between the two groups. The structured-writing group improved more in holistic ratings of their writing, but this change may have been due to the fact that the free-writing group received higher ratings in overall quality from the beginning (in other words, there was less room for them to improve). There were no differences in productivity.

In summary, the differences that were found favored the structured-writing group. This finding is similar to that reported by Hillocks (1986) for native-English-language writers. Although some educators have urged that free-writing approaches be used in the elementary grades with native speakers, research has not demonstrated clear superiority for these methods when the measure is quality of writing. The results of this single study are consistent with that finding.

A second study of writing (Prater & Bermúdez, 1993) examined the impact of peer response in conference groups on the writing development of English-language learners in fourth grade. Two teachers participated, each of whom taught a control and an experimental section. Students in the experimental classes were assigned to four- to five-member response groups, each including one or two English-language learners. The control students worked on writing by themselves during the same period. Students were required to develop one composition per week. The response groups made topic suggestions, responded to first drafts (which were then revised), and cooperatively edited the papers, with group members taking on different editorial responsibilities. Students completed an initial composition on their own, which was used as a pretest measure. After 3 weeks of writing, they were asked to produce another composition on their own (the posttest). Compositions were scored holistically on a 6-point scale, and the numbers of words, sentences, and idea units in each composition were counted. The authors provided no pretest data, so it is uncertain whether all of the comparisons were statistically appropriate. The data show that there was no improvement in quality of writing during these 3 weeks, but the amount of writing increased for the treatment group (both more words and more idea units).

A different finding emerged from a second study of peer support in writing (Franken & Haslett, 1999). This study of high school students in New Zealand focused on the writing of arguments. Two groups were formed-one in which the students worked alone and another in which they worked in pairs. Identical amounts of writing time were provided to the groups for 6 weeks (three 2-hour periods per week), with students writing about different topics each week. By the end of the study, students who had written alone did better; they wrote more complex texts and with better grammatical accuracy than the students who conferred with each other about writing. In other words, peer discussion failed to improve the quality of the writing in this case. In this study, all of the participants in the groups were English-language learners in contrast with the previous study, in which learning may have resulted from increased communication with native English speakers. Paired work has been successful in improving first-language writing, math, and oral-reading fluency, but these two studies of second-language writing suggest that the benefits are less consistent, at least when none of the students can serve as an English resource to the others.

We found only one other experimental study of writing instruction for English-language learners (Sengupta, 2000). This study examined the impact of revision training on the writing performance of secondary-level ESL students in Hong Kong. One group of writers continued with traditional instruction (students wrote papers that were corrected by the teachers), whereas the other group wrote together, discussed the quality of their paper, and revised the paper. Holistic evaluations of pre- and post-instruction essays found that this year-long revision training led to greater writing improvement than the traditional instruction.

In a meta-analysis of writing studies involving native speakers, Hillocks (1986) considered whether revision as conducted in these studies provides any learning benefit. He found that revision did help students improve their writing—to a small extent. The Sengupta (2000) study found a much larger effect of revision than was evident in the studies of native speakers. However, it should be noted that Hillocks examined 11 such studies and that they were not homogeneous; in other words, there was substantial variability in this finding. Sengupta's results are within the range of the findings with native speakers.

Summary and Conclusions

With so few experimental studies on instruction in any of the individual components of literacy and with such great variability in study designs, it is difficult to generalize from the findings. It appears fair to say that the 17 studies discussed in this section—whatever their strengths and weaknesses—yielded results that are largely consistent with the findings for native-speaking populations. Although these results are insufficient to prove that the same instructional routines found to benefit native speakers are equally effective with English-language learners, they in no way contradict this idea (Fitzgerald, 1995a, 1995b).

Of the 17 studies synthesized here, however, only 6 employed comprehension measures. When comprehension was measured, the studies often found no significant improvement in that outcome due to the instruction (e.g., Denton, 2000); when such improvement was observed, it was less pronounced than was the case for other measures (e.g., Gunn, Biglan, et al., 2000; Gunn, Smolkowski, et al., 2002). Generally, the effects observed in these studies were smaller than those found by the comparable National Reading Panel studies, and this was true particularly for reading comprehension.

The limited English proficiency of the language-minority students may be implicated in these findings. In the area of phonics instruction, for example, the National Reading Panel found that for English-speaking students, phonics instruction was found to have a consistently positive impact on all literacy measures for beginning readers, but only on decoding outcomes for students in the upper elementary grades. Accordingly, to build overall reading skill, it may be wise to provide phonics support for these older students who are struggling with reading, but only in the context of instruction in other literacy elements (e.g., vocabulary, comprehension). Phonics shows students how to decode, which helps them as long as the words they are trying to decode are in their oral language. English-language learners may lack oral counterparts for the words they decode; under such circumstances, the impact of phonics on text comprehension will be more variable and less certain. The same could be said of oral reading fluency instruction, which shows a substantial impact on the reading comprehension of native English speakers, but a much smaller, although still positive, impact on English-language learners. This pattern appears to hold with the teaching of comprehension strategies such as summarization or questioning because the use of these techniques may not result in as thorough an analysis of meaning as would be possible if students had greater facility with oral English.

The positive findings for this entire set of studies suggest that teaching specific reading and writing elements can be beneficial to second-language students. The smaller effect sizes, however, particularly for reading comprehension, suggest the potential importance of building greater knowledge of oral English simultaneously so the literacy tools provided by instruction can be used to maximum advantage. Chapter 5 showed the implications of oral language proficiency in reading comprehension, and those findings suggest the potential necessity of greater oral language development in order to obtain maximum benefit from the types of instruction evaluated here.

Furthermore, that instruction in the components of literacy benefits English-language learners does not mitigate the need to adjust these instructional approaches for use with these students (Gersten & Baker, 2000). Indeed, some of the studies reviewed here allude to such adjustments. For example, it may be useful to give greater attention to particular sounds (those not in the first language) when working to build auditory discrimination skills in English-language learners (Kramer et al., 1983). Similarly, teaching English vocabulary is effective, but progress may be most rapid when this instruction is connected to the students' home language, such as by providing a home-language equivalent or synonym for new words or focusing on shared cognates when available. (The issue here is not whether the students' home language should be taught as part of literacy instruction, but whether it should be used as the basis for some aspects of this instruction.) Future research needs to be more explicit about the kinds of adjustments for English-language learners that are made in successful programs.

Our review of the literature on explicit instruction in the literacy components, then, yields the following conclusions:

- Too few studies have examined the benefits of teaching the components of literacy considered here—phonological awareness, phonics, vocabulary, oral reading fluency, reading comprehension, writing, and spelling—to English-language learners. This situation is different from that for native-

English-speaking students. The National Reading Panel examined more than 400 studies on these topics, not including writing or spelling, and its search was limited to published journal articles over a well-defined time span. This panel, with more liberal and extensive search procedures, was able to identify only 17 analogous studies. Future research is needed to address effective literacy instruction for English-language learners.

- There are too few high-quality studies of English-language learners on any of these literacy components to allow specific conclusions about what works best with any element or component.
- In the aggregate, however, it appears that what works with native-speaker populations *generally* works with English-language learners. In fact, instruction that emphasizes literacy components confers a learning advantage to English-language learners. The effect sizes for such teaching tend to be in the moderate range, meaning that its benefits are large enough to be important.
- Effect sizes for English-language learners are lower and more variable than those for native-English-speaking students, suggesting that such teaching is likely to be necessary, but insufficient, for improving literacy achievement among the English-language learners. It is possible that combining high-quality instruction in the literacy components with efforts to enhance oral language development in English would lead to higher effect sizes. Research is needed to test that hypothesis.
- Common instructional routines may need to be adjusted to make instruction in the literacy components maximally effective with English-language learners. Unfortunately, authors often have been silent in describing such adjustments, or have done no more than mention them, rather than providing a thorough description or explanation. Future research needs to be explicit in this regard.

COMPLEX APPROACHES TO LITERACY TEACHING

Some experimental studies have addressed multiple literacy components simultaneously or aimed at less targeted outcomes. Here we evaluate experimental, quasi-experimental, and single-subject studies of the effectiveness of more complex approaches to enhancing literacy development for English-language learners. Again, average effect sizes were calculated for these studies as reported in Table 15.2. Appendix 15.A provides additional information about the study samples and interventions.

Success for All

One example of a complex instructional program is Success for All (SFA). SFA provides professional development for teachers, instructional time standards, a curriculum that addresses key literacy components, instructional materials, and assessment and remediation routines, including tutoring programs for low achievers. SFA has been widely used with high-poverty students. However, most studies of SFA have been conducted with native-English-speaking students or have not differentiated ethnicity from second-language status.[3] This distinction is important because students may be of a particular ethnicity without being language minority. Results from this research with nonlanguage-minority student populations have demonstrated that the program is effective (Slavin & Madden, 2001).

SFA is the only school-wide intervention that has been studied experimentally with language-minority students. One study with this population was documented in a technical report (Dianda & Flaherty, 1995; see also Livingston & Flaherty, 1997; Slavin & Madden, 1998); it focused on the effects of SFA on primary-grade children who were native Spanish speakers. Children from three schools were tested on the Spanish version of the PPVT at the beginning of kindergarten—when they entered the SFA program—and on the Spanish version of the Woodcock–Johnson Reading Tests at the conclusion of Grade 1. These performances were compared with those of children drawn from matched schools (in terms of poverty, language status, and ethnicity). The SFA children outperformed the comparison group on letter–word identification, word attack, and passage comprehension. The differences were greatest for children in the lowest quartile, and in all cases the comparisons significantly favored the SFA group. The study results indicate that SFA gave these students a faster start in learning to read Spanish; however, the study did not follow these students through the transition to English.

A second study of the effectiveness of SFA with first-grade English-language learners is known as the Arizona Evaluation (Slavin & Madden, 1998). The evaluation compared results for two SFA schools with those of four control schools. This analysis focuses on the data drawn from the first-grade classroom comparisons. Because the two SFA schools differed markedly from each other in poverty statistics and percentage of Hispanic children, two separate analyses were conducted: one for the high-poverty schools and one for the less impoverished ones. The results for both analyses with the Spanish-dominant portions of the school populations indicate SFA students scored better on word attack, with no significant group differences on any of the other outcomes (word identification, passage comprehension, or oral reading). However, multiple control groups were used, and these varied in comparability to the experimental treatment groups. Although the overall average effect size across all comparisons was large and significant, this was due to some extent to the nature of the comparisons (e.g., for the high-poverty analysis, the SFA school was compared to one control group that had similar pretest performance, as well as to a control group that differed from it in initial achievement by almost a full standard deviation).

A third SFA study with English-language learners—the Fairhill evaluation, drawn from the same technical report as the Arizona study (Slavin & Madden, 1998)—examined Grade 3 reading performance across two matched schools, one using SFA. The study involved Spanish speakers who were tested at the beginning of Grade 1 on the PPVT and at the end of Grade 3 on the Woodcock–Johnson. An analysis of covariance (ANCOVA) design was used to correct for initial differences on the PPVT. No mobility data were provided. The

---

[3]SFA has conducted additional evaluations of its program with language-minority students subsequent to 2002.

SFA students far outperformed the comparison group in reading, as measured by the Spanish-language version of the Woodcock–Johnson letter–word identification, word attack, and passage comprehension subtests, although it should be noted that the control group received no school instruction in Spanish over the 3 years. In English (again, the Woodcock–Johnson subtests), the SFA students showed no advantage over the control students in word identification or passage comprehension, although they did significantly better on word attack. In other words, the SFA students read about as well as the controls in English, except they were superior with regard to word attack in English and outperformed the controls in Spanish reading. The authors described these findings as *speculative* and *worthy of further investigation*.

From these three studies, it is evident that more research is needed. A large-scale experimental analysis of the effectiveness of SFA that follows children through the transition to English would be informative. In one of the studies done so far (Dianda & Flaherty, 1995), the SFA first graders did better in Spanish reading, whereas in another they did better in English word attack (Arizona data; Slavin & Madden, 1998). In the Fairhill study (Slavin & Madden, 1998), which followed students through the third-grade transition to English, SFA students performed better than the controls on English word attack and Spanish reading.

Encouraging Reading and Writing

Another approach to enriching the literacy development of English-language learners has been to encourage reading and writing. In one study, for example, six second-, third-, and fourth-grade teachers in two schools (one high-income, one low-income) were provided with extensive collections of children's books in Spanish (Schon, Hopkins, & Davis, 1982). One teacher dropped out of the study because she did not think it was a good idea to teach Spanish to the children. The teachers made available at least 60 minutes of free-reading time per week. The control group consisted of the students of seven teachers from two other schools who continued their regular program of teaching reading in English. The study found that encouraging students to read in their home language made no difference in their English literacy skills, compared with those of the control group.

In another study that involved encouraging reading in the home language (Schon, Hopkins, & Vojir, 1985), the effect of special reading time was evaluated with seventh- and eighth-grade students. Students were provided 45 minutes of reading time each week, along with Spanish reading materials. The experimental and control students were compared on Spanish and English reading comprehension, speed, and vocabulary, as well as attitude toward reading and academic self-concept. The two grade levels were handled separately, with eight comparisons being made for each; thus, there were 16 comparisons. For the eight seventh-grade comparisons, only one difference was found: The control group outperformed the experimental group in English reading comprehension. For the eighth-grade comparisons, four significant differences were found: The experimental group did better in Spanish reading, vocabulary, and reading speed, whereas the control group did better in English reading comprehension. Having students practice Spanish reading had an impact on

Spanish reading achievement, but appeared to limit or reduce the growth in English reading comprehension.

In a third study, students who were encouraged to read in their native language (Schon, Hopkins, & Vojir, 1984) were compared with two groups of Hispanic high school students. Low-achieving readers in all three groups were assigned to remedial reading classes (55 minutes per day). The experimental students were released for 55 minutes of free-reading time each week; they were provided with libraries of Spanish books and magazines and were encouraged to read. In one experiment, 168 low-income high school students (Grades 9–12) were assigned to the experimental and control groups. Students took pre- and posttests in English and Spanish reading. After 4 months, no differences were apparent. In a second experiment, conducted in a middle-class high school, 21 experimental English-language learners were compared with 30 controls. Attrition was considerable in this experiment, but was not analyzed. Yet it was especially important because if students made positive gains, they were removed from the special program, thereby reducing the chances of measuring the program's effectiveness. Again, no differences on any measure of Spanish or English reading or of reading interest were found, but whether this result was due to attrition cannot be determined.

The impact on English reading outcomes of encouraging students to read may be more positive when the reading takes place in English. This is the major message of Tudor and Hafiz's (1989) study of the benefit of encouraging sixteen 10- and 11-year-old students to read more in English. The students were English-language learners from Pakistan. They were placed in a classroom in the United Kingdom, and their performance was compared with that of two other classrooms of English-language learners (one from the same school and one from a different school). The average performances on the various pretest measures were similar, but consistently lower for the experimental group, so regression to the mean could be a problem. No standard deviations were provided to allow the appropriateness of the data treatment to be examined. In the study, which was carried out for 12 weeks, the experimental subjects were given additional reading time (1 hour per day after school on a voluntary basis). The teacher supervised the students at his home and helped them with word meanings as needed. In a series of independent *t* tests using two reading and three writing tests, the experimental group consistently showed gains during the experimental period, whereas the control group did not. The results of this study are more positive than those of the Schon et al. (1985) study. There are many possible reasons for this difference: a greater amount of reading, an emphasis on English as opposed to native-language reading, reading time that extended the school day rather than replacing school reading, or the motivation resulting from going to the teacher's home. In any event, the extensive additional English reading time beyond the school day had a positive impact on English literacy.

Elley (1991) reports on three studies in which students in various countries were provided Book Floods (i.e., many books were made available) and additional reading time. English was not the societal language in one of the studies, and no information is provided in a second study on the selection of the groups or whether there was any pre-intervention testing. For these reasons, only one of the studies is included here, although the findings of all three studies were consistent. The study included here was conducted in Fiji with English-language learners, children ages 9 to 11. Extensive pretesting took place in 16 rural schools. Eight schools were assigned to the Book Flood groups, and eight used an English-language instructional program (Tate Audiolingual). The author indicates that there were initial differences among the groups (in reading, racial composition, and resources) that were controlled for statistically. Half the Book Flood group was randomly assigned to a shared-book program; the other half was assigned to a sustained silent reading program for an equivalent 20 to 30 minutes per day. The program continued daily over 2 school years (there were initially 535 students, and this number fell to 459 by the end of the second year). Both Book Flood groups outperformed the Tate Audiolingual groups in reading comprehension and understanding of English-language structures at the fourth-grade level in Year 1, in reading and listening comprehension in fifth grade in Year 1, and on all measures in both grades in Year 2.

Unfortunately, confidence in these findings is limited because of the reporting flaws in this study. It is not possible to tell whether the pretest was in the students' native language or English. There was attrition over the 2 years, but the author does not report what was done, if anything, to account for it. The tests were developed specifically for the study, and no evidence of their validity or reliability is reported. Finally, this is a special instance of English-language learning. English is a societal language in Fiji, but the subjects attended rural schools, and their contact with English probably was quite limited, which may have made the intervention more like foreign-language study than second-language learning.

Tsang (1996) compared the impact of encouraging students to read with that of encouraging students to write. This study examined the literacy development of 144 secondary students, all of whom were speakers of Cantonese learning English in Hong Kong. All the students received regular English instruction—seven to nine times for 40 minutes over 6-day cycles. In addition, they were randomly assigned to three treatment conditions, which operated over a 24-week period. In one group, the students were given eight books to read for homework and wrote book reports about each. In a second group, students were assigned to write eight essays. Students in the control group did math homework. Results were measured in terms of improvement in essay writing (content, organization, vocabulary, language use, mechanics, and total impression). The group that did extra reading performed better than both of the other groups on English essay writing. More specifically, for the reading group, there were improvements in content and language use and overall improvement in writing; there were no gains in vocabulary, organization, or mechanics. It was evident that students were learning something about English from reading that was not being learned from writing or math. This study was like that of Tudor and Hafiz (1989), discussed earlier, in that students did the extra reading away from school, so the extra reading time was an extension rather than a replacement of other academic learning time.

Caution is necessary in interpreting the results of these studies of encouraging reading because of their limited quantity and quality. The results do offer some suggestions, however at the time of the inter-vention. Although reading in a home language in some cases contributes to better reading in that language, it does not lead to improved English literacy, at the time of the intervention, whereas extra time in English reading may have a beneficial effect on English reading outcomes. This benefit appears particularly likely when the reading time extends beyond the school day or provides students with an opportunity to use English that may be unavailable during daily schoolwork. More evidence is required both to replicate these findings and to determine just what is effective in terms of amount of reading, nature of materials and routines, context and long-term consequences.

Reading to Children

Reading aloud to children has been suggested as an approach to improving the literacy of English-language learners. For example, Hastings-Góngora (1993) trained parents in read-aloud techniques for use with their kindergarten children. A group of six parents attended a single training workshop, and another group of similar size did not. The parents who attended the workshop were provided with Spanish-language books for 5 weeks and encouraged to read them to their children. Given the brief period involved, it is not surprising that no significant gains due to this treatment were found on a standardized vocabulary test. Moreover, the lack of monitoring makes it impossible to know whether the parents actually read to their children.

In a better-designed study of reading to children (Ulanoff & Pucci, 1999), the effect of a single lesson was examined. Third-grade English-language learners were randomly assigned to one of three groups: a control group that heard a story in English with no discussion of the story, and two treatment groups that heard the same story—one group in which the teacher built background knowledge and previewed the difficult vocabulary in Spanish, read the book in English, and reviewed the story in Spanish, and one group in which the teacher read the book aloud in English and concurrently translated the story into Spanish. In each of the three treatments, student knowledge of specific words from the story was tested both before and after reading. The preview–review group learned significantly more words than the other two groups and maintained this superiority 1 week later. The implication is that reading to English-language learners with preview–review of selected words and content may improve vocabulary development, but of course this effect has yet to be tested over any meaningful period of time.

Finally, Hancock (2002) examined the impact of the language of books read by parents to their kindergarten-age children. Fifty-two native-Spanish-speaking kindergarten children were randomly assigned to one of two conditions: Their parents were provided with either Spanish-language books or English-language books to share with them. Students were pre- and posttested on a standardized measure of print awareness. The results indicate that students who worked with books in their own language came away knowing more about print concepts than those whose parents shared the books in English. The results of this study suggest that, at least early on, sharing books with a child in the native language is more helpful than sharing books in English if the goal is learning how print works (e.g., directionality, formatting).

Tutoring and Remediation

Two studies examined the impact of tutoring (or of being tutors) on the learning of English-language learners. Such studies have usually focused on individual children who have learning problems or are at risk. A good example of this kind of study is one that examined the impact of Descubriendo La Lectura, a Spanish version of Reading Recovery, on the literacy learning of first graders (Escamilla, 1994). In this program, at-risk readers, usually the lowest performing 20% at the beginning of the year, are taught one on one by a highly trained teacher for 30 minutes per day until they reach the average performance level for their classroom. The literacy achievement (letter identification, word reading, concepts about print, writing vocabulary, dictation, and text-level reading) of 23 experimental English-language learners from four schools was compared with that of 23 control students from two other schools that did not have the program. The Descubriendo children performed significantly better than the controls on all variables by the end of the year. The extra, intensive instruction provided those children with a clear learning advantage in Spanish reading at the end of first grade.

Syvanen (1997) examined the impact of cross-age tutoring on 16 fourth- and fifth-grade English-language learners (home languages unspecified). The students were tutored in reading in kindergarten and Grade 1 for 19 weeks. They showed no apparent gains in their reading achievement, compared with other English-language learners in the same school.

Other Investigations

One study analyzed experimental data within an ethnographic analysis of the home literacy environments of 10 kindergarten children (Goldenberg, Reese, & Gallimore, 1992). The purpose of the study was to better understand the home literacy experiences of children from non-English-language backgrounds and how school affects those experiences. To create an appropriate context for the study, kindergarten classes were assigned to one of two treatment groups: an experimental group that received copies of 12 stories to work with in school, along with associated workbook pages; and a control group that received worksheets paralleling the school's phonics program. The storybooks being read in the experimental classes were sent home with the children, and workbooks made up of phonics materials were sent home with control group children. Extensive observations were carried out in the homes of 10 children— 5 from the experimental group and 5 from the control group. Differences were evident in the literacy activities in the two sets of homes: There were more text-reading activities in the experimental group and more letter-teaching activities in the control group, but the patterns were complex, and, according to the authors, neither group was doing much with meaning. The materials sent home influenced home literacy environments, but not in ways the researchers expected. There were no statistical differences between the two groups of five children on various reading measures, possibly due to the lack of statistical power with such a small sample.

In another investigation, Cohen and Rodríquez (1980) examined the impact of a direct instruction/mastery learning model on the English literacy learning of 150 English-language learners in first grade, approximately half of whom were assigned to the experimental group. That group received direct instruction in behavioral objectives tied to beginning literacy learning. Although the control group instruction is not described, the experimental students did better on an English silent-reading comprehension test after 90 lessons.

In another study of young children, Tharp (1982) examined the impact of a complex instructional approach in which first graders, in a year-long intervention, received enhanced reading comprehension instruction (delivered in small groups), reduced phonics instruction, and frequent criterion-referenced testing. Three experiments were conducted, only one of which met the design criteria, allowing it to be analyzed here (the other two experiments had positive results, but lacked adequate control groups). This experiment was carried out in classrooms in which all children spoke Hawaiian Creole. Students were randomly assigned to two experimental and two control classrooms at each of two schools. At one site, research team teachers instructed the two experimental classrooms, and regular classroom teachers instructed the two control classrooms. At the other site, two regular classroom teachers who had been trained in the research-designed program instructed the experimental classrooms, and two regular classroom teachers instructed the control classrooms. Six critical elements of the experimental classrooms that differentiated them from the control classrooms included: (a) more time spent on reading comprehension and relatively less time on decoding; (b) more frequent criterion-referenced testing to monitor student progress; (c) classes that relied entirely on small-group discussion for reading lessons in which the "dominant participation structure was highly informal, continuing overlapping speech, mutual participation by teacher and students, co-narration, volunteered speech, instant feedback, and lack of penalty for wrong answers" (p. 519); (d) child motivation maintained through high rates of praise and other forms of positive interpersonal reinforcement; (e) individualized diagnostic prescriptive instruction; and (f) a quality control system in which the program characteristics are measured, rated, and used to monitor program implementation.

On the vocabulary subtest of the Gates–MacGinitie Reading Tests, which, according to the test manual, is a measure of decoding at the first-grade level, the experimental groups significantly outperformed the control groups despite the reduction in phonics instruction. On the comprehension subtest of the same battery, the differences favoring the experimental groups nearly reached the .05 significance level, but full-scale scores on the Metropolitan Reading Tests showed no differences.

An investigation of the impact of cooperative grouping procedures (Calderón, Hertz-Lazarowitz, & Slavin, 1998) found benefits for such procedures relative to basal instruction for Spanish-background students. The study involved 222 students from three experimental schools and four comparison schools in El Paso, Texas. Each group received 2 hours per day of reading and language arts instruction, with 30 minutes devoted daily to ESL instruction. The two groups used the same Spanish and English text materials. However, the experimental students were placed in groups of four: They carried out cooperative work during the lessons, and they received specialized teaching in comprehension, vocabulary, oral reading fluency, and writing. No pretest data are reported, so it is impossible to evaluate the appropriateness of the statistical comparisons. However, the investigators found that, by the end of second grade, there was no difference in Spanish reading comprehension between the two groups, although the cooperative-grouping students did better in Spanish writing. By the end of third grade, there was no difference on a test of English writing, but the experimental subjects did significantly better in English reading.

Waxman et al. (1994) studied the learning of 325 English-language learners in Grades 1 to 5. These students were assigned to four conditions: (a) a control group that continued with their regular instruction, (b) a second group that received ESL instruction in the content areas (including explanations in the home language and graphic mapping and problem solving in science, math, and reading), (c) a third group that received Effective Use of Time training (pretesting, informing, guided practice, posttesting), and (d) a fourth group that received a combination of the two programs. Each treatment group participated in fifteen 3-hour instructional sessions delivered by special teachers. Students were pre- and posttested on the Iowa Test of Basic Skills (ITBS). Despite the researchers' concern about the appropriateness of the procedures, ANCOVA was used to correct for the sizable initial achievement differences among the groups (particularly for the Effective Use of Time group). The Effective Use of Time group outperformed all the other groups in reading, but we cannot determine whether this result was due to the enhanced instructional routine or the initial differences among the groups. Because the two treatments in this study were not just variants of a single instructional approach, effect sizes for each of the separate treatments are included in Table 15.2.

The next two studies examined a series of improvements to literacy and language arts lessons that were related to the comprehension enhancements in the Tharp (1982) study. Two of these studies were of limited scope and short term, with one considering five lessons and the other a 5-day lesson sequence; neither looked at improvements in general literacy achievement. The third study examined the long-term benefits of such instruction over several years.

Saunders and Goldenberg (1999) presented 116 fourth and fifth graders with four different lesson formats. Students in the control group read a story from a basal reader and were given time to study the story and complete worksheets based on it; in addition to the control group activities, the other three groups discussed and/or wrote about the story. Each group included native speakers and English-language learners. The lessons took 1 week to complete. The results reveal that, overall, the native English speakers scored higher than the English-language learners in comprehension. However, for both native English speakers and English-language learners, the discussion-only and discussion and writing groups outperformed both the writing-only and control groups on factual and interpretive comprehension of the story. Existing differences in writing scores made it impossible to determine the impact of the treatment on theme writing. Students who discussed what they read had better comprehension than those who only read or who read and wrote. Thus, the instructional conversations in this study had a positive impact.

In a related, but more ambitious, study, Saunders (1999) examined the literacy learning of English-language learners in Grades 2 to 5 that resulted from the long-term use of enhanced literacy instruction. In this study, literacy learning was compared for 61 experimental students and 64 control group students from a different school. All the students were participating in a Spanish transitional bilingual program and remained in the same schools from Grades 1 to 5. This was not a prospective study; that is, data were selected for use *after* students had completed fifth grade, and it is possible that the selection procedures biased the results. All comparisons were based on matched samples of subjects (students who scored within 5 percentile points of each other on first-grade Spanish reading and language scores).

In this study, 12 instructional components were used to build the students' literacy and language skills: literature units that employed an experience–text relationship method of presentation, literature logs, instructional conversations, writing as a process, direct teaching of comprehension strategies, assigned independent reading, dictation, lessons in written conventions, English-language development through literature, pleasure reading, teacher read-alouds, and interactive journals. On both the Comprehensive Test of Basic Skills (CTBS) and a district assessment battery (a combination of measures of oral English proficiency, Spanish reading, and Spanish writing), the experimental students increasingly outperformed the control students from one grade to the next, with statistically significant differences evident at fifth grade, when most students were tested in English. The enhanced language arts instruction led to higher achievement in literacy for these students, but it is unclear whether sample selection procedures biased these results in any way.

Neuman and Koskinen (1992) examined the impact of using captioned TV as a way to build word knowledge for second-language learners. This study focused on the learning of English within three content areas among 129 English-language learners in seventh and eighth grades who represented several first languages. Students received 9 weeks of instruction (3 weeks for each content unit). A control group simply read the textbook, whereas the experimental groups watched TV presentations of content with captions, without captions, or in concert with texts that were based on the captions. Pretest differences were adjusted statistically, but it is not possible to evaluate the appropriateness of this adjustment. Generally, captioned TV outperformed just reading in all three units and did better than TV without captions, although not for all units. Hearing the language or seeing the physical representations on film along with seeing captions or other text helped the students learn key vocabulary, which was measured in isolation or in context.

Summary and Conclusions

Overall, there were few experimental studies that examined the effectiveness of complex innovations aimed at improving the literacy performance of English-language learners. With so few studies of any given approach—even when the results were promising—it is currently not possible to conclude that any of these approaches consistently confer an advantage to learners. We would characterize the quality of research evidence in this area as weak to moderate in terms of rigor of design and certainty of conclusions the studies would allow.

SFA was examined in three separate studies that met our selection criteria, and a positive impact was demonstrated in each of these. The results from studies on encouraging students to read indicate that, in some cases, reading in a home language contributes to better reading in that language, but not to improved English literacy. However, extra time in English reading may have a beneficial effect on English reading outcomes. As noted earlier, this benefit appears particularly likely when the reading time extends beyond the school day or provides students with an opportunity to use English that may be unavailable during daily schoolwork. Reading aloud to children is widely touted, but the quality of the evidence here is so limited that the best we can say is that students may be able to develop English vocabulary through this approach. Enhanced literature discussions and language arts routines showed promise, but three of the four studies of these approaches examined only the immediate impacts of single lessons, rather than overall improvements in literacy, although the one that looked at overall improvement had positive results. The impact of Descubriendo was evident in the children's native language. Cooperative grouping conferred a benefit, as did captioned TV, but these results were drawn from single studies, so further investigation is needed to confirm these findings.

Some important insights into effective instruction for English-language learners can be drawn from the pattern of results obtained when improvement in reading comprehension was the outcome measure. Eighteen of the 22 studies reviewed here measured comprehension outcomes. The 18 studies that measured reading comprehension had less positive results than the 4 that did not. Even more telling than this is the fact that, for any comparison made in these 22 studies, all failures to accomplish significant differences were for reading comprehension. Two of the three studies with positive results that included reading comprehension as an outcome measure (Dianda & Flaherty, 1995; Elley, 1991; Tharp, 1982) reported less improvement on comprehension than on the other measures used. It is fair to say that sizable positive reading comprehension outcomes were relatively rare in the studies reviewed in both portions of this chapter. Generally, the advantages conferred on English-language students by the approaches to literacy instruction reviewed here were greater for such measures as preliteracy skills and decoding than for reading comprehension. This finding is consistent with findings reported in Part II of this volume, which indicate that, although language-minority students and their native-speaking peers perform at similar levels on measures of phonological processing and word reading, their performance on measures of comprehension falls far below their native-speaking peers. This finding is not surprising given the multidimensional nature of reading comprehension, the language demands involved, and the background knowledge required for success on many of these tasks.

Our review of the literature on complex approaches to literacy instruction yields the following conclusions:

- Given the positive findings and sizable effects reported for many of these interventions, it is evident that we can enhance the literacy development of English-language learners with better instruction.
- Although many of the studies reviewed here found positive results, none of these innovations was examined thoroughly or across enough studies for us to conclude that they provide a certain avenue to better achievement for English-language learners.

- As previously noted, the interventions in these studies generally had a greater impact on decoding and fluency than on reading comprehension. As is evident from the studies reviewed in this chapter, to provide maximum benefit to language-minority students, instruction must do more than develop a complex array of reading skills; these instructional approaches typically had smaller effects with language-minority students than with first-language learners. This means that providing high-quality instruction in these skills alone would be insufficient to support equal academic success for language-minority students. It may be that what is needed is sound reading instruction combined with simultaneous efforts to increase the scope and sophistication of these students' oral language proficiency. There is a need for research testing that hypothesis.

- Efforts to provide students with substantial experience with English (such as by encouraging them to read English-language materials beyond the instructional day or reading to them to build their vocabulary) has shown some value. This pattern of results is evident in studies that encouraged students to read as well as in those aimed at developing more thorough discussion routines around literature.

- There is a need for research to further examine the value of the promising programs discussed in this section. Replication provides important evidence of the efficacy of an approach, and such studies are needed to increase the confidence with which we can implement the findings reviewed here in policy and practice.

APPENDIX 15–A

Table 15–A–1.

Distinguishing two types of studies – explicit instruction in literacy components and complex approaches – with studies listed by skill or approach, as in Chapter 15[1].

Study	Sample		Language Status Definition	Intervention Duration & Routine	Instructional Practices	Materials	Professional Development	Delivery
	N	Grade						

Explicit Instruction in Literacy Components

Phonemic Awareness & Phonics

| Gunn et al., 2000 | 184 | K–3 | Determined by ethnicity: Hispanic and non-Hispanic 84% of Hispanic students spoke only or mainly Spanish | 4–5 months and 15–16 months (up to 2 years) 25–30 minutes daily Pull-out Small group and one-on-one | 2 instructional groups Reading Mastery (RM; Engelmann & Bruner, 1988) group, used in 1st and 2nd grades: Emphasizes phonemic awareness, sound-letter correspondence, sounding out and blending words Corrective Reading (CR; Engelmann, Carnine, & Johnson, 1988) group, used in 3rd and 4th grades: Emphasizes phonics, decoding, fluency, and comprehension | Typical Reading Mastery materials Typical Corrective Reading materials Decodable texts | 10 hours of pre-service training in testing, grouping, presenting lessons, signaling for student responses, correcting errors, motivating students with clear expectations and feedback, and theoretical framework of effective reading instruction Twice monthly meetings | Instructors: Assistants hired for project Fidelity: Weekly observations |

(Continued)

[1] If the literacy outcome measures were in the students' home language, the study is printed in italics.

*No information provided in the study

	Sample			Intervention				
Study	N	Grade	Language Status Definition	Duration & Routine	Instructional Practices	Materials	Professional Development	Delivery
					Both methods used direct, explicit instruction, with modeling, practice, and feedback and skills taught until demonstrated mastery		Observed trainer teaching lessons as needed	
Gunn et al., 2002	117	K-3	(see Gunn et al., 2000 above)	(see Gunn et al., 2000 above)	(see Gunn et al., 2000 above)	(see Gunn et al., 2000 above)	(see Gunn et al., 2000 above)	(see Gunn et al., 2000 above)
Kramer et al., 1983	15	1–3	Mexican American students who could speak both Spanish and English	4 weeks 30 minutes per session, 4 days a week Pull-out Unspecified grouping	Phonemic awareness 1 new minimal contrast pair per week First 2 days of week, new sounds taught (one per day), and second 2 days of week previously taught pairs reviewed	Picture cards Other materials not specified	Not applicable	Instructor: Researcher Fidelity: Not applicable

(Continued)

Sample			Language Status	Intervention				
Study	N	Grade	Definition	Duration & Routine	Instructional Practices	Materials	Professional Development	Delivery
					Sounds taught using names (e.g., Chile Choo for /ch/) and reviewed in oral and written exercises and games			
					Individual, self-directed practice as free time allowed			
Larson, 1996	33	1	Bilingual and second year ESOL Puerto Rican students	5–7 weeks	Phonemic awareness	Elkonin boxes	Not applicable	Instructor: Researcher
				15 minutes per session, 2–3 times weekly	Letter-sound correspondences	Plastic letter tiles		Fidelity: Not applicable
				Pull-out	Modeling and practice in pointing to Elkonin boxes while pronouncing CVC words until 80% correct criterion met			
				One-on-one				
					Then modeling and practice in moving letter tiles into Elkonin boxes while			

(Continued)

451

(Continued)

Study	N	Grade	Language Status Definition	Duration & Routine	Instructional Practices	Materials	Professional Development	Delivery
					pronouncing CVC words until 80% correct criterion met			
					Training occurred either in English only, or in Spanish until 80% criterion met and then in English			
Stuart, 1999	112	Pre & K	English as a Second Language learners	12 weeks 1 hour daily In-class Whole class	Phonological awareness Letter-sound correspondences Whole class instruction with small group follow-up activities	Phonics Handbook (Lloyd, 1992), photocopied worksheets, phonics workbooks, "finger" phonics books (small decodable texts), phonics wall chart, phonics jigsaw puzzles, stencils, videos	Researcher met with teachers Teachers given Phonics Handbook, training video, and option to attend training seminar by program author (2 out of 3 attended)	Instructors: Classroom teachers Fidelity:*

Sample — Intervention

452

			Intervention				Professional Development	Delivery
Study	N	Grade	Language Status Definition	Duration & Routine	Instructional Practices	Materials		

Oral Reading Fluency

Study	N	Grade	Language Status Definition	Duration & Routine	Instructional Practices	Materials	Professional Development	Delivery
De La Colina et al., 2001	74	1–2	Spanish-English bilingual students enrolled in ESL program who scored at lowest ESL category (beginning or non-English speaker)	8, 10, and 12 weeks 45 minutes per session, 3 days per week In-class One-on-one	Read Naturally (RN; Ihnot, 1997): Instruction focuses on building fluency and comprehension; Repeated readings, modeling, and self-monitoring (students graphed their fluency before and after repeated reading practice) with a few comprehension questions following each passage	Translated RN passages (60-350 word passages at mid-1st grade through 6th grade reading levels, 24 per level)	*	Instructors: Classroom teachers Fidelity: Weekly observations by researchers; Self-monitoring with implementation checklist
Denton, 2000	93	2–5	Spanish-English bilingual students in bilingual classrooms, adequately fluent in both languages, average reading skills in Spanish,	8 weeks 40 minutes per session, 3 days per week Unclear if pull-out or in-class	2 instructional groups Read Well (RW; Sprick, Howard, & Fidanque, 1998): Emphasizes phonics, vocabulary, and comprehension;	RW: Small books with decodable text, some of which are "duet" texts with more sophisticated language that teacher read	Each tutor trained in both methods (RN for 2 hours; RW for 4 hours), which included viewing videos of methods and	Instructors: Undergraduate students with a special education major

(Continued)

	Sample				Intervention			Professional Development	Delivery
Study	N	Grade	Language Status Definition	Duration & Routine	Instructional Practices	Materials			
			poor reading skills in English	Small group (2–4 students) and one-on-one	Explicit, systematic phonics instruction, practice in fully decodable texts, during-reading discussion and questioning designed to build vocabulary and comprehension, and post-reading comprehension worksheets Read Naturally (RN; Ihnot, 1992): Emphasizes fluency, vocabulary, and comprehension; Student selects passage, pre-reading vocabulary and comprehension activities, student reads passage aloud, graphs fluency, rereads with and without	aloud for students RN: Short, interesting texts, presumably leveled	hands-on practice Tutors taking school-based practicum in reading instruction and received ongoing instruction in principles of reading instruction including Direct Instruction for students at-risk and with learning disabilities	Fidelity: Supervised by graduate students including researcher with 1–6 observations of tutoring sessions; Self-monitoring with implementation checklists

(Continued)

454

(Continued)

Sample			Intervention					Delivery
Study	N	Grade	Language Status Definition	Duration & Routine	Instructional Practices	Materials	Professional Development	
					audio-tape modeling until fluency goal met, answers multiple choice questions on passage, tutor times and quizzes student, and final fluency rate graphed			
Vocabulary								
Carlo et al., 2004	142	5	Spanish-speaking students in bilingual or mainstream programs and monolingual English-only students	15 weeks 30–45 minutes, four days per week In-class Whole group, small group, individual	Text-centered vocabulary instruction Day 1: Spanish-speaking students given Spanish-language text (in written and audio-taped format) Day 2: English-language text introduced to whole group, target words identified and vocabulary activity	Detailed lesson plans Newspaper articles, diaries, first hand documents, and historical accounts on immigration	Curriculum materials provided, which included detailed lesson plans and quasi-scripted lesson guides Biweekly learning community meetings in which coming weeks' materials were previewed	Instructor: Classroom teachers Fidelity: Three lessons filmed and coded for fidelity with reliability estimates

Sample				Intervention				
Study	N	Grade	Language Status Definition	Duration & Routine	Instructional Practices	Materials	Professional Development	Delivery
					Days 3 & 4: Small groups complete vocabulary activity with words from text Day 5: Direct instruction and activities in high utility vocabulary learning topics, such as awareness of cognates and polysemy or derivational word analysis		and previous weeks' experiences were reflected on	
Pérez, 1981	75	3	Mexican-American students with low reading achievement scores	3 months 20 minutes daily In-class Unspecified grouping	Oral Language Activities: Reading is presented as a step in a process of communication with its foundation in oral language	Teacher packets with oral language activity guides and materials, covering idiomatic expressions, riddles, analogies, compound words, polysemous words, etc.	Training included packets with instructional materials and suggestions, demonstration of using materials, and workshops on teaching ELLs	Instructor: Classroom teachers Fidelity: *

(Continued)

Sample				Intervention				
Study	N	Grade	Language Status Definition	Duration & Routine	Instructional Practices	Materials	Professional Development	Delivery
Vaughn-Shavuo, 1990	30	1	Spanish dominant bilingual students, as determined by district criteria	3 weeks 30 minutes daily Pull-out Small group	2 instructional groups Intervention group: Vocabulary taught using sentences that formed narratives Control group: Vocabulary taught using unconnected sentences Both groups engaged in the same follow-up writing activities involving the target vocabulary words	Steps to English Vocabulary Cue Card #1–7 (Kernan, 1983) Steps to English, Teacher's Manual, Level One (Kernan, 1983) Story grammar cards	Not applicable	Instructor: Researcher Fidelity: Not applicable

(Continued)

Sample				Intervention				
Study	N	Grade	Language Status Definition	Duration & Routine	Instructional Practices	Materials	Professional Development	Delivery
Reading Comprehension								
Bean, 1982	45	4–5	Orally fluent Spanish-English bilingual students according to scores on bilingual language proficiency test	1 day Session length uncertain Pull-out One-on-one	3 groups Each group read one version of experimental text, gave free recall retelling and then prompted retelling targeting ten key ideas in story	583 words from the opening of the story entitled "The Chase Twins" from Miami Linguistic Readers (D.C. Heath, 1966) reading series (third grade readability level) Version of story edited to make anaphoric pronoun references more explicit (624 words; fourth grade readability level) Version of story edited to omit trivial events to make	Not applicable	Instructor: Not applicable Fidelity: Not applicable

(Continued)

Sample			Intervention					
Study	N	Grade	Language Status Definition	Duration & Routine	Instructional Practices	Materials	Professional Development	Delivery
						problem-solving macropropositional structure more apparent and anaphoric pronoun references also made more explicit (427 words; fifth grade readability level)		
Shames, 1998	58	9–11	ESOL students in their first or second year of ESOL	1 year 51 minutes daily In-class Whole group	3 instructional groups Community Language Learning (CLL; Curran, 1972): Cooperative learning of second language using student-generated stories and dialogs; Students discuss a topic of interest to them, conversation is audio-taped, listened to,	CLL; CLL+CPS: Student-generated stories and dialogs CPS; CLL+CPS: American history textbook written especially LEP students, also some student-generated texts from CLL group	Research assistant and facilitators attended training in CLL for 4 hours Research assistant also attended CPS training for 4 hours	Instructors: Research assistant delivered primary instruction 3 days a week and set up follow-up activities; Classroom teacher delivered

(Continued)

Sample			Intervention					
Study	N	Grade	Language Status Definition	Duration & Routine	Instructional Practices	Materials	Professional Development	Delivery
					written down, and read; students then reflect on learning process			follow-up activities; Two bilingual community language facilitators present at all times
					Comprehension Processing Strategies (CPS): Comprehension strategies (K-W-L charts and Question-Answer-Relationships) introduced and modeled in three languages, and practiced each week with new texts; Vocabulary and sight words reviewed prior to reading, with letter-sound correspondences reviewed as needed			Fidelity: *
					CLL + CPS: Methods alternated every two weeks beginning with CLL			

(Continued)

	Sample				Intervention				
Study	N	Grade	Language Status Definition		Duration & Routine	Instructional Practices	Materials	Professional Development	Delivery
Swice-good, 1990	95	3	Bilingual Spanish-dominant Hispanic students enrolled in bilingual Spanish-English classes		6 weeks 90 minutes daily In-class Whole group	Self-generated questioning strategies Definition, modeling, and practice of strategy Practice occurred independently and in pairs and small groups	Third grade basal reader: Lima, Naranja, Limon (Flores, Guzman, Long, Macias, Somoza, & Tinajero, 1987)	Orientation, question-and-answer, and training sessions (unclear length)	Instructors: Classroom teachers Fidelity: Unscheduled classroom observations and visits; Teachers kept anecdotal logs
Writing									
Franken et al., 1999	20	9–12*	Diverse students from a variety of countries (Taiwan, Hong Kong, Malaysia, Korea, India, Mexico, Macedonia, Fiji, etc.) learning English as a Second Language (ESL)		6 weeks 2 sessions amounting to a total of 2.5 hours per week In-class Whole group and student pairs	Instruction and practice in writing argumentative essays 2 groups of students: on alternate weeks one group of students worked with a self-selected peer and the other group worked independently	Sample texts and writing prompts written on cue cards	*	Instructors: Classroom teacher and researcher Fidelity: *

(Continued)

Study	Sample			Intervention				
	N	Grade	Language Status Definition	Duration & Routine	Instructional Practices	Materials	Professional Development	Delivery
					First session was a double period in which students completed prewriting tasks, including study of a sample argumentative text, brainstorming, and mapping			
					Second session was a single period in which students wrote their own argumentative essays using a cue card with a writing prompt			
					First two weeks spent writing on general topics without outside textual support; second two weeks used more specific science topics and lists of facts; and third week used most specific topics and written texts as resources			

(Continued)

Sample			Intervention					
Study	N	Grade	Language Status Definition	Duration & Routine	Instructional Practices	Materials	Professional Development	Delivery
Gómez et al., 1996	72	5	Students classified as Level I, II, and III in English language proficiency based on cumulative files, standardized achievement tests, informal assessments, and an interview	6 weeks 4.5 hours daily, 2–4 days per week In-class Whole group	2 instructional groups Free Writing (FW): Students selected their own topics and wrote for as long as they wanted; Teachers wrote responses to content of writing rather than correcting errors, engaging students in written dialogs; Students encouraged to plan and share their writing in small groups Structured Writing (SW): Topics assigned by teachers; Students wrote for 9 minutes; Students worked alone and quietly; Teachers corrected errors, focusing on those deemed most important	*	FW and SW teachers and assistants trained separately in 2 3-hour sessions Received ongoing direction and support from researcher	Instructor: Classroom teachers and instructional assistants Fidelity: Supervision by researchers with daily monitoring using checklists Minor corrective consultations as needed

(Continued)

| Sample | | | | Intervention | | | | Delivery |
Study	N	Grade	Language Status Definition	Duration & Routine	Instructional Practices	Materials	Professional Development	
					All students permitted to write in English and Spanish			
Prater et al., 1993	46	4–6	Students in general education classrooms who had previously been in ESL or bilingual classrooms, who were judged limited English Proficient by their teacher	3 weeks Daily (session length uncertain)In-class small group and individual	Students wrote one composition per week by selecting a writing topic, writing a first draft, revising, editing, and completing a final rewrite	*	*	Instructor: Classroom teachers Fidelity:*
					Students in the small group condition discussed their potential topics and shared their first and revised drafts; also received instruction and modeling in group processes and responding to others' writing			
					Students in the individual condition			

(Continued)

	Sample			Intervention				
Study	N	Grade	Language Status Definition	Duration & Routine	Instructional Practices	Materials	Professional Development	Delivery
					completed all steps individually with only traditional written corrective feedback from the teacher			
Sengupta, 2000	100	9–12	Bilingual students in English programs in Hong Kong	1 year 80-minute lesson, weekly In-class Whole group	Revision Instruction: Focus on making texts more 'reader-friendly' in both organization and content through addition, deletion, re-ordering, and substitution during the production of multiple drafts Teachers gradually released responsibility by first offering extensive guidance, and then moving to peer-evaluation and finally self-evaluation with little scaffolding	Researcher provided lesson plans, pre-writing input for topics for all classes, and related teaching materials and guidelines	*	Instructors: Classroom teachers Fidelity: *

(Continued)

Sample			Intervention					Professional	
Study	N	Grade	Language Status Definition	Duration & Routine	Instructional Practices	Materials		Development	Delivery

Complex Approaches

Encouraging Reading & Writing

Study	N	Grade	Language Status Definition	Duration & Routine	Instructional Practices	Materials	Professional Development	Delivery
Elley, 1991	535 459	4–5 5–6	Fiji students learning to read in English after several years of Fijian or Hindi reading instruction	2 years SBE: Daily (session length uncertain) SSR: 20–30 minutes, daily In-class Whole group	2 instructional groups Shared Book Experience (SBE; Holdaway, 1979): Teacher reads book over several days with students increasingly joining in and lots of free-ranging discussion; Follow-up extension activities involving artistic interpretation, paired rereading, and acting Sustained Silent Reading (SSR): Students encouraged to read silently for pleasure; Teachers motivated reading by displaying, talking about, and reading from books	250 new books, mainly illustrated storybooks	SBE: 3 day in-service SSR: Notes outlining approach and its principles distributed	Instructor: Classroom teachers Fidelity: Researchers visited schools every two months

(Continued)

	Sample				Intervention				
Study	N	Grade	Language Status Definition		Duration & Routine	Instructional Practices	Materials	Professional Development	Delivery
Schon et al., 1982	114	2-4	Hispanic students in bilingual classrooms		8 months At least 60 minutes weekly In-class Whole group	Provided free reading time Developed positive attitudes toward reading through fun and social activities, such as read alouds and book sharing	Extensive collection of Spanish-language books, selected for attractive illustrations, simple texts, and high interest	*	Instructors: Classroom teachers Fidelity: *
Schon et al., 1984	272	9-12	Hispanic students in remedial reading classes		4-7 months At least 12 minutes daily, or 55 minutes weekly In-class Whole group	Provided free reading time	Extensive collection of Spanish-language newspapers, magazines, and books, selected for range of readability and high interest	*	Instructors: Remedial reading teachers Fidelity: Bilingual resource person visited classes biweekly to guide and monitor teachers

(Continued)

	Sample			Intervention				
Study	N	Grade	Language Status Definition	Duration & Routine	Instructional Practices	Materials	Professional Development	Delivery
Schon et al., 1985	400	7–8	Hispanic students in homogeneously grouped reading classes	8.5 months At least 45 minutes weekly In-class Whole group	Provide free reading time Encourage interested students to read Spanish materials	Extensive collection of Spanish-language newspapers, magazines, and books, selected for range of readability and high interest	*	Instructors: Reading teachers Fidelity: Bilingual resource person visited classes biweekly to guide and monitor teachers and update materials
Tudor et al., 1989	45	4–5	Panjabi-speaking ESL students	3 months 1 hour daily After-school Individual	Sustained silent reading Students chose their own books and could take books home Students gave oral reports on their reading selection about once a week	Leveled books (104 titles, many with multiple copies) Dictionaries	Not applicable	Instructor: Researcher Fidelity: Not applicable

(Continued)

Sample				Intervention				
Study	N	Grade	Language Status Definition	Duration & Routine	Instructional Practices	Materials	Professional Development	Delivery
Tsang, 1996	144	8–12	Cantonese students in English programs in Hong Kong	20 weeks	3 instructional groups	In extensive reading group: Leveled books, including simplified classics, original books, and information-based books representing a variety of interests	*	Instructors: Classroom teachers
				40 minute sessions, 7–9 times every six days	Traditional Writing Instruction plus Unrelated Enrichment: Students required to complete 8 math assignments with minimal English required; Assignments marked and returned to students by researcher			Fidelity: Researcher verified teacher fidelity every 2 weeks for first 2 months and weekly thereafter
				In class				
				Individual	Traditional Writing Instruction plus Extensive Reading: Students required to read 8 books from a list a leveled books available in the school library; Students completed brief book review forms after reading each book,			

(Continued)

Sample				Intervention				
Study	N	Grade	Language Status Definition	Duration & Routine	Instructional Practices	Materials	Professional Development	Delivery
					graded on details and persuasiveness by researcher			
					Traditional Writing Instruction plus Frequent Practice: Students required to write 8 essays of varying content and genres; Essays graded impressionistically by researcher			
					Best math assignments, reviews, and essays displayed and commented on publicly every 3 weeks			

(Continued)

Sample			Intervention					
Study	N	Grade	Language Status Definition	Duration & Routine	Instructional Practices	Materials	Professional Development	Delivery

Reading to Children

Study	N	Grade	Language Status Definition	Duration & Routine	Instructional Practices	Materials	Professional Development	Delivery
Hancock, 2002	77	K	Monolingual Spanish- and English-speaking children	1 semester (75 days) Daily Home-based Individual	Teachers sent home a book each day The treatment group received Spanish language books, while controls received English language books Instructions in same language as book sent home asking parents to read the book to their child	Families Read Every Day (FRED) books 30 new Spanish-language FRED books distributed to each classroom	Parents asked to read a short paragraph aloud in either Spanish or English during parent/teacher conference Paragraph emphasized benefits of reading aloud to children	Instructor: Parent or guardian Fidelity: Parents asked to note their reading in a log kept in each book
Hastings-Góngora, 1993	11	K	Bilingual Spanish-dominant students in a bilingual classroom (degree of proficiency unclear)	5 weeks * Home-based One-on-one	Parents encouraged to read aloud to children at home Packets of children's books with a book-reading log sent home	Packets of 7 Spanish-language children's books Spanish-language article on importance of reading to children (Trelease, 1992)	1 2-hour training workshop for parents and their children Bilingual teacher modeled reading aloud to children, shared	Instructor: Parents Fidelity: Parents given a book-reading log

(Continued)

Sample			Intervention					
Study	N	Grade	Language Status Definition	Duration & Routine	Instructional Practices	Materials	Professional Development	Delivery
					to two groups of parents: one group received training in reading aloud, the other did not		and discussed an article on the benefits of parents reading to children, and provided a practice opportunity and feedback	
Ulanoff et al., 1999	60	3	English learners for whom Spanish was their first language	1 day 1 session (session length uncertain) In-class Whole group	3 instructional groups Preview/Review: Teacher built background knowledge and previewed difficult vocabulary in Spanish, then children listened to teacher read book aloud in English, and teacher reviewed the story in Spanish Translation: Children listened to teacher read book aloud in English	Children's book: The Napping House (Wood & Wood, 1984)	*	Instructor: Classroom teacher Fidelity: *

(Continued)

Study	Sample			Intervention					
	N	Grade	Language Status Definition	Duration & Routine	Instructional Practices	Materials	Professional Development	Delivery	

| | | | | | and concurrently translate the story into Spanish | | | |
| | | | | | Control: Students listened to teacher read book aloud in English with no intervention or discussion of story | | | |

Tutoring and Remediation

Escamilla 1994	46	1	Spanish-dominant students receiving initial reading instruction in Spanish and scoring low on 2 Spanish-language literacy measures (Spanish dominance determined using Home Language Survey and Language Assessment Scales)	12–16 weeks 30 minutes daily Pull-out One-on-one	Descubriendo la Lectura: Spanish version of Reading Recovery; Students receive short-term, individualized tutoring in becoming independent readers and writers; Activities are not prescribed, but include guided reading, problem solving, and daily writing; Instruction often builds on student writing	300 Spanish-language children's books at 28 levels of difficulty Spanish Observation Survey	1 year of training in Descubriendo la Lectura	Instructor: Descubriendo la Lectura teachers

(Continued)

Sample				Intervention				
Study	N	Grade	Language Status Definition	Duration & Routine	Instructional Practices	Materials	Professional Development	Delivery
Syvanen, 1997	16	4–5	Intermediate ESL students	19 weeks 70–80 minutes, twice weekly In-class Whole group, individual	Students met with a reading buddy/tutee in kindergarten or first grade twice a week for 30 minutes Each tutoring session preceded by 20-30 minutes of preparation and training and 20 minutes of writing reflectively about and sharing experience Preparation and training included demonstrations of oral reading techniques, choosing appropriate books, and giving positive feedback	Children's books Reflective journals	*	Instructor: Classroom teachers Fidelity: *

(Continued)

	Sample			Intervention				
Study	N	Grade	Language Status Definition	Duration & Routine	Instructional Practices	Materials	Professional Development	Delivery

Other Investigations

Calderón et al., 1998	222	2–3	Bilingual students enrolled in transitional bilingual program	2 years 2 hours daily In-class (and pull-out) Whole group and small group	2 instructional groups using same basal materials (see Materials column) Traditional basal group: 90 minutes of largely whole group reading language arts instruction and 30 minutes pull-out ESL class; Activities included round-robin reading and workbook practice; Spanish basal used all year; English text introduced midyear and alternated daily with Spanish basal	Spanish basal reading series: <u>Campanitas de Oro</u> (Long & Tinajero, 1989) English transitional text: <u>Transitional Reading Program</u> (Tinajero, Long, Calderón, Castagha, & Maldonaldo-Colón, 1989)	Teachers of BCIRC students received extensive professional development and collaborated with researchers; Training in integration of first- and second-language development and transition principles, theories, and practices, as well as student-centered, constructivist philosophy	Instructor: Classroom teachers Fidelity: *

(Continued)

475

Sample				Intervention				
Study	N	Grade	Language Status Definition	Duration & Routine	Instructional Practices	Materials	Professional Development	Delivery
					Bilingual Cooperative Integrated Reading and Composition (BCIRC): 120 minutes direct instruction in reading comprehension and integrated writing and language arts, supplemented by worksheets; Each activity introduced by teacher to whole group and practiced in small groups and individually; Spanish basal used all year; English text introduced midyear and alternated every 2 weeks with Spanish basal			

(Continued)

	Sample			Intervention					
Study	N	Grade	Language Status Definition	Duration & Routine	Instructional Practices	Materials	Professional Development	Delivery
Cohen et al., 1980	150	1	Bilingual Mexican-American students competent enough in spoken English to handle English-language reading instruction (monolingual Spanish students excluded)	4 weeks 90 45-minute daily lessons In-class Whole group and/or small group	2 instructional method using same basal series (see Materials column) High Intensity Learning: Students pre-tested and placed at points in curriculum aligned to their performance; Students work individually at a self-directed pace until they demonstrate mastery in workbook before progressing to reading from reader; Reading occurs individually or in small teacher-led groups Ramirez and Castaneda Model (1974): Culturally-based instruction designed for Mexican-American students using whole and small groupings;	The Reading House Comprehension and Vocabulary (Lime) Series (Cohen & Hyman, 1977), which included taped lessons, 200-page workbook with 5 lessons on 18 instructional objectives, pre and post criterion-referenced tests, and a reader with a reading selection for each objective	All teachers received regular training provided by publisher in using the basal series, although teachers of two groups were trained separately Ramirez and Castaneda teachers additionally trained in this model using the model's manual; Trainer selected by model authors	Instructor: Classroom teachers Fidelity: *

(Continued)

Sample			Intervention					
Study	N	Grade	Language Status Definition	Duration & Routine	Instructional Practices	Materials	Professional Development	Delivery
					Instruction is teacher-directed and sensitive to students' culture			
Golden-berg et al., 1992	10	K	Spanish-speaking students of Latin-American-born parents enrolled in Spanish-language kindergarten	1 year * Home-based One-on-one	2 instructional groups Reading Encouraged: New booklet sent home every 3 weeks; Parents encouraged to read aloud to children at home; Identical booklets used in classrooms Phonics Worksheets: Packets of phonics worksheets sent home; Packets approximately same length as booklets; Packets aligned with classroom instruction	Set of 12 Spanish-language black-and-white booklets with simple plots and progressively more complex language Phonics worksheets focused on developing letter and syllable knowledge through phonological activities and writing	Teacher training unclear Parents in Reading Encouraged group told booklets would be sent home, encouraged to treat them like any other children's book, and told not to teach word reading or decoding Training of parents in Phonics Worksheets group unclear	Instructor: Parents Fidelity: Home observations conducted twice monthly

(Continued)

Sample				Intervention				Delivery
Study	N	Grade	Language Status Definition	Duration & Routine	Instructional Practices	Materials	Professional Development	
Neuman et al., 1992	129	7–8	Students enrolled in various stages of transitional bilingual program	12 weeks 15–20 minute lessons, each lesson given twice weekly In-class Unspecified grouping	4 instructional groups Traditional TV: Students watched original versions of episodes after a one-sentence introduction; Lesson ended with a brief summary and no instruction of target vocabulary words Captioned TV: Students watched captioned versions of episodes after a one-sentence introduction; Lesson ended with a brief summary and no instruction of target vocabulary words Script: Students read and listened to other read aloud a script of the captioned episodes	Nine video segments of 3-2-1 Contact a Children's Television Workshop science program; Segments organized in 3 units of 3 segments each on survival, protection, and breathing Captioned version of video segments Texts with no pictures based on captioned versions of video segments	*	Instructor: Classroom teachers Fidelity: Researchers monitored conditions via informal classroom visits and weekly teacher meetings

(Continued)

Sample			Intervention					
Study	N	Grade	Language Status Definition	Duration & Routine	Instructional Practices	Materials	Professional Development	Delivery
					Textbook: Regular science instruction; Oral lessons in first language followed by reading from English-language textbooks; Topics differed from episodes			
Saunders, 1999	125	2–5	Spanish-speaking LEP students enrolled in transitional bilingual program	4 years

Daily (session length uncertain)

In-class

Unspecified grouping | Multi-year Transition Program: Comprehensive Language arts program with 12 components and 4 principles designed to transition students to English instruction; 1st 2 years reading and writing instruction occurs in Spanish except for oral English language development; 3rd year English reading and writing introduced, while Spanish reading | * | * | Instructor: Classroom teachers, who are members of a collaborative research team

Fidelity: * |

(Continued)

480

| | Sample | | | | Intervention | | | | |
Study	N	Grade	Language Status Definition		Duration & Routine	Instructional Practices	Materials	Professional Development	Delivery
						and writing instruction continues; 4th and final year language arts instruction entirely in Spanish			
Saunders et al., 1999	116	4–5	Limited English proficient (LEP) students and fluent English-speaking students (both monolinguals and former LEPs)		4 days 90 minutes, daily In-class Small group	4 instructional groups All 4 within Multi-year Transition Program (see Saunders, 1999 above) and used rotating heterogeneous small groups, with 2 seen each day for 45 minutes Read + Study: Students worked independently on unrelated reading and writing activities Literature Logs (LL): Students prompted twice to write about experiences they have had that are similar	Children's book: Louella's Song (Greenfield, 1993)	Teachers function as part of research team, which meets monthly to study instructional components, view videos and demonstrations, plan units, and analyze student work Teachers helped plan research	Instructor: Classroom teachers, who are members of a collaborative research team Fidelity: Researchers had daily contact with teachers

(Continued)

Study	Sample			Intervention				
	N	Grade	Language Status Definition	Duration & Routine	Instructional Practices	Materials	Professional Development	Delivery
					to two of the protagonist's; Writing shared in two small group meetings with teacher			
					Instructional Conversation (IC): Students met twice with teacher in small groups to discuss the factual content and abstract concepts in the story			
					LL + IC: Students met with teacher 4 times in small groups and completed all activities the LL and IC groups did			

(Continued)

	Sample				Intervention			
Study	N	Grade	Language Status Definition	Duration & Routine	Instructional Practices	Materials	Professional Development	Delivery
Tharp, 1982	204	1	Bidialectical students speaking Hawaiian Creole English and standard English and 'other' students (from a wide variety of linguistic and cultural background and unclear linguistic proficiency)	1 year Daily (session length uncertain) In-class Small groups	KEEP Comprehension Program: Comprehension dominates reading curriculum; Students alternately read and discuss what they read with the teacher; Teacher guides discussions to promote connections with students' experiences and generate engagement in reading; Phonics, decoding, and vocabulary also taught, but within context of material also being read for comprehension	*	'Brief' training with follow-up supervision in KEEP comprehension approach	Instructor: Classroom teachers Fidelity: Follow-up supervision
Waxman et al., 1994	88 52	1–5 1–5	Hispanic LEP students with low achievement as identified by the district	6 months 15 3-hour sessions In-class Whole group	4 instructional groups Each group was taught by a teacher trained in 1 of 4 ways (see Professional Development column)	*	ESL in Content Areas (Chamot & O'Malley, 1986; 1987): Model builds English-language	Instructor: Classroom teachers Fidelity: *

(Continued)

	Sample			Intervention					
Study	N	Grade	Language Status Definition	Duration & Routine	Instructional Practices	Materials	Professional Development	Delivery
							and content knowledge through context-embedded problem solving; Concepts, problem-solving skills, and cognitive and metacognitive techniques (e.g. graphic mapping) taught in science, math, and reading using Spanish and English; Training focuses on verbalization, problem solving, imagery, and other cognitive heuristics, as well as cognitive and metacognitive learning strategies	

(Continued)

484

Sample			Intervention					
Study	N	Grade	Language Status Definition	Duration & Routine	Instructional Practices	Materials	Professional Development	Delivery
							Effective Use of Time (Stallings, 1980; 1986): Model focuses on using classroom time effectively; Its four steps are pre-testing, informing, organizing instruction through guided practice, and post-testing	
							Combination: Training time split equally between the ESL in Content Areas and Effective Use of Time models	
							Control: No training	

(Continued)

Sample			Intervention					
Study	N	Grade	Language Status Definition	Duration & Routine	Instructional Practices	Materials	Professional Development	Delivery
Success for All								
Dianda et al., 1995	147	K–1	Spanish-dominant students, Spanish ESL students, and 'other' ESL students	2 years	Comprehensive school reform program that focuses on prevention, early intervention, and long-term professional development	Exito para Todos (Spanish language) materials Success for All materials	*	Instructor: * *Fidelity: *
Slavin et al., 1998:AZ	138	1	Spanish-dominant students	1 year Reading period: 90 minutes daily, in-class, whole group Tutoring: 20 minutes, uncertain frequency, pull-out, individual	Homogeneous reading groups of 15 students in which oral reading, story structure and comprehension, and integrated reading and writing are emphasized Beginning reading instruction also addresses phonological awareness, letter-sound correspondence, and decoding	Exito Para Todos (Spanish language) materials	Teachers received detailed teacher manuals and 2 days of in-service training at beginning of year Several follow-up in-service sessions during the year reviewed classroom management, instructional pacing, and curriculum implementation	Instructor: Spanish-English bilingual classroom teachers Fidelity: On-site program facilitator visited classes and tutoring sessions frequently

(Continued)

	Sample			Intervention				
Study	N	Grade	Language Status Definition	Duration & Routine	Instructional Practices	Materials	Professional Development	Delivery
Slavin et al., 1998: Fairhill	50	1–3	Limited English Proficient Hispanic students, as defined by district criteria	2 years Reading period: 90 minutes daily, in-class, whole group Tutoring: 20 minutes, uncertain frequency, pull-out, individual	Student progress assessed every 8 weeks, at which point students may move to different reading groups One-on-one tutoring for students having difficulty keeping up with their homogeneous reading group	Success for All materials	Teachers received detailed teacher manuals and 2 days of in-service training at beginning of year Several follow-up in-service sessions during the year reviewed classroom management, instructional pacing, and curriculum implementation	Instructor: Classroom teachers and ESL teachers Fidelity: On-site program facilitator visited classes and tutoring sessions frequently

* Insufficient information provided in the article to allow determination.

REFERENCES

Chamot, A., & O'Malley, J. (1986). *A cognitive academic language learning approach: An ESL content-based curriculum.* Wheaton, MD: National Clearinghouse for Bilingual Education.

Chamot, A., & O'Malley, J. (1987). The cognitive academic language learning approach: A bridge to the mainstream. *TESOL Quarterly, 21,* 227-249.

Cohen, S. A., & Hyman, J. S. (1977). *The reading house comprehension and vocabulary (lime) series.* New York: Random House.

Curran, C. A. (1972). *Counseling-learning: A whole-person model for education.* New York: Grune & Stratton.

Miami Linguistic Readers. (1966). Lexington, MA: D.C. Heath.

Engelmann, S., & Bruner, E. C. (1988). *Reading Mastery.* Chicago: Science Research Associates.

Engelmann, S., Carnine, L., & Johnson, G. (1988). *Corrective Reading: Word-attack basics. Teacher presentation book, decoding A.* Chicago: Science Research Associates.

Flores, J., Guzmán, A., Long, S., Macías, R., Somoza, E., & Tinajero, J. (1987). *Lima, naranja, limón. Student's book.* New York: Macmillan.

Greenfield, E. (1993). Louella's song. In J. Pikulski (Sr. Author), *Dinosauring* (4th grade reader), 430–436. Boston: Houghton-Mifflin.

Holdaway, D. (1979). *Foundations of literacy.* Sydney, New South Wales: Ashton Scholastic.

Ihnot, C. (1992). *Read naturally.* St. Paul, MN: Read Naturally.

Ihnot, C. (1997). *Read naturally.* St. Paul, MN: Read Naturally.

Kernan, D. (1983). *Steps to English Vocabulary Cue Cards #1-7.* New York: McGraw-Hill.

Kernan, D. (1983). *Steps to English, Teacher's Manual, Level One.* New York: McGraw-Hill.

Lloyd, S. (1992). *The phonics handbook.* UK: Jolly Learning.

Long, S. & Tinajero, J. (1989). *Campanitas de oro.* New York: Macmillan.

Ramírez, M., III, & Castaneda, A. (1974). *Cultural democracy, bi-cognitive development, and education.* San Francisco, CA: Academic.

Sprick, M. M., Howard, L. M., & Fidanque, A. (1998). *Read well: Critical foundations in primary reading.* Longmont, CO: Sopris West.

Stallings, J. (1980). *Effective use of time program.* Unpublished training manual. Houston: University of Houston.

Stallings, J. (1986). Using time effectively: A self-analytic approach. In K. Zimwalt (Ed.), *Improving teaching* (pp. 15-27). Alexandria, VA: Association for Supervision and Curriculum Development.

Tinajero, J., Long, S., Calderón, M., Castagha, C., & Maldonado-Colón, E. (1989). *Transitional reading program.* New York: Macmillan.

Trelease, J. (1992). Léeme un cuento. *Ser Padres, 8,* 18–23.

Wood, D., & Wood, A. (1984). *The napping house.* San Diego, CA: Harcourt Brace, Jovanovich.

16

Qualitative Studies of Classroom and School Practices

Diane August with Frederick Erickson

This chapter includes four sections that examine schooling practices and contexts related to literacy development in language-minority students. They address, respectively, (a) instructional techniques designed to improve specific components of literacy, (b) comprehensive instructional programs designed to build literacy, (c) effective classrooms and schools, and (d) school change. The chapter does not include studies focusing on language of instruction (comparing bilingual with English-only instruction).[1] Such studies are covered in chapter 14, which examines evaluation studies comparing programs that used the native, nonsocietal language to some extent with those that used only the societal language. Although some studies in this chapter examine factors addressed in chapters 14 and 15, they differ in that this chapter reviews case studies and ethnographic research rather than experimental and quasi-experimental studies.

The following research question is addressed in this chapter:

What do we know about classroom and school practices and contexts designed to build literacy in language-minority students?

METHODS

We used a systematic interpretive procedure (Fitzgerald, 1995a, 1995b; Glaser, 1978) to analyze studies and summarize findings across studies. First, studies that focused on instruction and employed qualitative study designs were located through systematic searches of the research literature. Second, all studies were

---

[1]Ethnographic studies that focus on use of the children's first (non-English) language as a sociocultural variable are included in the section on context.

thoroughly read and coded with a coding instrument developed by the panel (see chap. 1). Third, using an iterative process, studies were categorized by outcomes of interest. This process resulted in the four categories into which the chapter is divided. Studies within the first category were further subdivided into strategies designed to build word-level skills, build text-level skills, build both kinds of skills, and develop literacy-related outcomes such as increases in student interaction in English. Within each of the four major categories, studies were ordered by age of the subjects. Fourth, studies in each group were reread and analyzed with regard to similarities, differences, and results to determine cross-cutting themes, as well as methodological strengths and weaknesses.

INSTRUCTIONAL TECHNIQUES DESIGNED TO IMPROVE SPECIFIC COMPONENTS OF LITERACY

In this section, we begin by examining approaches designed to build basic, word-level skills (word recognition, decoding, and spelling). We then turn to approaches designed to build text- or discourse-level skills (vocabulary, reading comprehension, reading fluency, and writing). Next, we describe studies that target both of these components concurrently. Finally, we review studies designed to increase students' participation in classroom discourse and literacy-related behavior. Where appropriate, we have organized the studies according to the language that was the target of instruction—students' native language or English.

The teaching methods examined in these studies varied widely. They included a Spanish version of Reading Recovery called *Descubriendo la Lectura* (Escamilla & Andrade, 1992); a phonological awareness and phonics program (Hus, 2001); instruction in reading strategies, in some cases using reciprocal teaching as a method of developing students' strategy (Hernández, 1991; Wright, 1997); collaborative strategic reading (discussed further later), intended to promote content learning, language acquisition, and comprehension (Klingner & Vaughn, 2000); sustained silent reading (also discussed later; Pilgreen & Krashen, 1983); reading clubs (Kreuger & Townshend, 1997); paired reading (Li & Nes, 2001); and literacy activities designed to increase student discourse (Martínez-Roldan & López-Robertson, 2000) or literacy-related outcomes (Genishi, Stires, & Yung-Chan, 2001; Kenner, 1999; Ramos & Krashen, 1998). Some studies investigated whether methods of instruction used with native speakers of English helped Spanish-speaking language-minority students if the instructional materials or techniques were translated and used in the students' first language—in these cases, Spanish (Escamilla & Andrade, 1992; Hernández, 1991). The remaining studies investigated instructional methods derived from research and theory on language acquisition for native English speakers; this instruction was delivered in English.

Studies focused on a spectrum of grade levels, from kindergarten through high school. Those examining primarily word-level skills targeted children in kindergarten through third grade, whereas those emphasizing text-level skills targeted children in the upper elementary grades and high school. There was also variation in the student samples. Studies included students struggling in their regular classes (Escamilla & Andrade, 1992; Kreuger & Townshend, 1977; Wright, 1997), those limited in English proficiency (Hernández, 1991; Li & Nes, 2001), and those with a mix of proficiency levels (Genishi et al., 2001; Hus, 2001; Kenner, 1999; Martínez-Roldan & López-Robertson, 2000; Pilgreen & Krashen, 1983; Ramos & Krashen, 1998; Wolf, 1993).

Developing Spanish Word-Level Skills

To support reading development for Spanish-speaking students learning to read in Spanish, Escamilla and Andrade (1992) developed a Spanish version of Reading Recovery—*Descubriendo la Lectura (DLL)*. *DLL* was developed for Spanish-speaking students who were receiving Spanish language (native-language) instruction, but were nonetheless struggling to become proficient in reading. As in Reading Recovery, *DLL* lessons are provided daily and are tailored to the individual student's needs and interests. The researchers report that daily tutoring sessions consisted of "(a) rereading aloud of two or more familiar books, (b) rereading of a book introduced the day before so the teacher can reinforce strategies and assess comprehension (c) word analysis or letter identification, (d) writing a story, (e) rearranging a cut-up story into the correct order and re-reading it, and (f) new book introduced and attempted" (p. 217).

The researchers illustrate *DLL* through a description of the experiences of Javier, the first Spanish-speaking student to participate in the program and in first grade at the time of the study. He is described by the authors as low achieving, based on his results on the Spanish Diagnostic Survey, an observational tool developed and tested by the researchers for identifying students for the *DLL* program. After 20 weeks of *DLL* instruction, "scores on the Spanish Diagnostic Survey indicate Javier went from being a non-reader, able to read only three words on a page and unable to self-monitor or self-correct...to a situation in which he could read an unfamiliar 194-word book with 99% accuracy and could self-monitor and self-correct" (p. 230). Javier made similar progress in writing. Although his progress was impressive, it is unclear whether it was due to regular classroom Spanish instruction (which he was also receiving), *DLL*, or a combination of the two. Moreover, *DLL* is intended for students who remain in the bottom 20% of their first-grade class after 1 year of instruction. This was not the case for Javier, who began *DLL* in October of his first-grade year.

Developing English Word-Level Skills

Hus (2001) investigated the reading levels of first-grade bilingual and multilingual students who received no early explicit reading instruction and compared their outcomes with those attained by bilingual and multilingual kindergartners who were given explicit instruction in the alphabetic principle, or phonics. Her participants included 68 boys and girls enrolled in four kindergarten classes and 50 students enrolled in two first-grade classes. During their kindergarten year, the first-grade students received regular classroom instruction that included no explicit reading instruction, whereas the focal group of kindergarten children was taught phonics over a 9-week period using the *Jolly Phonics* program.

Hus (2001) found that whereas the kindergarten students were able to make "significant gains in phonological processing, including phonological memory, and reading decoding skills in only 9 weeks, the grade 1 students (who had not been exposed to systematic phonics instruction)…clearly demonstrated a serious reading lag" (p. 179). Hus believes this lag may be due to the struggles these students had with sounding out words. Thus, she argues for teaching phonics to language-minority students at an earlier age to "catch them before they fall" (p. 181) and provide them with decoding skills that will enable them to build vocabulary and language proficiency through reading. Her suggestion is consistent with findings from the five studies on phonics and phonological awareness reported in chapter 15 that indicate systematic instruction in these areas confers benefits on language- minority students' reading development.

Developing Spanish Text-Level Skills

Hernández (1991) developed and investigated a modified reciprocal teaching format for building text-level skills in middle-school children's native language. Prior research had demonstrated the effectiveness of this approach for poor readers, but had not focused specifically on Spanish-speaking English-language learners (Palincsar & Brown, 1984; Paris, Cross, & Lipson, 1984; Paris & Jacobs, 1984). Reciprocal teaching is a method in which

> the teacher uses scaffolding techniques to demonstrate and use…specific reading strategies the student is supposed to learn, e.g., question generating, summarizing, and predicting, while the student is basically a spectator and novice responsible for little of the work. As students are assisted and become more competent in the use of the various comprehension strategies, they also begin to assume more leadership responsibility, modeling and assisting other students in using the comprehension strategies. (p. 93)

The participants in this study were seven Spanish-speaking students who were reading near grade level in their native language, but were not proficient in English. They were recent immigrants, all having lived in the United States for less than 19 months. They were enrolled in summer school prior to entering the seventh grade.

Over the six lessons, the students' scores on the daily comprehension questions increased by 25%. Students were also given identical pre- and posttest assessments of their Spanish comprehension using fourth-grade Spanish stories; the students' mean number of correct responses increased from 3.8 to 6.0, an increase of 37%, which was statistically significant on the Wilcoxon matched-pairs test ($p < .001$). A third assessment, also given pre and post, evaluated the students' use of strategies when attempting to read in English rather than Spanish. The prompts and student responses were in Spanish and were tape recorded for transcription. Hernández reports that analysis of the transcripts from these sessions "revealed that all of the students were able to demonstrate use of the comprehension strategies [question generating, summary, and prediction] even when they could not decode the English text aloud" (p. 101). Hernández also found that students used pictures when they were unable to make sense of the text.

A major goal of the study was to determine whether strategy use would transfer from students' native language, Spanish, to their second language, English. Given that Hernández assessed strategies and not comprehension in

English, it is not at all clear that using these strategies improved children's comprehension of the English stories. In fact, the examples provided appear to indicate that, before students could take advantage of strategies, they needed to be able to decode the text. Two examples are provided to illustrate this finding (R/T = researcher/teacher; S = student):

R/T: What did you do when you couldn't read the story?
S: I just looked at the picture.
R/T: When you were reading the story, how did you know what was happening?
S: The pictures, like when the elephant went into the hole and when they were throwing the coconuts and when the elephant got out. (p.103)

Second, although the approach is described as focusing on the use of strategies, the teacher spent considerable time actually helping students understand the text by using such strategies as framing questions for group response and summarizing part of the text for group response. The teacher's help (and later the direction of the student leader), rather than students' own strategy use, may explain the students' gains from pre- to posttest assessments. Finally, with regard to performance on the Spanish reading measures, although the students are described as having a mean grade equivalent of 6.26 on the Spanish version of the California Test of Basic Skills (CTBS), at the beginning of the study, the pre- and posttest Spanish assessments were at the fourth-grade level (and the level of the materials that were used is not specified). It is not clear whether student outcomes resulted from better strategy use or just from their reading text at a much easier reading level. It would also be interesting to know how they would do on comprehension of text more aligned with their reading level.

Developing English Text-Level Skills

Klingner and Vaughn (2000) conducted a study of the effects of collaborative strategic reading (CSR) on the peer group participation and vocabulary development of language-minority students. The study was conducted in a fifth-grade classroom in the southeastern United States. All but two of the students spoke Spanish as their native language or had learned both Spanish and English in their homes. On the basis of Language Assessment Scale scores (De Avila & Duncan, 1978, 1991), 16 of the 35 language-minority students were classified as limited in English proficiency. The researchers developed CSR to "promote content learning, language acquisition, and reading comprehension in diverse classrooms" (p. 70). Following a phase devoted to learning CSR, the approach was used for 2 or 3 days a week over a 4-week period during a science unit on the systems of the human body. In CSR, students work on content-area texts in heterogeneous cooperative groups using four specific strategies: previewing, identifying difficult words or concepts, getting the gist, and summarizing.

The primary focus of this study was on identifying the number of utterances students devoted to oral reading, each of the four comprehension strategies, and attending to procedures. About 20% of student utterances were devoted to reading aloud from their texts, and all six groups spent approximately half their discussion time identifying and clarifying chunks or difficult words or concepts in the passage; more variation among groups was apparent in the other strategies. By including a measure of vocabulary growth, the researchers were able to investigate students' vocabulary acquisition. Two researcher-designed 25-word tests, based on the two textbook chapters that were covered, were administered before and after the reading of each chapter. The tests revealed that the students made statistically significant gains in vocabulary. However, when the data are broken down into the groups of students who were English-language learners, high achieving, average achieving, and low achieving, it becomes clear that the high-achieving students made the greatest gains, whereas the English-language learners made the smallest gains.

Like others, Wright (1997) examined how strategy training influenced students' reading ability. The strategies the students were taught had elsewhere been identified as effective for students learning to read in their native language, but had not been investigated with students learning to read in a second language. Seven boys enrolled in Grade 10 participated in 2 weeks of reading strategy training. The participants were all students at a secondary boys' school, and all came from non-English-speaking backgrounds, although their first languages differed. Teachers identified the students as having poor reading skills that interfered with learning.

The approach consisted of eight 50-minute strategy training lessons. Results of the needs assessment dictated the four strategies, which included the (a) metacognitive strategies of overviewing, (b) self-evaluation, (c) inferencing, and (d) deducing the meaning of unknown words. It was hoped that a by-product of conscious strategy use would be increased learner autonomy. Most activities were tailored to the students, using reading texts from magazines, popular fiction, and newspapers, as well as from published reading texts.

For the Response to Literature (RL) task, the average length of students' responses increased from 362 words to 716 words, and the average number of correct statements increased from 17 to 39. The breakdown of scores on this task revealed significant gains for all sections except the interpretive statements. The researchers also report that diary entries and statements made during the postcourse interview revealed students' positive perceptions of the course. Students reported that the course was useful and that they had gained valuable skills from participating.

Interestingly, although students showed significant gains in their ability to determine whether statements they read were interpretive (rather than factual or evaluative), this was the single component on which students did not show significant gains on an assessment that required them to produce a 500-word narrative. One explanation is that students can recognize but not as readily produce interpretive statements. Issues related to the study include the small number of subjects; the low scores of some students, attributed by the authors to factors unrelated to the instructional approach (intellectual and social difficulty); the short duration of the training; use of measures of unknown validity or reliability; and the lack of a measure of interrater reliability on the RL assessment, the scoring of which leaves room for considerable subjectivity.

Pilgreen and Krashen (1983) studied the effects of providing sustained silent reading (SSR) to high school students studying English as a second language

(ESL). *SSR* is defined in this study as "quiet time, usually five to fifteen minutes per day, for self-selected reading [in which students] are not held accountable for what they read—no comprehension questions or book reports are required" (p. 21). The study participants were 125 high school students—in Grades 10 to 12—enrolled in five different ESL classes, as well as sheltered subject area classes. The students spoke 30 different first languages, with Spanish, Armenian, and Korean predominating. The Stanford Diagnostic Reading Comprehension Test revealed these students' reading ability to be at the fourth-grade level.

The outcomes for this study were two measures of reading ability— self-report and the standardized Stanford Diagnostic Reading Comprehension Test—as well as student reports of their interest in reading and reading habits (all of which were given both before and after the 16 weeks of SSR). After the SSR, students reported reading outside of school with greater frequency ($X^2 =$ 27.574, $df = 2$, $p < .001$) and having a greater liking for leisure reading ($X^2 =$ 27.574, $df = 2$, $p < .001$), although there was considerable variation across the classes on this latter measure. The students also reported using a wider range of sources to acquire books. A majority (77%) reported that their reading had improved a great deal, 56% claimed to enjoy the SSR sessions very much, and 68% thought the time devoted to SSR had been just right. The Stanford Diagnostic Reading Comprehension Test showed that students had gained an average of 15 months in their reading level by the end of the 16 weeks, averaging nearly 1 month for every week spent in the program. The gains were statistically significant ($p < .001$). As the authors note, "the gains are very encouraging, but can only be considered suggestive given the lack of a control group" (p. 23). In fact, the results could be attributable to instructional components other than SSR in the school the students attended. The authors plan future research using comparison groups from other schools.

Developing a Combination of Word- and Text-Level Skills

Kreuger and Townshend (1997) designed an instructional approach for use with first-grade English-language learners who had been identified as at risk with regard to learning to read in English. The 23 first-grade students were attending school in the Eastern Townships in Quebec, Canada, where 75% to 80% of students are English-language learners, with French as their native language. The students were divided into six groups of three to four students each and were coached every day for 30 minutes. The groupings were allowed to be flexible to meet shifting student needs. Students were removed from French instruction classes to maximize their exposure to English.

The program was called Reading Clubs and borrowed from the Reading Recovery work of Marie Clay (1993a, 1993b). Each Reading Club session began with a warm-up that introduced and reviewed the names and sounds of letters. The warm-up was followed by a quick review of the previous day's lesson or homework. Next, the day's lesson took up the major segment of time and varied from day to day. For instance, Monday's lesson involved introducing the week's story, playing word games, and reviewing names and sounds of letters; Tuesday's lesson involved working with sentence strips and modeling writing. On Wednesdays, the lesson involved making sentences out of word cards. Thursday's lesson involved storytelling and story writing, and Friday's lesson involved summarizing the story and playing more word games. In addition, every Tuesday, a running record for each child for the previous week's story was administered to assess whether the children could read the story. The program followed the same format each week.

The researchers deem the program successful, saying that,

> ...of the 23 children enrolled in the Reading Clubs, 19 made enough progress to read and write independently and moved with their peers into the second grade. On average, based on the Durrell Analysis of Reading Difficulty, Oral Reading subtest, these 19 students had progressed in one term from being too low to register on the test to a measurement of 1M or the middle of Grade 1. (pp. 126–127)

According to the researchers, the remaining four children had multiple learning problems, and their ability to read and write never extended past the controlled vocabulary of the Reading Clubs. An interesting observation is that, although all the students began the year at risk, only four students failed to respond to the program. It has been suggested that one method of distinguishing truly learning-disabled students from those who have not had an opportunity to learn is to undertake an intensive intervention; the children who do not respond are likely to have learning disabilities. The results of this study suggest that such an approach is worth exploring.

It would have been helpful if the author had provided student writing samples or other details about the students' writing to support narrative statements made throughout the report of the study. For example, in referring to the quality and amount of students' writing in daily journals, weekly stories, and books written throughout the year and on structured phonics worksheets, the authors report: ...children's writing began to emerge. Nineteen of the 23 students were confident enough in their writing to write what they wanted to say. This writing was not always spelled correctly and, in fact, not always readable, but children viewed themselves as writers and, for the most part, could communicate what they intended their audience to know. (p. 127) However, there is not sufficient information about the quality and quantity of children's writing ability to substantiate this claim. The same is true for the researchers' assertions about a "positive transference to their daily journal writing as these children started using their Reading Club vocabulary in their daily classroom writing" (p. 127). Finally, even with intensive small-group instruction, in addition to regular classroom instruction, the students on average ended the year at the middle, not at the end, of grade level for Year 1, suggesting the need to explore lengthening the time allotted to the intervention or fine-tuning it.

Li and Nes (2001) explored whether paired reading could help English-language learners become fluent and accurate readers. The researchers define *paired reading* as

> an instructional method that involves the pairing of a skilled reader with a less-skilled reader. The skilled reader demonstrates appropriate reading rate, inflection, and pausing for the less-skilled reader. In paired reading, the skilled reader in each pair reads the connected text first. Then the less-skilled reader reads the same text. Thus, the less-skilled reader has a role model of fluent reading, as well as repeated exposure to text. (p. 51)

The researchers identified four students ages 7 to 9 for participation in their program. The students were all recent immigrants of Chinese origin who were enrolled in public schools and received daily 40-minute pullout ESL classes. These four students participated in daily paired reading sessions that lasted approximately 20 minutes. The paired reading sessions were all conducted in the students' homes. The students then shifted to a maintenance period, during which they participated in paired reading approximately once every 10 days. The daily paired reading lasted for 8 months for three students (one student moved after 5 months). The materials used were children's storybooks, which were "selected in accordance with the students' reading levels" (p. 53).

The paired reading gave students an opportunity to read more with modeling and feedback from a skilled reader, and fluency and accuracy scores increased dramatically. One student, for example, read at an average rate of 34 words per minute (wpm) at the start of the study. While she was participating in paired reading, her average rate increased to 86 wpm; this rate rose again during the maintenance phase to 112 wpm. Her accuracy rate began at 85% and rose to 99%. The other three students posted similar gains: A second student read an average of 36 wpm at the outset; this rate rose to 69 wpm during the paired reading and then dipped to 66 wpm during maintenance. Her rate of accuracy began at 75 % and rose to 87%. A third student read less than 15 wpm initially; this rate increased to nearly 65 wpm during paired reading and rose again to 96 wpm during maintenance. His rate of accuracy began at 52% and rose to 96%. Finally, a fourth student read 35 wpm at the outset of the study; this rate rose to 55 wpm during paired reading and again to 67 wpm during maintenance. His rate of accuracy began at 57% and rose to 97%. As the authors point out, "their overall language skills had improved as a result of school learning and exposure to English" and this may "have contributed to students' increase in reading fluency and accuracy" (p. 60).

Beyond Word- and Text-Level Skills: Students' Participation in Classroom Discourse and Literacy-Related Behaviors

In this section, we describe one study that examined students' discourse related to classroom literacy activities. The study examined a primary-grade classroom and focused on a single activity—literature circles—that occurred as just one of a series of events experienced by students throughout the school day. The next two studies reviewed here examined literacy-related outcomes extending beyond classroom discourse. The final study looked at how prekindergarten children new to English learned English vocabulary in the context of literacy activities.

Martínez-Roldan and López-Robertson (2000) transcribed and analyzed 19 audiotapes of Literature Circles in a bilingual classroom. During the weekly Literature Circle, students participated in small-group discussions of high-quality children's literature; the Literature Circle provided a forum in which students could share their perspectives on the stories and listen to one another's ideas. The books were available in the students' dominant language; thus, language-minority students who were Spanish dominant and instructed in Spanish participated in Spanish, whereas students dominant and instructed in English participated in English. The authors indicate that students, despite low levels of English proficiency and literacy, were able to have meaningful discussions about books and identified the types of literature responses made by first-grade students in the Literature Circle: living through the experience (i.e., responding intimately and spontaneously to the literature); looking closely at the text and illustrations; exploring social issues; and making connections with other books, life experiences, and oral stories. In examining differences between the two language groups, the authors found the English group focused more on text and the Spanish group focused more on storytelling related to their frightening experiences as recent immigrants.

As noted, we reviewed two studies concerned with literacy-related outcomes that extend beyond classroom discourse. Kenner (1999) examined a prekindergarten class composed mostly of language-minority students who were given opportunities to use literacy materials commonly found in homes. She found that when these materials were present in the classroom, the children engaged in playacts that mimicked adult literate behaviors, showing the children's literacy awareness. Similarly, Ramos and Krashen (1998) report that increasing Hispanic inner-city students' exposure to books by taking them on weekly trips to the public library had positive results; most students reported that "they read more, that reading was easier, and that they wanted to return to the library," and "67% of the students asked their parents to take them back to the library" (p. 614).

The last study reviewed in this section examined how English-language learners acquired vocabulary in a full-day urban prekindergarten classroom (Genishi et al., 2001). The majority of students (14 of 16) spoke Chinese as their first language. The researchers collected handwritten notes, audiotapes, videotapes, the teacher's anecdotes and portfolio of practices and philosophy, and samples of students' work. They identified four classroom behaviors: conferring, sharing, responding to the physical world, and enacting an integrated curriculum. Two themes related to English vocabulary development emerged: A core vocabulary had developed among the students, and it was related to classroom routines and expectations. Although peer interactions were valuable, student's vocabulary development in English was more related to their interactions with the teachers in part because many student–student interactions took place in Chinese.

Summary and Conclusions

In general, the findings of these studies parallel those reported in chapter 15. However, because these were case studies and ethnographies, the findings are only suggestive. Other factors may have contributed to positive student outcomes, including, for example, regular classroom instruction (many of the instructional approaches were delivered outside of regular classroom instruction) or students' natural maturation. With regard to word-level skills, students involved in explicit phonics instruction improved their phonological awareness and decoding skills (Escamilla & Andrade, 1992; Hus, 2001). Instructional practices aimed at building text-level skills suggest that language-minority students may benefit from instructional approaches that are effective with monolingual students (Palincsar & Brown, 1984, 1985; Paris et al., 1984). For example, in all three studies in which an effort was made to help students take charge of their comprehension processes, through reciprocal teaching (Hernández, 1991), collaborative group work (Klingner & Vaughn, 2000), or teaching of metacognitive strategies (Wright, 1997), students' success in the skills targeted by the instruction improved (comprehension in Spanish; English vocabulary; ability to identify factual, interpretive, and evaluative statements; and response to literature in English). The students in the other studies that also borrowed from the first-language literacy research—SSR (Pilgreen & Krashen, 1983), an approach modeled on Reading Recovery (Kreuger & Townshend, 1997), and the use of paired reading (Li & Nes, 2001)—also improved in the targeted skills (reading ability, interest in reading and reading habits, oral English reading, English reading accuracy and fluency).

As with the findings of quasi-experimental research reported in chapter 15, however, some of the approaches found to be successful have attributes that would make them suitable for English-language learners. Two studies (Escamilla & Andrade, 1992; Hernández, 1991) provided instruction in students' native language—in this case, Spanish. In addition, several studies focused on making English word meanings clear through picture cues (Hus, 2001) and other techniques (Kreuger & Townshend, 1997); extracting meaning from text by identifying and clarifying difficult words and passages (Klingner & Vaughn, 2000); consolidating text knowledge through summarization (Klingner & Vaughn, 2000); providing extra practice reading words, sentences, and stories (Pilgreen & Krashen, 1983; Wright, 1997); as well as in the strategies taught (Klingner & Vaughn, 2000).

An issue that emerges from these studies has to do with strategy use versus teacher's scaffolding of text as a mechanism for improving students' comprehension. For example, Hernández (1991) presumably focused on teaching students strategy use. However, the teacher did many things that scaffolded instruction: The researcher/teacher started the lesson by discussing students' experiences related to the story content and introducing new vocabulary, and concluded the lesson by framing questions for group response, summarizing part of the text for group response, prompting predictions, and clarifying ambiguities. Student leaders gradually took over this role. Future studies on strategy use would benefit from clearly distinguishing the two methods of building comprehension, as well as pairing assessments of strategy use with measures of actual literacy skills (e.g., comprehension or writing) to look at outcomes more broadly.

Another issue relates to differential effects of the approaches studied on students with varying degrees of English proficiency (Klingner & Vaughn, 2000) and capability, with some students possibly needing more intensive or qualitatively different types of instruction (Kreuger & Townshend, 1997; Wright, 1997). For example, in the Kreuger and Townshend study, four students do not benefit from the intervention because they had multiple learning problems. In the Wright study, the low scores of some students are attributed to students' intellectual and social difficulties. The English-language learners in Klingner and Vaughn's study made the smallest gains in vocabulary. Language-minority students are a highly heterogeneous group, and the various approaches studied must be interpreted in this light and designed to take these differences into account.

A subset of the studies reviewed in this section examined instructional techniques focused on a specific component or components of literacy. These studies can help inform the design of instructional methods and strategies. However, because the studies were prospective case studies, and as such did not employ control groups, the findings are only suggestive. Approaches that appear to effect positive change should be submitted to more rigorous evaluations using experimental or quasi-experimental designs. Other methodological issues that weaken these studies include the brief duration of the instructional approach used in many of the studies and the use of researcher-developed outcome measures with no reported information about validity or reliability or the relationship to standardized assessments commonly used to measure the same literacy constructs in children.

This section has also reviewed one study that explored students' participation in classroom discourse related to literacy events (Martínez-Roldan & López-Robertson, 2000) and two studies involving unique classroom situations associated with literacy development (Kenner, 1999; Ramos & Krashen, 1998). The rich detail provided by the authors of the subset of ethnographic studies reported in this section provides a window into how students engage in classroom literacy events. However, as with the studies reported in Part III, there is scant information about how representative examples were selected or about their frequency or typicality, which makes it difficult to corroborate the authors' findings. Finally, as with studies reported in Part III, connecting the dimensions of interest (such as student discourse) with valid data about important student outcomes would further our understanding of literacy development. As an example, one cannot assume that increased discourse in English or increased discourse in general necessarily means improved literacy outcomes. In examining child–child interactions, Saville-Troike (1984) found that "three of the five highest achieving students (in English) used their native languages with peers to the virtual exclusion of English, while the other two top achievers rarely spoke to other children during ESL or regular classroom sessions" (p. 209).

COMPREHENSIVE INSTRUCTIONAL PROGRAMS DESIGNED TO IMPROVE MULTIPLE COMPONENTS OF LITERACY

This section focuses on comprehensive instructional programs designed to improve multiple components of literacy. As with the preceding section, many of the programs discussed are based on models developed for native-English-speaking students, with accommodations based on the needs and strengths of language-minority students. The programs encompass balanced-literacy, whole-language, and whole-literacy approaches.

Although all the studies reviewed here examined comprehensive programs, the nature of the programs and their goals varied considerably. Three of the studies examined students' overall literacy development and attainment in balanced-literacy programs (Fitzgerald & Noblit, 1999, 2000; Kucer & Silva, 1999). A fourth study (Araujo, 2002) explored kindergarten English-language learners' development in a curriculum consisting of circle reading, phonics/handwriting, and journal writing. A fifth study (Kucer, 1999) compared the responses of two students to whole-language instruction they received in the same class.

A sixth study (Kuball & Peck, 1997) considered students' writing development in whole-language instruction. A seventh study (Pérez, 1994) examined what Spanish-dominant students learned during whole-language Spanish instruction. The remaining studies focused on the development of specific aspects of students' reading and writing performance when exposed to specific instructional techniques delivered within the context of the designated instructional model. These instructional techniques and the instructional goals include strategy wall charts and students' use of strategies for overcoming blocks when reading, writing, or spelling (Kucer, 1995); dialogue journals and literature logs and students' writing (Reyes, 1991); a writer's workshop and students' ownership of writing and engagement in the writing process (Au & Carroll, 1997); and cloze lessons and students' understanding of their purpose (Kucer, 1992).

Although the participants in these studies represent a range of language backgrounds (Portuguese, Spanish, Native Hawaiian) and ages (kindergarten through sixth grade), most of the studies focused on children whose home language was Spanish, and no studies addressed middle- or high school students. The approaches to studying these programs were varied, reflecting the primary concerns of the investigators. In most cases, both qualitative and quantitative data were gathered in the same classrooms so that researchers could construct hypotheses about classroom practices and measure students' literacy growth and ultimate attainment. These studies' careful examination of the details of the practices teachers used, as well as multiple assessments of students' responses to these practices, contributes to our understanding of the complexity involved in developing literacy in a diverse group of learners and helps us understand the nature of the techniques that have potential for addressing student literacy needs.

Balanced Literacy

Araujo (2002) first identified the literacy events taking place in a Portuguese–English bilingual kindergarten classroom composed of language-minority children of Portuguese background. She describes how the teacher used two approaches—emergent literacy (whole-language approach) and conventional literacy (phonics)—as frames for the three types of literacy events that occurred in the classroom (circle reading, phonics/handwriting, and journal writing). The two literacy approaches might be enacted during the same literacy event. At the end of the kindergarten year, 13 of the 20 children were at various stages of writing development (9 were transitional spellers, 1 was a letter-name speller, 3 were at the early phonemic stage of writing development, and 7 did not experiment with writing[2]). With regard to reading, the class as a whole recognized 34 words in January and 171 words in June. (It should be noted that examples of these words indicated they were a mix of sight and decodable

---

[2]According to Gillet and Temple (1990), early phonemic spellers represent a word with a single letter, usually the first recognizable sound. Letter-name spellers use the names of letters to represent sounds, representing all the consonants in a word, but do not use vowels. Transitional spellers use vowels, and the words they write resemble real words (Araujo, 2002).

words.) However, there was a large range in gains per child, with six children gaining 10 to 14 words and six gaining 0 to 4 words over this time.

Fitzgerald and Noblit (2000) report findings from a naturalistic study of first-grade children's emergent reading development in a year-long balanced-reading-instruction program. Participants were students in a first-grade class in a rural area of the southeastern United States. Of the 30 children who attended this class over the year, 20 were included in the study. Of these, 11 were English-language learners. The balanced-reading program was designed to help children acquire both local (phonological awareness, knowledge of sound–symbol relationships) and global (understanding, interpretation, reading strategies, motivation to read) knowledge about reading. To achieve these goals, four central components were provided:

1. word study—learning sight words and various word-recognition strategies, including using context, phonics, and structural analysis (e.g., using analogous words to figure out an unknown word), learning cross-checking to figure out a new word, and, for some children, learning new word meanings;
2. responding to good literature during or after reading or listening;
3. writing; and
4. guided and unguided reading practice, which provided opportunities for students to use all of the dynamic features of the reading process while reading.

"'Local' knowledge about reading was most emphasized in word study, and 'global' knowledge and 'sentiments' about reading were most emphasized in responding to good literature" (p. 8).

On the basis of a wealth of data they collected, the researchers articulate four themes that emerged from analysis of these data. First, the children began to construct knowledge about local aspects of reading, including phonological awareness, knowledge of sight words, ability to match correct letters to sounds and identify orthographic patterns in words, and use of word-recognition and word-meaning strategies. Second, the children began to construct global knowledge about reading, including knowledge that reading and writing were about understanding and communicating. Third, the children were developing sentiments of wanting to read, and they were learning about giving and taking from reading (response). Fourth, transitional moments signaled children's movement toward more mature communicative competence.

A significant finding of this study was that, although the students progressed at different rates, in most cases their growth followed similar paths; some students took longer than others to acquire reading skills, but they eventually acquired the same skills. The implication is that, over time and with good instruction, lower level readers, including English-language learners, can attain the same goals as higher level readers. However, this was not the case with vocabulary. All but one of the English-language learners scored in the bottom half of the class on one test of knowledge of English word meanings. Although the researchers recognize that the time required to acquire a new language may explain this outcome, they also acknowledge not having had a plan for addressing vocabulary development, particularly for English-language learners. Major strengths of this study are that a variety of measures and methods were used to assess student progress over time and that the instruction occurred over the course of a year.

Fitzgerald and Noblit (1999) compared the reading development of two of the English-language learners in this same class. Both students had had year-long kindergarten experiences, yet both began the first-grade school year as barely emergent readers. Both students made remarkable progress in their reading and writing over the first-grade school year. Although their rates of progress differed, with one finishing the year far more advanced than the other, the researchers note a marked similarity in their paths. The researchers conclude that the developmental paths to reading they identified in these students were similar to those identified in research on native English speakers. This finding led the researchers to question the extent to which this path was influenced by the instruction received—instruction that had been designed with this model of development in mind. They are careful to acknowledge, however, the efforts made by the teacher to identify the students' needs and to support their growth when those needs became apparent, and they assert their belief that the students' development might not have occurred had such careful efforts not been made.

A study conducted by Neufeld and Fitzgerald (2001) examined the English reading development of three Latino English-language learners who were members of the low reading group in a first-grade all-English classroom located in rural North Carolina. These Latino students also participated in the free or reduced-price lunch program. At the beginning of the school year, the teacher created two reading groups—high and low. The low reading group was formed around the three boys who were the subject of the study. The teacher believed that students in the low group were not ready to read at all. Her goals for them included learning to say and spell the alphabet, learning to spell a few words, learning to write neatly, and improving their English oral language. The researchers found the three boys' reading development to be highly similar across the school year; they gradually developed an awareness of concepts important to reading. However, none of the three could pass the preprimer passage on a running record in June, nor did they demonstrate any noticeable gains in their English oral proficiency.

Although the path of development for the three students in this study was similar and their reading development remained in its early phases during the school year, the researchers found similarities between the path these boys followed and that described for native English speakers. The researchers explore two hypotheses for the boys' lack of reading development: that low English oral proficiency inhibited their reading growth, and that their slow growth resulted from the instruction they received—instruction that stemmed from the teacher's belief that the students needed to develop their English oral abilities before being able to succeed at reading.

Whole-Language Programs

According to Riches and Genesee (2006), a defining characteristic of whole-language programs is their emphasis on the integrity of reading, writing, speaking, and listening (and the respective subskills). Whole-language philosophy asserts that the acquisition of literacy skills occurs naturally, like the acquisition of oral and aural language, through involvement in authentic, meaningful uses of written language. However, in the studies we reviewed, there is wide variation among whole-language programs with respect to the language in which the program is conducted (i.e., Spanish or English), the age of the students, as well as the outcome measures used. Various socioaffective variables (e.g., attitudes toward reading and self-concept as a reader/writer) figure in a number of these studies, along with more conventional outcome measures such as spelling, grammar, and standardized reading test scores.

Kuball and Peck (1997) studied the development of writing in classrooms that used a whole-language approach. According to the authors, "the classroom was a print-rich environment in which skills were learned within the context of a whole....Skills were presented to students in context" (p. 217). In addition, they compared the writing performance of English-speaking children receiving whole-language instruction in English with that of Spanish-speaking children receiving whole-language instruction in Spanish. The study participants were 16 kindergarten students attending a large public school in the greater Los Angeles area. Eight students were Spanish speakers and classified as limited English proficient; they attended an afternoon kindergarten class, where they received whole-language instruction in Spanish. The other eight students were native speakers of English and attended the morning kindergarten class, where they received whole-language instruction in English.

The study was conducted over a 1-year period. Data were collected during the 3rd and 32nd weeks of the school year. The study findings indicate that both groups of students made progress (in their respective languages) in all areas examined. For instance, all of the study participants went from having the self-concept of nonwriters on the pretest to having the self-concept of writers on the posttest. On the Lamme/Green Scale of Children's Development in Composition,[3] the Spanish-speaking students improved in compositional skills between the pretest (on which 75% of the Spanish-speaking students received low ratings in compositional skills) and the posttest (on which all students received advanced ratings). All of the English-speaking children received advanced ratings in compositional skills on both pre- and posttest. All of the students were rated at the lowest levels of the 8-point scale of graphophonemic development on the pretest. The average ratings for the groups increased on the posttest, with 75% of the Spanish-speaking students receiving scores of 4 and the remaining 25% scores of 7, while 100% of the English-speaking children received scores of 4.[4] Although students' graphophonemic scores improved over the course of the year, their progress was less notable than English-language learners exposed to systematic phonics instruction (Stuart, 1999). It is interesting that, with regard to progression

---

[3]The Lamme/Green Scale defines four compositional stages: 0–child writes a one-word statement; 1–child writes simple messages and/or a list of 10 or more words; 2–child writes a complete thought, a message of two or more sentences, or a list of short sentences; and 3–child writes a long story of four or more sentences with a plot or a long letter that focuses on a single subject.

[4]Note, however, that "a rating of 1-4 represented the pre-phonemic stages in which a graphophonemic relationship has not yet been obtained. A rating of 5-6 indicated application of average graph-phonemic literacy skills for a kindergarten child, and a 7-8 rating represented possession of advanced grapho-phonemic literacy skills" (Kuball & Peck, 1997, p. 219).

through levels of these graphophonemic literacy skills, 25% of the Spanish-speaking group progressed through three to four stages, compared with none of the English-speaking group. This result is probably related to the graphophonemic regularity of the Spanish language.

Pérez (1994) studied the Spanish literacy development of Spanish-dominant students of low socioeconomic status (SES) receiving Spanish literacy whole-language instruction. In this study, Pérez used Stahl and Miller's (1989) definition of *whole language* to select four bilingual Spanish–English whole-language teachers for participation:

> (a) the medium of instruction is the children's own language, using dictated story charts, class and student published books, and, through their individual writing, using invented spelling; (b) instruction is child-centered rather than teacher-centered; (c) language is viewed as communicative; (d) there is an emphasis on trade books, rather than on basals; and (e) lessons in decoding are given as the need arises in the context of reading whole text. (p. 78)

The teachers were selected from two schools—one an urban school and the other a rural school with a large migrant population. Twenty students were selected from the four teachers' classrooms for participation in the study: four from kindergarten, six from first grade, six from second grade, and four from fourth grade.

Over the course of a single semester, Pérez collected classroom observation field notes, audiotapes and reading transcripts, and samples of in-class writing from the four classrooms and 20 students included in the study. Pérez found that the children and teachers in her study spent far more of the allocated reading/writing instruction time (50%–70%) talking about, rather than engaging in, reading and writing. *Talking about* included student discussion, asking and answering questions, and predictions about what the students were going to read. However, there was considerable variation in the kinds of talk at each grade level. Pérez found that all students participated in writing, but that the first-grade children did the least amount of writing, while the second- and fourth-grade students did the most. Although code switching was used by all but one child during the pre- and postreading and writing discussions, only six of the children used code switching in their writing. Children's most common strategy for invented spelling was sounding out of words and syllabification; children who attended to more graphophonic skills in reading appeared to use more invented spelling in their writing samples.

Miscue analysis[5] was used to assess children's reading, phonological awareness, and meaning construction. This analysis revealed that 14 of the children increased their meaning construction and knowledge of grammatical relations by more than 5 percentage points (6 did not) between March and June. Thus, the 16 children used "all the cues of language to produce syntactically and semantically acceptable miscues...and selected and used graphophonic cues

---

[5]Miscue analysis evaluates the degree to which students use semantic, syntactic, and graphophonic systems of language when reading" (Goodman, Watson, & Burke, 1987).The sentences that students read were judged in terms of their syntactic and semantic acceptability, as well as whether the miscues resulted in changing the meaning of the sentence.

(sounding out letters, syllables, and words), although they did not depend on this strategy to the exlusion of others such as context" (p. 88). Retelling scores increased for all the students. Given that about one third of the sample did not progress in some of the instructed skills, we agree with Pérez, who concludes that "whole language and phonics can form a complementary basis for literacy instruction. In this scheme, whole language involves using quality children's literature, writing, and assuring that skills are applied in the context of reading/ writing, rather than treated as isolated exercises" (pp. 91–92). She adds, "quality phonics instruction need not be synonymous with excessive worksheets, nor must it exclude the use of quality literature" (p. 92). As in studies reviewed previously, additional outcome data that would help benchmark student achievement against a normative sample would be valuable. It should also be noted that students were reading in Spanish, which was their first language. In addition, Spanish has a much more shallow orthography than English, which may necessitate less extensive phonics instruction.

Kucer and Silva (1999) examined the English literacy development of bilingual students receiving whole-language instruction in the context of a transitional bilingual education program. In this study, *whole language* was defined through the teacher's beliefs about literacy instruction, which are stated as follows:

> The teacher [the second author on this study] believed that by providing literacy instruction in an environment rich in contextual support, she could facilitate learning for her second language students and thought that the use of thematic units provided such a context. She defined herself as a whole-language advocate and, being opposed to the explicit teaching of skills in isolation, felt that reading and writing strategies were best taught within contextualized situations. (p. 351)

The participants in this study were 26 third-grade Mexican American bilinguals, all from working-class homes. In the first and second grades, these students received language and literacy instruction designed to provide them with a foundation in spoken English and written Spanish. They had all been identified by the second-grade bilingual teacher at their school as ready for transition to English-only instruction. Thus, during the third grade, these bilingual students attended all but language arts classes with native-English-speaking peers. For language arts, the students attended class with the bilingual teacher, whose expressed commitment to whole-language instruction is described earlier.

The researchers used identical pre- and posttests of students' reading, writing, and spelling to assess their literacy growth. The assessments asked students to (a) orally read and retell a short story, (b) write a story about an exciting experience, and (c) spell 57 words from the third-grade speller. All assessments were conducted in English. The data analysis reveals areas of both growth and stagnation. For instance, the students' scores on the miscue analysis and the retelling taxonomy posted statistically significant increases. However, for the holistic writing analysis, the students' mean score did not show statistically significant growth; the authors note that "the lack of significance is noteworthy, given the frequency with which students drafted, conferred, revised, and published their writing" (p. 362). For the analytic analysis of students' writing, the researchers report statistically significant growth in students' mean story word length (35.68 in the fall, 57.37 in the spring), as well as spelling and capitalization. They also note growth in the mean number of sentences that students produced, as well as their use of periods, but these changes were not statistically significant. The students' mean scores for the spelling word list assessment also showed statistically significant growth, with the spring assessment mean score increasing from 21.26 in the fall to 32.84 in the spring.

Although students showed progress in reading, they were reading texts that generated approximately 25 miscues, and on average this text was at the 2.5-grade level. At the conclusion of the study, however, students should have been able to read text close to the 4.0 grade level. Improvement to considerably below the students' grade level may indicate progress, but this achievement may not be sufficient for them to succeed with grade-appropriate text. As with other studies, assessments that would have enabled comparisons with normative samples would have helped in benchmarking student progress. With regard to the mixed progress in writing, the authors note the general nature of the students' writing conferences and the lack of direct and explicit instruction focused on distinct aspects of writing. We would concur with the authors who suggest the use of focused mini-lessons to build writing skills. In such lessons, one particular dimension of writing is highlighted for students needing extra support. During these lessons, not only is this dimension discussed, but students are also shown explicitly how to use it. Following the lessons, students apply what they have learned to drafts they are revising for publication.

In a separate analysis, Kucer (1999) examined the interaction of individual bilingual students enrolled in this class with the whole-language curricula to document the lived-through experiences of the students receiving whole-language instruction. To this end, the researcher focused on two students who responded differently to the curricula. Data collected included both descriptive and focused ethnographic field notes, interviews, oral readings, story writing, and spelling. Students were also given the pre- and posttest assessments described previously.

Analysis of the data revealed three types of student interactions with the curricula: engagements, conflicts, and avoidances. "Engagements reflected student behaviors that were aligned with the intention of the activity.... Behaviors that interfered with or negated the intention of the activity were categorized as conflicts...[and] behaviors that circumvented the focus of the activity were categorized as avoidances" (p. 240). One of the focal students, Jose Antonio, was engaged with the curriculum in 91% of his interactions. In contrast, his classmate, Angie, was engaged in just 48% of her interactions, and 36% of her interactions were avoidances. Jose Antonio's literacy growth, on all measures, exceeded Angie's, suggesting that Angie was unable to respond to the curricula as they were presented. The teacher assumed that identifying a problem or repeating the activity throughout the semester was enough to assist Angie. In fact, this was not the case. Although Angie knew what to do, she did not know how to do it. The data show that, rather than providing more scaffolding for how to do an activity, the teacher simply repeated the same instructions when Angie's performance was lacking. According to the author, a related reason Angie resisted and avoided the structures provided by the teacher was that "she had little input into the focus of the lessons; she was concerned with graphophonics and conventional spelling, while the teacher was concerned with context and writing for meaning" (p. 252). The study suggests that teachers need to be attuned to individual differences in learning styles and to scaffold instruction for students who are having difficulty mastering particular concepts. It also highlights the important contribution that qualitative research makes to understanding individual differences in achievement.

Kucer (1992) also studied students' understanding of one of the literacy activities to which they were exposed in this class-the cloze lesson. The purpose of this lesson was "to increase the students' ability to use context clues when they encountered words they did not know how to read" (p. 557). To create the cloze lessons, "words were deleted at points in text where there was sufficient contextual information to lead to the generation of meaningful predictions on the part of the students" (p. 561). For this study, Kucer selected six bilingual Mexican American children—three boys and three girls—who were "highly verbal, proficient in oral English, were comfortable interacting with [him], and represented the range of English literacy abilities in the class: fairly proficient in reading, two somewhat proficient, and two nonproficient" (p. 559).

Analysis of the literacy artifacts suggests that the students performed the cloze task well—93% of their responses were contextually appropriate. Of additional interest is what caused the errors in 7% of the instances: students' difficulty in seeing their responses as tentative and in need of ongoing monitoring, their difficulty with adverbial deletions, and their lack of background knowledge about particular topics. However, interviews with the students and their teacher following the lessons revealed that students could not articulate an understanding of the purpose of the cloze lesson that matched the teacher's, even when the teacher explained the purpose at the start of and during the lesson. Kucer proposes that students' previously developed schema for schooling may have predisposed them to assume that the purpose of this task was learning new words, making words rhyme, or sounding out words, rather than helping them deal with alternatives to sounding out words. Of interest would be some link between students' ability to use context to fill in the blanks in the cloze activity and improvements in their word reading ability, which was the purpose of the cloze activity.

Kucer (1995) also examined the effects of a series of lessons involving strategy wall charts on bilingual students' engagement with literacy processes. The charts were part of a curriculum he developed together with the teacher of the third-grade transitional bilingual classroom he observed. The purpose of the charts was to offer children easy access to strategies they could use when they became blocked during reading or writing. The strategies were demonstrated during conferences with groups of four to seven students. During the conferences, students shared problems they were having, after which the teacher and other students in the group attempted to solve the problems using various solutions from the strategy charts. Response conferences were similar, in that students used the strategy charts to discuss something they had read. Over time, the teacher became a less active participant in these conferences. Kucer spent 1 year in this classroom as a participant observer. He found that students' reader response strategies had developed the most and their writing strategies the least. It would have been interesting if the author had presented information on whether strategy use actually made a difference in student performance on word reading, comprehension, and writing because previous work with English-language learners indicates that strategy instruction absent teacher support in helping students understand the content they read may be of limited value given their lack of English proficiency (August & Hakuta, 1997).[6]

Reyes (1991) examined the influence of holistic process approaches to literacy that are common in whole-language programs to learn their effects on the development of sixth-grade Hispanic students' Spanish- and English-language writing fluency. Specifically, she examined the work produced in dialogue journals and literature logs by 10 English-language learners enrolled in the sixth grade at a middle school in a large urban school district in the southwest. These students were enrolled in bilingual classes and received instruction in Spanish and English. All 10 students spoke Spanish as their native language and lived in homes where Spanish was the primary language spoken. The attendance area of the school included a large low- to middle-income Mexican-origin Hispanic community.

Reyes examined students' work to determine "how...the construction of meaning [differed] in native (Spanish) and English [second language] using dialogue journals and literature logs" and "what features of written discourse: topic choice, code-switching, sensitivity to audience, writer's voice, grammatical structures, and spelling [indicated] marked improvement using dialogue journals and literature logs" (p. 293). To this end, she observed students for 4 intensive days, followed by weekly observations throughout the year, to determine the various kinds of writing in which they engaged. She analyzed 261 samples of students' journal writing and 96 pages of their writing in literature logs. The analysis focused on themes/topics and their effect on the length and complexity of the students' writing, the language used by the students and that used by the teacher to respond, code switching (alternation between Spanish and English in writing), positive and negative self-concepts and attitudes toward school, and writing skills (spelling inventions and grammatical structures).

Three major findings emerged from this study. First, Reyes found that English-language learners can and do attempt to write in English *before* they have complete control over the oral and written systems of the language. Second, although English-language learners may write in English, their development of complex ideas and the construction of meaning may suffer considerably. Third, the students were not successful in their literature logs, in that they had difficulty writing more reflective entries. The author attributes this difficulty to the requirement that the program be conducted in English, the lack of teacher mediation during reading and writing, and the teacher's hesitancy in helping students select English trade books that were appropriate for their reading level and in monitoring their reading. The author attributes these teacher shortcomings to professional development in whole-language and process writing, in which it was assumed that what works for native English speakers will also work for English-language learners with no cultural or linguistic modifications. Other findings include (a) students' lack of attention to correct form in both the dialogue journals and literature logs, even over time and despite the

---

[6]Kucer (personal communication, March 5, 2005) reports that the Kucer and Silva (1999) article presents this information; the author was unable to report these data in the 1995 article due to page-length restrictions.

fact that the teacher conducted daily writing conferences with individual students, peer conferences, and mini-lessons, in which she focused on specific errors students were committing in their writing, modeled correct form, and used the students' own inventive spellings in conventional form; (b) students' better control of journal writing when topics were self-selected, culturally relevant, familiar, personal, or important than when they were imposed by the teacher; and (c) students' more negative feelings when writing in their literature logs than in response journals.

Whole-Literacy Programs

Au and Carroll (1997) describe the outcomes of a 2-year demonstration classroom project designed to help teachers implement a whole-literacy approach to instruction. The whole-literacy curriculum was developed to improve the effectiveness of services to teachers and students in the Kamehameha Elementary Education Program (KEEP), which, according to the authors, had eroded over time, in part, because of the use of a mastery learning approach to skills. The project took place in a school district where more than 60% of the students enrolled spoke Hawaiian-Creole English as their first language. Most of the students came from low-income families. Demonstration classrooms were selected to implement the constructivist approach to literacy education. As part of this implementation, classroom teachers developed their instructional expertise by working with KEEP staff. One element of the project was the placement of KEEP staff members, known as consultants, in schools to provide teachers with in-service training. Each consultant worked with one to three project teachers. They observed in the classroom about twice a week, sometimes conducting demonstration lessons. Consultants also met with teachers individually and in small groups for networking. In addition, they supported other teachers who might become project teachers in future years.

   According to the authors,

> ownership of literacy was the overall goal, and the curriculum emphasized reading and writing rather than placing equal emphasis on all the language arts, including speaking and listening. Second, [project] teachers in primary-grade classrooms continued to use ability grouping for reading instruction, at least part of the time. Third, the curriculum stressed the use of culturally appropriate instructional strategies as described in Au and Mason, 1983. Fourth…the curriculum included grade-level benchmarks designed to focus instruction and facilitate program evaluation. (p. 205)

Instruction in literacy occurred in readers' and writers' workshops and included a portfolio assessment system anchored to the standards. Because of implementation problems,[7] the authors focused on writing, using classroom

---

[7] Because data from the first 2 years suggested that student achievement was unaffected by the efforts to implement a whole-literacy curriculum, project staff reexamined their approaches to providing faculty development and support. This review resulted in giving the teachers the option to focus on either reading or writing in their classrooms, rather than having to learn and implement new approaches to teaching both reading and writing in a single year. The majority of the teachers in the project chose to focus on writing.

observations to document the degree of implementation and portfolio assessments to assess student achievement.

A detailed analysis of the implementation data revealed a growth trend in the number of items implemented from the beginning to the end of the year. In analyzing the four categories of program features, researchers found that "classroom organization items were most readily implemented, followed by items related to student opportunities for learning. The instructional practices items were more challenging to implement because they required teachers to participate as learners and writers in the classroom. Assessment items proved the most difficult to implement" (p. 216). The findings also show that teachers who had greater experience with the whole-literacy approach, and thus were able to implement more of its features, had greater success with their students and ended the school year with fewer students below and more students above grade average.

Student scores were derived from a portfolio assessment system developed by KEEP. This assessment was anchored to standards and described the desired achievement of the hypothetical average student at the end of each grade. Four sources provided information about these standards: "(1) the Hawaii state department of education's language arts curriculum guide, (2) the reading objectives of the National Assessment of Educational Progress, (3) the standardized test series used in the state's evaluation program, and (4) recently published basal reading and language arts programs" (p. 205). In areas not traditionally evaluated, such as ownership and voluntary reading, benchmarks were based on published research and observations in KEEP classrooms.

Teachers provided ratings for six students from their classrooms—two representative of students achieving in the top third of the class, two in the middle third, and two in the lowest third—who had been present for writing instruction for at least half the school year. Students were rated on all the benchmarks for their grade level (and for the grade level above, in the case of advanced students). KEEP benchmarks fell into two categories: ownership of writing (i.e., enjoys writing, shows interest in others' writing, writes inside and outside of class for own purposes) and writing process (a holistic score for quality of writing, and ratings for carrying out key components of writer's workshop—planning, drafting, revising, editing, publishing, and research strategies). Although many of the benchmarks addressed processes, others dealt with products. For example, one benchmark required the holistic quality of students' writing samples to be judged at grade level. Teachers were asked to make these judgments by referring to a scoring manual that included anchor pieces for each grade level. Ratings were based on evidence in students' portfolios indicating that students had or had not met this benchmark. An audit of portfolio results for each classroom was conducted to ensure that ratings were reliable. The audit team consisted of two KEEP members from outside the school and the site manager. During Year 1, the auditor's ratings matched those of the consultants, KEEP staff who had been involved at the school helping teachers implement the KEEP curriculum, 98% of the time in the case of writing benchmarks; during Year 2, the rate of agreement was 94%.

Student achievement data revealed a drop in the number of students scoring below grade level for both ownership of writing and writing process. For instance, at the beginning of Year 1, 42% of students scored below grade level for ownership of writing, and 60% scored below grade level for writing process. By the end of Year 1, these numbers had declined to 15% and 31%, respectively. These numbers were lower still at the end of the second year: 6% and 28%, respectively.

The KEEP experience highlights the importance of supporting teacher change and the need for systems that are intensive, elaborate, and enduring to accomplish this change. According to the authors, "teachers relied heavily on the instructional advice and moral support offered by the KEEP consultants" (p. 218). "Some teachers said they could not have made as many changes in their classrooms, or achieved such positive results, without the consultants' help" (p. 218; cited in Au & Scheu, 1996). Two critical tools in supporting teacher change were the classroom implementation checklist and grade-appropriate benchmarks used to assess student progress.

This study has many strengths, among them detailed information about program implementation and audits to check portfolio results for each classroom to ensure that ratings were reliable. It indicates that whole-literacy instruction is a promising approach for developing high levels of writing competence in English-language learners. However, it also highlights the importance of intensive support that promotes fidelity to the model and the use of a carefully crafted assessment system aligned with instructional goals.

Summary and Conclusions

The studies reviewed in this section provide insights into the role of an instructional model as a whole or an instructional strategy carried out as one element of a model on the literacy development of language-minority students. Three studies took place in classrooms that used a balanced approach to literacy development (Araujo, 2002; Fitzgerald & Noblit, 2000; Neufeld & Fitzgerald, 2001). Seven studies took place in whole-language classrooms (Kuball & Peck, 1997; Kucer, 1992, 1995, 1999; Kucer & Silva, 1999; Pérez, 1994; Reyes, 1991). Finally, one study was conducted within the context of a whole-literacy program (Au & Carroll, 1997).

The studies described (a) document activities intended to promote extended oral and written discourse; (b) create venues where speaking, reading, and writing are interrelated; and (c) provide opportunities for students to actively construct knowledge using authentic literature, rich discussions around text and process approaches to writing. They are grounded in the theory that language mediates learning (Vygotsky, 1978), and that children construct knowledge through their engagement in peer interactions and through scaffolded interactions with adults (Spivey, 1997). Many of the programs document improvement in selected facets of children's language and literacy development: spelling and word recognition (Araujo, 2002), phonological awareness, word-recognition strategies, word meaning, global knowledge of reading, sentiments of wanting to read, and more mature communicative competence (Fitzgerald & Noblit, 2000); compositional skills for Spanish-speaking students and graphophonemic literacy for some students (Kuball & Peck, 1997); meaning construction and knowledge of grammatical relations, as well as retelling ability (Pérez, 1994); language sense (production of more syntactically and semantically acceptable sentences) and improvements in story retelling, writing, and spelling (Kucer & Silva, 1999); and writing (Au & Carroll, 1997).

Differential Language and Literacy Development. However, although the studies document the progress that some students make in developing literacy, they also highlight that this progress is not uniform, with the same instructional program producing differential student outcomes. These findings are consistent with findings reported in Chapter 15. Some students develop language and literacy skills, whereas others do not progress at the same pace. For example, Araujo (2002) indicates that, "while most children made some progress, the range between modest and dramatic improvement was widespread" (p. 244). Fitzgerald and Noblit (2000) document the differential growth in reading in which "at the end of the year, lowest readers performed as their better-reading counterparts did at midyear" (p. 17). Kuball and Peck (1997) indicate that, although 25% of the students achieved advanced-level graphophonemic literacy skills for kindergarten children, 75% of the English-language learners remained at the prephonemic level. Pérez (1994) notes that, although 16 students improved in their use of meaning construction and grammatical relations, 6 students did not.

Two conclusions might be drawn from these findings. The first is that, in the best of circumstances, some children need additional support to keep pace with their classmates. This conclusion is consistent with findings from research on the development of literacy in first-language learners (National Institute for Child Health and Human Development, 2000). Second, although some authors argue that some children do not make progress "because they were not developmentally ready" (Kuball & Peck, 1997, p. 227), others (Kucer & Silva, 1999; Pérez, 1994) call for a more balanced approach that includes direct instruction in phonics and writing. The value of direct instruction in these areas is consistent with findings reported in chapter 15.

Elements That Influence Literacy Development. Descriptions of balanced-literacy, whole-language, and whole-literacy classrooms provide insights into the elements that may promote literacy growth in English-language learners, as well as possible obstacles that hinder this growth. One important theme in this regard is the need to attend to the individual needs of students. English-language learners are not a homogeneous group. For example, Fitzgerald and Noblit (2000) used varied approaches to meet the needs of all students. First, the teacher provided, on a daily basis, variety in both reading activities and the settings in which those activities took place. Second, the teacher held reading meetings with students grouped according to their reading achievement level. Third, she provided a library organized by reading level in the classroom from which children could choose books to read. Fourth, during writing, each child was given individual attention by either the teacher or her instructional aide. Finally, for the English-language learners in the class, the teacher altered her instruction by incorporating such tactics as speaking more slowly and using simpler vocabulary, but she did not alter her expectations and did not change the language of instruction for these students. When teachers do not accommodate individual differences, students may have more difficulty acquiring literacy. Kucer (1999) found that two English-language learners responded differently to whole-language curriculum because of different interests and concerns. One child responded well to the teacher's whole-language approach, but another student was unable to respond to the curricula as presented.

Teachers' expectations for students with differing levels of English proficiency, and instructional approaches aligned with the expectations, may influence students' literacy development. In another study conducted by Neufeld and Fitzgerald (2001), the teacher's expectations for the English-language learners in her low reading group (that they could not learn to read before they had requisite levels of oral proficiency) and her aligned curriculum (learning to say and spell the alphabet, learning to spell a few words, learning to write neatly, and improving their English oral language, rather than systematic and sustained practice in word reading) resulted in students' inability to pass the preprimer passage when a running record was taken in June.

Throughout these studies, teaching is shown to play an important role in students' success. For example, Kucer (1999) attributes one child's failure with the curriculum in part to its delivery, described as routinized and unchanging throughout the school year. Although the instructional mediations offered by the teacher appeared to be sufficient for one child, the researcher suggests that the other student might have benefited from "instructional detours," events that focus on a particular difficulty a child is having (Cazden, 1992). The data show that, rather than taking these detours, the teacher simply repeated the same instructions when the child's performance was lacking. The results of these studies also indicate that the level of teacher scaffolding may be important during whole-language instruction. For example, in Kucer's (1995) study, although the focus of instruction was ostensibly on student strategy use, the teacher spent a lot of class time working with students to ensure they understood the text; in response groups, the teacher read the book chorally with the students a second time and then discussed the text from a variety of perspectives, clarifying things students did not understand.

Finally, the nature of the language in which children are learning to read matters. Spanish-speaking children instructed in Spanish mastered graphophonics more easily than did English-speaking children instructed in English (Kuball & Peck, 1997). This is likely related to the differences between English and Spanish in the depth of the orthography of the respective languages.

Developmental Paths.   A significant finding from two studies (Fitzgerald & Noblit, 2000; Neufeld & Fitzgerald, 2001) is that, with the exception of vocabulary, although students may progress at different rates, their growth follows similar paths. The implication is that, over time, with good instruction, lower level readers will ultimately attain the same goals as higher level readers. As noted previously, this may be the case, but some children may need more intensive and qualitatively different kinds of interventions (National Institute for Child Health and Human Development, 2000) if they are going to catch up more quickly to their monolinqual peers, an important goal in that it will enable them to fully benefit from mainstream classroom instruction. Moreover, although they may eventuall catch up in other literacy skills, it was not the case for vocabulary. At the end of first grade, all but one of the English-language learners scored in the bottom half of the class on one test of knowledge of English word meanings.

Importance of Ongoing Mentoring and Professional Development. The research cited earlier also indicates the important role that professional development might play in improving instruction. Several of the studies document teachers using classroom routines and strategies that appeared ineffective with English-language learners (Kucer, 1999; Reyes 1991). The authors suggest that mentoring and professional development may have made a difference in these circumstances. For example, in the study by Reyes, "although the literature journals and logs indicated that the students either did not comprehend or could not produce in English what they did comprehend" (p. 309), the teacher did not modify her teaching to accommodate students' needs. More specifically, she did not help students select books that were at an appropriate reading level or monitor and scaffold their reading. The KEEP experience (Au & Carroll, 1997) highlights the importance of supporting teacher change and the need for systems that are intensive, elaborate, and enduring to accomplish this change. In the KEEP program, there was intensive mentoring by the KEEP consultants; as noted in the study description, each consultant worked with only one to three project teachers and observed and mentored in classrooms twice a week. This level of support is considerably more than occurs in most schools. The authors advocate providing teachers with sustained coaching so they can develop the practices necessary to succeed, including organizing the classroom to support a constructivist approach, creating opportunities for student-centered learning, employing appropriate instructional practices, and developing an assessment system tied to instruction. Two critical tools in supporting teacher change were the classroom implementation checklist and grade-appropriate benchmarks used to assess student progress.

The studies also demonstrate that teachers may have received professional development in implementing popular programs like Writer's Workshop. However, because the workshops did not focus on how to modify the approaches to suit the linguistic needs of English-language learners, the instructional strategies that teachers learned and were implementing may not have been appropriate (Reyes, 1991).

Methodological Issues. When considering study findings, it is also important to keep in mind the attributes of each particular program, rather than defining a program according to its generic label (e.g., whole language). Fortunately, the rich descriptions of classroom events provided by these authors enable readers to understand more fully what is happening in these classrooms. For example, although a defining characteristic of whole-language programs is their emphasis on the integrity of reading, writing, speaking, and listening (and their respective subskills), there is wide variation among whole-language programs with respect to instruction in the component skills of reading and writing, with some programs providing a fair amount of direct teacher instruction of various subskills. In whole-literacy programs that use Writer's Workshop (Au & Carroll, 1997), for example, mini-lessons provide instruction in specific skills related to writing. There is also wide variation in the amount of teacher support; in some programs, but not in others, teachers provide a great deal of targeted support during instruction to help students deal with learning difficulties and improve in reading and writing skills.

Because these are prospective case studies, it is important to consider alternative explanations when interpreting study findings. The alternative explanations may be related to the background knowledge of the subjects, the language being studied, or the classroom instructional context. For example, children already literate in their native language may need less explicit instruction in English phonics (Kucer & Silva, 1999) as a result of transfer effects noted in Part II of this volume. Children learning to read in Spanish (Pérez, 1994) may need less explicit print-sound code instruction because Spanish has a very shallow orthography. Strong teaching may contribute to student outcomes, as in a study by Kucer and Silva (1999), where the teacher was described as

> bi-literate and bilingual in English and Spanish, had taught elementary school for 11 years mostly in bilingual settings and at the time of the study, was finishing her Ph.D. in a university language, literacy, and culture program that was whole language oriented...She was experienced in working with transitional students and in the assessment of their English literacy behaviors-oral readings and retellings, written stories, spelling samples, and informal observations of the students as they engaged in classroom literacy activities. (p. 351)

Finally, as is the case with all research on comprehensive instructional programs, the programs combine many elements, and it is difficult to determine exactly what it is about the programs that encouraged or detracted from literacy development.

RESEARCH ON EFFECTIVE
CLASSROOMS AND SCHOOLS

Largely in response to findings by researchers (Coleman et al., 1966; Jencks et al., 1972) who suggested that differences in student achievement were due to factors outside the control of schools (e.g., home environment), studies appeared (e.g., Edmonds, 1979, Purkey & Smith, 1983) that challenged this conclusion by identifying effective schools and the characteristics that made them effective. In this section, we review eight studies that follow this tradition. However, unlike the original effective schools research that designated schools as effective based on measures of school achievement; the authors of these studies employed a theoretical framework and previous research findings to define *effective literacy instruction* and then used this framework to observe instruction. In some cases, while observing, the researchers also refined their framework. One study (Padrón, 1994) used a previously designed observation instrument to gather data on classrooms with language-minority students.

Gersten and Jiménez (1994) examined the reading instruction provided by three intermediate-grade (Grades 3–5) teachers from different schools, all of whom had large numbers of English-language learners in their classes. The teachers were observed over a 2-year period. Data collected from the observations were analyzed from the perspective of research on second-language learning and bilingual education, the contemporary research base on effective literacy instruction, and general principles of effective instruction for low-income students. These three knowledge bases led to the development of a unified framework of eight constructs that the researchers used for "considering practices and approaches for promoting literacy and academic achievement of ESL students" (p. 440): implicit and explicit challenging of students, active involvement of all students, providing activities that students can complete successfully, scaffolding instruction for students through such techniques as building and clarifying student input and using visual organizers, teacher mediation/feedback to students, classroom use of collaborative/cooperative learning, techniques for second-language acquisition/sheltered English, and respect for cultural diversity. The researchers identify productive practices as those that "(a) led to high levels of student involvement, (b) fostered higher order cognitive processes, and (c) enabled students to engage in extended discourse" (p. 439). Vignettes reveal the ways in which the teaching of the two most experienced teachers aligned with the constructs defining effective practice and show the limitations of the teaching of the third, novice teacher.

As part of the same project, Gersten (1996) studied language arts and literacy instruction in 18 classrooms over a period of 2 years to refine his model of effective instruction, as well as to document instructional practices that facilitate learning and language development for language-minority students. The 18 classrooms were selected from three schools within the same district in Southern California. The schools were characterized by their large populations of language-minority students (60%–85%), the majority of whom were from low-income families. Students in two of the schools were primarily Latino from Spanish-speaking backgrounds. The third school was more diverse; approximately 44% of the students were Latino, and another 30% came from several Southeast Asian cultures. Teachers in all the classrooms were observed and interviewed. The effective practices identified by Gersten include

> checking students' comprehension of new vocabulary introduced in a story, providing opportunities for meaningful use of new vocabulary, presenting new ideas both verbally and in written form, using reasonably consistent language for a series of lessons, paraphrasing students' remarks and encouraging them to expand on their responses in English. [Moreover], intentional use of redundancy, more frequent use of simple or declarative sentences, frequent checks for student comprehension, and the use of physical gestures and visual cues appears to help students understand the concepts being taught. (pp. 238–239)

Using a nearly identical framework as that described earlier, Jiménez and Gersten (1999) examined the teaching practices of two Latino teachers, both of Mexican origin and both working in an elementary school in a large, urban school district in Southern California. The teachers each had more than 7 years of teaching experience and used innovative approaches for teaching literacy or language development. Both taught large classes of students of Mexican origin, all of whom spoke Spanish as their native language. Both used high-quality children's literature as the core of their reading/language arts curriculum. One teacher taught third graders in their transition year of school who were being prepared to enter classes taught only in English after having received the majority of their education in Spanish. The other taught a group of newly arrived fifth- and sixth-grade immigrants who were attending school in the United States for the first time.

The teachers were observed and interviewed over a period of 2 years. The researchers followed the approach to analyzing the data described previously (Gersten & Jiménez, 1994). Their analysis of the data allowed them to charac- terize the third-grade teacher's approach as one of infusion; that is, they found that this teacher was able to enhance her existing knowledge of teaching with new knowledge she acquired about providing effective instruction for language-minority students. This teacher's approach also met the constructs for effective instruction described before (Gersten & Jiménez, 1994). The fifth/ sixth-grade teacher appeared to reject traditional models of instruction in favor of a more contemporary whole-language approach—one that appeared to increase student engagement, but decreased the amount of academic content that was covered. For instance, the fifth/sixth-grade students engaged in less reading and writing than did the third-grade students. Furthermore, only four of the nine constructs for effective instruction were found to be present in this teacher's more contemporary approach. Thus, even when well implemented, the whole- language curriculum used by the second teacher was deemed ineffective by the researchers based on their theoretical framework. However as the authors note, "one particular area of disappointment for us was that we could not indepen- dently confirm through more traditional measures of assessment, student acade- mic achievement" (p. 294).

Gersten (1999) studied four teachers who were relatively inexperienced in working with English-language learners to document the challenges they faced when teaching this population. The teachers taught students in Grades 4 to 6 at three large, low-income schools. All of the teachers had been with their current district for less than 5 years, and none had received any formal training in teaching English-language learners. The teachers were observed over a period of 4 months, and segments of their lessons were recorded verbatim. Teachers were also interviewed after classroom observations and during breaks. A mod- ified version of the constructs described earlier was used for coding the data. This version consisted of three primary areas: (a) challenge, involvement, and success of students; (b) teacher scaffolding, mediation, and feedback; and (c) teacher respect for cultural diversity.

The study findings suggest that these teachers faced a tension between the need to engage in a productive and meaningful learning process and the need to receive student products that demonstrated knowledge of the conventions of English grammar and spelling. This tension frequently caused teachers to rely on instructional practices that involved little risk or challenge, such as having students copy text from the board, the dictionary, or a book. Gersten discusses why teachers resort to this type of instruction and offers his vision of a profes- sional development program designed to address the needs of teachers of English-language learners who have received no training in teaching this popu- lation. This program would reduce "the professional isolation of teachers through activities that connect them to other professionals…[and would support] teachers in developing their instructional repertoire (i.e., how to systematically develop written and oral English-language competence, how to build vocabulary, how to design lessons in literature that engage students and foster analysis and comprehension)... [and would address] reducing the distance between teachers and students" (pp. 51–52). According to the author, an English-language-development curriculum with a scope and sequence that resulted in systematic instruction and reading is critically important, especially for early-career teachers.

McLeod (1995) examined the school reform efforts of four elementary schools selected for their exemplary language arts programs.[8] The schools were screened and selected through nominations, telephone interviews, and field visits. Despite unfavorable conditions (e.g., poor neighborhood and lack of resources), these schools were innovative in finding resources and developing curriculum and instruction. The schools were characterized by making English-language learners an integral part of the school through such efforts as a two-way bilingual program, sheltered instruction, and creative groupings of students at the class and school levels. These schools focused on the delivery of high-quality instruction, so that while developing English literacy, English-language learners were challenged with high-quality literacy instruction instead of receiving a basic skills curriculum. They read and wrote across genres and were involved in discussing, interpreting, and analyzing literature. These schools also valued students' first language and culture as an asset, and students were engaged in intellectually challenging work in both their native language and English. Furthermore, teachers of English-language learners and native English speakers collaborated and became more efficient through common planning time.

Short (1994) identified features of instructional materials and classrooms that are beneficial for building literacy in the context of teaching social studies to middle-school language-minority students. Her research began with analysis of middle-school American history textbooks and observations of social studies classes with English-language learners. An integrated language and content curriculum unit was then developed and piloted the following school year. Participating teachers and students were observed, recorded, and interviewed. At the end of the school year, the curriculum was revised, and the new materials were presented the following school year in schools in Virginia, Maryland, New York, Florida, Nebraska, and California. During this year, teachers were interviewed and observed, and samples of student work were gathered. Teachers also maintained logs describing their implementation processes, students' reactions to lessons, modifications to planned activities, and suggestions for improvement. Short's investigation led to the identification of promising practices, which include the use of graphic organizers, hands-on and cooperative learning activities, activities designed to teach and reinforce the use of signal words that cue relationships in reading and writing, definition of new vocabulary through discussion and in context, interpretation of timelines and maps, examination of information from a historical perspective, and com-

---

[8] The study also examined four middle schools selected for their science and math programs.

parisons of historical events and people. Short also found that teachers must be able to recognize the limitations of published social studies materials and be willing to address these with their students.

Several other researchers have documented the results of poor instructional support. These authors consider their findings in light of recent theories of high-quality instruction for English-language learners and conclude that the instruction these students are receiving may not be of high quality. Padrón (1994) used a previously designed classroom observation instrument, the Classroom Observation Schedule, to gather data about reading instruction in fourth- and fifth-grade classes across 15 elementary schools. Some of the schools were designated as having large Hispanic English-language learner populations; the rest were classified as inner-city schools with ethnically diverse populations. Students were observed for their interactions with peers and teachers, and teachers were observed for their interactions with students; the settings of the interactions and the types of activities and materials used were also noted. Padrón found that, although passive instruction with little teacher–student and student–student interaction was present in all the schools she studied, those with majority Hispanic populations had more passive instruction than the others.

Summary

In their series of studies, Gersten and Jiménez (1994), Jiménez and Gersten (1999), Short (1994), and Padrón (1994) examine the quality of instruction by using a framework they have developed. A theme that runs through these studies is that teaching within these frameworks and implementing these techniques are not easy.

To a great extent, these attributes overlap with those of effective instruction for nonlanguage-minority students. For example, attributes identified by the researchers include implicit and explicit challenging of students, active involvement of all students, providing activities that students can complete successfully, and scaffolding instruction for students through such techniques as building and clarifying student input and using visual organizers, teacher mediation/feedback to students, and classroom use of collaborative/cooperative learning. In many cases, however, there are techniques related to second-language acquisition such as sheltered English and respect for cultural diversity

The value of these studies is that they identify potential explanatory factors. These factors need to be either bundled and tested experimentally as an intervention package or examined as separate components to determine whether they actually lead to improved student performance—a point reinforced by the authors (Gersten & Jiménez, 1994).

STUDIES OF SCHOOL CHANGE

In this section, we review two studies that examined how school staff worked together to implement changes designed to improve literacy outcomes for language-minority students. The first of these studies (Weaver & Sawyer, 1984) documented the process of change that occurred at a small rural elementary school with a predominantly Anglo student population when teachers sought outside assistance from a local university to support the language growth of two Vietnamese students who arrived at the school not yet speaking English. The second study (Goldenberg & Gallimore, 1991) examined changes that occurred at Benson Elementary School, located in a district with a 90% Hispanic student enrollment, where 80% of the Hispanic students had limited English proficiency.

Weaver and Sawyer (1984) describe the efforts made in a rural school district in central New York State to provide language and literacy instruction for two non-English-speaking students—Ben, a third grader, and Tina, a first grader—whose family had come to the United States as refugees from Vietnam. Their teachers, who had been relying on their intuition, did not experience success with the older child in his first year at the school. The district reading specialist took charge of creating an approach that involved first providing professional development to five teachers who would be working with the students. The focus was on building awareness of the challenges involved in language acquisition and cultural problems experienced by English-language learners, as well as strategies for promoting oral-language development and comprehension. The approach also called for the specialist and teachers to work together to develop a reading program for the two children. Assessments of the children were used to inform instruction, which was provided by both the classroom teachers and the reading specialist. The teachers and the specialist also met on a regular basis to discuss the children's progress. Instructional materials selected to address the weaknesses identified by the assessments focused on vocabulary development and reading comprehension. Posttests given at the end of the school year indicated that both children had reading achievement on a par with average and above-average achievers in their classes. Although both children grew in comprehension of spoken English, the assessments indicated the children required further development in this area. For example, Ben was in the 24th percentile in auditory vocabulary on the Stanford Diagnostic Reading Test (having begun in the 14th percentile).

Goldenberg and Gallimore (1991) report on efforts made by the staff at Benson Elementary School in southern California, to improve the Spanish literacy attainment of their primarily Hispanic students. Applying the findings of a 1983 to 1984 study (Goldenberg, 1984), the staff at Benson worked together over a 3-year period (1985–1987) in collaboration with university researchers to improve reading achievement. According to the authors, the changes were not the result of implementing a particular model or program; rather, they can be characterized as "a shift in the school's early literacy culture that transformed norms and expectations" (p. 4). The end result was a marked improvement in students' Spanish literacy attainment. The researchers summarize the changes that occurred at Benson in 1987 and after as follows:

> literacy in kindergarten greatly emphasized, before it was de-emphasized; children thought to benefit from literacy opportunities in kindergarten, before children considered not ready to read; more balanced literacy program in first grade with greater emphasis on comprehension, meaning, and reading connected text, before a one-dimensional system dominated by phonics; home and parent involvement greatly emphasized with books and other materials sent home regularly for parents and children to work on, before parents considered

incapable of helping children academically; greatly emphasized: goal to adhere to publisher's norms with respect to pacing of instruction, before publisher's norms considered unrealistic for this population. (p. 5)

These changes in the school's philosophy and approach to early literacy instruction had a profound influence on the students. By the second and third grades, the level of student achievement at Benson had risen dramatically relative to both local and national norms; the improvement occurred throughout the achievement range, but particularly among the lowest achieving students. In the fall of 1985, second-grade students at Benson ranked below students at other schools on the California Test of Basic Skills (CTBS) Spanish norms by nearly 10 percentage points. By the fall of 1989, whereas other schools' average percentile rank for second graders was just above 30, the percentile rank of Benson second graders was nearly 60. Third-grade scores showed similar growth. The authors conclude that a dynamic interplay of local and research knowledge[9] created change, and this change was gradual, "resembling an evolutionary process driven by obtaining and demonstrating desirable results at the local level" (p. 11).

Summary and Conclusions

The two studies reviewed in this section demonstrate the progress schools can achieve when staff work together to address specific issues. These studies highlight the importance of mobilizing staff to focus on the needs of language-minority students, even when such students are few in number in a school or classroom, and provide heartening evidence that a concerted school effort involving outside agents (researchers and specialists) and school personnel (principals, specialists, and classroom teachers) can make a difference. These studies also point to the importance of sustained and comprehensive efforts because change is slow and circuitous, and language-minority students, especially those who live in poverty, face many challenges in achieving grade-level standards of literacy. Noteworthy in these studies is that all the schools worked with staff at local universities, who assisted with staff development and school change efforts and documented the process of the changes that occurred, for both the students and the school, over time.

---

[9]One of the teachers was also the first author of this article and a researcher.

17

Literacy Instruction for Language-Minority Children in Special Education Settings

Diane August with Linda S. Siegel

This chapter reviews the limited number of studies addressing literacy instruction conducted with language-minority students in special education settings; only 12 such studies were located.[1] These studies focus on the context in which language-minority students with special needs are educated and the instructional approaches for improving literacy outcomes among these students. One study (Maldonado, 1994) whose subjects were in special education classes examined the benefits of instruction that involved some use of Spanish instruction compared with English-only instruction. This study is described in chapter 14 because its primary focus is on language of instruction. As with the studies reviewed in the previous chapters of this part of the report, students in these studies represented a full range of ages and grade levels, and the studies occurred in a variety of contexts. Methods used to identify students for special education settings are presented in Appendix 17.A. Appendix 17.B includes additional information about instructional approaches and assessments for selected studies.

The following research question is addressed in this chapter:
What do we know about literacy instruction for language-minority students in special education settings?

METHODS

The studies described in this chapter employed diverse research methods, including ethnography (Hughes, Vaughn, & Schumm, 1999; Jiménez, 1997;

---

[1] The studies had to appear in peer-reviewed journals; there are references to other studies in these articles, but they are to book chapters, technical reports, and meeting presentations.

Ruiz, 1995; Wolf, 1993)[2] and case studies (Fawcett & Lynch, 2000; Graves, Valles, & Rueda, 2000), as well as methods typical of the literature on children educated in special settings, including multiple-baseline designs (Rousseau, Tam, & Ramnarain, 1993; VanWagenen, Williams, & McLaughlin, 1994), parallel- treatment designs (Rohena, Jitendra, & Browder, 2002),[3] and alternating- treatment designs (Echevarría, 1996; Perozzi, 1985). Two studies were quasi-experiments (Bos, Allen, & Scanlon, 1989; Klingner & Vaughn, 1996).

In the following sections, we review studies examining the context in which language-minority students with special needs are educated and those examining instructional approaches designed for students with special needs. The final section presents a summary and conclusions that cut across both of the previous sections of the chapter.

THE CONTEXT IN WHICH LANGUAGE-MINORITY STUDENTS WITH SPECIAL NEEDS ARE EDUCATED

Review of the Research

In this section, we examine literacy practices in classroom and home contexts. Ruiz's (1995) study of a bilingual, self-contained classroom for students identified as language- and learning-disabled examined the different opportunities for student participation created in various instructional contexts in the same classroom. Ruiz drew the study data from 28 day-long observations of the classroom, 32 hours of audiotaped classroom interactions, and field notes. To analyze these data, she first identified interaction sequences and then selected "contextual features used by other ethnographers to identify classroom events." She further identified classroom events as being typical or atypical. She also used other ethnographic methods of analysis to "describe and explain the particulars of interaction in this bilingual special education classroom" (p. 492).

One focus of the analysis was on the features of classroom events associated with formality (Dickinson, 1985; Irvine, 1979). *Formal events* are defined as those with "increased structuring of the rules governing communicative behavior" (p. 4). Ruiz identified three classroom events that exhibited varying degrees of formality: class openings (most formal), lessons (moderately formal), and sociodramatic play (least formal). Through vignettes of students' language use and examples of their

---

[2]Jiménez (1997) used qualitative techniques described by Glesne and Peshkin (1992), Patton (1990), and Taylor and Bogdan (1984) that involved data collection through a variety of methods.

[3]A multiple probe across participants with a parallel-treatment design (PTD) was used to evaluate and compare the effectiveness and efficiency of two instructional conditions with respect to reading sight words. According to the authors, the PTD is "well suited for comparing the effectiveness and efficiency of instructional procedures" and "combines elements of the multiple probe (multiple baseline) design and uses random assignment and counterbalancing to control for extraneous variables for the purpose of comparing two antecedent manipulations with independent responses of equal difficulty" (Rohena et al., 2002, p. 174; cited in Sindelar et al., 1985; see also Tawney & Gast, 1984).

writing, Ruiz demonstrates that less formal contexts lead to "more frequent initiation of conversational turns, production of longer turns of speech, and production of a greater range of language forms and functions" (p. 496).

Ruiz also identified three types of students in this class: those with moderate to severe disabilities (Type 1), those with mild disabilities to normal abilities (Type 2), and those with normal abilities (Type 3). She found that certain features of classroom events covaried by type of student. In lessons, for instance, the most disabled students were given (a) more flexibility to engage in activities centered on students' background knowledge and experiences; (b) opportunities for verbal activity versus passivity (student initiations, longer conversational turns, greater range of functions and forms); and (c) an emphasis on communicating meaningful messages, not on language forms. For moderately disabled and nondisabled students, in contrast, lessons stressed linguistic form over meaning. She reports some data across students (i.e., student initiation rates in certain contexts) and provides examples of types of student discourse in the three different classroom events to highlight her findings. It would have been informative to know how typical or atypical these discourse patterns were. The same is true for the type of teacher discourse patterns across events.

Hughes et al. (1999) examined Hispanic parents' perceptions and practice of literacy-related activities at home. Surveys and interviews were completed by 40 parents of high-achieving children and 40 parents of learning-disabled children in grades 3–5. It was found that most of the parents had interest in and awareness of the importance of literacy activities at home. Regardless of their children's achievement status, Hispanic parents read books to them and took them to the library frequently, but writing activities were less emphasized than book reading. Many parents expressed a need for better communication between school and home and a wish to be informed of home literacy practices and strategies that would be beneficial for their children. Parents felt that, overall, the main barrier to their furthering their children's literacy development was their lack of English-language proficiency. In addition, parents of children with learning disabilities pointed to their children's problems in reading and writing as a barrier to home literacy activities, whereas parents of high achievers expressed the difficulty of motivating their children to engage in such activities.

In summary, according to the first study, the context in which children with special needs learn influences their discourse and development. Ruiz (1995) found that students initiate conversational turns more often, produce longer turns, and produce more diverse language forms and functions in less formal contexts. This finding also emerges for the studies in the next section, which report on instructional approaches. The second study (Hughes et al., 1999) found that, regardless of their children's achievement status, most parents had interest in and awareness of the importance of home literacy activities. Future intervention work might build on these findings by engaging parents' support in promoting the literacy development of struggling readers. Given the findings from this chapter, as well as chapters 9 and 14, parents might be encouraged to support children's native-language literacy development when they are not fully proficient in English literacy.

INSTRUCTIONAL APPROACHES DESIGNED FOR STUDENTS WITH SPECIAL NEEDS

Review of the Research

In this section, we turn to a wide variety of instructional approaches designed for language-minority students with a range of special needs. To facilitate the comparison of studies, effect sizes were computed for each study if sufficient data were available. They are reported in Table 17.2. Perozzi (1985) conducted a pilot study to explore the facilitation effect of the native language on English-language learning. The subjects were three Spanish-speaking and three English-speaking 4- and 5-year-old students. On the basis of interviews and formal assessments, one of the Spanish-speaking students was identified as having a language disorder, two (one English-speaking, one Spanish-speaking) were identified as having mild language delay, and three (two English-speaking, one Spanish-speaking) were identified as having normal language ability for their age. Although only six subjects participated, the within-subject design allowed for a detailed examination of the performance of each. The inclusion of three Spanish-speaking and three English-speaking students served as a cross-check for determining whether a facilitation effect would occur from majority to minority language (English to Spanish), as well as from minority to majority language (Spanish to English).

To determine which vocabulary items to teach, Perozzi obtained vocabulary items from Levels 1 and 2 of the Peabody Picture Vocabulary Test (PPVT) cards that each subject could not recognize in either Spanish or English. The examiner placed the pictures of a set (four words) in a row in front of the child, named each picture in the language appropriate to the given condition as she pointed to the picture names, and then requested that the child point to the picture. The words were reshuffled for each new trial. The examiner provided positive reinforcement for each response. Perozzi describes the procedure as follows:

> A set of words was taught first in the native language (L1) and then in the second language (Condition A). Another set was taught first in the second language (L2) and then in the native language (Condition B). For each subject the sequencing of the conditions was alternated. Thus, a subject learned a set of words in the native language then in the second language...and a set in the second language then in the native language. The conditions were then reversed for the remaining two sets yielding an A (L1–L2), B (L2–L1), B (L2–L1), A (L1–L2) sequence.... Number of trials to and including three consecutive correct responses (pointing to the picture requested by the examiner) for each word in a set served as the criterion. Words for which the criterion had been met continued to be named as foils during the learning of a set when one or two words in a set had not yet met criterion. Trials to criterion for each word in a set were totaled. (p. 405)

Only one student failed to follow the pattern of learning vocabulary faster in the second language when it was already known in the native language. This student, an English speaker identified as having normal language development, may have lacked motivation to learn a second language or experienced anxiety in the testing situation. The researchers also found that when vocabulary was taught in the native language before the second language, students learned both languages more rapidly than when this sequence was reversed.

The findings of this study, although preliminary, suggest that language-handicapped students whose native language is Spanish benefit from remediation in their native language. All three subjects, each with a different pattern of language development—normal, mild delay, and disordered—learned English receptive vocabulary more rapidly when it was first taught in Spanish. In addition, two of the subjects learned both Spanish and English more rapidly when Spanish was taught first than when English was taught first. The same facilitation effect was found for the English-speaking students.

Echevarría (1996) studied the effects of the instructional conversations (IC) approach on the Spanish language and concept development of five 7- and 8-year-old Latino English-language learners enrolled in special education because of identified learning handicaps. The study employed an alternating-treatments design (Barlow & Hersen, 1984). The students received five instructional conversation lessons designed to encourage their participation in thoughtful discussion of the materials they were reading, followed by five basal reading lessons. Teachers implementing an instructional conversations approach selected a theme as a starting point for the discussion and formulated a general plan for how the theme would unfold, including how to *chunk* the text to permit optimal exploration of the theme. They used a variety of methods, including

> activation and use of background knowledge; direct teaching of a skill or concept when necessary; elicitation of extended student contributions through invitations to expand, questions, restatements, and pauses; probes for the basis of students' statements; use of few known-answer questions; responsiveness to students' contributions; encouragement of general participation and self-selected turns; and creation of a challenging, nonthreatening environment. (pp. 342–343)

For the basal lessons, the teacher followed the guidelines from the publisher. The teacher introduced the stories as the manual suggested and asked the questions specified by the manual. All lessons were conducted in Spanish, the students' native language, as were the assessments.

Six measures were used[4]: a measure designed to assess fidelity of treatment (Elements of Instructional Conversation Measure); an assessment of the alignment of student responses during the lesson with the presentation of instructional conversations approach elements (Student Outcome Measure); a tally and analysis of all utterances made during the lesson (Analysis of Utterances); an assessment of students' ability to retell the story, apparently focused on narrative ability rather than comprehension (Narrative Competence Measure); a measure of students' understanding of the central concept of the story (Thematic Concept Development); and a measure of literal recall (Literal Recall). The relative effectiveness of the two conditions for a single subject was determined by t tests. The Teacher Rating Scale indicated that the teacher had implemented the instructional conversations approach and basal lessons in significantly different ways, indicating an ability to shift from one approach to the other effectively.

---

[4] More detailed information about the measures can be found in Appendix 17.B.

Several findings emerged from this study. First, students exhibited more instructional conversations approach-related outcomes, termed *academic discourse* by the researcher, during the instructional conversation lessons (e.g., using the text as a basis for a comment, relating background experiences to the story, and using complete sentences and more complex language). Second, there were more utterances in the instructional conversation condition than in the basal condition. Moreover, the instructional conversation condition yielded more self-initiated scripted as well as nonscripted utterances, indicating not only more frequent participation without teacher prompting, but also more original contributions. Third, the narrative analysis revealed no differences in story structure or number and category of propositions between students in the two conditions. Fourth, students in the instructional conversation condition demonstrated greater understanding of the story's thematic content (72% of these students mentioned the concept, compared with 20% of those in the basal condition). Fifth, literal recall and narrative construction did not differ between the two groups. Finally, the presence of lesson features characteristic of instructional conversations tended to encourage student participation; the higher the teacher's implementation score was, the higher the students' score on the Student Outcome Measure was. The small number of subjects makes it impossible to derive statistical significance.

Wolf (1993) describes Reader's Theater, an activity that requires students to work together to create textual interpretations so they can perform a significant scene from a story. In depicting the ways in which a group of three third- and fourth-grade remedial reading students who had been placed in a resource specialist program engaged with this task, she demonstrates these children's abilities to engage with literacy in meaningful ways that transcended the labels they had been assigned. For instance, the task of selecting a single scene required students not only to draw on their understanding of the text they had read, but also to use their imaginations to envision how the characters in the scene would appear at the point in the story that was being depicted. The students also had to draw on their ability to develop well-supported arguments to convince their peers to adopt their suggestions when agreement could not initially be reached on which scene to present.

Rousseau and colleagues (1993) examined the effects of two instructional approaches to teaching reading to language-minority students with speech and language impairments: *listening previewing*, defined as "the student's listening to the teacher read a passage aloud and pointing to the words being read while he or she read silently," and *discussion of key words*, defined as "the teacher's discussing the meanings of key words from the reading passage prior to the student's reading the passage aloud" (p. 255). The study was conducted to learn which of the two approaches was "more effective in increasing the oral reading proficiency and reading comprehension of [language-minority] students, and...to compare the more effective individual treatment to the two treatments together" (p. 256). Two dependent measures were used: words read correctly and correct answers to comprehension questions.

Study participants included five Hispanic students enrolled in an inner-city elementary school in a large metropolitan area in a special education class for language-minority students with speech and language deficits. Although all five students were enrolled in Grade 6, diagnostic evaluations of their abilities revealed them to be at a third- to fourth-grade reading level. In the key words condition, each student read a story orally following the discussion of key words. In the listening previewing condition, following the teacher's reading, each student read the story orally. In the combined approach, both key words and listening previewing were presented in a single group lesson during each session, in that order. Regardless of condition, students' oral reading and question-answering abilities were assessed after each lesson in individual sessions held in a quiet corner of the room. During these sessions, students read the story orally and answered eight comprehension questions asked by the teacher. These individual sessions were recorded for later analysis.

The study consisted of a baseline period and three subsequent phases and used a combined alternating-treatment and reversal design. The baseline and Phase 1 were used to address the question of which treatment was more effective, whereas Phases 2 and 3 were used to compare the more effective treatment, as identified in Phase 1, with the effect of the two treatments used together. In Phase 2, the treatments were combined for several days. In Phase 3, the students received only the more effective treatment as identified in Phase 1 for several days, after which the combined treatments were again offered. Throughout the study, the order in which students participated in individual oral reading sessions was systematically rotated each session to avoid the possibility that any student might have the potential advantage of always being the first to read.

The findings reveal that, at baseline, students were poor oral readers and lacked story comprehension. During Phase 1 of the study, discussion of key words improved students' oral reading and comprehension. During Phase 2, when both treatments were offered, students' scores on oral reading and comprehension improved dramatically. Their scores dropped again during Phase 3, when only the key words treatment was provided, but improved again when instruction returned to including both treatments. Thus, the study results indicate that the two treatments presented together were more effective than either treatment presented alone in increasing oral reading proficiency and reading comprehension. According to the authors, the discrepancy between oral reading proficiency and comprehension indicates that, for language-minority students with speech and language deficits, oral reading proficiency is not a valid indicator of comprehension, as they assumed it would be.

To study the writing development of language-minority students with diagnosed learning disabilities, Graves et al. (2000) investigated how four teacher interns, each in a different setting, implemented approaches to interactive writing with such students. They also examined student outcomes on a number of words written and quality of compositions after 10 weeks and 1 year. Although the four teachers taught at different schools, the majority of the students at these schools (80% or more) came from low socioeconomic backgrounds. The students were in Grades 2 to 6. In three of the classrooms, students spoke Spanish in addition to English; in the fourth classroom, students spoke Spanish, Lao, Vietnamese, Cambodian, and Tagalog. The data for this study came from weekly teacher logs; four random observations of writing instruction over the 10-week study period; samples of student work (submitted twice during the 10-week observation period); and student responses to a writing prompt taken from the Test of Written Language II (Hammill & Larsen, 1993) and administered at the start of the 10-week period, at the end of that period, and again after 1 year. The weekly teacher logs included information on the number of hours spent on writing instruction each week, student attendance, teaching techniques used, student assignments, and the amount of time students spent in writing activities.

The researchers provide four vignettes to illustrate the different ways in which process approaches to writing were implemented in each of the classrooms. The teachers' approaches appear to reflect the opportunities and limitations created by the settings in which they worked, as well as the needs of their students. The four writing interventions and settings were (a) use of interactive journals in Spanish in a self-contained classroom for bilingual students; (b) use of optimal learning environment (OLE)[5] in Spanish in a resource program for primarily bilingual students; (c) use of writer's workshop with a focus on expository writing (initially in Spanish) in a resource program for both Spanish and English speakers; and (d) use of a combination of journal writing, brainstorming and planning, and spelling practice in English in a resource program for English as a second language. Observations confirmed that teachers were implementing the approaches. In addition, researchers found that in all classrooms, "teachers spent at least one hour per week teaching writing, taught students to write for real audiences, provided instruction on mechanics, and tried to create a community of learners in the classroom" (p. 8).

Analysis of the data collected through the writing prompt was done only for the students who participated at all stages of the data collection. Student essays were analyzed for word count and quality. The quality of the compositions was measured by using a Story Quality Scale, which "consists of scores from 1 to 5 for coherence, organization, and episodic structure, for a possible total score of 15. Based on the scoring criteria, a score of 0 to 4 is considered a weak composition; a score of 4.1 to 8 is considered moderately good; a score of 8.1 to 12 is good; and a score of 12.1 to 15 is excellent" (Graves et al., 2000, p. 3). The study findings suggest that, after 10 weeks, students in all four classes made some improvement in the quality of their writing, but this progress was minimal (see Table 17.1). In two classes (OLE and writer's workshop), students' compositions remained weak, and in the other two classes, the quality of writing was at the low end of moderately good. After 1 year, students in the interactive writing class scored lower than at the first posttest; students in the writer's workshop and mixed-approach classes made minimal progress during this time. Only the students in the OLE program showed more substantial improvement, scoring at the high end of moderately good.

In interpreting the study findings, it should be noted that students in the mixed-approach class were judged in English at all three time points. Students in the writer's workshop class were judged in either their native language

---

[5]OLE is a writing-as-a-process instruction program that includes the following elements: interactive journals; writer's workshop; mini-lessons, including strategic writing; patterned writing and reading; creation of text for wordless books; shared reading with predictable text, literature conversations, and read-alouds; literature study with response journals; student-made alphabet charts; and drop-everything-and-read (DEAR) time.

TABLE 17.1
Results of Four Approaches to Writing

Program	Preintervention	10 Weeks Later	1-Year Follow-up
Interactive journals (Approach 1)	3.44	4.33	3.60
OLE (Approach 2)	3.36	4.00	7.00
Writer's workshop with expository text (Approach 3)	3.40	3.73	3.91
Combination (Approach 4)	4.08	4.54	4.89

(Spanish) or English at the three time points. Only in the interactive journals and OLE classes were students judged at all time points in their native language, in which their writing would be expected to be stronger. In addition, other factors differentiating the classrooms besides instructional model may have influenced learning outcomes, including time in the particular setting and age of the students. In all cases, there was substantial attrition between the end of the 10-week intervention and the 1-year follow-up.

Follow-up interviews with the teachers after 1 year revealed that they had concerns about the effects of school initiatives on their students' progress; some felt that changes in their school's procedures for educating language-minority students with learning disabilities explained, at least in part, the lack of growth in students' writing. In Approach 1, for instance, students began the study in a self-contained classroom, taught by the teacher intern, for approximately 3 hours each morning. The time was reduced to 1 hour the following school year, which limited the teacher's ability to provide regular writing instruction and maintain interactive journals. These students also began the study using Spanish, their native language, but in the second year the teacher was forced to switch the children to English. Yet the children were tested in Spanish at the 1-year follow-up. A similar switch was made by the Approach 3 teacher, who also reported a change in her instructional delivery in Year 2 that resulted in fewer writing projects. The Approach 4 teacher reported that students were generally unmotivated and hated to write. The Approach 2 teacher (OLE) reported that she was able to use the same approach during the follow-up year that she had used the first year.

Bos, Allen, and Scanlon (1989) used an experimental design to teach vocabulary. The extent to which the results report second-language English learning or first-language Spanish learning is not clear because students' recall was evaluated in "the language in which their reading was more proficient" (p. 175). In the study, 42 upper elementary learning-disabled students were assigned to one of four instructional groups. The vocabulary instruction for each group was a 3-day study of a list of words from a third-grade social studies chapter. Instruction was in their preferred language. One group received instruction in pronunciation of the words and memorization of definitions. A second group used the same list of words and focused on creating semantic maps and predicting word meanings. A third group developed a matrix showing the relationships among the words and predicted word meanings. A fourth group completed the same chart as the third group and also completed cloze sentences. The children in all groups were asked to complete written recalls in their language of preference about the social studies chapter on the second and third days of the lessons and again 4 weeks later. They also completed multiple-choice vocabulary tests in the language in which they read better. The group that constructed relationship maps and completed cloze sentences outperformed the group that worked on pronunciation and memorization of definitions. The former group also outperformed the pronunciation and memorization group on text recall. The results of this study are consistent with the proposition that active processing of word meanings leads to greater recall and understanding of word meanings; however, this was only a brief learning trial using one list of words.

Jiménez (1997) investigated what teachers can do to meet the multiple needs of low-literacy Latino students. The sample consisted of five Latino language-minority seventh-grade students, three of whom were enrolled in a special education classroom and two of whom attended a self-contained at-risk bilingual classroom.[6] Data collection consisted of four observations of students in their classroom environment, think-aloud data collected prior to the instructional component of the study, teacher interviews to learn more about the two teachers' approach to instruction, and transcripts of the taped lessons. The researcher and a graduate assistant taught eight lessons over a 2-week period designed to increase students' use of cognitive strategies. The three students from the special education class were taught mainly in English, whereas the two students from the bilingual classroom were taught mainly in Spanish. Using a language experience text and three books about a Mexican staple, corn, Jiménez emphasized three key reading strategies: how to approach unknown vocabulary, how to integrate prior knowledge with text information, and how to formulate questions. Using qualitative analysis techniques, Jiménez learned that the students held limited views of reading before receiving the cognitive strategy instruction, but subsequently appeared to have a better idea of what reading was about. The students appreciated the use of Spanish and were willing to try out the various cognitive strategies.

Rohena et al. (2002) investigated the effectiveness and efficiency of a constant time-delay instructional approach and language of instruction for teaching of sight words in English to four Puerto Rican middle-school students with mental retardation. The students were schooled in the continental United States. The goals of their study were

(a) to evaluate and compare the effectiveness of Spanish and English constant time delay instruction on English sight word acquisition; (b) to examine the

---

[6] Not all the students in the study sample had been identified as learning disabled. Three students were from a special education classroom; two were from a self-contained at-risk classroom. The students had been identified as at risk for referral to special education.

effects of the instructional conditions (i.e., Spanish and English time delay) on the generalization of English sight words and incidental information from the classroom to the community setting (i.e., grocery, department, and hardware stores); and (c) to compare the efficiency of the instructional conditions with respect to the percentage of errors, number of sessions, and number of minutes of instructional time to criterion in learning to read English sight words. (p. 170)

Time-delay instruction consisted of requiring students to wait 4 seconds before responding to a sight word they were to read (*sporting goods, fresh meats*), with incidental information provided in either English (*baseball* for the sight word *sporting goods*) or Spanish (*chuletas* for the sight word *fresh meats*). A list of 15 words (5 from each of three stories) was selected for the study. The children were taught to read the sight words, which were all English words, although the language of instruction (English or Spanish) was counterbalanced. The researcher presented the word card, provided a cue (look at the word), waited 4 seconds, and scored the response before presenting the next word.

A multiple probe across participants with a parallel-treatment design was used to evaluate and compare the effectiveness of the two instructional conditions: English time delay and Spanish time delay. The two comparison conditions, Spanish and English, and the no-treatment condition were presented daily and were counterbalanced, with at least 2 hours allowed between the presentations of the conditions. In the no-treatment condition, the same procedure was used without incidental information. Reinforcement in the form of pennies was presented to the child when he or she attended to the task.

The investigators measured the percentage of words read correctly in each condition, the number of instructional sessions required for the child to achieve the criterion, the percentage of errors in each condition, and the number of minutes required to achieve the criterion. Generalization was measured by the number of words that were read correctly in the community setting; however, generalization to new words was not measured. The results indicate that, before the treatment, students read few if any of the words correctly. All the children showed some improvement after the intervention, although some improvement levels were minimal. In terms of accuracy and efficiency of reading, both conditions appeared to produce similar results. In addition, reading of the words generalized from the classroom to the stores in the community in both conditions, and there appeared to be no significant differences between the two conditions in this regard. The results of this study indicate that it is possible to teach sight word-reading skills to some language-minority students with mental retardation, and that the language of instruction does not appear to make a difference, provided the instructional language is closely matched to the child's level of language comprehension.

VanWagenen et al. (1994) developed an assisted-reading intervention in English for middle-school students (12 years old). This intervention, designed to build word-reading and comprehension skills, was given to three Spanish-speaking students from backgrounds of extreme poverty, situational conflicts, and forms of abuse who saw a special education teacher for daily reading instruction. For the intervention,

TABLE 17.2
Effect Sizes for Instructional Approaches Designed for Language-Minority Students in Special Education Settings

Study	N	Grade	Home Language	Type of Study	Pretest Differences	Treatment Duration	Effect Size	Confidence Interval	Signif.
Alternating treatment									
Echevarría, 1996	5	2-3	Spanish	ATD	Not appropriate for effect size calculations				
Perozzi, 1985	6	Pre-K	Spanish/English	ATD	Not appropriate for effect size calculation				
Multiple baseline									
Rousseau et al., 1993	5	6	Spanish	MB	Not appropriate for effect size calculation				
VanWagenen et al., 1994	3	7	Spanish	MB	Not appropriate for effect size calculation				
Parallel treatment									
Rohena et al., 2002	4	7-8	Spanish	PT	Not appropriate for effect size calculation				
Quasi-experiments									
Klingner & Vaughn, 1996	26	9-11	Spanish	Quasi-Exp.	Yes				
• Gates-MacGinitie							-.03	-.8 - .74	No
• Comprehension							-.39	-1.17 - .38	No
• Strategy							-.58	-1.36 - .21	No
Randomized control trial									
Bos et al., 1989	42	4-6	Spanish	RCT		3 days	.81	.47-1.16	Yes

(1) the teacher tape-recorded her reading of each new passage from the text for four minutes, (2) the students silently read the same passage while listening to the teacher's prerecorded reading of the passage (taped at about 128 words per minute), (3) the students read the same passage a second time...aloud, (4) the students [read] the passage silently three times without the tape recording and (5) the students [read] the passage orally a second time. (p. 228)

Students were assessed on pre- and posttests for reading rate, error rate, and reading comprehension. In calculating reading errors, mispronunciations attributed to dialect, repetition, and self-correction were not counted. Evaluation of comprehension was based on the percentage correct on the written activities following each story and on criterion-referenced tests for each unit. The students completed written work over an entire story on an average of every 6 to 8 days depending on the length of each story.

The researchers employed a multiple-baseline design to evaluate the effectiveness of the intervention. Following the intervention, the students demonstrated improvement on measures of reading rate, error rate, and comprehension. According to the authors, these results indicate the benefit of using assisted-reading techniques with English-language learners to facilitate an increased rate of reading and comprehension while reducing the number of errors made by students while reading. It should be noted that, during baseline, teachers spent considerable effort on developing students' comprehension of the story. It is unclear given the study design, however, whether assisted-reading practice absent the initial focus on comprehension would have been beneficial for these English-language learners.

Klingner and Vaughn (1996) intervened with 26 seventh- and eighth-grade Hispanic learning-disabled students who were English-language learners. As a first step, the students received 15 days of reciprocal teaching instruction to learn the following six strategies (expanded from Palincsar & Brown, 1984): predict what a given passage is about, brainstorm what they already know about the topic of a passage, clarify words and phrases they did not understand while reading, highlight the main idea of a paragraph, summarize the main ideas and the important details in a paragraph or passage, and ask and answer questions about a passage. The reciprocal teaching consisted of teacher modeling of strategies using social studies passages, followed by students' gradually taking over the role of teacher. Although the instruction was in English, students were encouraged to use Spanish when they felt it might increase their understanding of key passages. At the end of this period, the students were randomly assigned to either a cooperative grouping condition, where they followed essentially the same procedures as in the reciprocal teaching phase but without the teacher as a facilitator, or a cross-age tutoring condition (the experimental students were providing the tutoring to sixth-grade students) for 35 to 40 minutes a day for 12 days.

Analysis indicated no significant between-group differences on the three dependent measures—the Gates–MacGinitie Reading Comprehension Test (MacGinitie & MacGinitie, 1989), Passage Comprehension Tests (Palincsar & Brown, 1984), and a strategy interview—but significant pre- to posttest gains on these measures. Of note is the pattern of change over the course of the intervention and individual differences in this pattern. Growth increases in comprehension were greatest during the phase that included intensive input from the researchers. Moreover, the distribution of change scores on the Gates–MacGinitie test indicated substantial variability, with three students showing declines, two showing a gain of more than 26 percentile points, and the remaining students showing pre- to posttest differences of 0 to 9 points. When students were divided into *more growth* and *less growth* students, each made up about 40% of the sample. "The factors that seemed to relate to students' potential profit from the intervention included: initial reading ability and oral language proficiency" (p. 285). "Students with low decoding skills were least likely to show improvement. All of the students who showed the most growth (except for one) had either decoding scores or comprehension scores at a fourth grade level or higher" (p. 286). For the most part, students who scored 3 or lower (on a scale of 1–5) on the Language Assessment Scales (LAS) were in the less growth group.

Fawcett and Lynch (2000) used a case study approach to examine why two secondary-level Somali students who were English-language learners failed to benefit from an intervention that was successful with students who were not English-language learners, but had been identified as needing intensive extra literacy support. The Somali students were severely impaired in reading and spelling, as measured by the Wechsler Objective Reading Dimension Reading and Spelling Test; both children showed evidence of risk on the Dyslexia Screening Test.

The researchers examined the effectiveness of using a computer-based intervention, Readers' Interactive Teaching Assistants (RITA), which in previous research had led to highly effective and cost-efficient support for 6- and 8-year-old children (Fawcett, Moss, Nicolson, & Reason, 1999). The RITA system provides an alphabetical display on the screen, which enables children to type using the mouse as an alternative to the keyboard. Output is via pictures, graphics, and high-quality computer synthesized speech or digitized human speech in addition to text. The teacher can specify activities from the menu, with RITA first providing a series of suggestions (based on the child's current progress and the program's guidelines) that the teacher can select or discard as appropriate. The RITA system was specifically designed so that teachers can make their own work cards for a particular activity, which can then be integrated into the system. The children participated in three 20-minute sessions per week for 10 weeks. During this time, the researchers carried out the interventions while interacting with the Special Educational Needs Coordinator.

Pre- and postmeasures included various subtests of the Dyslexia Screening Test—1-minute reading, phonemic segmentation, 2-minute spelling, nonsense passage reading, and 1-minute writing (Fawcett & Nicolson, 1996)—and the subtests of the Neale Analysis of Reading Ability (Neale, 1989). The latter test allows reading accuracy, reading rate, and reading comprehension to be assessed separately. Overall, the findings indicate that progress for the two English-language learners was poor.

According to the authors, the main difficulty was that these children, whose native language was Somali, had difficulty distinguishing key English phonemes—primarily /b/, /p/, and /d/, which are not differentiated in

Somali. The most successful approach adopted for the children was to select the problem sounds and support sound differentiation, and explicitly train the children in phoneme–grapheme conversion. They note that the RITA system was well liked by both the teachers and the students, who remained highly motivated throughout.

SUMMARY AND CONCLUSIONS

The samples in a majority of the studies are small; of the 10 studies examining instructional approaches, 8 had five or fewer subjects. As Rohena and colleagues (2002) suggest, "the small number of participants in a study limits the findings, and additional research is needed to extend the findings to a larger sample and diverse groups of individuals (other language minority background students)" (p. 182).

The studies reviewed in this section investigated a variety of techniques designed to improve the language and literacy development of language-minority students with special needs. Of interest is that approaches grounded in different theoretical models were found to be promising. Examples are behavioral approaches to developing sight word reading (Rohena et al., 2002) and vocabulary (Perrozi, 1985), as well as cognitive or learning strategy approaches (Klingner & Vaughn, 1996) and more holistic, interactive approaches that encourage thoughtful discussion of ideas (Echevarría, 1996). Given the small sample sizes and lack of controls in some of the studies, however, more research is needed to explore the effectiveness of these approaches.

Although all the studies reviewed here involved language-minority students in special education settings, a wide range of students is represented across the studies. In some cases, the children may not have been learning disabled, but poor readers as a consequence of their limited English proficiency or lack of exposure to reading instruction in their second language[7] (see Appendix 17.A for a description of identification procedures). In the study of VanWagenen et al. (1994), for example, children were assigned to the special education teacher because of the need for intensive instruction in word-recognition meaning, pronunciation, and application of grammatical structures. The designation was based solely on scores on the Woodcock Reading Mastery Test. Although the two students studied by Fawcett and Lynch (2000) scored very low on the reading and spelling subtests of the Dyslexia Screening Test, they demonstrated strengths on the nonverbal subtests (postural stability and bead threading), compared with norms for their age. They also achieved high scores on the semantic fluency test, which measures speed of access to information within a specified category (in this case, animals) and is considered indicative of verbal intelligence (Frith, Landerl, & Frith, 1995). In addition to cross-study differences, there appears to have been a range of levels of disability within studies[8] because students differed greatly in the progress they achieved in

---

[7] The authors do not claim that these students were learning disabled.

[8] There were some studies in which having a range was intentional; these are not the studies referred to here.

response to the same instructional approach. Thus, in interpreting the study findings, it is essential to consider students' individual profiles and how these profiles interact with particular instructional approaches.

Of note is that approaches that have been found effective in English may also work for children learning in their native language. For example, Echevarría (1996) found that instructional conversations implemented in Spanish with Spanish-speaking children were effective; these approaches have been found to be effective with students learning in English as a second language as well (Saunders & Goldenberg, 1999). The study findings also suggest that modifications designed to make English instruction more comprehensible for language-minority students are helpful. For example, VanWagenen et al. (1994) used an assisted-reading approach that introduced vocabulary and comprehension first; Rousseau et al. (1993) found that teaching key vocabulary was more effective than listening previewing in enhancing literal recall, and that the combination of the two strategies was more effective than either alone; and Klingner and Vaughn (1996) allowed students to use their first language to clarify meaning. Clearly, more research is needed to determine whether these findings will hold up in studies explicitly designed to investigate them, comparing tailored and untailored interventions, rather than tailored interventions and instruction as usual.

Students' native language appeared to help them in learning a second language. Perrozi (1985) found that three children, each with a different pattern of language development—normal, mild delay, and disordered—learned English receptive vocabulary more rapidly when the vocabulary was initially taught in the child's native language, Spanish. Although Rohena et al. (2002) did not find that language of instruction had a differential effect on sight word acquisition and generalization, they remind readers that the verbal prompts in English were simple (several words) and within participants' level of English proficiency. They also note that language of instruction may be less important in developing sight word reading than in developing text-based components of literacy, such as comprehension. In a study more fully described in chapter 14, Maldonado (1994) found that second- and third-grade Spanish speakers with learning disabilities taught initially in Spanish and transitioned into English outperformed a control group that received traditional special education in English. The students in the two groups had similar characteristics, including age, education, experience, learning disability, language proficiency, and socioeconomic status (SES). See also findings reported in chapter 9 that indicate transfer from first- to second-language literacy.

The level of students' English-language proficiency appears to interact with the instructional approach employed. Several studies found that instructional approaches were successful only if students had requisite levels of English. For example, Klingner and Vaughn (1996) found that children with the potential to benefit most from the intervention had some initial reading ability and fairly high levels of second-language oral proficiency.

These studies also indicate that the context in which children learn influences their discourse and development. As noted earlier, Ruiz (1995) documents differences in students' performance in less formal contexts. Echevarría (1996) demonstrates that, during instructional conversation lessons, significantly higher levels of academic discourse occurred, and students attained a higher level of conceptual development. The broader school context can also influence children's literacy development. Graves et al. (2000) report that teachers believed school-level initiatives (reduction in time allocated to writing, uniform switch to English) had a detrimental effect on students' writing progress. Wolf (1993) found that, through Reader's Theater, students labeled at risk were able to interpret text and perform a scene from a story they were reading.

One important issue raised by these studies is the manner in which students are identified as learning disabled and the assessments used to track their progress. In some cases, limited information about the selection process is provided (although the measures are reported, the criteria for inclusion are not; individual student scores are not provided). With regard to identification and tracking student progress, in many cases the information that is presented is difficult to interpret because it is based solely on researcher-developed assessments, and no information is given about what the scores mean—more specifically, how these students compare with other children with similar needs or with children without learning issues (however, this information can be found in Fawcett & Lynch, 2000; Graves et al., 2000). Many of the authors fail to provide information about the reliability or validity of the assessments used or about interrater reliability when more open-ended assessments were used. The authors of two studies (Rohena et al., 2002; Rousseau et al., 1993) caution that, although the data may suggest that the instructional approaches employed had powerful effects on students' reading ability, it is important to examine whether those effects were long-lasting, as well as whether they generalize to other reading materials, tasks, or situations. Finally, studies should be designed to differentiate between a language delay and a reading disability.

In several studies (Bos et al., 1989; Hughes, Vaughn, & Schumm, 1999; Klingner & Vaughn, 1996), intelligence tests were used to determine which students were placed in special education settings. It is common to use intelligence (IQ) tests in the diagnosis of learning disabilities and other educational difficulties; in many cases, the so-called discrepancy definitions used. According to this definition, to be considered *learning disabled*, an individual must have a discrepancy between a score on an IQ test and an achievement test. Serious questions have been raised about this practice in the case of individuals who are being assessed in their first language (e.g., Siegel, 1989, 1992). The use of IQ tests may be even more inappropriate in the case of language-minority children and youth. It is often assumed that so-called intelligence tests measure reasoning and problem-solving ability independently of specific knowledge and cultural norms. However, most IQ tests have a language component that requires the vocabulary and knowledge of complex syntax in English. In addition, most IQ tests require background knowledge that is culture specific. The most recent empirically based definition of learning disabilities does not use a discrepancy between IQ and achievement as an indicator of a disability, but instead focuses on students' ability to learn given appropriate schooling. If achievement in reading, spelling, and/or arithmetic is low despite appropriate schooling, it is more reasonable to assume that there is a learning difficulty or disability.

APPENDIX 17.A STUDY SAMPLES AND METHODS USED TO IDENTIFY THE SAMPLES

Author	Study Sample	Methods Used to Identify Study Sample
Ruiz, 1995	A bilingual (Spanish–English) self-contained classroom for students identified as language learning disabled.	Not described here—see Ruiz (1988) for the complete ethnographic investigation of this classroom.
Wolf, 1993	Three limited-English-proficient third- and fourth-grade students.	Not described, but author indicates the boys had all received a Resource Specialist Program label that caused retention and special classroom placement throughout their careers.
Hughes, Vaughn, & Schumm, 1999	80 language-minority Hispanic parents.	Forty of the parents were selected based on their children having been identified by the school district as learning disabled (LD). School district criteria for LD identification included a discrepancy of one or more standard deviations between IQ and an academic score in reading, writing, arithmetic, or spelling; evidence of a disorder in one or more of the basic psychological processes; LD not due to second-language learning or other exclusionary criteria.
Perozzi, 1985[9]	Three English-speaking (ES) and three Spanish-speaking (SS) preschool	The diagnosis of the Spanish-speaking subjects was based on the clinical

(Continued)

[9]Although they were administered standardized scales of language functioning, details of the scores are not presented, making it difficult to understand the nature and degree of their deficit.

Author	Study Sample	Methods Used to Identify Study Sample
	children; one SS student was diagnosed as having mild language delay, one as being language disordered, and one as having normal language. One ES student was diagnosed as having mild language delay and two as having normal language.	impression of the diagnostician using the pooled information described below. The diagnoses for the English-speaking children were substantiated by scores on the Test of Language Development (TOLD).
		A bilingual/bicultural American Speech-Language–Hearing Association (ASHA) certified speech-language pathologist with 10 years experience working with communicatively handicapped bilingual children conducted an extensive interview with the parents of the subjects wherein a case history was obtained and a determination of the subjects' native language was made. A language-use matrix, which assesses the language of interaction between a child and parents, siblings, and others in the home environ ment, was used. Subjects were designated as Spanish speakers if only Spanish was used in the home and as English speakers if only English was used. If both languages were used, the subjects were dropped from the study.

(Continued)

Author	Study Sample	Methods Used to Identify Study Sample
		Diagnosis of level of language function ing was conducted in Spanish for the SS children and in English for the ES children. SS subjects were administered a locally translated Spanish adaptation of the Assessment of Children's Language Comprehension (ACLC) (Foster, Giddan, & Stark, 1973). ES children were adminis tered the standard (English) version of the ACLC and TOLD (Newcomer & Hammill, 1977). An expressive language sample was obtained by the diagnostician for all six subjects in two contexts—child–clinician and child–parent conversations. Mean length of utterance, semantic content categories, and morphosyntactic forms were described and analyzed for each sample.
Echevarría, 1995, 1996[10]	The subjects in the study were classified as Learning Handicapped and had been placed in a self-contained special education classroom, Special Day Class (SDC)	Brigance, a criterion-referenced test to measure decoding and comprehension, was used to identify children who had poor decoding and comprehension.

(Continued)

---

[10]Specific details regarding identification have not been provided.

Author	Study Sample	Methods Used to Identify Study Sample
		Eligibility statements from Individualized Education Program (IEP) data indicate the following[11]:
		1. Elena is eligible for special education due to learning disabilities in auditory memory, visual motor integration, and attention deficits affecting her educational performance in reading and written language.
		2. Fernanda has multiple handicaps, concomitant impairment, mental retardation, and orthopedic impairment, the combination of which causes such educational problems that she cannot be accommodated in a program solely for the impairments.
		3. Juan qualifies for special education due to a significant discrepancy between demonstrated ability and current academic performance in reading and language as related to auditory processing deficits and visual

(Continued)

---

[11] Information about the assessments used to provide the IEP data is not provided.

Author	Study Sample	Methods Used to Identify Study Sample
		4. Laura is eligible for special education services based on a discrepancy between her low average ability and achievement in the areas of reading and written language due to auditory sequential memory deficits and visual processing.
		5. Salvador is eligible for special education based on learning disabilities in the area of auditory processing and memory. These deficits affect his academic performance in all areas.
Bos, Allen, & Scanlon, 1989	Forty-two fourth- to sixth grade students with learning disabilities whose first language was Spanish and who spoke Spanish at home.	"Learning disabilities were identified according to a school district criteria including a discrepancy between intellectual ability and reading achievement" (p. 174).
Jiménez,1997	Five Latino middle school students who were reading up to four grade levels below their current Grade 7 placement when the study began. Students' low levels of reading ability held true regardless of whether their dominant language was English or Spanish. Three students were drawn from a self-contained special education classroom and two from a self-contained at-risk bilingual education classroom.	Students in the special education class were administered the Total Reading Battery for the Metropolitan Achievement Test (MAT 6, Form L, 1986); Woodcock Spanish Psycho-Educational Battery (Form A, 1986); Receptive and Expressive One-Word Picture Vocabulary Tests (ROWPVT, EOWPVT-R).
		Students in the self-contained at-risk bilingual education class had been

(Continued)

Author	Study Sample	Methods Used to Identify Study Sample
		identified by school personnel as at risk for referral to special education. One had taken the Spanish language academic achievement test, La Prueba Riverside de Realización en Español, Form A, Level 12.
Rohena, Jitendra, & Browder, 2002	Four Puerto Rican middle school students (two girls and two boys) with moderate mental retardation.	Each participant met the state criteria for mental retardation and district eligibility criteria for placement in life skills classrooms. Eligibility criteria included evidence of "impaired mental development which adversely affects the educational performance of a person. The term includes a person who exhibits a significantly impaired adaptive behavior in learning, maturation, or social adjustment as a result of subaverage intellectual functioning. The term does not include persons with IQ scores of 80" (Special Education Standards and Regulations of the Pennsylvania Department of Education, 1990, § 342). This determination was made through a full assessment and comprehensive report by a certified school psychologist. Determination of mental retardation was based on formal measures of intelligence, such as the Wechsler Intelligence Scale

(Continued)

Author	Study Sample	Methods Used to Identify Study Sample
		for Children-Third Edition (WISC-III; Wechsler, 1991) or the Stanford-Binet Intelligence Scale (Thorndike, Hagen, & Sattler, 1986), and of adaptive behavior, such as the Vineland Adaptive Behavior Scales (Sparrow, Balla, & Cichetti, 1984).
Rousseau, Tam, & Ramnarain, 1993[12]	Five Hispanic students, two males and three females, ages 11 years, 10 months to 12 years, 3 months (mean age = 12 years, 0 months) with speech and language deficits.	All students attended the same special education class for language-minority students with speech and language deficits and received speech and language therapy three times per week. Diagnosis of speech and language deficits was made by a bilingual speech and language therapist using a test battery consisting of the Goldman-Fristoe Test of Articulation Skills (Goldman & Fristoe, 1986), the Clinical Evaluation of Language Fundamentals-Revised

(Continued)

[12] The School Board did not allow specific scores for the children to be released. Thus, no information is presented on the actual test scores of the children, although they were tested in both English and Spanish (if Spanish was their first language). It would be interesting and important to know more about these children because it is not clear how the diagnosis of learning disability was made.

Author	Study Sample	Methods Used to Identify Study Sample
		(Semel, Wiig, & Secord, 1987), and the Language Processing Test (Richard & Hanner, 1985). Additional diagnostic evaluation included the Degrees of Reading Power (DRP; Touchstone Applied Science Associates, 1990), administered annually to all elementary school students in Grades 3 through 6, and subtests of the Brigance Diagnostic Comprehensive Inventory (Brigance, 1983); the Kaufman Test of Educational Achievement (Kaufman & Kaufman, 1985), and the Woodcock-Johnson Psycho-Educational Battery-Revised (Woodcock & Johnson, 1989).
Graves, Valles, & Rueda, 2000	Four volunteers from a pool of 10 interns in the Bilingual Personnel Preparation Program in Special Education at San Diego State University, each working as a teacher intern, and their students.	All students were English-language learners with a learning disability, according to specific school district labeling processes. All students were tested in both Spanish and English and labeled because of a significant lag in both languages. All students had specific individualized education program goals in written expression.

(Continued)

547

Author	Study Sample	Methods Used to Identify Study Sample
VanWagenen, Williams, & McLaughlin, 1994[13]	Three Spanish-speaking students—one 12-year-old girl from Colombia, one 12-year-old boy from El Salvador, and one 12-year-old boy from Mexico—assigned to the special education teacher because of the need for intensive instruction on word recognition and meaning and pronunciation drill, with instruction in and application of grammatical structures.	Woodcock Reading Mastery Test Form A (Woodcock, 1973).
Fawcett & Lynch, 2000[14]	Children in their first year at a mixed-ability comprehensive school in Sheffield. Although the two English-language learners were identified as needing intensive literacy support because of reading and spelling performance 4 years behind their chronological age, it is not clear that their deficits were due to a learning disability.	Wechsler Objective Reading Dimension (WORD; Psychological Corporation, 1993) reading and spelling tests; the Dyslexia Screening Test (Fawcett & Nicolson, 1996); the British Picture Vocabulary Scale (BPVS; Dunn, Dunn, Whetton, & Pintillie, 1982).

(Continued)

[13] The diagnosis of reading difficulties was based on the Woodcock Reading Mastery Test. However, the scores of the children are not presented, so it is difficult to know the nature and extent of their reading difficulties.

[14] The Dyslexia Screening Test has poor validity.

Author	Study Sample	Methods Used to Identify Study Sample
Klingner & Vaughn, 1996[15]	The sample included 26 seventh- and eighth-grade students with learning disabilities.	Students selected to participate met the following criteria: a significant discrepancy of at least 1.5 standard deviations between standard scores on an intelligence test and an achievement test (both administered in English) and evidence that their learning disabilities were not due to other conditions (e.g., English language learning, sensory handicap, physical handicap); Spanish spoken as their first language; English decoding skills at least at the second grade level; scores at least 2 years below grade level on the Woodcock-Johnson passage comprehension subtest.

[15] The diagnosis of learning disabled is especially problematic in this study because the researchers used the discrepancy between IQ and reading to identify students with learning disabilities; the use of the IQ test with language-minority children is inappropriate. In addition, the discrepancy definition should not be used to diagnose learning

APPENDIX 17. B ELABORATION ON THE APPROACHES AND MEASURES USED IN THE CITED STUDIES

Echevarría (1996)

Teacher Rating: Elements of Instructional Conversation (IC) Measure. This was used to measure fidelity to treatment by raters who were blind to the conditions of the study. Each lesson (IC and basal) was rated with the IC Rating Scale, scoring the number of elements instantiated in the lessons. Interrater reliability at the start of the rating was 80%; midway through the tapes, it was 100%.

During the Lesson: Student Outcome Measure. In an effort to assess the student response during the lesson, students were rated with the Student Outcome Measure (SOM). The scale was designed by the researcher and was based on probable responses to the presentation of IC elements. For example, the raters assessed whether the subject used the text as a basis for a statement or position at least once during the lesson. Students were individually assessed on their performance during the lesson through analysis of videotaped lessons and were rated on a 3-point scale by raters blind to the conditions of the study. Reliability was established through training sessions, wherein the trainer (researcher) and two blind raters collectively scored a videotape from pilot data. The trainer then went through each item to ensure agreement between the raters. Once the raters were in close agreement on each item during the training session, they independently rated two videotaped lessons (double rated) to establish reliability. The results of the rating yielded a reliability rating of 87%.

During the Lesson: Analysis of Utterances. For each of the students, the raters tallied and categorized every utterance the subject made during the lesson. Each utterance was categorized as follows: self-initiated nonscripted (an original comment made by the student without teacher prompting), self-initiated scripted (a comment related to a teacher question made by the student without teacher prompting), teacher prompted (teacher calls on a student), unrelated to lesson content (comment about something other than the lesson), and asked for attention (e.g., called the teacher's name). The raters then tabulated the total number of utterances in each category, as well as total number of utterances overall.

After the Lesson: Narrative Competence Measure. According to the study's authors, research indicates that the school environment demands specific kinds of discourse or communication, one of which is narrative ability. Following each lesson, each of the five students was asked to retell the story, using the prompt, "You have just finished reading a story. Now tell me the whole story." The audiotaped narratives were transcribed into written form. Two bilingual speech pathologists were trained to segment the narratives into propositions, or simple clauses, to categorize each proposition, and to score each narrative according to the story structure guidelines discussed in Peterson and McCabe

(1983). The raters participated in three practice sessions prior to the calculation of interrater agreement. Agreement percentages indicated a level of reliability ranging between 85% and 89%. The narratives were also segmented into propositions and classified into categories, following the procedure developed by Jax (1989) on the basis of proposition characteristics specified by Stein and Glenn (1979) and modified by Roth and Spekman (1986).

After the Lesson: Thematic Concept Development.   All of the stories had a discernible idea or theme, either stated explicitly in the story (basal treatment) or introduced by the teacher (IC treatment). If students mentioned the theme in their retelling of the story, this was seen as an indicator that they understood the central concept to some extent. For example, in reference to one story, the teacher's manual explicitly stated that the students would read about a fox fooling other animals and the word *fooled* was found throughout the story. If the student used the word *fooled* in the narrative, it was assigned a score of 1. Such language, referred to as *the tracer* (Newman, Griffin, & Cole, 1989; Saunders & Goldenberg, 1992), provides a trace of the differentiated understanding of the thematic concept that IC was hypothesized to promote. Those narratives with no such evidence were assigned a 0.

After the Lesson: Literal Recall.   Following the lesson, the examiner asked students questions about the story. Questions were taken from the text and were generally literal recall or opinion in nature. The teacher scored the comprehension questions. She was instructed to score each answer on a 3-point scale developed by Saunders and Goldenberg (1992): 0, incorrect–inconsistent with the story; .5, partially correct–consistent with the story but not a complete answer; 1, correct–consistent with the story and a complete answer. There were five possible correct answers for each lesson.

Rousseau, Tam, and Ramnarain (1993)

Materials used in the sessions were taken from *Vocabulary Development* (Frank Schaffer Publications, 1980) and *Reading for Meaning* (Frank Schaffer Publications, 1989).

Discussion of Key Words.   Key words were words essential to understanding the meaning of the passage that the teacher thought the students would not know or be able to read in English. Some key words were *legend, receiver, nominated,* and *refused.* These words had been identified prior to data collection. During a key words session, the teacher presented a group lesson in which she wrote 10 to 12 preselected words from the story on the chalkboard for discussion. Next, the teacher read the first word to the students and asked them to repeat the word chorally. Then she explained the word's meaning through verbal explanations, gestures, pictures, modeling, or some combination of these to convey the meaning of the word. The teacher answered any questions the students asked about the words. Each key word was presented in the same manner. Following the discussion of key words, each student read the story orally and answered the comprehension questions.

Listening Previewing.   The teacher read aloud the story for the session while the students read silently. The teacher told the students to listen carefully as she read the story, to read silently while she read aloud, and to follow by pointing to each word on their own copies as she read. Pointing to the words was required to help ensure that the students were attending to the teacher's reading. The teacher and a paraprofessional monitored the students to ensure that they were pointing to each word as the teacher read. Following the teacher's reading, each student read the story orally and answered the comprehension questions.

Key Words and Listening Previewing.   Both treatments were presented in a single group lesson each session. Key words were always presented first because it made logical sense to discuss the meanings of the new words before reading them in context. The teacher followed the same procedure as described earlier. Immediately following the presentation of the key words, the teacher read the story aloud and followed the procedures described before for listening previewing. Following the group lesson, each student read the story orally and answered the comprehension questions, as described later.

Assessment.   Two dependent measures were used: words read correctly and correct answers to comprehension questions. Words read correctly were words the student pronounced correctly that corresponded to words in the printed passage; incorrect words were mispronunciations, omissions of words, substitutions, hesitations, and unknown words. Correct answers to comprehension questions were defined as oral answers to literal comprehension questions based on information in the stories. Two researchers scored the first minute of each recorded session, circling each error in oral reading and marking the comprehension questions as correct or incorrect. Interrater agreement was 96% for oral reading and 100% for comprehension.

Graves, Valles, and Rueda (2000)

Essay quality was measured with the Story Quality Scale (Graves & Montague, 1991), which is described as follows:

> The Story Quality Scale...consists of scores from 1 to 5 for coherence, organization, and episodic structure, for a possible total score of 15. Based on the scoring criteria, a score of 0 to 4 is considered a weak composition; a score of 4.1 to 8 is considered moderately good; a score of 8.1 to 12 is good; and a score of 12.1 to 15 is excellent. The authors report that in previous research studies, students with LD [learning disability] in sixth grade often were able to produce stories in the 6 to 7 range whereas their general education counterparts almost always produced stories rated between 10 and 15. (Graves, Semmuel, & Gerber, 1994, p. 3)

VanWagenen, Williams, and McLaughlin (1994)

Students were assessed on pre- and posttests for reading rate, error rate, and reading comprehension as follows: "Reading rate was the number of words read correctly per minute. Error rate was measured by counting the number of errors, which included (1) insertions of extra words, (2) omissions of words or word parts, (3) mispronunciations of whole words or word parts, (4) word or sound reversals, and (5) substitutions of words or word parts" (Savage & Mooney, 1979). Mispronunciations attributed to dialect, repetitions, and self-corrections were not counted as errors. Comprehension was evaluated as the percentage correct on the written activities following each story and from criterion-referenced tests for each unit. The students completed written work over an entire story on an average of every 6 to 8 days depending on the length of each story.

Following the intervention, the students demonstrated improvement on measures of reading rate, error rate, and comprehension. For instance, the mean number of words read correctly by Student A increased by 24; her mean number of errors (including insertions of extra words, omissions of words or word parts, mispronunciations of whole words or word parts, word or sound reversals, and substitutions of words or word parts) decreased by 5; and her comprehension score, based on the percent correct answers given on written activities that followed each story and on criterion-referenced tests for each unit, increased by 3. Student B's reading rate increase by 7, her error rate decreased by 1, and her comprehension increased by 9. Student C's reading rate increased by 14, her error rate decreased by 10, and her comprehension increased by 30.

Fawcett and Lynch (2000)

On the Neale comprehension subtest, one student (GA) improved by 0.5 year per 10 weeks of instruction, and the other (SA) improved by 0.17. Both subjects' scores decreased on the Neale rate and accuracy subtests. Given the improvement in comprehension, it may be that students benefit from slower reading. On the Dyslexia Screening Tests (DST), one student (GA) showed modest gains in three areas (1-minute reading, phonemic segmentation, and 1-minute writing), but remained in the at-risk category in these three areas. His scores decreased in 2-minute spelling and nonsense passage. Although he showed decreases on the nonsense passage reading subtest, his scores remained in the normal range. The other student's (SA) scores decreased on three subtests of the DST; they increased marginally on one subtest (phonemic segmentation) and more substantially on another (1-minute writing). On three subtests (1-minute reading, phonemic segmentation, and 2-minute spelling), she ended up in the at-risk range, whereas on nonsense passage and 1-minute writing, she ended up in the normal range.

18

Teacher Beliefs and Professional Development

Diane August and Margarita Calderón

This chapter briefly reviews seven studies that examine teachers' beliefs and attitudes, which are thought to influence how teachers perceive, process, and act on information in the classroom (Clark & Peterson, 1986; Mangano & Allen, 1986). The chapter then turns to five studies of professional development for teachers who work with language-minority children to develop their literacy skills. Three studies (Calderón & Marsh, 1988; Saunders & Goldenberg, 1996; Hoffman et al., 1988) focused on professional development for English-as-a-second-language (ESL) and bilingual education teachers, and two examine training programs for teachers of language-minority students with learning disabilities (Haager & Windmueller, 2001; Ruiz, Rueda, Figueroa, & Boothroyd, 1995). To be included in this chapter, studies had to meet the inclusion criteria established for the panel as a whole (see chap. 1). However, the reporting of student outcomes was not a requirement.

The National Staff Development Council (NSDC) developed standards that provide guidelines for the context, process, and content of professional development (National Staff Development Council, 2001). As defined by NSDC, *staff development* is the continuous education of teachers, administrators, and other employees; it often incorporates collaborative work among teachers and principals; and it applies to specific learning strategies, as well as to planning and decision making. A recent research report on professional development from the American Educational Research Association (2005) asserts that professional development leads to better instruction and improved student learning when it ... focuses on how students learn particular subject matter, instructional practices that are specifically related to the subject matter and how students understand it, and strengthening teachers' knowledge of specific subject matter content. [Moreover], effective professional development helps teachers apply what they learn to their teaching...connects to the curriculum materials that teachers use, the district and state academic standards that guide their work, and the assessment and accountability measures that evaluate their success (p. 4). For example, when teaching bilingual teachers to teach math in Spanish, it would be appropriate to conduct the professional development sessions in Spanish, using the district's math curriculum.

The two research questions related to teacher beliefs and professional development are the following:

1. What does the research tell us about teachers' beliefs and attitudes related to literacy development in language-minority students?
2. What does the research tell us about the kinds of professional development that have been provided to teachers and how this professional development relates to teachers' beliefs and practices?

TEACHER BELIEFS AND ATTITUDES

A variety of qualitative, descriptive studies in a range of settings that focused on literacy development have considered teachers' beliefs and attitudes, especially beliefs and attitudes related to issues of language, culture, and achievement. Two researchers examined teachers' beliefs and attitudes as one aspect of effective schooling for language-minority students. Pease–Alvarez, García, and Espinosa (1991) conducted a case study of two primary-grade teachers whose instruction in bilingual settings was deemed to be effective. Both teachers "believed strongly that classroom practices that reflect the cultural and linguistic background of minority students are important ways of enhancing student self esteem" (p. 353). Gersten (1996) identifies teachers' respect for and responsiveness to cultural diversity as one critical instructional practice that appears in classrooms nominated as effective.

Five studies focused exclusively on teachers' beliefs and attitudes. Orellana (1995) investigated gendered aspects of literacy in two Spanish–English bilingual primary classrooms and described how teachers' beliefs and attitudes about gender influence literacy practice. For example, one teacher used gender as "an integral factor in achieving the control that was central to literate practice" (p. 696). In the context of Anglo-Hispanic bilingual classrooms, Franklin (1986) examined first-grade teachers' expectations and assumptions about literacy instruction, with particular attention to their beliefs regarding the role of students' language and cultural background for students experiencing difficulty acquiring literacy skills. In this study, teachers blamed the English-language learners' difficulty with reading skills on their cultural and language backgrounds, rather than on teaching methods, materials, and teacher assumptions. Johnson (1992) studied the influence of teachers' theoretical beliefs about teaching ESL on their instructional practices within literacy contexts. She found that the majority of the lessons teachers taught were aligned with their theoretical beliefs, and because the theoretical beliefs differed from teacher to teacher (skill-based, rule-based, and function-based), the teachers provided "strikingly different English-as-a-second language instruction" (p.101). Rueda and García (1996) examined the beliefs of three groups of ESL teachers (fully credentialed ESL, emergency-credentialed ESL, and credentialed special education), focusing on their perspectives on bilingualism and methods for teaching and assessing reading. Their findings indicate that the fully credentialed and emergency-credentialed teachers held slightly more positive views of bilingualism and biliteracy, whereas the special education teachers tended to favor a transmission model of reading instruction and a discrete-skills perspective on reading assessment. Browne and Bordeaux (1991) surveyed Native American and Euro-American elementary teachers in South Dakota to elicit their views on factors contributing to low reading achievement among Native American students. There was a significant difference between the two groups in beliefs about learning styles, with significantly more Native American teachers believing that Native American children have different learning styles. There were also significant differences in beliefs about the impact of bilingualism on reading achievement, with significantly more Native American teachers rating it as negative. However, significantly more Native American teachers believed a mismatch between learning styles and teaching styles to be a negative influence on reading achievement.

In summary, two studies examined teacher beliefs in classrooms deemed to be effective and found that teachers in these classrooms had high expectations for language-minority learners and valued cultural differences. There were five studies that focused solely on teacher beliefs. Two studies (Johnson, 1992; Orellana, 1995) suggest that teachers' beliefs and theoretical orientation influence their classroom practices. One author (Johnson, 1992) recommends that teacher training "create opportunities for teachers to explore various theoretical and methodological orientations as well as become aware of how their own beliefs relate to the way they perceive, process, and act upon information in literacy instruction"(p. 101). Teacher training may influence teacher beliefs (Rueda & García, 1996), and this may help teachers become more aware of how their attitudes and beliefs influence their instruction. The studies also found that teachers teaching in similar contexts may hold different beliefs about the students they teach (Browne & Bordeaux, 1991)—a difference that may be related to the match between teachers' and students' cultural backgrounds.

PROFESSIONAL DEVELOPMENT

A variety of qualitative, descriptive studies have examined the professional development of ESL, bilingual, and special education teachers who work with language-minority students. The professional development is focused on the development of literacy alone or in the context of teaching content to these students.

Bilingual and ESL Teachers

A study (Hoffman et al., 1988) investigated professional development to improve the strategies teachers use when reading aloud to young children. Sixteen kindergarten and first grade teachers from six schools with very high concentrations of Hispanic English-language learners participated in the study. Information about base-line book reading practices was based on audiotapes of teachers' book sharing sessions in their classrooms immediately prior to the training. A two-day training provided teachers an opportunity to: "develop a rationale for reading to children in terms of its importance to literacy acquisition, identify effective literature sharing strategies, and inspect representative samples of the 70 units [the authors] had developed "p. 352. Teachers also viewed videotapes of differing examples of story reading and developed guidelines for effectively sharing books in their classrooms. Teachers began to use the literature units in their classroom on a regular basis in February and on average taught a different unit every two weeks; they continued into the next school year. Audiotapes of teachers during book sharing sessions in their classrooms collected in October served as posttests. Results indicated that prior to the training, teachers demonstrated use of effective strategies on a total of 174 occasions (7 before reading, 138 during reading, and 29 after reading); this increased to 392 after the training (29 before reading, 323 during reading, and 40 after reading). The differences were statistically significant. The authors did not directly explore how changes in teacher behavior influenced student behavior; this would have contributed to the study findings and it was authors' intention to explore this line of research in a subsequent study.

One study worked with teachers to convey the value of constructivism and teacher-directed learning in order to determine implications for teacher assessment. Saunders and Goldenberg (1996) analyzed discussions among a group of teachers and a researcher working together to implement instructional conversations, a form of constructivist teaching, in language arts instruction for English-language learners. In instructional conversations,

> teacher and students engage in discussion about something that matters to the participants, has a coherent and discernible focus, involves a high level of participation, allows teacher and students to explore ideas and thoughts in depth, and ultimately helps students arrive at higher levels of understanding about the topics under discussion (e.g., content, themes, and personal experiences related to a story). (p. 142)

The study took place as part of a university and school collaboration to improve language arts instruction at a predominantly Latino school in the Los Angeles area at a time when project participants were focused on modes of teaching to promote higher levels of comprehension. The participants were one kindergarten, one first-grade, and two second-grade teachers. Three of the four taught in Spanish. The study reported the analysis of discussions from the first 9 of 30 meetings.

The authors found that teachers' conception of effective practice changed over time. They moved from operating "from a dichotomy based on an implicit understanding of traditional and alternative modes of teaching" to a more explicit understanding of the modes. This understanding provided the basis for synthesis, recognizing that each mode was effective in particular areas and that even during alternative teaching (instructional conversations) more traditional teaching, such as direct teaching, would still be needed. In summary, as a result of professional development, the teachers arrived at a more balanced notion of reading instruction. It would be interesting to find out whether the teachers' changed notions influenced their practice, and whether any changes in practice resulted in changes in student literacy outcomes.

The purpose of a study by Calderón and Marsh (1988) was to describe professional development institutes and their impact on bilingual teachers and other school personnel who participated in them, and to analyze them as a model for staff development. The professional development consisted of multidistrict trainer of trainers institutes that focused on literacy development, conducted throughout California from 1980 to 1986. The institutes took place 12 to 15 days a year for 3 years and were designed to (a) integrate theory/research on oral language, reading, and writing with demonstrations of specific teaching models in different contexts; (b) introduce participants to principles of effective professional development and coaching; (c) provide time for practice of the instructional models at the training sessions; and (d) encourage the use of new models in the classroom through coaching checklists and the collection of information about implementation.

Three cohorts of teachers were studied. For the first cohort, questionnaires were administered to 621 participants from 10 regional county offices of education. A subsample of 40 participants was also interviewed. In addition, formal and informal interviews were conducted with and questionnaires administered to the institutes' trainers during each year. The study of the second cohort focused on how well 100 teachers in five counties had been trained. A multi-method procedure, consisting of questionnaires, interviews, videotaping of classrooms and training sessions, coaching logs, and observation protocols, was used to collect data from 1982 to 1986. The third cohort consisted of a subsample of five teachers. The in-depth ethnographic study of these five teachers identified the fidelity, adaptation, and frequency of use of each instructional model through observation/coaching protocols, and it used this information to help the teachers know when they needed assistance the most and forecast for new teachers when they would benefit most from assistance.

Findings are reported for several levels: impact on teachers, school administrators, personnel in county offices of education, and researchers. Teachers reported that they used the teaching strategies and materials and the achievement of their language-minority students improved; they acquired leadership skills, as well as the skills necessary to help other teachers learn effective strategies; a network and buddy system had developed that promoted professional growth; and administrators supported the bilingual program. Administrators sent increasingly larger cohorts of teachers to the institutes each year and funded 95% of the cost. Regarding areas of improvement, lack of administrative support for peer coaching was ranked as most troublesome, followed by inadequate administrative knowledge of bilingual instruction and supervisory skills.

The authors conclude that the extensive role played by facilitators, who brokered the knowledge to be used, how its use was to occur, and the institutional arrangements necessary helped in the implementation of the model. In addition, because the training was often "halfway inside/halfway outside" (p. 148) the district, committed teachers could participate without interference from less committed peers. Finally, the implications from this professional development model were that, to ensure that the training would be used, it is necessary to present theory, model the instructional strategies, and give teachers the opportunity to practice with feedback and extensive support.

Special Education Teachers

Haager and Windmueller (2001) report on a professional development program consisting of intensive workshops followed by classroom-based teaching and consultation. The goal of the program was to improve early reading intervention practices for 17 first- and second-grade teachers working in an urban elementary school with a 98% Hispanic student population. The project was a partnership designed to join university and school personnel in a collaborative effort to improve reading outcomes for English-language learners at risk for experiencing reading failure and being placed unnecessarily into special education.

Results of research were used to prepare a training module that included the research base for teaching specific skills, as well as a collection of practical, hands-on strategies that teachers could implement in their classrooms with small groups of students. Professional development consisted of instruction in teaching phonemic awareness, the alphabetic principle, oral reading fluency, and English-language development, as well as assessment. Teachers examined their students' test scores and engaged in collaborative planning for interventions. Another important component of the intervention was collaboration between the special education teacher, who was the project coordinator, and the school's primary resource specialist, who provided classroom teachers with instructional advice for both learning-disabled students and other students who were having difficulties.

Data on the effectiveness of the professional development intervention were both qualitative and quantitative. The qualitative data consisted of teachers' perceptions of the intervention and self-reports of the extent to which they used the information from the workshops. Teachers reported that Dynamic Indicators of Basic Early Literacy Skills (DIBELS) developed by Kaminski and Good (1996) was a powerful tool for change. The DIBELS test results helped them focus on the needs of individual students and modify the instruction they provided (moving from whole-group to small-group and individual instruction). In addition, teachers reported reteaching lessons when students were not making progress, holding parent conferences, and using flashcards to teach high-frequency words. It should be noted that about half the teachers felt they would have benefited from ongoing consultation with a coach. Data on student outcomes were collected three times during the school year on 335 first- and second-grade students enrolled in the school using DIBELS. The skill areas assessed include phonological awareness, the alphabetic principle (letter–sound relationships), and fluency with connected text. The results indicate that students progressed in all the areas measured, although they did not reach the established benchmarks as early as expected. Because the school had a history of low achievement in reading (the exact details of which are not provided), the authors conclude that the professional development approach is promising, given that patterns of growth in all areas of reading development were noted for all study participants. Because there was no matched control group of students instructed by teachers who did not participate in the training, however, it is difficult to assess whether the changes in student outcomes are attributable to the professional development.

Ruiz and colleagues (1995) report on the process of change experienced by five teachers in bilingual special education classrooms as they participated in a professional development program. The program was designed to introduce the teachers to the Optimal Learning Environment (OLE) project, "an innovative curriculum with a record of success with Latino children in special education" (p. 623). Drawing on the work of Poplin (1988), the researchers framed their investigation around opposing education paradigms. The first, known as either reductionism or the medical model, is one the researchers believe has long dominated special education. Reductionism "considers learning disabilities to be a definable phenomenon, essentially unaffected by contextual learning variables and exclusively 'owned' by the student. In contrast to this paradigm is one in which context plays an important role in mediating student performance" (p. 623). A second organizing principle consists of a belief in "the value of instructional contexts in which students interact with teachers and peers in holistic constructivist contexts of instruction" (p. 623).

To investigate changes in teachers' paradigmatic orientation, five teachers and the paraprofessionals who worked with them were selected to participate in a 3-year study. The teachers and paraprofessionals attended 5 to 10 OLE workshops, whose structure changed during the course of the project. Originally, the workshops were presented by using a transmission model; over time, however, a holistic/constructivist approach was adopted. That is, educators with experience in holistic instructional methods originally presented this information to the teachers, whereas later on the OLE teachers became the major providers of the information, sharing their students' work products and their successes/problems with the holistic instructional strategies they were implementing. In addition to the workshops, the OLE literacy consultants assisted the teachers in their classrooms when invited to do so.

Data were gathered from field notes taken during monthly classroom visits, formal annual interviews with the teachers, informal interviews with the teachers and paraprofessionals, videotapes of classrooms recorded approximately every 6 weeks, videotapes of OLE project meetings, and student work. These data enabled the researchers to identify three patterns that characterized the change process: (a) The amount of special education training affects teachers' paradigmatic orientation with more special education training resulting in a stronger "reductionist" orientation; (b) change involves shifts in instructional practices and shifts in beliefs, and they do not automatically go hand in hand; (c) change is most facilitated at the beginning stages of collaboration by including practicing members of the teachers' occupational community as agents of change. (p. 622)

Summary

In many cases, the data collected were suitable for answering the research questions posed. For example, the goal of two interventions (Saunders & Goldenberg, 1996; Ruiz et al., 1995) was to examine changes in teachers' instructional paradigms. In both cases, researchers used transcriptions of professional development sessions and teacher interviews to document this change. In addition, Ruiz et al. (1995) documented teachers' classroom practices before and after the professional development to examine the congruence between the professional development and practice. However, in cases where the focus of the professional development was on providing teachers with strategies for changing student performance, it is important to examine both changes in teachers' instructional methods and changes in student performance as a means of validating that both the content and delivery of the professional development were appropriate.

The attributes of professional development deemed important for all teachers (American Educational Research Association, 2005) were affirmed as important in these studies. All the studies entailed extensive professional development lasting for at least a year; the professional development consisted of ongoing meetings between teachers and those providing the professional development, opportunities for classroom practice coupled with mentoring and coaching, and teacher learning communities. It was always focused on learning specific strategies for improving instruction for language-minority students, the theory that informs the strategies, and how to apply the strategies in classrooms: improving strategies teachers use when reading aloud to young children (Hoffman, et al., 1988); combining direct and constructivist methods (Saunders & Goldenberg, 1996); teaching oral language, reading, and writing in different instructional contexts (Calderon & March, 1988); improving early reading interventions (Haager & Windmueller, 2001); and introducing a specific literacy curriculum for learning disabled students (Ruiz, et al, 1995).

However, the studies reviewed in this chapter also suggest what might be unique to professional development focused on teachers who work with language-minority students. Calderón and Marsh (1988) highlight the importance of staff development that builds on theory, effective teacher craft, and close collaboration between researchers and teachers given the paucity of experimental research on literacy instruction for this group of students (see chap. 15 for a discussion of the research on effective practice). Professional development for mainstream teachers has a much more robust research base from which to draw (National Institute of Child Health and Human Development, 2000). In addition, the studies suggest that, to develop a coherent program of instruction for language-minority students, it is important to involve all staff concerned with their education (i.e., bilingual and English-language specialists, learning disabilities specialists if called for, and classroom teachers) in the same professional development efforts (Haager & Windmueller, 2001; Ruiz et al., 1995). Although this may be important for all students, it is especially important for language-minority students who tend to be served by multiple school personnel.

The findings also demonstrate that creating change in teachers is a time-consuming process that requires considerable investment on the part of the change agents, as well as the teachers. Four of the professional development efforts studied took place over extended periods of time (1–3 years); all involved many meetings and workshops or an intensive summer program (32 hours of contact time) and, in some cases, follow-up in classrooms. In addition, all the efforts involved an outside collaborator with expertise—in the case of these studies, there was close collaboration with university researchers.

The studies suggest that, "regardless of the specific research questions posed, it is best to think of professional development as including three outcomes: change in teachers' classroom practices, change in their beliefs and attitudes, and change in students' learning outcomes" (Guskey, 1986; cited in Ruiz et al., 1995, p. 622). However, they also suggest that change in these outcomes is not unidirectional. For example, although some researchers suggest that changing teachers' perceptions may be the first step in this process (Richardson, 1991; cited in Haager & Windmueller, 2001, pp. 247–248), Calderón and Marsh (1988) found that changing teacher practice and producing positive student outcomes changed teachers' beliefs. Ruiz et al. (1995) found that there were two dimensions of change—practices and beliefs; both involved transitional processes, and during the transition there was no particular order in which they occurred. The authors indicate further that such factors as teachers' ethnic background and students' background may influence the directionality of the relationship between these factors.

Finally, in using student outcomes to assess effective professional development, it is critical to ensure that teacher effectiveness is not confounded with student capacity. Value-added assessment systems have been developed to examine the relationships among school systems, schools, teachers, and students' academic growth over time (Sanders & Horn, 1998), taking into account student capacity. In examining links between professional development and student performance, other factors should be considered, including school and district policies that influence learning (e.g., class size, allocation of teachers to classrooms, and required curricular materials). To gauge effectiveness, most studies reviewed here examined teachers' reports of change or actual changes in their teaching behavior. Larger scale studies employing more complex designs are needed to examine the relationship between professional development for teachers and the progress of their language-minority students.

Database References
for Part IV

Alvarez, J. (1975). *Comparison of academic aspirations and achievement in bilingual versus monolingual classrooms.* Unpublished doctoral dissertation, University of Texas, Austin.

Anderson, P. J. (1997). Professional development schools: A balanced wheel makes it better for everyone. *TESOL Journal, 7*(1), 19–24.

Araujo, L. (2002). The literacy development of kindergarten English-language learners. *Journal of Research in Childhood Education, 16*(2), 232–247.

Au, K. H., & Carroll, J. H. (1997). Improving literacy achievement through a constructivist approach: The KEEP demonstration classroom project. *Elementary School Journal, 97*(3), 203–221.

Barik, H., & Swain, M. (1975). Three year evaluation of a large-scale early grade French immersion program: The Ottawa study. *Language Learning, 25*(1), 1–30.

Barik, H., & Swain, M. (1978). Evaluation of a bilingual education program in Canada: The Elgin study through grade six. *Bulletin CILA, 27*, 31–58.

Barik, H., Swain, M., & Nwanunobi, E. A. (1977). English–French bilingual education: The Elgin study through grade five. *Canadian Modern Language Review, 33*, 459–475.

Barrera, M., Jr., Biglan, A., Taylor, T. K., Gunn, B. K., Smolkowski, K., Black, C., Ary, D. V., & Fowler, R. C. (2002). Early elementary school intervention to reduce conduct problems: A randomized trial with Hispanic and non-Hispanic children. *Prevention Science, 3*(2), 83–94.

Bean, T. W. (1982). Second language learners' comprehension of an ESL prose selection. *Journal of the Linguistic Association of the Southwest, 4*(4), 376–386.

Bos, C. S., Allen, A. A., & Scanlon, D. J. (1989). Vocabulary instruction and reading comprehension with bilingual learning disabled students. *Yearbook of the National Reading Conference, 38*, 173–179.

Browne, D. B., & Bordeaux, L. (1991). How South Dakota teachers see learning style differences. *Tribal College, 2*(4), 24–26.

Calderón, M., Hertz-Lazarowitz, R., & Slavin, R. E. (1998). Effects of Bilingual Cooperative Integrated Reading and Composition on students making the transition from Spanish to English reading. *Elementary School Journal, 99*(2), 153–165.

Calderón, M., & Marsh, D. (1988, Winter). Applying research on effective bilingual instruction in a multi-district inservice teacher training program. *NABE Journal*, pp. 133–152.

Carlo, M. S., August, D., McLaughlin, B., Snow, C. E., Dressler, C., Lippman, D., Lively, T., & White, C. (2004). Closing the gap: Addressing the vocabulary needs of English language learners in bilingual and mainstream classrooms. *Reading Research Quarterly, 39*(2), 188–215.

Cohen, A. D., Fathman, A. K., & Merino, B. (1976). *The Redwood City bilingual education report, 1971–1974: Spanish and English proficiency, mathematics, and language use over time.* Toronto: Ontario Institute for Studies in Education.

Cohen, S. A., & Rodríquez, S. (1980). Experimental results that question the Ramírez–Castaneda model for teaching reading to first grade Mexican Americans. *Reading Teacher, 34*(1), 12–18.

Covey, D. D. (1973). *An analytical study of secondary freshmen bilingual education and its effects on academic achievement and attitudes of Mexican American students.* Unpublished doctoral dissertation, Arizona State University.

Danoff, M. N., Coles, G. J., McLaughlin, D. H., & Reynolds, D. J. (1978). *Evaluation of the impact of ESEA Title VII Spanish/English bilingual education programs: Vol. I. Study design and interim findings: Vol. III. Year two impact data, educational process, and in-depth analyses.* Palo Alto, CA: American Institutes for Research.

De la Colina, M. G., Parker, R. I., Hasbrouck, J. E., & Lara-Alecio, R. (2001). Intensive intervention in reading fluency for at-risk beginning Spanish readers. *Bilingual Research Journal, 25*(4), 503–538.

De la Garza, V. J., & Medina, M., Jr. (1985). Academic achievement as influenced by bilingual instruction for Spanish-dominant Mexican American children. *Hispanic Journal of Behavioral Sciences, 7*(3), 247–259.

Denton, C. A. (2000). *The efficacy of two English reading interventions in a bilingual education program.* Unpublished doctoral dissertation, Texas A&M University, College Station.

Dianda, M. R., & Flaherty, J. F. (1995). *Report on workstation uses: Effects of Success for All on the reading achievement of first graders in California bilingual program.* (No. 91002006). Los Alamitos, CA: Southwest Regional Laboratory (ERIC Document Reproduction Service No. ED394327).

Doebler, L. K., & Mardis, L. J. (1980-81). Effects of a bilingual education program for Native American children. *NABE Journal, 5*(2), 23–28.

Echevarría, J. (1995). Interactive reading instruction: A comparison of proximal and distal effects of instructional conversations. *Exceptional Children, 61*(6), 536–552.

Echevarría, J. (1996). The effects of instructional conversations on the language and concept development of Latino students with learning disabilities. *Bilingual Research Journal, 20*(2), 339–363.

Elley, W. B. (1991). Acquiring literacy in a second language: The effect of book-based programs. *Language Learning, 41*(3), 375–411.

Escamilla, K. (1994). Descubriendo la lectura: An early intervention literacy program in Spanish. *Literacy Teaching and Learning, 1*(1), 57–70.

Escamilla, K., & Andrade, A. (1992). Descubriendo la lectura: An application of reading recovery in Spanish. *Education and Urban Society, 24*(2), 212–226.

Fawcett, A. J., & Lynch, L. (2000). Systematic identification and approach for reading difficulty: Case studies of children with EAL. *Dyslexia, 6*(1), 57–71.

Fitzgerald, J., & Noblit, G. W. (1999). About hopes, aspirations, and uncertainty: First-grade English language learners' emergent reading. *Journal of Literacy Research, 31*(2), 133–182.

Fitzgerald, J., & Noblit, G. (2000). Balance in the making: Learning to read in an ethnically diverse first-grade classroom. *Journal of Educational Psychology, 92*(1), 3–22.

Franken, M., & Haslett, S. J. (1999). Quantifying the effect of peer interaction on second language students' written argument texts. *New Zealand Journal of Educational Studies, 34*(2), 281–293.

Franklin, E. A. (1986). Literacy instruction for LES children. *Language Arts, 63*(1), 51–60.

Genishi, C., Stires, S. E., & Yung-Chan, D. (2001). Writing in an integrated curriculum: Prekindergarten English language learners as symbol makers. *Elementary School Journal, 101*(4), 399–416.

Gersten, R. (1996). Literacy instruction for language-minority students: The transition years. *Elementary School Journal, 96*(3), 227–244.

Gersten, R. (1999). Lost opportunities: Challenges confronting four teachers of English-language learners. *Elementary School Journal, 100*(1), 37–56.

Gersten, R., & Jiménez, R. T. (1994). A delicate balance: Enhancing literature instruction for students of English as a second language. *Reading Teacher, 47*(6), 438–449.

Gersten, R., & Woodward, J. (1995). A longitudinal study of transitional and immersion bilingual education programs in one district. *Elementary School Journal, 95*(3), 223–239.

Goldenberg, C., & Gallimore, R. (1991). Local knowledge, research knowledge, and educational change: A case study of early Spanish reading.improvement. *Educational Researcher, 20*(8), 2–14.

Goldenberg, C., Reese, L., & Gallimore, R. (1992). Effects of literacy materials from school on Latino children's home experiences and early reading achievement. *American Journal of Education, 100*(4), 497–536.

Gómez, R., Jr., Parker, R., Lara-Alecio, R., & Gómez, L. (1996). Process versus product writing with limited English proficient students. *Bilingual Research Journal, 20*(2), 209–233.

Graves, A. W., Valles, E. C., & Rueda, R. (2000). Variations in interactive writing instruction: A study in four bilingual special education settings. *Learning Disabilities Research & Practice, 15*(1), 1–9.

Gunn, B., Biglan, A., Smolkowski, K., & Ary, D. (2000). The efficacy of supplemental instruction in decoding skills for Hispanic and non-Hispanic students in early elementary school. *Journal of Special Education, 34*(2), 90–103.

Gunn, B., Smolkowski, K., Biglan, A., & Black, C. (2002). Supplemental instruction in decoding skills for Hispanic and non-Hispanic students in early elementary school: A follow-up. *The Journal of Special Education, 36*(2), 69–79.

Haager, D., & Windmueller, M. P. (2001). Early reading approach for English language learners at-risk for learning disabilities: Student and teacher outcomes in an urban school. *Learning Disability Quarterly, 24*(4), 235–249.

Hancock, D. R. (2002). The effects of native language books on the pre-literacy skill development of language minority kindergartners. *Journal of Research in Childhood Education, 17*(1), 62–68.

Hastings-Góngora, B. (1993). The effects of reading aloud on vocabulary development: Teacher insights. *Bilingual Research Journal, 17*(1/2), 135–138.

Hernández, J. S. (1991). Assisted performance in reading comprehension strategies with non-English proficient students. *Journal of Educational Issues of Language Minority Students, 8*, 91–112.

Hoffman, J.V., Roser, N.L., & Farest, C. (1988). Literature-sharing strategies in classrooms serving students from economically disadvantaged and language different home environments. *Yearbook of the National Reading Conference, 37*, 331–337.

Hughes, M. T., Vaughn, S., & Schumm, J. S. (1999). Home literacy activities: Perceptions and practices of Hispanic parents of children with learning disabilities. *Learning Disability Quarterly, 22*(3), 224–235.

Hus, Y. (2001). Early reading for low-SES minority language children: An attempt to "catch them before they fall." *Folia Phoniatrica et Logopedica, 53*(3), 178–182.

Huzar, H. (1973). *The effects of an English–Spanish primary grade reading program on second and third grade students.* Unpublished master's thesis, Rutgers University.

Jiménez, R. T. (1997). The strategic reading abilities and potential of five low-literacy Latina/o readers in middle school. *Reading Research Quarterly, 32*(3), 224–243.

Jiménez, R. T., & Gersten, R. (1999). Lessons and dilemmas derived from the literacy instruction of two Latina/o teachers. *American Educational Research Journal, 36*(2), 265–301.

Johnson, K. E. (1992). The relationship between teachers' beliefs and practices during literacy instruction for non-native speakers of English. *Journal of Reading Behavior, 24*(1), 83–108.

Kaufman, M. (1968). Will instruction in reading Spanish affect ability in reading English? *Journal of Reading, 11*, 521–527.

Kenner, C. (1999). Children's understandings of text in a multilingual nursery. *Language and Education, 13*(1), 1–16.

Klingner, J. K., & Vaughn, S. (1996). Reciprocal teaching of reading comprehension strategies for students with learning disabilities who use English as a second language. *Elementary School Journal, 96*(3), 275–293.

Klingner, J. K., & Vaughn, S. (2000). The helping behaviors of fifth graders while using collaborative strategic reading during ESL content classes. *TESOL Quarterly, 34*(1), 69–98.

Kramer, V. R., Schell, L. M., & Rubison, R. M. (1983). Auditory discrimination training in English of Spanish-speaking children. *Reading Improvement, 20*(3), 162–168.

Kreuger, E., & Townshend, N. (1997). Reading clubs boost second-language first graders' reading achievement. *Reading Teacher, 51*(2), 122–127.

Kuball, Y. E., & Peck, S. (1997). The effects of whole language instruction on the writing development of Spanish-speaking and English-speaking kindergartners. *Bilingual Research Journal, 21*(2/3), 213–231.

Kucer, S. B. (1992). Six bilingual Mexican-American students' and their teacher's interpretations of cloze literacy lessons. *Elementary School Journal, 92*(5), 557–572.

Kucer, S. B. (1995). Guiding bilingual students through the literacy process. *Language Arts, 72*(1), 20–29.

Kucer, S. B. (1999). Two students' responses to, and literacy growth in, a whole language curriculum. *Reading Research & Instruction, 38*(3), 233–253.

Kucer, S. B., & Silva, C. (1999). The English literacy development of bilingual students within a transitional whole language curriculum. *Bilingual Research Journal, 23*(4), 347–371.

Lampman, H. P. (1973). *Southeastern New Mexico Bilingual Program: Final report*. Artesia, NM: Artesia Public Schools.

Larson, J. C. (1996). *Impact of phonemic awareness training in Spanish and English on Puerto Rican first-grade Chapter I students*. Unpublished doctoral dissertation, Temple University, Philadelphia, PA.

Li, D., & Nes, S. (2001). Using paired reading to help ESL students become fluent and accurate readers. *Reading Improvement, 38*(2), 50–61.

Maldonado, J. A. (1994). Bilingual special education: Specific learning disabilities in language and reading. *Journal of Education Issues of Language Minority Students, 14*, 127–147.

Maldonado, J. R. (1977). *The effect of the ESEA Title VII program on the cognitive development of Mexican American students*. Unpublished doctoral dissertation, University of Houston, Houston, TX.

Martínez-Roldan, C. M., & López-Robertson, J. M. (2000). Initiating literature circles in a first-grade bilingual classroom. *Reading Teacher, 53*(4), 270–281.

McLeod, B. (1995). *School reform and student diversity: Exemplary schooling for language minority students* (NCBE Resource Collection Series No. 4). Washington, DC: National Clearinghouse for Bilingual Education.

Medina, M., Jr., & de la Garza, J. V. (1989). Initial language proficiency and bilingual reading achievement in a transitional bilingual educational program. *NABE Journal, 13*(2), 113–125.

Morgan, J. C. (1971). *The effects of bilingual instruction of the English language arts achievement of first grade children*. Unpublished doctoral dissertation, Northwestern State University of Louisiana.

Neufeld, P., & Fitzgerald, J. (2001). Early English reading development: Latino English learners in the "low" reading group. *Research in the Teaching of English, 36*, 64–109.

Neuman, S. B., & Koskinen, P. (1992). Captioned television as comprehensible input: Effects of incidental word learning from context for language minority students. *Reading Research Quarterly, 27*(1), 94–106.

Orellana, M. F. (1995). Literacy as a gendered social practice: Tasks, texts, talk, and take-up. *Reading Research Quarterly, 30*(4), 674–708.

Padrón, Y. N. (1992). The effect of strategy instruction on bilingual students' cognitive strategy use in reading. *Bilingual Research Journal, 16*(3/4), 35–51.

Padrón, Y. N. (1994). Comparing reading instruction in Hispanic/limited-English-proficient schools and other inner-city schools. *Bilingual Research Journal, 18*(1/2), 49–66.

Pease-Alvarez, L., García, E. E., & Espinosa, P. (1991). Effective instruction for language minority students: An early childhood case study. *Early Childhood Research Quarterly, 6*(3), 347–363.

Pérez, B. (1994). Spanish literacy development: A descriptive study of four bilingual whole-language classrooms. *Journal of Reading Behavior, 26*(1), 75–94.

Pérez, E. (1981). Oral language competence improves reading skills of Mexican American third graders. *Reading Teacher, 35*(1), 24–27.

Perozzi, J. A. (1985). A pilot study of language facilitation for bilingual, language-handicapped children: Theoretical and approach implications. *Journal of Speech & Hearing Disorders, 50*(4), 403–406.

Pilgreen, J. K., & Krashen, S. (1983). Sustained silent reading with English as a second language high school students: Influence on reading comprehension, reading frequency, and reading enjoyment. *School Library Media Quarterly, 22*(1), 21–23.

Plante, A. J. (1976). *A study of effectiveness of the Connecticut "Pairing" model of bilingual/bicultural education*. Hamden, CT: Connecticut Staff Development Cooperative.

Prater, D. L., & Bermúdez, A. B. (1993). Using peer response groups with limited English proficient writers. *Bilingual Research Journal, 17*(1/2), 99–116.

Ramos, F., & Krashen, S. (1998). The influence of one trip to the public library: Making books available may be the best incentive for reading (Rapid Research Report). *Reading Teacher, 51*(7), 614–615.

Reyes, M. D. L. L. (1991). A process approach to literacy using dialogue journals and literature logs with second language learners. *Research in the Teaching of English, 25*(3), 292–313.

Rohena, E. I., Jitendra, A. K., & Browder, D. M. (2002). Comparison of the effects of Spanish and English constant time delay instruction on sight word reading by Hispanic learners with mental retardation. *Journal of Special Education, 36*(3), 169–184.

Rousseau, M. K., Tam, B. K. Y., & Ramnarain, R. (1993). Increasing reading proficiency of language-minority students with speech and language impairments. *Education and Treatment of Children, 16*(3), 254–271.

Rueda, R., & García, E. (1996). Teachers' perspectives on literacy assessment and instruction with language-minority students: A comparative study. *Elementary School Journal, 96*(3), 311–332.

Ruiz, N. T. (1995). The social construction of ability and disability: II. Optimal and at-risk lessons in a bilingual special education classroom. *Journal of Learning Disabilities, 28*(8), 491–502.

Ruiz, N. T., Rueda, R., Figueroa, R. A., & Boothroyd, M. (1995). Bilingual special education teachers' shifting paradigms: Complex responses to educational reform. *Journal of Learning Disabilities, 28*(10), 622–635.

Saldate, M., Mishra, S. P., & Medina, M. (1985). Bilingual instruction and academic achievement: A longitudinal study. *Journal of Instructional Psychology, 12*(1), 24–30.

Saunders, W. M. (1999). Improving literacy achievement for English learners in transitional bilingual programs. *Educational Research & Evaluation (An International Journal on Theory & Practice), 5*(4), 345–381.

Saunders, W. M., & Goldenberg, C. (1996). Four primary teachers work to define constructivism and teacher-directed learning: Implications for teacher assessment. *Elementary School Journal, 97*(2), 139–161.

Saunders, W. M., & Goldenberg, C. (1999). Effects of instructional conversations and literature logs on limited- and fluent-English proficient students' story comprehension and thematic understanding. *Elementary School Journal, 99*(4), 277–301.

Schon, I., Hopkins, K. D., & Davis, W. A. (1982). The effects of books in Spanish and free reading time on Hispanic students' reading abilities and attitudes. *NABE: The Journal for the National Association for Bilingual Education, 7*(1), 13–20.

Schon, I., Hopkins, K. D., & Vojir, C. (1984). The effects of Spanish reading emphasis on the English and Spanish reading abilities of Hispanic high school students. *The Bilingual Review, 11*(1), 33–39.

Schon, I., Hopkins, K. D., & Vojir, C. (1985). The effects of special reading time in Spanish on the reading abilities and attitudes of Hispanic junior high school students. *Journal of Psycholinguistic Research, 14*(1), 57–65.

Sengupta, S. (2000). An investigation into the effects of revision strategy instruction on L2 secondary school learners. *System, 28*(1), 97–113.

Shames, R. (1998). *The effects of a community language learning/comprehension processing strategies model on second language reading comprehension.* Unpublished doctoral dissertation, Florida Atlantic University, Boca Raton.

Short, D. J. (1994). Expanding middle school horizons: Integrating language, culture, and social studies. *TESOL Quarterly, 28*(3), 581–608.

Siegel, J. (1992). Teaching initial literacy in a pidgin language: A preliminary evaluation. *Australian Review of Applied Linguistics, 12,* 53–65.

Slavin, R. E., & Madden, N. A. (1998). *Success for All/Éxito Para Todos: Effects on the reading achievement of students acquiring English* (Report No. 19). Baltimore, MD: The Johns Hopkins University, Center for Research on the Education of Students Placed at Risk.

Stuart, M. (1999). Getting ready for reading: Early phoneme awareness and phonics teaching improves reading and spelling in inner-city second language learners. *British Journal of Educational Psychology, 69*(4), 587–605.

Swicegood, M. A. (1990). *The effects of metacognitive reading strategy training on the reading performance and student reading analysis strategies of third grade Spanish-dominant students.* Unpublished doctoral dissertation, Texas A&M University, College Station.

Syvanen, C. (1997). English as a second language students as cross-age tutors. *ORTESOL Journal, 18,* 33–41.

Tharp, R. G. (1982). The effective instruction of comprehension: Results and descriptions of the Kamehameha Early Education Program. *Reading Research Quarterly, 17*(4), 503–527.

Tsang, W. K. (1996). Comparing the effects of reading and writing on writing performance. *Applied Linguistics, 17*(2), 210–233.

Tudor, I., & Hafiz, F. (1989). Extensive reading as a means of input to L2 learning. *Journal of Research in Reading, 12*(2), 164–178.

Ulanoff, S. H., & Pucci, S. L. (1999). Learning words from books: The effects of read-aloud on second language vocabulary acquisition. *Bilingual Research Journal, 23*(4), 409–422.

Valladolid, L. A. (1991). *The effects of bilingual education of students' academic achievement as they progress through a bilingual program.* Unpublished doctoral dissertation, United States International University.

VanWagenen, M. A., Williams, R. L., & McLaughlin, T. F. (1994). Use of assisted reading to improve reading rate, word accuracy, and comprehension with ESL Spanish-speaking students. *Perceptual and Motor Skills, 79*, 227–230.

Vaughn-Shavuo, F. (1990). *Using story grammar and language experience for improving recall and comprehension in the teaching of ESL to Spanish-dominant first-graders.* Unpublished doctoral dissertation, Hofstra University, Hempstead.

Waxman, H. C., Walker de Felix, J., Martínez, A., Knight, S. L., & Padrón, Y. (1994). Effects of implementing classroom instructional models on English language learners' cognitive and affective outcomes. *Bilingual Research Journal, 18*(3/4), 1–22.

Weaver, B., & Sawyer, D. J. (1984). Promoting language and reading development for two Vietnamese children. *Reading Horizons, 24*(2), 111–118.

Wolf, S. A. (1993). What's in a name? Labels and literacy in Readers Theatre. *Reading Teacher, 46*(7), 540–545.

Wright, L. (1997). Enhancing ESL reading through reader strategy training. *Prospect, 12*(3), 15–28.

Background References
for Part IV

Adams, M. J., Foorman, B. R., Lundberg, I., & Beeler, T. (1998). *The nature and importance of phonemic awareness.* Baltimore, MD: Paul H. Brooks.

Alanis, I. (2000). A Texas two-way bilingual program: Its effects on linguistic and academic achievement. *Bilingual Research Journal, 24*(3), 225–248.

American Educational Research Association. (2005, Summer). Teaching teachers: Professional development to improve student achievement. *Research Points, 3,* 1–2, 4.

American Institutes for Research. (1975). Bilingual education program (Aprendamos en dos idiomas), Corpus Christi, Texas. In American Institutes for Research (Ed.), *Identification and description of exemplary bilingual education programs.* Palo Alto, CA: Author.

Ames, J., & Bicks, P. (1978). *An evaluation of Title VII Bilingual/Bicultural Program, 1977–1978 school year, final report, Community School District 22.* Brooklyn, NY: School District 22.

Ariza, M. (1988, April). *Evaluating limited English proficient students' achievement: Does curriculum content in the home language make a difference?* Paper presented at the meeting of the American Educational Research Association, New Orleans, LA.

Au, K. H., & Scheu, J. A. (1996). Journey towards holistic instruction. *Reading Teacher, 49*(6), 468–477.

August, D. (2002). *English as a second language instruction: Best practices to support the development of literacy for English language learners.* Baltimore: The Johns Hopkins University, Center for Research on the Education of Students Placed at Risk.

August, D., & Hakuta, K., (1997). *Improving schooling for language-minority children: A research agenda.* Washington, DC: National Research Council.

Bacon, H. L., Kidd, G. D., & Seaberg, J. J. (1982). The effectiveness of bilingual instruction with Cherokee Indian students. *Journal of American Indian Education, 21*(2), 34–43.

Baker, K., & de Kanter, A. (1981). *Effectiveness of bilingual education: A review of the literature* (Final draft report). Washington, DC: U.S. Department of Education, Office of Technical and Analytic Systems.

Baker, K., & Pelavin, S. (1984). *Unique problems and solutions in evaluating bilingual programs.* Paper presented at the annual meeting of the American Educational Research Association, New Orleans, LA.

Baker, S., & Smith, S. (1999). Starting off on the right foot: The influence of four principles of professional development in improving literacy instruction in two kindergarten programs. *Learning Disabilities Research and Practice, 14*(4), 239–253.

Balasubramonian, K., Seelye, H., & de Weffer, R. E. (1973). *Do bilingual education programs inhibit English language achievement: A report on an Illinois experiment.* Paper presented at the 7th annual convention of Teachers of English to Speakers of Other Languages, San Juan.

Barclay, L. (1969). *The comparative efficacies of Spanish, English and bilingual cognitive verbal instruction with Mexican American Head Start children.* Unpublished doctoral dissertation, Stanford University.

Barlow, D. H., & Hersen, M. (1984). *Single case experimental designs: Strategies for studying behavior change* (2nd ed.). New York: Pergamon.

Bates, E. M. B. (1970). *The effects of one experimental bilingual program on verbal ability and vocabulary of first grade pupils.* Unpublished doctoral dissertation, Texas Tech University.

Becker, W. C., & Gersten, R. (1982). A follow-up of follow through: The later effects of the Direct Instruction Model on children in fifth and sixth grades. *American Educational Research Journal, 19,* 75–92.

Board of Education of the City of New York. (1994). *Educational progress of students in bilingual and ESL programs: A longitudinal study, 1990–1994.* New York: Author.

Borenstein, M. (n.d.). *Comprehensive meta-analysis: Study database analyser.* Retrieved September 22, 2005, from http://www.assess.com/Software/Meta-Analysis.htm

Brigance, A. H. (1983). *Brigance Diagnostic Comprehensive Inventory of Basic Skills.* North Billerica, MA: Curriculum Associates.

Brisk, M. E. (1998). *Bilingual education: From compensatory to quality schooling.* Mahwah, NJ: Lawrence Erlbaum Associates.

Bruck, M., Lambert, W. E., & Tucker, G. R. (1977). Cognitive consequences of bilingual schooling: The St. Lambert project through grade six. *Linguistics, 24,* 13–33.

Burkheimer, G. J., Conger, A. J., Dunteman, G., Elliott, B., & Mowbray, K. (1989). *Effectiveness of services for language-minority limited-English-proficient students.* Washington, DC: U.S. Department of Education.

Burnham-Massey, L., & Pina, M. (1990). Effects of bilingual instruction on English academic achievement of LEP students. *Reading Improvement, 27*(2), 129–132.

Calderón, M., & Minaya-Rowe, L. (2003). *Designing and implementing two-way bilingual programs.* Thousand Oaks, CA: Corwin.

Campeau, P. L., Roberts, A., Oscar, H., Bowers, J. E., Austin, M., & Roberts, S. J. (1975). *The identification and description of exemplary bilingual education programs.* Palo Alto, CA: American Institutes for Research.

Carlisle, J. F., & Beeman, M. M. (2000). The effects of language of instruction on the reading and writing achievement of first-grade Hispanic children. *Scientific Studies of Reading, 4*(4), 331–353.

Carsrud, K. E., & Curtis, J. (1979). *ESEA Title VII Bilingual Program. Final report.* Austin, TX: Austin Independent School District.

Carsrud, K. E., & Curtis, J. (1980). *ESEA Title VII Bilingual Program. Final report.* Austin, TX: Austin Independent School District.

Cazabon, M., Lambert, W. E., & Hall, G. (1993). *Two-way bilingual education: A progress report on the Amigos program.* Santa Cruz, CA, and Washington, DC: National Center for Research on Cultural Diversity and Second Language Learning. Available at http://www.ncbe.gwu.edu/miscpubs/ncrcdsll/rr7/index.htm

Cazabon, M., Nicoladis, E., & Lambert, W. E. (1998). *Becoming bilingual in the Amigos two-way immersion program* (Research Report No. 3). Santa Cruz, CA and Washington, DC: Center for Research on Education, Diversity & Excellence. Available at http:// www.cal.org/crede/pubs/research/rr3.htm

Cazden, C. (1992). *Language minority education in the United States: Implications of the Ramírez report.* Santa Cruz, CA, and Washington, DC: National Center for Research on Cultural Diversity and Second Language Learning. Available at www.ncbe.gwu.edu/miscpubs/ncrcdsll/epr3/

Christian, D., & Genesee, F. (Eds.). (2001). *Bilingual education.* Alexandria, VA: Teachers of English to Speakers of Other Languages.

Ciriza, F. (1990). *Evaluation report of the Preschool Project for Spanish-Speaking Children 1989–90.* San Diego, CA: San Diego City Schools.

Clay, M. M. (1993a). *An observation survey of early literacy achievement.* Portsmouth, NH: Heinemann.

Clay, M. M. (1993b). *Reading Recovery: A guidebook for teachers in training.* Portsmouth, NH: Heinemann.

Clark, C. M., & Peterson, P. L. (1986). Teachers' thought processes. In M. C. Wittrock (Ed.), *Handbook of research on teaching* (pp. 255–296). New York: Macmillan.

Clerc, R., Webb, J., & Gavito, A. (1987). *Houston Independent School District: Comparison of bilingual and immersion programs using structural modeling.* Houston, TX: Houston Independent School District.

Cohen, A. D. (1975). *A sociolinguistic approach to bilingual education.* Rowley, MA: Newbury House.

Coleman, J., Campbell, E. Q., Hobson, C. J., McPartland, J., Mood, A. M., Weinfeld, F. D., & York, R. L. (1966). *Equality of educational opportunity.* Office of Education, U.S. Department of Health, Education, and Welfare. Washington, DC: U.S. Government Printing Office.

Cooper, H. (1998). *Synthesizing research* (3rd ed.). Thousand Oaks, CA: Sage.

Cooper, H. M., & Hedges, L. V. (Eds.). (1994). *The handbook of research synthesis*. New York: Russell Sage Foundation.

Cottrell, M. C. (1971, April). *Bilingual education in San Juan Co., Utah: A cross-cultural emphasis*. Paper presented at the annual meeting of the American Educational Research Association, New York.

Croft, D., & Franco, J. N. (1983). Effects of a bilingual education program on academic achievement and self concept. *Perceptual and Motor Skills, 57*, 583–586.

Curiel, H. (1979). *A comparative study investigating achieved reading level, self-esteem, and achieved grade point average given varying participation*. Unpublished doctoral dissertation, Texas A & M University.

Curiel, H., Stenning, W., & Cooper-Stenning, P. (1980). Achieved ready level, self-esteem, and grades as related to length of exposure to bilingual education. *Hispanic Journal of Behavioral Sciences, 2*, 389–400.

Day, E. M., & Shapson, S. M. (1988). *Provincial assessment of early and late French immersion programs in British Columbia, Canada*. Paper presented at the annual meeting of the American Educational Research Association, New Orleans, LA.

Danoff, Malcom N., Arias, B.M., Coles, Gary J., and Others. 1977a. *Evaluation of the Impact of ESEA Title VII Spanish/English Bilingual Education Program*. American Institutes for Research. Palo Alto.

Danoff, Malcom N., Coles, Gary J., McLaughlin, Donald H., and Reynolds, Dorothy J. 1977b. *Evaluation of the Impact of ESEA Title VII Spanish/English Bilingual Education Programs, Vol. I: Study Design and Interim Findings*. American Institutes for Research. Palo Alto. Redundant with Danoff et al 1977a.

De Avila, E., & Duncan, S. (1978, 1991). *Language Assessment Scales*. San Rafael, CA: Linguametrics.

Díaz, J. O. P. (1979). *An analysis of the effects of a bicultural curriculum on monolingual Spanish ninth graders as compared with monolingual English and bilingual ninth graders with regard to language development, attitude toward school, and self-concept*. Unpublished doctoral dissertation, University of Connecticut.

Díaz, J. O. P. (1982). The effects of a dual language reading program on the reading ability of Puerto Rican students. *Reading Psychology, 3*(3), 233–238.

Dickinson, D. K. (1985). Creating and using formal occasions in the classroom. *Anthropology and Education Quarterly, 16*, 47–62.

Dunn, L. M., Dunn, L. M., Whetton, C., & Pintillie, D. (1982). *The British Picture Vocabulary Scale (BPVS)*. Berks, UK: National Foundation of Educational Research-Nelson.

Edmunds, R. (1979). Effective schools for the urban poor. *Educational Leadership, 37*(1), 15–24.

Educational Operations Concepts. (1991). *An evaluation of the Title VII ESEA bilingual education program for Hmong and Cambodian students in kindergarten and first grade*. St. Paul, MN: Author.

Ehri, L. C. (1997). Sight word learning in normal readers and dyslexics. In B. A. Blachman (Ed.), *Foundations of reading acquisition and dyslexia: Implications for early intervention* (pp. 163–189). Mahwah, NJ: Lawrence Erlbaum Associates.

El Paso Independent School District. (1987). *Interim report of the five-year bilingual education pilot 1986–1987 school year*. El Paso, TX: Office for Research and Evaluation.

El Paso Independent School District. (1990). *Bilingual education evaluation: The sixth year in a longitudinal study*. El Paso, TX: Office for Research and Evaluation.

El Paso Independent School District. (1992). *Bilingual education evaluation*. El Paso, TX: Office for Research and Evaluation.

Elizondo de Weffer, R. (1972). *Effects of first language instruction in academic and psychological development of bilingual children*. Unpublished doctoral dissertation, Illinois Institute of Technology, Chicago.

Engelmann, S. E., & Bruner, E. C. (1988). *Reading mastery: DISTAR reading*. Chicago, IL: Science Research Associates.

Engelmann, S., Carnine, L., & Johnson, G. (1999). *Corrective reading*. Columbus, OH: SRA McGraw-Hill.

Fawcett, A. J., & Nicolson, R. I. (1996). *The Dyslexia Screening Test*. London: The Psychological Corporation.

Fawcett, A.J., Nicolson, R.I., Moss, 5H., Nicolson, M.K., & Reason, R. (1999). Effectiveness of reading intervention in junior school. School Psychology International

Fitzgerald, J. (1995a). English as a second language instruction in the United States: A research review. *Journal of Reading Behavior, 27*, 115–152.

Fitzgerald, J. (1995b). English-as-a-second-language learners' cognitive reading processes: A review of research in the United States. *Review of Educational Research, 65*, 145–190.

Fitzgerald, J., & Noblit, G. (2000). Balance in the making: Learning to read in an ethnically diverse first-grade classroom. *Journal of Educational Psychology, 92*(1), 3–22.

Foorman, B. (1999). Why direct spelling instruction is important. In B. Honig, L. Diamond, & R. Nathan (Eds.), *Reading research anthology: The why? of reading instruction* (pp. 116–119). Novato, CA: Arena.

Foster, R., Giddan, J. J., & Stark, J. (1973). *Assessment of children's language comprehension.* Palo Alto, CA: Consulting Psychologists Press.

Frank Schaffer Publications. (1980). Vocabulary development. Grand Rapids, MI: Author.

Frank Schaffer Publications. (1989). *Reading for meaning.* Grand Rapids, MI: Author.

Friedenberg, J. E. (1984). The effects of simultaneous bilingual reading instruction on the development of English reading skills. *Acta Paedologica, 1*(2), 117–124.

Frith, U., Landerl, K., & Frith, C. (1995). Dyslexia and verbal fluency: More evidence for a phonological deficit. *Dyslexia, 1*, 2–11.

Fulton-Scott, M. J., & Calvin, A. D. (1983). Bilingual multicultural education vs. integrated and nonintegrated ESL instruction. *NABE: The Journal of the National Association for Bilingual Education, 7*(3), 1–12.

Gándara, P., Maxwell-Jolly, J., García, E., Asato, J., Gutiérrez, K., Stritikus, T., & Curry, J. (2000). *The initial impact of Proposition 227 on the instruction of English learners.* Davis, CA: Linguistic Minority Research Institute, University of California.

García, G. (2000). Bilingual children's reading. In M. L. Kamil, P. B. Mosenthal, P. D. Pearson, & R. Barr (Eds.), *Handbook of reading research* (Vol. III, pp. 813–834). Mahwah, NJ: Lawrence Erlbaum Associates.

Genesee, F., Holobow, N. E., Lambert, W. E., & Chartrand, L. (1989). Three elementary school alternatives for learning through a second language. *The Modern Language Journal, 73*, 250–263.

Genesee, F., & Lambert, W. E. (1983). Trilingual education for majority-language children. *Child Development, 54*, 105–114.

Genesee, F., Lambert, W. E., & Tucker, G. R. (1979). An experiment in trilingual education: Report 4. *Language Learning, 28*, 343–365.

Genesee, F., Sheiner, E., Tucker, G. R., & Lambert, W. E. (1976). An experiment in trilingual education. *Canadian Modern Language Review, 32*, 115–128.

Genesee, F., Sheiner, E., Lambert, W. E., & Tucker, G. R. (1997). An experiment in trilingual education (Report 4). Montreal, Canada: McGill University. (ERIC Document Reproduction Service NO. ED150884)

Gersten, R. (1985). Structured immersion for language minority students: Results of a longitudinal evaluation. *Educational Evaluation and Policy Analysis, 7*(3), 187–196.

Gersten, R., & Baker, S. (2000). What we know about effective instructional practices for English-language learners. *Exceptional Children, 66*(4), 454–470.

Gersten, R., & Woodward, J. (1995). A longitudinal study of transitional and immersion bilingual education programs in one district. *Elementary School Journal, 95*(3), 223–239.

Gillet, J. W., & Temple, C. (1990). Understanding reading problems (3rd ed.). Glenview, IL: Scott Foresman.

Glaser, B. G. (1978). *Theoretical sensitivity.* Mill Valley, CA: Sociology Press.

Glenn, J. L. (2000). *Environment-based education: Creating high performance schools and students.* Washington, DC: The National Environmental Education and Training Foundation.

Glesne, C., & Peshkin, A. (1992). *Becoming qualitative researchers: An introduction.* White Plains, NY: Longman.

Goldenberg, C. (1984). *Roads to reading: Studies of Hispanic first graders at risk for reading failure.* Unpublished doctoral dissertation, Graduate School of Education, University of California, Los Angeles.

Goldenberg, C. (1996). The education of language-minority students: Where are we, and where do we need to go? *Elementary School Journal, 36*(4), 715–738.

Goldman, R., & Fristoe, M. (1986). *Goldman–Fristoe Test of Articulation Skills.* Circle Pines, MN: American Guidance Service.

Goodman, Y., Watson, D., & Burke, C. (1987). *Reading Miscue Inventory.* New York: Owens.

Graves, A., & Montague, M. (1991). Using story grammar cueing to improve the writing of students with learning disabilities. *Learning Disabilities Research and Practice, 5*, 88–93.

Graves, A., Semmuel, M., & Gerber, M. (1994). The effects of store prompts on students with and without learning disabilities. *Learning Disabilities Quarterly, 17*, 154–164.

Greene, J. P. (1997). A meta-analysis of the Rossell and Baker review of bilingual education research. *Bilingual Research Journal, 21*(2/3), 1–22.

Guskey, T. R. (1986). Staff development and the process of teacher change. *Educational Researcher, 15,* 5–12.

Hakuta, K., Butler, Y. G., & Witt, D. (2000). *How long does it take English learners to attain proficiency?* (Policy Report 2000-1). Santa Barbara, CA: The University of California Linguistic Minority Research Institute.

Hammill, D., & Larsen, S. (1993). *Test of Written Language II*. Austin, TX: Pro-Ed.

Hedges, L. V. (1981). Distribution theory for Glass's estimator of effect size and related estimators. *Journal of Educational Statistics, 6*(2), 107–128.

Hillocks, G., Jr. (1986). *Research on written composition*. Urbana, IL: National Conference on Research on English.

Howard, E. R., Sugarman, J., & Christian, D. (2003). *Two-way immersion education: What we know and what we need to know*. Baltimore, MD: Johns Hopkins University, Center for Research on the Education of Students Placed at Risk.

Ihnot, C. (1997). *Read naturally*. St. Paul, MN: Read Naturally.

Irvine, J. T. (1979). Formality and informality in communicative events. *American Anthropologist, 81,* 773–790.

Jax, V. A. (1989). Understanding school language proficiency through the assessment of story construction. In A. A. Ortiz & B. A. Ramírez (Eds.), *Schools and the culturally diverse exceptional student*. Reston, VA: The Council for Exceptional Children.

Jencks, C. M., Ackland, H., Bane, M. J., Cohen, D., Ginitis, H., Heyns, B., & Michelson, (1972). *Inequality: A reassessment of the effect of family and schooling in America*. New York: Harper & Row.

Johnson, B. T. (1989). *DSTAT: Software for the meta-analytic review of research literature*. Hillsdale, NJ: Lawrence Erlbaum Associates.

Kaminski, R., & Good, R. (1996). Toward a technology for assessing basic early literacy skills. *School Psychology Review, 25*(2), 215–227.

Kaufman, A. S., & Kaufman, N. L. (1985). *Kaufman Test of Educational Achievement*. Circle Pines, MN: American Guidance Service.

Kiss, G. R., & Savage, J. E. (1977). Processing power and delay: Limits on human performance. *Journal of Mathematical Psychology, 16,* 68–90.

Kuhn, M. R., & Stahl, S. A. (2003). Fluency: A review of developmental and remedial practices. *Journal of Educational Psychology, 95,* 3–21.

LaBerge, D., & Samuels, S. J. (1974). Toward a theory of automatic information processing in reading. *Cognitive Psychology, 6,* 293–323.

Lambert, W. E., & Tucker, G. R. (1972). *Bilingual education of children: The St. Lambert experience*. Rowley, MA: Newbury House.

Layden, R. G. (1972). *The relationship between the language of instruction and the development of self-concept, classroom climate, and achievement of Spanish speaking Puerto Rican children*. Unpublished doctoral dissertation, University of Maryland.

Legarreta, D. (1979). The effects of program models on language acquisition by Spanish-speaking children. *TESOL Quarterly, 13*(4), 521–534.

Levy, B. A., Abello, B., & Lysynchuk, L. (1997). Transfer from word training to reading in context: Gains in reading fluency and comprehension. *Disabilities Quarterly, 20,* 173–188.

Lipsey, M. W., & Wilson, D. B. (2001). *Practical meta-analysis*. Thousand Oaks, CA: Sage.

Livingston, M., & Flaherty, J. (1997). *Effects of Success for All on reading achievement in California schools*. Los Alamitos, CA: WestEd.

Lum, J. B. (1971). *An effectiveness study of English as a second language (ESL) and Chinese bilingual methods*. Unpublished doctoral dissertation, University of California, Berkeley.

MacGinitie, W. H., & MacGinitie, R. K. (1989). *Gates-MacGinitie Reading Comprehension Test* (3rd ed.). Itasca, IL: Riverside.

Malherbe, E. C. (1946). *The bilingual school*. London: Longmans Green.

Mangano, N., & Allen, J. (1986). Teachers' beliefs about language arts and their effects on students' beliefs and instruction. In J. Niles & R. Lalik (Eds.), *Solving problems in literacy: Learners, teachers, and researchers. Thirty-fifth yearbook of the National Reading Conference* (pp. 136–142). Rochester, NY: National Reading Conference.

Matthews, T. (1979). *An investigation of the effects of background characteristics and special language services on the reading achievement and English fluency of bilingual students*. Seattle, WA: Seattle Public Schools, Department of Planning, Research, and Evaluation.

McConnell, B. B. (1980a). *Effectiveness of individualized bilingual instruction for migrant students.* Unpublished doctoral dissertation, Washington State University.

McConnell, B. B. (1980b). *Individualized bilingual instruction. Final evaluation, 1978–1979 program.* Unpublished manuscript.

McSpadden, J. (1979). *Acadiana bilingual bicultural education program: Interim evaluation report, 1978–79.* Lafayette, LA: Lafayette Parish School Board.

McSpadden, J. (1980). *Acadiana bilingual bicultural education program: Interim evaluation report, 1979–80.* Lafayette, LA: Lafayette Parish School Board.

Medina, M., & Escamilla, K. (1992). Evaluation of transitional and maintenance bilingual programs. *Urban Education, 27*(3), 263–290.

Medrano, M. F. (1988). The effects of bilingual education on reading and mathematics achievement: A longitudinal case study. *Equity and Excellence, 23*(4), 17–19.

Meléndez, W. A. (1980). *The effect of the language of instruction on the reading achievement of limited English speakers in secondary schools.* Unpublished doctoral dissertation, Loyola University of Chicago.

Meyer, M. M., & Fienberg, S. E. (1992). *Assessing evaluation studies: The case of bilingual education strategies.* Washington, DC: National Academy of Sciences.

Moore, F. B., & Parr, G. D. (1978). Models of bilingual education: Comparisons of effectiveness. *The Elementary School Journal, 79*, 93–97.

Mortensen, E. (1984). Reading achievement of native Spanish-speaking elementary students in bilingual vs. monolingual programs. *Bilingual Review, 11*(3), 31–36.

Murillo, H. A. (1987). *A comparison of the effects of dual language and intensive English instruction on kindergarten students in the Laredo Independent School District.* Unpublished doctoral dissertation, University of Nebraska, Lincoln.

National Institute of Child Health and Human Development. (2000). *Report of the National Reading Panel. Teaching children to read: An evidence-based assessment of the scientific research literature on reading and its implications for reading instruction* (NIH Publication No. 00-4769). Washington, DC: U.S. Government Printing Office.

National Staff Development Council. (2001). *NSDC Standards for Staff Development.* Available at www.nsdc.org/standards/index.cfm

Neale, M. D. (1989). *The Neale analysis of reading ability* (rev. British ed.). Windsor, UK: National Foundation of Educational Research-Nelson.

Newcomer, P. L., & Hammill, D. D. (1977). *Test of Language Development—2 Primary (TOLD–2).* Austin, TX: Pro-Ed.

Newman, D., Griffin, P., & Cole, M. (1989). *The construction zone: Working for cognitive change in school.* Cambridge: Cambridge University Press.

Nicolson, R. I., Fawcett, A. J., Moss, H., Nicolson, M. K., & Reason, R. (1999). An early reading intervention study: Evaluation and implications. *British Journal of Educational Psychology, 69*, 47–62.

Olesini, J. (1971). *The effect of bilingual instruction on the achievement of elementary pupils.* Unpublished doctoral dissertation, East Texas State University, Commerce, TX.

Oudeans, M. K. (2003). Integration of letter–sound correspondences and phonological awareness skills of blending and segmenting: A pilot study examining the effects of instructional sequence on word reading for kindergarten children with low phonological awareness. *Learning Disabilities Quarterly, 26*, 258–280.

Palincsar, A. D., & Brown, A. L. (1984). Reciprocal teaching of comprehension-fostering and comprehension-monitoring activities. *Cognition and Instruction, 1*(2), 117–175.

Palincsar, A. D., & Brown, A. L. (1985). *Reciprocal teaching of comprehension strategies: A natural history of one program for enhancing learning* (Technical Report No. 334). Urbana: University of Illinois Center for the Study of Reading.

Pan, M. L. (2004). *Preparing literature reviews: Qualitative and quantitative approaches* (2nd ed.). Glendale, CA: Pyrczak.

Paris, S. G., Cross, D. R., & Lipson, M. Y. (1984). Informed strategies for learning: A program to improve children's reading awareness and comprehension. *Journal of Educational Psychology, 76*(6), 1239–1252.

Paris, S. G., & Jacobs, J. E. (1984). The benefits of informed instruction for children's reading awareness and comprehension skills. *Child Development, 55*, 2083–2093.

Patton, M.W. (1990). *Qualitative evaluation and research methods.* Newbury Park, CA: Sage.

Pedhazur, E.J. (1997). *Multiple Regression in Behavioral Research* (3rd ed.). Orlando, FL: Harcourt Brace.

Pena-Hughes, E., & Solis, J. (1980). *ABC's: McAllen's immersion system*. McAllen, TX: McAllen Independent School District.

Perfetti, C. A., & Hogaboam, T. (1975). Relationship between single word-decoding and reading comprehension skill. *Journal of Educational Psychology, 67,* 461–469.

Peterson, C., & McCabe, A. (1983). *Developmental psycholinguistics: Three ways of looking at a child's narrative*. New York: Plenum.

Poplin, M. (1988). The reductionist fallacy in learning disabilities: Replicating the past by reducing the present. *Journal of Learning Disabilities, 21,* 389–400.

Powers, S. (1978). *The influence of bilingual instruction on academic achievement and self-esteem of selected Mexican American junior high school students*. Unpublished doctoral dissertation, University of Arizona.

Psychological Corporation (1993). Wechler Objective Reading Dimension. Sidcup: Psychological Corporation

Prewitt-Díaz, J. (1979). *An analysis of the effects of a bilingual curriculum on monolingual Spanish ninth graders as compared with monolingual English and bilingual ninth graders with regard to language development, attitude toward school and self-concept*. Unpublished doctoral dissertation, University of Connecticut, Storrs.

Purkey, S., & Smith, M. (1983). Research on effective schools: A review. *Elementary School Journal, 83,* 427–452.

Ramírez, J., Pasta, D. J., Yuen, S., Billings, D. K., & Ramey, D. R. (1991). *Final report: Longitudinal study of structural immersion strategy, early-exit, and late-exit transitional bilingual education programs for language-minority children* (Report to the U.S. Department of Education). San Mateo, CA: Aguirre International.

Ramos, M., Aguilar, J. V., & Sibayan, B. F. (1967). *The determination and implementation of language policy* (Monograph Series 2). Quezón City, Philippines: Philippine Center for Language Study.

Rasinski, T. V. (2003). *The fluent reader: Oral reading strategies for building word recognition, fluency, and comprehension*. New York: Scholastic Professional Books.

Richard, G., & Hanner, M. (1985). *Language Processing Test*. East Moline, IL: LinguiSystems.

Richardson, V. (1991). Significant and worthwhile change in teaching practice. *Educational Researcher, 19*(7), 10–18.

Riches, C., & Genesee, F. (in press). Crosslanguage and crossmodal influences. In F. Genesee, K. Lindhold-Leary, W. Saunders, & D. Christian (Eds.), *Educating English language learners: A synthesis of research evidence*. New York: Cambridge University Press.

Rosier, P., & Holm, W. (1980).*The Rock Point experience: A longitudinal study of a Navajo school program (Saad Naaki Bee Na nitn)* (Bilingual Education Series #8. Papers in Applied Linguistics). Washington, DC: Center for Applied Linguistics. (ERIC Document Reproduction Service No. ED195363)

Rossell, C. H. (1990). The effectiveness of educational alternatives for limited-English-proficient children. In G. Imhoff (Ed.), *Learning in two languages*. New Brunswick, NJ: Transaction.

Rossell, C. H. (2000). Educating limited English proficient students. *American Language Review, 4,* 15–19.

Rossell, C. H., & Baker, K. (1996). The educational effectiveness of bilingual education. *Research in the Teaching of English, 30*(1), 7–69.

Roth, F. P., & Spekman, N. (1986). Narrative discourse: Spontaneously generated stories of learning disabled children and normally achieving students. *Journal of Speech and Hearing Disorders, 51,* 8–23.

Rothfarb, S. H., Ariza, M., & Urrutia, R. (1987). *Evaluation of the Bilingual Curriculum Content (BCC) project: A three-year study. Final report*. Miami: Office of Educational Accountability, Dade County Public Schools.

Ruiz, N.T. (1988). Language for learning in a bilingual special education classroom, Unpublished doctoral dissertation, Stanford University.

Sanders, W. L., & Horn, S. P. (1998). Research from the Tennessee Value-Added Assessment System (TVAAS) database: Implications for educational research and evaluation. *Journal of Personnel Evaluation in Education, 12*(3), 247–256.

Saunders, W., & Goldenberg, C. (1992, April). *Effects of instructional conversations on transition students' concepts of "friendship": An experimental study*. Paper presented at the annual meeting of the American Educational Research Association, San Francisco, CA.

Savage, J. F., & Mooney, J. F. (1979). *Teaching reading to children with special needs*. Boston: Allyn & Bacon.

Saville-Troike, M. (1984). What really matters in second language learning for academic achievement? *TESOL Quarterly, 18*(2), 199–219.

Secada, W. G., Chávez-Chávez, R., García, E., Muñoz, C., Oakes, J., Santiago-Santiago, I., et al. (1998). *No more excuses: The final report of the Hispanic Dropout Project.* Madison, WI: University of Wisconsin. (ERIC Document Reproduction Service No. ED461447)

Semel, E., Wiig, E., & Secord, W. (1987). *Clinical evaluation of language fundamentals—revised.* San Antonio, TX: Psychological Corporation.

Shadish, W. R., Robinson, L., & Lu, C. (1999). *ES: A computer program and manual for effect size calculation.* St. Paul, MN: Assessment Systems Corporation.

Siegel, J. (1997). Using a pidgin language in formal education: Help or hindrance? *Applied Linguistics, 18*(1), 86–100.

Siegel, L. S. (1989). IQ is irrelevant to the definition of learning disabilities. *Journal of Learning Disabilities, 22,* 469–478, 486.

Sindelar, P. R., Rosenburg, M. S., & Wilson, R. J. (1985). An adapted alternating treatments design for instructional research. *Education and Treatment of Children, 8,* 67–76.

Skoczylas, R. V. (1972). *An evaluation of some cognitive and affective aspects of a Spanish bilingual education program.* Unpublished doctoral dissertation, University of New Mexico.

Slavin, R. E., & Cheung, A. (2004). *A synthesis of research on language of reading instruction for English language learners.* Baltimore, MD: Johns Hopkins University.

Slavin, R. E., & Madden, N. A. (Eds.). (2001). *One million children: Success for All.* Thousand Oaks, CA: Corwin.

Snow, C. E., Burns, S. M., & Griffin, P. (Eds.). (1998). *Preventing reading difficulties in young children.* Washington, DC: National Academy Press.

Sparrow, S., Balla, D., & Cichetti, D. (1984). *Vineland Adaptive Behavior Scales.* Circle Pines, MN: American Guidance Service.

Spivey, N. N., & King, J. R. (1989). Readers as writers composing from sources. *Reading Research Quarterly, 24*(1), 7–26.

Spivey, N.N. (1997). *The construction metaphor: Reading, writing, and the making of meaning.* San Diego: Academic Press.

Stahl, S. A., & Miller, P. D. (1989). Whole language and language experience approaches for beginning reading: A qualitative research synthesis. *Review of Educational Research, 59*(1), 87–116.

Stanovich, P. J., & Stanovich, P. J. (2003). *Using research and reason in education.* Washington, DC: Partnership for Literacy.

Stebbins, L. B., St. Pierre, R. G., Proper, E. C., Anderson, R. B., & Cerva, T. R. (1977). *Education as experimentation: A planned variation model: Vol. IV-A. An evaluation of follow through.* Cambridge, MA: Abt Associates.

Stein, N. L., & Glenn, C. G. (1979). An analysis of story comprehension in elementary school children. In R. O. Freedle (Ed.), *Advances in discourse processes: Vol. 2. New directions in discourse processing.* Norwood, NJ: Ablex.

Stern, C. (1975). *Final report of the Compton Unified School District's Title VII bilingual-bicultural project: September 1969 through June 1975.* Compton City, CA: Compton City Schools.

Stuart, M. (2004). Getting ready for reading: A follow-up study of inner city second language learners at the end of Key Stage 1. *British Journal of Educational Psychology, 74,* 15–36.

Tawney, J. W., & Gast, D. L. (1984). *Single-subject research in special education.* Columbus, OH: Charles E. Merrill.

Taylor, S., & Bogdan, R. (1984). *Introduction to qualitative research methods: The search for meanings* (2nd ed.). New York: Wiley.

Teschner, R. V. (1990). Adequate motivation and bilingual education. *Southwest Journal of Instruction, 9*(2), 1–42.

Thomas, W. P., & Collier, V. (1997). *School effectiveness for language minority students.* Washington, DC: National Clearinghouse for Bilingual Education. Available at http://www.ncbe.gwu.edu/ncbepubs/resource/effectiveness/index.htm

Thomas, W. P., & Collier, V. (2002). *A national study of school effectiveness for language minority students' long-term academic achievement.* Santa Cruz, CA: University of California at Santa Cruz, Center for Research on Education, Diversity, and Excellence.

Thorndike, R. L., Hagen, E. P., & Sattler, J. M. (1986). *Stanford-Binet Intelligence Scale* (4th ed.). Itasca, IL: Riverside.

Tierney, R. J., & Shanahan, T. (1992). Research on the reading–writing relationship: Interactions, transactions, and outcomes. In R. Barr, M. L. Kamil, P. Mosenthal, & P. D. Pearson (Eds.), *Handbook of reading research* (Vol. II, pp. 246–280). Mahwah, NJ: Lawrence Erlbaum Associates.

Tivnan, T., & Hemphill, L. (2005). Comparing four literacy reform models in high-poverty schools: Patterns of first-grade achievement. *The Elementary School Journal, 105,* 419–441.

Touchstone Applied Science Associates. (1990). *Degrees of reading power.* Brewster, NY: Author.

Vásquez, M. (1990). *A longitudinal study of cohort academic success and bilingual education.* Unpublished doctoral dissertation, University of Rochester, NY.

Vaughn, S., Elbaum, B., Schumm, J., & Hughes, T. (1998). Social outcomes for students with and without learning disabilities in inclusive classrooms. *Journal of Learning Disabilities, 31,* 428–436.

Vaughn, S., & Schumm, J. S. (1995). Responsible inclusion for students with learning disabilities. *Journal of Learning Disabilities, 28,* 264–270, 290.

Vygotsky, L. S. (1978). *Mind and society: The development of higher mental processes.* Cambridge, MA: Harvard University Press.

Wechsler, D. (1991). *Wechsler Intelligence Scale for Children—Third Edition.* San Antonio, TX: Psychological Corporation.

Wechsler, D. (1993.) *Wechsler Objective Reading Dimension.* New York: Psychological Corporation.

Willig, A. (1985). A meta-analysis of selected studies on the effectiveness of bilingual education. *Review of Educational Research, 55*(3), 269–317.

Woodcock, R. W. (1973). *Woodcock Reading Mastery Test.* Circle Pines, MN: American Guidance Service.

Woodcock, R.W. & Johnson, M.B. (1989). Woodcock-Johnson Psyco-Educational Battery-Revised. Allen, TX: Developmental Learning Materials

Yap, K. O., & Enoki, D. Y. (1988). *LEP student achievement: Some pertinent variables and policy implications.* Paper presented at the annual meeting of the American Educational Research Association, New Orleans, LA.

Yeung, A. E., Marsh, H. W., & Suliman, R. (2000). Can two tongues live in harmony? Analysis of the National Education Longitudinal Study of 1988 (NELS88) longitudinal data on the maintenance of home language. *American Educational Research Journal, 37*(4), 1001–1026.

Zirkel, P. A. (1972). *An evaluation of the effectiveness of selected experimental bilingual education programs in Connecticut.* Unpublished doctoral dissertation, University of Connecticut.

V

Student Assessment

19

Synthesis: Language and Literacy Assessment

Georgia Earnest García, Gail McKoon, and Diane August

The literature on language and literacy assessment reviewed in Part V covers a broad variety of measures that are used to evaluate students' oral language, reading, and writing performance—some employed as national, state, district, and classroom assessments to assess student performance and others developed for research purposes.

The following research questions are addressed in Part V:

1. What assessments do states and school districts use with language-minority students for identification, program placement, and reclassification purposes? Are the assessments used for these purposes useful and appropriate?
2. What do we know about alternative assessments of oral English proficiency and literacy?
3. What first- and second-language vocabulary and wide-scale literacy assessments for language-minority students have been investigated? What does the research tell us about accommodations for language-minority students taking these assessments?
4. Are the assessments currently used to predict the literacy performance of language-minority students (including those with reading disabilities) useful and appropriate?
5. What research has focused on language and literacy measures or methods developed for the identification of language-minority students eligible for special education services (including speech and hearing)?
6. What standardized (commercial) and researcher-developed oral proficiency, literacy, and literacy-related assessments have been used by the researchers whose work is reviewed throughout this volume?

Appropriate, valid, and reliable language and literacy assessments are keys to understanding the literacy development of language-minority students, improving classroom instruction, and policy and research purposes.

We begin this synthesis chapter by presenting pertinent background information. We then describe the methodology of our review. Next, we summarize the findings of the literature on the research questions addressed by our review. After identifying methodological issues, we recommend directions for future research. Chapter 20 follows and is the full review of the research.

BACKGROUND

A myriad of concerns have been raised by educators and researchers about the use of language and literacy assessments with language-minority students. A major concern is that the validity and reliability of assessments administered in English to language-minority students may be seriously compromised when the students are not sufficiently proficient in English (American Educational Research Association, American Psychological Association, & National Council on Measurement in Education, 1999; Durán, 1989). Concerns related to possible cultural and linguistic biases and the validity and reliability of tests used with language-minority students are discussed later. In addition, because of the influence of the No Child Left Behind (NCLB) Act on district and state policy, the provisions of the law that relate to English-language learners are described.

Linguistic and Cultural Bias

Assessments developed for monolingual populations generally do not take into account important issues related to English-language learners' second-language status (García, 1994; García & Pearson, 1994; Valdés & Figueroa, 1994). For example, as a result of differences in receptive and productive development in the second language, English-language learners may comprehend more than they can demonstrate when their test responses are in the second language (Lee, 1986). Second-language learners may need more time than monolingual students to complete written tests because they tend to process text in a second language more slowly (Mestre, 1984). They may know different vocabulary items in each of their languages, making it difficult to assess their total vocabulary knowledge with an assessment in only one of the languages (García, 1994; García & Pearson, 1994). They may have well-developed cognitive skills that underlie comprehension, such as integrating background knowledge with textual knowledge or drawing inferences across propositions, but they cannot apply these skills to text because their limited English proficiency interferes with their accessing enough of the text's meaning to apply the skills. Similarly, assessments developed for and/or normed on the dominant group in a society may pose issues of cultural bias for language-minority students from different ethnic/racial/national groups and socioeconomic classes (García & Pearson, 1994; Mercer, 1979; Samuda, 1975).

Validity and Reliability

Knowing when English-language learners are proficient enough in English to participate in English assessments is an issue that still needs to be addressed (Figueroa, 1989; Hakuta & Beatty, 2000). When English-language learners are in the process of acquiring English, written tests in English may pose reading challenges that interfere with the assessment of the content they have learned, making their test scores invalid as indicators of content knowledge or achievement (Butler & Stevens, 2001). One response to this concern has been the use of testing accommodations with English-language learners. As reported in a recent National Academy of Sciences report (Koenig & Bachman, 2004), a review of research on the effects of accommodations on the wide-scale test performance of English-language learners (Sireci & Scarpati, 2003) found that "the most common accommodations studied were linguistic modification, provision of a dictionary or bilingual dictionary, provision of dual-language booklets, extended time, and oral administration. Most studies examined the effects of multiple accommodations" (p. 89). With regard to studies that examine linguistic modifications, Abedi, Hofstetter, Baker, and Lord (2001) claim that this type of accommodation was the most effective method in reducing the score gap between English-language learners and native English speakers. However, Sireci and Scarpati (2003) point out that in this study, "the gap was narrowed because native-English speakers scored worse on the linguistically modified test, not because the English language learners performed substantially better" (p. 65). In a study by Abedi (2001), significant but small gains were noted for eighth-grade but not for fourth-grade students. Sireci and Scarpati indicate that Abedi explains this finding by hypothesizing that, "with an increase in grade level, more complex language may interfere with content-based assessment" (p. 13), and "in earlier grades, language may not be as great a hurdle as it is in the later grades" (p. 14). With regard to research on other accommodations provided for English-language learners, Sireci et al. note that providing English-language learners with customized dictionaries or glossaries appeared to improve their performance (e.g., Abedi, Lord, Boscardin, & Miyoshi, 2001). Two studies available on dual-language test booklets revealed no gains (Anderson, Liu, Swierzbin, Thurlow, & Bielinski, 2000; García et al., 2000).

Another issue that has been raised is the appropriateness of testing English-language learners with standardized tests that are normed on populations that do not represent the group being tested (Butler & Stevens, 2001; García & Pearson, 1994; Mercer, 1979; Valdés & Figueroa, 1994). A number of researchers have pointed out that few English-language learners, if any, are included in the norming samples for standardized tests developed in English (Butler & Stevens, 2001; García & Pearson, 1994). According to the Standards for Educational and Psychological Testing (American Education Research Association, American Psychological Association, & National Council on Measurement in Education, 1999), serious test bias occurs when measures normed on native English speakers are used with English-language learners:

> test norms based on native speakers of English either should not be used with individuals whose first language is not English or such individuals' test

results should be interpreted as reflecting in part current level of English proficiency rather than ability, potential, aptitude, or personality characteristics or symptomatology. (p. 91)

The standards further state that when a test is

administered in the same language to all examinees in a linguistically diverse population, the test user should investigate the validity of the score interpretations for test takers believed to have limited proficiency in the language of the test [because] the achievement, abilities, and traits of examinees who do not speak the language of the test as their primary language may be seriously mismeasured by the test. (p. 118)

As is the case for English assessments normed on populations that do not include English-language learners, native-language assessments may not have appropriate norming samples either (American Educational Research Association, American Psychological Association, & National Council on Measurement in Education, 1999; August & Hakuta, 1997), such as a standardized test in Spanish normed on students from Mexico City or on Cuban American students from Miami that is administered to Mexican American students in the United States.

Assessment of English-language learners in their native language raises other issues as well. Hakuta and Beatty (2000) note that assessing a student in the native language may mean providing the student with a *parallel version* of the English assessment or providing an assessment in the native language that focuses on the "same or closely related constructs as the original English version of the [assessment]" (p. 25). However, developing native-language assessments that are equivalent or parallel versions of English assessments is not an easy task (American Educational Research Association, American Psychological Association, & National Council on Measurement in Education, 1999; August & Hakuta, 1997; García & Pearson, 1994). For example, translated vocabulary items may differ in their word frequency or difficulty from the original items and, as Olmeda (1981) explains, "may exhibit psychometric properties substantially different from those of the original English items" (p. 1083). Deciding which English-language learners should take a particular assessment in the native language is also tricky because it is difficult to determine language dominance, and English-language learners may acquire some concepts in one language and others in the other language (García & Pearson, 1994). Some states address these concerns by providing side-by-side versions of tests in English and the native language, a technique used successfully for math assessment in Oregon (Durán, Brown, & McCall, 2002).

A final validity issue relates to language proficiency measures (August & Hakuta, 1997; Durán, 1989; García, 1994). Language proficiency measures typically sample students' knowledge and use of a particular language. They often include skills considered necessary for oral language proficiency, such as those related to phonology, morphology, syntax, and lexicon. However, they do not necessarily measure students' ability to use the language in real-life settings or for academic purposes. Moreover, many language proficiency measures were developed to determine the appropriate placement for English-language learners, rather than to track their progress in component skills over time. In recent years, both researchers and policymakers have called for language proficiency measures that assess how well students can perform and learn in academic classrooms where instruction is conducted in English and that allow for assessing development over time.

Assessment and Educational Policy

The standards-based accountability reform movement, with its emphasis on high academic standards and high expectations for all students and the use of assessments to measure students' attainment of such standards, has led to mandates to include English-language learners in assessments sooner and more broadly than in the past. In the policy context when this research review was undertaken, the NCLB Act holds states and school districts accountable for all students by requiring English-language learners to be assessed and assessment data to be disaggregated to show how well specific groups of students, including English-language learners, are meeting state and district standards. Testing requirements under Title I and Title III of NCLB require school districts and states to provide for an annual assessment of English proficiency in the four domains of reading, writing, speaking, and listening. Title III also requires the assessment of comprehension. The Title III integrated system of standards and assessments requires that language proficiency assessments are aligned with state language proficiency standards, which in turn are aligned with state academic content and achievement standards. In addition, Title I stipulates that

> States may not exempt [limited English-proficient] students from participating in the State assessment system in their first three years of attending schools in the United States. Inclusion in the State academic assessment system must immediately begin when the student enrolls in school. No exemptions are permitted based on level of English proficiency. (U.S. Department of Education, 2003, p. 19)

However, for English-language learners who have been in U.S. schools for fewer than 3 years, district personnel may provide accommodations that are appropriate linguistic accommodations and/or use an assessment in the students' native language that is aligned with the state content and achievement standards. English-language learners who have attended schools in the United States for at least 3 consecutive years (except those living in Puerto Rico) are subject to the same types of assessments, including literacy assessments, in English as native-English-speaking students.

In specific situations, districts may use an assessment in a language other than English for up to 2 additional years. Moreover, schools are required to show adequate yearly progress (AYP) in making sure that all students achieve academic proficiency in order to close the achievement gap. NCLB requires states to include the academic achievement results of all students, including English-language learners, in AYP calculations.

In 2004, then Secretary Paige announced two new policies related to the implementation of NCLB. The new policies allow limited-English-proficient (LEP) students who are new arrivals to us public schools during their first year of enrollment in U.S. schools to have the option of taking the reading/language arts content assessment in addition to the English-language proficiency assessment. Previously, they were required to take both assessments. They are required to take the mathematics assessment, with accommodations as appropriate. In addition, states are now permitted to exclude for 1 year results from the mathematics and, if given, the reading/language arts content assessments in AYP calculations. The other new policy change allows states, for the purpose of AYP calculations for up to 2 years, to include in the LEP subgroup students who have attained English proficiency and are no longer considered LEP according to the district/state's definition. According to the press release (U.S. Department of Education, 2004), the intent of this change is to "give states the flexibility to allow schools and local education agencies (LEAs) to get credit for improving English language proficiency from year to year" (p. 1).

METHODS

Our review of the literature on student assessment includes studies that evaluate and measure students' oral proficiency (listening and speaking), as well as their reading and writing proficiencies. As with other chapters in this review, studies were identified through electronic searches. We also identified technical reports on the language and literacy assessment of English-language learners by contacting the National Center for Research on Evaluation, Standards, and Student Testing; examining the references cited in studies already included in our database; and reviewing the references cited in key syntheses and theoretical works on the assessment of language-minority children. Finally, we performed a manual search of articles on assessment in the *National Reading Conference Yearbook*.

The initial search resulted in 115 peer-reviewed journal articles and technical reports. After reading them, we removed 77 from consideration because they were not empirical, did not directly relate to language or literacy assessment, did not focus on the appropriate population of language-minority children, or did not meet the agreed-on quality control standards for the research. Our review, reported in chapter 20 and summarized here, focuses on findings from the remaining 37 studies. This number of studies is remarkably small given the importance of assessing language-minority children's command of language, literacy, and content knowledge in their first language and in English.

As described in chapter 1, we conducted a qualitative analysis of the empirical literature. The 38 studies do not lend themselves to meta-analysis because there are at most three or four studies on any one issue, and within an issue the studies vary in the questions addressed and the methods used.

SUMMARY OF EMPIRICAL FINDINGS

Our review of research on the assessment of literacy with language-minority students was organized into six topics, covering all 38 studies that met our inclusion criteria.

Assessments to Identify, Place, and Reclassify Language-Minority Students

First, although educators rely on assessment data to identify, place, and reclassify English- language learners as fully English proficient, research conducted on the different types of assessments commonly used for these purposes is extremely limited. Only one national survey reports on the methods used across the states and governing bodies. Second, researchers found that the Language Assessment Scales (LAS; De Avila & Duncan, 1990; Duncan & De Avila, 1988), a commonly used measure of oral language proficiency, should not be used to predict students' academic language proficiency in English because in their studies it did not predict how well English-language learners performed on reading or content area assessments in English. Additionally students' academic and reading performance in Spanish, their oral English development, and teachers' judgments should have been taken into account in determining academic proficiency in English. However, given the small number of studies, considerably more research is needed to validate these methods.

Alternative Assessments of Oral Language Proficiency and Literacy

Research related to alternative assessments of oral proficiency used cloze tests and language observation to assess students' actual use of language to communicate in social or academic contexts. Alternative measures of literacy emphasized the development of cloze tests, curriculum-based measures, and sentence verification tests that could be used by educational personnel in lieu of time-consuming tests such as standardized reading tests. Findings indicate these alternative assessments are promising but additional research is necessary however, because of the limited number of studies and, in the case of cloze tests, because the extent to which the usefulness, reliability, and validity of such tests depends on the choice of items is unknown.

Vocabulary and Wide-Scale Literacy Assessments

Four groups of researchers investigated the use of both the English (PPVT, PPVT–R; Dunn & Dunn, 1981) and Spanish (Test de Vocabulario en Imágenes Peabody [TVIP]–H) (Dunn, Padilla, Lugo, & Dunn, 1986) versions of the Peabody Picture Vocabulary Test (PPVT) with samples of language-minority children in the United States who spoke Spanish (Cuban American, Mexican American) and Native American languages (predominantly Yaqui). In all four studies, the language-minority children scored lower than corresponding samples of native-English-speaking children on the PPVT. In a Canadian study, a sample of English-language learners also performed lower on the PPVT–R than a sample of native-English-speaking children. Three groups of researchers identified test bias issues related to using the PPVT or word frequency tests in English and Spanish with Spanish-speaking students. For example, findings from two studies suggest that the underlying structure of both the PPVT and the TVIP–H, which emphasizes increasingly difficult and less frequent words and the stopping of the test after a student has missed a certain number of words in a row, may constitute a bias when the order of the words is not based on a word frequency measure from the student's first language or cultural group. These issues may make it inappropriate to use these tests to assess language-minority students' vocabulary knowledge. However, a few researchers have found that when they tested the use of an English version of the PPVT with small samples of Spanish speakers, psychometric properties, such as temporal stability and internal item consistency, indicated that the measure was reliable. Finally, versions of the PPVT may appropriately estimate how well language-minority children's recognition of mainstream English vocabulary matches that of native-English-speaking students.

A second set of studies focuses on the use of wide-scale and standards-based reading tests in English with language-minority students in the United States— how the English proficiency of language-minority students affects their performance on content area assessments and testing accommodations. When traditional psychometric properties are examined relative to the reliability of wide-scale English reading tests used with language-minority students, the tests typically are found to be reliable. However, the studies reported in this section also substantiate a concern that language factors may be a source of construct-irrelevant variance in standardized reading achievement tests, affecting the construct validity of the tests.

Assessments Used to Predict the Literacy Performance of Language-Minority Students

Five groups of researchers tested how well literacy measures in English predicted the English reading performance of language-minority students. Some studies have found that measures of phonological and graphophonological processing, including letter naming, letter naming fluency, rapid letter naming, and phonological awareness, were good predictors of English reading performance within the English-language learner population. Because some of the researchers did not control for students' oral English proficiency or examine their native literacy development or performance on the same measures, however, the findings of these studies must be qualified. Nonetheless, the fact that others obtained similar results with English measures adapted for English-language learners suggests that these findings should be tested by other researchers, taking into account students' oral English proficiency and native-language literacy development. Although several of the studies we reviewed used criterion measures to determine low performers or students with reading disabilities, the finding of one study that some low-performing Hispanic students substantially improved their reading performance with instruction suggests that additional longitudinal studies are needed to test the predictors against language-minority students' actual reading performance.

Finally, one group of researchers focused on teachers' identification of students considered at risk for dropping out of school. Their findings suggest that teachers' nominations may be more reliable when they are asked to respond thoughtfully to specific criteria, rather than express their opinions spontaneously. Because teacher judgment plays a significant role in the education of language-minority students, additional research is needed to explore its use as an assessment tool.

Measures and Methods Used to Identify Students Eligible for Special Services

Another important issue is the accurate identification of language-minority students with language and/or learning difficulties. Studies addressing this issue have focused on the types of language proficiency assessments school psychologists have reported using for the placement of language-minority children in special education, the identification of language-minority children with language disorders, and the identification of learning disabilities in older language-minority children. Researchers voice concerns about the measures that some school psychologists report using most frequently because they sample only students' receptive vocabulary acquisition, providing a limited view of their language development. One study found that teacher nominations combined with ratings of academic skills were better predictors of the students with reading disabilities, as determined by their standardized reading scores, than teachers' nominations alone.

Three groups of researchers who investigated the identification of language disorders in language-minority children emphasize the importance of conducting assessments in the children's home language. Although none of the researchers actually tested a protocol that could easily be used by speech and language pathologists in the field, Restrepo (1998) found that parents' report of a speech-language problem, the number of errors students make in spontaneous speech, and the length of their clauses appear to provide some direction for such an effort.

Little research has focused on identifying older language-minority students with learning difficulties. Weak story retelling schema may be one way to identify language-minority students with learning disabilities; however, students' low performance may be associated with low English proficiency rather than a learning disability. Miramontes (1987) also found that the limited English proficiency of middle-school students in her sample may result in overidentifying these students as learning disabled.

Assessments Used in the Research Included in This Volume

To aid future research on English-language learners, this volume describes the assessments used in the research reviewed in the report. Table 20.1 provides the frequencies of use of various literacy assessments by literacy component. The searchable database that accompanies this volume provides information on all the measures used in each study. Across all the studies included in chapters 3 to 20, the greatest number of measures focused on reading comprehension (79). This was followed by phonemic and phonological awareness (77) and vocabulary (51). The fewest measures addressed pragmatics (1), morphology (3), and discourse (2). Interestingly, with regard to frequency of use, there were more researcher-developed (240 English measures and 65 Spanish measures) than standardized/commercial measures (110 in English and 41 in Spanish); many studies relied solely on researcher-developed measures to assess students' language and literacy skills. In the research studies reviewed, few state standards/accountability measures were used in either Spanish (10) or English (28). Of note is that few researchers report information on the validity or reliability of the researcher-developed measures used in the studies. An effort should be made in future research to determine this information. Moreover, as mentioned earlier, studies should include standardized measures of literacy to help benchmark results obtained from researcher-developed instruments.

METHODOLOGICAL ISSUES

A major concern is the limited number of studies that address any given research question. For example, only four studies examined whether a measure used for placement decisions was useful or appropriate. None of these studies was of sufficient magnitude to allow decisive or comprehensive conclusions to be drawn.

In addition, the studies do not represent sufficiently high-quality research to permit firm conclusions about the validity of specific assessment instruments for language-minority children, the reliability of those instruments, or their contextual or cultural appropriateness. First, many of the 37 studies reviewed are essentially pilot efforts; the number of subjects or the number of items is too small for us to assume that the findings are generalizable. Second, the data for some of the studies are reported in summary forms that do not allow scrutiny of essential features. Third, in many studies, the assessment items are not reported, so that independent evaluation of the assessment instrument on which the study focused is not possible. The number of variables that are potentially relevant to the acquisition and assessment of English skills is extremely large; thus, it is necessary that items be reported, both for evaluation and replication by other researchers. Overall, there has been little effort to achieve replicability, an essential aspect of high-quality research. For example, researchers have not typically included in their studies the measures used by other researchers addressing similar research questions. It is only with such efforts that the construction of a base of high-quality research is possible and the systematic development of a body of research findings advanced.

RECOMMENDATIONS FOR FUTURE RESEARCH

Methodological Recommendations for Improving the Research Base

Our first recommendation is that future empirical investigations of language and literacy assessments for language-minority students incorporate necessary expertise from a range of disciplines: linguistics, cognitive psychology, education, and psychometrics. Linguists are necessary because of the importance of assessing language-minority children's knowledge of aspects of first and second languages adequately and accurately. For example, the phonology and word structures of English and how they map to those of other languages are complex issues that have been the subject of considerable research in linguistics. In turn, whether and how these structures are projected in the human lexicon has been the subject of a great deal of research in psychology. In cases where the assessments are used to assess instruction and development within classroom contexts, educators can help ensure that they will be useful and easy to administer. Psychometric expertise helps ensure that the assessments are valid and reliable.

The second recommendation is that, when reporting on their studies, researchers publish an appendix containing the items used in the assessment measures they investigated (or archive them on an accessible Web site). Without complete knowledge of the materials used in a study, other researchers cannot evaluate the study findings with respect to potentially relevant variables not considered by the original investigators, nor can they carry out the replications essential for building a strong body of empirical knowledge.

Our third recommendation is that researchers make every effort to include in their experimental designs at least some of the same measures used by other researchers to investigate similar questions and found to be valid and reliable with language-minority students. For example, if earlier work on reading comprehension used a particular assessment, future research should include it along with whatever other measures are important to the study. We reiterate here the necessity for a systematic, progressive accumulation of empirical findings.

Substantive Recommendations for Improving the Research Base

In research on assessment, it is essential to address two different but related goals: (a) the use of assessments to understand the development of first- and second-language oral proficiency and literacy, and (b) the use of assessments for making placement and policy decisions, such as choice of learning environment. With regard to the former, research should provide an array of demonstrably valid and reliable measures that characterize exactly what a language-minority child knows and can do—including knowledge of all facets of English, from oral proficiency through orthographic, phonological, morphological, and lexical knowledge to sentence and discourse comprehension—with an appropriate range of developmental points. The measures should also be designed to measure English proficiency within academic contexts. Such measures would provide the information needed to monitor student's development, assess instructional techniques and conduct sound research. The development effort would benefit from replication across minority languages. Wherever possible, it would be beneficial to explore what existing measures allow accurate, practical decisions about language and literacy development. The searchable database, which describes the assessments used in this review, is a good starting place to locate such assessments. In the following sections, we outline some of the requirements and considerations that would define a research agenda in this area. A second area of research is how such assessments should be used to make placement and policy decisions.

Assessing Language Proficiency and Literacy. To assess a language-minority child's language, literacy, and content knowledge, we need to understand the linguistic and psychological structures he or she has in both the minority and majority languages and how they interact. We also need to understand how and to what degree the linguistic and psychological structures differ for fluent bilingual and fluent monolingual speakers. Interactions can take place at many levels—from the specific constructs of languages (e.g., phonemes, words) to abstract linguistic structures to metacognitive processes. See Part I of this volume for a discussion of literacy development, and see Part II for a discussion of cross-language relationships. We also need to understand the influence of culture. The studies reported in Part III make a modest case for the proposition that language-minority students' literacy achievement improves when they read or otherwise use culturally familiar materials.

Even a simple task such as assessing children's ability to read a list of individual words aloud requires knowing enough about the similarities and differences between the two languages involved to take into account, for example, which English words will be especially difficult for a child acquiring English and which will be especially easy and how this compares with ease or difficulty for fluent monolinguals. Moreover, accurate understanding of the similarities and differences between the two languages and between bilingual and monolingual language processing is essential if lists of words that will assess the whole range of the child's ability are to be constructed.

Vocabulary is also an important component of oral language proficiency and literacy for second-language learners and is crucial to reading comprehension. For vocabulary tests normed on monolingual populations, the frequency ordering of words may be different for second-language learners than for the norming population. Whether or how language-minority children's performance on vocabulary tests can be mapped to monolingual academic literacy performance is an important question. There have been no studies of sufficient breadth to address these issues convincingly.

In cognitive psychology, the last 20 years of research have shown that language comprehension is not a unidimensional construct. Advances in theory have come to depend on several structural dimensions. One is the distinction among what a reader or listener brings to the comprehension process, what the text or discourse brings, and what the reader or listener takes away. Another is the distinction between the processes in which the reader or listener engages during comprehension and the products of those processes that can be remembered later. Still another is the distinction among various levels of information that a reader or listener may comprehend, including the words in which information was expressed, the ideas embodied in those words, and a mental model of how those ideas could combine into a real-life situation. We assume that the goal of educating language-minority children is for them to comprehend the second language as effectively as a fluent speaker does. What it means for a fluent speaker to comprehend, however, cannot be defined outside the context of the overall propositional structure of a discourse and the context of the comprehender's purposes. A fluent first-language reader is likely to remember the highest level propositions in a discourse better than lower level, detailed propositions, and he or she will not draw inferences and structural connections that require more than passive automatic processing unless there is some purpose for learning the information (e.g., real-life applications or exams). The types of inferences needed to connect pieces of information and the types of surface structures with which meanings and structures are signaled may differ between second and first languages. Outcomes on measures of comprehension are certainly influenced by proficiency in first- and second-language proficiency and literacy. See Parts I and II of this volume for additional discussion of this topic. They are influenced by cultural differences as well (see Part III). Thus, in developing robust measures of comprehension for second-language literacy, contributions from cognitive psychology, linguistics, and disciplines that examine sociocultural aspects of learning are needed.

Assessment for Making Placement and Policy Decisions. More research is needed to document and evaluate methods used at the district level to classify, track, and reclassify English-language learners as well as assess them for accountability. What types of assessments do districts use, singly or in combination, to place students in bilingual education or ESL instruction? What types of assessments do they use to identify language-minority students eligible for services, such as Title I and special education? How do they determine when students are ready to be placed in all-English instruction without special support? What methods and standards are used to determine whether English-language learners are retained in grade, can graduate from high school, or be tested solely in English? Are the instruments used valid and reliable across the range of types of students with whom they are used? How well do the assessments currently employed actually predict the literacy performance of language-minority students?

For example, experts in second-language acquisition often warn that data from oral language proficiency measures in English should not be the only basis for exit decisions (August & Hakuta, 1997; Collier, 1995; Cummins, 1984). Drawing on Cummins' theoretical distinction between conversational and academic language skills (Collier & Thomas, 1989; Cummins, 1981, 1984), they recommend that decisions about reclassification and assessment policies be based on measures of students' academic language proficiency in English.[1] Considerable future research is needed to develop valid and reliable measures. Especially important is the question of whether any single measure can provide sufficient information about all the component skills needed by an English-language learner to do well in an unsupported English classroom or on English content area assessments without accommodations. We stress that research must specifically examine the relationship between any measure used for placement decisions or policy decisions and the performance of children who are assessed on the basis of that measure.

One goal of assessing English-language learners' literacy performance is the identification of students who have special needs in learning to read beyond those imposed by learning a second language. Identification of such problems as dyslexia is difficult when assessments are administered in English and English-language learners' preliteracy skills in that language are minimal or nonexistent. Educators are required by law to assess these children in their first language, but there have been no broad or longitudinal studies to enable firm conclusions about what first-language assessments are effective for diagnosing various kinds of impairments. Although several studies explored this issue by examining whether such indexes as knowledge of letter names, knowledge of letter–sound correspondences, and teacher judgments can adequately predict which children will have severe or continued difficulty, all were limited in their sample of students, the measures chosen for investigation, and the conclusions that can be drawn from their findings. In future research, a wide range of measures needs to be examined across a broad spectrum of abilities (in English and in the first language), and the predictive validity of these measures must be examined longitudinally.

---

[1]Academic language proficiency in English refers to students' ability to read and write in English, learn from English text, and comprehend and participate in classroom instruction on content area topics conducted in an all-English classroom.

An Illustrative Example

The complexity of the measurement problem is well illustrated in the study of Holm, Dodd, Stow, and Pert (1999). Their goal was to identify bilingual language-minority children with speech disorders in language production. To this end, the children's language production abilities were compared with those of normal children, both bilingual and monolingual, in both their first language and English. The comparison was carried out with a test in which the children were asked to name pictured objects aloud. A full comparison required that the words to be spoken capture a range of similarities and differences in the phonological and word structures of the first language and English, so the word lists were constructed only after a careful linguistic investigation of the similarities and differences in fluent adult speech. The resulting list of words was pilot tested and refined to ensure that the test givers who worked with the children could score their pronunciations accurately.

The results of this study show the importance of measuring language structures in both the native language and English and comparing them with the structures of fluent monolingual children. The distributions of the speech errors made by the bilingual children were different in the two languages. When speaking English, for example, the most frequent error the children made involved cluster reduction; when speaking their native language, the most frequent error involved voicing. Moreover, the frequency orderings of errors for these children speaking English were different from those for monolingual children speaking English, and they were different for the bilingual children speaking their native language and monolingual children speaking the native language. These differences demonstrate that the bilingual children had a different structure of phonology for their first language than for English, and that both of these structures differed from those of monolingual children.

The essential point for the present purpose is that accurate information about these children's speech production abilities could be obtained only in the context of knowledge of first- and second-language phonological systems. The study of Holm et al. (1999) also drives home one of our methodological recommendations: Measurement of language-minority children's language abilities requires linguistic expertise. This study also illustrates a second methodological recommendation for future research: that all the items used in experiments be published. Given all that is and is not known about the phonological and word structures of English and other languages, it is possible (even likely) that any experiment, regardless of how carefully designed, will overlook variables related to its items that could confound the results and conclusions drawn from those results. Publication of the items used would enable other researchers to consider possible uncontrolled variables, as well as variables that might be discovered to be significant at later points in time; it would also allow other researchers to attempt to replicate the experiment.

20

Language and Literacy Assessment of Language-Minority Students

Georgia Earnest García, Gail McKoon, and Diane August

Many of the uses of assessment are common to all students, but some uses are unique to language-minority students (August & Hakuta, 1997). Common purposes of language and literacy assessments are to inform instruction, monitor and compare student performance, and identify students eligible for special services (e.g., Title I, speech and hearing services, special education, enrollment in accelerated or gifted programs). Unique purposes of language and literacy assessments for language-minority students include the identification of students with limited English proficiency (LEP), placement in instructional programs designed for English-language learners (e.g., bilingual education and programs in English as a second language [ESL]), monitoring or evaluation of English-language development, and decisions on when English-language learners should be reclassified as fully proficient.

The research questions addressed in this chapter focos on assessments states and school districts use with language-minority students for identification, program placement, and reclassification purposes; alternative assessments of oral language proficiency and literacy; first- and second-language vocabulary and wide-scale literacy assessments for language-minority students; the assessments used to predict the literacy performance of language-minority students (including those with reading disabilities); language and literacy measures or methods developed for the identification of language-minority students eligible for special education services (including speech and hearing); and standardized (commercial) and researcher-developed oral proficiency, literacy, and literacy-related assessments used by the researchers whose work is reviewed throughout this volume.

ASSESSMENTS TO IDENTIFY, PLACE, AND
RECLASSIFY LANGUAGE-MINORITY STUDENTS

In this section, we review the findings of studies related to the first part of research question 1: What assessments do states and school districts use with language-minority students for eligibility identification, program placement, and reclassification purposes?

Kindler (2002) presents information on the types of assessments used by states in the United States and other governing bodies with English-language learners for placement and exit decisions. Kindler's report is based on a national survey of the 50 states and 8 other governing bodies (e.g., American Samoa, Guam, Puerto Rico).[1] According to Kindler, 94% of the states and other governing bodies indicated that they used a commercial language proficiency test in English to help identify limited-English proficient students eligible for bilingual education or ESL services. The most commonly used were the Language Assessment Scales (LAS, 85%; De Avila & Duncan, 1990; Duncan & De Avila, 1988), IDEA Language Proficiency Tests (IPT, 70%; IDEA, 1978, 1994), and Woodcock–Muñoz Language Survey (52%; Woodcock & Muñoz–Sandoval, 1993). More than three fourths of the states/governing bodies indicated that they used other sources of information, in addition to commercial language proficiency tests, to identify limited-English proficient students. These included home language surveys, information from parents, teacher observations, student records, teacher interviews, referrals by educational personnel, student grades, language samples, and/or a commercial achievement test. More than one third of the states/governing bodies reported taking into account students' performance on a criterion-referenced achievement test, although no one such test was used by a majority of the states/governing bodies. For example, 30% reported using a state achievement test, 28% the Stanford Achievement Test (SAT 9; Stanford Achievement Test, 1996), 26% the Iowa Test of Basic Skills (ITBS; Hoover, Dunbar, & Frisbie, 2001), and 20% the Comprehensive Test of Basic Skills (CTBS; CTB McGraw-Hill, 1986b), Gates–MacGinitie Reading Tests (MacGinitie & MacGinitie, 1989), or Terra Nova (CTB McGraw-Hill, 1997, 2001). How districts across the states or states themselves, in cases where identification and placement decisions were at the state level, used the commercial assessments (oral language proficiency tests and/or achievement tests) in combination with these other types of indicators or what weight they gave to each type of assessment is not explained.

In terms of reclassification (the determination of which students previously classified as limited-English proficient are sufficiently proficient in English to participate fully in an all-English mainstream classroom; Kindler, 2002), most states reported using more than one form of assessment. More than half reported

---

[1]The volume is based on information submitted by all 50 states to the U.S. Department of Education for the 2000-2001 school year. It should be noted that these data are reported for students in public schools only.

using student grades, teacher observations, informal assessment, and student records for reclassification decisions, with more than one third using teacher interviews, information from parents, referrals, and home language surveys. Almost all respondents reported using a wide-scale assessment, although it is difficult to know from the data presented whether this assessment was an oral proficiency measure or a language arts measure administered in English. More than half of the respondents reported that they used an oral proficiency measure, such as the LAS, the IPT, or the Woodcock–Muñoz Language Survey. Other tests used for reclassification were the SAT 9 and Terra Nova; more than 25% of respondents stated that they used their state achievement tests. Again, no information was provided on how information from the different types of assessments and other indicators employed were combined to make reclassification decisions.

With data available from only one national survey (Kindler, 2002), too little information is available to report definitively on how states use assessments to identify, place, and reclassify English-language learners. Moreover, the data reported by Kindler are state-level summary data that do not capture the nuances of practice at the local education agency level; more specifically, the data do not specify how the local education agencies combine various assessments and other indicators to place and reclassify students. It is also important to note that these data were collected prior to the No Child Left Behind (NCLB) Act, which resulted in dramatic changes in states' assessment activities (see chap. 19). The NCLB requires states to measure the English proficiency of English-language learners in reading, writing, and listening and speaking, as well as to assess their content knowledge in reading/language arts and math; these legislative requirements have created changes in state and district student identification and reclassification procedures. In accordance with Section 3123 of the act, states are now required to submit a report on programs and activities carried out by the state education agency (SEA) every second year.

Language Proficiency Measures for Screening and Reclassification

In this section, we review the findings of studies addressing the second part of research question 1: Are the assessments used by states and school districts with language-minority students for eligibility identification, program placement, and reclassification purposes useful and appropriate?

Although educators rely on assessment data to identify, place, and reclassify English-language learners as fully English proficient, research conducted on the different types of assessments commonly used for these purposes is extremely limited. With regard to screening, Quinn (2001) found that using language measures developed for monolingual English speakers to screen English-language learners for special programming was of questionable validity. In a study that assessed the English-language development of English-language learners in Great Britain (ages 5–11, predominantly from South Asia), Quinn found that two screening instruments developed for native English speakers—the Test for

Reception of Grammar (TROG; Bishop, 1983) and the South Tyneside Assessment of Syntactic Structures (STASS; Armstrong & Ainley, 1986)—revealed no clear developmental patterns for the English-language learners. Also, the English-language learners did not appear to acquire the same structures in the same developmental sequence as the native English speakers. Quinn concludes that the receptive and expressive developmental patterns of the English-language learners were substantially different from those reported as typical of native-English-speaking students. Given these findings, Quinn recommends that if the TROG is used with English-language learners, researchers and educators should disregard the rules provided for discontinuing the test because they will not be appropriate.

A major problem faced by educational personnel is how to determine when English-language learners should exit bilingual education or ESL instruction and be placed in all-English classrooms with no additional support. In the preceding section, we pointed out that some states use English proficiency measures to assess students' readiness to enter mainstream English programs. Yet only three groups of researchers investigated the relationship between English-language learners' performance on English proficiency measures and on academic measures in English, generally reading achievement tests (Laesch & Van Kleeck, 1987; Stevens, Butler, & Castellón-Wellington, 2000) or how the various assessments used for program placement relate to each other and to student placement (Nadeau & Miramontes, 1988).

Some language proficiency measures, such as one version of the LAS, include brief assessments of students' English reading and writing performance in addition to assessments of their oral English proficiency. The use of these types of proficiency measures to determine when English-language learners should exit bilingual or ESL programs has been criticized because such measures do not fully demonstrate students' academic language proficiency in English (i.e., show students' ability to read and write in English, learn from English text, and comprehend and participate in classroom instruction on content area topics conducted in an all-English classroom). Two groups of researchers attempted to show the limitations of using language proficiency measures, such as the LAS, for reclassification purposes by analyzing how well English-language learners' scores on the LAS predicted their scores on an English standardized achievement test in reading or a content area such as social studies (Laesch & Van Kleeck, 1987; Stevens et al., 2000). The rationale for this type of comparison is that if students are considered to be fluent on the language proficiency measure, and if such a measure is used for reclassification purposes, then presumably the students should be able to perform at grade level on an academic (e.g., reading) or a content area (e.g., social studies) test in English. Stevens et al. (2000) also analyzed the type of language (everyday or academic) measured on the LAS as compared with that measured on a content area test in social studies. Both groups of researchers (Laesch & Van Kleeck, 1987; Stevens et al., 2000) conclude that the LAS should not be used to predict students' academic language proficiency in English because in their studies it did not predict how well English-language learners performed on reading or content area assessments in English. In a study focused on Mexican American third graders enrolled in a bilingual education classroom, Laesch and Van

Kleeck found that the students' scores on the LAS, on which they had been classified as fluent English speakers, did not correlate significantly with their performance in English on the CTBS, a standardized reading achievement test.[2] Although Stevens et al. report that the LAS reading test scores of seventh-grade English-language learners enrolled in sheltered social studies classes were correlated significantly ($r = .448$) with their performance on a standardized social studies test (the ITBS), the magnitude of the correlation was weak, with the LAS scores accounting for 20% of the ITBS variance. The researchers also noted that the LAS and the ITBS social studies tests differed in the types of vocabulary, linguistic structures, and content emphasized, with the LAS emphasizing everyday life and the ITBS emphasizing academic discourse, vocabulary, and topics.

Only Nadeau and Miramontes (1988) attempted to examine the interrelationships among a district's use of assessments (oral English proficiency assessment, criterion-referenced achievement tests [CRT] in Spanish and English, English and Spanish reading and vocabulary tests of the CTBS, and teacher judgment), the placement of Spanish-speaking students in a four-stage bilingual education program (K–6), and students' reclassification. However, the scope of the study findings was limited, in that the majority of the 2,100 students involved in the study were enrolled in Grades K to 3 and in the first stage of the program (they had been in the program for only 2 years). Nonetheless, the authors report that those students who scored high on the criterion-referenced and standardized tests in Spanish also scored high on similar measures in English ($r = .66$ between English and Spanish CTBS vocabulary; $r = .83$ between English and Spanish CTBS reading; and $r = .86$ between English CTBS reading and Spanish CTBS vocabulary). For students in Stage 1, there was a correlation of .535 between English oral language and Spanish reading scores. Finally, for Stage 2 students, there were moderate correlations between English oral language and CTBS Spanish vocabulary ($r = .50$), English oral language and CTBS Spanish reading ($r = .68$), CTBS English vocabulary and CTBS Spanish reading ($r = .64$), and English CRT reading and CTBS Spanish reading ($r = .57$). In addition, students who scored high on the oral English proficiency measures scored higher than the 50th percentile on the English CTBS tests. As a result of these two findings, the authors conclude that students' academic and reading performance in Spanish and their oral English development were key factors in their English academic performance and should have been taken into account in determining their reclassification. The authors conclude further that the teachers' determination of students' readiness for reclassification did correlate with the students' performance on academic measures, with higher performing students being recommended for reclassification. This finding suggests that teacher judgment also was a valid indicator of student readiness for placement in the all-English classroom.

---

[2]Hence, $r = .18$ for Total CTBS, $r = .22$ for CTBS Reading Total, $r = .11$ for CTBS Language Total, and $r = .22$ for CTBS Math Total.

ALTERNATIVE ASSESSMENTS OF ORAL
LANGUAGE PROFICIENCY AND LITERACY

In this section, we present the findings of studies addressing research question 2: What do we know about alternative assessments of oral language proficiency and literacy?

Most research related to alternative assessments of oral proficiency (Brown, 1983; Gómez, Parker, Lara-Alecio, Ochoa, & Gómez, 1996) used cloze tests to assess students' use of language to communicate in social or academic contexts. Alternative measures of literacy emphasized the development of low-cost alternatives (cloze tests, curriculum-based measures, and sentence verification tests) that could be used by educational personnel in lieu of time-consuming tests such as the LAS or standardized reading tests (Baker & Good, 1995; Baldauf, Dawson, Prior, & Propst, 1980; Laesch & Van Kleeck, 1987; Ozete, 1980; Royer & Carlo, 1991; Royer, Carlo, Carlisle, & Furman, 1991).

Oral Language Proficiency Measures

Research on oral language proficiency measures has examined alternatives to the commercial proficiency measures commonly used in the field (Brown, 1983; Gómez, Parker, Lara-Alecio, Ochoa, & Gómez, 1996) and the use of English developmental screening measures with English-language learners (Quinn, 2001). Many commercial oral language proficiency tests have been criticized because they do not assess students' actual use of the language to communicate in social or academic contexts. One researcher (Brown, 1983) tested how well a conversational cloze test (Hughes, 1981), in which every seventh word was deleted from transcripts of simulated authentic conversations, matched the oral interview performance of 30 English-language learners from diverse language backgrounds in Great Britain. Brown found that the correlation between students' performance on the conversational cloze tests and their participation in two 5-minute oral interviews was .80. Although he concludes that the conversational cloze test had the potential to provide a useful estimate of students' oral communication, that estimate appeared to be limited to conversational English (Cummins, 1981) within a narrow social context. No detailed information is available about the choice of the cloze items or the contents of the interviews.

Another group of researchers (Gómez et al., 1996) developed and tested a language observation procedure for assessing students' actual use of language to communicate in an academic setting. The authors document how fifth graders from six different bilingual classrooms in the United States used English in pairs to communicate while solving problems in mathematics. The authors report that their instrument allowed them to observe and evaluate seven social language attributes based on Hatch's (1992) definition of *social language* in terms of cognitive, linguistic, and social facets. Although their results correlate with those from the IDEA Language Proficiency Tests and may be consistent with second-language acquisition theory, the practicality of their instrument for classroom use and the generalizability of the instrument to other classrooms and observers are issues that need to be considered.

Literacy Measures

Several groups of researchers investigated the validity and reliability of alternative literacy measures that could be used by teachers to assess the literacy progress of language-minority students. Laesch and Van Kleeck (1987) and Baldauf et al. (1980) investigated the validity and reliability of cloze tests in which students filled in the missing words for a passage in which the fifth word had been deleted from every sentence. Laesch and Van Kleeck investigated how well Mexican American third graders performed on multiple-choice cloze tests, in which the students underlined their choice of a word to fill in the blank for a missing word; Baldauf et al. investigated how well secondary students from a range of language backgrounds in Australia and Papua New Guinea performed on matching cloze tests, in which the words deleted from a passage were presented in the margins of the text, and the students chose which words fit into which blanks. Correlations among the four cloze tests analyzed ranged from .66 to .83. Laesch and Van Keeck performed a qualitative analysis of students' errors and found that the errors corresponded with differences in the students' academic language proficiency. Baldauf et al. conducted a factor analysis of performance on their cloze test and standardized reading tests, and concluded that the tests were measuring the "same underlying construct" (p. 437); moreover, performance on the cloze test was significantly correlated with teachers' judgments of reading performance. These results must be viewed with caution, however, because the total numbers of students in the two studies were small, and the words deleted for the cloze tests are not specified by the authors. Further research is needed to support the possible use of cloze tests as alternatives to standardized tests and to determine exactly how deleted words should be chosen to provide an accurate, valid, and reliable measure.

Baker and Good (1995) tested another type of alternative literacy assessment that they believe teachers could easily develop, administer, and score: a curriculum-based measure of students' oral English reading fluency, in which the number of errors made by a student while reading aloud a passage randomly selected from the school curriculum for 1 minute is counted. They report that this measure was valid and reliable for both bilingual (Spanish–English) and native-English-speaking second graders. The native English speakers scored significantly higher than the Spanish-speaking students on the Stanford Diagnostic Reading Comprehension Test (SDRT; Karlsen & Gardner, 1985), but they did not score significantly higher on the oral reading fluency measure, although their mean score appeared to be higher. Baker and Good speculate that the Spanish-speaking students may have performed better on the oral reading fluency measure than on the SDRT because the fluency measure was based on the curriculum they were explicitly being taught (Reading Mastery Level II; Engelmann & Bruner, 1974). They also report that the Spanish-speaking students' scores on the SDRT and the fluency measure were significantly and positively correlated ($r = .59$), and that these correlations were of much greater magnitude than those between the students' scores on the English LAS and the fluency measure ($r = .26$). This finding led them to conclude that the curriculum-based oral reading fluency measure assessed students' English reading as measured by the SDRT rather than their oral English language development.

A limitation of the curriculum-based oral reading fluency measure tested by Baker and Good (1995), however, is that students' scores on repeated administration of the measure did not reflect continued progress for the native English speakers, suggesting a ceiling effect. Given that Baker and Good did not control for differences in the bilingual students' English proficiency, it is also possible that English proficiency was a confounding variable.

Royer et al. (Royer & Carlo, 1991; Royer et al., 1991) tested a sentence verification technique (SVT) designed to measure English reading ability for Spanish-speaking students enrolled in transitional bilingual education programs. Students responded to four types of test sentences after reading English passages: a veridical copy of a passage sentence; a paraphrased version of a passage sentence that did not change meaning; a sentence in which the use of one or two new words changed the meaning of the passage sentence; and a sentence in which the meaning and wording were similar to a passage sentence, but differed in theme, vocabulary, and syntax. In one study with Spanish-speaking students in Grade 5 (Royer et al., 1991) and in another with Spanish- and English-speaking students in Grades 3 to 6 (Royer & Carlo, 1991), a significant source of variance in the Spanish-speaking students' performance on the English SVT was their placement in a three- or four-stage transitional bilingual education program. This finding suggests that the SVT was able to differentiate English-language learners according to their English academic performance, as indicated by their program placement. Although concurrent validity with other reading or listening measures was not established for the SVT, the authors conclude that both the English and Spanish versions of the test provided valid and reliable measures of students' English and Spanish reading and language development that teachers could use to place the students in the appropriate curriculum. Moreover, similar to Baker and Good's (1995) curriculum-based oral reading fluency measure, the SVT is based on reading passages in the students' curriculum and, according to Royer et al., can easily be constructed, administered, and scored by teachers. However, the validity and reliability of the measure have not been established. In addition, a number of theoretical and empirical issues must be considered in choosing test sentences to determine what level of comprehension as well as kind of comprehension (e.g., integrating propositions within text or integrating textual propositions with background knowledge) is being tested, and these considerations would have to guide future research on the utility of this technique.

Only two groups of researchers investigated the use of low-cost assessments to monitor the Spanish reading performance of language-minority students (Ozete, 1980; Royer & Carlo, 1991). Ozete examined Spanish-speaking students' reading performance in Spanish with cloze tests. He investigated various types of cloze tests (the deletion of every fifth word vs. every eighth word; the inclusion of similar syntactic distractors vs. different syntactic distractors) and scoring procedures (exact word completions vs. semantically acceptable completions) with third- and sixth-grade Mexican American and Puerto Rican students enrolled in a dual-language maintenance program. For both groups, he found that students' reading levels in Spanish, as determined by their performance on a Spanish reading comprehension assessment and on the Spanish vocabulary and reading sections of the Language Assessment Battery (Board of Education of the City of New York, 1976), were significantly correlated with their performance on the cloze tests (ranging from .400–.691), and that test reliabilities were higher when cloze scoring was based on semantically acceptable words. There were no significant differences in the sixth graders' performance on the four types of cloze tests. Differences in the third graders' performance, however, led Ozete to recommend that third graders be given multiple-choice cloze tests that delete every fifth word rather than every eighth word and that include different rather than similar syntactic distractors.

In other work, Royer and Carlo (1991) worked with 49 native-Spanish-speaking sixth-grade students, conducting assessments at three different time points—February of Year 1, May of Year 1, and June of Year 2—for listening and reading comprehension skills. Researchers used the SVT tests in Spanish and English, in which students listened or read original sentences and were then presented with four possible representations of the target sentence: (a) original sentence, (b) paraphrases, (c) meaning changes, or (d) distractors. Examinees decided whether a test sentence had the same meaning as a sentence read or heard in a passage by responding "yes" to (a) or (b) and "no" to (c) or (d). Results show that, by the third data-collection point, Spanish and English reading comprehension correlated .18.

Like the research described earlier, Ozete's study suggests the need for further exploration of cloze tests for determining academic language proficiency. No firm conclusions can be drawn at this point, however, because the articles reporting on studies of the cloze procedure do not include sufficient information about the reading materials or the choices of deleted words.

VOCABULARY AND WIDE-SCALE LITERACY ASSESSMENTS

This section presents the results of studies addressing research question 3: What first- and second-language vocabulary and wide-scale literacy assessments for language-minority students have been investigated? What does the research tell us about accommodations made for language-minority students taking these assessments? We first examine studies investigating the performance of language-minority children on the PPVT (PPVT–R; Dunn & Dunn, 1981), commonly used in the field to assess language-minority students' receptive vocabulary knowledge. Next, we look at studies examining language-minority students' reading performance on wide-scale measures such as standardized and standards-based literacy tests, as well as content area tests that involve reading. Finally, we turn to research on testing accommodations.

English and Spanish Versions of the PPVT

All the research on standardized vocabulary tests has dealt with versions of the PPVT in English and/or Spanish (Argulewicz & Abel, 1984; Fernàndez, Pearson, Umbel, Oller, & Molinet-Molina, 1992; Geva et al., 2000; Sattler & Altes, 1984; Scruggs, Mastropieri, & Argulewicz, 1983; Tamayo, 1987). Both the English (PPVT, PPVT–R) and the Spanish (Test de Vocabulario en Imágenes

Peabody [TVIP–H]; Dunn, Padilla, Lugo, & Dunn, 1986) versions of the test are administered individually to children to estimate their receptive language development. The tests consist of words of decreasing frequency as established by word frequency lists in the respective languages. When students respond incorrectly (by not identifying the appropriate picture) to six items in a block of eight questions, the test administration is discontinued (Geva, Yaghoub-Zadeh, & Schuster, 2000). A limitation of the PPVT is that the "standardization sample did not include individuals [showing] evidence of . . . limited ability in English" (Bessai, 2001, p. 909). Current standards for assessment call for piloting and norming tests on the relevant populations.

Four groups of researchers (Argulewicz & Abel, 1984; Fernández et al., 1992; Sattler & Altes, 1984; Scruggs et al., 1983) investigated the use of English versions of the PPVT with samples of language-minority children in the United States who spoke Spanish (Cuban American, Mexican American) and Native American languages, predominantly Yaqui Indians. In all four studies, the language-minority children scored lower than corresponding samples of native-English-speaking children on the PPVT. In a Canadian study (Geva et al., 2000), a sample of English-language learners also performed lower on the PPVT–R than a sample of native-English-speaking children.

What the PPVT and TVIP actually measure has been a major focus of concern. Three groups of researchers identified test bias issues related to the use of the PPVT or other word frequency tests in English and Spanish with Spanish-speaking students. These bias issues may make it inappropriate to use such tests to assess language-minority students' conceptual and vocabulary knowledge (Fernández et al., 1992; Sattler & Altes, 1984; Tamayo, 1987). Findings from two studies (Fernández et al., 1992; Tamayo, 1987) suggest that the underlying structure of both the PPVT and the TVIP–H, which emphasizes increasingly difficult and less frequent words and the stopping of the test after a student has missed a certain number of words in a row, may constitute a bias when the order of the words is not based on a word frequency measure from the student's first language or cultural group. In a study with Spanish-speaking preschoolers in Miami (67% Cuban American), Fernández et al. (1992) found that when they divided the students into Spanish monolingual and Spanish–English bilingual groups based on other measures of their language proficiency, both groups scored lower than the respective norms on English and Spanish versions of the PPVT. In examining their total sample's performance on the English version of the PPVT, the authors found that the order of difficulty as reflected by the Miami sample's English performance was different from that reported for the norming sample, indicating potential test bias. The authors also conclude that assessing the vocabulary knowledge of preschool language-minority students in each language, and not across both languages, results in seriously underestimating the children's vocabulary knowledge when they have singlet words—words they may know in one language, but not the other. Preschoolers in their study knew both words only about half of the time but knew the word in one or the other language about a third of the time.

Sattler and Altes (1984) point out that the PPVT–R tends to underestimate the knowledge of Spanish-speaking children. They compared the performance of 31 Mexican American students who were either monolingual Spanish speakers or English–Spanish bilinguals on Spanish (translated) and/or English versions of the PPVT–R with their performance on a nonverbal measure of ability in Spanish (translated) or English, the McCarthy Scales of Children's Abilities (McCarthy, 1972). They did this because the students' performance on the McCarthy Scales showed that both groups were of normal intelligence, even though their performance on the PPVT–R in English and/or Spanish was below the 3rd percentile. The authors specifically warn that the PPVT–R, in English or Spanish, "should not be used to assess the intellectual capacities of Hispanic children" (p. 315).

Although the previous research studies indicate that the PPVT may underestimate students' word knowledge, the PPVT may appropriately estimate how well language-minority children's recognition of mainstream English vocabulary matches that of native-English-speaking students. In hierarchical regression analyses conducted by Geva et al. (2000), native English speakers' and English-language learners' scores on the PPVT were comparably predictive of word-identification skills. After controlling for age and nonverbal intelligence, the authors found that the PPVT–R explained between 4% and 6% of unique variance in word recognition for both English-language learners and native-English-speaking students. This is the case regardless of the students' language proficiency status. Some researchers found that when they tested the use of English versions of the PPVT with small samples of Spanish speakers, psychometric properties, such as temporal stability (Scruggs et al., 1983) and internal item consistency (Argulewicz & Abel, 1984), indicated that the measure was reliable.

Regardless of a study's purpose, however, using versions of the PPVT without acknowledging the language of instruction or the second-language status of participating students violates the standards (American Educational Research Association, American Psychological Association, & National Council on Measurement in Education, 1999) by excluding key information that may explain the students' test performance. For example, Argulewicz and Abel (1984) acknowledge that all the Mexican American students in their study came from homes in which Spanish was spoken, but the authors did not take the students' possible second-language status into account in interpreting their results.

Wide-Scale Reading Tests, Content Area Assessments, and Testing Accommodations

In this section, the first set of studies focuses on the use of wide-scale reading tests in English with language-minority students in the United States (Davidson, 1994; García, 1991) and the use of a state-level, standards-based reading test with this population (Pomplun & Omar, 2001). The second set of studies focuses on how the second-language status of language-minority students affects their performance on content area assessments (e.g., mathematics, science, social studies; Abedi, 2002; Davies, 1991; Stevens et al., 2000). Finally, we turn to one study that examines testing accommodations (Hannon & McNally, 1986). Although federal policy allows the use of testing accommodations with English-language learners with limited-English proficiency, only one study that met inclusion criteria for this volume looked specifically at such accommodations, and its focus was on a reading test not commonly used in the United States.

When traditional psychometric properties were examined in terms of the reliability of wide-scale English reading tests used with language-minority students (Davidson, 1994), the tests typically were found to be reliable, although variance discrepancies due to possible linguistic or cultural differences were noted. For example, Davidson reports that use of the 3 Rs reading test (Riverside Publishing Company, 1983) with Hispanic English-language learners enrolled in bilingual education/ESOL programs in Illinois (testing at one grade level below that of the students) did not violate two tests of norms appropriacy (reliability with published scores and internal trait structure). Nonetheless, the author was concerned about large variance differences in the Hispanic sample, which he thought might be related to language and reading skills.

García (1991) used what is known about second-language/bilingual reading and the test performance of language-minority students to design a study that specifically investigated linguistic and cultural test bias issues. In a study comparing the standardized reading test performance of Hispanic fifth and sixth graders with that of native-English-speaking fifth and sixth graders enrolled in the same classrooms, García identified linguistic and cultural factors that affected the test performance of the two groups of students differentially. She reports that the Spanish-speaking students' test performance was adversely affected by too little time to complete the test, less familiarity with the passage topics, less familiarity with the test vocabulary, and lower performance on test questions that required them to integrate background knowledge with test information. She speculates that the latter difficulty could have been due to the type of instruction received by the low- or average-performing Spanish speakers or to a tendency of some of the low- and average-scoring language-minority students not to diverge too far from the literal meaning of the English test passages.

When García (1991) gave a small sample of the Spanish-speaking students (of all reading levels) the opportunity to respond to test questions in Spanish and/or the questions were posed to them in oral Spanish, they revealed much greater comprehension of the English test passages than was indicated by their original test answers. She notes that when students had to respond in their second language, English, they sometimes successfully figured out the meanings of unfamiliar English vocabulary in the test passages, but answered the test questions incorrectly because of the paraphrasing that occurred in the test questions and items. Whereas other researchers, such as Davies (1991) and Abedi (2002), found that the linguistic complexity of test items adversely affected the performance of language-minority students on standardized mathematics tests, García reported that unfamiliar English vocabulary was the major linguistic factor adversely affecting the English reading test performance of the Hispanic students in her study.

Pomplun and Omar (2001) tested the extent to which a standards-based state reading test (with fewer, longer authentic passages than are normally found on standardized tests and some constructed responses) reliably predicted the performance of native-English-speaking students, English-language learners (Hispanic and Asian) and former English-language learners (Hispanic and Asian) in Kansas.[3] They report that the reliability of the standards-based state test was high for the English-language learners, but there were differences between the narrative scores of those students and native-English-speaking students that could be attributable to differences in the English-language learners' cultural and language backgrounds.

Abedi (2002) compared the standardized test performance in mathematics, science, and reading of English-language learners and non-English-language learners from four different sites in the United States to test whether performance differences across the content areas could be tied to language factors. He found differences in the performance gap across the three content areas, with the English-language learners scoring higher in mathematics and science and lower in reading, language, and spelling. Abedi argues that the English-language learners' second-language status and the higher language demands inherent in the reading test relative to the mathematics and science tests accounted for this discrepancy in performance.

Abedi (2002) and Stevens et al. (2000) attempted to tease out the role of reading and language factors in the content area assessment of language-minority students. In examining structural equation models for two of the four testing sites in his larger study, Abedi found that the relationships among individual items, between items and the total test score, and between items and the external criteria were higher for non-English-language learners than for English-language learners, and that the structural models indicated a better fit for non-English-language learners than for English-language learners. Test item responses for English-language learners with lower English proficiency also showed low reliability, suggesting that language background may be a source of measurement error for English-language learners. Abedi concludes that his "data substantiate the concern of Messick's (1994) that language factors may be a source of construct-irrelevant variance in standardized achievement tests, affecting the construct validity of the tests themselves" (p. 232).

Davies (1991) found better performance among the third- and sixth-grade native English speakers than among English-language learners on literacy and numeracy measures. His analysis of lexical difficulty and conceptual structure suggests that the difference does not result from specific cultural biases in the tests, but from a general lack of English-language proficiency among the English-language learners. The items that were most difficult for the English-language learners were also those most difficult for the language-majority students. Many of the word problems were judged unclear and more difficult than necessary. Some items were judged at a level for adult text. He argues that greater attention be given to improving proficiency in English as a second language for English-language learners because inadequate language proficiency seems responsible for depressed achievement.

---

[3]The authors used confirmatory factor analysis that compared general education students with current and former Hispanic and Asian English-language learners who were disaggregated for all analyses with the goal of determining whether students should participate in large-scale standards-based assessments. The authors found few differences in the narrative and expository latent constructs that were derived through LISREL programming, suggesting that the assessment was capturing comparable constructs irrespective of language background.

Stevens et al. (2000) analyzed the test performance of seventh-grade English-language learners on a standardized achievement test in social studies (the ITBS). They report that the reliability coefficient for the students' performance (.569) was below that of the norming sample (.87), indicating low test reliability. When they compared the item-response profiles of the top one third and the bottom one third of the English-language learners on the ITBS, they discovered that the profiles of the top scorers were much more similar to those of the native English speakers than to those of the bottom scorers. The scores of the top one third appeared to be adversely affected by a lack of specific social studies knowledge, whereas the scores of the bottom third appeared to be adversely affected by low English proficiency. The authors recommend that researchers recognize the diversity of performance and language proficiency within the English-language learner population.

In the studies that met inclusion criteria for this report, only Hannon and McNally (1986) investigated the use of a testing accommodation with English-language learners. They report that English-language learners (ages 7–8) from Asian backgrounds in Britain made significantly fewer errors when a standardized, multiple-choice sentence completion test was read aloud to them individually than when they read the test silently, whereas there were no significant differences in errors under the two conditions for middle-class, English-speaking students. The authors speculate that the oral test may have indicated the upper limit of the English-language learners' reading level because it relied on students' comprehension of oral English in an individual administration rather than of written English. However, they note that the English-language learners still missed one third of the items on the oral test, whereas working-class students missed one quarter of the items and middle-class students missed very few. A content analysis of the items missed by the English-language learners and working-class students indicated that cultural bias and differential experiences may have accounted for their lower performance on the oral test, compared with the middle-class students. Hannon and McNally call for criterion-referenced tests that are tied to a common curriculum learned by all students, rather than norm-referenced tests.

ASSESSMENTS USED TO PREDICT THE LITERACY PERFORMANCE OF LANGUAGE-MINORITY STUDENTS

Studies reviewed in this section addressed research question 4: Are the assessments currently used to predict the literacy performance of language-minority students (including those with reading disabilities) useful and appropriate? Five groups of researchers tested how well literacy measures in English predicted the English reading performance of language-minority students (Chiappe, Siegel, & Gottardo, 2002; Everatt, Smythe, Adams, & Ocampo, 2000; Geva et al., 2000; Jansky, Hoffman, Layton, & Sugar, 1989; Stage, Sheppard, Davidson, & Browning, 2001). Geva et al. (2000) adapted English measures originally developed for monolingual English speakers for use with English-language learners. One other group of researchers focused on teachers' identification of students considered at risk for dropping out of school (Frontera & Horowitz, 1995).

Everatt et al. (2000) investigated what types of screening measures differentiated Sylheti–English bilingual children and native-English-speaking children who were low versus normal readers as determined by a passing score on the Raven's Coloured Progressive Matrices (Raven, 1995), scores on an English spelling test, and judgments of their classroom and special needs teachers. Although some of the children spoke Sylheti (an oral dialect of Bengali that does not have a written form) at home, they all received instruction in English at school. When *t* tests were conducted and the alpha rate of .05 was split according to the number of *t* tests (16) conducted across a range of measures, the Sylheti students' performance on word reading, nonword reading, and a rhyme task significantly differentiated those students who scored poorly on the criterion measures from those who scored higher. Everatt et al. claim that their findings identified Sylheti–English bilingual students with dyslexia. However, the number of students in the study was too small to allow generalization of the findings; moreover, whether the low performers actually had dyslexia is a question not really addressed by the researchers.

Stage et al. (2001)[4] measured English oral reading fluency at four different times (T1–T4) during the first-grade year of a diverse group of children in the United States (70% Native American, 18% Hispanic, 12% Euro-American) and found that growth in oral reading fluency in English (between kindergarten and first grade) was predicted by the students' end-of-year kindergarten performance on letter-naming measures (r = .62, .71, .70, and .69 for T1–T4, respectively) and letter–sound fluency measures (r = .72, .77, .73, and .71 for T1–T4, respectively). When they controlled for students' initial oral reading fluency in first grade, however, letter-naming fluency was the best predictor (ß = .360 for letter-naming fluency and .251 for letter–sound fluency). In addition, the authors report that students who scored in the 10th percentile or lower on the growth of oral reading fluency measure also scored below the 25th percentile on the kindergarten letter-naming fluency measure (i.e., they identified eight or fewer letters). On the basis of this finding, the authors conclude that the letter-naming fluency measure may be particularly useful for students having limited letter–sound knowledge because, even with students of limited reading ability, it was successful in identifying those who did not make progress over the course of first grade.

Two studies (Chiappe et al., 2002; Geva et al., 2000) investigated the use of English measures as predictors of early reading with English-language learners and native-English-speaking kindergartners, first graders, and/or second graders in Canada. Chiappe et al. compared how well different types of measures in English—an environmental print task, five measures of phonological processing, an oral cloze task for syntactic awareness, and a verbal short-term memory task (Memory for Sentence subtest, Stanford Binet; Thorndike, Hagen, & Sattler, 1986)—developed for monolingual English speakers predicted the English early reading performance (as measured by the Wide Range Achievement Test [WRAT; Stone, Jastak, & Wilkinson, 1995], a letter identification task, and a spelling test) of language-minority versus native-English-speaking kindergartners.

---

[4] Although minority, these students may not be language minority.

Although the authors did not include a measure of the students' oral English proficiency in their analysis, they did divide the language-minority students into two groups: those who entered kindergarten knowing some English and a language other than English (termed bilinguals), and those who entered kindergarten speaking a language other than English at home (termed non-English speakers). Similar to the findings of Stage et al. (2001), this study showed that measures of alphabetic knowledge, such as letter naming, and phonological processing in November were significant predictors of all of the children's performance in May on the WRAT–3. (Among bilinguals, $r = .84$; among non-English speakers, $r = .82$; among native speakers of English, $r = .80$ for letter identification. For phonological processing [i.e., phoneme deletion], $r = .30$ for bilinguals, .46 for non-English speakers, .40 for native speakers of English.) As a result, the authors conclude that letter naming and phonological processing may be reliable predictors of reading disability for both native English speakers and English-language learners. Although it is impossible to know the actual effect of students' limited English proficiency or native-language literacy on the various measures employed, the authors acknowledge that the students' status as English-language learners (i.e., bilingual or non-English speakers) appeared to influence their lower performance on some of the measures.

In a study of English-language learners with varying levels of English proficiency and native-English-speaking students in Canada, Geva et al. (2000) employed hierarchical regression techniques and found that phonological awareness (PA) and rapid automatized naming (RAN) assessed at the end of first grade and the beginning of second grade were significant predictors of English word recognition among both groups of students at the end of Grade 2.[5] The researchers also found that the profiles of the native English speakers and English-language learners with word-recognition difficulties (at least 1 standard deviation below the mean during the spring of Grade 2) on the phonological awareness and RAN measures were similar. They conclude that, "despite the absence of fully developed proficiency in the second language, it is feasible to use these measures [adapted measure of phonological awareness and RAN] as reliable indicators of potential reading disability among ESL students" (p. 149).

In contrast, Jansky et al. (1989) report that different types of test batteries had to be developed for Hispanic bilingual and native-English-speaking students. They had previously found that a five-test screening battery (Bender Motor Gestalt Test [Bender, 2004], Gates Word-Matching Test [MacGinitie & MacGinitie, 1989], and Binet Sentence Memory Test [Thorndike, Hagen, & Sattler, 1986]) administered in first grade predicted the later reading

---

[5]To offset test bias for the English-language learners, the researchers used the students' raw scores on the WRAT<-15->R and PPVT–R, rather than using the norms, which were not standardized on samples that included English-language learners, and they adapted several of the measures. For example, they included only high-frequency English words on the phonological awareness measure, and they used a Hebrew pseudoword-recognition task for the phonological memory task so it would be equally challenging for both groups of students. To compute word-recognition scores, they combined students' scores on the WRAT–R (which is stopped after students have made a certain number of errors) with those on an experimental word-recognition task, in which students were given the opportunity to identify all the high-frequency words on the measure.

performance of native English speakers, in addition to identifying students at risk for reading failure. Only two factors, however, embedded in a battery of eight tests predicted the Grades 2 to 6 reading performance of first-grade bilingual Hispanic students: their oral language and prereading skills. They also found that the measures identified fewer than 40% of the children who became failing readers and classified as high-risk children who became middle-level readers. The researchers speculate that many of the Hispanic readers identified in first grade as at risk for reading failure based on their low preliteracy skills did not really have reading disabilities because they subsequently improved their reading performance with instruction.

One group of researchers investigated how well teachers could predict the academic or reading performance of language-minority students. Frontera and Horowitz (1995) found that U.S. fourth-grade teachers' answers on a questionnaire about their students' study habits and content area reading and writing behaviors significantly predicted those students who demonstrated high dropout characteristics, as measured by their grade point average (GPA; correlations ranged from .31 to .57), overage status (correlations ranged from .33 to .59), and reading and science test scores on the Stanford Achievement Test (SAT; correlations ranged from .39 to .51). However, only 57 children were included in the study. Although the teachers' answers were correlated with the students' later behaviors, the authors do not specify false alarm or miss rates.

MEASURES AND METHODS TO IDENTIFY STUDENTS ELIGIBLE FOR SPECIAL SERVICES

In this section, we review studies addressing research question 5: What research has focused on language and literacy measures or methods developed for the identification of language-minority students eligible for special education services (including speech and hearing)?

When English measures normed on native English speakers are used with language-minority students, it is difficult to know whether low scores are due to the students' second-language or dialect status or to an actual language or learning problem. Public Law 94-142, the Education for All Handicapped Children Act, states that an oral proficiency assessment in the home/native language is required before language-minority students are identified as eligible for special education services. Our discussion of this research question is divided into three parts: The first focuses on the types of language proficiency assessments used by school psychologists for the placement of language-minority children in special education, the second on the identification of language-minority children with language disorders, and the third on the identification of learning disabilities in older language-minority children.

Assessments Used for Placement in Special Education

Ochoa, Galarza, and González (1996) surveyed the types of language proficiency assessments used by 859 school psychologists from eight different states to help decide which language-minority students should be placed in special education. The authors point out the importance of school psychologists determining whether language-minority children's academic difficulties are due to a real disability or to factors related to second-language acquisition. According to the results of a self-report survey (with a 29% response rate), 48% of the school psychologists who used district data (i.e., they did not conduct their own assessments) used the LAS and 24% the IPT. Of those psychologists who reported conducting their own assessments (62% of the total sample), 85% used the PPVT–R to help determine English-language proficiency, and 67% used the Spanish version of the PPVT–R or the TVIP to help determine students' Spanish-language proficiency. The authors note that a small percentage (35%) of school psychologists used a test such as the Woodcock Language Proficiency Battery (Woodcock, 1991) to assess students' academic English proficiency.

Ochoa et al. (1996) voice concerns about the number of school psychologists who did not conduct their own language assessments and those who conducted their own assessments, but used assessments such as the PPVT–R and TVIP. They note that using district data is unreliable because the qualifications of the district examiners and testing contexts are usually unknown. The measures that the school psychologists reported using most frequently sample only students' receptive vocabulary acquisition, providing a limited view of their language development. The researchers recommend that school psychologists assess the language dominance of language-minority students so they know which language should be used in conducting further assessments.

Limbos and Geva (2001) investigated how well teachers' assessments (i.e., teacher nominations, ratings of specific skills, and spontaneous expressions of concern) of first- and second-grade English-language learners and native English speakers in Canada correctly identified the students as being at risk for a reading disability. Students' designation as reading disabled was determined by a combined standardized reading score (based on students' raw scores on the WRAT–3, Word Attack [Woodcock & Johnson, 1985], and Rapid Automatized Naming Test [RAN; Wolf & Denckla, 2005]), with students scoring at or below the 10th percentile being considered reading disabled. Limbos and Geva found that teacher nominations and ratings of academic skills individually were better predictors of students' reading disability than teachers' spontaneous expressions of concern. Correlations between teacher ratings and objective test results ranged from .44 to .71. Further, teacher ratings were more highly correlated with the oral language outcomes for the English-language learners ($r = .55$) than for the native English speakers ($r = .44$). Teacher ratings correlated only .27 with grammar and sentence repetition for native-English-speaking students, but .55 for the English-language learners. When assessments based on teacher nominations and ratings of academic skills were combined, all of the students with reading disability, as determined by their standardized reading scores, were identified. However, Limbos and Geva also report that when teachers made errors in determining English-language learners' reading performance, their assessment usually was adversely affected by their overreliance on students' oral language proficiency in English. For all the measures, the teachers missed some children who should have been identified as at risk and did identify as at risk some children who were not.

The Identification of Language Disorders

Of the four studies we reviewed that focused on language disorders, one was a survey of the types of assessments used by a small sample of speech and language pathologists in California to identify such students (Langdon, 1989). In the other three studies, researchers investigated different ways to identify such students (Ambert, 1986; Holm, Dodd, Stow, & Pert, 1999; Restrepo, 1998). Langdon's findings are similar to those of Kindler (2002), in that the responding speech and language pathologists reported placing the most importance on students' discrete-point language proficiency test scores. In contrast to Kindler's data, many also reported that they assessed students' language proficiency in both languages and that they used language samples.

All three groups of researchers who investigated the identification of language disorders in language-minority children emphasize the importance of conducting assessments in the children's home language (Ambert, 1986; Holm et al., 1999; Restrepo, 1998). Their findings appear to lay the groundwork for the development of future assessments. For example, Ambert (1986) relied on the collection and analysis of spontaneous speech samples in Spanish, an approach used by many speech and language pathologists (Langdon, 1989). However, Ambert used the developmental stages of normal Spanish-language acquisition (Gili-Gaya, 1974), along with results she had previously obtained with normal Spanish-speaking children, to analyze the receptive and expressive language of Spanish-speaking English-language learners (ages 5–12) with language disorders. On the basis of her findings, she attempted to provide a definition of Spanish-speaking children with language disorders that could be used by other researchers and educational personnel. According to Ambert, "the Spanish-speaking children with language disorders could not process what they heard, had difficulty establishing associations between words and meaning and in understanding questions, and had problems with auditory discrimination, word retrieval, and gender agreement" (p. 28).

Restrepo (1998) used discriminant analysis to identify measures that differentiated a small sample of nondisabled Spanish-speaking students (ages 5–7) from a small sample of Spanish-speaking students with severe to moderate language impairments (as determined by certified bilingual speech and language pathologists). Restrepo found that parents' report of a speech–language problem, the number of errors students made per *t* unit in their spontaneous speech (as judged by the Developmental Assessment of Spanish Grammar [Toronto, 1976]), the mean length of the *t* unit, and a history of speech–language problems in the family accounted for 79% of the variance and had a sensitivity of 91.3% for the differentiation of students with speech–language problems. Although Restrepo does not present a protocol that could be used by speech and language pathologists, the findings he reports suggest that such a protocol could be developed. However, Restrepo did not investigate the relationship between children's language impairments and current or future reading performance.

Holm et al. (1999) studied children ages 4 to 7 in England who spoke Mirpuri, Punjabi, or Urdu at home, but were instructed in English at school. Their findings emphasize the importance of defining the normal phonological development of bilingual children in contrast to that of monolingual children. The researchers attempted to develop a common phonological assessment procedure for the three languages a non-native speaker of those languages could use, with the assistance of a bilingual coworker, to identify English-language learners with speech disorders. However, they discovered that the normal phonological development of bilingual children in each of the languages appeared to differ from that of monolingual English-speaking children. The authors suggest that, "researchers need to investigate whether bilingual children differentiate the two phonological systems, and if so, to identify phonological error patterns in each language and compare those patterns with data on normal bilingual development for each language" (p. 286).

The Identification of Older Language-Minority Students With Learning Disabilities

Two groups of researchers investigated the identification of older language-minority students with learning disabilities (Goldstein, Harris, & Klein, 1993; Miramontes, 1987). Goldstein et al. conclude that weak story retelling schema (in English) may be one way to identify such students (in their case, Mexican Americans ages 12–16). This hypothesis initially appeared promising because it coincides with data on the weak story schema of native English speakers with learning disabilities. However, there was a large amount of variance in their study that was not accounted for by the correlation between the students' retelling performance and their performance on the Peabody Individual Achievement Test (Markwardt, 1989; $r = .12$). A contributing factor may have been students' limited oral English proficiency. The researchers did not assess how well students could retell stories written in English when they were allowed to use Spanish, the language they used at home, or how well they could retell stories written in Spanish.

Miramontes (1987) assessed Latino students' oral reading in Spanish and English by using the Reading Miscue Inventory (Goodman & Burke, 1972) to analyze the miscue patterns (oral variations from the text) of four groups of Latino readers in fourth, fifth, and sixth grades—those considered to be good Spanish readers, those considered to be good English readers, those considered to be learning disabled in Spanish, and those considered to be learning disabled in English. She found that the strategies used by 50% of the Spanish learning-disabled group while reading in Spanish actually resembled those of the good Spanish readers. In addition, when she looked at the miscue data within groups, there were clear differences within the learning-disabled categories. Of the 10 students classified as learning disabled in Spanish, 7 could read at a fourth-grade level in Spanish. This finding led Miramontes to speculate that 50% of the students classified as learning disabled in Spanish may have been misclassified because of their limited oral English proficiency. She concludes that "a process-oriented assessment procedure conducted in each language might be a more useful way to determine students with learning disabilities because students' strengths and weaknesses could then be compared in each language to provide a more accurate view of reading proficiency" (p. 631). However, it is not possible to draw conclusions from this study because the numbers of children in the groups were small, and it is not clear how the children's performance was scored.

ASSESSMENTS USED IN THE RESEARCH CITED IN THIS VOLUME

In this section, we present the findings of studies addressing research question 6: What standardized (commercial) and researcher-developed oral proficiency, literacy, and literacy-related assessments have been used by the researchers whose work is reviewed throughout this volume? In the CD that accompanies this volume, a description of the measures used in each study is provided. Table 20.1 provides the frequencies of the use of various literacy assessment by literacy component.

Standardized Assessments

The Woodcock–Johnson Letter–Word Identification Test (Woodcock & Johnson, 1985) and the Wide Range Achievement Test were the primary instruments used to assess letter identification skills across the studies with each being referenced two times.

Only two standardized measures of morphological skill were used in the research we reviewed: the Mechanics and Usage subtest of the LAS for Reading and Writing, and the Spanish Structured Photographic Expressive Language Test (Werner & Kresheck, 1983). The former, conducted in English, is a silent measure with textual prompts (the subject is required to write answers); the latter, conducted in Spanish, is administered orally with visual stimuli (pictures).

Four measures of oral reading fluency were used: the LAS, the Reading Miscue Inventory, the Woodcock Language Proficiency Battery, and the Record of Oral Language (Clay, 1983). Each measure was used once in the research. Of these, one was administered in English, two in Spanish, and one—the Reading Miscue Inventory—in both languages.

Phonemic and phonological awareness were measured across studies with instruments designed specifically for this purpose, as well as with more broadly focused assessment batteries. The Sound Mimicry subtest of the Goldman–Fristoe–Woodcock Auditory Skills Test Battery (Goldman, Fristoe, & Woodcock, 1973) and the Phonological Abilities Test (Muter, Hulme, & Snowling, 1997) were the only measures used in multiple studies, each being referenced three times. Other instruments used to assess these constructs included subtests developed by the Dutch National Institute for Educational Measurement, as well as subtests of the Gates–MacGinitie Reading Tests, Reading Edge (Scientific Learning, 1998), Test of Auditory Analysis Skills (Rosner, 1979), Woodcock Reading Mastery Tests (Woodcock, 1998), and Word Recognition and Phonics Skills (Carver & Mosley, 2000). Dutch, English, and Spanish were the languages of measurement, with English predominating.

Although print concepts were assessed in just three studies, the assessments were conducted in both English and Spanish. The Concepts About Print Test (Clay, 1972), Test of Early Reading Ability (Reid, Hresko, & Hammill, 2002), and Prueba de Lectura Inicial (Editest, 1967a) were each employed once in the research.

A wide variety of assessment devices were used to measure reading ability (broadly defined). Most assessments integrated some evaluation of vocabulary knowledge and reading comprehension skill. Other subskills assessed by these measures include spelling, oral reading, listening comprehension, reading rate, and phonetic analysis. The most frequently used instruments were the CTBS (four times), the ITBS (three times), the Metropolitan Achievement Test (two times; Prescott, Balow, Hogan, & Farr, 1993), and the Inter-American Test of Reading (two times; Guidance Testing Associates, 1967). English, Spanish, and Urdu were the languages of measurement for this construct.

Reading comprehension assessments are reported frequently in the research. Most of these assessments either were of the cloze variety or consisted of a short passage followed by multiple-choice questions. The most frequently used measures of this construct were the CTBS (four times), the Gates–MacGinitie Reading Tests (three times), and the Stanford Diagnostic Reading Test (three times). Other measures used repeatedly include the California Achievement Test (CTB McGraw-Hill, 1986a), Test de Lecture (Editest, 1967b), Test de Rendement en Français (Commission des Ecoles Catholiques de Montreal, 1974), LAS Reading and Writing, Stanford Achievement Test, Woodcock Language Proficiency Battery, and the Woodcock Reading Mastery Tests, each used twice. These assessments were conducted in English, Spanish, and French.

A number of diverse assessments were classified as *reading unspecified*. Although captured predominantly through tests of achievement, this construct was also assessed through receptive vocabulary measures (e.g., British Picture Vocabulary Scale [Dunn, Dunn, Whetton, & Burley, 1982]), reading comprehension tests, and oral reading instruments (e.g., Durrell Analysis of Reading Difficulty [Durrell, 1955], Neale Analysis of Reading Ability [Neale, 1989], and Slosson Oral Reading Test [Slosson, Jensen, & Armstrong, 1983]). The most frequently used instruments were the CTBS (seven times) and the Metropolitan Achievement Test (four times); the Neale Analysis of Reading Ability, Tests of Basic Experiences (Moss, 1978), and Stanford Achievement Test were each used twice. Assessments were conducted in English, Spanish, Japanese, and Urdu.

In the area of spelling, the Wide Range Achievement Test was used most frequently (four times). Other measures of this construct include the appropriate subtests of the Canadian Tests of Basic Skills (Thomson Nelson, 1998) and two spelling tests administered in Dutch. English and Spanish were the other languages of assessment for this construct.

The *Bilingual Syntax Measure* (1975), referenced in two studies, was the only assessment used repeatedly as a measure of syntax. Some of the other assessments used to measure this construct include the Clinical Evaluation of Language Fundamentals (Semel, Wiig, & Secord, 1995), the Mechanics and Usage subtest of the LAS for Reading and Writing, the Spanish Structured Photographic Expressive Language Test, the Test de Rendement en Francais, and the Test for the Reception of Grammar (Bishop, 1983). Dutch, English, French, and Spanish were the languages of assessment for this construct.

Vocabulary was a construct frequently measured across these studies. The PPVT was the most common instrument used for this purpose, being administered in English, French, Hebrew, and Swedish (referenced 20 times) and Spanish (TVIP, referenced 12 times). Another instrument used repeatedly as a measure of vocabulary was the British Picture Vocabulary Scale (four times). The following measures were each used twice in the research: ITBS, CTBS, the California Achievement Test, the Test de Rendement en Francais, the Gates–MacGinitie Reading Tests, the Stanford Achievement Test, and the Stanford Diagnostic Reading Test.

Word and pseudoword reading was measured with a variety of assessments that employ word attack and word identification tasks, either as part of a larger battery or as the focus of the instrument. The Wide Range Achievement Test and the Woodcock Reading Mastery Tests were by far the most frequently reported measures of this construct, with the former being referenced in 11 studies and the latter in 10. The Woodcock Language Proficiency Battery was used twice. These measures were administered predominantly in English and in a few cases in Spanish.

Writing was assessed in six studies using six distinct instruments (two Texas state assessments were used in a single study—one for English and one for Spanish). Most of these instruments were proficiency batteries used to assess multiple constructs, including a variety of reading and writing skills. The instruments used included the IDEA Reading and Writing Proficiency Test and the Correctness and Appropriateness of Expression subtest of the Iowa Test of Educational Development (Forsyth, Ansley, Feldt, & Alnot, 2001), the Prueba de Lectura Inicial, and the California Standardized Testing and Reporting (STAR) program tests. English was the predominant language of assessment for this construct, although Spanish was also assessed in two cases (Texas Assessment of Academic Skills [Texas Education Agency, 2000], Prueba de Lectura Inicial).

Researcher-Developed Assessments

The quality of empirical research on literacy clearly depends on researchers' selection, development, and use of specific assessments. Issues of validity, reliability, and linguistic and cultural bias that apply to standardized assessments also apply to researcher-developed assessments.

Letter identification skills were measured by 15 different researcher-developed assessments across 14 studies. Tasks included naming upper- and lowercase letters in random order, identifying letters as they appeared within words, physically pointing to letters that were named by an administrator, and writing words. These assessments were conducted in English, Spanish, Greek, Urdu, and Persian.

Morphology was assessed in just one study using the Writing Vocabulary Assessment. This instrument was administered in English, and it provided a sample of words that students could use to write independently.

Fourteen researcher-developed measures were used to assess oral reading fluency across 11 studies. Oral reading accuracy and rate were the primary tasks designed to assess this construct. Cloze procedures were also employed. These measures were administered in English, Spanish, and Dutch.

Twenty-four measures of oral language proficiency (broadly defined) were employed. Tasks included use of the oral cloze tasks, teacher ratings of competence, sentence verification technique (SVT) in both English and Spanish, listening comprehension activities, ratings of students' oral responses to interview and comprehension questions, sentence imitation, self-report questionnaires, and story retelling. In addition to English and Spanish, languages of assessment included Italian, Dutch, Hebrew, and Portuguese.

Oral language (unspecified) was assessed with 11 measures. Tasks included researcher observations of classrooms, cloze procedures, verbal identification of pictures, a language survey completed by parents, teacher questionnaires, student questionnaires, judgment of grammatical correctness, and construction of questions from words given in random order. This construct was measured in English, Spanish, French, Hebrew, and Arabic.

Phonemic and phonological awareness was the most frequently assessed construct in the research we reviewed. To evaluate this construct, 68 measures were employed across 25 studies. Phoneme segmentation, pseudoword repetition, and RAN were the only tasks used repeatedly. Other tasks consisted of requiring subjects to segment, delete, and blend syllables and phonemes in both words and pseudowords. Manipulation of the onset and coda was also required, along with alliteration and rhyme judgment and generation tasks. These researcher-developed assessments were administered in English, Spanish, Punjabi, Urdu, Chinese, Hebrew, Dutch, and Turkish.

Concept of print was measured with six assessments across five studies. Tasks included the naming of environmental print, use of an observation survey, moving word problems, and word size problems. These assessments were administered in English, Spanish, Chinese, French, and Turkish.

Thirteen measures of reading (broadly defined) were employed across 14 studies. These assessments included the use of writing samples, questionnaires, and rating scales (for students and teachers); listening comprehension tasks; and error analysis during oral reading, reading comprehension, and single-word reading tasks. English, Spanish, Italian, Náhuatl, and Urdu were the languages of assessment for this construct.

Reading comprehension was assessed with 46 researcher-developed measures across 30 studies; 2 measures were used repeatedly. The English and Spanish versions of the SVT were each used in three studies. In addition to these measures, oral reading rate and accuracy, cloze procedures, oral and written comprehension questions, inference tasks, and oral and written retellings were used to assess this construct. Languages of assessment included English, Spanish, Náhuatl, Dutch, Urdu, Hebrew, Korean, Arabic, Yoruba, French, and Turkish.

Five measures were used to assess reading (unspecified). Tasks included multiple-choice sentence completion cloze tests and several tests about which little or no information is provided. English and French were the languages used to administer these assessments.

Spelling ability was assessed with 25 researcher-developed measures. Spelling tests of real and pseudowords, spelling recognition tasks, and writing samples were also used to assess this construct. English, Spanish, Chinese (in one instance using Hanyu Pinyin, a phonetic spelling system for Chinese), Hebrew, Persian, and Turkish were the languages of assessment.

Syntax was assessed with 30 researcher-developed measures. Oral cloze tasks were used to assess this construct, as well as tasks involving sentence

TABLE 20.1
Frequencies of Standardized/Commercial, Researcher-Developed, and State-Standards/Accountability Measures by Literacy Component

Literacy Component	Total Measures of Component in Database		Standardized/ Commercial Measures-English		Standardized/ Commercial Measures-Spanish		Researcher-Developed Measures-English		Researcher-Developed Measures-Spanish		State Standards/ Accountability-English		State Standards/ Accountability-Spanish	
	Freq	Studies	Freq	Studies	Freq	Studies	Freq	Studies	Freq	Studies	Freq	Studies	Freq	Studies
Print concepts	8	(7)	2	(2)	1	(1)	4	(3)	2	(2)	0	(0)	0	(0)
Letter identification	23	(24)	6	(8)	1	(1)	12	(11)	3	(3)	1	(1)	0	(0)
Word or pseudoword reading	47	(59)	12	(21)	6	(17)	23	(15)	5	(5)	1	(1)	0	(0)
Oral reading fluency	20	(17)	2	(2)	3	(3)	12	(9)	2	(2)	1	(1)	0	(0)
Reading comprehension	79	(71)	21	(25)	7	(11)	34	(22)	12	(8)	4	(4)	1	(1)
Reading broadly defined	42	(50)	14	(18)	7	(10)	9	(9)	4	(5)	6	(6)	2	(2)
Reading unspecified	30	(39)	14	(19)	4	(9)	5	(5)	0	(0)	5	(4)	2	(2)
Vocabulary	51	(69)	16	(33)	6	(12)	12	(9)	9	(7)	5	(5)	3	(3)
Spelling	31	(28)	2	(4)	1	(3)	24	(17)	1	(1)	2	(2)	1	(1)
Writing proficiency	39	(30)	4	(4)	2	(2)	25	(16)	5	(5)	2	(2)	1	(1)

(Continued)

TABLE 20.1
(Continued)

Literacy Component	Total Measures of Component in Database		Standardized/ Commercial Measures-English		Standardized/ Commercial Measures-Spanish		Researcher- Developed Measures-English		Researcher- Developed Measures- Spanish		State Standards/ Accountability- English		State Standards/ Accountability- Spanish	
	Freq	Studies	Freq	Studies	Freq	Studies	Freq	Studies	Freq	Studies	Freq	Studies	Freq	Studies
Phonemic/ phonological awareness	77	(35)	9	(10)	0	(0)	55	(18)	13	(7)	0	(0)	0	(0)
Morphology	3	(3)	1	(1)	1	(1)	1	(1)	0	(0)	0	(0)	0	(0)
Syntax	40	(34)	7	(7)	2	(3)	22	(19)	8	(4)	1	(1)	0	(0)
Discourse	2	(2)	0	(0)	0	(0)	1	(1)	1	(1)	0	(0)	0	(0)
Pragmatics	1	(1)	0	(0)	0	(0)	1	(1)	0	(0)	0	(0)	0	(0)

Note. The numbers of studies in the database that measured the literacy component are in parentheses.

analysis, vocabulary knowledge, grammar judgment, story recall, simulated conversation, and analysis of oral and written language. In addition to English, assessments of syntax were conducted in Spanish, Náhuatl, Russian, Dutch, Turkish, Punjabi, Hebrew, Greek, and Chinese.

Vocabulary knowledge was assessed with 21 measures used across 16 studies. Tasks evaluated both productive and receptive vocabulary knowledge and included categorization, cognate circling, verbal definition, picture identification, disambiguation tests, novel bound-morpheme generalization, matching tests, and multiple-choice tests. These assessments were administered in English, Spanish, Dutch, and Turkish.

Word and pseudoword reading ability was assessed by 28 researcher-developed measures across 20 studies. This construct was measured by employing tasks that required the subject to read words in isolation and in context and by analyzing the errors made during the completion of these tasks. Sight word and pseudoword reading was assessed in both timed and untimed conditions. English, Spanish, Chinese, Persian, Portuguese, Dutch, Turkish, and Hebrew were the languages used to assess this construct.

Writing proficiency was assessed with 30 measures in 21 separate studies. Rating scales applied to samples of student work, essay and composition tests, responses to literature, written story retellings, and written instructions were all evaluated. Writing proficiency was assessed in terms of ability to convey meaning, mechanics/grammar, organization of thoughts, sentence construction, topic development, productivity, and linguistic complexity and variety. These measures were administered in English, Spanish, and Náhuatl.

Discourse was assessed with two measures. One study employed three measures. The assessments involved analyzing utterances and student responses to questions that followed the reading of a passage, evaluating story writing and retelling ability, and administering the anaphoric reference test. English, Spanish, Dutch, and Náhuatl were the languages in which these assessments were conducted.

Two tasks were used to assess metalinguistic knowledge across two studies. This construct was measured in Spanish and Náhuatl.

Two researcher-developed measures were used to assess pragmatic competence. The first, a metaphor task, was administered in English and required subjects to provide a possible interpretation for randomly constructed metaphors. The second evaluated spontaneous speech in Turkish and Dutch, computing proficiency on the basis of the number of different content words occurring in 75 utterances of speech and the mean number of morphemes in the longest utterance recorded from subjects' speech samples.

Content knowledge was assessed in two studies, with measures administered in both English and Spanish in each case. One measure was a survey to which teachers responded regarding aspects of student performance in school. The other was a prior-knowledge test administered before the intervention.

Summary

It is hoped that in the future researchers will use the information reported in this part of the volume as a starting place for selecting measures for their research and developing a research agenda on assessments for language-minority students. Of note is the prominence given to measures of phonemic and phonological awareness and comprehension. Across all the studies included in chapters 3 to 20, the greatest number of measures focused on phonemic and phonological awareness (77) and reading comprehension (79), followed by vocabulary (51). The fewest measures addressed pragmatics (1), morphology (3), and discourse (2). Interestingly, with regard to frequency of use, there were more researcher-developed (240 English measures and 55 Spanish measures) than standardized/commercial measures (103 in English and 41 in Spanish); many studies relied solely on researcher-developed measures to assess students' language and literacy skills. At the time the research was reviewed, few state standards/accountability measures were used in either Spanish (10) or English (28) in the research studies reviewed.

Few researchers report information on the validity or reliability of the researcher-developed measures used in their studies. An effort should be made in future research to determine and report this information. Moreover, as mentioned earlier, studies should include standardized measures of literacy to help benchmark results obtained from researcher-developed instruments.

Database References
for Part V

Abedi, J. (2002). Assessment and accommodations of English language learners: Issues, concerns, and recommendations. *Journal of School Improvement, 3*(1), 83–89.

Ambert, A. N. (1986). Identifying language disorders in Spanish-speakers. *Journal of Reading, Writing, and Learning Disabilities International, 2*(1), 21–41.

Argulewicz, E. N., & Abel, R. R. (1984). Internal evidence of bias in the PPVT–R for Anglo-American and Mexican-American children. *Journal of School Psychology, 22*(3), 299–303.

Baker, S. K., & Good, R. (1995). Curriculum-based measurement reading with bilingual Hispanic students: A validation study with second-grade students. *School Psychology Review, 24*(4), 561–578.

Baldauf, R. B., Jr., Dawson, R. T., Prior, J., & Propst, I. K., Jr. (1980). Can matching cloze be used with secondary ESL pupils? *Journal of Reading, 23*(5), 435–440.

Brown, D. (1983). Conversational cloze tests and conversational ability. *ELT Journal, 37*(2), 158–161.

Chiappe, P., Siegel, L. S., & Gottardo, A. (2002). Reading-related skills of kindergartners from diverse linguistic backgrounds. *Applied Psycholinguistics, 23*(1), 95–116.

Davidson, F. (1994). Norms appropriacy of achievement tests: Spanish-speaking children and English children's norms. *Language Testing, 11*(1), 83–95.

Everatt, J., Smythe, I., Adams, E., & Ocampo, D. (2000). Dyslexia screening measures and bilingualism. *Dyslexia, 6*(1), 42–56.

Fernández, M. C., Pearson, B. Z., Umbel, V. M., Oller, D. K., & Molinet-Molina, M. (1992). Bilingual receptive vocabulary in Hispanic preschool children. *Hispanic Journal of Behavioral Sciences, 14*(2), 268–276.

Frontera, L. S., & Horowitz, R. (1995). Reading and study behaviors of fourth-grade Hispanics: Can teachers assess risk? *Hispanic Journal of Behavioral Sciences, 17*(1), 100–120.

García, G. E. (1991). Factors influencing the English reading test performance of Spanish-speaking Hispanic children. *Reading Research Quarterly, 26*(4), 371–392.

Geva, E., Yaghoub-Zadeh, Z., & Schuster, B. (2000). Part IV: Reading and foreign language learning: Understanding individual differences in word recognition skills of ESL children. *Annals of Dyslexia, 50*, 121–154.

Goldstein, B. C., Harris, K. C., & Klein, M. D. (1993). Assessment of oral storytelling abilities of Latino junior high school students with learning handicaps. *Journal of Learning Disabilities, 26*(2), 138–132.

Gómez, L., Parker, R., Lara-Alecio, R., Ochoa, S. H., & Gómez, R., Jr. (1996). Naturalistic language assessment of LEP students in classroom interactions. *Bilingual Research Journal, 20*(1), 69–92.

Hannon, P., & McNally, J. (1986). Children's understanding and cultural factors in reading test performance. *Educational Review, 38*(3), 237–246.

Holm, A., Dodd, B., Stow, C., & Pert, S. (1999). Identification and differential diagnosis of phonological disorder in bilingual children. *Language Testing, 16*(3), 271–292.

Jansky, J. J., Hoffman, M. J., Layton, J., & Sugar, F. (1989). Prediction: A six-year follow-up. *Annals of Dyslexia, 39*, 227–246.

Laesch, K. B., & Van Kleeck, A. (1987). The cloze test as an alternative measure of language proficiency of children considered for exit from bilingual education programs. *Language Learning, 37*(2), 171–189.

Langdon, H. W. (1989). Language disorder or difference? Assessing the language skills of Hispanic students. *Exceptional Children, 56*(2), 160–167.

Limbos, M., & Geva, E. (2001). Accuracy of teacher assessments of second-language students at risk for reading disability. *Journal of Learning Disabilities, 34*(2), 136–151.

Miramontes, O. B. (1987). Oral reading miscues of Hispanic students: Implications for assessment of learning disabilities. *Journal of Learning Disabilities, 20*(10), 627–632.

Nadeau, A., & Miramontes, O. (1988). The reclassification of limited English proficient students: Assessing the inter-relationship of selected variables. *NABE: The Journal for the National Association for Bilingual Education, 12*(3), 219–242.

Ochoa, S. H., Galarza, A., & González, D. (1996). An investigation of school psychologists' assessment practices of language proficiency with bilingual and limited-English-proficient students. *Diagnostique, 21*(4), 17–36.

Ozete, O. (1980). Modified cloze and cloze testing in Spanish. *Bilingual Review/Revista Bilingue, 7*(3), 203–211.

Pomplun, M., & Omar, M. H. (2001). The factorial invariance of a test of reading comprehension across groups of limited English proficient students. *Applied Measurement in Education, 14*(3), 261–283.

Quinn, C. (2001). The developmental acquisition of English grammar as an additional language. *International Journal of Language & Communication Disorders, 36*(Suppl.), 309–314.

Restrepo, M. A. (1998). Identifiers of predominantly Spanish-speaking children with language impairment. *Journal of Speech, Language, and Hearing Research, 41*(6), 1398–1411.

Royer, J. M., & Carlo, M. S. (1991). Assessing the language acquisition progress of limited English proficient students: Problems and a new alternative. *Applied Measurement in Education, 4*(2), 85–113.

Royer, J. M., Carlo, M. S., Carlisle, J. F., & Furman, G. A. (1991). A new procedure for assessing progress in transitional bilingual education programs. *Bilingual Review/Revista Bilingue, 16*(1), 3–14.

Sattler, J. M., & Altes, L. M. (1984). Performance of bilingual and monolingual Hispanic children on the Peabody Picture Vocabulary Test–Revised and the McCarthy Perceptual Performance Scale. *Psychology in the Schools, 21*(3), 313–316.

Scruggs, T. E., Mastropieri, M. A., & Argulewicz, E. N. (1983). Stability of performance on the PPVT–R for three ethnic groups attending a bilingual kindergarten. *Psychology in the Schools, 20*(4), 433–435.

Stage, S. A., Sheppard, J., Davidson, M. M., & Browning, M. M. (2001). Prediction of first-graders' growth in oral reading fluency using kindergarten letter fluency. *Journal of School Psychology, 39*(3), 225–237.

Stevens, R. A., Butler, F. A., & Castellón-Wellington, M. (2000). *Academic language and content assessment: Measuring the progress of English-language learners* (CSE Technical Report No. 552). Los Angeles: University of California, National Center for Research on Evaluation, Standards, and Student Testing.

Tamayo, J. M. (1987). Frequency of use as a measure of word difficulty in bilingual vocabulary test construction and translation. *Educational and Psychological Measurement, 47*(4), 893–902.

Background References for Part V

Abedi, J. (2001). *Assessment and accommodation for English language learners: Issues and recommendation* (Policy Brief 4). Los Angeles: University of California, Center for the Study of Evaluation/National Center for Research on Evaluation, Standards, and Student Testing.

Abedi, J., Hofstetter, C., Baker, E., & Lord, C. (2001). *NAEP math performance and test accommodations: Interactions with student language background* (Technical Report No. 536). Los Angeles: University of California, Center for the Study of Evaluation/National Center for Research on Evaluation, Standards, and Student Testing.

Abedi, J., Lord, C., Boscardin, C. K., & Miyoshi, J. (2001). *The effects of accommodations on the assessment of limited English proficient (LEP) students in the National Assessment of Educational Progress (NAEP)* (Technical Report No. 537). Los Angeles: University of California, Center for the Study of Evaluation/National Center for Research on Evaluation, Standards, and Student Testing.

American Educational Research Association, American Psychological Association, & National Council on Measurement in Education. (1999). *Standards for educational and psychological testing 1999*. Washington, DC: American Educational Research Association Publications.

Anderson, M., Liu, K., Swierzbin, B., Thurlow, M., & Bielinski, J. (2000). *Bilingual accommodations for limited English proficient students on statewide reading tests: Phase 2* (Minnesota Report No. 31). Minneapolis, MN: University of Minnesota, National Center on Educational Outcomes.

Armstrong, S., & Ainley, M. (1986). *South Tyneside assessment of syntactic structures*. Ponteland, Northumberland, UK: STASS Publications.

August, D. L., & Hakuta, K. (Eds.). (1997). *Improving schooling for language-minority learners*. Washington, DC: National Academy Press.

Bender, L. (2004). *The Bender visual motor gestalt test* (2nd ed.). Itasca, IL: Riverside.

Bessai, F. (2001). *Review of the Peabody Picture Vocabulary Test–III*. Retrieved September 28, 2005, from http://www.unm.edu/~fv3003/shs533/ppvt%20IIIdoc

Bilingual syntax measure. (1975). San Antonio, TX: Psychological Corporation.

Bishop, D. (1983). *Test for reception of grammar*. London: Medical Research Council.

Board of Education of the City of New York. (1976). *Language assessment battery*. New York: Author.

Butler, F. A., & Stevens, R. (2001). Standardized assessment of the content knowledge of English language learners K–12: Current trends and old dilemmas. *Language Testing, 18*(4), 409–427.

Carver, C., & Mosely, D. (2000). *Word recognition and phonics skills (WRaPS)*. London: Hodder & Stoughton Educational.

Clay, M. M. (1972). *The concepts about print test*. Auckland, New Zealand: Heinemann.

Clay, M. M. (1983). *Record of oral language*. Auckland, New Zealand: Heinemann.

Collier, V. P. (1995). Acquiring a second language for school. *Directions in Language & Education, 1*(4), 1–12.

Collier, V. P., & Thomas, W. P. (1989). How quickly can immigrants become proficient in English? *Journal of Educational Issues of Language Minority Students, 5*, 26–38.

Commission des Écoles Catholiques de Montreal. (1974). *Test de rendement en francais.* Montreal: Author.

CTB McGraw-Hill. (1986a). *California achievement tests.* Monterey, CA: Author.

CTB McGraw-Hill. (1986b). *Comprehensive test of basic skills.* Monterey, CA: Author.

CTB McGraw-Hill. (1997, 2001). *Terra nova.* Monterey, CA: Author.

Cummins, J. (1981). The role of primary language development in promoting educational success for language minority students. In California State Department of Education (Ed.), *Schooling and language minority students: A theoretical framework.* Los Angeles, CA: National Dissemination and Assessment Center.

Cummins, J. (1984). *Bilingualism and special education: Issues in assessment and pedagogy.* Clevedon, UK: Multilingual Matters.

Davies, A. (1991). *The native speaker in applied linguistics.* Edinburgh: Edinburgh University Press.

De Avila, E., & Duncan, S. (1990). *Language assessment scales–oral.* Monterey, CA: CTB McGraw-Hill.

Duncan, S., & De Avila, E. (1988). *Language assessment scales–reading and writing.* Monterey, CA: CTB McGraw-Hill.

Dunn, L. M., & Dunn, L. M. (1981). *Peabody picture vocabulary test.* Circle Pines, MN: American Guidance Service.

Dunn, L. M., Dunn, L. M., Whetton, C., & Burley, J. (1982). *British picture vocabulary scale.* Swindon, Wiltshire, UK: NFER-Nelson.

Dunn, L. M., Padilla, E. R., Lugo, D. E., & Dunn, L. M. (1986). *Test de vocabulario en imágenes Peabody.* Circle Pines, MN: American Guidance Service.

Durán, R. P. (1989). Testing of linguistic minorities. In R. L. Linn (Ed.), *Educational measurement* (3rd ed., pp. 573–587). New York: American Council on Education.

Durán, R. P., Brown, C., & McCall, M. (2002). Assessment of English-language learners in the Oregon statewide assessment system: National and state perspectives. In G. Tindal & T. M. Haladyna (Eds.), *Large-scale assessment programs for all students.* St. Paul, MN: Assessment Systems Corporation.

Durrell, D. D. (1955). *Durrell analysis of reading difficulty.* New York: Harcourt, Brace, & World.

Editest. (1967a). *Prueba de lectura inicial.* Brussels: Author.

Editest. (1967b). *Test de lecture California.* Brussels: Author.

Engelmann, S., & Bruner, E. C. (1974). *Reading mastery, level II.* DeSoto, TX: SRA.

Erickson, F. (1998). Qualitative research methods for science education. In B. J. Fraser & K. G. Tobin (Eds.), *International handbook of science education* (pp. 1157–1173). Dordrecht, The Netherlands: Kluwer.

Figueroa, R. A. (1989). Best practices in the assessment of bilingual children. In A. Thomas & J. Grimes (Eds.), *Best practices in school psychology* (pp. 93–106). Washington, DC: National Association of School Psychologists.

Forsyth, R. A., Ansley, T. N., Feldt, L. S., & Alnot, S. D. (2001). *Iowa tests of educational development.* Itasca, IL: Riverside.

García, E. (1994). *Understanding and meeting the challenge of student cultural diversity.* Boston: Houghton-Mifflin.

García, G. E., & Pearson, P. D. (1994). Assessment and diversity. In L. Darling-Hammond (Ed.), *Review of research in education* (Vol. 20, pp. 337–392). Washington, DC: American Educational Research Association.

Gili-Gaya, S. (1974). *Estudios de lenguaje infantil.* Barcelona, Spain: Bibliograph.

Goldman, R., Fristoe, M., & Woodcock, R. W. (1973). *Goldman–Fristoe–Woodcock auditory skills test battery.* Circle Pines, MN: American Guidance Service.

Goodman, Y. M., & Burke, C. (1972). *Reading miscue inventory.* New York: Macmillan.

Guidance Testing Associates. (1967). *Inter-American test of reading.* Austin, TX: Author.

Hakuta, K., & Beatty, A. (2000). *Testing English language learners in U. S. schools.* Washington, DC: National Academy Press.

Hatch, E. (1992). *Discourse and language education.* New York: Cambridge University Press.

Hoover, H. D., Dunbar, S. B., & Frisbie, D. A. (2001). *Iowa tests of basic skills.* Itasca, IL: Riverside.

Hughes, A. (1981). Conversational cloze as a measure of oral ability. *English Language Teaching Journal, 35,* 161–168.

IDEA language proficiency tests. (1978, 1994). Brea, CA: Ballard & Tighe.

Karlsen, B., & Gardner, E. (1985). *Stanford diagnostic reading test* (4th ed.). San Antonio, TX: Psychological Corporation.

Kindler, A. L. (2002). *Survey of the states' limited English proficient students and available educational programs and services, 2000–2001 summary report*. Washington, DC: National Clearinghouse for English Language Acquisition and Language Instruction Educational Programs.

Koenig, J. A., & Bachman, L. F. (2004). *Keeping score for all: The effects of inclusion and accommodation policies on large-scale educational assessment*. Washington, DC: National Academy Press.

Lee, J. F. (1986). Background knowledge and L2 reading. *Modern Language Journal, 70*, 350–354.

MacGinitie, W. H., & MacGinitie, R. K. (1989). *Gates–MacGinitie reading tests*. Itasca, IL: Riverside.

Markwardt, F. C. (1989). *Peabody individual achievement test–revised*. Circle Pines, MN: American Guidance Service.

McCarthy, D. (1972). *McCarthy scales of children's abilities*. New York: Psychological Corporation.

Mercer, J. R. (1979). In defense of racially and culturally nondiscriminatory assessment. *School Psychology Digest, 8*, 89–115.

Messick, S. (1994). The interplay of evidence and consequences in the validation of performance assessments. *Educational Researcher, 23*(2), 13–23.

Mestre, J. P. (1984, Fall). The problem with problems: Hispanic students and math. *Bilingual Journal*, pp. 15–20.

Moss, M. H. (1978). *Tests of basic experiences*. Monterey, CA: CTB McGraw-Hill.

Muter, V., Hulme, C., & Snowling, M. (1997). *Phonological abilities test*. London: Harcourt Assessment.

National Reading Conference Yearbook. (various years). Oak Creek, WI: Author.

Neale, M. D. (1989). *Neale analysis of reading ability*. Swindon, Wiltshire, UK: NFER-Nelson.

No Child Left Behind Act of 2001, 20 U.S.C. 6301 et seq. (2002).

Olmeda, E. L. (1981). Testing linguistic minorities. *American Psychologist, 36*, 1078–1085.

Prescott, G., Balow, I., Hogan, T., & Farr, R. (1993). *Metropolitan achievement tests* (7th ed.). San Antonio, TX: Psychological Corporation.

Raven, J. C. (1995). *Raven's coloured progressive matrices*. San Antonio, TX: Psychological Corporation.

Reid, D. K., Hresko, W., & Hammill, D. (2002). *Test of early reading ability* (3rd ed.). Austin, TX: PRO-ED.

Riverside Publishing. (1983). *3–R's reading test*. Itasca, IL: Author.

Rosner, J. (1979). Test of auditory analysis. In J. Rosner (Ed.), *Helping children overcome learning difficulties: A step-by-step guide for parents and teachers* (pp. 77–80). New York: Academic Therapy Publications.

Samuda, R. J. (1975). *Psychological testing of American minorities*. New York: Dodd Mead.

Scientific Learning. (1998). *Reading edge*. Berkeley, CA: Author.

Semel, E., Wiig, E. H., & Secord, W. A. (1995). *Clinical evaluation of language fundamentals*. San Antonio, TX: Psychological Corporation.

Siegel, L. S., & Ryan, E. B. (1988). Development of grammatical sensitivity, phonological, and short-term memory skills in normally achieving and learning disabled children. *Developmental Psychology, 24*, 28–37.

Sireci, S., Li, S., & Scarpati, S. (2003). *The effects of test accommodation on test performance: A review of the literature* (Center for Educational Assessment Research Report No. 485). Amherst, MA: School of Education, University of Massachusetts.

Slosson, R. L., Jensen, J. A., & Armstrong, R. J. (1983). *Slosson oral reading test*. East Aurora, NY: Slosson Educational Publications.

Stanford Achievement Test. (9th ed.). (1996). San Antonio, TX: Psychological Corporation.

Stone, M. H., Jastak, S., & Wilkinson, G. (1995). *Wide range achievement test—3*. Wilmington, DE: Wide Range.

Texas Education Agency. (2000). *Texas assessment of academic skills*. Austin, TX: Author.

Thomson Nelson. (1998). *Canadian tests of basic skills*. Scarborough, Ontario, Canada: Author.

Thorndike, R. L., Hagen, E. L., & Sattler, J. M. (1986). *Stanford–Binet* (4th ed.). Itasca, IL: Riverside.

Toronto, A. S. (1976). Developmental assessment of Spanish grammar. *Journal of Speech and Hearing Disorders, 41*, 150–171.

U.S. Department of Education. (2004, February 19). *Secretary Paige announces new policies to help English language learners* (Press release). Retrieved September 28, 2005, from http://www.ed.gov/news/pressreleases/2004/02/02192004.html

U.S. Department of Education. (2003). Title I, *Standards and assessment, non-regulatory draft guidance*. Retrieved September 28, 2005, from http://www.ed.gov/policy/speced/guid/nclb/standass-guidance03.pdf

Valdés, G., & Figueroa, R. (1994). *Bilingualism and testing: A special case of bias.* Norwood, NJ: Ablex.

Werner, E. O., & Kresheck, J. D. (1983). *Spanish structured photographic expressive language test.* DeKalb, IL: Janelle.

Wolf, M., & Denckla, M. B. (2005). *Rapid automatized naming test.* Hydesville, CA: Psychological and Educational Publications.

Woodcock, R. W. (DATE). *Woodcock language proficiency battery–revised.* Itasca, IL: Riverside.

Woodcock, R. W. (1998). *Woodcock reading mastery tests–revised.* Circle Pines, MN: American Guidance Service.

Woodcock, R., & Johnson, M. B. (1985). *Woodcock–Johnson revised.* Itasca, IL: Riverside.

Woodcock, R., & Muñoz-Sandoval, A. (1993). *Woodcock–Muñoz language survey.* Itasca, IL: Riverside.

21

Cross-Cutting Themes and Future Research Directions

Catherine Snow

Summarizing research on a topic as complex as second-language literacy is a Herculean task. The complexity of the panel's work is revealed in the topic-based organization of this volume and in the richness of the synthesis chapters provided in each part. Understanding the development of second-language literacy skills requires at least the following subtasks:

- *Understanding the complexity of the reading process.* The contributions to successful reading made by accuracy and fluency in word reading, control over the requisite language skills (vocabulary, syntax, discourse structures), and world knowledge have all been richly documented for monolingual readers. Although the reading process is complex for all students, the individual differences among English-language learners greatly increase the complexity of the task of understanding the reading process for these students.
- *Understanding individual differences.* Any learner brings certain strengths and weaknesses to the task of learning to read. However, English-language learners are more variable by far in the kinds of knowledge they bring to the literacy classroom than are English-only children. Some English-language learners know how to read in their first language and some do not. English-language learners are also likely, for example, to fall below the range of monolingual English-speaking children on measures of English-language knowledge, and some may fall below that range on knowledge of the Roman alphabet and other aspects of English orthography.
- *Understanding development.* Dynamic models of development view the acquisition of any complex skill as successive restructurings, not just accretions of knowledge. There is good evidence that children adopt, abandon, and reformulate their theories of how English is spelled and read as they develop from novice to skilled readers.

- *Understanding the context in which second-language learners develop reading.* English-language learners vary tremendously in their conditions of learning— classrooms where everyone else is a monolingual English speaker; mixed first-language classrooms learning exclusively in English; and bilingual classrooms, where the first language may be used a little or a lot. Their home environments are also varied with regard to language use (i.e., monolingual first language or bilingual) and literacy practices. Even describing these many variations is a massive task, let alone understanding how they interact with literacy outcomes.

The panel reviewed information relevant to each of these four dimensions of second-language literacy. We start this concluding chapter by presenting those propositions that, according to the research reviews in the preceding chapters, could be defended with the available evidence. Associated with each of those propositions, we note a set of claims we would like to be able to make that are not yet sufficiently supported by the available evidence.

We highlight what appears to be the most important subset of true knowledge gaps—areas that simply have not received enough research attention. Many of the suggestions for future research presented in this chapter—both in areas in which we have partial knowledge and areas that have thus far been largely ignored—come directly from the preceding chapters. A list of all the valuable suggestions for future research formulated by the authors of those chapters would, unfortunately, be much longer than the list of propositions for which we have reasonably convincing research evidence. Therefore, we limit our suggestions here to the most salient of those made previously.

In the next section, we delineate themes that cut across the preceding chapters, noting how the findings presented in one chapter illuminate those discussed in others. We argue for the need to use data from all the chapters in an integrated fashion in an effort to understand the complexities of literacy development in a second language. In the process, we bring into the discussion a few studies outside the scope of those reviewed by the panel that we would argue are highly relevant to our charge. This is not to criticize the scope of the panel's work, but to highlight the inherently multidisciplinary nature of work on second-language literacy. The panel focused for the most part on research related to the literacy development of language-minority children and youth that had been published in peer-reviewed journals and included literacy outcomes. But data of relevance to understanding the issues addressed in this volume also come from anthropological, linguistic, discourse-analytic, and applied linguistic work that may have appeared in books rather than journals and that reflect different perspectives on literacy development. In addition to studies discussed later in this chapter, the huge literature on foreign-language teaching, whose roots predate the interest in second-language literacy acquisition, is of considerable potential relevance and yet fell largely outside the panel's purview.

WHAT WE KNOW

The research reviewed in previous chapters has yielded a number of conclusions on second-language reading about which we can have a fair degree of certainty. These conclusions are presented in this section, together with some indication of the major limitations on how far we can take them.

Domains of Achievement

Second-language readers are more likely to achieve *adequate performance* (defined as performance that either is equivalent to that of monolinguals or meets local educational standards) on measures of word recognition and spelling than on measures of reading vocabulary, comprehension, and writing. Adequate performance on word-level skills in the second language can be achieved either through bilingual instruction or instruction exclusively in the target language. Obviously, excellent instruction (systematic, intensive, differentiated) is more likely than poor instruction to generate expected levels of performance on word-level skills. But instruction good enough to produce expected levels of second-language performance on word-level skills does not ensure expected levels of performance on text-level skills. The research reviewed in this volume provides few descriptions or evaluations of programs that have generated expected levels of performance on comprehension for the majority of second-language readers studied.

In all, there were only three experimental studies that focused on vocabulary, three that examined methods to improve comprehension, and four that focused on writing. These small numbers contrast markedly with the National Reading Panel's summary of research (National Institute of Child Health and Human Development, 2000) on literacy instruction for monolinguals, which had available approximately 45 experimental studies focused on vocabulary and 205 experimental studies focused on comprehension.[1]

Although the capacity of English-language learners to achieve adequate word reading may be the most robust conclusion identified by the panel, it is important to note that almost all the available studies of word reading were carried out with elementary school learners[2] who are typically asked to read only relatively short, regular, and frequent words. Despite the clear strengths in word reading displayed by English-language learners, for example, in many cases we do not know how fluently they read, nor do we know how they perform when expected to read novel, multisyllabic, technical vocabulary in the middle and secondary grades.

Findings from studies on reading comprehension paint a different picture from the one that emerges from studies focused on word reading and spelling. The few available studies, many carried out in the Netherlands, yielded highly consistent results, indicating that the reading comprehension performance of language-minority students falls well below that of their native-speaking peers. Studies of comprehension have similarly been limited largely to students in the elementary and middle grades, leaving open the possibility that English-language learners take longer to catch up on comprehension, but eventually do arrive at the levels of native speakers. This optimistic conclusion, unfortunately,

---

[1]According to the National Reading Panel, it did not include studies of English-language learners in its review and did not examine writing.

[2]Two studies of middle-grades learners were reviewed.

is not supported by the National Assessment of Educational Progress (NAEP) data or available research on older second-language readers. For example, Barnitz and Speaker (1991) found that intermediate-level English-as-a-second-language (ESL) university students and secondary-level English-language learners failed to draw even fairly obvious inferences when reading a poem rich in figurative language, although their literal comprehension was adequate; advanced-level ESL university students drew some inferences, but not to a degree that would be considered satisfactory in a literature class.

Factors Influencing Literacy: The Same and Maybe Some More

The same societal, familial, and individual factors that predict good literacy outcomes for monolingual readers do so for second-language readers as well:

- Societal/cultural factors related to literacy outcomes for both first- and second-language readers include supportive communities, stable economic prospects, effective schools, high educational standards, high teacher expectations for student performance, and good instruction.
- Familial/cultural factors include socioeconomic status (SES), parental education and literacy levels, and home support for literacy development.
- Individual factors include school readiness skills, phonological processing skills, oral language proficiency (including vocabulary), and use of comprehension strategies.

It is widely assumed that additional societal, familial, and individual factors not relevant to the literacy development of monolingual readers may come into play in predicting literacy outcomes for second-language readers. Indeed, the greater complexity of predicting outcomes for the latter readers is one reason they are the focus of research. Unfortunately, strong research evidence does not exist to support the impact of many societal/familial factors that one might predict would be related to second- but not first-language outcomes. The weak evidence concerning certain societal/familial factors and the stronger evidence concerning individual factors that are particularly relevant to predicting second-language outcomes are briefly summarized here.

- One might expect societal factors, both institutional and cultural, to influence second-language outcomes, but evidence supporting this expectation is scarce. For example, research has not demonstrated an impact of such factors as the history of the second-language group's immigration (voluntary or forced, economically or politically motivated), the status of the first-language group in the second-language setting (e.g., Koreans in the United States have high status, but in Japan have low status), and the history and nature of literacy within the first language (Chinese has a long and revered literacy tradition, whereas Hmong does not). One fairly consistent finding across a number of studies is that language-minority students' reading comprehension performance improves when they read culturally familiar materials. However, the language of the text appears to be a stronger influence on reading performance: Students perform better when they read or use material in the language they know better. Although the general hypothesis that the sociocultural context influences literacy outcomes remains highly plausible, limitations in the design, systematicity, instrumentation, and, most important, theoretical grounding of the available research limit the strength of the basis for this interpretation. Moreover, students' cultural affiliations are frequently confounded with SES, for which, as discussed earlier in the report, there is strong evidence of an impact on literacy outcomes, rendering interpretation even more problematic.

- Familial factors, like societal factors, incorporate economic, legal, and cultural influences. Remarkably, there is little evidence of influence of such likely determinants of child outcomes as immigration status (documented or not), commitment to maintaining the first language as a home language, parental literacy in either the first or second language, capacity and opportunity to select educational programs for the child, and presence in the home of highly proficient first-language (e.g., grandparents) and second-language (e.g., older siblings schooled in the United States) speakers.

- Individual factors relevant to second-language reading include, in addition to school readiness and emergent literacy skills, level of language and literacy knowledge in the first language, background knowledge, metacognitive capacity to treat those first-language skills as resources in learning the second language, strategies to approach text comprehension, and motivation to succeed academically and socially in the second-language setting. Age of onset of second-language learning is widely thought to influence second-language outcomes, but its influence cannot be easily disentangled from the impact of factors that happen to correlate with age, such as motivation, access to social contacts, commitment to maintaining the first language, and grade-level task demands.

The Sorry State of Assessment

Our review of assessments used with English-language learners in Part V clearly leads to the conclusion that more work remains to be done. The lack of diagnostic assessments in the domain of reading comprehension (see Snow, 2003) is particularly poignant for second-language readers, whose sources of difficulty with comprehension may be different from those of monolingual readers. The state of the art of oral proficiency and academic-language assessment is far behind that of phonological awareness, word reading accuracy, and fluency assessment. Finally, little research has focused on identifying older English-language learners with learning disabilities. Serious attention to these issues is prerequisite to making real progress in understanding second-language literacy development and in helping teachers monitor and improve instructional outcomes for second-language learners.

Transfer Cannot Be Ruled Out

The concept of transfer from a first to a second language or from a first to a second literacy system has an honored, but contested, place in thinking about language learning. The classic definition of *transfer*, derived from the tradition of behaviorist psychology and contrastive analysis (Lado, 1964), suggests that strongly developed first-language habits are hardest to overcome in a second language—in other words, transfer is considered to be mostly negative in its impact. In contrast, the potential for transfer is a major plank in many arguments favoring bilingual over purely second-language education. A somewhat moderated potential for transfer is a central claim in Cummins' (1979) influential notions about the threshold hypothesis.

It is thus striking that there has been so little research speaking directly and unequivocally to the existence, role, or strength of transfer in second-language literacy development. Much of the evidence reviewed in Part II is consistent with the transfer of knowledge from the first to the second language in specific domains. However, most of the research findings do not unequivocally support the conclusion that transfer exists because alternative explanations are not systematically ruled out.

The evidence does show that:

- Word reading in the second language correlates with that in the first language, but to a greater or lesser extent, depending on the orthographic relationships between the first and second languages.
- Spelling in the second language shows the influence of first-language orthographic knowledge at the early stages of second-language development if second-language orthographic knowledge is limited.
- Vocabulary knowledge in the second language can be enhanced by the use of vocabulary knowledge from the first language in cases where etymological relationships between the first and second languages exist, with positive consequences for second-language reading comprehension. At the later stages of second-language development, however, the enhancement is more powerful for metalinguistic aspects of word knowledge and often requires mediation through first-language literacy.
- Reading comprehension in the second language correlates with that in the first language, but perhaps more strongly at later grades, when comprehension tasks are more challenging.
- Use of reading strategies in the first language correlates with their use in the second language once second-language reading has developed sufficiently so such strategies can be used.
- Strategic aspects of writing are closely related in the first and second languages, although again probably only after some threshold of second-language knowledge has been achieved.

Overall, correlations across languages in performance on particular tasks certainly are consistent with the claim that there is transfer from the first to the second language, but they hardly constitute strong proof of any causal relation implicating transfer. Perhaps performance in both languages is accounted for by some third factor, such as intelligence, speed of processing, visual memory, phonological sensitivity, or metalinguistic skill. In fact, there is good evidence (reviewed in chap. 7) that phonological recoding, phonological memory, and phonological awareness are strongly related across languages, suggesting that such tasks draw on the same abilities no matter the language in which they are performed. Perhaps the impact of instruction in the second language changes the nature of processing in the first language, a phenomenon that might be seen as transfer, but not of the type in which most researchers or educators are interested.

Conversely, the conditional nature of most of these documented transfer candidates could be regarded as support for the claim that these are true examples of transfer. We would hardly expect transfer of word reading skill from Chinese to English to be as strong as that from Spanish to English. It makes sense that transfer of vocabulary knowledge from Spanish to English is mediated by literacy knowledge in Spanish because Spanish–English cognates are more similar in written than in spoken form. It also makes sense that more meta-linguistic tasks constitute sites for transfer. Following Bialystok and Bouchard Ryan (1985), we define *metalinguistic* as encompassing two dimensions: control of processing and analysis of knowledge. Control of processing is not a specifically linguistic capacity, and thus should be equally available across languages. Analysis skills, similarly, are language neutral; the knowledge to be analyzed, in contrast, is highly language specific, so we cannot expect that analysis of knowledge tasks will show transfer until there is some second-language knowledge to which analysis skills can be applied. This is precisely the pattern that has been documented for transfer in the domains of lexicon and reading comprehension. But the case remains somewhat circumstantial.

What would constitute stronger proof of transfer? Unequivocal proof of transfer would come from intervention studies in which some fairly specific skill was taught in the first language to one group of learners and their performance in the second language on some related skill was compared with that of another group not receiving the first-language instruction. Yet designing such a study would require having a theory of what may transfer and to what, of how language and literacy skills relate to one another, and of what aspects of first-language knowledge may be usable for the second language. It is not certain that we have a sufficiently well-developed theory to test a full array of specific hypotheses in this domain.

To take a simple example, we might hypothesize that learning to spell in Spanish will generate skills that transfer to English. Thus, we would provide a group of learners with systematic Spanish spelling instruction and then assess their English spelling. Evidence reviewed in chapter 9 indeed suggests that the students would make many errors influenced by Spanish spelling and pronunciation—for example, *"Guen mi mami smail her aic ar beri briti"* ("When my mommy smiles her eyes are very pretty"). This would constitute presumptive evidence of transfer, especially if the comparison group made few such errors, and the transfer would appear to be entirely negative. But what if the two groups of learners were assessed on phonological analysis of words—for example, were asked to count phonemes? On that task, the children who had been taught to spell in Spanish might well perform better than those who had not because they would be relying much less on memorized spellings (sight words are a big part of early literacy instruction in English) or visual memory, and because they would have had instruction that systematically linked letters to sounds. Does this situation provide evidence in support of positive or negative transfer?

To take another example based on real but perplexing data, most studies of immigrant children growing up bilingual show negative correlations between first- and second-language vocabulary. On the face of it, those negative correlations appear to exclude the possibility of positive transfer. However, classroom teachers are unanimous in noting that children who arrive in the United States with strong first-language vocabularies have little difficulty in acquiring English words. The mechanism widely suggested for this phenomenon is that knowledge of the concepts need not be reacquired; all that is needed is new labels for those concepts already present. In other words, conceptual knowledge is available in the first language and facilitates vocabulary acquisition in the second language. Is this evidence of transfer from the first to the second language, or is the conceptual knowledge nonlinguistic? If the availability of conceptual knowledge promotes second-language acquisition for older learners, why does the same not hold true for younger children growing up bilingual? Or is the more rapid second-language acquisition of children with large first-language vocabularies simply a reflection of the fact that they are more likely to have had excellent first-language schooling?

The intriguing lack of a documented relationship in the studies reviewed in this volume between oral language proficiency in the first language and second-language literacy suggests the value of a double-dissociation design for identifying cases of true transfer. If one teaches Skill X in the first language as part of a study designed to test for transfer, perhaps one should be required to predict not just what second-language skill will be influenced, but also what second-language skill will *not* be influenced. Returning to the earlier Spanish spelling example, we would interpret findings such as those we have imagined to be a demonstration of positive transfer from Spanish spelling to English phonological analysis, possibly mediated by Spanish phonological analysis. But if the children who had received Spanish spelling instruction also showed greater improvement than controls on English oral language proficiency, it would be difficult to attribute these changes to any well-specified transfer mechanism. Such findings would appear to suggest a prima facie case that the effects in English resulted from something other than pure transfer because no hypothesized mechanism links Spanish spelling to English oral proficiency.

In short, then, on the basis of the available evidence, transfer cannot be ruled out as a factor in second-language literacy development, but neither is the evidence demonstrating its impact strong or unequivocal. Most discouraging, despite the recurrent invocation of transfer as an argument for bilingual instruction and the long history of its use as a central theoretical concept, there is still remarkably little clarity about how to define transfer operationally, what evidence would count as demonstrating its existence, or the range of phenomena for which it might be expected to operate.

We Have to Believe Instruction Is Important

The literature we reviewed reveals remarkably little about the effectiveness of different aspects of instruction, and it provides only limited guidance about how good instruction for second-language speakers might differ from that for first-language speakers. Many of the instructional components known to be effective with monolingual English speakers—enhancing children's phonological awareness before or while teaching letter–sound relationships, teaching letter–sound relationships systematically, integrating letter–sound instruction with use of meaningful and engaging texts, providing extra help immediately to students who are falling behind—appear to be effective as well with English-language learners. Adapting instruction to specifics of the child's knowledge base (e.g., focusing phonological awareness instruction on phoneme distinctions not made in the child's first language, pointing out cognates, drawing contrasts between the first and second language in preferred discourse structures) has sometimes proved helpful, but English-language learners in heterogeneous classrooms where such first-language-specific help is unavailable can be successful if provided high-quality instruction in their second language. Some evidence exists concerning the value of specific instructional approaches to well-defined learning challenges (e.g., using more elaborated, context-enriched methods for teaching vocabulary; see chap. 15). Although the qualitative studies suggest that high-quality comprehensive literacy programs promote second-language literacy development, there is limited quasi-experimental research on the value of these more comprehensively defined approaches to literacy instruction for second-language learners (e.g., Success for All). Given the importance of concurrently developing a multitude of skills in second-language learners, much more research is needed in this area.

Most discouraging, the research we reviewed provides little basis for deciding whether or what kinds of accommodations or adaptations are most helpful to second-language learners. The research does suggest, however, that one kind of accommodation—developing English oral proficiency in the context of literacy instruction—would help. Part IV indicates that effect sizes for English-language learners are lower and more variable than those for native-English-speaking students, suggesting that the teaching of component skills is likely to be necessary, but insufficient, for improving literacy achievement among the English-language learners, and the research in Part I indicates that second-language oral language proficiency influences text-level skills.

Just as the studies cited in Part II highlight cross-language relationships, the studies in chapter 14 demonstrate that language-minority students instructed in their native language (primarily Spanish) as well as English perform, on average, better on English reading measures than language-minority students instructed only in their second language (English in this case). This is the case at both the elementary and secondary levels. The strongest evidence supporting this claim comes from the randomized studies that indicate a moderate effect in favor of bilingual instruction. Nonetheless, the advantage of bilingual over English-only instruction is moderate, so lower expectations for learners without access to native-language literacy instruction are unjustified. Obviously, if there is political or educational value attached to bilingualism and biliteracy, then bilingual programs are to be preferred even more strongly because there is no basis in the research findings to suggest that they are in any way disadvantageous to English academic outcomes.

A logical case could be made that factors shown to promote monolingual children's literacy development, such as the capacity of the teacher to adapt instruction to the child's needs, are even more important to children learning to read in a second language. The quantitative data needed to support this statement are not directly available, however, and collecting them would require a complex study to test what is, in effect, an interaction hypothesis: Differentiation of instruction according to individual learner needs accounts for a larger proportion of the variance in reading outcomes for students learning to read in a second than a first language. But if we accept that learning to read in a second language is more difficult than learning to read in a language one already speaks, it appears obvious that this is also a task whose outcome is more determined by quality of teaching. Thus, it is surprising that we do not have more robust findings concerning the relationship of high-quality instruction to good outcomes for second-language learners. A first step might be simply to expand the available database of descriptions of instruction demonstrated to be highly effective with second-language readers. The currently available descriptive studies of instruction (see chap. 16) do not provide empirical warrants that the instruction described generates excellent outcomes for bilingual learners.

In chapters 16 and 17 (focusing on children educated in special education settings), we review studies offering rich descriptions of promising instructional practices. These descriptions can provide considerable guidance to educators about what kinds of practices might be used with second-language readers, even in the absence of incontrovertible evidence that these are the best possible practices. For example, studies in both chapters indicate that students' English-language proficiency appears to interact with the instructional approach employed; accordingly, teachers may need to differentiate instruction depending on student proficiency levels. Use of student assessment data to focus instruction and collaboration between special education teachers and resource specialists was also deemed important in meeting student needs. It appears obvious that understanding something about cultural differences is important for educators working with such students; case studies of classroom practice (e.g., Au & Mason's [1981] study of the Kamehameha School) suggest that adapting instruction to the cultural and linguistic characteristics of learners has positive effects on students' level of engagement and participation during reading lessons. But the studies lack measures of literacy achievement or comprehension, or are not designed in ways that allow causal inferences attributing improvement in reading to cultural accommodations. Clearly, more research is needed in this area.

Some sparse evidence suggests that features of effective professional development are not specific to teachers of second-language learners. More specifically, it suggests that creating change in teachers is a time-consuming process that requires considerable investment on the part of the change agents as well as the teachers. Consistent with previous findings (Baker & Smith, 1999), teachers found the professional development to be most helpful when it provided hands-on practice opportunities with teaching techniques readily applicable to their classrooms or in-class demonstrations with their own or a colleague's students. In addition, teachers requested more personalized coaching—a time-tested method for improving teaching practices (Gersten, Morvant, & Brengelman, 1995). Unfortunately, large-scale evaluations of professional development that focus on issues specific to English-language learners are not available. However, many features of good instruction are as useful to teachers of English-language learners as to teachers of monolingual children, and of course many classrooms contain both types of students. Thus, professional development that attends to the need for differentiated instruction should be available to all teachers in U.S. schools, and issues of second-language acquisition and second-language reading should not be restricted to professional development for ESL or bilingual teachers.

THE KEY GAPS

In the preceding section, we note not just what we know about various topics, but also where conclusions are limited or where research has thus far failed to confirm reasonable expectations. In this section, we focus on the true gaps—the topics that have been neglected almost entirely, in some cases in the research literature in general and in others in the work selected for review in this volume.

Whole Chunks of Development

It is striking how little systematic attention has been paid to school readiness, the course of emergent literacy skills, or the design of optimal preschool programs for English-language learners. Prevention has become a slogan for good literacy practice, and it is widely acknowledged that prevention is most effective if begun during the preschool period. Yet it appears that the field is ignoring the needs of a group that is at high risk of literacy difficulties by failing to focus on efforts to understand or enhance their development during the preschool years. The topic of simultaneous bilingual development is frequently visited in the field of child language; it has generated dozens of case studies and some small-group analyses. A smaller number of studies have addressed the development of incipiently bilingual children in the preschool period (see Tabors & Snow, 1994, 2001, for reviews), but those studies for the most part have not addressed questions related to designing optimal preschool environments for these second-language learners.

The vast majority of the studies reviewed in this volume focus on kindergarten through fifth-grade students. Middle- and secondary-grade students are not included in most of the studies reviewed. Hence, research has paid far too little attention to issues that become increasingly important in those grades: vocabulary development, oral language proficiency, comprehension of challenging texts, instruction for dealing with academic text structures, interactions between reading comprehension and content area learning, and so on.

The topic of age differences in second-language learning and the related topic of the impact of varying levels of first-language literacy cannot be addressed systematically without more studies providing comparable cross-age data. Questions about the existence of and explanations for age differences in second-language/second-literacy acquisition have generated an extensive literature (see Marinova-Todd, Marshall, & Snow, 2000, for a highly partial review). Although much of that literature might be regarded as tangential to issues of literacy development, a little probing makes clear that literacy in the first and second languages interacts with age in complex ways. Jia and Aaronson (2003), for example, showed that Chinese immigrant children under the ages of 10 and 11 switched toward dominance in English relatively quickly, in part, because their access to literacy in Chinese was still quite limited. Slightly older immigrants who had mastered full literacy in Chinese and who had more autonomy selected Chinese-focused activities at a much higher rate, choosing to read Chinese books and magazines, listen to Chinese music, view Chinese videos, and associate with Chinese-speaking peers. Needless to say, their progress in English was slower than that of the younger immigrants, but their maintenance of Chinese was much greater. Greater attention to age differences is consistent with the dynamic, developmental dimension of the model that provides the framework for this volume. Such an emphasis also has enormous importance for practice if the evidence suggests that younger and older English-language learners benefit from different emphases in instruction.

Practitioners are desperate for information about how best to serve older immigrant students, particularly those who have experienced poor and/or interrupted schooling, whose first-language academic skills are low or indeterminate, and who come from language and schooling backgrounds about which little is known. A much greater focus on postprimary English-language learners is needed to provide a research basis for improved practice in the middle and secondary grades.

Aspects of Literacy

New instructional topics would emerge into sharper focus with greater research attention to older learners, including the challenges of comprehension, learning from text, understanding and producing academic language, genre differentiation, and academic writing. These tasks receive little attention in the early grades, where word reading and initial vocabulary learning shape the instructional agenda. Yet they are the key challenges for later arrivals, who must tackle them simultaneously with learning basic vocabulary and the basics of reading English words.

Questions about factors that influence the development of academic language skills and the possibility of transfer of these skills from the first to the second language need to take into account cultural differences, individual differences, home language influences, and educational settings and goals.

There is actually a good deal of information available about the production and comprehension of extended discourse by second-language learners. Much of this information comes from the ESL or foreign-language field, and thus deals mainly with students outside the 3- to 18-year age range on which we focus in this volume. Nonetheless, this work holds considerable relevance for understanding the reading development of older English-language learners. For example, Maeno (2000, 2004) found that college-age Japanese second-language speakers learned relatively quickly some key rules for successful Japanese narrative discourse (e.g., to avoid excessive detail), but did not appear to notice other rules adhered to by native speakers (e.g., that information is typically organized in stanzas of three lines). Kang (2003) found that Korean college students writing English narratives tended to underuse orientation and character delineation (by native English speakers' standards) and were much more likely than native English speakers to draw explicit morals from each narrative. Hu-Chou (2000) found that advanced foreign-language students of

Chinese failed to organize information in the way expected by Chinese readers when writing academic essays. These examples (all taken from recent Harvard dissertations; dozens more such studies could be cited with a broader and more systematic search) offer some indication of contrasts in textual or extended-discourse rules that could well interfere with comprehension, as well as with the evaluation of students' written output, thereby suggesting some specific targets for instruction.

The impacts of such variations in cultural schemata on second-language reading comprehension and writing have been documented repeatedly since the work of Kintsch and Greene (1978), Kaplan (1966), and Carrell (1983; see also Barnitz, 1986; Devine, Carrell, & Eskey, 1987, for reviews). Much of that work, however, has been published in journals devoted primarily to adult second- and foreign-language learning (*Language Learning, Studies in Second Language Acquisition*), in which learning to read is viewed as a secondary goal or inevitable consequence of language learning, rather than a major task in its own right.

There is also a small body of work on the acquisition of features of academic or distanced discourse among second-language learners. This work is important because of evidence showing that control over academic discourse features relates to reading comprehension (Snow, 1990; Velasco, 1989). In the areas of development and instruction, the panel limited its review to studies in which reading and writing were outcomes, but a broader definition of *literacy* could defensibly encompass the oral language skills that relate closely to reading. Velasco (1989), for example, showed that poor readers were less likely than good readers to produce formal word definitions (i.e., ones that included a superordinate) and provided less differentiating information about target words both in Spanish (their first language) and English (the language they were learning).

One can also see the use of language skills in distanced communication as requiring metalinguistic skill—in particular, control of processing skills (Snow, Cancino, De Temple, & Schley, 1991), in which case metalinguistic skill is a possible site for transfer from the first language. In giving definitions, one must suppress the natural, narrative mode and provide information that appears obvious (e.g., "A cat is a small animal that purrs" rather than "I have a cat and she likes to eat cucumbers") to satisfy the task demands. In providing picture descriptions, children are often asked to describe the picture to an imagined listener/reader who cannot see it, thus requiring them to anticipate the communicative needs of a distant audience. The general picture that can be gleaned from this work is that second-language speakers, like first-language speakers, differentiate face-to-face from distanced communication; even in the early grades, English-language learners understand both the need to adapt and the kinds of adaptations that may be helpful. For example, Rodino and Snow (1997) found that Spanish–English bilingual fifth graders in mainstream classrooms produced more words, different words, clarificatory markers, adjectives, specific locatives, and references to internal states when describing a picture to a distant rather than a present audience; these differences held across languages, but were much stronger in English, as was performance overall, suggesting that these learners were forgetting their Spanish. A similar group of learners still in bilingual classrooms showed poorer performance in English, but better performance in Spanish on these measures. Comparable adjustments were made in the content of picture descriptions produced in English (De Temple, Wu, & Snow, 1991) and French (Wu, De Temple, Herman, & Snow, 1994) by elementary students in an international school. In English, the longest and most detailed descriptions were produced orally for the distant audience; in French, the written descriptions were longer and more specific, even when the instructions did not mention the need for distanced communication.

Home exposure to English had limited effects on the quantity or quality of picture descriptions among these students (Ricard & Snow, 1990), about one third of whom came from non-English-speaking homes. Home exposure related more strongly to the quality of formal definitions. Students who spoke French at home produced longer and more complex picture descriptions in French than those who did not, but not more specific or adapted descriptions and not better formal definitions, suggesting indeed that control of processing is independent of language proficiency.

Cross-language correlations in performance on academic language tasks have been found to be quite high in some cases (Davidson, Kline, & Snow, 1986; Velasco, 1989), but rather low in the international-school students studied by other researchers (De Temple et al., 1991; Snow, 1990; Wu et al., 1994). That disparity may be related to the different educational settings of these two groups of students: The first set of studies examined students in truly bilingual programs attempting to promote literacy and academic language use in both languages, whereas the international school, which was the site of the second set of studies, used English as the medium of instruction, offered ESL to students low in English proficiency, and taught French as a foreign language.

Attrition and Bilingualism

Given our focus on English literacy outcomes, it is not surprising that the panel paid little attention to studies of first-language attrition and the limits on bilingualism under different educational and societal conditions. Language attrition is a complex field in its own right, and one that would not have been easy to incorporate into this review. It is relevant, however, as an aspect of thinking about the value of first-language support in instructional settings and about transfer. After all, if the system from which transfer is meant to occur is withering, what are the implications for the possibility of optimizing transfer effects?

Understanding Where They Start

Reading research conducted in North America has paid remarkably little attention to the reading processes of monolingual readers in other languages. Yet understanding the word- and text-level processing in which both skilled and developing readers of Chinese, Japanese, Arabic, Hindi, Spanish, and other languages engage appears crucial if we are to develop explicit theories of transfer and of universal versus particular processes involved in literacy development. Every orthography poses its own challenges and offers unique mechanisms for representing words graphically, and every language similarly creates specific challenges and offers its own preferred mechanisms for organizing information into literate structures. Research has focused on the psycholinguistic processes involved in reading Chinese (e.g., Chen & Shu, 2001; Perfetti & Tan, 1998), and European researchers have exploited variation in orthographic depth in the study of word-reading development (e.g., Goswami & Bryant, 1990). However, the implications of this work for second-language reading development have been underemphasized.

In addition to arguing for systematic exploitation of what we know about early reading development in other languages, we would argue for much more cross-linguistic analysis that incorporates attention to grammar and discourse as well as orthography. One might argue that proponents of contrastive analysis conducted all the cross-linguistic analysis ever needed. Yet their analyses could be better characterized as *cross-language* than *cross-linguistic*; that is, their work was not sufficiently informed by a sophisticated understanding of linguistic systems.

A lesson to be learned from studying first-language acquisition across a wide range of languages is that each language has a domain of relative elaboration or complexity: Spanish has its multiple verb forms, Russian nouns must be marked simultaneously for one of six cases in a way that differs in each of four declensions, Hebrew marks gender on all nouns and on verbs that agree with them, and so on. To the foreign-language learner of any of these languages, these systems seem impossibly complex, and the naive prediction is that they will be acquired late and with difficulty by the young first-language learner. Yet nothing could be further from the truth; children are more likely to make errors with verbs in English than in Spanish and take longer to learn pronominal cases in English than noun cases in Russian. The complexity of the target system becomes a spur to the learner, rather than an obstacle: It defines a problem space that children learning a language encounter early and thus work on diligently.

Our understanding of literacy acquisition can be informed by these findings from cross-linguistic studies of language acquisition. The task of learning to read in any language is defined by the orthographic system of that language. To learn to read in Chinese, one must solve the presenting problem of visual discrimination and visual memory, and all the evidence suggests that Chinese children do so rather efficiently. To learn to read in Arabic, one must solve the presenting problem of selecting from among a small set of possible pronunciations of the written form by using syntactic and meaning cues. To learn to read in English, one must solve the presenting problem of orthographic depth and the identification of both phonological and morphological units. A successful course of acquisition is driven by the nature of the skilled processes needed. This is the insight provided by truly cross-linguistic analyses.

Thus, it is not surprising that the individual skills that predict good reading outcomes for English-learning versus monolingual English readers are so similar—they are the skills that help children solve the particular challenges of reading English. Nor is it surprising that features of instruction that work well for English monolingual children also work for English-learning children, who must learn the same skills because they are ultimately faced with the same task. These understandings would be more accessible if the research being done on second-language reading were informed more systematically by the linguistic and orthographic challenges of the target language.

This same argument, of course, should apply equally, although perhaps even more complexly, to the processes involved in comprehension. As discussed earlier, we know that there are language-specific rules for organizing information in text and differentiating genres. There are also culture-specific rules for what it means to comprehend—how much work is meant to be the responsibility of the reader versus the writer. These are systems that reveal themselves in differences among the narratives of Asian, Latino, and Anglo preschool children (McCabe, 1996; McCabe & Bliss, 2003), in school-age children's science reasoning (Ballenger, 1997; Hudicourt-Barnes, in press), and in extended written and oral discourses (Hu-Chou, 2000; Kang, 2003; Maeno, 2000, 2004). These systems need to be understood on their own terms before it becomes possible to see how any two of them contrast, where the potential for positive and negative transfer lies, and what aspects of the contrasts can be targeted most helpfully in instruction.

Finally, second-language literacy instruction ideally should be designed with some understanding of the literacy practices and preferences of English-language learners. Rubinstein-Avila (2001) found that Dominican- and Mexican-origin Latino English-language-learning adolescents read, in both Spanish and English, materials that could have been used as a resource in their literacy instruction had their teachers known more about the students' preferred literacy activities. The students in Rubinstein-Avila's sample who read the most outside of school were also those whose mothers had higher educational levels and who defined themselves as better readers. Survey information from a wider range of English-language learners about their out-of-school literacy practices could be of great value in adapting literacy instruction to these students' needs and interests.

The complex model of influences on reading that informed the panel's work notes the importance of having available data about both monolingual and fluent bilingual readers to allow for comparison with English-language learners learning to read in their first language, their second language, or both. Clearly, in this view, studies of literacy development in languages other than English constitute part of the research agenda for understanding second-language literacy development.

Learning to Read in a Second Language, the First Time or the Second?

Finally, a key issue that needs more attention in both research and theory on biliteracy is the difference between learning to read *in* a second language and learning to read a second language. Learning to read for the first time in a second language is arguably a difficult task, particularly for children who have limited oral skills in that language and limited emergent literacy skills in any language. For such children, the task of literacy development is unsupported by a well-developed understanding of the nature and purposes of literacy, and the potential for self-monitoring and self-teaching (Share, 1995) is absent because these processes presume access to meaning via decoding. Children with limited vocabulary knowledge who try to apply initial knowledge of letter–sound correspondences to printed forms will have little basis for knowing whether they are performing this task correctly, and thus they will be unable to progress without constant access to instructional guidance.

Weber and Longhi-Chirlin (2001) present case studies of two Spanish-speaking first graders in an English-only classroom. Both children were making slow progress in comprehending spoken English and in decoding and spelling in English. But they linked the words they were reading only minimally to their oral comprehension skills. Their reading was not informed by the expectation of meaning that is present among first-language readers, and thus the course of literacy development they experienced was quite different from (and likely to be slower and/or less successful than) that of English-only speakers learning to read in a language they already speak.

THEMES THAT CUT ACROSS THE CHAPTERS OF THIS VOLUME

Inevitably in the process of trying to organize and synthesize a sprawling literature, it is necessary to put studies into categories, formulate specific questions, and in other ways simplify the task. The result is that studies that could inform one another sometimes end up being discussed in isolation.

In chapter 15, we review research suggesting that certain literacy instructional practices are quite effective with second- and first-language readers. But to understand those practices and how to avoid ones that are less effective, we must have information of the type discussed in chapter 16, including rich descriptions of what teachers actually do in classroom settings to engage learners, present lessons, organize the classroom to make differentiated instruction possible, and so on. Thus, there is value in linking studies of instructional effectiveness explicitly to rich descriptions of those effective strategies, rather than isolating impact studies from descriptive studies.

In Part II, it makes perfect sense as an organizational strategy to separate studies that identify the predictors of second-language oral proficiency from those that identify the predictors of second-language literacy. But this separation promotes the notion that second-language oral and literacy skills develop independently of one another—that they have separate ontogenies. In fact, language and literacy skills in either the first or second language have a transactional relationship with one another: The development of each depends on and contributes to the development of the other. Thus, it is useful to study first- and second-language oral proficiency and literacy skills together so that transactional links among them can be studied.

Most distorting, however, is the division of topics resulting in the presence in this volume of two chapters focused on the sociocultural context, separating the treatment of language and literacy development from the web of meaning in which it occurs. We would argue that this convenient and perhaps inevitable separation is particularly disorienting when discussing language minorities living in a traditionally monolingual society that is widely committed to monolingual schooling and places little value on bilingualism. The challenge of being, becoming, or remaining a bilingual has an entirely different character in the United States than in the highlands of Peru, in Stockholm, or in Riga; even within the United States, the challenge is quite different in National City, California, than it is in Des Moines, Iowa. We are failing to understand the phenomenon of biliteracy development if we do not integrate the sociocultural context with developmental and instructional data. Thus, it is important to connect the topic of sociocultural context to the treatment of language and literacy development, integrating data about the sociocultural context with developmental and instructional data.

Yet we do not believe we are misrepresenting the field by separating these topics, which tend to be treated in different bodies of work, approached with different methods, and even published in different journals. We are struck (and discouraged) by the degree to which research reports on the literacy development of bilingual children ignore the nature of the communities in which they live, the quality of the instruction they receive, the language-learning goals their parents hold for them, and the daily opportunities they experience to speak English or another tongue. We are equally troubled by how often we encounter descriptions of the context of second-language/literacy acquisition unaccompanied by data about the outcome of the acquisition process.

Building on the previous chapters that link language to literacy and on the synthesis that appears earlier in the present chapter, we discuss here a few further specific cases of the need for integration. In doing so, we explore in greater detail how integrating information across levels, disciplines, and settings—something seldom done because it requires a level of collaboration and cross-fertilization that goes beyond the capacity of most research—could lead to a comprehensive picture of second-language and second-literacy learning.

The Link Between English Proficiency and the First-Language Context

In one scenario, adolescent immigrants from China, the Dominican Republic and Mexico, and Haiti all arrive in the United States at about the same time, with parents who have immigrated for more or less the same reasons (Páez, 2001). They all attend similar sorts of schools, sometimes even the same schools. Yet 4 years later, there are significant differences in the levels of English spoken by members of the three groups and in the degree to which they have maintained their home language. The Haitian adolescent immigrants speak English best, but are least likely to have maintained their parents' language. The Spanish speakers are most likely to continue to use Spanish regularly, but their skills in English fall far short of what we might expect. The Chinese adolescent immigrants' scores on a measure of oral English are, on average, slightly below those of the Haitians, but only in the Chinese group do any students score at a level indicating adequate English proficiency. In other words, the process of learning English is related to the likelihood of maintaining the home language, and that in turn is influenced by such factors as the history of literacy and education in the home language (which promote home language maintenance for Chinese immigrants) and the ease of travel to and continued political participation in the home country (which promote home language maintenance for Spanish-speaking immigrants).

The Link Between English Proficiency and the Second-Language Context

In another scenario, Spanish-speaking children are learning to read and write in English in a number of different settings: in English-only instructional settings in Seattle, Washington; in transitional bilingual programs in New York City; in two-way bilingual programs in Boston, Massachusetts; and in bilingual schools in Bogotá, Colombia. In the second and fourth cases, all the children in the class are native Spanish speakers, whereas in the first and third, half or fewer are. The children in Bogotá are probably more middle class than those in the other settings. The children in the three U.S. settings hear quite a lot of English outside of school, whereas the children in Bogotá rarely do. From one perspective, the tasks of learning to speak, understand, read, and write English are the same for all these children. All must grapple with the problem spaces defined by English vocabulary, phonology, grammar, and orthography.

From other perspectives, however, these learners have quite different tasks ahead of them. Spanish speakers in Seattle are a minority of the non-English speakers in the city's schools; the faster they learn English, the sooner they assert their dominance within the immigrant community. By fourth grade, most of these students are essentially monolingual English speakers, but many are still reading poorly in English. Spanish speakers in New York are given little support for Spanish literacy development, but they code mix Spanish and English daily with family members and neighbors, and they visit Puerto Rico or the Dominican Republic regularly; thus, their oral Spanish skills continue to develop even as they learn English. Furthermore, the variety of English they learn is heavily influenced by Spanish, just as their variety of Spanish is heavily influenced by English. The Spanish speakers in Boston have access to support for Spanish literacy development, but their opportunities for rich oral Spanish are constrained by the limited Spanish of their English-speaking classmates. By fourth grade, quite a lot of English is spoken by everyone in their classes, even during Spanish time. Several of the Spanish speakers are resisting returning to the bilingual fifth grade, saying they would rather go to a regular school. The children in Bogotá continue to speak Spanish with each other; by fourth grade, some of them are competent English readers, whereas others are still struggling in English, although they read well in Spanish. A few of the children have been pulled out of the school and placed in all-Spanish educational settings by their parents in response to their struggles. Although they have been exposed to as much English instruction as the children in Boston, on average their English is much less developed. In contrast, the Spanish-speaking parents in Boston are worried that their children do not speak English well enough, whereas the parents in Bogotá are thrilled at their children's English skills.

All these children faced the same tasks from a purely psycholinguistic perspective, from a cross-linguistic perspective, and from an instructional perspective. But these perspectives are not enough. The political perspective that defines English as the national language of the United States and Spanish as the national language of Colombia cannot be ignored. Also relevant is the economic perspective—that immigrants must learn English to survive in the United States and gain little additional value from their home language, whereas Colombians must speak Spanish but gain an advantage in the labor market if they also speak English. The sociological perspective, which defines who interacts with whom and in what language(s), must be considered as well because opportunities for interaction also constitute opportunities for language learning. Nor can the cultural perspective, from which derive the value of bilingualism to children and their families and their sense of connection to the ancestral land, be forgotten, although it can be trumped by other considerations. As the students in these four settings grow older, the forces of adolescent development, identity formation, personal preferences, talents, and motivation start to play a role in their pursuit of English, Spanish, or bilingual outcomes. Most clearly, however, if they have not also learned to read well in either or both languages, their futures will be severely imperiled.

REFERENCES

Au, K. H.-P., & Mason, J. M. (1981). Social organizational factors in learning to read: The balance of rights hypothesis. *Reading Research Quarterly, 17*(1), 115–152.

Baker, S., & Smith, S. (1999). Starting off on the right foot: The influence of four principles of professional development in improving literacy instruction in two kindergarten programs. *Learning Disabilities Research and Practice, 14*(4), 239–253.

Ballenger, C. (1997). Social identities, moral narratives, scientific argumentation: Science talk in a bilingual classroom. *Language and Education, 11*(1), 1–14.

Barnitz, J. (1986). Toward understanding the effects of cross-cultural schemata and discourse structure on second language reading comprehension. *Journal of Reading Behavior, 18*, 95–118.

Barnitz, J., & Speaker, R. (1991). Second language readers' comprehension of a poem: Exploring contextual and linguistic aspects. *World Englishes, 10*, 197–209.

Bialystok, E., & Bouchard Ryan, E. (1985). Toward a definition of metalinguistic skill. *Merrill-Palmer Quarterly, 31*, 229–251.

Carrell, P. (1983). Three components of background knowledge in reading comprehension. *Language Learning, 33*, 183–207.

Chen, H.-C., & Shu, H. (2001). Lexical activation during the recognition of Chinese characters: Evidence against early phonological activation. *Psychonomic Bulletin and Review, 8*, 511–518.

Cummins, J. (1979). Linguistic interdependence and the educational development of bilingual children. *Review of Educational Research, 49*, 221–225.

Davidson, R., Kline, S., & Snow, C. E. (1986). Definitions and definite noun phrases: Indicators of children's decontextualized language skills. *Journal of Research in Childhood Education, 1*, 37–48.

De Temple, J., Wu, H. F., & Snow, C. E. (1991). Papa Pig just left for Pigtown: Children's oral and written picture descriptions under varying instructions. *Discourse Processes, 14*, 469–495.

Devine, J., Carrell, P., & Eskey, D. (Eds.). (1987). *Research in reading in English as a second language.* Washington, DC: Teachers of English to Speakers of Other Languages.

Gersten, R., Morvant, M., & Brengleman, S. (1995). Close to the classroom is close to the bone: Coaching as a means to translate research into classroom practice. *Exceptional Children, 52*, 102–197.

Goswami, U., & Bryant, P. (1990). *Phonological skills and learning to read.* Hillsdale, NJ: Lawrence Erlbaum Associates.

Hu-Chou, H.-L. (2000). *Toward an understanding of writing in a second language: Evidence and its implications from L2 writers of Chinese.* Unpublished doctoral dissertation, Harvard Graduate School of Education.

Hudicourt-Barnes, J. (in press). Argumentation in Haitian Creole classrooms. *Harvard Educational Review.*

Jia, G., & Aaronson, D. (2003). A longitudinal study of Chinese children and adolescents learning English in the United States. *Applied Psycholinguistics, 24*, 131–161.

Kang, J. Y. (2003). *On producing culturally and linguistically appropriate narratives in a foreign language: A discourse analysis of Korean EFL learners' written narratives.* Unpublished doctoral dissertation, Harvard Graduate School of Education.

Kaplan, R. B. (1966). Cultural thought patterns in intercultural education. *Language Learning, 16*(1), 1–20.

Kintsch, W., & Greene, E. (1978). The role of culture-specific schemata in the comprehension and recall of stories. *Discourse Processes, 1*, 1–13.

Lado, R. (1964). *Language Teaching: A Scientific Approach*, McGraw-Hill.

Maeno, Y. (2000). *Acquisition of Japanese oral narrative style by native English-speaking bilinguals.* Unpublished doctoral dissertation, Harvard Graduate School of Education.

Maeno, Y. (2004). *The acquisition of the Japanese oral narrative style by native English-speaking bilinguals.* Lewiston, NY: Edwin Mellen.

Marinova-Todd, S., Marshall, D. B., & Snow, C. E. (2000). Three misconceptions about age and second-language learning. *TESOL Quarterly, 34*, 9–34.

McCabe, A. (1996). *Chameleon readers: Teaching children to appreciate all kinds of good stories.* New York: McGraw-Hill.

McCabe, A., & Bliss, L. (2003). *Patterns of narrative discourse: A multicultural, life span approach.* Boston: Allyn & Bacon.

National Institute of Child Health and Human Development. (2000). *Report of the National Reading Panel. Teaching children to read: An evidence-based assessment of the scientific research literature on reading and its implications for reading instruction* (NIH Publication No. 00-4769). Washington, DC: U.S. Government Printing Office.

Páez, M. (2001). *Language and the immigrant child: Predicting English language proficiency for Chinese, Dominican, and Haitian students.* Unpublished doctoral dissertation, Harvard Graduate School of Education.

Perfetti, C., & Tan, L. H. (1998). The time course of graphic, phonological, and semantic activation in Chinese character identification. *Journal of Experimental Psychology: Learning, Memory, & Cognition, 24*, 101–118.

Ricard, R. J., & Snow, C. E. (1990). Language skills in and out of context: Evidence from children's picture descriptions. *Journal of Applied Developmental Psychology, 11*, 251–266.

Rodino, A. M., & Snow, C. E. (1997). "Y...no puedo decir mas nada": Distanced communication skills of Puerto Rican children. In G. Kasper & E. Kellerman (Eds.), *Communication strategies: Psycholinguistic and sociolinguistic perspectives* (pp. 168–191). London: Longman.

Rubinstein-Avila, E. (2001). *From their points of view: Literacies among Latino immigrant students.* Unpublished doctoral dissertation, Harvard Graduate School of Education.

Share, D. L. (1995). Phonological recoding and self-teaching: Sine qua non of reading acquisition. *Cognition, 55*, 151–218.

Snow, C. E. (1990). The development of definitional skill. *Journal of Child Language, 17*, 697–710.

Snow, C. E., Cancino, H., De Temple, J., & Schley, S. (1991). Giving formal definitions: A linguistic or metalinguistic skill? In E. Bialystok (Ed.), *Language processing and language awareness by bilingual children* (pp. 90–112). New York: Cambridge University Press.

Snow, C. E., (2003). Assessment of reading comprehension: Researchers and practitioners helping themselves and each other. In Sweet, A. & Snow, C. E. (Eds.). *Rethinking Reading Comprehension.* (pp. 192–206). New York: The Guilford Press.

Tabors, P. O., & Snow, C. E. (1994). English as a second language in pre-school programs. In F. Genesee (Ed.), *Educating second language children* (pp. 103–125). New York: Cambridge University Press.

Tabors, P. O., & Snow, C. E. (2001). Young bilingual children and early literacy development. In S. Neuman & D. K. Dickinson (Eds.), *Handbook of early literacy research* (pp. 159–178). New York: Guilford.

Velasco, P. M. (1989). *The relationship of oral decontextualized language and reading comprehension in bilingual children.* Unpublished doctoral dissertation, Harvard Graduate School of Education.

Weber, R.-M., & Longhi-Chirlin, T. (2001). Beginning in English: The growth of linguistic and literate abilities in Spanish-speaking first graders. *Reading Research and Instruction, 41*, 19–50.

Wu, H. F., De Temple, J. M., Herman, J. A., & Snow, C. E. (1994). L'animal qui fait oink! oink!: Bilingual children's oral and written picture descriptions in English and French under varying circumstances. *Discourse Processes, 18*, 141–164.

Biographical Sketches

DIANE AUGUST, PRINCIPAL INVESTIGATOR

Dr. August is currently a Senior Research Scientist at the Center for Applied Linguistics, where she is directing a large study funded by the National Institute of Child Health and Human Development (NICHD) and the Institute of Education Sciences (IES), which investigates the development of literacy in English-language learners. She is also co-principal investigator on two IES-funded studies: The first is to develop, implement, and evaluate two models of instruction for language-minority children; and the second is to develop a diagnostic assessment of reading comprehension. She is also a co-principal investigator for the Department of Education-funded National Research and Development Center for English Language Learners. Dr. August has worked for many years as an educational consultant in the areas of literacy, program improvement, evaluation and testing, and federal and state education policy. She has been a Senior Program Officer at the National Academy of Sciences and study director for the Committee on Developing a Research Agenda on the Education of Limited English Proficient and Bilingual Students. For 10 years, she was a public school teacher in California, specializing in literacy programs for language-minority children in Grades K to 8. Subsequently, she served as a legislative assistant in the area of education for a U.S. congressman from California, worked as a Grants Officer for Carnegie Corporation of New York, and was Director of Education for the Children's Defense Fund. Among her numerous publications are two volumes co-edited with Kenji Hakuta: *Educating English Language Learners* and *Improving Schooling for Language-Minority Children: A Research Agenda*.

TIMOTHY SHANAHAN, PANEL CHAIR

Dr. Shanahan is Professor of Urban Education at the University of Illinois at Chicago (UIC) and Director of the UIC Center for Literacy. He will be president of the International Reading Association (IRA) in 2006–2007. He was director of reading for the Chicago Public Schools, the nation's third largest school district. Dr. Shanahan was a member of the National Reading Panel that advised the U.S. Congress on reading research, and he is Chair of the National Early Literacy Panel. He has published more than 150 books, articles, and chapters on reading education, and he received the Albert J. Harris Research Award for his work on reading disabilities. Professor Shanahan co-designed Project FLAME, a family literacy program for Latino immigrants, which has received an Academic Excellence designation from the U.S. Department of Education. He has been editor of the *Journal of Reading Behavior* and the *Yearbook of the National Reading Conference*. He serves on the Board of Directors of the National Family Literacy Center.

ISABEL L. BECK

Dr. Beck is Professor of Education in the School of Education and Senior Scientist at the Learning Research and Development Center, both at the University of Pittsburgh. She has engaged in extensive research on decoding, vocabulary, and comprehension, and she has published approximately 100 articles and book chapters, as well as several books. Most recently, she co-authored *Bringing Words to Life: Robust Vocabulary Instruction* (with M. McKeown and L. Kucan, Guilford). Dr. Beck's work has been acknowledged with such awards as the Oscar S. Causey Award for outstanding research from the National Reading Conference and the Contributing Researcher Award from the American Federation of Teachers for "bridging the gap between research and practice." She is also a member of the International Reading Association's Hall of Fame, and most recently she received that organization's William S. Gray Citation. Among the criteria for which she received the latter was "initiation and development of original ideas that have…improved practices in reading."

MARGARITA CALDERÓN

Dr. Calderón, a native of Juárez, Mexico, is a Research Scientist at Johns Hopkins University's Center for Research on the Education of Students Placed at Risk (CRESPAR). She is co-principal investigator with Robert Slavin on the 5-year randomized evaluation of English immersion, transitional, and two-way bilingual programs, funded by the Institute of Education Sciences. Through a series of other grants from OERI/IES, the Texas Education Agency, the Texas Workforce Commission, and the Department of Labor, she is conducting longitudinal research and development projects in El Paso, Texas, regarding teachers' learning communities, bilingual staff development, and adult English-language learners. She conducts research on reading programs for the Success for All Foundation and is collaborating with the Center for Applied Linguistics in a longitudinal study investigating the development of literacy in English-language learners. She co-edited (with Robert Slavin) *Effective Programs for Latino Students*, co-authored (with Liliana Minaya-Rowe) *Implementing Two-Way Bilingual Programs*, and has published more than 100 articles, chapters, books, and teacher training manuals. Other professional activities include the research and development of the Bilingual Cooperative Integrated Reading and Composition (BCIRC) model and the Teachers' Learning Communities program.

CHERYL DRESSLER

Dr. Dressler is a literacy consultant. She was a teacher of English as a second language (ESOL) at the secondary level in Switzerland and at the primary and university levels in the United States. In 2002, Dr. Dressler received an EdD from the Harvard Graduate School of Education. During her doctoral study years, she assisted in a longitudinal, in-depth study of the vocabulary development of monolingual and bilingual fourth and fifth graders. Her doctoral thesis investigated the English spelling development of Spanish-speaking English-language learners. Dr. Dressler's current research interests include the development of vocabulary and word structure knowledge, including orthographic and morphological knowledge, both in children who are native English speakers and in English learners. She has published in *Reading Research Quarterly* and *Learning Disabilities Research & Practice,* and she recently authored a vocabulary program for students in kindergarten and first grade, *Wordly Wise 3000, Book K and Book 1* (Educators Publishing Service).

FREDERICK ERICKSON

Dr. Erickson is George F. Kneller Professor of Anthropology of Education at the University of California, Los Angeles, where he has also been director of research at the university's laboratory elementary school. Previously, he taught at the University of Illinois, Harvard University, Michigan State University, and the University of Pennsylvania. He has been involved in the development of theory and methods in contemporary ethnography, sociolinguistics, and discourse analysis, and he has been an innovator in video-based analysis of face-to-face interaction. His sponsored research includes support by the National Institute of Mental Health, the National Institute of Education, the Spencer Foundation, and the Ford Foundation, as well as grants from the Fulbright Commission and the British Council. He has published two books and numerous articles, including an essay on qualitative research on teaching for the third edition of the *Handbook of Research on Teaching,* and articles on ethnicity and ethnographic description in *Sociolinguistics: An International Handbook of the Science of Language and Society.* He has served on the editorial boards of several journals and was editor of *Anthropology and Education Quarterly.* He has been an officer of the American Anthropological Association, from which he received the George and Louise Spindler Award for outstanding scholarly contributions to educational anthropology, and of the American Educational Research Association (AERA), from which he received an award for distinguished research on minority issues in education. In 2000, he was elected a Fellow of the National Academy of Education. In 1998–1999, he was a Fellow at the Center for Advanced Study in the Behavioral Sciences in Stanford, California. He will return to the center as a Fellow in 2006–2007.

DAVID J. FRANCIS

Dr. Francis is Professor of Quantitative Methods and Chairman of the Department of Psychology at the University of Houston, where he also serves as Director of the Texas Institute for Measurement, Evaluation, and Statistics. He is a Fellow of Division 5 (Measurement, Evaluation, and Statistics) of the American Psychological Association and a member of the Technical Advisory Group of the What Works Clearinghouse. He has also served as Chairman of the Mental

Retardation Research Subcommittee of the National Institute of Child Health and Human Development (NICHD) and the Advisory Council on Education Statistics. He is a member of national advisory panels for several federally funded projects, research centers, and state departments of education. He is also a recipient of the University of Houston Teaching Excellence Award. His areas of quantitative interest include multilevel and latent variable modeling, individual growth models, item response theory (IRT), and exploratory data analysis. Dr. Francis is currently the principal investigator on three major research projects funded by the Institute of Education Sciences and NICHD that focus on language and literacy acquisition of language-minority children. He has collaborated for many years in research on reading and reading disabilities, attention problems, and developmental consequences of brain injuries and birth defects.

GEORGIA EARNEST GARCÍA

Dr. García is a Professor in the Language and Literacy Division, Department of Curriculum and Instruction, University of Illinois at Urbana–Champaign. She also holds an appointment in the Department of Educational Policy Studies and is a faculty affiliate with the Latinas/Latinos Studies Program. Dr. García was a Senior Research Scientist at the Center for the Study of Reading for 6 years and a Fellow in the Bureau of Educational Research from 1993 to 1996. She served on the Assessment Task Force, National Council on Education Standards and Testing and, most recently, was a member of the RAND Reading Study Group on Skillful Reading. She was named a College of Education Distinguished Scholar in 1997 and was awarded the Faculty Award for Excellence in Graduate Teaching, Advising, and Research by the Council of Graduate Students in Education in 1993. She was elected to the Board of Directors of the National Reading Conference from 1998 to 2000. Dr. García's research has been funded by the Office of Educational Research and Improvement (now the Institute of Education Sciences), the Office of Special Education Programs, and the Mellon Foundation. Her areas of research include the literacy development, instruction, and assessment of students from culturally and linguistically diverse backgrounds, with much of her current research focusing on bilingual reading and writing. She has published her work in the *American Educational Research Journal, Anthropology and Education Quarterly, Journal of Literacy Research/Reading Behavior, Reading Research Quarterly, Research in the Teaching of English,* and *Review of Research in Education.* She wrote the chapter on bilingual children's reading for the third volume of the *Handbook of Reading Research,* and she was co-guest editor for the themed issue on multicultural literacy research and practice for the Journal of Literacy Research.

FRED GENESEE

Dr. Genesee is a Professor in the Psychology Department at McGill University, Montreal, Canada. He is the author of nine books and numerous articles in scientific, professional, and popular journals and publications. He has carried out extensive research on alternative approaches to bilingual education, including second/foreign-language immersion programs for language-majority students and alternative forms of bilingual education for language-minority students. This work has systematically documented the longitudinal language development (oral and written) and academic achievement of students educated through the media of two languages. Along with Donna Christian and Elizabeth Howard, he has carried out a national longitudinal study of a number of two-way immersion programs in the United States. He has consulted with policy groups in Canada, Estonia, Germany, Hong Kong, Italy, Japan, Latvia, Russia, Spain, and the United States on issues related to second-language teaching and learning in school-age learners. Dr. Genesee's current research focuses on simultaneous acquisition of two languages during early infancy and childhood. His specific interests include language representation (lexical and syntactic) in early stages of bilingual acquisition, transfer in bilingual development, structural and functional characteristics of child bilingual code mixing, and communication skills in young bilingual children.

ESTHER GEVA

Dr. Geva is a Professor in the Department of Human Development and Applied Psychology at the Ontario Institute for Studies in Education of the University of Toronto. The bulk of Dr. Geva's research, publications, conference presentations, and workshops concerns issues in the development of second-language reading skills in children and adults from various linguistic backgrounds. In recent years, Dr. Geva's research interests have focused primarily on theoretical and clinical aspects of language and literacy development in primary-level English-language-learning children. Her research is funded by the Social Sciences and Humanities Research Council of Canada, the Ontario Ministry of Education, and the National Center of Excellence. Recently, Dr. Geva obtained (with Michal Shany from Haifa University) a grant to study developmental and instructional issues in the literacy development of Ethiopian children in Israel. This grant, funded by the Israeli National Research Council, was awarded the Chief Scientist prize for the best research grant. Dr. Geva is a member of the Highly Qualified Personnel Committee of the Canadian Language and Literacy Research Network and has served on various U.S. and Canadian committees concerned with literacy development in minority children. She has edited (with Ludo Verhoeven) a special issue of *Reading and Writing: An Interdisciplinary Journal*, entitled *Cross-Orthography Perspectives on Word Recognition*, and co-edited a special issue of the *Journal of Scientific Studies of Reading*, entitled *Basic Processes in Early Second Language Reading*. Her clinical and research work with minority children resulted in the book *Interprofessional Practice With Diverse Populations: Cases in Point* (co-edited with A. Barsky and F. Westernoff). Her articles have appeared in journals such as *Annals of Dyslexia, Language Learning, Applied Psycholinguistics, Reading and Writing: An Interdisciplinary Journal*, and *Dyslexia*.

CLAUDE GOLDENBERG

Dr. Goldenberg, a native of Argentina, is Executive Director of the Center for Language Minority Education and Research (CLMER) and Associate Dean of the College of Education at California State University, Long Beach. His research has focused on Latino children's academic development, home–school connections to improve achievement, home and school factors in Latino children's academic achievement, and the processes and dynamics of school change. Dr. Goldenberg was a National Academy of Education Spencer Fellow, received a Research Recognition Award from the University of California Office of the President, and was co-recipient (with Ronald Gallimore) of the International Reading Association's Albert J. Harris Award. He was on the National Research Council's Head Start Research Roundtable and on the Council's Committee on the Prevention of Early Reading Difficulties in Young Children. He has been on the editorial boards of *Language Arts, The Elementary School Journal,* and *Literacy, Teaching and Learning.* He is the author of *Successful School Change: Creating Settings to Improve Teaching and Learning* (Teachers College Press, 2004), which describes a 5-year project to improve teaching and learning in a predominantly Hispanic school.

MICHAEL L. KAMIL

Dr. Kamil is Professor of Education at Stanford University. He is a member of the Psychological Studies in Education Committee and is on the faculty of the Learning Sciences and Technology Design Program. His research explores the effects of computer technologies on literacy and the acquisition of literacy in first and second languages. For the past several years, he has been researching the effects of recreational reading on reading achievement for English-language-learner populations. His research is funded by the California Postsecondary Education Commission, Mid-Atlantic Regional Educational Laboratory, and Pacific Regional Educational Laboratory. Dr. Kamil has been editor of *Reading Research Quarterly, Journal of Reading Behavior,* and *The Yearbook of the National Reading Conference.* He currently serves on several editorial advisory boards for research journals. He was a member of the National Reading Panel and the RAND Reading Study Group. He was the lead editor of the *Handbook of Reading Research, Volume III,* and is the lead editor for *Volume IV.* He served as chair of the 2009 Reading Framework Committee for the National Assessment of Educational Progress. He serves as a member of the Advisory Panel for the National Evaluation of Educational Technology. In addition, he has edited, authored, or co-authored more than 100 books, chapters, and journal articles. His recent publications include a co-edited volume on professional development for reading instruction (with Dorothy Strickland) and a monograph reviewing the research on adolescent literacy.

KEIKO KODA

Dr. Koda is Associate Professor in the Department of Modern Languages at Carnegie Mellon University. Her major research areas include second-language reading, biliteracy development, psycholinguistics, and foreign language pedagogy. She has been widely published in refereed journals and has authored a number of book chapters. She recently completed a monograph, *Insights Into Second Language Reading* (Cambridge University Press, 2004). She has been a member of the editorial boards of *TESOL Quarterly, Research in Second Language Learning, International Review of Applied Linguistics in Language Teaching,* and *The Modern Language Journal.* She is a consultant for the Educational Testing Service and the American Council on the Teaching of Foreign Languages in second-language reading and assessment. She also serves as a member of the Test of English as a Foreign Language (TOEFL) Committee of Examiners at the Educational Testing Service. Her work has appeared in *Applied Psycholinguistics, Cognition, The Modern Language Journal, Journal of Child Language, Journal of Psycholinguistic Research, Language Learning, Second Language Research,* and *Studies in Second Language Acquisition.* Currently, she is involved in ongoing projects on cross-linguistic variations in reading acquisition, which will be published in a forthcoming volume, Learning to Read Across Languages (Lawrence Erlbaum Associates, 2006).

NONIE K. LESAUX

Dr. Lesaux is Assistant Professor of Human Development and Psychology at the Harvard Graduate School of Education. Her research focuses on the reading development and developmental health of children who are at risk for learning difficulties. These children include children from language-minority backgrounds, children from low socioeconomic backgrounds, and children with difficulties in language processing and other skills that influence reading development. Her doctoral research (University of British Columbia, 2003) reported on the findings of a 5-year longitudinal study that examined the development of reading, from kindergarten through Grade 4, of language-minority learners who entered mainstream classrooms with little or no proficiency in English, compared with their native-speaking peers.

Her current research projects are designed to continue to develop an understanding of reading development of language-minority learners, as well as to continue to examine the relationships among demographic, health, language, and reading-related variables in at-risk populations. Dr. Lesaux is currently principal investigator on a project funded by the NICHD that focuses on the relationship between Spanish and English oral language and literacy skills as they relate to reading comprehension for Spanish speakers developing literacy skills in English. In 2003, she was a finalist in the International Reading Association's Outstanding Dissertation Competition. Dr. Lesaux has published her work in *Developmental Psychology* and *Journal of Learning Disabilities,* and she is a member of the International Academy for Research in Learning Disabilities, Society for the Scientific Study of Reading, and Society for Research in Child Development.

GAIL MCKOON

Dr. McKoon is Professor of Psychology in the College of Social and Behavioral Sciences at Ohio State University. Her primary research interests are reading, human memory, and knowledge representation, and she is considered a leading expert in research on reading comprehension. She has served on advisory panels for the National Science Foundation and the National Institute of Mental Health, and she has published more than 80 articles in peer-reviewed journals. In 1985, she was designated by the Social Science Citation Indices as one of the 50 highest impact authors in psychology, and in 2002, she was honored by election to the prestigious Society for Experimental Psychology.

ROBERT S. RUEDA

Dr. Rueda is Professor of Psychology in Education at the Rossier School of Education at the University of Southern California. Dr. Rueda's research interests center on the sociocultural factors in learning and motivation, with a focus on reading and literacy in students in at-risk conditions, English-language learners, and students with mild learning disabilities. His recent work has been funded through the National Center for the Improvement of Early Reading Achievement, and the National Center for Research on Education, Diversity, and Excellence. His articles have appeared in journals such as the *Journal of Research in Education*, *Remedial and Special Education*, *Exceptional Children*, *Anthropology and Education Quarterly*, *Urban Education*, and *The Elementary School Journal*. Recently, in monographs and book chapters, he has collaborated with others in treating the sociocultural issues involved in the teaching of diverse learners. He has served as a reviewer for a wide variety of journals of education and psychology, and he has been a member of the editorial boards of *American Educational Research Journal*, *Journal of Literacy Research*, *NRC Yearbook*, *The California Reader*, *Review of Research in Education*, *Learning Disabilities Research and Practice*, *Exceptional Children*, and *Education and Training in Mental Retardation and Developmental Disabilities*. Dr. Rueda is a Fellow of the American Psychological Association.

LINDA S. SIEGEL

Dr. Siegel holds the Dorothy C. Lam Chair in the Department of Special Education and is Associate Dean for Graduate Studies and Research in the Faculty of Education at the University of British Columbia. She has published more than 130 peer-reviewed articles, as well as numerous other publications, on cognitive and language development (spanning oral language development as well as reading, writing, and spelling). She has received international recognition for her research in reading, learning disabilities (e.g., assessment and intelligence tests), bilingualism, ESOL, and language learning of French, Spanish, Chinese, Punjabi, Arabic, Italian, Portuguese, and other languages, and she has published articles in Italian, French, Spanish, and English. Dr. Siegel has been the Associate Editor of *Child Development* and the Editor of the *International Journal of Behavioral Development*, has served on the editorial boards of a number of journals, and has participated in research grant review panels in the United States, Canada, and Hong Kong. She is currently directing an English immersion program in Xian, China, and conducting research on English-language teaching in Hong Kong.

CATHERINE SNOW

Dr. Snow is the Henry Lee Shattuck Professor of Education at the Harvard Graduate School of Education. Her work focuses on language development in mono- and bilingual children, and on the role of language knowledge in literacy development. She has been a visiting professor or visiting scientist at several institutions, including the Universidad Autónoma de Madrid and New York University. She began her academic career in the Linguistics Institute at the University of Amsterdam. A leading authority in the field of reading and literacy, Dr. Snow has a list of publications that fills many pages. In 2001–2003 alone, she authored or co-authored more than a dozen articles and chapters and co-edited seven books. She chaired the Committee on the Prevention of Reading Difficulties in Young Children of the National Research Council and The RAND Reading Study Group, and currently chairs the Carnegie Corporation of New York's Advisory Council on Advancing Literacy.

Author Index

Subject Index

Opening the Database

Place the compact disk in the CD/DVD drive.
The program will load automatically.

Browse All Studies

This presents a list of all the studies in the database, showing Reference #, Author(s), Title, and Citation for
 each.
Click on Page Down to scroll down the list.
Click on Page Up to scroll up the list.
 (You can also use the scroll bar on the right to move up and down the list.)
Click on Detail View (to the right, above the study title) to examine a particular study in detail.
Click on Print This Study (to the right, above the Author name(s), to print out the complete record of the
 study.
Click on Previous Study to see the preceding study in the list.
Click on Next Study to see the following study in the list.
Click on Main Screen to return to the title page.

Search Studies

This permits searching for a specific study or studies in the database.
Enter search criteria in one or more areas, then click on Perform Search.
Click on Cancel Search to return to the title page and begin a new search.
When you obtain a list of studies from a search, click on Detail View (to the right, above the study title) to
 examine a particular study in detail.
Click on Print This Study (to the right, above the Author names) to print out the complete record of the
 study.
Click on Previous Study to see the preceding study in the list.
Click on Next Study to see the following study in the list.

Reference

If you know the reference number of a study (from having looked at the study previously), you can access
 the study quickly by entering the number in this field.

Authors

Entering the last name of an author in this field will call up all studies where that person is author or
 co-author. Use & to link the last names of two co-authors: Smith & Jones. For three or more co-authors,
 use & before the last name of the last author: Smith, Jones, & Brown.

Title

Entering a key word or phrase will call up all studies whose titles contain the word or phrase. Example:
 Entering "literacy" (without the quotation marks) will result in a list of 42 studies.

Citation

This field may be used in the same way as the Authors and Title fields to access specific studies. In addition, you can enter a year to get all studies for a given year. You can also enter all or part of a journal name to obtain a list of all studies from a specific journal.

Abstract

This field has the potential for a large variety of specific searches. Any key word or phrase may be entered, and if the abstract of a study contains the word or phrase, the study will be listed.

Research Domain

Click on this field to see a list of the seven research domains (plus Other) under which the studies of the database are classified. Select the domain that you want to investigate.

[Note: There is a bug in the program here. When you select the domain, you see an additional menu that gives the possible choices for Focus of Study. Just move your cursor outside the field and click on blank space to close this second menu.]

Focus of Study

Click on this field to see a menu of choices among focal areas related to literacy.

Sample Description

As with the Abstract field, the Sample Description permits a variety of specific searches. Try key words and phrases related to such topics as native language, age, grade level, geographical area, socioeconomic status, and the like.

Measures

Enter a key word or phrase to see a list of studies in which a given test or type of test was used. Try words and phrases such as the name of a language, an aspect of literacy (e.g., phonological awareness, reading comprehension), an aspect of language (e.g., syntax/ syntactic, morphology/morphological, vocabulary), a type of test (e.g., cloze), and the like.

Print

When you are looking at a particular study on the screen you can print out the complete record of the study by clicking on Print This Study (to the right, above the Author names).